Dictionary
of
Patron Saints' Names

Dictionary
of
Patron Saints' Names

Thomas W. Sheehan, M. Div.

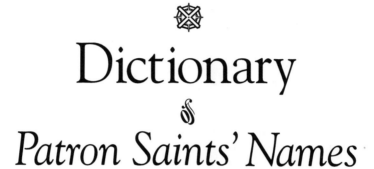

Our Sunday Visitor Publishing Division
Our Sunday Visitor, Inc.
Huntington, Indiana 46750

Copyright © 2001 by Our Sunday Visitor Publishing Division, Our Sunday Visitor, Inc.

Our Sunday Visitor Publishing Division
Our Sunday Visitor, Inc.
200 Noll Plaza
Huntington, IN 46750

ISBN: 0-87973-539-2
LCCCN: 2001-131189

Cover design by Monica Haneline
Interior design by Sherri L. Hoffman
PRINTED IN THE UNITED STATES OF AMERICA

Table of Contents

Introduction   7
- The Need for This Book   7
- The Purpose of This Book   8
- There Is a Patron Saint for Every Name   9
- Criteria Used for Choosing Patron Saints   9
- Criteria Used for Matching Saints' Names to
  Those of Modern Catholics   10
- Christian Names Among African-American and
  Hispanic-American Newly Invented Names   11
- How to Use This Book   13
- How Catholic Saints Are Made   14
- How the Saints' Feast Dates Were Chosen for This Work   15

Female Names   17
Male Names   305
Bibliography   591
About the Author   595

Introduction

The Need for This Book

Some years ago while making sick calls, I visited a very ill man who had arranged on his bedside stand small statues of six saints: Michael the Archangel, Teresa of Ávila, Joseph, Thomas, Bernadette of Lourdes, and the Blessed Virgin Mary of the Immaculate Conception. I inquired why he had these particular saints' statues. He told me that as each of his six children was born, he had a small statue carved of the saint after whom he had named the child.

He explained that for years these statues were displayed in little shrines above the couch in the family living room. Their purpose was to remind everyone, especially the children, that they were members of a greater Catholic family focused on Christ. Furthermore, the statues presented role models for the children to follow. They were now placed near his bed so that he could look upon them and remember his children and his Catholic treasures, especially when he was racked with pain.

It has been a long-standing custom with Catholic parents to name their children after the saints. This was done to commend the children to the protection of the saints, provide an example as to the best way to follow Jesus, and give the children a special Christian-Catholic identity.

However, this custom has been increasingly ignored. The African-American and Hispanic cultures in America have increasingly created new names, often from pretty sounds that have no meaning. Even the Anglo culture, by using surnames for first names, creates names that seem to have no Catholic roots. As a result, the Catholic population has slowly forgotten its moorings in the greater faith family of both the living and dead. Thus, we have a generation of Catholics for whom the saints are irrelevant. Our children increasingly do not know who they are, what they are supposed to be, or where they should be going.

Our secular pagan American culture, seeing the void, has labored mightily to substitute its own values and personalities. These include TV and film stars, music and sports personalities, business and political leaders, and even criminal elements (such as those involved in drugs). Their values and life-styles have increasingly become the guidelines for modern living.

This sad fact was brought home to me recently when I was walking across the parking lot of the parish to which I had been assigned. I met a parishioner who was well along in her pregnancy, exchanged greetings, and asked her if she knew the sex of the child. She did indeed know and was planning to name the baby "Tiffany Chanel" because the two names had the feeling of upper class and richness. I asked her how this helped the child know she was a special member of the Christian-Catholic family. We talked about this for a while and then I informed her that the names she had picked were perfectly fine. She just needed to know that Tiffany means "The Revealing of God" and that St. Peter Mary Chanel calls all Catholics to be missionaries.

The Purpose of This Book

In our modern world, most Muslims and Jews discover in their names that they belong somewhere. Christian-Catholics need to rediscover their connections to the Catholic family and take pride in being members of it. And there are ways to make it happen.

First: It is important to recognize that many more patron saints exist than those usually printed in all the old patron saints' books. For example: There is a St. Chastity, St. Fawn, St. October, St. Hope, St. Logan of Dillon, St. Thomas More of Chelsea, Bl. Page, St. Tiger, Bl. Taylor, Bl. Ashley, and so many more. We only need to take the time to be introduced and to get to know them.

Second: It is important to recognize that the mission of the Church is to "baptize" everything in the world for the service of God and salvation. Thus, if parents fail to give familiar Christian names to their children, then the clergy should take care to "Christianize" the name. Knowing the meaning of a name often allows bridges to be built from one culture to another, and a name that was not thought to be Christian suddenly becomes a vehicle for making Catholic connections.

There Is a Patron Saint for Every Name

In one way or another, a Catholic connection can be made with just about every name on the planet. All that is needed is a little research. This book provides about two thousand patron saints matched to some six thousand male and eight thousand female names. It is the goal of this book to provide patron saints for:

- English and Irish surnames, nicknames, place names, and occupation names that are now first, or given, names.
- African-American alternate spellings and inventions.
- Spanish names and nicknames.
- Hispanic-American alterations and new creations.
- Arabic, African, Native American, European, Hindu, and Japanese names found in America.

Criteria Used for Choosing Patron Saints

1. The Blessed Virgin, St. Joseph, and the Apostles are always the first choice for patrons. Being the closest to Jesus on the earth, they forever remain excellent guides for us to follow.
2. The saints, blesseds, venerables, and servants of God of North America, England, and Ireland are the next to be chosen. Often we tune out a saint's example because he lived in a time and culture that is distant to us in time or place. But to find role models in our own North American culture and from relatively recent times closes that gap and makes the saint more relevant.
3. The saints, blesseds, venerables, and servants of God of Central and South America are the third choice. These saints, living in recent times, also help to close the distance between them, God, and us. This makes the attainment of heaven seem a reasonable daily task.
4. Single and married saints of the recent past, from all cultures, are the fourth choice. As most Catholics who read about the saints are destined to follow the single or married vocation, it seems the emphasis on these saints is a wise choice.
5. Bible saints mentioned in the Old and New Testaments are the fifth choice. They provide an opportunity to introduce everyone to our biblical heritage. Also, by including Jewish

saints, one comes to realize that one is a part of a very large and diverse family of believers.

6. Religious and priest saints of the recent past are the sixth choice. The closer the saint's time is to our modern time, the easier it is to make the necessary connections.

7. All saints from ancient times and places — these are pressed into service when necessary. After all, our faith family reaches across the centuries and around the world.

8. Jesus, the Holy Spirit, and God the Father may also serve as patrons. They are pressed into service when no other saints are available.

Criteria Used for Matching Saints' Names to Those of Modern Catholics

1. An exact name match is always the best. Thus, the Blessed Virgin Mary is an excellent choice for a person who bears the name of Mary.

2. Matching the meaning of the names is always the second choice. For example: A person named Modesty could adopt St. Modesta as a patron. After all, *modestia* is the Latin word for "modesty." Sometimes, however, names have the same meaning but do not look related. Thus, St. Ingenuinus, whose name means "ingenious," can serve as patron for Cassidy, whose name means "the clever one."

   In our modern age this may be the best approach when receiving African-American, Arab, Hindu, American Indian, and other converts into the Church. By not imposing a European name and embracing a name from non-Christian culture, the Church baptizes (makes Christian) a pagan name and shows respect for the culture of the convert. Thus, an Arab named Hakeem could keep his name. He would also know that his name's meaning, "The Ruler," would find a Christian connection in the Christian name Richard.

3. Saints whose names are variants of modern names can also be pressed into service. Thus, it is acceptable for St. Anne to be named patron of someone named Nancy, and St. Margaret can be accepted as a patron for person named Maggie, Rita, or Peggy.

4. A saint's name in one language may have an entirely different spelling in another language, but it may still serve. Thus, a St. Drostan can serve as patron for a person named Dustie.

5. The saint's occupation or place of birth (or where he preached, died, etc.) can be considered a person's patron. It is a popular practice to name St. John of Beverly as patron for Beverly. It is just as acceptable to recognize Bl. William Way of Devon as a patron for a person named Devonna. A person named Melody can claim St. Romanus the Melodist for a patron. Remember, in later ages, place and occupation names became surnames.

6. Saints who are officially appointed by the Catholic Church to do a particular job. For example, St. Barbara has been officially named patron of storms. Thus, someone named Storm, Stormy, or Tempest can call St. Barbara her patron saint.

7. Saints with a similar names can be pressed into service. For example: All saints' books suggest that St. Brice can be accepted as a patron for a person named Bruce even though they are two entirely different names. This would justify the adoption of St. Sandila as a patron for a person named Sandra and St. Malo for a person named Mallory. Further, Bl. Taylor can stand in for a person named Tyler.

8. Jesus and Mary, under one title or another, can be also adopted as patrons. Thus, Jesus the Healer can be patron for a person named Marva or Milagros. Both names mean "miracle" or "healer."

9. The sex of the name and the patron are matched whenever possible. Following this last criterion has often led to choosing an ignored female saint over a well-known male saint. This has often meant a saint is chosen about whom very little has been recorded.

Christian Names Among African-American and Hispanic-American Newly Invented Names

The process of discovering Christian connections to African-American and Hispanic-American newly invented names is much easier then it would seem at first glance.

It helps to remember that most of these names find their roots in western Christian culture. Thus, the African-American name Dwalou sounds very African but is actually constructed out of the English names Dwayne+Louis. Some Hispanic inventions do the same. The only difference is that they use Spanish names as roots. Thus, Solivia is merely the marriage of Solana+Olivia. Such compound words are called "doubles" in this work. ("Doubles" are not new. The Anglo community has been doing the same for many years. An example is the name Rosemary.) Among both Hispanics and African-Americans such combining of names is a way of giving the child both of its parents' names.

Also, African-American names are often phonetic spellings or a creative reworking of a common American name. Thus, among African-Americans Feeby is a simplified spelling of Phoebe, and Semaj is James spelled backwards. Among Hispanics, Shelsy is a simplified spelling of Chelsea and Nohely is simply a fancy spelling of Noel.

It is also helpful to know that certain sounds are considered beautiful among each of these American subcultures. African-Americans prefer De, La, Sha, and Na, while Hispanics seem to have a soft spot for Ja, Je, Ya, and Za. While they mean nothing in themselves, they almost always lead to a Christian connection. An African-American example is LaShana (Lashawna) and a Hispanic example is Yanice (Janice).

Sometimes it takes a little contemplation and word surgery to find the Christian pearl buried in a name originally constructed out of nice sounds. For example the Hispanic name Yamilet is really Ya+Amile+T and leads to St. Amelia. Yadira is a triple combination, Ya+Adi+Ira, which leads to Sts. Adelaide and Irene. A beautiful modern Hispanic invention, Aracelis, is really just two Latin words, *ara+caelestis*. Together they mean "altar of heaven." Together they lead one to Sts. Araba and Celestine.

Members of both subcultures feel free to draw names from non-Christian roots. Thus, Tamika is an African-American adaptation of the Japanese name Tamiko. And Hispanics have admitted the Arabic word Yesenia to its dictionary of names. Making a Christian connection can range from easy to difficult. Happily, Tamiko and Yesenia find easy connections to Christian names through Tammy and Arsenia.

However, it is sometimes impossible to make a connection through similar-sounding names. That is when it is necessary to know the meaning of an Arabic, African, Hindu, or other non-Christian name. Only then can a match be made across cultures to an existing Christian name. Thus, the Arabic Nasser can be served by a saint named Victor, for both names mean about the same thing. (See "Criteria Used for Matching Saints' Names to Those of Modern Catholics," starting on page 10, for a fuller explanation.)

How to Use This Book

The Book Plan

It is extremely simple:

1. As the table of contents shows, all female and male names are listed separately, but in alphabetical order. However, some names are used by both genders, so there are duplications of some of those entries. The following abbreviations are used with their names: SG (Servant of God; plural, SsG), Bl. (Blessed; plural, Bls.), Ven. (Venerable; plural, Vens.), and St. (Saint; plural, Sts.).
2. Both sets of names present information within minor and major entries (see following).

Minor Entries

Each minor entry is usually only one line long. It presents:

1. A name variant.
2. The nationality of the name, if known.
3. Directions to a major entry where more information can be found.
4. In rare instances, a minor entry, which sometimes refers the reader to another minor entry.

Major Entries

This entry may be only a few lines or several paragraphs. It presents:

1. The name, its meaning, and its nationality, which appear in the first line or two.

2. The rationale for choosing a patron (or patrons), which is given next.
3. A short biography of the chosen patron, which follows.
4. The feast date of the patron, which is then given.
5. Additional patron(s) and date(s), which may occasionally be provided.

When an entry refers you to another name, keep in mind that the other name may be either a female or male appellation so that you must check both sections as needed.

The reader should also keep in mind that historians and other scholars do not agree entirely on dates, the spelling of names, and events in connection with the entries appearing in this work. Therefore, it is a good idea to consult at least three or more references to determine the "accuracy" of a given "fact."

How Catholic Saints Are Made

In the modern Catholic Church the process of canonization involves a number of steps.

The First Step: This involves an expression of interest in a deceased Catholic's life. At this point, no title is given to the person proposed for sainthood. Sometimes such a person is referred to as a "candidate."

The Second Step: Involves an active collecting and organizing of information about the life of the proposed saint. The title "servant of God" is often used informally and unofficially.

The Third Step: Involves the presenting and acceptance of the researched information in Rome. At this point, the prospective saint is officially recognized as a "servant of God."

The Fourth Step: Roman Catholic Church authorities issue a decree that the proposed saint's life is praiseworthy and is eligible for further investigation. At this point the person is declared "venerable" and local honor is allowed.

The Fifth Step: With the approval of one miracle brought about through the prayers of the proposed saint, the candidate is beatified by the Pope and is declared "blessed," at which point local and/or national veneration is allowed.

The Sixth Step: Involves the actual canonization of the individual as a saint. The Holy Father publicly and infallibly recognizes that the "saint" is in heaven and is worthy of honor by the whole world after two more miracles have been verified.

How the Saints' Feast Dates Were Chosen for This Work

Many of the saints presented in this book have more than one feast day. As a recording of every date would take an inordinate amount of space and also make for tedious reading, certain criteria had to be established to help the compiler of this work select one acceptable date for each saint.

The dates with the highest priority are those officially listed on the modern revised calendar of the Roman Catholic Church. However, the number of these saints whose feasts have been moved to new dates is relatively small.

For the others, the dates assigned to them long ago in the Roman Martyrology and other ancient works are still valid. Moreover, they are helpful in finding a day for the faithful to remember and give thanks to God for the living examples of the saints, for they continue to teach believers how to follow Christ.

From the most ancient times, the date of death of a saint was the date usually chosen as that saint's feast date. This was done by local religious authority or by public acclamation or sometimes by both. The day of death was widely regarded as the birth date of the new saint into his or her heavenly home. The death date remains the single most popular date for modern saints' feast days.

This fact has helped the compiler of this volume when presenting a saint who is so little known that either the feast date has been forgotten or no official feast date had ever been established. In these cases the date of death, when known, is offered as a feast date. When the death date is unknown, November 1, the Feast of All Saints, is presented as an acceptable alternate.

Thus, it may seem that choosing a death date would seem to be a simple matter, but in reality it is not. This is because many ancient and medieval saints were honored by different countries on different dates. For example, St. Adalbert, bishop of Prague, was killed on April 23, 997. His relics were honored by the Prussians on April 23, by Bohemia on August 25, by Poland on October 20, and by Hungary on November 6. In such a case the compiler would first choose to follow the old Roman calendar. Lacking that, he would choose the date of death.

Things get more complicated when a saint is presented who is honored by different branches of the Church. For example, St. Addai, one of the original seventy-two disciples of Jesus, was honored in the ancient Syrian Church on January 23, April 5, October 18, and October 30. The modern Syrian Church remembers him on May 14 and the first Monday in August. The Armenian Church celebrates his feast on December 21. The Roman Church honors him on August 1. The first choice of the compiler would be a Roman date if there is one.

Lacking a Roman feast date, a date suggested by the Eastern Churches united to Rome or by the Orthodox Churches is quite acceptable. For instance, St. Isaiah, the Old Testament prophet, is not officially recognized as a saint by the Roman Church. However, he is considered one by the Greek Church and his feast date is given as July 6.

This information should help the reader realize that a number of feast dates cited in this book may be unfamiliar. This is probably because the compiler, as explained above, has chosen to present only one of several possible dates. Alternate dates, even though not included in this work, are still valid.

Female Names
A-Z

𝒜

Aakusta (Finnish) See Augusta.

Aaren (American) See Erin.

Aarika (American) See Erica.

Abagail (Hebrew) See Abigail.

Abaigail (Hebrew) See Abigail.

Abaigeal (Irish) See Abigail.

Abarena (African-American) See Abra, Abina.

Abbe (nickname) See Abigail.

Abbey (nickname) See Abigail.

Abbi (nickname) See Abigail.

Abbie (nickname) See Abigail.

Abby (nickname) See Abigail.

Abbye (nickname) See Abigail.

Abegael (variant) Abigail.

Abela (Hispanic-American double) See Abbe+Bella.

Abianne (American double) Abigail+Anne.

Abigael (variant) Abigail.

Abigail "The Cause for Father's Joy" (Hebrew).

> *Patron Saints:* Christian tradition does not provide a St. Abigail, but the Bible does. She is Abigail, Jewish laywoman and matriarch, wife of King David, who lived in about 1000-950 B.C.
>
> *Feast Dates:* November 1 — St. Abigail.

Abigale (variant) See Abigail.

Abigayle (variant) See Abigail.

Abina (Ghanian) See Thursday.

Abismael "The Cause for a Father's Joy+The One Whom God Hears" (Hispanic-American double).

> *Patron Saints:* Abismael is a modern Hispanic-American invention created by joining the names of the mother and father, Abbie (a nickname for Abigail) and Ismael (or Ishmael).

Two Sts. Ismael can be found in the saints' books. One of them was a martyr who gave his life for Christ in ancient Chalcedon.

> *Feast Dates:* November 1 — St. Abigail; June 16 — St. Ismael.

Abra "The Mother of Multitudes" (Modern English feminine form of Abraham).

> *Patron Saints:* The Jewish patriarch Abraham is the most obvious choice for patron. However, one should not forget St. Abra, 342-360, a daughter born to St. Hilary of Poitiers before he became a bishop. At his advice she became a religious sister. She died at the age of eighteen.
>
> *Feast Dates:* October 9 — St. Abraham; December 12 — St. Abra.

Abrena (African-American) See Abra.

Abriana (Italian) See Abra.

Acacia "The Guileless One" (Greek) or "The Thorny One" (Greek).

> *Patron Saints:* There is one male saint, a martyr in ancient times, named Acacius. It might also be helpful to know that the acacia tree is a symbol of resurrection and eternal life in Christian art. Thus the most obvious choice of patron saint for Acacia is the risen Christ. The Blessed Virgin, assumed into heaven, is another choice.
>
> *Feast Dates:* June 22 — St. Acacius; Easter Sunday — The Risen Lord; August 15 — Assumed Virgin Mary.

Ada "An Ornament" (Hebrew variant of Adah) or "One of Red Earth" (Phoenician for Adamah) or "The Happy One" (English variant of Aida) or "The

Noblewoman" (German short form of Adelaide).

Patron Saints: There are three known Sts. Ada, one of whom was a seventh-century French Benedictine religious abbess. It is also good to know that Ada is a short feminine form of Adam. The Bible tells us that Adah was one of the daughters of Adam and Eve. She later became the wife of Cain. Finally, Ada is also recognized as a short form of Adelaide. This leads to another two dozen saints.

Feast Dates: December 4 — St. Ada; December 24 — St. Adam.

Adabella (Spanish double) See Ada+Bella.

Adal (German) See Ada, Adela, Adeline.

Adala (variant) See Ada, Adela, Adeline.

Adalene (Spanish) See Ada, Adela, Adeline.

Adalia (German, Spanish) See Ada, Adela, Adeline.

Adalie (variant) See Ada, Adela, Adeline.

Adalina (variant) See Ada, Adela, Adeline.

Adall (variant) See Ada, Adela, Adeline.

Adalle (variant) See Ada, Adela, Adeline.

Adan (variant) See Aidan.

Adana (Spanish) See Adalene.

Addi (nickname) See Ada, Adela, Adelaide, Adeline, Adrienne.

Addie (Greek, German) See Ada, Adelaide, Adeline, Adrienne.

Addison (Old English double) See Adeline+Son.

Addy (nickname) See Ada, Adela, Adelaide, Adeline, Adrienne.

Adel (nickname) See Ada, Adela, Adelaide, Adeline.

Adela "The Noblewoman" (German, Spanish, English variant of Adelaide, Adeline).

Patron Saints: There are a few Sts. Adela. One of them was a married lay-woman and grandmother of St. Gregory of Utrecht. She later became a religious abbess in 725.

Feast Dates: December 24 — St. Adela.

Adelaida (Italian, Spanish, Portuguese variant) Adela, Adelaide.

Adelaide "The Noblewoman" (German variant of Ada, Adela, Adeline).

Patron Saints: There are about two dozen Sts. Adela, Adelaide, Adelina, Adelindis, and Adeltrudis. The most famous St. Adelaide was a married noblewoman, 931-999. She had five children, became a widow, and suffered much from palace intrigues. She is remembered for helping the poor.

Feast Dates: December 16 — St. Adelaide.

Adele (French) See Ada, Adela, Adeline.

Adelheid (Old German) See Ada, Adela, Adelaide, Adeline.

Adelia (Latin) See Ada, Adela, Adeline.

Adelice (variant) See Alice.

Adelina (Latin, Spanish, French, Italian) See Ada, Adela, Adeline.

Adelind (English) See Ada, Adela, Adeline.

Adelinda (Latin) See Ada, Adela, Adeline.

Adeline "The Noblewoman" (English variant of Ada, Adela, Adelaide).

Patron Saints: There are two medieval Sts. Adeline. One was the sister of St. Vitalis of Savigny and the other was a niece of St. Bernard of Clairvaux. Both were abbesses.

Feast Dates: August 28 and October 20 — St. Adeline.

Adella (English) See Ada, Adela, Adeline.

Adelle (French) See Ada, Adela, Adeline.

Adelyne (English) See Ada, Adela, Adeline.

Adena (Hebrew) See Ada, Adela, Adeline.

Adey (nickname) See Ada, Adela, Adeline, Adelaide, Adrienne.

Adi (nickname) See Ada, Adrienne.

Adie (nickname) See Ada, Adrienne.

Adina (Spanish) See Ada, Adeline.

Adonia "The Beautiful One" (Spanish).

Patron Saints: There are a half-dozen Sts. Donata and Donatilla.

Feast Dates: November 1 — St. Dona of Llandona; All Saturdays — The Blessed Virgin Mary, Our Lady (see Madonna).

Adora "The Adored One" (Latin).

Patron Saints: There is one St. Adorator who lived in the 300s. He worked hard all of his life to make converts to Christianity, which included his parents.

Feast Dates: October 22 — St. Adorator.

Adrea (English) See Adrienne.

Adria (Latin, Italian, Spanish) See Adrienne.

Adrian (Italian, Spanish) See Adrienne.

Adriana (English, Italian, Spanish) See Adrienne.

Adriane (German) See Adrienne.

Adrianna (Italian) See Adrienne.

Adriena (variant) See Adrienne.

Adrienna (Italian) See Adrienne.

Adrienne "The Dark One" (French) or "The One from the Adriatic Sea" (French).

Patron Saints: Both a St. Adria and a St. Adriana can be found, and both were laywomen. The first was a martyr for Christ in Rome in about 250. The second is remembered for her great holiness.

Feast Dates: December 2 — St. Adria; August 10 — St. Adriana.

Adrina (African-American) See Adrienne.

Adriyanna (American) See Adrienne.

Aedan (Irish) See Aidan, Eden.

Aedhan (Irish) See Aidan, Eden.

Aerial (Hebrew) See Ariel.

Aeriel (Hebrew) See Ariel.

Aeriela (variant) See Ariel.

Aeriella (variant) See Ariel.

Aesha (African-American) See Aisha.

Afee (African-American) See Afi.

Affrica (variant) See Africa.

Afi (Yoruba) See Psyche.

Afi (West African) See Friday.

Afra (variant) See Africa.

Africa "Pleasant One" (Latin, Irish) or "The Sun" (Spanish).

Patron Saints: There are more than five thousand black African saints. In fact, the story of Catholicism in Africa is one of great sacrifice. It spans from the most ancient times to modern day. And there are six Sts. Afra. One of them was the daughter of St. Hilaria. She was a single woman who worked as a madam for a local brothel. At one point she hid a fleeing Catholic bishop. She and many of her girls were converted to faith in Jesus by him. Her mother and friends were massacred by soldiers when they tried to bury her martyred body. She is informally known as the "Patron of Prostitutes."

Feast Dates: August 5 — St. Afra.

Africah (variant) See Africa.

Afrika (Irish) See Africa.

Afrodite (Greek) See Aphrodite.

Ag (nickname) See Agatha, Agnes.

Agace (variant) See Agatha.

Agata (Italian, Irish, Polish, Czech) See Agatha.

Agate (Latvian, Norwegian) See Agatha.

Agatha "The Good, Kind One" (Greek).

Patron Saints: There are about a half-dozen Sts. Agatha. The most popular is a young (teen to twenties), single woman who died a martyr's death in 251 in Sicily. She is the patron of bell makers, bell ringers, jewelers, and nurses, as well as against breast diseases, fires, and volcanic eruptions.

Feast Dates: February 5 — St. Agatha.

Agathe (French, German) See Agatha.

Agathi (Modern Greek) See Agatha.

Agda (Swedish, Danish) See Agatha.

Aggi (nickname) See Agatha, Agnes.

Aggie (nickname) See Agatha, Agnes.

Aggy (nickname) See Agatha, Agnes.

Agna (Norwegian) See Agnes.

Agne (Lithuanian, Greek) See Agnes.

Agnella (nickname) See Agnes.

Agnes "The Pure One" (Greek) or "The Lamb" (Latin).

Patron Saints: There are about a dozen Sts. Agnes. The one most remembered by modern Catholics is a teenager (believed to be thirteen years old) and virgin who was martyred in 305. St. Ambrose tells us that "Agnes was holy beyond her years and courageous beyond human nature." Christian art shows her holding an *agnus* (Latin for "lamb"). She was like Christ, a "pure lamb sacrificed." She is patron of chastity, young girls, Girl Scouts, and virgins.

Feast Dates: January 21 — St. Agnes.

Agnesa (Ukrainian, Bulgarian) See Agnes.

Agnese (Italian) See Agnes.

Agnessa (Russian) See Agnes.

Agnesse (nickname) See Agnes.

Agneta (Swedish) See Agnes.

Agnete (German) See Agnes.

Agnieszka (nickname) See Agnes.

Agnola (nickname) See Agnes.

Agota (Hungarian) See Agatha.

Agueda (Spanish) See Agatha.

Agusta (variant) See Augusta.

Aida "The One Arriving" (Egyptian) or "Happy One" (Italian) or "An Ornament" (Hebrew).

Patron Saints: There are two male Sts. Aida. Both died in the battle at Ebstorf in 880, fighting pagan Norse invaders, and both are recognized as martyrs.

Feast Dates: February 2 — both Sts. Aida.

Aidan "The Fiery Little One" (Irish Gaelic).

Patron Saints: There are almost two dozen Sts. Aidan (Aedhan). The most famous was St. Aidan the Elder. A follower of St. David, he also became a bishop and made many converts. He died around 600.

Feast Dates: January 31 — St. Aidan; August 31 — St. Eden, also known as Aidan (see Eden).

Aigneis (Irish) See Agnes.

Aila (variant) See Aileen, Helen.

Ailbhe (Irish) See Elva.

Ailee (variant) See Aileen.

Aileen "The Light" (Scottish form of Helen through Eileen).

Patron Saints: Aileen is a form of Eileen, which, in turn, is a form of Helen. There are about a half-dozen Sts. Helen. The greatest is St. Helena, the Roman empress.

Feast Dates: August 18 — St. Helena of Constantinople (see Helen).

Ailene (English) See Aileen, Eileen, Helen.

Ailey (English) See Aileen.

Aili (Scottish) See Aileen.

Ailis (Irish) See Adelaide.

Aime (French) See Aimee.

Aimee "The Beloved One" (French).

Patron Saints: There are about a half-dozen Sts. Ama and Amata. One of them, a single woman, died a martyr's death in Persia in about 250. Aimee can also be a short form of Amelia and leads to many patrons.

Feast Dates: June 6 — St. Ama; May 31 — St. Amelia (see Amelia).

Aimil (Scottish Gaelic) See Emily.

Aindrea (Irish) See Andrea.

Aingeal (Irish Gaelic) See Angela, Angelica.

Airika (variant) See Erica.

Airzena (African-American double) See Arizona, Airika+Xenia.

Aisha "The Woman Who Is Alive and Well" (Arabic) or "The Living One" (Swahili).

Patron Saints: There is no St. Aisha. However, if Asha is accepted as a variant of Aisha, then a saint with a very similar name can be pressed into service. She is St. Ashkhenia, a queen in Armenia, who lived in the fourth century. She and her husband, St. Tindat III, were converts who took the Catholic faith very seriously. Furthermore, if Aisha is accepted as a form of Isha, then a St. Isha becomes available.

Feast Dates: November 29 — St. Ashkhenia; December 24 — St. Eve (see Isha).

Akilah "The Bright, Logical One" (Arabic).

Patron Saints: Akilah means the same thing as Alberta.

Feast Dates: March 11 — St. Alberta.

Akusta (variant) See Augusta.

Alaine (English) See Aileen, Alana.

Alana "The Fair, Beautiful One" (Irish Gaelic) or "The Light" (variant of Aileen, Helen).

Patron Saints: Alaina seems to be a modern blend of Alana and Elaine. This leads to a dozen Sts. Alan and one North American female saint-in-the-making. Because Alaina can also be accepted as a form of Helen, this makes three dozen Sts. Helen available as patrons. The American saint-in-the-making is SG Frances Allen, the daughter of Ethan Allen. Born in 1784, she grew up in a Protestant and anti-Catholic atmosphere, but this did not stop her from becoming a convert and a religious sister in Montreal. It was the Catholic teaching on the Real Presence of Jesus in Holy Communion that attracted her to Catholicism. She died at the age of thirty-four years in 1810 and has long been considered a candidate for canonization.

Feast Dates: September 10 — SG Frances Allen of Montreal; August 18 — St. Helena (see Helen).

Alanah (variant) See Alana, Lana.

Alane (English) See Alana, Lana.

Alanza (Spanish) See Alphonsa.

Alayna (variant) See Alana, Lana.

Alayne (variant) See Alana, Lana.

Alba (variant) See Albina.

Alberika (variant) See Aubrey.

Alberta "The Noble Brilliant One" (Old English).

Patron Saints: There are about a dozen Sts. Albert but only one known St. Alberta. She was the sister of St. Fides of Agen. She remained single and died a martyr in 303.

Feast Dates: March 11 — St. Alberta.

Albertina (English, Portuguese, Spanish, Swedish) See Alberta.

Albertine (English, French) See Alberta.

Albina "The White One" (Latin) or "The Fair Blond One" (variant form of Elvira).

Patron Saints: There are about a half-dozen Sts. Albina. One St. Albina was a prominent matron in ancient Rome. After raising her daughter, St. Marcella, she renounced her wealth and position and built the first convent in Rome. She embraced a life of prayer and died in 370.

Feast Dates: March 4 — St. Albina.

Albinia (Italian) See Albina.

Albreanna (African-American double) See Alberta+Breanna.

Alecia (Greek) See Alice.

Aleece (nickname) See Alice.

Aleena (Dutch) See Aileen, Helen.

Aleesha (nickname) See Alice.

Aleethia (African-American) See Aletha.

Alegra (Latin) See Alana.

Alegria (Spanish) See Alana.

Alejandra (Spanish) See Alexandra.

Alejandrína (Spanish) See Alexandra.

Aleka (Greek, Hawaiian) See Alexandra, Alexis, Alice.

Alelia (African-American) See Lelia.

Alena (variant) See Adelina, Alana, Helena, Lana, Madelina.

Alene (English) See Adeline, Aileen, Helene, Madeline.

Alesa (American) See Alice.

Alesha (English) See Alice.

Alessandra (Spanish, Italian) See Alexandra.

Aleta (Spanish) See Aletha, Alice.

Aletea (Spanish) See Aletha, Alice.

Aletha "The Truthful One" (Greek).

Patron Saints: St. Alethius died a martyr in ancient Nicaea.

Feast Dates: July 8 — St. Alethius.

Alethea (African-American) See Aletha.

Alethia (African-American) See Aletha.

Alex (nickname) See Alexandra, Alexis.

Alexa (Greek, French) See Alexandra, Alexis.

Alexandra "The Helper and Defender of Humanity" (Greek).

Patron Saints: There are at least two Sts. Alexandra. The better-known St. Alexandra was a single woman, who with six Christian lady-friends was tortured and killed by being thrown into a blazing furnace during Roman times. For more patrons, one must turn to the hundreds of unnamed saints of Alexandria.

Feast Dates: March 20 — St. Alexandra.

Alexandria (French) See Alexandra.

Alexandrina (French) See Alexandra.

Alexandrine (French) See Alexandra.

Alexi (Greek) See Alexandra, Alexis.

Alexia (Greek) See Alexandra, Alexis.

Alexina (variant) See Alexandra, Alexis.

Alexine (variant) See Alexandra, Alexis.

Alexis "The Helper and Defender of Humanity" (Greek).

Patron Saints: There are about a dozen male Sts. Alexius and one female, Bl. Alix Le Clercq. She was born in 1576 and grew into an attractive and intelligent young lady. When she was nineteen, she began having vivid dreams of the Blessed Virgin and became convinced that it was her heaven-sent job to form a new religious community. Slowly, people came into her life to help her accomplish this goal. By 1598 three ladies began to lodge with her and together they planned to educate children. However, there was also opposition and misunderstandings. The new order of sisters became known as the Augustinian Canonesses Regular of the Congregation of Our Lady.

Feast Dates: January 9 — Bl. Alix Le Clercq.

Aleyah (Hispanic-American) See Alejandra.

Alfa (nickname) See Alfreda.

Alfi (nickname) See Alfreda.

Alfie (nickname) See Alfreda.

Alfreda "The Wise, Diplomatic Counselor" (Old English).

Patron Saints: There is one St. Alfrida, also known as Etheldritha. A single noblewoman, Alfrida lived in England during the Middle Ages. She refused to marry as her father wished, fled his court, and became a hermit. She died in about 795.

The Blessed Virgin under the title of "Our Lady of Good Counsel" might prove to be a good choice. Under this title, Mary is also known as the "Patron of Enlightenment." Also see Avery.

Feast Dates: August 2 — St. Alfrida; April 25 — Our Lady of Good Counsel (see Consuelo).

Alfy (nickname) See Alfreda.

Ali (nickname) See Alberta, Albina, Alexandra, Alexis, Alfy, Alice, Allison.

Alice "The Truthful One" (Greek form of Althea) or "Of Noble Rank" (German form of Adelaide).

Patron Saints: There are a couple of Sts. Alice. There are also a few Sts. Adelaide and a St. Aletheus. The best-known St. Alice was born in Belgium and was given to the local Cistercian convent to be cared for. She was a bright, pretty, and happy child, always helpful and caring. But while still a child, Alice contracted leprosy and was isolated from the sisters. Cut off from family, friends, and the sisters, she looked to God for consolation. Her one comfort was Holy Communion. However, because of the fear of spreading leprosy, Alice was not allowed to receive the cup with the other sisters. Jesus appeared to her and comforted her by teaching this truth: "Where there is a part, there is the whole of me." Her health grew steadily worse, and during the last year of her life she suffered even more and lost her eyesight. She offered all to God for the souls in purgatory. She died a teenager in 1250.

Feast Dates: June 15 — St. Alice.

Alicea (English) See Alice.

Alicia (Italian, Spanish, Swedish) See Alice.

Alie (nickname) See Alberta, Albina, Alexandra, Alexis, Allison.

Alike (variant) See Alice.

Alina (variant) See Helen, Ada, Adela, Adeline, Adelaide.

Aline (variant) See Ada, Adela, Adeline, Adelaide, Aileen.

Alis (variant) See Alice.

Alisa (Russian) See Alice.

Alisandra (Spanish) See Alexandra.

Alisen (variant) See Allison.

Alisha (variant) See Alice, Allison, Isha, Louise.

Alishia (variant) See Alice.

Alison (French) See Alice, Allison, Louise.

Alissa (nickname) See Alice.

Alita (Spanish) See Adelaide.

Alithia (African-American) See Alethea.

Alix (French) See Alexandra, Alexis, Alice.

Alixy (nickname) See Alexandra, Alexis.

Alla (variant) See Alexandra, Alexis, Alice.

Allena (variant) See Alana, Lana.

Allene (variant) See Alana, Lana.

Alli (variant) See Alberta, Alana, Allison, Alexandra, Alexis, Alfreda, Alice.

Allie (nickname) See Alberta, Allison, Alexandra, Alexis, Alfreda, Alice.

Allina (variant) See Alana, Lana.

Allison "The Son of Al" (English).

Patron Saints: Allison can be a variant form of Alice, Adelaide, and Louise, which leads to many patrons.

Feast Dates: June 15 — St. Alice (see Alice); March 15 — St. Louise de Marillac (see Louise).

Allson (English) See Allison, Louise.

Allsun (Irish) See Allison.

Ally (nickname) See Alberta, Allison, Alexandra, Alexis, Alfreda, Alice.

Allyce (variant) See Alice.

Allys (variant) See Alice.

Allyson (English) See Alice, Allison, Louise, Son.

Alma "Gentle, Loving, Bounteous One" (Latin) or "The Spiritually Supportive One" (Latin) or "Faithful Maiden" (Hebrew, Greek) or "Learned One" (Arabic) or "The Spirit [Soul]" (Italian, Spanish).

Patron Saints: There is one known St. Alma Pompa. She was the wife of King Hoel in Brittany and died in 450. Three of her children were also declared to be saints. The name Alma also leads to the Blessed Virgin. Remember the Latin hymn *Alma Redemptoris Mater?* In English, this can be loosely translated as "gentle, loving bounteous mother." The Hebrew meaning of Alma provides even more information about Mary. Isaiah 7:14 reads, "The maiden is with child" *(Jerusalem Bible).* When this passage was translated into Greek in Matthew, "maiden" was read as "virgin."

Feast Dates: July 26 — St. Alma Pompa; January 1 — The Blessed Virgin Mary, Mother of God.

Almera (variant) See Almira.

Almeta (African-American) See Alma.

Almetta (African-American) See Alma.

Almira "The Very Truthful One" (Arabic) or "The Exalted Princess" (Spanish).

Patron Saints: There is at least one saint with a similar name. St. Almirus served as a religious bishop in France. After resigning his post he became a hermit and founded a religious community. He died in 560.

Feast Dates: September 11 — St. Almirus.

Almire (variant) See Almira.

Aloisa (German) See Louise.

Aloisia (Spanish) See Louise.

Aloismal (Hispanic-American double) See Aloisia+Mal.

Aloma (Latin) See Paloma.

Alonza (English) See Alphonsa.

Aloysia (English) See Louise.

Alphonsa "The Noble Ready One" (Latin).

Patron Saints: There is no female saint named Alphonsa. However, there are three male saints and a half-dozen blesseds named Alphonsus. The best known is St. Alphonsus Mary Liguori, 1696-1787, a bishop and Doctor of the Church. He died at the age of ninety-one in Italy.

Feast Dates: August 1 — St. Alphonsus Liguori.

Alta "The Elevated Lofty One" (Latin).

Patron Saints: St. Alten is remembered as an "Irish saint."

Feast Dates: January 11 — St. Alten.

Altha (African-American) See Althea.

Althea "The Wholesome Healer" (Greek).

Patron Saints: St. Altheus served as the bishop of Sion in the eighth century. Jesus, as the "Miracle Worker and Healer," can also be drafted as patron.

Feast Dates: September 23 — St. Altheus; All Sundays — Jesus, Miracle Worker (see Marva).

Altheda (variant) See Althea.

Altovise (African-American double) See Alta+Visa.

Alura "The Divine Counselor" (Old English) or "The Attractive One" (Middle English).

Patron Saints: There is no St. Alura, but there are two Sts. Attracta. One lived in medieval Ireland. She founded a convent in Killaraght and is famous as the patron of the "Men of Lugna."

Feast Dates: August 11 — St. Attracta.

Alva "The Blond One" (Latin, Spanish).

Patron Saints: St. Alvera was a martyr in ancient Luxeuil.

Feast Dates: March 6 — St. Alvera.

Alverta (variant) See Alberta.

Alvina "The Friend to All" (Old English, Spanish).

Patron Saints: There is one known saint with this name. St. Alvenera was martyred in ancient France.

Feast Dates: March 6 — St. Alvenera.

Alvinia (variant) See Alvina.

Alvira (variant) See Elvira.

Alyce (variant) See Alice.

Alycia (variant) See Alice.

Alyna (variant) See Aileen, Alana.

Alyne (variant) See Aileen, Alana.

Alys (variant) See Alice.

Alyse (variant) See Alice.

Alysha (Hispanic-American) See Alice.

Alysia (variant) See Alice.

Alyson (English) See Allison.

Alyss (variant) See Alice.

Alyssa "The Sane One" (Greek, Spanish).

Patron Saints: Besides being a name in its own right, Alyssa can be a variant of Alice, Allison, Elyse, and Melissa. This makes many patrons available.

Feast Dates: June 15 — St. Alice (see Alice); June 1 — St. Melosa (see Melissa).

Alyx (variant) See Alexandra, Alexis.

Alzetta (African-American double) See any "Al" name+Zetta.

Ama (variant) See Aimee.

Amabel (Latin) See Mabel.

Amada (Spanish) See Aimee.

Amalea (variant) See Amelia, Emily.

Amalee (variant) See Amelia, Emily.

Amaleta (variant) See Amelia, Emily.

Amalia (Spanish, Italian, Polish, German, Dutch) See Amelia, Emily.

Amalie (German) See Amelia, Emily.

Amalija (Serbian, Bulgarian) See Amelia, Emily.

Amalita (Spanish) See Amelia, Emily.

Amanda "The One Worthy of Love" (Latin) or "The Adorable One" (Spanish).

Patron Saints: There are about two dozen ancient male saints named Sts. Amand and Amandus. St. Amand of France, 584-679, became a monk, and his father threatened to disinherit him unless he left the monastery. His cheerful reply to his father was, "Christ is my only inheritance." A little later he was ordained a priest and then was consecrated a missionary bishop for Flanders. When he heard how hostile the people of Ghent were toward preachers, he went to preach to them and was occasionally beaten and once he was thrown into the river. But in due time, large crowds of people came to him to be baptized.

Feast Dates: February 6 — St. Amand.

Amandi (variant) See Amanda.

Amandine (French) See Amanda.

Amandy (English) See Amanda.

Amara "The Glorious, Beautiful One" (Greek, Spanish).

Patron Saints: St. Amaranthus died a martyr in ancient Africa.

Feast Dates: November 8 — St. Amaranthus.

Amarilys (Hispanic-American) See Flora.

Amata (Spanish) See Amanda.

Amata (Italian, German, Swedish, Polish, Hungarian) See Aimee.

Amatia (Latin) See Aimee.

Amber "The Firelike Jewel" (Old French, Arabic) or "The Fierce Burning One" (Gaelic).

Patron Saints: There is no St. Amber. However, in the Bible the word "amber" leads to a multitude of angelic patrons called the seraphim. This, in turn, leads to St. Seraphina.

"Amber" is mentioned only in the Old Testament. It appears in a vision that God gave the prophet Ezekiel. "Then I looked, and behold, a whirlwind was coming out of the north, a great cloud with raging fire engulfing itself; and brightness was all around it and radiating out of its midst like the color of amber, out of the midst of the fire" (Ezekiel 1:4, *King James Version*; see also Ezekiel 1:27 and 8:2). The ancient Jews understood Amber to be "a fire-speaking being," which can lead to the highest order, or choir, of angels, the seraphim. The seraphim are the angels closest to God. They are angels of love, light, and fire (purity). It is their job to unceasingly praise God: "Holy, holy, holy is the Lord of hosts" (Isaiah 6:3).

Feast Dates: September 29 and October 2 — The Holy Seraphim; March 12 — St. Seraphina (see Seraphina).

Amberly (American) See Amber.

Amberlynne (American double) See Amber+Lynn.

Ambia (American) See Amber, Ambrosia.

Ambre (Old French) See Amber.

Ambrosia "The Sweet Nectar" (Greek) or "The Immortal One" (Greek).

Patron Saints: There are almost a dozen-and-a-half Sts. Ambrose. One of them was a teenage page in King Mwunga of Uganda's court. He converted to Catholicism in the fall of 1885. Soon, he and twenty-one other members of the king's court came under persecution because they opposed the king's homosexual advances. This led to their martyrdom. Ambrose was burned alive in 1886.

Feast Dates: June 3 — Bl. Ambrose Kibuka.

Ambur (variant) See Amber.

Amby (nickname) See Amber, Ambrosia.

Ame (variant) See Aimee.

Amee (variant) See Aimee, Ame, Amey.

Amelia "The One Who Flatters" (Italian, Portuguese) or "The Hardworking One" (form of Emily).

Patron Saints: There are about two dozen Sts. Amelia, Aemilia, Aemiliana, Emilian, Emiliana, and Emily. One St. Amelia gave her life at Gerona in order to remain faithful to the Catholic religion.

Feast Dates: May 31 — St. Amelia.

Amelija (Russian) See Amelia, Emily.

Amelina (English) See Amelia, Emily.

Ameline (English) See Amelia, Emily.

Amelita (Spanish double) See Amelia+Ita, Emily+Ita.

Amenda (Spanish variant) See Amanda.

America (Teutonic) See Amelia, Emily.

Amey (variant) See Aimee, Amelia, Emily.

Ami (variant) See Aimee.

Amia (Norwegian) See Aimee.

Amie (variant) See Aimee.

Amil (variant) See Aimee.

Amile (Hispanic-American) See Amelia.

Amilia (variant) See Amelia, Emily.

Ammy (Norwegian) See Aimee.

Amy (English) See Aimee, Amelia, Emily.

Amye (variant) See Aimee.

Ana (Spanish, Portuguese, English) See Ann, Anastasia.

Anabella (Spanish double) See Anna+Bella.

Anabelle (French double) See Anna+Belle.

Anahid (Hispanic-American double) See Anna+Hilda.

Anaias (Provençal) See Ann.

Anaka (African-American) See Ann.

Anastasia "The Resurrected One" (Greek).

Patron Saints: There are about a dozen Sts. Anastasia. One Anastasia is patron against poisoning and is mentioned in Eucharistic Prayer I. The daughter of a Roman nobleman, she married a pagan. When persecution of the Christians began, she went to the prisons to minister to those held there. Her husband, learning of this, forbade her to continue her work with the imprisoned. When he died, she continued her ministry and was arrested, put aboard a ship, and abandoned at sea. However, she survived and converted

28

to Christianity all the pagans on the ship. She was taken to the island of Palmaria with her converts. They were killed in 304.

Feast Dates: December 25 — St. Anastasia; Easter Sunday — The Risen Christ.

Anastasie (French) See Anastasia.

Andee (variant) See Andrea.

Andela (Czech, Croatian) See Angela, Angelica.

Anderea (variant) See Andrea.

Andi (nickname) See Andrea.

Andie (nickname) See Andrea.

Andona (variant) See Antonia.

Andra (variant) See Andrea.

Andrea "The Womanly One" (Latin) or "A Man's Woman" (Greek) or "Beautiful One" (Spanish).

Patron Saints: There are about two dozen Sts. Andrew. The greatest is St. Andrew the Apostle, who has been named patron of single women and women who wish to conceive. However, a lesser known Andrew is presented here. He is Andrew Chakichi, an eight-year-old Japanese boy who was beheaded with his father, mother, and brother in Japan in 1622. All are recognized as "blessed."

Feast Dates: October 2 — Bl. Andrew Chakichi; November 30 — St. Andrew, Apostle.

Andreana (variant) See Andrea.

Andreanna (French-Latin double) See Andrea, Ann.

Andree (French) See Andrea.

Andreina (Italian) See Andrea.

Andrel (variant) See Andrea.

Andresa (Latvian) See Andrea.

Andri (English) See Andrea.

Andria (English) See Andrea.

Andriana (English-Latin double) See Andrea, Ann.

Andrina (variant) See Andrea.

Andy (nickname) See Andrea.

Andzela (Latvian) See Angela, Angelica.

Ane (Danish) See Ann.

Aneesa (Arabic) See Mina.

Aneesha (African-American) See Aneesa.

Anele (Lithuanian) See Angela, Angelica.

Anelja (Ukrainian) See Angela, Angelica.

Anessa (Greek) See Agnes.

Anestassia (nickname) See Anastasia.

Anet (variant) See Ann.

Anete (variant) See Antonia.

Anett (English) See Ann.

Anette (variant) See Ann.

Anezka (Czech) See Agnes.

Ange (nickname) See Angela, Angelica.

Angee (nickname) See Angela, Angelica.

Angel (English) See Angela, Angelica.

Angela "The Swift Messenger" (Greek, Spanish).

Patron Saints: There are three known Sts. Angela and a half-dozen Sts. Angelina. To these must be added the uncountable angels. The pages of the Bible overflow with angels. These pure spirits guide human beings and they minister at God's throne. They can take on a human or animal form when appearing to people. Catholic tradition also suggests that there are nine choirs, or classes, of angels. The most important, for us, are the guardian angels, who have been assigned to us.

While actually superior to humanity, angels seem to have been given the job of serving mankind. This seems strange at first, but it really is not. For is not a teenager cared for by an adult? Is not a child cared for by both the teen and adult? And is not the baby served by the child, teen, and adult? In our world, the right ordering of things demands that the greater serve the lesser. Thus, "If any one would be first, he must be last of all and servant of all" (Mark 9:35).

Feast Dates: October 2 — The Holy Guardian Angels.

Angele (French) See Angela, Angelica.

Angelica "The Swift Messenger" (Greek, Spanish).

Patron Saints: There are about six Sts. Angelina, one St. Angelico, and one St. Angelica. The last is simply remembered as an Italian virgin and martyr.

Feast Dates: First Sunday of September — St. Angelica; October 2 — Guardian Angels (see Angela).

Angelika (German) See Angela, Angelica.

Angelina (Italian, Portuguese) See Angela, Angelica.

Angeline (French) See Angela, Angelica.

Angelique (French) See Angelica.

Angelita (Spanish double) See Angela+Ita.

Angelle (variant) See Angela, Angelica.

Angie (nickname) See Angela, Angelica.

Angil (variant) See Angela, Angelica.

Angy (nickname) See Angela, Angelica.

Ania (variant) See Ann.

Anica (Spanish) See Ann.

Anice (English) See Agnes.

Aniceta (variant) See Anisette.

Anicete (variant) See Anisette.

Anicetta (variant) See Anisette.

Anicette (variant) See Anisette.

Aniela (Polish) See Angela, Angelica.

Anika (African-American) See Ann.

Aniko (Hungarian) See Ann.

Anilla (Hungarian) See Ann.

Anisetta (variant) See Anisette.

Anisette "An Aromatic Herb+The Little One" (Middle English double).

Patron Saints: St. Anicetus and a few of his relatives died for the faith in ancient Nicomedia in 305.

Feast Dates: August 12 — St. Anicetus.

Anissa (variant) See Ann.

Anissa (African-American) See Aneesa, Anisette.

Anita (Spanish double) See Ann+Ita.

Anitra (variant) See Ann.

Anjanette (African-American double) See Ann+Janet.

Anjela (German) See Angela, Angelica.

Anjelica (German) See Angelica.

Anka (Croatian, Slovenian) See Ann.

Anke (German) See Ann.

Ann "The God-Graced One" (English form of Hannah).

Patron Saints: There are about two dozen Sts. Anne. The most famous is the mother of the Blessed Virgin. She is recognized as patron of grandmothers, mothers, housewives, housekeepers, women in labor, horsemen, cabinetmakers, Canada, and to find a good husband.

An ancient tradition insists that Anne married Joachim when she was about twenty years old and for the next twenty years was unable to conceive a child. Both Anne and Joachim were publicly embarrassed because they had no children. Therefore, Joachim prayed and fasted for forty days and Anne prayed. Then an angel appeared to Anne and told her that God had heard their prayers and that she would bear a child. The child would be called "blessed" throughout all time. Anne was so happy that she offered to give the child as a gift to God and God accepted. In time, Mary made them grandparents of the Son of God.

Feast Dates: July 26 — St. Anne.

Anna (Latin, Germanic, Slavic) See Ann.

Annabal (English double) See Anna+Belle.

Annabel (English double) See Anna+Belle.

Annabell (English double) See Anna+Belle.

Annabella (Italian double) See Anna+Bella.

Annabelle (variant double) See Anna+ Belle.

Annag (Scottish Gaelic) See Ann.

Annah (Dutch) See Ann.

Annamaria (Latin double) See Anna+ Maria.

Anne (English, French) See Ann.

Anneke (Dutch) See Ann.

Annelisa (English double) See Anne+ Lisa.

Annemarie (French double) See Anne+ Marie.

Annetta (English double) See Anne+Etta.

Annette (French double) See Anne+Ette.

Anni (nickname) See Ann.

Annice (English) See Agnes, Ann.

Annie (nickname) See Ann.

Annik (Breton) See Ann.

Annika (Danish, Swedish) See Ann.

Annikki (Finnish) See Ann.

Annina (Russian, Czech) See Ann.

Anninka (Russian, Czech) See Ann.

Annis (English) See Agnes, Ann.

Annora (English double) See Ann+Nora.

Annunciata "The Announcer" (Latin) or "The Bearer of News" (Latin).

> *Patron Saints:* The Blessed Virgin, under the title of the Annunciation, can be patron. The great teaching of this event is based on Mary's words of acceptance (see Luke 1:38). This reply witnesses to great faith and challenges us all to trust in God as we take each new step into the unknown of our lives.
> *Feast Dates:* March 25 — Annunciation of the Blessed Virgin.

Annunziata (Italian) See Annunciata.

Anny (nickname) See Ann.

Anora (variant) See Ann/Ann+Nora.

Anselma (variant) See Selena.

Anstey (Polish) See Anastasia.

Anstice (variant) See Anastasia.

Antalka (variant) See Antonia.

Antane (variant) See Antonia.

Antje (Frisian) See Ann.

Antoinette (French double) See Antonia+ Ette.

Antonetta (Swedish-Slavic double) See Antonia+Etta.

Antonia "The Priceless One" (Latin).

> *Patron Saints:* There are almost a dozen Sts. Antonia. St. Antonia of Florence married, bore a son, and became a widow. Then in 1429, when two Franciscan religious came to town to found a convent, she was the first to join them. Three years later she was made superior of the convent. From about 1430, she suffered a most painful disease, her spiritual life underwent severe trials, and her son created nothing but trouble for her. However, God granted her patience and humility, which helped her to endure the sufferings that came to her.
> *Feast Dates:* February 28 — St. Antonia of Florence.

Antonie (German) See Antonia.

Antonietta (Italian) See Antonia.

Antoniette (variant) See Antonia.

Antonina (Spanish) See Antonia.

Antuca (Spanish) See Antonia.

Antwanette (Arabic) See Antonia.

Antwonette (Arabic) See Antonia.

Anula (Polish) See Ann.

Anunciación (Spanish) See Annunciata.

Anusia (Polish) See Ann.

Anuska (Czech) See Ann.

Anya (Russian) See Ann.

Aparicia "The One Who Appears" (Spanish).

> *Patron Saints:* One North American saint, Bl. Sebastian de Aparicio, was born a peasant in Spain. At the age of thirty-one, he sailed to the recently discovered New World to make his fortune. In Mexico he worked as a field laborer, transported grain, and was hired by the government to build a road between Zacatecas and Mexico City.

He became very rich. However, he used his money to help the poor.

He also married — twice — and both wives died. After the death of his second wife, he gave all his possessions to the poor and to a convent of Poor Clare nuns. Then at the age of seventy-three he became a Franciscan brother. For the next twenty-five years he did menial tasks and collected alms for the poor.

Feast Dates: February 25 — Bl. Sebastian de Aparicio, O.F.M.

Aphra "This Is Dust" (Hebrew) or "Young Doe" (Hebrew).

Patron Saints: Because the name means "dust," one can adopt St. Eve, whom God made out of the dust of Adam. St. Aphraates might also be put to work. He lived in ancient Edessa in about 350. He was a convert who fled persecutions a few times. In time, he became a bishop and fought many heresies.

Feast Dates: April 7 — St. Aphraates; December 24 — Sts. Adam and Eve (see Eartha).

Aphrodite (Greek) See Aphra, Venus.

Apolline (variant) See Apollonia.

Apollonia "The Sunlight" (Greek) or "The Giver of Life" (Greek).

Patron Saints: There are at least two Sts. Apollonia. One was an aged, single deaconess in Alexandria. In about 249 she was attacked by a pagan mob, arrested, and tortured because she had allowed her home to be used as a refuge by Christians. Her teeth were slowly pulled out with pincers and she was threatened by fire. Eventually she was burned to death. She is now patron of dentists and against toothaches.

Feast Dates: February 9 — St. Apollonia.

Apriel (African-American) See April.

April "Born in April" (Latin) or "The One Open to New Life [The Sun]" (Latin).

Patron Saints: There are two Sts. April. Both died martyrs, one in Nicomedia, the other in Africa.

Feast Dates: March 18 and March 24 — both Sts. April.

Aprilette (English double) See April+Ette.

Apryl (American) See April.

Ara "The Altar" (Latin).

Patron Saints: St. Araba died a martyr in ancient Nicaea.

Feast Dates: March 13 — St. Araba.

Arabella (Latin double) See Ara+Bella.

Araceli (Hispanic-American double) See Aracelis.

Aracelis "The Altar+Of Heaven" (Hispanic-American double).

Patron Saints: Aracelis can be created out of the Latin words *ara* and *caelestis*.

Feast Dates: March 13 — St. Araba; June 22 — St. Thomas More of Chelsea.

Ard (nickname) See Ardella.

Arda (nickname) See Ardella.

Ardeen (English) See Ardella.

Ardelia (English) See Ardella.

Ardella "The Warm, Enthusiastic One" (Latin).

Patron Saints: One saint with a variant name, St. Ardo, served the Church as an abbot in France in 843.

Feast Dates: March 7 — St. Ardo.

Ardene (English) See Ardella.

Ardine (English) See Ardella.

Ardis (English) See Ardella.

Areta (Spanish) See Aretha.

Aretha "The Virtuous One" (Greek).

Patron Saints: There are two Sts. Arethas. One lived in about 340 when the Jewish king Dhu Nowas mounted a persecution against Christians. This led to the murder of Arethas, the governor of the Christian city of Nedshran in Arabia. About five hundred citizens died with him. Arethas was ninety-six years old.

Feast Dates: July 27 — St. Arethas.

Aretta (variant double) See Aretha+Etta.

Arette (French double) See Aretha+Ette.

Aria "The Song" (Latin).

Ariadne (variant) See Ariana.

Patron Saints: There is one St. Aria, who died a martyr in ancient Rome, and two Sts. Ariadne.

Feast Dates: August 21 — St. Aria.

Arian (variant) See Ariana.

Ariana "The Holy, Pleasing One" (Latin).

Patron Saints: There is no St. Ariana, but we can call on St. Arianell to be the patron. St. Arianell was the daughter of a man belonging to a royal family in Gwent, Wales. At some point in time, an evil spirit possessed her, and St. Dyfrig exorcised her. She then became a religious sister. St. Dyfrig served as her spiritual director.

Feast Dates: June 27 — St. Arianell.

Ariane (French) See Ariana.

Arianell (French) See Ariana, Ariel.

Arianie (variant) See Ariana.

Ariann (variant) See Ariana.

Arianne (variant) See Ariana.

Ariel "The Lion of God" (Hebrew).

Patron Saints: There is a St. Arialdus, and a St. Ariel can be found among the angels in the Bible. The Bible mentions an "Ariel" in the Book of Isaiah: "Look, Ariel is lamenting in the streets, the ambassadors of peace weep bitterly" (Isaiah 33:7, *Jerusalem Bible*). Some Jewish scholars insist that this refers to an angel. Both Jewish and Christian traditions report that Ariel is a member of the angelic choir of virtues. This choir looks after the day-to-day functioning of creation. Thus Ariel is sometimes said to rule the waters, be in charge of the winds, or assist Raphael in curing diseases.

Feast Dates: September 29 — The Holy Archangels; October 2 — The Holy Guardian Angels.

Ariela (variant) See Ariel.

Ariella (variant) See Ariel.

Arielle (variant) See Ariel.

Arizona "From the Place of Few Springs" (Spanish).

Patron Saints: One man has been named the "Apostle to Arizona." Born in 1645, Ven. Eusebio Kino grew up in northern Italy. In 1681, four years after he was ordained, he and a number of companions sailed for Mexico. At the age of thirty-eight, he went to southern California. A year later he went to Arizona. For the next thirty years he ministered to the Indians in that area. He taught them to farm, to care for cattle, and to read and write; he also instructed them in the Catholic faith and built churches. Moreover, he made forty exploratory expeditions into the Southwest and mapped the region. He died in 1711 while celebrating Mass.

Feast Dates: March 15 — Ven. Eusebio Kino, S.J.

Arlana (variant) See Arleen.

Arlee (nickname) See Arleen.

Arleen "A Pledge" (Irish Gaelic) or "The Noblewoman" (variant of Earlene).

Patron Saints: Arleen can be accepted as the female form of Arlen, and there is one St. Harlindis of Arland. Harlindis was the sister of St. Belindis. They were the daughters of Count Arland and became religious sisters who founded an abbey in Belgium. Harlindis became its first abbess. She also exchanged letters with St. Boniface and St. Willibrord for many years. She died in 745.

Feast Dates: March 22 — St. Harlindis of Arland.

Arlen (variant) See Arleen.

Arlena (English) See Arleen.

Arlene (Irish) See Arleen.
Arleta (English) See Arleen.
Arlette (French) See Arleen.
Arleyne (English) See Arleen.
Arlie (nickname) See Arleen.
Arliene (variant) See Arleen.
Arlina (variant) See Arleen.
Arlinda (American double) See Arleen+Linda.
Arline (English) See Arleen.
Arluene (variant) See Arleen.
Arly (nickname) See Arleen.
Arlyn (English) See Arleen.
Arlyne (English) See Arleen.
Armanda (American double) See Arleen+Amanda.
Arnita (American double) See Arleen+Anita.
Artisha (African-American double) See Arleen+Leticia/Isha.
Aryka (variant) See Erica.
Aryn (variant) See Erin.
Asha (variant) See Aisha.
Ashely (English) See Ashley.
Ashia (variant) See Aisha.
Ashla (English) See Ashley.
Ashlan (English) See Ashley.
Ashlea (English) See Ashley.
Ashlee (English) See Ashley.
Ashleigh (English) See Ashley.
Ashlen (English) See Ashley.
Ashley "From Ash Tree+Meadow" (Old English double).

Patron Saints: The only saint named Ashley is an English male martyr. In 1606 Bl. Edward Oldcorne was discovered in a "priest hole," a hiding place in English Catholic homes, and was arrested. Ralph Ashley, a Jesuit lay brother, who acted as his servant, was also arrested. Both were tried and convicted of treason. They were later hanged, drawn, and quartered.

Feast Dates: April 7 — Bl. Ralph Ashley, S.J.

Ashli (English) See Ashley.
Ashlie (English) See Ashley.
Ashly (English) See Ashley.
Asia "From the East" (Greek).

Patron Saints: Some think Asia means "east." Others think it is a nickname for Anastasia and Athanasia. Still others insist it is an Arabic form of *aisha*, meaning "alive and well." This leads to St. Asja, who served God in ancient Syria as a layman, hermit, physician, ascetic, and disciple of St. Mark.

Feast Dates: October 15 — St. Asja; August 14 — St. Athanasia of Timia (see Athanasia).

Asja (English) See Asia.
Aslin See Asia+Lynn, Astera+Lynn (Hispanic-American double).
Assumpta "The One Taken to Heaven" (Latin).

Patron Saints: There is a missionary to China, Bl. Mary Assunta Pallotta, F.M.M., 1878-1905, who can serve as a patron. However, we should not overlook the greatest patron of them all. On November 1, 1950, Pope Pius XII declared that "the Immaculate Virgin, preserved free from all stain of original sin, was taken up body and soul into heavenly glory, when her earthly life was over, and exalted by the Lord as 'queen over all things.' " The primary foundation for this is found in the faith of the people who have consistently embraced this teaching since the most ancient times. The Holy Spirit can move the Church to truth not only from the top down but also from the bottom up.

Feast Dates: August 15 — Assumption of the Blessed Virgin.

Assunta (variant) See Assumpta.
Asta (English) See Astera.
Astera "The Star" (Greek).

Patron Saints: There is one St. Asteria and a dozen Sts. Asterius. This St. Asteria was a citizen of ancient Bergamo. She refused to sacrifice to Jupiter and was beheaded in about 305. Two more great patrons are still available. They are Jesus the Morning Star and his mother.

Feast Dates: August 10 — St. Asteria; All Saturdays — The Blessed Virgin Mary, Star of the Sea (see Star).

Asteria (English) See Astera.

Astra (English) See Astera.

Astra (Spanish) See Star.

Astraea (English) See Astera.

Astrea (English) See Astera.

Astrid "The One with Divine Strength" (Old Norse) or "The One Strong in Love" (Norse).

Patron Saints: St. Astricus was a holy archbishop in Bohemia who died in 1007.

Feast Dates: November 12 — St. Astricus.

Astrud (English) See Astrid.

Astryr (English) See Astrid.

Asya (African-American) See Asia.

Athana (English) See Athanasia, Athena.

Athanasia "The Wise One" (Greek).

Patron Saints: There are a half-dozen Sts. Athanasia. One of them, St. Athanasia of Timia, lost her husband just seventeen days after her wedding. He was killed defending his country against an Arabic invasion. She was soon forced to marry again, but she and her second husband mutually agreed to enter religious life. She built a nunnery at Timia and prayed much. Her advice was much sought after by people of all social classes. She died in 860.

Feast Dates: August 14 — St. Athanasia of Timia.

Athena "The Wise One" (Greek) or "The Wise One" (short form of Athanasia).

Patron Saints: St. Athena is remembered as an "Irish virgin."

Feast Dates: February 26 — St. Athena; August 14 — St. Athanasia (see Athanasia).

Athina (English) See Athanasia, Athena.

Auberta (English, French) See Alberta.

Aubina (variant) See Albina.

Aubine (French) See Albina.

Aubree (variant) See Aubrey.

Aubrette (variant) See Aubrey.

Aubrey "The Elf Ruler" (Old French) or "The Noble Bearlike One" (German).

Patron Saints: Alberik is the Swedish form of Aubrey, and there are about a dozen Sts. Alberic. One was a bishop in ancient Asia Minor. During a persecution by Emperor Maximilian, he refused to offer sacrifice to the pagan god Juno and was burned alive with some of his followers.

Feast Dates: May 4 — St. Aubrey, also known as Alberic.

Aubriana (English double) See Aubrey+Ana.

Aubrie (variant) See Aubrey.

Aubry (variant) See Aubrey.

Audey (English) See Audrey.

Audi (variant) See Audrey.

Audie (variant) See Audrey.

Audra (French) See Audrey.

Audreanne (English double) See Audrey+Anne.

Audree (English) See Audrey.

Audrey "The Noble Strong One" (Old English).

Patron Saints: There is one St. Audrey. She married, but in three short years her husband died and she retired to the Isle of Ely. For the next five years she prayed and led a secluded life. Then she was asked to enter a political marriage with a boy. When the boy grew up, he demanded a sexual relationship. Audrey refused, entered a convent, and did penance. She died in about 679. She is patron against neck and throat injuries.

Feast Dates: June 23 — St. Audrey of Ely.

Audrie (variant) See Audrey.

Audry (variant) See Audrey.

Audrye (variant) See Audrey.

Augusta "The Majestic One" (Latin).

Patron Saints: There are about six Sts. Augusta. One of them converted to Catholicism while still a teenager. She was soon put in jail and her father had her beheaded.

Feast Dates: August 22 — St. Augusta.

Auguste (German, Estonian) See Augusta.

Augustina (English feminine form of Augustine) See Augusta, Austin.

Auli (Estonian) See Aurelia.

Aundrea (Greek) See Andrea.

Auno (Finnish) See Agnes.

Aura (variant) See Aurelia.

Aurea (variant) See Aurelia.

Aurel (variant) See Aurelia.

Aureleaa (variant) See Aurelia.

Aurelia "The Golden One" (Latin).

Patron Saints: There are about a dozen Sts. Aurelia. One lived in about 1050. She and a female friend made a pilgrimage to the Holy Land and then went to Rome. While in Capua, the Saracens (Muslims) captured the city and persecuted the Christians. Both women suffered much; but, in time, they moved to Anagni and led solitary lives devoted to prayer.

Feast Dates: September 25 — St. Aurelia.

Aurelie (French) See Aurelia.

Aurelle (variant) See Aurelia.

Aurellia (variant) See Aurelia.

Auria (variant) See Aurelia.

Aurica (Romanian) See Aurelia.

Aurie (variant) See Aurelia.

Aurilla (variant) See Aurelia.

Aurora "The Dawn, Sunrise" (Latin, Spanish) or "The Golden One" (variant form of Aurelia).

Patron Saints: The fact that Aurora means "dawn" leads to patrons. For example, Oriana also means "dawn," and this leads to Rori, which is a short form of Aurora, Oriana, or Roricius. There is a St. Roricius.

Feast Dates: July 21 — St. Roricius (see Oriana).

Aurore (French) See Aurora, Zona.

Austen (French) See Augusta, Augustina, Austin.

Austin "The Majestic Little One" (English short form of Augusta, Augustina).

Patron Saints: It is helpful to know that Austin is a modern form of Augustine or Augusta. There are about six Sts. Augusta and many more Sts. Augustine.

Feast Dates: October 22 — St. Augusta (see Augusta).

Austina (English) See Augusta, Augustina, Austin.

Austine (Latin) See Augusta, Augustina, Austin.

Auston (English) See Augusta, Augustina, Austin.

Austyn (English) See Augusta, Augustina, Austin.

Autum (variant) See Autumn.

Autumn "The Fall Season" (Latin).

Patron Saints: Autumn is the time for vegetation's glorious color and death. It seems that the act of dying reveals the hidden qualities of life. This helps discover the poor souls in purgatory as patrons. The Old Testament warns us that "at the close of a man's life his deeds will be revealed" (Sirach 11:27). The Bible adds that death is followed by judgment leading to punishment or reward. Jesus tells us: "As you go with your accuser before the magistrate, make an effort to settle with him on the way, lest he drag you to the judge, and the judge hand you over to the officer, and the officer put you in prison. I tell you, you will never get out till you have paid the very last copper" (Luke 12:58-59).

Jesus is talking about facing judgment beyond life. Since heaven is not jail and hell is a prison with no release, he must be talking about purgatory. The Old Testament tells us we can help the poor souls pay this "last copper" through prayer and sacrifice: "Therefore he made atonement for the dead, that they might be delivered from their sin" (2 Maccabees 12:45).

Feast Dates: November 2 — The Poor Souls in Purgatory.

Ava "The Happy Greeting" (Old German).

Patron Saints: Besides being a name in its own right, Ava is also an Irish form of Eve and a variant of Avis. St. Ava is remembered for being one of the companions of St. Ursula. However, she was the only one to escape death near Cologne. But she did not escape severe torture, maiming by lions, starvation, mutilation, and imprisonment. She is patron of children learning to walk.

Feast Dates: May 6 — St. Ava.

Avan (variant) See Ava.

Ave (Latin) See Ava.

Aveline (Irish) See Eve, Evelyn, Hazel.

Avelyne (variant) See Evelyn.

Aven (variant) See Ava.

Averi (variant) See April, Avery.

Averil (variant) See April, Avery.

Avery "Born in April" (Middle English for April).

Patron Saints: Some think that Avery is an alternate form of Alfreda, April, Aubrey, Audrey, or Everard.

These leads to about a dozen patrons. One of them is Father Everard Hanse, who was born and raised Protestant in England and became a popular Anglican preacher. However, after suffering a serious illness, he joined the Catholic Church, traveled to France, and was ordained. One month later he returned to England and was almost immediately thrown into prison. He was treated very cruelly because he had turned against his Anglican heritage. In 1581 he was hanged, drawn, and quartered as required by law.

Feast Dates: July 30 — Bl. Everard Hanse; March 18 and 24 — both Sts. April (see April).

Averyl (variant) See April, Avery.

Avgusta (Russian) See Augusta.

Avis (Latin) See Bird.

Aviva "The Youthful, Live-Giving One" (Hebrew).

Patron Saints: Vita means "life" and is the Latin word for Aviva. There are about a dozen Sts. Avitus. One was a martyr in Africa in ancient times.

Feast Dates: January 22 — St. Avitus; June 15 — St. Vitus (see Vita).

Avon (variant) See Ava.

Avrey (variant) See Ava, Avery.

Avril (variant) See April, Avery.

Ayan (Somali) See Dawn.

Ayania (African-American) See Ayan, Dawn.

Ayanna (African-American) See Ayan, Dawn.

Ayannia (African-American) See Ayan, Dawn.

Ayeisha (African-American) See Aisha.

Ayesha (African-American) See Aisha.

Ayiesha (African-American) See Aisha.

Ayisha (African-American) See Aisha.

Aysha (African-American) See Aisha.

Azania Meaning unknown (South African).

Patron Saints: There are a half-dozen Sts. Aza. One of them died a martyr in ancient Persia.

Feast Dates: April 10 — St. Aza.

Azie (African-American) See Aziza.

Azisa (African-American) See Aziza.

Aziza "The Precious, Beautiful One" (Swahili) or "The Dignified One" (Arabic).

Patron Saints: St. Azi was known as a "Wonderworker" because of the miracles he worked in Roman times. After he converted, he quit soldiering and became a hermit in the desert. He was beheaded for converting.

Feast Dates: November 19 — St. Azi; August 8 — Bl. Jane of Aza (see Jane).

B

Bab (nickname) See Barbara.
Babara (variant) See Barbara.
Babb (nickname) See Barbara.
Babbie (variant) See Barbara, Elizabeth.
Babe (American) See Barbara.
Babette (French-English double) See Barbara+Ette.
Babita (Spanish double) See Barbara+Ita.
Babs (nickname) See Barbara.
Bahaki (African-American) See Bahati.
Bahati (East African) See Lucky.
Bahiyah (Arabic) See Joy.
Bailey "From the Wood Clearing" (Old English) or "Where Berries Grow" (Old English) or "The Porter" (Old English) or "From Outside the Castle Wall" (Middle English) or "The Bailiff" (Old English).

Patron Saints: There is one ancient St. Balay, who was a hermit at Ploermellac in Brittany. Also available is one modern North American: St. Elizabeth Bayley Seton, 1774-1821. She was born into a wealthy Episcopal family in New York City. Shortly before she turned twenty, she married William Seton, who was wealthy, and they raised a large family. William's business ventures took a downturn and, soon after, his health began to decline. So in 1803 Elizabeth, William, and their eldest daughter traveled to Italy, hoping that the mild weather there would cure what ailed him, but he soon died. Elizabeth was helped through this difficult time by the Filicchis, the Catholic Italian family with whom they stayed. And she was so impressed by their faith that she eventually converted to Catholicism. The Real Presence in the Eucharist was the biggest attraction for her.

Returning to New York, she found distrust among her Protestant friends and relatives after she was baptized Catholic in 1805. Not long after opening a girls' school in Baltimore, she founded the Sisters of St. Joseph, of which she was named superior by Archbishop John Carroll. A year later, in 1810, at Emmitsburg, Maryland, Mother Seton opened a free school for poor children, the beginning of the Catholic parochial school system.

She contracted tuberculosis and died in 1821, just short of her forty-seventh birthday.

Feast Dates: July 12 — St. Balay; January 4 — St. Elizabeth Bayley Seton.

Bailie (Scottish, English) See Bailey.
Baillie (Scottish, English) See Bailey.
Baily (Scottish, English) See Bailey.
Bairbre (Irish) See Barbara.
Balenda (African-American) See Belinda.
Bambi "The Little Baby" (Italian).

Patron Saints: The newly born Christ Child makes the perfect patron.

Feast Dates: December 25 — The Birth of Jesus Christ.

Baptista "The Baptizer" (Latin).

Patron Saints: John the Baptizer, 4 B.C.-A.D. 30, was born of elderly parents three months before Jesus.

Ancient tradition tells us that Zachary, John's father, was murdered by King Herod's soldiers while officiating at the altar during the massacre of the Holy Innocents. Zachary died because he would not reveal where he had hidden his son. Elizabeth, his mother, died of old age when John was only seven years old and John became an orphan. It is said that he was cared for in the desert by God and his angels.

Feast Dates: June 24 — The Birth of John the Baptizer.

Baptiste (French) See Baptista.

Barabal (Scottish Gaelic) See Barbara.

Barb (nickname) See Barbara.

Barbara "The Stranger [or Foreigner]" (Latin, Spanish).

Patron Saints: There are a couple of Sts. Barbara. The most famous is the teen convert who died a martyr's death in about 300. She was the beautiful daughter of a pagan man, and marriage proposals piled up. Her father wished her to marry, but she refused and an argument followed.

She insisted that she would give herself only to Jesus. Then her father accused her of the "crime" of being a Christian before a judge, and the judge ordered her beaten and tortured and killed. Her father then secured her release and, still in a rage, took her up a high mountain and killed her. She was a most popular saint in medieval times and was made patron of architects, builders, brass workers, miners, stoneworkers, ammunition workers, artillerymen, gunners, prisoners, the impenitent, fortifications, and warehouses. She is also patron for protection from lightning, thunder, storms, fire, accidents, and sudden death.

Feast Dates: December 4 — St. Barbara; August 9 — Ven. Marianne (Barbara) Cope, O.S.F.

Barbe (French) See Barbara.

Barbee (variant) See Barbara.

Barbel (German) See Barbara.

Barbette (English) See Barbara.

Barbey (variant) See Barbara.

Barbi (variant) See Barbara.

Barbie (variant) See Barbara.

Barbora (Czech) See Barbara.

Barbra (English) See Barbara.

Barbro (Swedish) See Barbara.

Barby (variant) See Barbara.

Barica (Slovakian) See Barbara.

Baruska (Czech) See Barbara.

Basha (Polish) See Barbara.

Basia (Polish) See Barbara.

Basilia (Spanish) See Basil.

Batista (Italian) See Baptista.

Bautista (Spanish) See Baptista.

Baylay (variant) See Bailey.

Bayley (variant) See Bailey.

Bea "The One Who Makes Others Happy" (English short form of Beatrice).

Patron Saints: There are a half-dozen Sts. Beatrice and a few Sts. Bee. One St. Bee was a beautiful Irish princess who gave herself to Christ from childhood. Reaching adulthood, she was told she had to marry. Not wishing to do so, she slipped out of the castle and sailed to a foreign land while everyone was occupied with the revelry in progress. Eventually she became the abbess of Egremont. She is remembered as patron of laborers.

Feast Dates: September 6 — St. Bee; September 1 — St. Beatrice da Silva Meneses (see Beatrice).

Beah (African-American) See Bea.

Bearnard (variant) See Bernadine.

Beata "The Blessed Happy One" (Latin, Spanish).

Patron Saints: There are a few Sts. Beata. One lived in ancient times. She and her brother, St. Sanctianus, with some other Christians, were beheaded in Spain by order of Emperor Aurelian.

Feast Dates: September 6 — St. Beata.

Beathag (Scottish) See Sophie.

Beatrica (variant) See Beatrice.

Beatrice "One Who Makes Others Happy" (French).

Patron Saints: There are a half-dozen Sts. Beatrice. The most recent is St. Beatrice da Silva Meneses, born in Portugal in 1424 and was raised in the home of Princess Isabel. As a young adult, she was a servant to Isabel, who was now a queen, having married King John II of Castile, Spain. But Queen Isabel, who was very jealous, was also prone to listening to gossip. Hearing false reports about the beautiful Beatrice, she had her thrown into prison for three days and starved. This made a deep impression on Beatrice. Upon her release, she left the royal court and entered a Cistercian convent in Toledo, Spain. Later she founded her own religious order, whose first house was a gift of a repentant Queen Isabel. St. Beatrice died in 1490 at the age of sixty-six.

Feast Dates: September 1 — St. Beatrice da Silva Meneses.

Beatrisa (variant) See Beatrice.

Beatrix (German) See Beatrice.

Beatriz (Spanish) See Beatrice.

Beatryks (variant) See Beatrice.

Beattie (variant) See Beatrice.

Bebe (Spanish) See Bibi, Beatrice.

Becca (English) See Rebecca.

Becki (English) See Rebecca.

Beckie (English) See Rebecca.

Becky (English) See Rebecca.

Bee (nickname) See Bea, Beatrice.

Begga (variant) See Bea.

Begonia "The Flower" (Spanish).

Patron Saints: Two of the many saints who qualify are St. Flora and Bl. Richard Flower.

Feast Dates: November 24 — St. Flora; May 4 — Bl. Richard Flower (see Lotus).

Beitris (Scottish) See Beatrice.

Beki (variant) See Rebecca.

Bekie (variant) See Rebecca.

Bekkee (variant) See Rebecca.

Bekki (variant) See Rebecca.

Bekkie (variant) See Rebecca.

Bel (variant) See Belinda, Belle, Isabel.

Belanca (variant) See Bianca, Blanche.

Belicia (Spanish) See Belle.

Belinda "Beautiful+Pretty One" (Spanish double) or "A Bear+Linden Wood Shield" (German double).

Patron Saints: Although no saints are named Belinda, there are three Sts. Belina, one St. Berlindis, and a few Sts. Isabel from which to choose. St. Belina was born of peasant parents at Landreville in France. She tended sheep. One day in 1135 the local feudal lord made sexual advances toward her. She refused him and he killed her.

Feast Dates: February 19 — St. Belina; February 3 — St. Berlindis (see Linda).

Belissa (variant double) See Belle+Isa.

Belita (Spanish double) See Elizabeth/Isobel+Ita.

Bell (English) See Belinda, Belle, Isabel.

Bella (Italian, Latin, Spanish) See Belinda, Belle, Isabel.

Bellah (African-American) See Belinda, Belle.

Bellanca (variant) See Bianca, Blanche.

Belle "The Beautiful One" (French) or "Consecrated to God" (Spanish form of Isabel through Elizabeth).

Patron Saints: Belle can be a short form of Isabel, and there are a half-dozen Sts. Isabel.

Feast Dates: September 10 — Bl. Isabel Fernandez (see Isabel).

Bellina (variant) See Belle.

Belva (variant) See Belle.

Belvia (variant) See Belle.

Benedetta (Italian) See Benedicta.

Benedicta "Blessed and Blessing One" (Latin, Spanish).

Patron Saints: There are about a dozen Sts. Benedicta. One of them was an unmarried teenager, the daughter of St. Aufrid and Bl. Hilsindis. She helped her mother found a convent in Thorn in the eleventh century.

Feast Dates: May 3 — St. Benedicta; September 6 — St. Beata (see Beata).

Benedikta (German) See Benedicta.

Benicia (Spanish) See Benedicta.

Benita (Spanish double) See Benedicta+ Ita.

Bennie (nickname) See Benedicta.

Benny (variant) See Benedicta.

Benoite (French) See Benedicta.

Beonca (variant) See Bianca.

Beoncha (variant) See Bianca.

Beonka (variant) See Bianca.

Berdella (nickname) See Bird.

Berdie (nickname) See Alberta, Bertha, Bird.

Berdy (nickname) See Alberta.

Berenice (variant) See Bernice.

Berenika (Czech) See Bernice.

Berenike (German) See Bernice.

Beret (variant) See Brigid.

Berget (Dutch) See Brigid.

Bergetta (Dutch double) See Brigid+Etta.

Bergette (French-German double) See Brigid+Ette.

Berit (Scandinavian) See Brigid.

Berlinda (variant) See Belinda.

Berlynn (English double) See Bertha+ Lynn.

Bern (nickname) See Bernadette, Bernadine, Bernice.

Berna (variant) See Bernadette, Bernadine, Bernice.

Bernadette "Brave as a Bear+Little One" (French double).

Patron Saints: There is only one St. Bernadette. She is Marie Bernarde Soubirous, born in Lourdes, France, on January 7, 1844. Nicknamed "Bernadette," she survived the cholera epidemic of 1854 but was frail most of her life, suffering from asthma and eventually tuberculosis. Having received no education, she was not thought to be very bright but was known to be exceptionally kind and obedient.

It was in these poor circumstances that the Blessed Virgin Mary found Bernadette on February 11, 1858. Bernadette, only fourteen years old, was collecting firewood on the banks of the Gave River near Lourdes. She looked up and saw Mary in a cave above. She reported her experience and was laughed at.

However, some people believed her. From that day in February through March 4 she experienced daily visions, and the crowds accompanying her grew. On February 25 a spring began to flow where none had been before. On March 25 the Blessed Virgin asked that a chapel be built on the site and identified herself as the "Immaculate Conception." This doctrine had only been officially declared in 1854 and Bernadette had never heard of it.

In 1866 Bernadette became a religious sister, but her poor health continued and she died at the age of thirty-five.

Feast Dates: April 16 — St. Bernadette Soubirous of Lourdes.

Bernadine "The One Who Is Brave as a Bear" (French).

Patron Saints: There are about a half-dozen Sts. Bernardine, all male. The best remembered is St. Bernardine of Siena, the son of the governor of Massa Marittima, Italy, orphaned when seven years old.

He joined the Franciscans and, at twenty-three, he became a priest. By his thirty-seventh year he had became well known for his long, fiery, and eloquent sermons. He traveled all over Italy preaching missions and denouncing gambling. When asked to become a bishop on three different occasions, he refused. He felt that this would keep him from reaching souls.

The last two years of his life he devoted to his favorite occupation — preaching missions. He did this even though he was emaciated. He is recognized as patron of those addicted to compulsive and uncontrolled gambling.

Feast Dates: May 20 — St. Bernardine of Siena.

Bernarda (Italian) See Bernadette, Bernadine.

Bernardene (English) See Bernadette, Bernadine.

Bernardette (Italian) See Bernadette.

Bernardina (Italian, Spanish) See Bernadine.

Berne (nickname) See Bernice.

Berneen (Irish) See Bernadette, Bernadine.

Bernelle (variant) See Bernice.

Bernetta (German, Norwegian) See Bernice, Bernadette, Bernadine.

Bernette (variant) See Bernice.

Bernharda (German, Norwegian) See Bernadette, Bernadine.

Berni (nickname) See Bernice. Bernadette, Bernadine.

Bernice "The Bringer of Victory" (Greek).

Patron Saints: There are almost a half-dozen Sts. Bernice. One of them was a citizen in ancient Antioch. She led a group of fifty-nine Christians to martyrdom. The most popular St. Bernice is also known as St. Veronica.

Feast Dates: October 19 — St. Bernice of Antioch; July 12 — St. Bernice, also known as Veronica (see Veronica).

Bernie (nickname) See Bernice, Bernadette, Bernadine.

Bernike (Latvian) See Bernice.

Bernita (Modern Greek, English) See Bernadette, Bernadine.

Berny (nickname) See Bernice, Bernadette, Bernadine.

Berri (nickname) See Beryl.

Berrie (nickname) See Beryl.

Berry (nickname) See Beryl.

Bert (variant) See Alberta, Bertha, Gilbertine.

Berta (German, Italian, Slavic, Spanish) See Alberta, Bertha, Gilbertine, Roberta, Robin.

Berte (nickname) See Alberta, Bertha, Gilbertine.

Bertha "The Shining, Glorious One" (Old German).

Patron Saints: There are almost a half-dozen Sts. Bertha. Among the better known is St. Bertha of Lorraine, a noblewoman who married a pagan man and bore one son. Her husband died in battle when her child was still an infant. She raised him according to Catholic teachings and taught him to have special concern for the poor. Together, mother and son built a convent. The son died at the age of twenty. St. Bertha lived for twenty-five more years, until 840, widowed and childless, dedicated to prayer and the poor.

Feast Dates: May 15 — St. Bertha.

Berthe (French) See Bertha.

Berthena (African-American double) See Bertha+Athena.

Berti (nickname) See Berty.

Bertice (nickname) See Berty.

Bertie (nickname) See Berty.

Bertille (variant) See Bertha.

Bertina (German) See Bertha.

Bertine (nickname) See Bertha.

Berty (nickname) See Alberta, Bertha, Gilbertine, Roberta.

Beryl "The Sea-Green Jewel" (Greek).

Patron Saints: There is one St. Beryl of Antioch. He heard St. Peter preaching and converted. In the year 44 St. Peter consecrated him a bishop. He served as the first bishop of Catania.

Also note that, according to ancient superstition, beryl was thought to afford victory and protection to those involved in sports, law courts, and on the battlefield. In the Bible the gemstone beryl is mentioned in reference to three different things: the Jewish high priest's breastplate, the earth in the Garden of Eden, and the walls of heavenly Jerusalem. Thus it symbolically represents all saints.

Feast Dates: March 21 — St. Beryl; November 1 — All Saints.

Beryle (variant) See Beryl.

Bess (nickname) See Bessie, Elizabeth.

Besse (Norwegian) See Elizabeth.

Bessia (variant) See Bessie.

Bessie "The One Consecrated to God" (Old English form of Elizabeth).

Patron Saints: There are two saints whose names probably inspired the name Bess or Bessie. Both died martyr's deaths in ancient times. The first, St. Bessa, was probably black and was executed in Africa. The other, St. Bessia, was killed near Laodicea. And, because Bess is a familiar form of Elizabeth, someone named Bess can also turn to two dozen Sts. Elizabeth.

Feast Dates: December 18 — St. Bessa; July 27 — St. Bessia; January 4 — St. Elizabeth Bayley Seton (see Bailey).

Bessy (variant) See Bessie, Elizabeth.

Bet (variant) See Bessie, Bethany, Bethia, Elizabeth.

Beth (nickname) See Bethany, Bethia, Elizabeth.

Bethany "From the House of Sorrow" (Hebrew) or "From the House of Poverty" (Hebrew).

Patron Saints: There are three saints mentioned in the New Testament who bear the name of Bethany. The Gospel writer relates: "Now a certain man was ill, Lazarus of Bethany, the village of Mary and her sister Martha" (John 11:1). Lazarus, Mary, and Martha were among Jesus' best friends. Thus when Lazarus died, "Jesus wept" (John 11:35). Jesus probably met them while having dinner at the home of Simon the Leper in Bethany. "It was Mary who anointed the Lord with ointment and wiped his feet with her hair, whose brother Lazarus was ill" (John 11:2).

According to ancient legend, after the ascension of Jesus, these three — Mary, Martha, and Lazarus — were put in a leaky, rudderless, oarless boat and set adrift by Jewish enemies. They wanted to remove all evidence of Jesus' power on earth. However, these sisters and brother survived the ordeal and eventually traveled to France and worked as missionaries. Lazarus worked there as a bishop for almost thirty years.

Feast Dates: July 29 — St. Martha (see Martha); July 22 — St. Mary Magdalen; July 29 — St. Lazarus.

Bethena (variant) See Bethany, Bethia.

Bethia "From the House of God" (Hebrew).

Patron Saints: One person, St. Bethlin, can be adopted. A religious bishop, he lived in the eighth century and is remembered for his prayerfulness. Any of a number of Sts. Elizabeth can also be adopted.

Feast Dates: September 9 — St. Bethlin; January 4 — St. Elizabeth Bayley Seton (see Bailey).

Bethina (variant) See Bethany, Bethia.
Betina (Spanish) See Betty.
Betrys (variant) See Beatrice.
Betse (variant) See Betty, Elizabeth.
Betsey (variant) See Betty, Elizabeth.
Betsi (variant) See Betty, Elizabeth.
Betsy (variant) See Betty, Elizabeth.
Bett (variant) See Betty, Elizabeth.
Betta (nickname) See Elizabeth.
Bette (nickname) See Elizabeth.
Betti (variant) See Betty, Elizabeth.
Bettie (variant) See Betty, Elizabeth.
Bettina (American double) See Benedicta/Beth+Tina.
Bettine (variant) See Elizabeth.
Bettsy (variant) See Betty, Elizabeth.
Betty "The One Consecrated to God" (English form of Elizabeth).
  Patron Saints: Two saints are available. One is St. Betse, a French priest. The other is St. Bettelin, also known as St. Bethlin. He was a hermit bishop and lived in the 700s in Mercia. Also, Betty is an accepted familiar form of Elizabeth, and this makes about two dozen Sts. Elizabeth available.
  Feast Dates: April 22 — St. Betse; September 9 — St. Bettelin (see Bethia); January 4 — St. Elizabeth Bayley Seton (see Bailey).
Bev (nickname) See Beverly.
Beverle (variant) See Beverly.
Beverlee (variant) See Beverly.
Beverley (variant) See Beverly.
Beverlie (variant) See Beverly.
Beverly "From the Beaver+Meadow" (Old English double).
  Patron Saints: St. John of Beverly was born in Yorkshire, England. He studied at the school of St. Theodore in Kent. Then he entered a monastery as a monk and soon became bishop of Hexham in 687. While he was a great administrator, he also made time for prayer and ministering to the poor.

Later, in 705, he became the bishop of York. He was known for his sanctity and miracles performed. By 717 he was worn out and resigned his bishopric and retired to Beverly. During the last four years of his life, he performed simple monastic duties. He died there on May 7, 721, at the age of fifty-five.
  Feast Dates: May 7 — St. John of Beverly; August 30 — Bl. Leigh.
Bevvy (variant) See Beverly.
Bianca "The Fair White [or Blond] One" (Italian).
  Patron Saints: This name leads to Bl. Blanca, 1249-1309. She and her husband were citizens of Siena. They chose to live a marriage without sexual relations in order to honor God. After her husband died, Blanca joined a Third Order and devoted herself to serving the poor and doing penance. She died at the age of sixty.
  Also remember that Blanche, Bianca, and Gwen all mean "white." There are about a dozen female Sts. Gwen as well as an English martyr named Eustace White.
  Feast Dates: April 26 — Bl. Blanca.
Bianka (Italian) See Bianca.
Bibi "The Lady of the House" (Arabic) or "Lively One" (variant short form of Bibiana).
  Patron Saints: Besides being an Arabic name in its own right, Bebe is a familiar form of Beatrice and Vivian.
  Feast Dates: August 16 — Bl. Beatrice (see Beatrice); March 15 — St. Lady (see Lady).
Bibiana (Spanish) See Vivian.
Bice (variant) See Beatrice.
Biddie (variant) See Brigid.
Biddy (variant) See Bianca, Brigid.
Bijou (Old French) See Jewel.
Bill (variant) See Belle, Billie, Wilhelmina.

Billi (variant) See Belle, Billie, Wilhelmina.

Billie "The Resolute Protector" (English form of Wilhelmina) or "The Beautiful One" (English form of Belle).

Patron Saints: Billie is a form of Wilhelmina (Vilhelmina), which is the feminine form of William. There are no Sts. Wilhelmina. But there are over fifty Sts. William from which to choose, and there is a St. Bilhildis, who can serve as a patron. She was the wife of the pagan duke of Thuringia, who was killed in battle. After his death, she entered a convent. Later, she founded a monastery and became its first abbess. She died in 660 at about thirty years of age.

Feast Dates: November 27 — St. Bilhildis; February 29 (28) — Bl. Villana de' Botti (see Wilhelmina).

Billiejean (American double) See Billie+Jean.

Billiejo (American double) See Billie+Jo.

Billy (variant) See Belle, Billie, Wilhelmina.

Bina (nickname) See Sabina.

Binni (variant) See Belinda, Benedicta.

Binnie (English) See Belinda, Benedicta.

Bionca (Italian) See Bianca.

Bird "The Birdlike One" (English) or "The Bright Ruler" (German).

Patron Saints: Besides serving as a nickname for Alberta and Bertha, Bird serves as a name by itself. One English martyr who has this name is Bl. James Bird, a nineteen-year-old native of Winchester, England. He converted to Catholicism and quit attending Protestant services. For this he was hanged in 1593.

Feast Dates: March 25 — Bl. James Bird.

Birdie (nickname) See Alberta, Bertha, Bird, Brigid.

Birdy (nickname) See Alberta, Bertha, Bird, Brigid.

Birgit (Scandinavian) See Brigid.

Birgitta (French, German) See Brigid.

Birte (Danish) See Brigid.

Blaine "The Thin One" (Irish Gaelic).

Patron Saints: There is one St. Blane. He was born and raised in Scotland. However, he spent eleven years in Ireland under the instruction of Sts. Comgall and Canice. He probably became a monk.

Returning to Scotland, he placed himself under the guidance of his saintly uncle-bishop and was ordained a priest. Eventually he also became a bishop, worked many miracles, and made many converts. He died an old man in 590 and was buried in the monastery-cathedral that he had built.

Feast Dates: August 10 — St. Blane.

Blair (variant) See Blaire.

Blaire "The Dweller on the Plain" (Celtic).

Patron Saints: Patrons can be found by making two connections. First, it is good to know that Blaire means the same thing as Sharon. This leads us to the Blessed Virgin Mary. Second, Sharon is also a form of Sarah, and this leads us to Sarah, the wife of Abraham, whom God named. There are also a couple of Christian Sts. Sarah.

Feast Dates: Month of May — The Blessed Virgin Mary, Rose of Sharon (see Sharon); August 19 — St. Sarah (see Sarah).

Blaise "The Stammerer" (Old German, French).

Patron Saints: There are about a half-dozen saints named Blaise, all male. The most famous is St. Blaise in whose name throats are blessed every February 3. There is also a North American saint-in-the-making, a martyr from the state of Georgia, SG Blas

46

de Rodríguez, O.F.M. There is also a St. Blaesilla.

St. Blaesilla was born in ancient Rome between 363 and 367, shortly after the persecutions ended. She was the daughter of St. Paula, grew up, married, and became a follower of St. Jerome. Later, when her mother moved to Palestine to assist Jerome, Blaesilla accompanied her. She died there at the age of twenty-five.

Feast Dates: January 22 — St. Blaesilla.

Blanca (Italian, Spanish) See Bianca, Blanche.

Blanche "The White One" (Old French).

Patron Saints: Remember that Blanche, Bianca, and Gwen all mean "white." There are about a dozen female Sts. Gwen. There is also an English martyr named Eustace White.

Feast Dates: April 26 — Bl. Blanca (see Bianca).

Blane (variant) See Blaine.

Blanka (variant) See Bianca, Blanche.

Blas (variant) See Blaise.

Blase (variant) See Blaise.

Blasia (variant) See Blaise.

Blayne (variant) See Blaine.

Blaze (variant) See Blaise.

Blinni (variant) See Blanche.

Blinnie (variant) See Blanche.

Blinny (variant) See Blanche.

Bliss "The Very Happy [Joyous] One" (Old English).

Patron Saints: Bliss means "joyous." This is essentially the same thing as the Latin *gaudentia*. St. Gaudentia was a single woman in ancient Rome who dedicated her vocation as a single person to God. In time, she and three companions were arrested for being Christian and were killed by the pagan government.

There are about two dozen Sts. Gaudens, Gaudentia, Gaudentius, Gaudinus, Gaudiosus, and Gaudola.

Feast Dates: August 30 — St. Gaudentia.

Blisse (variant) See Bliss.

Blithe (variant) See Blythe.

Blossom "The Flowering One" (Old English) or "The Blooming One" (Old English).

Patron Saints: There is no St. Blossom, but there are a half-dozen Sts. Flora, which means "flower." Thus they can serve as patrons for anyone who has a flowerlike name.

Feast Dates: November 24 — St. Flora (see Flora); May 4 — Bl. Richard Flower (see Lotus).

Blyss (variant) See Bliss.

Blythe "The Very Happy [Joyful] One" (Old English).

Patron Saints: There are two saints with similar names: Sts. Blath and Blaithmaic. St. Blath served as a humble lay sister and did housekeeping and cooking chores for Ireland's great St. Brigid in the fifth century.

Moreover, Blythe means "joyous." In Latin the word is *gaudium* and it leads to two dozen saints.

Feast Dates: January 29 — St. Blath; August 30 — St. Gaudentia (see Bliss).

Bo (variant) See Bonnie.

Bobbe (variant) See Roberta, Robin.

Bobbee (variant) See Barbara, Bobbie, Roberta.

Bobbi (nickname) See Barbara, Bobbie, Roberta, Robin.

Bobbie "The [Bright] Famous One" (English) or "The Stranger" (English nickname for Barbara).

Patron Saints: There is one St. Bobilia. She was a companion of St. Ursula when she made her pilgrimage to Rome. She was martyred with her near Cologne, Germany, by a pagan chieftain.

Also, because Bobbie can serve as a familiar form of Roberta, Robin, and Barbara, one is led to about two dozen more patrons.

Feast Dates: October 16 — St. Bobilia; September 17 — St. Robert Bellarmine (see Roberta).

Bobby (nickname) See Bobbie, Roberta, Robin.

Bobbye (nickname) See Roberta, Robin.

Bobette (English double) See Barbara/ Bobbie/Roberta/Robin+Ette.

Bobey (variant) See Barbara, Bobbie, Roberta.

Bobina (variant) See Roberta, Robin.

Bobine (variant) See Roberta, Robin.

Bobinette (English double) See Roberta/ Robin+Ette.

Bonelle (African-American double) See Bonnie+Elle.

Bonfilia (Spanish) See Bonnie+Filia.

Bonita (Spanish double) See Bonnie+Ita.

Bonnee (variant) See Bonnie.

Bonni (variant) See Barbara, Bonnie.

Bonnibelle (English double) See Bonnie+ Belle.

Bonnie "The Good One" (Middle English) or "The Good and Pretty One" (Spanish).

Patron Saints: There is one known St. Bonita and a couple of Sts. Bonitus. St. Bonita lived in Auvergne, France, and had a great devotion to St. Julien. She dedicated her single lifestyle to God.

Bonnie can also serve as a nickname for Barbara.

Feast Dates: October 16 — St. Bonita of Alvier; December 4 — St. Barbara (see Barbara).

Bonny (variant) See Barbara, Bonnie.

Borbala (Hungarian) See Barbara.

Brana (variant) See Breanna.

Brandais (variant) See Brandy.

Brandea (variant) See Brandy.

Brandee (Dutch) See Brandy.

Branden (English) See Brandy.

Brandi (English) See Brandy.

Brandice (variant) See Brandy.

Brandie (variant) See Brandy.

Brandon (variant) See Brandy.

Brandy "The Burnt Wine" (Dutch) or "The Brave One" (Irish) or "The Little Raven" (Irish Gaelic).

Patron Saints: Some think that Brandy is the feminine form of the Irish Brandon or Brendan. This would lead one to a half-dozen Sts. Brendan. Others point out that brandy is the name of an alcoholic drink, and this would lead to drafting Bl. Matt Talbot as a patron. He is patron of alcoholics.

St. Brendan, 484-577, the most popular saint of Ireland, founded a great many monasteries. The one at Clonfert became a center of missionary activity for many centuries. During his lifetime, about three thousand monks lived and prayed there under his direction. The founder of many dioceses, he is remembered for making many missionary journeys to England, Ireland, and Scotland.

The stories about his many voyages became very popular reading in the Middle Ages. Some modern scholars think that Brendan could have discovered North America on one of his trips. He could very well have traveled to Newfoundland via Iceland and Greenland. He died at the age of ninety-three while visiting his sister at her convent. He is patron of sailors and against ulcers.

Feast Dates: May 16 — St. Brendan the Voyager; June 7 — Bl. Matt Talbot (see Sherry, Talbot).

Breana (Irish) See Breanna.

Breane (variant) See Breanna.

Breanna "The Strong, Virtuous+God-Graced One" (Irish Gaelic double).

Patron Saints: Breanna is a combination of two names, Brian and Anna. There are a few Sts. Brian or Bryan and a dozen-and-a-half Sts. Anna from which to choose. Then there is St. Bryenna. Bryenna was a virgin who is remembered for dying as a martyr at Sarmata in ancient times.

Feast Dates: August 30 — St. Bryenna; July 26 — St. Ann, Mother of Mary (see Ann).

Breanne (variant) See Breanna.

Bree (variant) See Brandy, Breezy, Breanna, Brigid.

Breena (variant) See Breanna.

Breeze (variant) See Breezy.

Breezie (variant) See Breezy.

Breezy "The One Like the Wind" (Modern English).

Patron Saints: The Latin word for "breeze" or "wind" is *zephyr*, and there is one St. Zephyrinus. He served God and the Church as pope from 198 to 217. It was his job to deal with many Christological errors.

Feast Dates: August 26 — St. Zephyrinus.

Bregetta (Dutch double) See Brigid+Etta.

Bren (nickname) See Brenda.

Brenda "Like a Sword" (Old Norse) or "The Brave One" (Irish) or "The Little Raven" (Irish Gaelic).

Patron Saints: There is one known St. Brenda and about a dozen Sts. Brendan from which to choose. All the Sts. Brendan are males as is the one St. Brenda. He was one of twelve sons of Heligab-Blannog of Wales. He is remembered for being a very holy and pious monk at the monastery at Bangor.

Feast Dates: November 1 — St. Brenda; May 16 — St. Brendan the Voyager (see Brandy).

Brendan (variant) See Brandy.

Brenden (variant) See Brandy.

Brenn (variant) See Brenda.

Brenna (variant) See Breanna, Brenda.

Brett (Irish) See Brittany.

Breyona (Irish) See Breanna.

Bria (American) See Breanna.

Briana (variant) See Breanna.

Brianca (variant) See Breanna.

Brianna (variant) See Breanna.

Brid (Irish Gaelic) See Brigid.

Bride (Irish) See Brigid.

Bridey (variant) See Brigid.

Bridget (English) See Brigid.

Bridgett (English) See Brigid.

Bridgette (English) See Brigid+Ette.

Bridie (English) See Brigid.

Brie (Irish) See Brigid.

Brietta (variant double) See Brigid+Etta.

Brighid (Gaelic) See Brigid.

Brigid "The Strong, Protective One" (Irish Gaelic) or "The High One" (Celtic).

Patron Saints: There are about twenty Sts. Brigid. St. Brigid, 450-525, is the most honored female saint of Ireland. St. Patrick had baptized her parents.

From a very early age Brigid took an interest in religion. Still a teenager (about eighteen years of age), she became the abbess of her own convent. By any standard, Brigid was a remarkable woman. She exhibited great prayerfulness, self-discipline, patience, charity, and compassion. She is also remembered for many fantastic miracles. Brigid died at the age of seventy-five. She is patron of poultry workers, dairy workers, milkmaids, newborn babies, religious sisters, New Zealand, and Ireland.

Feast Dates: February 1 — St. Brigid of Ireland.

Brigida (Italian, Portuguese, Russian, Spanish) See Brigid.

Brigit (variant) See Brigid.

Brigita (Czech, Latvian, Lithuanian, Croatian) See Brigid.

Brigitta (Estonian) See Brigid.

Brigitte (French double) See Brigid+Ette.

Brilla "The Light of Dawn" (Spanish).

Patron Saints: Brilla means the same thing as "dawn."

Feast Dates: Fifth and Eighteenth Sundays of the Year — Jesus the Morning Star (see Danica); July 21 — St. Roricius (see Oriana).

Brina (nickname) See Breanna, Sabrina.

Brinie (variant) See Breanna.

Briny (variant) See Breanna.

Briseida (Spanish) See Dionysia.

Bristy (variant) See Brittany.

Brit (nickname) See Brittany.

Brita (Swedish) See Brigid.

Britanee (variant) See Brittany.

Britani (variant) See Brittany.

Britany (variant) See Brittany.

Britney (variant) See Brittany.

Britni (variant) See Brittany.

Britny (variant) See Brittany.

Britt (variant) See Brigid, Brittany.

Britta (Polish, Ukrainian) See Brigid.

Britta (variant) See Brittany.

Brittani (English) See Brittany.

Brittanie (English) See Brittany.

Brittany "The One from England [Brittany]" (Latin).

Patron Saints: Brittany has long been the name of a French province, and some saints who bear this name find their origin in Brittany. They are Sts. Brittan of Rath, Brito, and Britwin.

Two women have very similar names: Sts. Brita and Britta. St. Brita was a native of Sweden and a widow most of her life. She was executed because of her Catholic faith.

This name is also a short form of Bridget.

Feast Dates: October 8 — St. Brita; January 11 — St. Britta.

Brittney (English) See Brittany.

Brittni (English) See Brittany.

Brittnie (English) See Brittany.

Britton (English) See Brittany.

Brogan "The Heavy Workshoe" (Irish).

Patron Saints: There are about a dozen Sts. Brogan. One was an abbot in Ireland in the seventh century.

Feast Dates: September 17 — St. Brogan.

Bron (Welsh) See Bronwyn.

Bronnie (nickname) See Bronwyn.

Bronny (nickname) See Bronwyn.

Bronwen (Welsh) See Bronwyn.

Bronwyn "The White-Breasted One" (Welsh).

Patron Saints: There is a St. Bron who is remembered for being a bishop and a disciple of St. Patrick in the fifth century. And there is a St. Wynnin. Together, they provide the needed patrons.

Feast Dates: June 8 — St. Bron; January 21 — St. Wynnin of Holywood (see Wynne).

Brook (variant) See Brooke.

Brooke "From the Small Stream" (Old English).

Patron Saints: Brook means "a stream" and because Bourne means "stream," Bl. Thomas Welbourne can serve as patron. Furthermore, the Spanish word for brook is *arroyo.* This leads to Bl. Joachim Royo, a Dominican priest who preached in China. In 1746 a persecution broke out over a simple matter.

The local Chinese viceroy was a bitter enemy of Christianity, and a false complaint was a welcome tool to be used to destroy the missionaries. Father Royo, his bishop, and fellow priests were arrested, put in chains, and starved; but this barbarous treatment only won more sympathy from the people. They remained in prison for a year, then Bishop Sanz was beheaded. The priests were executed a short time later.

Feast Dates: May 27 — Bl. Joachim Royo, also known as Brook; August 1 — Bl. Thomas Welbourne.

Brooks (Old English double) See Brooke+Son.

Brosa (variant) See Ambrosia.

Brose (English) See Ambrosia.

Brosia (variant) See Ambrosia.

Bryana (English) See Breanna.

Bryanna (English) See Breanna.

Bryenna (variant) See Breanna, Brynne.

Brygida (Polish, Ukrainian) See Brigid.

Bryn (Latin) See Breanna, Brynne.

Bryna (variant) See Breanna, Brynne.

Bryndon (variant) See Brynne, Brendan.

Bryne (English) See Breanna, Brynne.

Brynn (English) See Breanna, Brynne.

Brynne "The Mountaineer" (Welsh) or "The Burning One" (Saxon).

Patron Saints: Four ancient saints with similar names can be adopted: Sts. Brynach, Brynolph, Bryenna, and Buan. Furthermore, some think Brynne is a form of Briana or Breanna.

Brynach was often called Gwyddel, which means "The Irishman." Upon reaching adulthood, he embraced the life of a religious monk and moved to England to live as a hermit. He built a simple dwelling on the River Cledda, and another on the River Gwam. Then he began to work as a missionary. Soon he had a number of young men gathered around him and he became their abbot. He died in 470.

Feast Dates: April 7 — St. Brynach; August 30 — St. Bryenna (see Breanna).

Buena (Spanish) See Bonnie.

Buffi (nickname) See Beverly, Elizabeth.

Buffie (nickname) See Beverly, Elizabeth.

Buffy (American) See Beverly, Elizabeth.

Bunni (nickname) See Bernice, Bonnie, Bunny.

Bunnie (nickname) See Bernice, Bonnie, Bunny.

Bunny "Like a Cuddly Rabbit" (American).

Patron Saints: Many consider Bunny to be a nickname for Bernice. Others think it is a form of Bonnie. To many modern Americans, however, it simply means, "cuddly, like a rabbit."

Feast Dates: July 12 — St. Bernice (see Bernice); October 16 — St. Bonita of Alvier (see Bonnie).

Buny (English) See Bernice, Bonnie, Bunny.

Burdelle (African-American double) See Bird/Burtie+Della.

Burt (English) See Alberta, Gilbertine.

Burtie (nickname) See Alberta, Gilbertine.

Burty (nickname) See Alberta, Gilbertine.

Bushra (Arabic) See Evangeline.

Butterfly "The Butterfly" (Middle English).

Patron Saints: In Latin the word for "butterfly" is *papilio*. This leads to one St. Papylinus and two Sts. Papylus. One St. Papylus was a deacon who died a martyr in ancient Pergamum.

Feast Dates: October 13 — St. Papylus.

Byllye (American) See Billie.

Byrdie (nickname) See Alberta, Bird.

C

Cachet (French) See Désirée.

Caci (variant) See Acacia, Casey.

Cacia (English) See Acacia, Casey.

Cacie (English) See Acacia, Casey.

Cacilia (German) See Cecilia.

Caddy (English) See Kady.

Caela (variant double) See Catherine, Kay+Leigh.

Caelan (variant double) See Cailin, Catherine, Kay+Lynn.

Caelee (Irish-English double) See Cailin, Catherine, Kay+Leigh.

Caelie (Irish-English double) See Cailin, Catherine, Kay+Leigh.

Caelynn (English double) See Cailin, Catherine, Kay+Lynn.

Caila (Irish-English double) See Cailin, Catherine, Kay+Leigh.

Cailan (Irish-English double) See Cailin, Catherine, Kay+Lynn.

Cailee (Irish-English double) See Cailin, Catherine, Kay+Leigh.

Cailida (Spanish) See Kailida.

Cailin "A Girl" (Irish form of Colleen) or "The Pure One+From the Pool Below the Waterfall" (English double).

    Patron Saints: While Cailin is an old Irish name meaning "the girl," many modern Americans think of it as a combination of Katherine and Lynn. St. Cailan was the first bishop of Down, Ireland, in 520.

    Feast Dates: November 1 — St. Cailan.

Caily (Irish-English double) See Cailin, Catherine, Kay+Leigh.

Cailyn (Irish-English double) See Cailin, Catherine, Kay+Lynn.

Cailynn (English double) See Katherine, Kay+Lynn.

Cairistiona (Scottish Gaelic) See Christiana, Christine.

Cait (Irish) See Catherine.

Caitlan (Irish) See Catherine.

Caitlin (English double) See Catherine+Lynn.

Caitlynn (English double) See Catherine+Lynn.

Caitria (Irish) See Catherine.

Caitrin (variant) See Catherine.

Caitriona (Irish) See Catherine, Kay.

Cal (nickname) See Calandra.

Calandra "The Lark" (Greek).

    Patron Saints: One St. Calanus was martyred in ancient Thessalonica. There is also one English martyr who bears an English name with the same meaning.

    Feast Dates: February 27 — St. Calanus; March 7 — Bl. John Larke of Chelsea (see Lark).

Calandre (French) See Calandra.

Calandria (Spanish) See Calandra.

Calesta (variant) See Callista.

Caley (American double) See Calandra, Catherine, Kay+Leigh.

Calida "The Warm Ardent One" (Spanish).

    Patron Saints: One ancient saint, St. Kali, fits very nicely.

    Feast Dates: May 24 — St. Kali, also known as Sara (see Zara).

Calie (nickname, double) See Calandra, Calida, Catherine, Kay+Leigh.

Cali (variant double) See Calandra, Calida, Catherine, Kay+Leigh.

Calin (Irish, variant double) See Cailin, Calandra, Catherine, Kay+Lynn.

Calla (variant) See Callista.

Calli (nickname, double) See Cailin,

Calandra, Calida, Callista, Catherine, Kay+Leigh.

Callie (nickname, double) See Cailin, Calandra, Calida, Callista, Catherine, Kay+Leigh.

Calliope "The Poetic One" (Greek).
Patron Saints: There is one St. Calliope. She was tortured terribly and killed by enemies of the Christian faith in ancient Rome.
Feast Dates: June 8 — St. Calliope.

Callista "The Most Beautiful One" (Greek).
Patron Saints: There are at least four Sts. Callista. One was a woman who was beheaded for the Catholic faith in Nicomedia in 304.
Feast Dates: September 2 — St. Callista.

Cally (nickname, double) See Cailin, Calandra, Calida, Callista, Catherine, Kay+Leigh.

Calyn (American double) See Cailin, Catherine, Kay+Lynn.

Calynn (American double) See Cailin, Catherine, Kay+Lynn.

Calysta (variant) See Callista.

Cam (nickname) See Cameron, Camilla.

Camala (variant) See Camilla.

Camara (variant) See Camera.

Camberly (American) See Kimberly.

Camel (variant) See Camilla.

Camera "One Who Teaches from Experience" (West African) or "The One Who Photographs" (American).
Patron Saints: The ancient martyrs of Camerino are still remembered.
Feast Dates: May 19 — The Martyrs of Camerino; August 21 — St. Cameron (see Cameron).

Cameron "The One with a Crooked Nose" (Scottish Gaelic).
Patron Saints: There is one St. Cameron. He gave his life for Jesus as a martyr in ancient Cagliari in Italy.

Feast Dates: August 21 — St. Cameron.

Cami (French) See Cameron, Camilla.

Camila (Spanish, Italian) See Camilla.

Camilah (variant) See Camilla.

Camile (French) See Camilla.

Camilia (variant) See Camilla.

Camilla "The Perfect One" (Arabic) or "The Young Church Server" (Italian).
Patron Saints: There are a half-dozen Sts. Camella, Camilla, and Camillus. One St. Camilla remained single and dedicated her life to God in the 1300s. A second one lived her life in the 1300s as the abbess of a convent of Poor Clares, a religious order of sisters. She is remembered for possessing mystical gifts.
Feast Dates: July 27 — St. Camilla Rovellone; May 31 — St. Camilla Varani.

Camille (French) See Camilla.

Camira (Hispanic-American) See Camera, Cameron.

Camisha (African-American double) See Cameron/Camilla+Isha.

Cammie (nickname) See Camilla.

Cammy (nickname) See Camilla.

Camryn (American) See Cameron.

Canada "From the Village" (French).
Patron Saints: There is a St. Villanus, a St. Villicus, and a Bl. Villana whose names can mean "village."
Feast Dates: February 28 (29) — Bl. Villana de' Botti.

Candace "The Glowing White One" (Greek).
Patron Saints: Candace is a form of Candida, from the Latin for "glowing white." There are about thirty saints named Candida. One of them was a very old woman when she had the privilege of welcoming St. Peter the Apostle to her home in Naples. Peter cured her of a nagging illness during

his brief stay. She later converted St. Aspren to the faith. After her death, her house became a church.

Feast Dates: September 4 — St. Candida.

Candelaria "The Illuminated One" (Spanish).

Patron Saints: A convert from paganism, St. Illuminata died a martyr to the Catholic faith in ancient Rome.

Feast Dates: November 28 — St. Illuminata.

Candi (American) See Candace.

Candice (English) See Candace.

Candida (Latin) See Candace.

Candide (French) See Candace.

Candie (nickname) See Candace.

Candis (variant) See Candace.

Candra (Latin) See Candace.

Candy (nickname) See Candace.

Canzata (African-American double) See Candace+Zeta.

Capri (Italian) See Caprice.

Caprice (Italian) See Cassidy.

Cara (Latin) See Carissa, Catherine.

Caralee (English double) See Carissa+Leigh.

Care (variant) See Charity.

Caree (nickname) See Carey, Catherine.

Carel (English) See Carol, Caroline, Charlene.

Caren "The Pure One" (American short form of Catherine).

Patron Saints: St. Caron served God as a holy bishop in medieval Wales.

Feast Dates: March 2 — St. Caron.

Carena (variant) See Caren, Catherine.

Caressa (French) See Carissa.

Carey "The Strong Woman" (short form of Carey, Carla, Carol, Caroline, Charlene).

Patron Saints: Since Carey is a form of Caroline, one is led to about a dozen Sts. Charles. There is also an English martyr in 1594 who had this name.

Bl. John Carey worked as a servant of Bl. Thomas Bosgrave. He helped his master and fellow servants in giving shelter to Catholic priests. They were all executed for committing this "crime" against England.

Feast Dates: July 4 — Bl. John Carey; August 17 — St. Carolomann (see Carla).

Cari (variant) See Carey, Carla, Carol, Caroline, Charity, Charlene.

Carie (variant) See Carey, Carla, Carol, Caroline.

Carilyn (English double) See Catherine/Carey+Lynn.

Carilynn (English double) See Catherine/Carey+Lynn.

Carin (variant) See Catherine.

Carina (English, Italian, Greek, Spanish) See Carissa, Cora, Karina.

Carine (Italian) See Carissa, Cora.

Carisma (American) See Charisma.

Carissa "The Graced One" (Greek) or "The Dear Little One" (Latin).

Patron Saints: Some think the name is a combination of Carrie and Melissa. Others think it arises from the Greek *charis*, meaning "graced one." There are also a number of Sts. Carissa. One St. Carissa traveled to Rome with St. Ursula. She, Ursula, and some other young women were murdered by a pagan Hun chieftain near Cologne, Germany, on the return trip in about 1000.

Feast Dates: August 22 — St. Carissa; June 1 — St. Melosa (see Melissa).

Carita (Latin-Spanish double) See Carissa/Charity+Ita.

Caritina (Spanish) See Carissa.

Carla "The Strong Woman" (English and Spanish short forms of Carol).

Patron Saints: There is one Bl. Carolomann, 707-754. Also known as Karlmann, he became king of Austrasia,

Swabia, and Thuringia. As king, he was active in Church matters. He supported St. Boniface in Germany, founded abbeys, and tried to right the wrongs created by his father in regards to Church property. When he was about forty years old, a tragic slaughter of the Alemans led him to resign. Then he entered a Benedictine monastery, becoming a monk. He spent his time working in the kitchen and as a shepherd.

Feast Dates: August 17 — St. Carolomann; January 28 — Bl. Charlemagne (see Charlene).

Carlee (English) See Carla, Carol, Caroline.

Carleen (English) See Carla, Carol, Caroline.

Carlen (variant) See Carla, Caroline, Charlene.

Carlene (variant) See Carla, Carol, Caroline.

Carley (English) See Carla, Carol, Caroline.

Carli (English) See Carla, Carol, Caroline.

Carlie (English) See Carla, Carol, Caroline.

Carlin (Slavic, Latin) See Carla, Carol, Caroline.

Carlina (variant) See Carla, Carol, Caroline.

Carline (Spanish, Portuguese, Italian) See Carla, Carol, Caroline.

Carlisa (American double) See Carla+Lisa.

Carlita (Spanish double) See Carla/Carol/Caroline/Charlotte/Lottie+Ita.

Carlota (Spanish, Portuguese, Romanian) See Carla, Carol, Caroline, Charlotte, Lottie.

Carlotta (Italian) See Carla, Carol, Caroline, Charlotta, Lottie.

Carly (English) See Carla, Carol, Caroline.

Carlye (American) See Carla, Carol, Caroline.

Carlyn (variant double) See Carla/Carol/Caroline+Lynn.

Carlynn (variant double) See Carla/Carol/Caroline+Lynn.

Carlynne (variant double) See Carla/Carol/Caroline+Lynn.

Carm (nickname) See Carmella, Carmen, Karma.

Carma (nickname) See Carmella, Carmen, Karma.

Carmel (variant) See Carmen.

Carmela (Italian) See Carmella.

Carmelina (Spanish) See Carmella.

Carmelita (Spanish double) See Carmela+Ita.

Carmella "From the Garden" (Hebrew).

Patron Saints: The fact that Carmel means "garden" leads to the adoption of Sts. Adam and Eve who are patrons of gardeners. One could also adopt the Blessed Virgin as Our Lady of Mount Carmel. The story of Our Lady of Mount Carmel begins with St. Simon Stock, circa 1168-1265. As a poor boy, he lived in a hollowed-out trunk of a tree. Then as a teenager he traveled to the Holy Land, where he came into contact with and joined the Carmelites who lived on Mount Carmel. After he returned to Europe the Blessed Virgin appeared to him and gave him a scapular, promising that all who wore it in life would gain salvation in death.

Feast Dates: July 16 — The Blessed Virgin Mary, Our Lady of Mount Carmel; December 24 — Sts. Adam and Eve (see Eartha).

Carmen "The Song" (Middle Latin, Spanish) or "The Crimson Red One" (Middle Latin).

Patron Saints: As a name in its own right, Carmen can mean either "a song" or "crimson red." If one accepts "a song," then one is led to Bl. Peter the Singer, St. Joseph the Hymn Writer, and St. Clement the Hymnographer. St. Clement was the abbot of the Studion monastery at Constantinople. He had a great devotion to the Blessed Virgin and wrote many hymns and canons in her honor. If one accepts "crimson red," then one is led to the many Sts. Rufina. Finally if Carmen is accepted as a Spanish form of Carmella, then one is led to Our Lady of Mount Carmel. Finally, it is good to know that there is one saint-in-the-making, SG Carmen Moreno.

Feast Dates: September 6 — SG Carmen Moreno (see Moreno); April 30 — St. Clement the Hymnographer.

Carmencita (Spanish double) See Carmen+Ita.

Carmia (variant) See Carmen, Karma.

Carmie (nickname) See Carmella, Carmen, Karma.

Carmina (English) See Carmella, Carmen, Karma.

Carmine (English) See Carmen, Karma.

Carmita (Spanish) See Carmella, Carmen.

Carmy (nickname) See Carmella, Karma.

Carna (variant) See Catherine.

Carnella (African-American) See Carmella, Catherine.

Carnetta (African-American double) See Carmella/Catherine+Etta.

Caro (nickname) See Carla, Carol, Caroline.

Carol "The Strong Woman" (English) or "A Joyful Song" (Old French).

Patron Saints: Carol is a short feminine form of Caroline and Charlene. There are a few patron saints.

Feast Dates: August 17 — Bl. Carolomann (see Carla); January 28 — Bl. Charlemagne (see Charlene).

Carola (Polish, Russian) See Carla, Carol, Caroline.

Carole (English) See Carla, Carol, Caroline.

Carolin (English) See Carla, Carol, Caroline.

Carolina (Spanish, Portuguese, Italian) See Carla, Carol, Caroline.

Caroline "The Strong Woman" (English) or "A Joyful Song" (Old French).

Patron Saints: Caroline is the feminine form of Charles. There are about a dozen Sts. Charles. And then there is St. Charlier, a priest of the French diocese of Bourges. This holy man lived in the 500s.

Feast Dates: February 1 — St. Charlier; August 17 — St. Carolomann (see Carla).

Carolyn (Polish, Russian) See Carla, Carol, Caroline.

Carolyne (English double) See Carla/Carol/Caroline+Lynn.

Carolynn (English double) See Carla/Carol/Caroline+Lynn.

Caron (Welsh) See Caren, Catherine.

Carone (variant) See Caren, Catherine.

Carree (American) See Carey, Carla, Carol, Caroline.

Carrie (English) See Carey, Carissa, Carla, Carol, Caroline.

Carroll (English) See Carla, Carol, Caroline.

Carry (English) See Carey, Carla, Carol, Caroline.

Cary (nickname) See Carey, Carla, Carol, Caroline.

Carye (nickname) See Carey, Carla, Carol, Caroline.

Caryl (English) See Carla, Carol, Caroline.

Carylin (variant) See Carla, Carol, Caroline.

Caryn (variant) See Carin, Catherine.

Casandra (variant) See Cassandra.

Casandre (French) See Cassandra.

Casandry (variant) See Cassandra.

Casey "The Watchful, Brave One" (Irish Gaelic) or "The Peacemaker" (short form of Casimira).

Patron Saints: Besides being a full name in its own right, Casey also serves as a nickname for Acacia and Cassandra. There is also one North American, Ven. Bernard Casey, 1870-1957, who can be a patron.

He was born in Wisconsin to Irish immigrant farmers, was poor, and worked at many different jobs including handyman, prison guard, brickmaker, and streetcar motorman. He proposed marriage to a girlfriend but was opposed by her mother. He entered the diocesan seminary but was asked to leave because of low grades. Then he was accepted by the Capuchin seminary in Detroit and took the name Solanus. He struggled through his studies and was ordained in 1904 at the age of thirty-three. Because of his low grades he was not allowed to preach or hear confessions. This positioned him for his life's work. Being a doorkeeper, he came into contact with all kinds of troubled people. Soon miracles began to happen. He served God in Wisconsin, New York, Michigan, and Indiana. He died at the age of eighty-six.

Feast Dates: January 6 — Ven. Solanus Casey, also known as Bernard "Barney" Casey, O.F.M. Cap.

Casi (variant) See Acacia, Casey, Casimira.

Casia (nickname) See Acacia, Casey, Catherine.

Casie (variant) See Acacia, Casey, Casimira, Catherine.

Casilda "The Hut [or Kiosk or Pigeonhole] Dweller" (Spanish, Italian, Latin).

Patron Saints: There is one St. Casilda, a daughter of a Saracen prince in Spain in the eleventh century. She is remembered for the great charity she showed to the Christian prisoners.

Feast Dates: April 9 — St. Casilda.

Casimira "The Peacemaker" (Slavic).

Patron Saints: The most similar name to this is St. Casimir of Poland, 1458-1484. He was born in Cracow, the third son of the king of Poland. He did not want to be king, and this infuriated his father. He could often be found in prayer, either praying the rosary or meditating on the passion of Jesus. He also had a deep devotion to the Eucharist and to the Blessed Virgin. He is patron of Poland and Lithuania.

After his brother became king of Poland, he was occasionally called upon for diplomatic service.

Feast Dates: March 4 — St. Casimir of Poland.

Casina (Greek) See Cinnamon.

Cass (nickname) See Cassandra, Casilda, Casimira, Cassidy, Catherine.

Cassandra "The Helper of Mankind" (Greek) or "The One Not Believed" (Greek).

Patron Saints: Cassandra is a form of Alexandra, and there is one St. Alexandra. There is also a St. Cas of Benchor (Bangor), Ireland. Very little is known about this particular saint.

Feast Dates: April 26 — St. Cas of Benchor; March 20 — St. Alexandra (see Alexandra).

Cassaundra (variant) See Cassandra.

Cassi (nickname) See Cassandra, Casimira, Cassidy, Catherine.

Cassia (nickname) See Acacia, Catherine.

Cassidy "The Clever One" (Irish Gaelic) or "The One Who Complains" (Gaelic).

Patron Saints: There are a half-dozen saints with similar names. One

St. Cassia was martyred at Thessalonica by Emperor Diocletian in the year 95.

Feast Dates: March 3 — St. Cassia.

Cassie (nickname) See Cassandra, Casilda, Cassidy, Casimira, Catherine.

Cassondra (variant) See Cassandra.

Cassy (nickname) See Cassandra, Casilda, Cassidy.

Castalia (Spanish) See Catherine.

Cat (nickname) See Catherine.

Catalin (American double) See Catherine+Lynn.

Catalina (Spanish) See Catherine.

Catalyn (American double) See Catherine+Lynn.

Catarin (variant) See Catherine.

Catarina (Italian, Portuguese, German) See Catherine.

Cate (nickname) See Catherine.

Catee (nickname) See Catherine.

Catelin (American double) See Catherine+Lynn.

Catelyn (American double) See Catherine+Lynn.

Catelyna (American double) See Catherine+Lynn.

Catelynn (American double) See Catherine+Lynn.

Caterina (Italian) See Catherine.

Caterine (variant) See Catherine.

Catey (nickname) See Catherine.

Cath (nickname) See Catherine.

Catharina (Dutch) See Catherine.

Catharine (variant) See Catherine.

Cathe (nickname) See Catherine.

Cathee (nickname) See Catherine.

Catherine "The Pure One" (French).

Patron Saints: There are a dozen Sts. Catherine. St. Catherine Labouré, 1806-1876, was the daughter of a farmer, was very poor, and was never able to go to school. Her mother died when she was only eight years old, and four years later, when an older sister who had been taking care of the family left to become a sister, Catherine had to take over the care of the family. Upon growing up, she joined the Sisters of St. Vincent de Paul and was sent to a convent in Paris. Almost at once she began to have visions of the Blessed Virgin in the convent chapel. In the visions, the Virgin asked her to have a religious medal made that proclaimed the Immaculate Conception. The words on the medal were to read, "O Mary, conceived free from sin, pray for us who have recourse to you!" Today the medal is known as the Miraculous Medal, and Our Lady of the Miraculous Medal is the patron of motorcyclists.

Feast Dates: November 28 — St. Catherine Labouré; March 3 — St. Katharine Drexel (see Katherine).

Catheryn (variant) See Catherine.

Cathi (nickname) See Catherine.

Cathie (nickname) See Catherine.

Cathleen (English, Irish) See Catherine.

Cathleena (English) See Catherine.

Cathlene (Irish) See Catherine.

Cathryn (English) See Catherine.

Cathryne (English) See Catherine.

Cathy (nickname) See Catherine.

Cathye (nickname) See Catherine.

Cathyleen (variant) See Catherine.

Cathylene (variant) See Catherine.

Cati (nickname) See Catherine.

Catie (nickname) See Catherine.

Catina (variant) See Catherine.

Catrin (Welsh) See Catherine.

Catrina (Romanian) See Catherine.

Catrine (variant) See Catherine.

Catriona (Scottish) See Catherine.

Catti (nickname) See Catherine.

Cattie (nickname) See Catherine.

Catty (nickname) See Catherine.

Caty (nickname) See Catherine.

Cay (variant) See Catherine, Kay.

Caye (variant) See Catherine, Kay.

Cayla (American double) See Cailin, Catherine, Kay+Leigh.

Caylee (American double) See Cailin, Catherine, Kay+Leigh.

Cayley (American double) See Cailin, Catherine, Kay+Leigh.

Cayli (American double) See Cailin, Catherine, Kay+Leigh.

Caylin (American double) See Cailin, Catherine, Kay+Lynn.

Caylyn (American double) See Cailin, Catherine, Kay+Lynn.

Caylynn (American double) See Calin, Catherine, Kay+Lynn.

Cayne (variant) See Catherine, Kay.

Ceanan (variant) See McKenna.

Ceara (Irish) See Ciara, Sierra.

Ceatta "Roman Goddess+Little One" (Latin) or "The Announcer" (nickname for Annunciata).

Patron Saints: There is no known St. Ceatta. However St. Ceara may be adopted. St. Ceara was born into Irish royalty in the 600s. She founded a nunnery at Tehelly, Ely O'Carroll, Munster. Furthermore, some have suggested that Ceatta is nothing more than a short form of Annunciata, and this leads directly to the Blessed Virgin as patron.

Feast Dates: January 5 — St. Ceara; July 10 — St. Etto (see Etta); March 25 — The Blessed Virgin Mary (see Annunciata).

Cecca (Italian) See Frances.

Cecelia (Latin) See Cecilia, Sheila.

Cecile (French) See Cecilia.

Cecilia "The Blind One" (Latin, Spanish).

Patron Saints: There are a few Sts. Cecilia. The best remembered lived in the 200s in Rome. She was raised a Catholic and as an adult she was forced to marry against her will. She was able to convince her husband to honor her virginity and she was also able to convert him and his brother to Christianity.

Her husband and brother devoted themselves to doing works of charity and were soon arrested for burying dead Christians. They were beheaded, Cecilia buried them, and she herself was arrested.

During her trial she debated with the judge, laughed at him, and tripped him up. This did not make the judge happy and he had her beheaded. She is now the patron of music, musicians, composers, poets, singers, vocalists, and organ makers.

Feast Dates: November 22 — St. Cecilia.

Cecilie (Polish) See Cecilia.

Cecily (Polish) See Cecilia.

Cecyle (variant) See Cecilia.

Cecylia (Polish) See Cecilia.

Cele (nickname) See Cecilia, Celeste.

Celena (variant) See Selena.

Celene (variant) See Selena.

Celesta (English) See Celeste.

Celeste "The Heavenly One" (Latin).

Patron Saints: There are about a half-dozen Sts. Celestine. One St. Celestine, named Pietro da Morrone, was born in 1210, the eleventh of twelve children of peasant parents in Abruzzi, Italy. By age twenty he was living as a hermit. Soon disciples gathered around him and he found himself the head of a monastery.

Many years later, after Pope Nicholas IV died in 1292 and the cardinals had failed to elect a successor for two years, Peter sent a message to them telling of God's anger. In response they chose him to be pope. He allowed himself to be elected but soon found himself unequal to the task. After only five months as pope, he resigned. He is the only pope ever to resign. He died in 1296.

Feast Dates: May 19 — St. Celestine V.

Celestia (English) See Celeste.

Celestina (Spanish) See Celeste.

Celestine (French) See Celeste.

Celestyn (variant) See Celeste.

Celestyna (variant) See Celeste.

Celia (Hungarian) See Cecilia.

Celia (variant) See Cecilia, Celestine, Selena.

Celie (variant) See Celeste, Selena.

Celina (variant) See Cecilia, Celeste, Selena.

Celinda (variant) See Celeste, Selena.

Celine (variant) See Cecilia, Celeste, Selena.

Celinia "The Moonlike One" (Latin).

 Patron Saints: St. Celinia was a virgin who became a religious sister. She died in 530.

 Feast Dates: October 2 — St. Celinia.

Celinia (variant) See Selena.

Celinka (variant) See Celeste.

Celisse (variant) See Celeste.

Celka (variant) See Celeste.

Ceryl (variant) See Cherise.

Cesarina (Spanish) See Caesar.

Cesya (French) See Alexandra.

Chabela (Spanish) See Elizabeth.

Chabi (Spanish) See Elizabeth.

Chaka (African) See Ignatia, Seraphina.

Chakra "The Point of Energy" (Sanskrit).

 Patron Saints: For a Christian the point of energy is Jesus, our risen Redeemer, as well as the Holy Spirit.

 Feast Dates: All Sundays — Jesus Christ, Our Savior.

Chalina (Spanish) See Rose, Rosalina.

Chana (Hebrew) See Hannah, Chiquita.

Chanda (African-American) See Chandra.

Chandal (variant) See Chantal.

Chandelle "The Candle" (French).

 Patron Saints: Every Holy Saturday a large candle called the Paschal, or Easter, Candle is lit in the darkness to proclaim the risen Lord. He is the light that shines in the darkness.

 Feast Dates: Holy Saturday — Jesus Christ, Light of the World.

Chandra "The Moonlike One [or Moonlight]" (Hindu).

 Patron Saints: As Chandra arises from Hindu origins, there is no St. Chandra. However, Chandra's meaning, "moonlike," is essentially the same as Celinia. There is one St. Celinia.

 Feast Dates: October 21 — St. Celinia (see Celinia); November 16 — SsG Elba and Celina Ramos (see Elba).

Chanel (variant) See Chanelle.

Chanell (variant) See Chanelle.

Chanelle "From the Canal" (French).

 Patron Saints: St. Peter Mary Chanel, 1803-1841, served God as a priest in a very poor area. Despite the grinding poverty, in three years he brought a religious revival to that area. His care of the sick impressed many people.

 However, his heart had long been set on becoming a missionary, so at the age of twenty-eight, he joined the Marists. They made him a seminary professor for five years. Then in 1836, at the age of thirty-three, he was sent to the missions in the East Indies. Soon, a local chieftain's jealousy was aroused, and a band of warriors was sent to kill Peter. This they did, with an axe. He was only thirty-eight years old. A few months later, the whole island, where he had ministered, had converted to Catholicism.

 Feast Dates: April 28 — St. Peter Mary Chanel.

Channa (variant) See Shannon.

Channel (variant) See Chanelle.

Chanta (African-American) See Chantal.

Chantae (African-American) See Chantal.

Chantal "The Singer" (French) or "The Stone" (Old French).

Patron Saints: There is one St. Jane Chantal, 1572-1641. At age twenty she was given in marriage to an officer in the French army. It was a good marriage and she was a baroness, but after nine years her husband was killed in a hunting accident and her grief knew no bounds. She experienced deep depression and only a letter from her father reminding her of her obligations to her children could rouse her from her state of depression.

She then doubled her efforts to care for them and practice her faith. She began to realize that divine love must consume the self-love in her life. She lived more simply and practiced penance. Then she met St. Francis de Sales, who encouraged her to found a new religious order dedicated to helping people on the streets and in their homes. With Francis de Sales' help, she accomplished this. By the time St. Jane Chantal died, the community, known as the Visitation Order, had sixty-six convents.

Feast Dates: December 12 — St. Jane Frances de Chantal.

Chantalle (variant) See Chantal.

Chantay (African-American) See Chantal.

Chantel (variant) See Chantal.

Chantell (variant) See Chantal.

Chantrice (French) See Chantal.

Char (nickname) See Chara, Charlotte, Charlene, Charla.

Chara (Spanish) See Rose.

Chara (variant) See Charlene, Charlotte.

Chareka (African-American) See Clare, Charlotte.

Charil (nickname) See Charlene, Charlotte.

Charin (nickname) See Sharon.

Charisa (variant) See Carissa.

Charisma "The One with Special Talent" (Greek) or "The One Who Inspires Allegiance" (Greek).

Patron Saints: See Carissa.

Feast Dates: August 22 — St. Carissa.

Charita (Spanish double) See Char+Ita.

Charity "The One Who Is Loving and Caring" (English) or "The Dear Little One" (Latin).

Patron Saints: There are a few Sts. Charity. In ancient times they were known as Sts. Agape and Charitina. Christian tradition tells the story of a woman, Sophia, who lived in about 130 and had three daughters named Pistis, Elpis, and Agape. In English the mother's name is "Wisdom" and the daughters' names are translated as "Faith, Hope, and Charity." They were condemned to death.

At that time Faith was only twelve years old, her sister Hope was ten, and Charity was nine. The oldest, Faith, was scourged, then thrown into boiling pitch, taken out while still alive and beheaded. Hope and Charity escaped the scourging, but not being dipped in the boiling pitch. They were also beheaded. Their mother, Sophia, suffered and watched all this barbarous activity. Then she was also killed.

Feast Dates: August 1 — St. Charity, also known as Agape.

Charla (variant) See Carla, Charlene, Charlotte.

Charlaine (variant) See Charlene, Charlotte.

Charlayne (African-American) See Charlene.

Charleen (English) See Charlene, Charlotte.

Charlemae (African-American double) See Charlene+Mae.

Charlena (variant) See Charlene, Charlotte.

Charlene "The Strong Woman" (French).

Patron Saints: It helps to know that Charlene is a feminine form of Charlemagne. Bl. Charlemagne, 742-814, learned how to fight and went on many campaigns. In 768 his father died and the kingdom, according to the custom of the time, was divided between Charlemagne (or Charles, as he is also known) and his brother, Carloman. When Carloman died three years later, Charlemagne became ruler of the entire kingdom.

He had a great interest in the Catholic Church and was usually involved in the deliberations at Church synods. On Christmas Day in 800, the pope crowned him "Roman Emperor." He founded churches, monasteries, and convents and helped introduce Gregorian chant in his kingdom.

Feast Dates: January 28 — Bl. Charlemagne; February 1 — St. Charlier (see Caroline).

Charleszetta (African-American double) See Charlene+Zetta.

Charlete (variant) See Charlene, Charlotte.

Charli (nickname) See Charlene, Charlotte.

Charlice (nickname) See Charlene, Charlotte.

Charlie (nickname) See Charlene, Charlotte.

Charline (English) See Charlene, Charlotte.

Charlotta (Finnish) See Charlene, Charlotte.

Charlotte "The Strong Woman+Little One" (French double).

Patron Saints: Charlotte is a feminine form of Charles with either Lottie or Etta added on.

Feast Dates: January 28 — Bl. Charlemagne (see Charlene); April 16 — St. Lota (see Lottie); July 10 — St. Etto (see Etta).

Charmaine "The Singer" (English variant of Carmen) or "The Delightful One" (Greek).

Patron Saints: There are a few Sts. Carmen and at the transfiguration on Mount Tabor (others say Mount Hermon) the Father called Jesus his "Delight."

Feast Dates: September 6 — SG Carmen Moreno (see Moreno); August 6 — The Transfiguration of Jesus (see Delight).

Charmian (African-American) See Charmaine.

Charmion (African-American) See Charmaine.

Charmona (African-American double) See Charmaine/Cherise+Monique/Monica.

Charnese (African-American) See Shanice.

Charniece (African-American) See Shanice.

Charo (Spanish) See Charlene, Charlotte.

Charry (nickname) See Charity.

Charshee (African-American double) See Charyl+Sheehan/Sheena/Sheeree/Sheereen.

Charyl (American) See Charlene, Charlotte, Cherise.

Charyll (American) See Charlene, Charlotte, Cherise.

Chastity "The Chaste One" (Latin).

Patron Saints: The Latin word for chastity is *castus,* and there is one St. Casta. She embraced martyrdom at Ain Ghorab, near Tebessa in Mauretania. The Catholic Church has also appointed another saint as patron of chastity. She is St. Agnes.

Feast Dates: February 23 — St. Chastity, also known as Casta; January 21 — St. Agnes (see Agnes).

Chauntay (French) See Chantal.

Chauntée (French) See Chantal.

Chauntel (French) See Chantel.

Chava (Hebrew) See Eve.

Checole (American double) See Chelsea/Cheryl+Nicole.

Chela (Spanish) See Cecilia.

Che-Lin (African-American double) See Ché+Lynn.

Chelsae (English) See Chelsea.

Chelsea "From Port of Chalk-Filled Ships" (Old English).

Patron Saints: For centuries Chelsea has been the name of a fashionable borough of London, England. Over the years many upper-class individuals have lived there. Two are saints. One of them was St. Thomas More, 1478-1535, who was the son of a lawyer and judge. He studied law and was admitted to the bar in 1501. He became England's leading literary light of that time.

Soon he became lord chancellor and had to face the king's divorce. After three difficult years he resigned his post and retired to his home in Chelsea. In 1534 he was arrested and imprisoned in the Tower of London. Fifteen months later he was beheaded. Today he is patron of lawyers and civil servants.

Feast Dates: June 22 — St. Thomas More of Chelsea; March 7 — Bl. John Larke of Chelsea (see Lark).

Chelsey (English) See Chelsea.

Chelsie (English) See Chelsea.

Chelsy (English) See Chelsea.

Cher (French) See Cherise.

Cheree (French) See Cherise.

Cherice (French) See Sharon.

Cherie (French) See Cherise, Sharon, Sherry.

Cherise "The Beloved One" (French).

Patron Saints: There is one medieval St. Chera. She is simply remembered as an "Irish virgin."

Feast Dates: October 16 — St. Chera.

Cherish (English) See Cherise.

Cherlyn (English double) See Charlene+Lynn.

Cherry "Like a Cherry" (Middle English) or "One Who Is Loving and Caring" (variant of Charity).

Patron Saints: In Latin the word for "cherry" is *cerasus*. This leads one to four Sts. Cera. One of them was born of royalty. She founded a nunnery in Munster and became the superior.

Feast Dates: January 5 — St. Cherry, also known as Cera.

Chery (variant) See Cherise.

Cherye (variant) See Cherise.

Cheryl (English) See Beryl, Charlene, Cherise.

Chesa (Slavic) See Selima.

Cheslie (variant) See Chelsea.

Chesna (Slavic) See Sheehan.

Chessa (American) See Cherise.

Chessie (Hispanic-American) See Cherise.

Cheyanne (variant) See Ann, Cheyenne.

Cheyenne "One Who Speaks Unintelligibly" (North American Indian).

Patron Saints: This name seems to have become popular for girls because it sounds like "shy Anne." Thus any St. Anne can be adopted as a patron. Furthermore, the fact that Cheyenne means "unintelligible speech" leads directly to a half-dozen Sts. Blaise or Blaesilla. The name Blaise means "the stammerer."

Feast Dates: July 26 — St. Anne (see Ann); January 22 — St. Blaesilla (see Blaise).

Cheyna (American) See Cheyenne.

Chi "The Life Force" (Chinese) or "The Christ" and "The Anointed One" (Greek).

Patron Saints: Chi is the "X," the twenty-second letter in the Greek alphabet. It was used by the ancients as a shorthand way of referring to Jesus Christ, the End-Time Messiah.

Feast Dates: Thirty-fourth Sunday of the Year — Christ the King.

Chiara (Italian) See Clare.

Chiarra (variant) See Clare.

Chica (Spanish) See Frances.

Chickie (nickname) See Chiquita.

Chicky (nickname) See Chiquita.

Chila (Spanish) See Frances.

China (American) See Chyna.

Chinue (Nigerian) See Ann.

Chinyere (African-American) See Chinue.

Chiquita "The Little One" (Spanish).

Patron Saints: The Spanish word *chiquita* means "little one," and this is the same meaning of the name Paula. There are a few Sts. Paula. One St. Paula was the daughter of poor parents in the 1300s, in Cardenosa, Spain. A young man who wished to have his pleasure with her relentlessly pursued her. In desperation she fled into a chapel and begged Jesus to help her. Immediately, she sprouted a beard. Needless to say, the young man lost interest in her.

Feast Dates: February 20 — St. Paula the Bearded; January 26 — St. Paula (see Paula).

Chita (variant) See Chiquita, Concepción, Conchita.

Chloe "The Young Green Growth" (Greek).

Patron Saints: There is no St. Chloe, but there are a few saints whose names contain the root *chlo*. They are Sts. Chlodoald, Chlodulf, Chlotilda, and Chlotar. And because *clo* is the Greek root for the word "green," Bl. Thomas Green might be adopted as a patron. He was a Carthusian monk in London at the beginning of the Catholic persecu-

tions under Henry VIII. He was imprisoned and starved to death in 1537.

Feast Dates: June 25 — Bl. Thomas Green; June 3 — St. Clotilda (see Clotilda).

Chloris "The Pale Green One" (Greek).

Patron Saints: Two saints with very similar names may be adopted. One was St. Choris. She was a young lady who died a martyr's death in ancient Nicaea.

Feast Dates: March 13 — St. Choris; June 3 — St. Chlotilda (see Chloe).

Chofa (Spanish) See Sophie.

Chofi (Spanish) See Sophie.

Chris (nickname) See Christine, Christy, Crystal.

Chriselda (variant) See Griselda.

Chrissie (nickname) See Christine, Christy, Crystal.

Chrissy (nickname) See Christine, Christy.

Christa (French) See Christine, Christy, Crystal.

Christabel (French double) See Christine+Belle.

Christabella (American double) See Christine, Christa+Bella.

Christal (variant) See Christine, Crystal.

Christan (variant) See Christiana, Christine.

Christean (variant) See Christiana, Christine.

Christel (French) See Christine, Crystal.

Christen (Greek) See Christiana, Christine.

Christi (nickname) See Christine, Christy, Crystal.

Christiana "The Anointed One" (Spanish).

Patron Saints: There are about a half-dozen Sts. Christiana. The best remembered is St. Christiana, 306-337. As a teenager, she was taken as a slave into what was then the kingdom of Georgia and later part of the former U.S.S.R. The people were very impressed by her virtue and prayer life. One day a woman brought her sick child and Christiana told her that Jesus could heal all things. She then said a prayer and returned the child to its mother in good health.

Rumors of the cure spread to the queen of Georgia, who was suffering from an ailment, and she sent for Christiana. She told the queen that Jesus accomplished the healing. The queen, in turn, told the king of the power in Jesus' name. Soon all of Georgia came to Jesus Christ.

Feast Dates: December 15 — St. Christiana, also known as Nino.

Christiane (German) See Christiana, Christine.

Christie (nickname) See Christine, Christy, Crystal.

Christin (Greek) See Christiana, Christine.

Christina (Spanish) See Christiana.

Christine "The Anointed One" (French).

Patron Saints: There are about a dozen Sts. Christine. One of the more colorful is St. Christina the Astonishing, 1150-1224. She was orphaned when she was only three years old. Raised by two older sisters, she had a seizure when she was about twenty-two. People thought her dead and carried her body to church in an open coffin. Mass was begun and suddenly Christina sat up. This thoroughly frightened everybody. She claimed to have actually died (probably what moderns call a "near-death experience"). She insisted that she saw hell, purgatory, and heaven and was given a choice of staying in heaven or returning to earth to pray and sacrifice for the dead. She chose to come back to earth. One story has it that she was called "The Astonishing" because of the various ways she tried to avoid other people, including one occasion when she reportedly flew like a bird to escape.

Feast Dates: July 24 — St. Christina the Astonishing.

Christmas "Anointed One+Been Sent" (Greek-Latin double).

Patron Saints: The finest patron is the Infant Jesus, born in Bethlehem. St. Francis of Assisi in the 1300s gave us the nativity scene to meditate upon. One Christmas Eve he took an infant, belonging to one of his friends, to a local cave and placed it in a rock crevice. Then in the cool darkness he thought about what God had to give up to become one of us. St. Francis believed that for the Christ-Child Christmas was an extreme sacrifice.

Feast Dates: December 25 — Birth of the Infant Jesus.

Christy "The Anointed One" (Greek).

Patron Saints: "The Christ" or "The Messiah" or "The Anointed One" is Jesus' royal title, for every king of Israel was recognized as the "anointed one." Jesus the Christ is the first and best patron. However, there is another. She is St. Christe. She died a martyr in ancient Caesarea.

Feast Dates: February 6 — St. Christe; December 25 — Birth of the Infant Jesus (see Christmas).

Christye (nickname) See Christine, Christy, Crystal.

Christyn (variant) See Christiana, Christine, Christy, Crystal.

Chrys (English) See Christine, Crystal.

Chrystal (variant) See Christine, Crystal.

Chrystyna (Ukrainian) See Christiana, Christine, Christy, Crystal.

Chyna "From China" (American) or "Fine Crockery from China" (English, Chinese).

Patron Saints: About a hundred Chinese have been officially recognized as saints in the Catholic Church. They include five Dominican martyrs in 1893, thirteen martyrs in 1900, fifty-six Boxer Rebellion martyrs in 1900, and seven martyrs in 1907.

It is estimated that more than thirty thousand Chinese Christians and foreigners were murdered during the Boxer Uprising in 1900. Among them were seven-year-old Paul Lang, nine-year-old Andrew Wang Tien-ching, eleven-year-old Andrew Wang Hsin-shih, seventy-nine-year-old Paul Lieu Chin-to, and Anna Wang (age unknown).

Feast Dates: July 20 — Boxer Rebellion Martyrs.

Ciara (Hispanic-American) See Sierra.

Ciata (nickname) See Annunciata.

Cicelie (variant) See Cecilia.

Cicelle (Hungarian) See Cecilia.

Cicely (Russian) See Cecilia.

Cidra (variant) See Sidra.

Cilla (nickname) See Priscilla.

Cinandrea (Hispanic-American double) See Cintia+Andrea.

Cinda (variant) See Cynthia, Lucinda.

Cindee (nickname) See Cynthia, Lucinda.

Cinderella "The One Who Rises from Ashes" (French).

Patron Saints: Patrons can be found in the nickname Ella. The name, meaning "one who rises from ashes," reminds one of the mythical phoenix that, in turn, is used to symbolize the resurrection of Christ.

Feast Dates: April 7 — Bl. Ralph Ashley; January 23 — St. Elli; Easter Sunday — The Risen Lord.

Cindi (variant) See Cinderella, Cynthia, Lucinda.

Cindie (nickname) See Cinderella, Cynthia, Lucinda.

Cindy (nickname) See Cinderella, Cynthia, Lucinda.

Cinnamon "The Yellow-Brown Spice" (Middle English).

Patron Saints: Casina is Greek for "cinnamon," and there is one St. Casina. She died a martyr in ancient Ancyra. There are also two saints whose names, when put together, sound much like Cinnamon. The first is St. Cinna, who was a black companion of St. Isidore in ancient times. St. Monan was a companion of St. Adrian and preached the Gospel in ancient Scotland. The pagan Danes killed him.

Feast Dates: November 7 — St. Casina, also known as Cinnamon; April 19 — St. Cinna; March 1 — St. Monan.

Cinny (nickname) See Cynthia.

Cinth (nickname) See Cynthia, Hyacinth.

Cinthea (nickname) See Cynthia, Hyacinth.

Cinthia (Spanish) See Cynthia, Hyacinth.

Cintia (Spanish) See Cynthia, Hyacinth.

Cinzia (Italian) See Cynthia.

Cissie (nickname) See Cecilia.

Cissy (nickname) See Cecilia.

Cita (nickname) See Teresita.

Citalia (Spanish) See Star.

Claartje (Dutch) See Clare.

Clair (French) See Clare.

Claire (French) See Clare.

Clara (Latin, Italian) See Clare.

Clarabelle (French double) See Clara+Belle.

Claramae (English double) See Clara+Mae.

Clare "The Brilliant One" (English).

Patron Saints: There are a half-dozen Sts. Claire and Clara. The greatest is St. Clare, 1193-1253, born in Assisi, Italy, to a rich family. At the age of eighteen she heard St. Francis of Assisi preach and was moved. Francis placed her in a convent and when this became known, her relatives tried to drag her away but could not. Soon, her sister and mother joined her. They practiced strict poverty, wore no shoes, slept on the floor, abstained from meat, did penance, and prayed. Clare, as the superior, always saw herself as a servant.

The power of her prayer was also well known. When an enemy army threatened her convent, she carried the Blessed Sacrament to the convent walls where the enemy could see it. She prayed and the army fled. She is considered patron of embroiderers, television, and against sore eyes.

Feast Dates: August 11 — St. Clare.

Clareta (Spanish double) See Clare+Ita.

Claretta (Latin double) See Clare+Etta.

Clarette (French double) See Clare+Ette.

Clarey (variant) See Clare.

Clari (variant) See Clare.

Clarice (English, French) See Clare.

Clarie (variant) See Clare.

Clarina (Dutch) See Clare.

Clarinda (German) See Clare.

Clarine (English) See Clare.

Clarissa (German, English, Spanish) See Clare.

Clarita (Slavic-Spanish double) See Clare+Ita.

Clary (Slavic) See Clare.

Claryssa (Hispanic-American) See Clare.

Claude (French) See Claudia.

Claudelle (variant) See Claudia.

Claudetta (variant double) See Claudia+Etta.

Claudette (French double) See Claudia+Ette.

Claudia "The Lame One" (Latin, German, Italian, Spanish).

Patron Saints: There are at least three Sts. Claudia. Paul writes: "Eubulus sends greetings to you, as do Pudens and Linus and Claudia and all the brethren" (2 Timothy 4:21). Christian tradition identifies her as the mother of St. Linus, the second pope. It also testifies that Claudia was the daughter of the British king Caractacus, who was defeated by the Roman general Aulus Plautius. The king and his family were sent to Rome in chains. Then Emperor Claudius released the family. Claudia remained in Rome, where she converted to Catholicism, was baptized, married Pudens, and gave birth to the future second pope.

Feast Dates: August 7 — St. Claudia.

Claudie (English) See Claudia.

Claudina (English) See Claudia.

Claudine (French) See Claudia.

Clea (nickname) See Cleopatra.

Clem (nickname) See Clementine.

Clemence (French) See Clementine.

Clementia (nickname) See Clementine.

Clementine "The Mild, Merciful One" (Greek).

Patron Saints: There are about a half-dozen Sts. Clementina and three dozen Sts. Clement. St. Clementina was one of the ten ladies-in-waiting who traveled with St. Ursula on a pilgrimage to Rome. Upon their return trip to Britain, a pagan Hun chieftain killed them near Cologne, Germany.

Feast Dates: October 21 — St. Clementina.

Clemmie (English) See Clementine.

Clemmy (English) See Clementine.

Cleo (nickname) See Cleopatra.

Cleopatra "The Father's Glory" (Greek) or "The Announcer" (from Clio, one of the Greek Muses).

Patron Saints: There are a couple of Sts. Cleopatra. One of them, in ancient times, suffered the loss of a child; but she persevered and had a church built near Mount Tabor in honor of St. Varus. On the day the church was dedicated, her twelve-year-old son, who had died, appeared to her in glory with St. Varus.

Feast Dates: October 19 — St. Cleopatra.

Clio (nickname, Spanish) See Cleopatra, Clara.

Cloe (variant) See Chloe.

Cloris (nickname) See Chloris.

Clotilda "The Famous Battle Maiden" (German).

Patron Saints: There are a few Sts. Clotilda. One lived from 474 to 545 and was married to Clovis, the king of the Franks. She was one of the primary reasons why her husband became a Catholic. Unfortunately, her husband died when she was only thirty-seven and she had to deal with many family feuds and much strife between her three sons and a daughter. Eventually she left Paris with a broken heart and took up residence at Tours in France. There, she spent the next thirty years of her life, helping the poor and sick and praying for her family. She died at the age of seventy-one.

Feast Dates: June 3 — St. Clotilda.

Clotive (African-American) See Chloe, Clotilda.

Clover "The Clover Blossom" (Old English) or "The Three-Leafed One" (Latin).

Patron Saints: Clover is often called a trefoil, from the Latin *trifolium.* This leads to Sts. Trea and Foila. St. Trea was an Irish convert to the faith who lived at Ardtree, Derry, in the 400s. She devoted her single life to prayer and solitude.

The clover also reminds one of St. Patrick, who used it to teach the doctrine of the Blessed Trinity.

Feast Dates: August 3 — St. Trea; March 3 — St. Foila; Trinity Sunday — Holy Trinity (see Trinidad).

Coco (Spanish) See Jacqueline.

Codi (variant) See Cody.

Codie (variant) See Cody.

Cody "The Cushion" (Old English).

Patron Saints: There are two Sts. Cody. St. Coddeus died a martyr's death in ancient Sicily.

Feast Dates: May 10 — St. Cody, also known as Coddeus.

Coleen (variant) See Colleen.

Colene (variant) See Colleen.

Coletta (variant) See Colette.

Colette "Little+Victorious One" (Greek-French double).

Patron Saints: Colette is a form of Nicole, and there is at least one St. Colette, 1381-1447, the patron of pregnant women. At age seventeen she gave what little she had to the poor and entered a convent. After embracing solitude for three years, she had a vision of St. Francis, who told her to restore the rule of St. Clare in all of it severity. She met with the Holy Father and received permission to do this. Then she traveled from convent to convent, reforming them. At first she met with opposition, but in time, her reforms gained sympathizers. Behind all her activity was a strong and deep life of prayer. She always prayed for sinners. And after foretelling her own death, she died at the age of sixty-seven.

Feast Dates: March 6 — St. Colette.

Colleen "The Young Girl" (Irish Gaelic) or "The Young Maiden" (Irish Gaelic).

Patron Saints: Knowing the Irish spelling is Cailin leads to a St. Collen who was born in Wales in about 600, and upon reaching adulthood, became a monk. He spent some time in Brittany and eventually became the abbot of a monastery in Wales. There is also a group of single women (Colleens) who were driven into exile because they insisted on burying Christian dead around the year 200.

Feast Dates: May 20 — St. Collen; October 17 — Holy Maidens; November 1 — St. Cailan (see Cailin).

Colleta (variant) See Colette, Nichole.

Collete (French) See Colette, Nichole.

Collie (variant) See Colleen.

Colline (variant) See Colleen.

Colly (variant) See Colleen.

Comfort (nickname) See Consolata.

Con (nickname) See Concepción, Conchita, Concordia, Consolata, Constance, Consuelo.

Concepción "The Conception" (Spanish).

Patron Saints: On December 8, 1854, Pope Pius IX infallibly declared the doctrine of the Immaculate Conception with these words: "We declare and define, by the authority of our Lord Jesus Christ, the doctrine that the Blessed Virgin Mary, in the first instant of her conception, was by the singular grace and privilege of God, in view of the merits of Christ . . . preserved free from every stain of original sin."

This is based upon the tradition of the Church and Scripture. St. Luke relates that the message of Gabriel to Mary was that she was "full of grace." To be "full of grace" means "never to be touched by sin." It was the constant tradition of the Church that Mary was ever-virgin and, in the Bible, "virgin" is symbolic of commitment. To be "ever-virgin" is to "always say yes" and "never sin." Finally, the Immaculate Conception provides an answer to the problem of abortion.

What God did for Mary, at the first moment of her conception, he does for all of us at baptism. He defeats sin and fills us with his presence. Only a person can be saved from sin. Thus preservation from sin, from conception, is another way of saying that persons really begin to exist at conception.

Feast Dates: December 8 — The Immaculate Conception of the Blessed Virgin Mary, Patron of the U.S.A.

Concha (variant) See Concepción, Conchita.

Conchita "The One Conceived" (Spanish).

Patron Saints: There is one Mexican-American saint-in-the-making available. SG Concepción Cabrera de Armida, 1862-1937, was known to everyone in Mexico as Conchita. She was destined to become the mother of nine children. However, her first child died at the age of six years. Then her husband and two more sons and a daughter died. She handled her pain by turning ever more toward the Lord. In 1889 she began having visions. At the request of her spiritual director she filled over one hundred volumes with her experiences. She reminded all that "no matter what path we take in life, it always passes by the Cross."

In the 1920s, when the Church was being persecuted in Mexico, she often risked death to hide clergy in her home. Only after reaching the age of seventy-five and suffering deep desolation, did she die at home and in bed.

Feast Dates: March 3 — SG Concepción Cabrera de Armida; December 8 — Immaculate Conception of the Blessed Virgin Mary (see Concepción).

Concordia "The Harmonious One" (Latin).

Patron Saints: There is at least one St. Concordia and almost a dozen Sts. Concordius. St. Concordia was the wife of a Roman jailer named Hippolytus. It was the duty of Hippolytus to imprison and torture Christians, including the deacon St. Lawrence in 258.

Hippolytus and Concordia were so impressed by Lawrence that they converted to Christianity. Then they converted nineteen members of their household to the Catholic faith. This did not set well with the emperor. He had the whole family executed.

Feast Dates: February 22 — St. Concordia; July 31 — St. Harmon (see Harmony).

Condoleeza "One Who Is Sympathetic+The Oath of God" (African-American double).

Patron Saints: This seems to be a modern compound name created by joining Condolence to Leeza (Elizabeth). There is a St. Conda. In ancient times he was the abbot of Boiredha-Conna in Ireland.

One could also adopt Our Lady of Consolation as a patron saint. See Consolata; also see Elizabeth.

Feast Dates: April 12 — St. Conda.

Congetta (variant) See Concepción.

Conni (nickname) See Concepción, Conchita, Concordia, Consolata, Constance, Consuelo.

Connie (nickname) See Concepción, Conchita, Concordia, Consolata, Constance, Consuelo.

Conny (nickname) See Concepción, Conchita, Concordia, Consolata, Constance, Consuelo.

Consolata "The One Who Comforts" (Italian).

Patron Saints: In addition to the Blessed Virgin Mary, as Our Lady of Consolation, one could pick an even more powerful patron. In the Book of Genesis God consoles our first parents by promising a Savior immediately after judging and condemning evil. Israel awaited the Divine Consolation, thus: "Now there was a man in Jerusalem, whose name was Simeon, and this man was righteous and devout, looking for the consolation of Israel" (Luke 2:25). Ultimately, Jesus the Divine Consolation came into our world and he expects humanity to cooperate in the process of salvation. Mary began the final defeat of evil by giving her "yes" to God and became the "Mother of Consolation." Through her, God brought us to Jesus and salvation.

Feast Dates: September 24 — Our Lady of Consolation.

Constance "The Firm One" (Latin, English).

Patron Saints: There are a half-dozen Sts. Constantia. When the French Revolution began in 1789, all religious orders were forced to close by the government, except those engaged in teaching and nursing. Thus the Carmelite sisters at Compiégne, who gave themselves mainly to prayer, were driven from their convent. However, they continued to meet and live the religious life in secret. In 1794 they were arrested and sentenced to death for this crime. One by one they climbed the steps of the guillotine proclaiming, "We are condemned for clinging to our religion. We have the happiness to die for God." Sixteen sisters died this way, the oldest was seventy-eight. St. Constance Meunier was the youngest, at only sixteen years of age.

Feast Dates: July 17 — St. Constance Meunier.

Constancia (Spanish) See Constance.

Constanta (Romanian) See Constance.

Constantia (Spanish, Romanian) See Constance.

Constanza (Spanish) See Constance.

Consuela (variant) See Consuelo.

Consuella (variant) See Consuelo.

Consuelo "The One Who Counsels" (Spanish).

Patron Saints: There is one St. Consul. But by far the best patron is the Blessed Virgin. St. Paul tells us that Christ is "the power of God and the wisdom of God" (1 Corinthians 1:24).

We must never forget that Jesus was also born of a woman. Her womb and lap were his home. Thus Mary became the "Seat of Wisdom." Furthermore, raising the Christ Child daily exposed Mary to the wisdom of God. Through Jesus, she became wise — thus the name "Our Lady of Good Counsel." This devotion to our Lady was begun in Genazzano, Italy, on April 25, 1467. Mary is revered as the patron of enlightenment.

Feast Dates: April 25 — Our Lady of Good Counsel.

Conswella (African-American) See Consuelo.

Cor (nickname) See Concordia, Cora, Coral, Cordelia.

Cora "The Maiden" (Greek) or "Loving Heart" (Latin).

Patron Saints: A few saints have Cor as part of their names, such as: St. Corebus and St. Thomas of Cori. Note that *cor* is Latin for "heart." There are also the two greatest "Hearts." One belongs to Jesus; the other to his Mother, Mary. Devotion to the Immaculate Heart of Mary is based on the Bible (see Luke 2:19). Devotion to Mary's Immaculate Heart rose as a very popular devotion from the 1100s to the 1400s and continues today.

Feast Dates: Saturday After the Second Sunday of Pentecost — The Immaculate Heart of Mary.

Corabel (Greek-French double) See Cora+Belle.

Corabele (Greek-French double) See Cora+Belle.

Corabella (Greek-Italian double) See Cora+Belle.

Coraima (Hispanic-American double) See Cora+Aimee.

Coral "The Gem from the Sea" (Latin).

Patron Saints: Many ancients prized coral, which was often used in the making of opaque and colored glass. In the Middle Ages it was used as medicine for the heart and fevers. Also, superstitious people wore coral necklaces to ward off evil spirits. For this reason a coral necklace often appears in medieval paintings on or near the Baby Jesus. It is the artist's way of saying that Jesus came to deliver us from evil. He did it by suffering.

Feast Dates: Good Friday — Jesus, Protector from Evil (see Griffin).

Coralie (French) See Coral.

Coraline (English) See Cora.

Corazón (Spanish) See Cora.

Cordelia "The Jewel of the Sea" (Middle Welsh) or "The Warm Heart" (Latin).

Patron Saints: There is one medieval St. Cordula who was one of ten ladies-in-waiting to St. Ursula. She accompanied her on a pilgrimage to Rome. She was killed with her in 360.

Feast Dates: October 22 — St. Cordula.

Cordelle (variant) See Cordelia.

Cordey (variant) See Cordelia.

Cordi (Welsh) See Cordelia.

Cordie (variant) See Cordelia.

Cordula (variant) See Cordelia.

Cordy (variant) See Cordelia.

Coreen (variant) See Cora.

Corella (variant) See Coral.

Corena (variant) See Cora.

Corenda (variant) See Cora.

Corene (variant) See Cora.

Coretta (Greek double) See Cora+Etta.

Corette (French double) See Cora+Ette.

Corey (Greek) See Cora, Cornelia.

Cori (Irish) See Cora, Coral, Cornelia.

Coriann (American) See Cora/Coral+ Ann.

Corie (variant) See Cora, Coral.

Corilla (variant) See Coral.

Corina (Greek, Spanish) See Cora.

Corinne (Irish) See Cora.

Corisa (variant) See Corissa.

Corissa "The Greatest Maiden" (Greek) or "The Greatest Loving Heart" (Latin).

Patron Saints: From ancient times, Catholics have been devoted to the love of God. This love took human form in Jesus. Thus in seeking to become one with the Sacred Heart of Jesus, the believer seeks union with God. He also seeks to be loved and understood by a God-Man, by a heart that truly understands the human condition. Devotion to the Sacred Heart became a very popular devotion in the 1200s and 1300s. It continues to be popular in modern times.

Feast Dates: Friday After the Second Sunday After Pentecost — The Sacred Heart of Jesus.

Corla (African-American) See Cora.

Corliss (English) See Cora.

Cornela (variant) See Cornelia.

Cornelia "The Yellow-Colored One" (Latin).

Patron Saints: There are a few ancient Sts. Cornelia and one modern American saint-in-the-making. Ven. Cornelia Peacock, 1809-1879, was the daughter of a prominent Protestant Philadelphia couple, but she was orphaned while young and raised by her sister. At the age of twenty-two she became an Episcopalian and married an Episcopal priest, Pierce Connelly. They had four children.

Moving to Natchez, Mississippi, they met Catholics and decided to convert to Catholicism. Soon Pierce felt called to be a priest. Cornelia, at the age of thirty-five, agreed to live apart, and in 1843 Rome also agreed. Pierce was ordained and Cornelia entered a Roman convent with her youngest child.

Later Pierce returned to the Anglican Church and made life miserable for her when she would not return to him. He even won custody of their children and turned them against her. She founded a religious order to teach young girls and remained faithful to her Catholic faith.

Feast Dates: April 18 — Ven. Cornelia Connelly, S.H.C.J.

Cornelie (variant) See Cornelia.

Cornie (nickname) See Cornelia.

Corny (nickname) See Cornelia.

Corona "The Crowned One" (Latin).

Patron Saints: There are a couple of ancient Sts. Corona. One was a single woman who died a martyr's death in Roman times. She is now patron of games of chance, lotteries, and hidden treasure.

Feast Dates: May 14 — St. Corona.

Corra (variant) See Cora.

Correa (Hispanic-American) See Cora.

Correy (nickname) See Cora.

Corrie (nickname) See Cora.

Corrina (variant) See Cora.

Corrine (variant) See Cora.

Corry (nickname) See Cora.

Corteney (English) See Courtney.

Cortnay (English) See Courtney.

Cortney (English) See Courtney.

Cortnie (English) See Courtney.

Cory (English) See Cora, Coral, Cornelia.

Cosette (French double) See Nichole+ Ette.

Costanza (Italian) See Constance.

Countess "The Noblewoman" (Middle English).

Patron Saints: There are many saints who held the royal rank of "Countess." One is Bl. Ela, countess of Salisbury, England. Another is St. Regina, countess of Ostrevent, wife of Bl. Count Aldebert, mother of ten daughters, and a relative of King Pepin of France in the 700s. Aldebert and Regina founded an abbey for their daughters. The oldest, St. Renfroy, became its first abbess.

Feast Dates: July 1 — St. Regina, Countess of Ostrevent; November 1 — Bl. Ela, Countess of Salisbury (see Elata).

Courtney "From the Law Court" (Old French) or "From the Short One's Manor" (Old English).

Patron Saints: Throughout history Christians found the civil courts to be tools that often condemned them to death. Testimony that they were Christian provided the evidence that brought death to the body.

For this reason, the Gospel of John uses "courtroom terms" throughout, such as: "testified," "witness," "judgment." It teaches that if one is condemned to be a "martyr" on earth for being a Christian, such a person will be found deserving of eternal life in heaven. This makes all the martyrs patron saints of Courtney.

Feast Dates: November 1 — All Holy Martyrs (Feast of All Saints).

Crecia (nickname) See Lucretia.

Creola "The One Native to the Region" (variant of the French-Spanish Creole).

Patron Saints: In the early 1800s, after overcoming many obstacles with the help of the Blessed Virgin Mary, Sister St. Michel arrived in New Orleans with a newly carved statue of Our Lady of Prompt Succor and immediately introduced this devotion.

The great test of Mary's power arrived on January 8, 1815. It seems that twenty thousand well-trained and well-equipped British troops were preparing to attack just south of New Orleans. Opposing them were six thousand ill-quipped American fishermen, farmers, flatboatmen, frontiersmen, and pirates under the command of General Andrew Jackson. The last battle of the War of 1812 was about to be fought.

The wives, mothers, and sisters of these men were terrified at the almost certain prospect of military defeat and the deaths of their menfolk. They quickly assembled at the Ursuline chapel and stormed heaven with continuous prayers for a night and a day.

Then news came of the miraculous American victory. A short time later General Jackson himself came to the chapel and admitted divine intervention in the American victory. The Ursuline sisters vowed to honor the Blessed Virgin, under the title of "Our Lady of Prompt Succor," every January 8, with a special Mass. In 1928 the archbishop and bishops of Louisiana officially recognized this native devotion and made Our Lady of Prompt Succor patron of New Orleans and of the state of Louisiana.

Feast Dates: January 8 — Our Lady of Prompt Succor.

Cricket "The One Who Echoes" (Old French).

Patron Saints: The Spanish (as well as Italian) word for "cricket" is *grillo*, and there are a half-dozen Sts. Grellan. One of them, St. Grellan Obelech, served God in Ireland while St. Columba of Iona was alive. There is also a St. Echa, who lived as a priest-hermit in York, England, and died in 767.

Feast Dates: April 15 — St. Grellen; May 5 — St. Echa.

Cris (nickname) See Christine, Christy, and Crystal.

Crishana (African-American double) See Chris+Shawna.

Crispina "The Curly-Haired One" (Latin).

Patron Saints: There are at least two Sts. Crispina and a dozen Sts. Crispinus. One St. Crispina was a rich black woman who lived in Numidia, Africa. In 304 she was arrested and tortured because she was a Christian Catholic. Eventually she was beheaded at Thebeste, Algeria.

Feast Dates: December 5 — St. Crispina.

Crissi (nickname) See Christine, Christy, Crystal.

Crissie (nickname) See Christine, Christy, Crystal.

Crissy (nickname) See Christine, Christy, Crystal.

Crista (variant) See Christine, Crystal.

Cristal (variant) See Christine, Crystal.

Cristel (variant) See Christine, Crystal.

Cristen (variant) See Christiana, Christine, Christy.

Cristi (nickname) See Christine, Christy, Crystal.

Cristie (nickname) See Christine, Christy, Crystal.

Cristin (Irish) See Christian, Christine.

Cristina (Spanish, Italian, Portuguese) See Christine.

Cristine (variant) See Christiana, Christine.

Cristiona (Irish) See Christiana, Christine.

Cristy (Spanish) See Christine, Christy, Crystal.

Crisy (nickname) See Christine, Christy, Crystal.

Crystal "The Anointed One" (English form of Christine) or "Fire in Ice" (Middle English).

Patron Saints: Some scholars think that Crystal is a form of Christine; others do not.

For the ancients, crystal, a type of quartz, was a wonderful mystery. It was clear to the eye and cold to the touch. Some thought it was permanently frozen water, yet light passing through it could be focused to make fire. Crystal is mentioned in the Bible several times. It links it with coral in Job 28:18. In Ezekiel 1:22 "the likeness of a firmament" is described as "shining like crystal." Revelation 22:1 tells us that "the river of the water of life" is as "bright as crystal." Thus crystal reminds one of purity, harmony, and eternal life in family.

Feast Dates: November 1 — The Heavenly Family; July 24 — St. Christine the Astonishing (see Christine).

Crystel (variant) See Christine, Crystal.

Crysti (variant) See Christine, Christy, Crystal.

Crystie (variant) See Christine, Christy, Crystal.

Crysty (variant) See Christine, Christy, Crystal.

Cutrina (African-American) See Katrina.

Cybele (French, Greek) See Sibyl.

Cybil (English) See Sibyl.

Cybill (variant) See Sibyl.

Cybille (variant) See Sibyl.

Cydney (French) See Sydney.

Cydnie (variant) See Sydney.

Cymbre (variant) See Kimberly.

Cyn (variant) See Cynthia.

Cyndi (English) See Cynthia, Lucinda.

Cyndia (variant) See Cynthia.

Cyndie (variant) See Cynthia, Lucinda.

Cyndy (English) See Cynthia, Lucinda.

Cynth (English) See Cynthia.

Cynthea (nickname) See Cynthia, Hyacinth.

Cynthia "The Moon" (Greek) or "The Blue Larkspur Flower" (short form of Hyacinth).

Patron Saints: For starters, Cynthia is recognized as a short form of Hyacinth. Furthermore, while there is no St. Cynthia, there are many other names that, like Cynthia, mean "moon." They include Diana and Luna. Many patrons can be found among them.

Feast Dates: June 9 — Bl. Diane d'Andalo; January 30 — St. Hyacintha de Mariscotti (see Hyacinth).

Cynthie (French) See Cynthia, Hyacinth.

Cynthy (nickname) See Cynthia, Hyacinth.

Cyntia (Polish) See Cynthia.

Cyrilla "The Regal One" (Greek) or "The Ladylike One" (Greek).

Patron Saints: There are six Sts. Cyrilla. One died a martyr in ancient Potenza.

Feast Dates: May 13 — St. Cyrilla.

𝒟

Dace (nickname) See Candace.

Dacey "The Southerner" (Irish Gaelic) or "The Bright White One" (nickname for Candace).

Patron Saints: One meaning makes Dacey a form of Candace or Candida. There are thirty Sts. Candida. Its other meaning, "the southerner," leads to Bl. William Southerne, a diocesan English Catholic priest. He was executed by the English government for being a Catholic and a priest in 1618.

Feast Dates: April 30 — Bl. William Southerne; September 4 — St. Candace (see Candida).

Dacia (Irish) See Dacey.

Dacie (variant) See Dacey.

Dacy (variant) See Dacey.

Dael (variant) See Dale.

Daffi (nickname) See Daffodil, Daphne.

Daffie (variant) See Daffodil, Daphne.

Daffodil "The Daffodil Lily Flower" (Old English).

Patron Saints: There is one St. Lily. Also, the name Daffodil, like Susanna, means "lily."

Feast Dates: March 2 — St. Lily, also known as Liliosa; August 11 — St. Susanna (see Susan).

Daffy (nickname) See Daffodil, Daphne.

Dafny (American) See Daffodil, Daphne.

Dagmar "The Day Maid" (Scandinavian) or "The Glorious Day" (Old German) or "The Glory of the Danes" (German) or "The Famous Thinker" (German) or "The Joy of the Land" (German).

Patron Saints: The various possible meanings of this name lead to many possible patrons. One candidate might be St. Day (also known as Dye). This saint is honored in a Cornish church near Redruth. Another candidate could be St. Zita, who has been named patron of maids.

Feast Dates: January 18 — St. Day, also known as Dye; April 27 — St. Zita (see Zita).

Dahlia "Flower from the Valley" (Swedish).

Patron Saints: Knowing that Dahlia means "from the valley" easily provides a patron.

Feast Dates: January 29 — St. Dallan Forgaill (see Dale).

Dain (variant) See Dana.

Dainnese (American double) See Danielle+Denise.

Daisie (English) See Daisy.

Daisy "The Eye of the Day" (Old English) or "The Pearl" (nickname for Margaret).

Patron Saints: Medieval Christian art used the daisy to symbolize the innocence of the Infant Jesus. As a result, the Infant of Prague is a good choice for patron. This devotion dates to 1556 when María Manríquez de Lara brought an eighteen-inch statue of the Baby Jesus with her to Bohemia. In 1637 the statue was in the possession of a Carmelite monastery in Prague. One day when a certain Father Cyrillus was meditating before it, he heard the words "Have pity on me, and I will have pity on you. Give me my hands and I will give you peace." The monk noticed the statue's hands had broken off. He eventually had the statue repaired even though his superior, the prior, created many obstacles. A short time later, when a plague spread through Prague, the prior became ill to the point of death. He then promised God to spread devotion to the Infant if he recovered and the plague ended. Both requests were granted and the prior kept his word.

Also, because Marguerite is the common name for the "daisy flower" in France, any saint named Margaret can serve as a patron for a person named Daisy. There are about two dozen Sts. Margaret.

Feast Dates: Christmas — The Infant of Prague; October 16 — St. Margaret Mary Alacoque (see Margaret).

Dakota "Thought of as a Friend" (North American Indian).

Patron Saints: There is no St. Dakota. However, patrons can be found if one realizes that Dakota means "thought of as a friend." The Latin word for "friend" is *amicus.* There are three Sts. Amicus and one St. Amicia. St. Amicia is remembered for living the life of a virgin. Her relics are venerated in France.

There is also one man, St. Abraham, who is officially named a "friend of God" in James 2:23.

Feast Dates: November 1 — St. Amicia; October 9 — St. Abraham, Patriarch (see Abra).

Dal (variant) See Dallas.

Dale "From the Valley" (Old English).

Patron Saints: There are a few ancient saints with names similar to Dale, such as Dallan, Dalmatius, and Dalua. Any of them can serve as patrons. One was St. Dale, born of royalty in Connaught, Ireland, in about 550. He was a great scholar. Later in life he went completely blind. Many thought this was due to his studying so hard. He died at the hands of pirates, while at sea, in 598.

Feast Dates: January 29 — St. Dale, also known as Dallan Forgaill.

Dalena (nickname) See Madeline, Magdalena.

Dalenna (variant) See Madeline, Magdalena.

Dalia (Spanish) See Dahlia, Dale.

Dalila (Swahili) See Damara, Delilah.

Dall (variant) See Dallas.

Dallas "The Wise One" (Irish Gaelic).

Patron Saints: There is no known St. Dallas. However, there is an ancient saint with a very similar name.

Feast Dates: January 29 — St. Dallan Forgaill (see Dale); September 30 — St. Sophia (see Sophia).

Damara "The Gentle Girl" (Greek) or "The Wife" (form of Mavis).

Patron Saints: There is at least one ancient saint with this name. St. Damaris is mentioned in Acts 17:34. She believed in the preaching of St. Paul the Apostle.

Feast Dates: October 4 — St. Damaris.

Damaris (Greek) See Damara, Mavis.

Dame (English) See Damara, Domina, Donna, Madonna, Martha, Mavis.

Damica (French) See Dakota.

Damita (Spanish double) See Damara+Ita.

Dan (variant) See Dana, Danielle.

Dana "From Denmark" (Scandinavian) or "God Is My Judge" (nickname for Danielle).

Patron Saints: There are about a half-dozen saints with similar names, including Sts. Danacha, Danax, and Danda. One of them, St. Danacha, suffered martyrdom in 344 during the persecution by King Shapur II.

Also, Dana can be identified as a variant of Daniel, which means "God is my judge."

Feast Dates: November 20 — St. Danacha; October 19 — St. Antoine Daniel (see Danielle).

Danae "Mother of Perseus" (Greek).

Patron Saints: There is a saint with a similar name who can be adopted.

Feast Dates: November 20 — St. Danacha (see Dana).

D'Andrea (African-American) See De+ Andrea.

Dane (variant) See Dana.

Daneen (variant double) See Danielle+ Ina.

Danella (American) See Danielle.

Danelle (Hebrew) See Danielle.

Danette (French double) See Danielle+ Ette.

Dani (variant) See Danica, Danielle.

Dania (Latin) See Dana.

Danica "The Morning Star" (Old Slavic) or "God Is My Judge" (Hebrew form of Danielle).

Patron Saints: There is one great patron who is known as the "Morning Star." The Old Testament uses the image of a "star" to foretell the coming of the Messiah. "I see him, but not now; I behold him, but not nigh: a star shall come forth out of Jacob" (Numbers 24:17). In the New Testament, Jesus declares: "I am the root and the offspring of David, the bright morning star" (Revelation 22:16). Thus Jesus as the "Morning Star" is the best patron. This title identifies him as the victor of life over death and God over Satan. We must keep our eyes on Jesus because as the "Morning Star" he is our guide and pathway to God the Father.

Feast Dates: Fifth and Eighteenth Sundays of the Year — Jesus the Morning Star.

Danice (American double) See Danica/ Danielle+Janice.

Daniela (Spanish, Italian) See Danielle.

Daniella (Estonian, Hungarian) See Danielle.

Danielle "God Is My Judge" (French).

Patron Saints: There are three dozen Sts. Daniel. One of them was St. Daniel, who with his wife, Varda, were martyrs in Persia in 344.

Feast Dates: February 25 — Sts. Daniel and Varda.

Danika (variant) See Danica.

Danila (Serbian, Slovakian, Slovenian) See Danielle.

Danina (variant double) See Danielle, Ina.

Danine (variant double) See Danielle, Ina.

Danisha (variant) See Danielle.

Danit (variant) See Danielle.

Danita (English) See Danielle.

Danni (variant) See Danielle.

Danny (variant) See Danielle.

Dannya (variant) See Dana, Danielle.

Dannye (variant) See Danielle.

Danula (African-American) See Danielle.

Danya (variant) See Dana, Danielle.

Danyalis (Hispanic-American) See Dana, Danielle.

Danyell (American) See Danielle.

Danyella (American) See Danielle.

Danyelle (American) See Danielle.

Daphna (variant) See Daphne.

Daphne "From the Laurel Tree" (Greek).

Patron Saints: There is one known St. Daphne. She is simply remembered as a "Roman virgin."

Feast Dates: November 1 — St. Daphne.

Dara "From the House of Compassion" (Hebrew).

Patron Saints: Daria could be the root of Dara, and there are about a half-dozen ancient Sts. Daria.

Feast Dates: August 8 — St. Daria (see Daria).

D'Arcey (variant) See Darcie.

Darci (Irish) See Darcie.

Darcie "Dark One" (Irish) or "From the Fortress" (Old French).

Patron Saints: A few ancient saints had names similar to Darcie. One is St. Darerca, who was the sister of St. Patrick and was married twice. Before her first husband died she gave him nine children; with her second husband she had six more. Ten of her children became bishops and all of her children are recognized as saints. Unfortunately, modern Americans remember only one child: St. Mel. St. Darerca died in 516.

It should also be remembered that Darcie can mean "dark." In English this is often equated with "brown"; therefore, someone named Darcie may consider the English martyr Bl. William Browne as a patron saint.

Feast Dates: February 13 — St. Darerca; September 5 — Bl. William Browne (see Mahogany).

Darda (variant) See Dara.

Dareen (variant) See Dara.

Dari (variant) See Dara.

Daria "The Queenly One" (Greek, Spanish).

Patron Saints: There are about a half-dozen ancient Sts. Daria. One of them was a woman who joined St. Brigid's religious order. Being blind from birth did not stop her from serving Jesus as a religious sister. She died in 480 at the age of eighteen. Keep in mind also that Regina in Latin means "queen," and this leads one to the Blessed Virgin Mary.

Feast Dates: August 8 — St. Daria; August 22 — The Blessed Virgin Mary, Queen of Heaven and Earth (see Queen).

Darian (Greek) See Dara.

Darileen (variant) See Daryl.

Darla (English) See Dara, Darleen.

Darleen "The Little Dear One" (Anglo-French) or "The Little Darling" (Old English).

Patron Saints: There is a saint by the name of Kentigern Mungo and *mungo* means "darling." He worked as a missionary bishop in medieval Scotland until he was driven into exile in Wales. After staying with St. David for a while, he returned to Scotland and continued his missionary efforts. He died in 603.

Feast Dates: January 13 — St. Kentigern Mungo.

Darlen (variant) See Darleen.

Darlene (French) See Darleen.

Darling (English) See Darleen, Daryl.

Darlyn (American) See Darleen.

Darlyne (American) See Darleen.

Darnella (American) See Darnell.

Darrelle (American) See Daryl.

Darryl (American) See Daryl.

Darta (Latvian) See Dorothy.

Darva (variant double) See Dara/Daria+Van/Vanessa.

Darya (variant) See Dara.

Daryl "The Little Darling" (Old French).

Patron Saints: There are a half-dozen ancient Sts. Daria.

Feast Dates: August 18 — St. Daria (see Dara); January 13 — St. Kentigern Mungo (see Darleen).

Dasha (Russian) See Dorothy.

Dashanica (African-American double) See Dasha+Nicki.

Dasi (variant) See Dacey, Daisy.

Dasie (variant) See Dacey, Daisy.

Dasya (variant) See Daisy, Dorothy.

Daughter "The Female Child of" (Middle English).

Patron Saints: While somewhat awkward, Daughter is used by some modern feminists like "son" in "Jackson," meaning "son of Jack." Thus Elizabethdaughter means "daughter of Elizabeth." The Latin for "daughter" is *filia nata*. There is one St. Fillian. He preached the Gospel in Ireland during the time of St. Patrick.

Feast Dates: June 20 — St. Fillian.

Daveen (English) See Davita.

Daveta (English) See Davita.

Davette (American double) See Davita+ Ette.

Davida (Hebrew) See Davita.

Davina (English, Scottish) See Davita.

Davisha (African-American double) See Davita+Aisha/Isha.

Davita "The Beloved One" (Hebrew, English).

Patron Saints: There is one St. Davita and about three dozen Sts. David. St. Davita was a member of a small group of Catholics who became the victims of the Arian king Huneric in the 400s in Carthage, Africa. It seems that their persecutors amused themselves by devising all sorts of exotic tortures for this group of martyrs, one of their methods involving Davita being skinned alive.

Feast Dates: December 6 — St. Davita.

Davonna (American double) See Davita/ Donna+Yvonne.

Dawn "From the Dawn" (Old English) or "From the Sunrise" (Old English).

Patron Saints: The fact that the name Dawn means "sunrise" leads to several patrons. It is important to know that the names Aurora and Oriana also mean "dawn." Rori is a nickname for these, and there is a St. Roricius.

Jesus, as the rising Morning Star, may also be adopted as a patron.

Feast Dates: Fifth and Eighteenth Sundays of the Year — Jesus the Morning Star (see Danica); July 21 — St. Roricius (see Oriana).

Dawna (English) See Dawn.

Dawnisha (African-American double) See Dawn+Aisha/Isha.

Dawnn (English) See Dawn.

Dayana (Latin) See Diana.

Dayle (English) See Dale.

Daysha (American) See Dorothy through Dasha.

De "From" (French prefix) or "The Fiery Little One" (nickname for the Irish name Edana).

Patron Saints: The French prefix *De* or *D'*, indicating origin, has been much preferred by modern African-Americans, usually when constructing male names. For example: DeShaun, DeWayne, and Devonne. It is sometimes used in female names such as Delita and DeVera. De can also be a form of Dee, and this leads to a patron.

Feast Dates: July 5 — St. De (see Edana); August 6 — The Transfiguration of Jesus (see Delight).

Dea "The Female Who Is Like God" (Spanish).

Patron Saints: God can also act as a patron.

Feast Dates: Trinity Sunday — The Divine Godhead.

Deafilia (Spanish double) See Dea+Filia.

Deana "The Divine One" (variant form of Diana) or "From the Valley" (a variant of Dale) or "From Indian Country" (American short form of Indiana).

Patron Saints: Deana finds its roots in three different names that provide many patrons. First, Deana may be a form of Diana. Second, it may be a variant of Dale. Third, it can be a short form of Indiana.

Besides, there is a Bl. William Dean, an English diocesan priest-martyr. As an adult, he converted to Catholicism, traveled to France, then studied for the priesthood and was ordained in due course. He immediately returned to England, where he was caught and banished. However, he returned and was sentenced to be hanged, drawn, and quartered. At his execution, when he tried to speak, he was choked into silence.

Feast Dates: August 28 — Bl. William Dean; June 9 — Bl. Diane d'Andalo (see Diana).

Deanna (variant) See Deana, Diana.

Deanne (variant) See Diana, Geraldine, Indiana.

Deb (nickname) See Deborah.

Debbee (nickname) See Deborah.

Debbi (nickname) See Deborah.

Debbie (nickname) See Deborah.

Debby (nickname) See Deborah.

Debera (variant) See Deborah.

Debi (nickname) See Deborah.

Debora (variant) See Deborah.

Deborah "The Bee" (Hebrew).

Patron Saints: It is good to note that the Greek word *melissa* means "honeybee," and there is a St. Melosa.

But more important, the Bible introduces a St. Deborah who served God in about 1200 to 1050 B.C. as a Jewish "judge." The Book of Judges tells the stories of twelve of these people. It seems that whenever the ancient Jews forgot about God, he let them be oppressed. When they repented, he would raise a judge to free them.

The Bible reveals something unusual (deplorable or otherwise) about each ancient judge: Ehud was left-handed; Gideon was the poorest of the poor; Jephthah was a robber; Samson was a brutal womanizing lout; and Deborah is included among the judges simply because she was a woman. The ancients considered females weak. But God chose the weak to reveal his power, not the human power.

Feast Dates: November 1 — St. Deborah; June 1 — St. Melosa (see Melissa).

Debra (American) See Deborah.

Debs (nickname) See Deborah.

December "Born in the Tenth Month" (Middle English).

Patron Saints: There is one ancient saint named Decima, which is from the Latin for "ten."

Feast Dates: April 14 — St. Decima (see Dixie).

Decima (Latin) See December, Dixie.

Dede (variant) See Dee, Deirdre, Delia, Diana.

Dedie (variant) See Deirdre, Delia, Diana.

Dedre (variant) See Deirdre.

Dedriana (African-American double) See Dedre+Adriana.

Dee "From the Sacred River" (Celtic) or "The Dark One" (modern variant of the Welsh *du*).

Patron Saints: Besides being a Celtic and a Welsh name in its own right, Dee may also serve as a nickname for Edana, Delia, Deirdre, Dolores, or Dorothy. This leads to many possible patrons.

Feast Dates: July 5 — St. De (see Edana); November 29 — SG Dorothy Day (see Dorothy).

Dee Dee (nickname) See Dee, Delia, Diana.

Deena (American) See Dena, Diana, Dinah, Indiana.

Deerdre (variant) See Deirdre.

Deetsje (Dutch) See Deborah.

Deeyn (variant) See Diana, Deana.

Dehlia (variant) See Delia.

Deidra (Irish) See Davita.

Deigh (nickname) See Dee.

Deirdre "The Sorrowful One" (Irish Gaelic) or "The Chatterer" (Irish Gaelic).

Patron Saints: One meaning of the name is "sorrow," and this leads directly to Mary, Mother of Sorrows.

Feast Dates: September 15 — Mary, Mother of Sorrows (see Dolores).

Del (nickname) See Dell.

Dela (variant) See Ardella, Delia.

Delcina (variant) See Delcine.

Delcine "The Sweet One" (English).

Patron Saints: There is at least one St. Dulcissima. She died for her faith in Jesus in ancient Sutri, Italy.

Feast Dates: September 16 — St. Dulcissima.

Delfeen (variant) See Delphine.

Delfeena (variant) See Delphine.

Delfine (variant) See Delphine.

Delia "The Moon Goddess of Delos" (Greek).

Patron Saints: For some, Delia refers to an ancient Greek moon goddess. For others, it is a short form of Adelaide, and this leads to two dozen saints.

Feast Dates: December 16 — St. Adelaide (see Adelaide); December 24 — St. Adela (see Adela).

Delicia (Latin) See Delight.

Delight "The Delightful One Who Gives Pleasure" (Old French).

Patron Saints: The Gospel of Matthew clearly indicates that it is Jesus, the Son of God, in whom God delights (see Matthew 17:5).

Feast Dates: August 6 — The Transfiguration of Jesus.

Delila (English) See Delilah.

Delilah "The Languishing, Brooding One" (Hebrew) or "The Gentle Girl" (Hebrew).

Patron Saints: The fact that the name can mean "the gentle one" leads to one patron.

Feast Dates: October 4 — St. Damaris (see Damara).

Delinda (variant) See Delia.

Delita (African-American) See Delight.

Delite (English) See Delight.

Dell (nickname) See Ada, Adela, Adelaide, Adeline, Ardella, Delia.

Della (nickname) See Dell.

Delly (nickname) See Dell.

Delois (African-American double) See Dolores, De+Lois.

Delora (variant) See Dolores.

Delores (Spanish) See Dolores.

Deloria (American double) See Dolores, De+Lois.

Deloris (variant) See Dolores.

Delphi (variant) See Delphine.

Delphina (Spanish) See Delphine.

Delphine "The Calm One" (Greek) or "The Delphinium Flower" (Greek).

Patron Saints: There is at least one known St. Delphina, who lived from 1284 to 1358. She was of royalty, born at Château-Pont-Michel. When she was only three years old, King Charles II of Naples engaged her to Elear. Upon growing up, this couple married but agreed to live a celibate union. Both became members of the Third Order of St. Francis. After her husband's death, she lived in retirement at the royal court in Naples.

Feast Dates: December 9 — St. Delphina.

Delphinia (variant) See Delphine.

Delta "The Greek Letter 'D'" (Greek) or "The Fourth One" (Greek) or "The Door" (Greek).

Patron Saints: There is no St. Delta, but the fact that *delta* means "door" makes a biblical connection. This leads the believer to recognize two patrons who act as "Doors." The first is the Lord, who said, " Truly, truly, I say to you, I am the door of the sheep" (John 10:7). The second are all believers who "open . . . a door, . . . to declare the mystery of Christ" (Colossians 4:3). Like St. Paul, we must all become missionaries, "doors" through whom the pagans come to know Jesus.

Feast Dates: All Sundays — Jesus the Door; November 1 — All Canonized Missionaries.

Demeia (African-American) See Demetria.

Demeter (variant) See Demetria.

Demetra (variant) See Demetria.

Demetria "The Goddess of the Harvest" (Greek, Spanish).

Patron Saints: Demetria, a black woman, was martyred for Jesus in ancient Africa.

Feast Dates: June 3 — St. Demetria.

Demetris (variant) See Demetria.

Demi (Greek) See Demetria.

Demita (nickname) See Demetria.

Demitria (African-American) See Demetria.

Dena (Hebrew) See Deana, Dinah.

Denae (Hebrew) See Danae.

Dene (variant) See Danae, Deana, Diana.

Denean (variant double) See Denise+Ina.

Denecia (variant) See Denise.

Deneen (variant double) See Denise+Ina.

Denese (variant) See Denise.

Deni (French) See Denise.

Denice (variant) See Denise.

Denika (Slavic) See Denise.

Denine (variant double) See Denise+Ina.

Denise "The Queen Goddess" (French).

Patron Saints: Denise is a form of Dionysia, and there are six Sts. Dionysia. During the persecution of Christians under the Roman emperor Decius (249-251), four women were arrested and imprisoned in Alexandria, Egypt, for "being Christians." Among them was Dionysia. They were all executed.

Feast Dates: December 12 — St. Dionysia.

Denisha (African-American double) See Denise+Sha.

Denna (variant) See Deana.

Denni (nickname) See Deana, Denise.

Dennicia (variant) See Denise.

Dennie (variant) See Denise.

Denny (variant) See Denise.

Deny (variant) See Denise.

Denyce (English) See Denise.

Denys (English double) See Denise+Son.

Denyse (English double) See Denise+Son.

Denzella (African-American double) See Denise+Ella.

Deonne (variant) See Dione.

Des (nickname) See Désirée.

Desa (African-American) See Désirée.

Desarae (French) See Désirée.

Desdemona "The Unlucky One" (Greek).

Patron Saints: Two saints with similar names may serve as patrons. They are Bl. Désirée and St. Mona.

Feast Dates: September 8 — Bl. Jacques Désiré Laval (see Désirée); February 26— St. Monas (see Mona).

Deseray (variant) See Désirée.

Desery (African-American) See Désirée.

Desiah (African-American) See Désirée.

Désirae (variant) See Désirée.

Desiray (variant) See Désirée.

Desire (English) See Désirée.

Désirée "The Longed-for One" (French).

Patron Saints: Désirée was originally a term of endearment, not a name. Thus there is only one Bl. Jacques Désiré Laval, a French priest who arrived in Mauritius in 1841. For the next twenty-three years, until his death in 1864, he devoted himself to helping the emancipated slaves. About thirty thousand attended his funeral.

Furthermore, the Bible provides a second very important patron, for 2 Timothy 4:8 recalls that the Lord "will award to me on that Day, and not only to me but also to all who have loved his appearing." Désirée's best patron is none other than Jesus the much-desired and coming end-time King.

Feast Dates: Advent Season — Jesus the Coming One; September 8 — Bl. Jacques Désiré Laval.

Desmona (variant) See Desdemona.

Dessie (American) See Desdemona, Désirée.

Destany (French) See Destinee.

Destinee "Fortune" (Latin) or "With a Destiny" (Old French).

Patron Saints: The Latin word *fortuna* has several meanings, including "destiny and fortune." There is one St. Fortuna and a half-dozen Sts. Fortunata.

Feast Dates: May 6 — St. Fortuna (see Fortuna).

Destini (variant) See Destinee.

Destiny (English) See Destinee.

Dette (nickname) See Bernadette.

Deva "The Moon Goddess" (Sanskrit).

Patron Saints: Deva means the same thing as Diana, and this leads to a half-dozen Sts. Diane.

Feast Dates: June 9 — Bl. Diane d'Andalo (see Diana).

Devan (English) See Devonna.

Deven (English) See Devonna.

DeVera (African-American double) See De+Vera.

Devin (Irish) See Devonna.

Devina (variant) See Davita.

Devine (variant) See Davita.

DiVinia (African-American) See Divina.

Devon (variant) See Devonna.

Devona (English) See Devonna.

Devondra (African-American) See Devonna.

Devonna "The Defender of Devonshire" (Old English-French) or "The Poet" (Old English).

Patron Saints: There are plenty of patrons for Devonna. Two ancient saints are Sts. Devinic and Devanick. There are also two English martyrs: Bl. William Way of Devon and Bl. Thomas Ford of Devon.

William Way, born in 1561, was ordained a priest at Rheims in 1586 and immediately sailed for England. Six months after his arrival, he was jailed in London and languished there from 1587 to 1588. Finally, he was convicted of being a Catholic priest and was executed at the age of twenty-seven.

Feast Dates: September 23 — Bl. William Way of Devon.

Devonne (Israeli) See Devonna.

Devora (Israeli) See Deborah.

DeWonda (African-American double) See De+Wanda.

Dézirae (variant) See Désirée.

Déziray (variant) See Désirée.

Dharma "One Who Lives Correctly" (Hindu) or "The Seeker of Justice" (Hindu).

Patron Saints: The two greatest "saints" can share in being patrons for Dharma. They are Jesus and the Blessed Mother.

Feast Dates: All Sundays — Jesus the Teacher of Righteousness (see Karma); April 25 — The Blessed Virgin Mary, Our Lady of Good Counsel (see Consuelo).

Di (nickname) See Diana.

Diahann (variant) See Diana.

Diamary (Hispanic-American double) See Diana+Mary.

Diamond "The Precious Diamond Gem" (Latin).

Patron Saints: While never very popular, Diamond is being used with more frequency by African-Americans. To find a patron saint, however, we must turn to the Book of Revelation (specifically 21:11, *Jerusalem Bible*). There we find it around the throne of God and in the walls of the heavenly city. It is symbolic of absolute purity and family harmony.

Feast Dates: November 1 — All Saints.

Dian (variant) See Diana.

Diana "The Moon Goddess" (Latin) or "From Indian Country" (American nickname for Indiana).

Patron Saints: Bl. Diane, 1201-1236, was an only daughter and as a teen listened intently to the Dominican preachers who came to town. She asked her father to allow her to become a Dominican nun, but he adamantly refused. Therefore, she took a secret vow of virginity and then fled to a convent. Much dissension followed. At one time her family forcibly removed her from a convent, breaking one of her ribs in the process. In the end her father consented and built her a convent.

Feast Dates: June 9 — Bl. Diane d'Andalo.

Diandra (variant) See Diana.

Diane (English) See Diana.

Dianna (variant) See Diana.

Dianne (variant) See Diana.

Diantha "The Moon Goddess+The Flower" (Greek double).

Patron Saints: Diantha is composed from two names: Diana, meaning "moon goddess," and Anthus, meaning "flower" or "blossom." This leads to a few Sts. Diane and to six Sts. Anthusa.

One St. Anthusa was privileged to become the mother of St. John Chrysostom. After her husband died in the 300s, she gave herself to a life of prayer in her own home.

Feast Dates: January 27 — St. Anthusa; June 9 — Bl. Diane d'Andalo (see Diana).

Dianthe (variant) See Diantha.

Dianthia (variant) See Diantha.

Didi (variant) See Dee, Deirdre, Delia, Diana.

Dido "The Teacher" (Greek).

Patron Saints: St. Didea is listed as an "Irish virgin."

Feast Dates: June 3 — St. Didea; All Sundays — Jesus the Teacher of Righteousness (see Karma).

Diedre (Irish) See Deirdre.

Diks (nickname) See Dixie.

Diksie (American) See Dixie.

Dilan (Irish) See Dylan.

Dillon (Irish) See Dylan.

Dimpna (Spanish) See Dymphna.

Dina (nickname) See Bernadine, Deana, Dinah, Geraldine.

Dinah "The Vindicated One" (Hebrew) or "From the Valley" (Old English).

Patron Saints: Christian tradition provides a few saints with similar names: Sts. Dinach and Dinara. It also calls St. Ann, the Blessed Virgin's mother, "St. Dina."

In addition, the Bible presents Dinah (daughter of Jacob and Leah), who lived in about 1700 B.C. Shechem, the son of a pagan chief, seduced her. When confronted with his transgression, Shechem offered to marry Dinah and pay a dowry. However, the brothers of Dinah were insistent upon revenge. First, they got Shechem and his men to agree to be circumcised. Then, while these men were in pain, two of Jacob's sons (Simeon and Levi) murdered all of them. (See Genesis 34.)

Feast Dates: November 1 — St. Dinah; July 26 — St. Dina, also known as Anne, mother of Mary (see Ann).

Dinnie (nickname) See Denise.

Dinny (nickname) See Denise.

Dinora (Spanish) See Dinah.

Dinoralys (Hispanic-American) See Dinah.

Dion (variant) See Dione.

Diona (Greek) See Dione.

Dione "The Queen Moon Goddess" (Greek).

Patron Saints: Dione is a modern form of Dionysia, and there are six Sts. Dionysia. In the 400s, when a persecution broke out in Africa, Catholics became the victims of the Arian king Huneric. Among them was a very beautiful young woman by the name of Dionysia. She was publicly scourged and her young son wept. She encouraged him and was burned at the stake with her son and her sister, St. Davita.

Feast Dates: December 6 — St. Dionysia; December 12 — St. Dionysia (see Denise).

Dionis (variant) See Dione.

Dionisia (variant) See Dione.

Dionne (Greek) See Dione.

Dionysia (Latin) See Dione.

Disa "The Active Spirit" (Old Norse) or "The One Worth Double" (Greek).

Patron Saints: There is one St. Diseus, a black man who died a martyr in ancient Africa.

Feast Dates: October 21 — St. Diseus.

Dita (Spanish) See Edith.

Divina (Hebrew) See Davita.

Dix (variant) See Dixie.

Dixie "She Is a Ten" (French) or "I Have Spoken" (Latin).

Patron Saints: Some argue that there is no St. Dixie. But they are wrong. For knowing that Dixie means "ten" or "tenth" and knowing that the Latin words for this are *decem* and *decimus*, one is led to St. Decima. To modern Americans, her name would be Dixie. St. Dixie died the death of a martyr in ancient Terni.

Feast Dates: April 14 — St. Dixie, also known as Decima.

Dixy (variant) See Dixie.

Djuana (African-American double) See De+Juana.

D'nette (African-American double) See Danielle+Ette.

Dode (variant) See Dora, Dorothy, Dottie.

Dodi (English) See Dora, Dorothy, Dottie.

Dodie (Greek) See Dora, Dorothy, Dottie.

Dody (English) See Dora, Dorothy, Dottie.

Doe (variant) See Dorothy.

Doll (English) See Dallas, Dorothy, Dottie.

Dolli (English) See Doris, Dorothy, Dottie.

Dollie (English) See Doris, Dorothy, Dottie.

Dolly (English) See Doris, Dorothy, Dottie.

Dolocitas (Spanish double) See Dolores+Ita.

Dolores "The Sorrowing One" (Spanish).

Patron Saints: There is no St. Dolores to be found. However, the meaning of the name is "Sorrow," and this leads us directly to "Our Mother of Sorrows." The Gospel presents us with this poignant line: "But standing by the cross of Jesus [was] his mother" (John 19:25). Mary's sharing the pain of the crucifixion was part of God's plan. What must her pain have been like? Imagine your loved one suffering and there is nothing that you can do about it.

The crucifixion was not the only sorrow Mary suffered. She also suffered when giving birth to Jesus in a cave, when having to flee to Egypt with Jesus and Joseph, and when searching for Jesus while he was lost for three days. Through the ages, Catholic appreciation reached its greatest import in the 1200s to 1300s.

Feast Dates: September 15 — The Blessed Virgin Mary, Mother of Sorrows.

Dolorita (Spanish double) See Dolores+Ita.

Doloritas (Spanish double) See Dolores+Ita.

Doloroza (Ukrainian, Hungarian) See Dolores.

Domenica (Italian) See Dominique.

Domeniga (variant) See Dominique.

Domina "The Lady" (Latin).

Patron Saints: There is one St. Dominata. She died a martyr in ancient Temesa.

Feast Dates: September 14 — St. Dominata.

Dominga (Spanish) See Dominique.

Domini (variant) See Dominique.

Dominica (variant) See Dominique.

Dominique "She Who Belongs to the Lord" (French).

Patron Saints: There are about three dozen Sts. Dominic and a few Sts. Dominica. In about 249, in Rome, the deacon St. Laurence was taking care of the needs of the local Catholic Church members. Dominica, a wealthy Roman woman, invited him to make her home the headquarters for his work. Dominica also gave shelter to the persecuted Christians and their families. When her sympathy for the Christians became known, she was arrested by the authorities and was put to death by scourging.

Feast Dates: August 21 — St. Dominica; July 6 — St. Dominica (see Sunday).

Domino (English) See Dominique.

Dona (Spanish, Italian) See Donna, Madonna.

Donaii (African-American) See Donna, Madonna.

Donata "The Offering [Gift]" (Latin).

Patron Saints: There are about eighty Sts. Donatus and ten Sts. Donata. A St. Donata was a martyr in Rome.

Feast Dates: August 8 — St. Donata.

Donella (variant) See Donna.

Donelle (variant) See Donna.

Donetta (English double) See Donna+Etta.

Donette (French double) See Donna+Ette.

Donia (variant) See Donna.

Donica (variant) See Donna.

Donielle (variant) See Donna.

Donna "The Lady" (Latin, Italian) or "My+Lady" (nickname for Madonna).

Patron Saints: There are a half-dozen Sts. Donata and Donatilla. One can also adopt the Blessed Virgin, who is known as the Madonna. There is also one ancient English saint by the name of Dona. However, he is a male. St. Dona of Llandona was the son of a local chieftain in western England and lived in about 600 to 650. He became a monk and was stationed for a while in England and then in Brittany.

Feast Dates: November 1 — St. Dona of Llandona; All Saturdays — The Blessed Virgin Mary, Our Lady (see Madonna).

Donnell (African-American double) See Donna+Elle.

Donni (variant) See Donna.

Donnie (variant) See Donna.

Donny (variant) See Donna.

Dora "The Gift" (short form of Adora, Dorothy, Endora, Isadora, Pandora, Theodora).

Patron Saints: There are many patrons available. Among them is St. Theodora, a beautiful young black girl who lived in Alexandria, Egypt, in 304. She was discovered to be a Christian during a Roman persecution and immediately sentenced to be a prostitute in a brothel. After all, Christians were thought to be immoral. Did they not preach "love"? However, she did not remain there long.

A pagan male friend, Didymus, rescued her in a very imaginative way. He visited her and traded clothes with her. She safely left the brothel as a man while he remained behind, dressed as a woman. Unfortunately, Theodora died soon after her escape and Didymus was discovered and beheaded for helping her. Both are now recognized as saints.

Feast Dates: April 28 — St. Theodora of Alexandria; May 14 — Bl. Theodore Guerin (see Theodora).

Doralia (variant) See Dora.

Doralin (variant double) See Dora+Lynn.

Doralynn (Greek double) See Dora+Lynn.

Dorcas (variant) See Tabitha.

Dorcey (African-American) See Dorcas.

Dorde (Norwegian) See Dorothy.

Dore (nickname) See Dora, Doreen, Isadora, Pandora, Theodora.

Doreen "The Sullen One" (Irish Gaelic) or "The Bountiful One" (Greek) or "The Golden One" (French) or "The Daughter of the Fair Hero" (Irish Gaelic) or "The Gift" (form of Doreen or Dorothy).

Patron Saints: Knowing that Doreen is accepted as a form of Dorothy leads to a half-dozen Sts. Dorothy.

Feast Dates: November 29 — SG Dorothy Day (see Dorothy).

Dorelia (variant) See Dora.

Dorella (variant) See Dora.

Dorelle (variant) See Dora.

Dorena (variant) See Dora.

Dorene (variant) See Dora.

Doreta (variant) See Dora, Dorothy.

Dorete (Danish) See Dora, Dorothy.

Doretta (English double) See Dora/Dorothy+Etta.

Dorette (English double) See Dora/Dorothy+Ette.

Dorey (variant) See Dora, Pandora, Theodora.

Dori (nickname) See Dora, Doris, Pandora, Theodora.

Dorian (Greek) See Doris.

Dorice (variant) See Doris.

Dorie (nickname) See Dora, Doris, Dorothy, Pandora, Theodora.

Dorina (variant) See Dora, Doreen.

Dorinda (Spanish) See Dora.

Doris "From the Sea" (Greek, Spanish) or "The Bountiful Ocean" (Hawaiian) or "A Gift of God" (Greek).

Patron Saints: Doris is a form of Dorothy, and this leads to a half-dozen Sts. Doris and Dorothy. Also knowing that Doris means "from the sea" leads to a half-dozen more Sts. Mares and Maris. And finally, there is one St. Dorostolus, who died a martyr's death in ancient Cappadocia.

Feast Dates: June 8 — St. Dorostolus; November 29 — SG Dorothy Day (see Dorothy).

Dorisa (variant) See Doris.

Dorita (Spanish double) See Dora/Doris+Ita.

Dorla (Czech) See Dora, Dorothy.

Dorli (Swiss) See Dora, Dorothy.

Dorlisa (variant) See Dora, Dorothy.

Doro (variant) See Dora, Dorothy.

Dorofija (Ukrainian) See Dora, Dorothy.

Dorolice (variant) See Dora, Dorothy.

Dorota (Polish, Czech) See Dora, Dorothy.

Dorotea (English, Italian, Spanish, Finnish, Swedish) See Dora, Dorothy.

Doroteya (Russian) See Dora, Dorothy.

Dorothea (German, Greek, French) See Dora, Dorothy.

Dorothée (French) See Dora, Dorothy.

Dorothy "A Gift of God" (English).

Patron Saints: There are a half-dozen Sts. Dorothy. Here is the story of an American saint-in-the-making.

Born in 1897 in New York City, she moved to San Francisco at six years of age. She experienced the Great Earthquake of 1906 during which she saw people helping people, and this made a lasting impression on her. Although her common-law husband opposed the idea of bringing children into the world, Dorothy gave birth to a baby girl in 1927. Shortly after that Dorothy was baptized a Catholic.

She met Peter Maurin, a former Christian Brother, who convinced her to start a publication that would promote Catholic social teaching. She became involved in many issues of the day, including civil rights and pacifism. But one of her main concerns revolved around the poor, and many homeless people found their way to her. She fed, clothed, and housed them, and this led to the founding of "hospitality houses." Every day she attended Mass and received Communion. She died at the age of eighty-three in 1980.

Feast Dates: November 29 — SG Dorothy Day.

Dorree (variant) See Dory.

Dorri (variant) See Dory.

Dorrie (nickname) See Dory.

Dorris (variant) See Doris.

Dorry (variant) See Dory.

Dorte (Danish, Norwegian) See Dorothy.

Dorthea (English) See Dorothy.

Dorthy (Polish) See Dorothy.

Dory (variant) See Dora, Doris, Dorothy, Pandora, Theodora.

Doryda (Polish) See Doris.

Dosi (nickname) See Dottie, Dorothy.

Dosia (Polish) See Dorothy.

Dosya (Russian) See Dorothy.

Dot (nickname) See Dottie, Dorothy.

Dotti (nickname) See Dottie, Dorothy.

Dottie "A Gift of God" (English nickname for Dorothy).

Patron Saints: There are many Sts. Dorothy and Theodora. There is also a Bl. Andrew Dotti, 1256-1315. As a young man he served as a captain in the military. Then he followed St. Philip Benizi into the Servite religious order. He lived the last years of his life in solitude.

Feast Dates: September 3 — Bl. Andrew Dotti; May 14 — Bl. Theodore Guerin (see Theodora).

Dotty (nickname) See Dottie, Dorothy.

Dovie (African-American) See Jemima, Paloma.

Drew (nickname) See Andrea.

Drinka (Spanish) See Alexandra.

Dru (nickname) See Drusilla.

Drucie (nickname) See Drusilla.

Drucilla (Latin) See Drusilla.

Drusa (nickname) See Drusilla.

Drusie (nickname) See Drusilla.

Drusilla "The Descendant of the Strong One" (Latin).

Patron Saints: There are two Sts. Drusilla (also known as Drosis). One was the daughter of the Roman emperor Trajan. She died a martyr in ancient Antioch.

Feast Dates: November 9 — St. Drusilla.

Duan (variant) See Duana.

Duana "The Little Dark One" (Irish Gaelic).

Patron Saints: There are a few ancient saints with similar names. One is the patron of true lovers and of sick animals. She is St. Dwyn, the daughter of St. Brychan. It seems she fell passionately in love with a man named Maelon Mafodril, who loved her. However, they had a major disagreement and canceled plans for their marriage. She settled near Llandwyn, Wales, and became a nun and later, in about 360, an abbess.

Feast Dates: January 25 — St. Dwyn, also known as Dwynwen.

Duchess "A Woman of Noble Rank" (Middle English).

Patron Saints: Many saints have held noble rank. For example: St. Wiltrudis, duchess of Bavaria; St. Hedwig, duchess of Silesia; and St. Olga, duchess of Kiev. Any can serve as patrons.

Feast Dates: January 6 — St. Wiltrudis of Bavaria (see Velma); October 15 — St. Hedwig of Silesia (see Hedwig).

Duchie (English) See Duchess.
Duchy (English) See Duchess.
Dulce (Spanish) See Delcine.
Dulcea (variant) See Delcine.
Dulci (nickname) See Delcine.
Dulcia (American) See Delcine.
Dulciana (variant) See Delcine.
Dulcie (American) See Delcine.
Dulcine (American) See Delcine.
Dulcinea (Spanish) See Delcine.
Dulcy (variant) See Delcine.
Dulsea (variant) See Delcine.
Dusten (English) See Dusty.
Dusti (English) See Dusty.
Dustie (English) See Dusty.
Dusty "Valiant Fighter" (American nickname for Dusten).

Patron Saints: There is one St. Dustin who spelled his name Drostan. There is also one female St. Drosis. It also helps to know that Dustin means "valiant fighter." And more patrons are found when one realizes that the name Louise means "famous warrior woman." Thus the dozen Sts. Louise can serve as patrons.

St. Dustin served God as a bishop and disciple of St. Columba of Iona in ancient Scotland. First he served as abbot for a monastery in Ireland, and then he became a hermit near Clenesk and then a monk at the Iona monastery. In the 500s he became the founding abbot of the monastery at Deer, Aberdeenshire, Scotland.

Feast Dates: July 11 — St. Dustin, also known as Drostan; March 15 — St. Louise de Marillac (see Louise).

Dvora (Israeli) See Deborah.
Dvorah (Israeli) See Deborah.
Dwana (variant) See Duana.
Dwyna (variant) See Duana.
Dyan (variant) See Diana.
Dyana (Latin) See Diana.
Dyane (English) See Diana.
Dyann (English) See Diana.
Dyanna (English) See Diana.
Dyanne (English) See Diana.
Dylan "The One from the Sea" (Old Welsh).

Patron Saints: There is one saint from Wales, St. Dilwar, whose name is similar. Also knowing that Dylan means "from the sea" leads directly to a half-dozen ancient Sts. Mares and Maris. These names are Latin for "the sea." Also, some scholars suggest that Dylan is a form of Dillon. This leads to St. Logan of Dillon, an Irishman who died in the late 500s. He was a member of the royalty but felt called to be a priest and was eventually ordained. For a period of time he served as a missionary priest at Disert Illadhan in Ireland. Today this is known as Castle Dillon.

Feast Dates: February 2 — St. Logan (also known as Illogan) of Dillon.

Dylana (variant) See Dylan.

Dylane (variant) See Dylan.

Dylis (African-American double) See Dylan/Diana+Lisa/Phyliss.

Dylon (variant) See Dylan.

Dymphna Meaning unknown (Old English).

Patron Saints: There is one St. Dymphna, who is patron of asylums, mental-health workers, against epilepsy, insanity, and sleepwalking. Dymphna was the daughter of a pagan king and a Catholic princess and was raised a Catholic. While in her teens, her mother died and her father searched for a woman like her. One day he realized how much Dymphna resembled her mother and he began making sexual advances. She took the matter to her confessor, St. Gerebran, and he sped her out of the country to Belgium, where she became a hermit devoted to prayer.

However, her father soon found her and begged her to return home and made more sexual advances. She refused him. Then St. Gerebran arrived to help and was murdered. The father, now in a rage, killed her on the spot with his sword. It was the year 650 and Dymphna was only a teenager.

Feast Dates: May 15 — St. Dymphna.

$\mathcal{E}$

Eabha (Irish) See Eve.
Eadaoine (Irish) See Euphemia.
Eadie (Irish) See Edith.
Eadith (Irish) See Edith.
Ealasaid (Scottish Gaelic) See Elizabeth.
Earla (variant) See Arleen, Earlene.
Earleen (English) See Arleen, Earlene.
Earlene "The Noblewoman" (Old English) or "The Pledge" (Irish Gaelic form of Arleen).

   Patron Saints: One saint has a similar name. St. Ealsitha was the daughter of the king and queen of Mercia in ancient England. When her parents killed her husband, she fled in horror and retired to the Isle of Croyland to pray, and there she stayed.

   Earlene also seems to have arisen from Arlene, which also means "the pledge." Furthermore, many saints bear names that mean "noblewoman," just like Earlene. This makes many saints available.

   Feast Dates: August 2 — St. Ealsitha; August 25 — St. Patricia (see Patricia).
Earley (English) See Arleen, Earlene.
Earlie (English) See Arleen, Earlene.
Earline (variant) See Arleen, Earlene.
Eartha "From the Earth" (Old English).

   Patron Saints: There is a St. Earthongata, but all that is known about her is her name. However, with the help of the Bible, two more very well-known and special patrons emerge. Genesis 1:27 tells us, "So God created man in his own image, . . . male and female he created them." The Hebrew word for "man" is *adamah*. It means "of the red earth" and refers to both Adam and Eve.

Almost every Christian and Jew knows how Adam and Eve lost paradise because of disobedience.

   Jewish tradition adds that after they left paradise, Adam and Eve settled in a cave, had many children, and faced continued temptations by the devil. They slowly learned that the devil was their worst enemy. They also learned that prayer and sacrifice (self-discipline) were their best weapons against him.

   Feast Dates: February 26 — St. Earthongata; December 24 — Sts. Adam and Eve (see Isha).
Earthalee (African-American double) See Eartha+Leigh.
Easter "Born at Easter" (Old English).

   Patron Saints: The primary patron of someone named Easter is Jesus the risen Lord. However, there is at least one other saint who bears this name. St. Easterwine was a kinsman of St. Benedict Biscop. In time, he became an abbot at Wearmouth and then traveled to Rome. He died in the year 686.

   Feast Dates: March 7 — St. Easterwine; Easter Sunday — The Risen Lord.
Eastre (variant) See Easter.
Eba (English) See Eve.
Ebana (African-American) See Ebony.
Ebba (English) See Eve.
Ebeny (African-American) See Ebony.
Ebonee (African-American) See Ebony.
Eboni (Greek) See Ebony.
Ebonie (African-American) See Ebony.
Ebony "The Hard Black Wood" (Middle English).

   Patron Saints: There is one saint with the name St. Ebana. She was the

92

daughter of St. Salaberga and served as an abbess in Laon, France, in the 600s.

Feast Dates: August 7 — St. Ebana; April 4 — St. Benedict the Black (see Jetta).

Ebyni (African-American) See Ebony.

Echo "The Repeating Voice" (Greek).

Patron Saints: There is one saint with a similar name, St. Echa. He was a priest who lived near York in medieval England, and gave his life to prayer and solitude.

Feast Dates: May 5 — St. Echa.

Ed (nickname) See Edana, Edel, Eden, Edith, Edmonda, Edna, Edwina.

Eda (Irish, English) See Edana, Edith.

Edana "The Fiery Little One" (Irish Gaelic) or "The Rejuvenated One" (variant form of Edna).

Patron Saints: St. Edana (also known as De) became a religious sister and lived the life of a hermit on an island in the middle of a river. Some think it was the Trent River in England. Others claim it was the Shannon and Boyle rivers in medieval Ireland. She is remembered for her prayerfulness.

Feast Dates: July 5 — St. Edana.

Edda (German) See Edith.

Eddi (nickname) See Edith, Edna, Edwina.

Eddie (nickname) See Edith, Edna, Edwina.

Eddy (American) See Edith, Edna, Edwina.

Ede (nickname) See Edith.

Edel "The Noblewoman" (Irish).

Patron Saints: There are two Sts. Adela and some Sts. Adelaide, Adelina, Adelindis, and Adeltrudis. There is also one woman named Bl. Edel Quinn, 1907-1944, who is being considered for sainthood. She wanted to become a nun, but poor health prevented her.

Therefore, she gave herself completely to the Dublin Legion of Mary.

Everything she did was marked by a childlike trust in God, and devotion to Mary was also constant. She would often say, "Mary loves us because we are Christ's gift to her." In 1936, at twenty-nine years of age, she became an envoy for the Legion, with the goal of establishing this organization in Africa.

Struggling against constant ill health, she met every challenge with unwavering faith and courage. She established hundreds of Legion branches and died in Nairobi in 1944 at the age of thirty-seven.

Feast Dates: May 12 — Bl. Edel Quinn; December 24 — St. Adela (see Adela).

Edeline (English) See Ada, Adela, Adelaide, Adeline.

Edell (variant) See Ada, Adela, Adelaide, Adeline.

Edella (variant) See Ada, Adela, Adelaide, Adeline.

Eden "In Paradise" (Latin) or "The Garden of Delight" (Hebrew) or "The Plain" (Babylonian).

Patron Saints: Sts. Adam and Eve are primary candidates for patrons because they actually lived in Eden for a short time. To them can be added almost two dozen male Sts. Eden. However, they are usually listed according to their Irish spelling, Aedhan. One St. Eden (Aedhan) lived the life of a monk at the Iona monastery in about 650. He was very holy, became a bishop, and worked many miracles. There are also Sts. Edain and Edentius. St. Edentius is remembered for preaching the Gospel in Gascony.

Feast Dates: August 31 — St. Eden, also known as Aidan, Aedan, or Aedhan; May 6 — St. Edentius.

Edi (nickname) See Edith, Edna.

Edie (English) See Edith, Edna.

Edina (English) See Edwina.

Edisa (African-American double) See Edith+Lisa.

Edit (Swedish, Hungarian) See Edith.

Edita (Italian, Spanish) See Edith.

Edith "The Rich Gift" (Old English).

Patron Saints: There are about a half-dozen Sts. Edith. The most recent is Edith Stein, 1891-1942. Born and raised Jewish, she was a brilliant scholar who became an atheist at age fifteen. Her first brush with Catholicism occurred when she was twenty-six years old. A friend, who was also her teacher, was killed. When Edith visited his widow, she found her completely calm. This was credited to the widow's faith. A few years later, in 1921, Edith noticed the autobiography of St. Teresa of Ávila in the home of a friend and she read it in a single night. Next she bought a Catholic catechism. This led to instructions and conversion. She was baptized in 1922.

When Hitler came to power in Germany in 1933, Edith entered a convent in Cologne, where she became a religious sister and changed her name to Sister Benedicta of the Cross. Because of anti-Semitism she was removed to Holland in 1938, but in 1942 all Jewish members of Dutch religious were arrested. Edith was sent to Auschwitz and died in a gas chamber at the age of fifty-one. Beatified in 1987, she was canonized in 1998.

Feast Dates: August 9 — St. Edith Stein.

Editha (Italian) See Edith.

Edithe (English) See Edith.

Editta (Italian) See Edith.

Ediva (English) See Edith.

Edmonda "The Prosperous Protector" (Old English).

Patron Saints: There are about a half-dozen Sts. Edmund. Among them is St. Edmund Campion, a Protestant deacon in London, England, who converted to Catholicism. He traveled to France, studied the faith, and was ordained a Catholic priest. Then he returned to England to preach the Gospel. This led to his arrest. In 1581 he was hanged, drawn, and quartered.

Feast Dates: December 1 — St. Edmund Campion.

Edmunda (English) See Edmonda.

Edna "The Rejuvenated One" (Hebrew, Spanish).

Patron Saints: There is one St. Edna. There is also a female St. Edwen and a male St. Edwin. St. Edna was born sometime in the 600s in England or Ireland. She is known by many different names, including Edana, Modwenna, and Moninne.

Feast Dates: July 5 — St. Edna (see Eden).

Edrianna (Greek) See Adrienne.

Edwina "The Rich Friend" (Old English).

Patron Saints: There are fewer than a handful of Sts. Edwina. One of them is thought to have been one of many daughters of St. Edwin, king of Northumbria in the 600s. She is patron of Llanedwen, Anglesey.

Feast Dates: November 6 — St. Edwen.

Edwyna (variant) See Edwina.

Edy (nickname) See Edith.

Edyta (Polish) See Edith.

Edyth (English) See Edith.

Edythe (variant) See Edith.

Effee (nickname) See Euphemia, Eve.

Effi (nickname) See Euphemia, Eve.

Effie (nickname) See Euphemia, Eve.

Effy (nickname) See Euphemia, Eve.

Egypt "The One from Egypt" (Egyptian).

Patron Saints: The Church honors two classes of Egyptian martyrs. The first are those killed in 303 under Diocletian. The second are those martyred in 357 during the Arian controversy.

Feast Dates: January 5 — Egyptian Roman Martyrs; May 21 — Egyptian Anti-Arian Martyrs.

Eibhilin (nickname) See Evelyn.

Eileen "The Light" (Irish form of Helen through Aileen) or "Mother of the Living" (variant of Evelyn).

Patron Saints: There is no St. Eileen, but Eileen is a variant of Helen, and there are more than a dozen Sts. Helen. The greatest is the empress St. Helena, who found the cross of Christ in about 325.

Feast Dates: August 18 — St. Helena (see Helen).

Eilene (variant) See Eileen, Helen.

Eilidh (Scottish Gaelic) See Helen.

Eilis (Irish Gaelic) See Elizabeth.

Eilish (Irish Gaelic) See Elizabeth.

Eimile (Irish) See Emily.

Eirena (variant) See Irene.

Eirene (Greek) See Irene.

Eiric (Scottish) See Henrietta.

Eirin (Norwegian) See Irene.

Eister (Irish) See Esther.

Ekaterina (Bulgarian, Russian) See Katherine.

El (nickname) See Elly, Elana, Elata, Eldora, Eleanor, Ella, Ellen, Eloise, Elone, Elsie, Elva, Elvira.

Elaina (variant) See Elaine.

Elaine "The Light" (Welsh, Norwegian form of Helen).

Patron Saints: Elaine is a variant of Helen, and there are more than a dozen Sts. Helen. There are also two Sts. Elena. One is remembered as the "Virgin of Padua."

Feast Dates: November 4 — St. Elena; August 18 — St. Helena (see Helen).

Elana (Greek) See Elaine, Helen.

Elane (variant) See Elaine, Helen.

Elata "The Lofty Elevated One" (Latin).

Patron Saints: Bl. Ela, the countess of Salisbury, was a prayerful religious sister in England in the 1200s.

Feast Dates: November 1 — Bl. Ela.

Elayna (variant) See Elaine, Helen.

Elayne (variant) See Elaine, Helen.

Elba "The Noble Bright One" (Spanish).

Patron Saints: Elba is a feminine form of Albert, and there are three dozen Sts. Albert. However, the story of an American saint-in-the-making follows.

Civil war raged in the little Central American country of El Salvador, and by 1989 over seventy-five thousand men, women, and children had been killed. The clergy of the Roman Catholic Church were particularly vulnerable, for they were misunderstood by both sides. When they spoke out for the rights of the poor, they were branded Communists by the government; and when they spoke out for law and order, they were seen as government agents by the rebels. Thus it was that in the morning hours of November 16, 1989, government troops forced their way into the Jesuit house of the Central American University in San Salvador. They killed six Jesuit priests and two housekeepers. The priests were SsG Ignacio Martín-Baro, Amando López, Ignacio Ellacuría, Juan Ramón Moreno, Joaquín López y López, and Segundo Montes. Celina and Elba Ramos, a daughter and mother, were murdered with them. All were shot in the head with M-16 rifles at close range.

Feast Dates: November 16 — SG Elba Ramos.

Elberta (English) See Alberta.
Elbertina (English) See Alberta.
Elbertine (English) See Alberta.
Elda (Spanish) See Hilda.
Eldora "The Gilded One" (Spanish).

Patron Saints: Eldora means the same as "Aurelia." There are about a dozen Sts. Aurelia.

Feast Dates: September 25 — St. Aurelia (see Aurelia).

Eleanor "The Light" (Old French, Welsh, Norwegian form of Helen) or "The Merciful One" (Greek).

Patron Saints: There are two Bls. Eleanora, one St. Elenara, and a dozen Sts. Helen.

St. Eleonora was the daughter of Count Raymond IV of Provence. She became queen of England when she married King Henry III in 1236 at the age of ten. After thirty-seven years of marriage, her husband died and she became a Benedictine nun. She lived a pious and prayerful life.

Feast Dates: May 25 — Bl. Eleonora.

Eleanora (Greek) See Eleanor, Helen.
Eleanore (variant) See Eleanor, Helen.
Electra "The Brilliant Shining One" (Greek).

Patron Saints: There is at least one saint with a very similar name. St. Electa was either a daughter or granddaughter of St. Brychan of Wales in medieval times. A young prince who was madly in love with her and whom she had rejected murdered her.

Feast Dates: August 1 — St. Electa.

Eleen (variant) See Ellen, Helen.
Elektra (American) See Electra.
Elen (Welsh, Norwegian) See Ellen, Helen.
Elena "The Light" (Italian, Spanish, Portuguese, Baltic, Russian form of Helen)

or "The Helper of Mankind" (short form of Alexandra).

Patron Saints: Elena finds its source on its own and in Alexandra and Helen (through Elaine). This makes many patrons available. St. Elena is one. Raised a pagan, she converted to Catholicism and was baptized without the knowledge of her parents. She was martyred while making a secret journey to attend Mass in 640.

Feast Dates: June 18 — St. Elena; November 4 — St. Elena (see Elaine).

Elene (English) See Aileen, Elena, Helen.
Eleni (Greek) See Helen.
Elenor (Swedish) See Elenore, Helen.
Elenora (Dutch, Italian) See Elenore, Helen.
Elenore (German, Danish) See Helen.
Eleonora (Italian, Polish, Russian) See Helen.
Eleonore (French, German, Spanish) See Helen.
Elffrieda (nickname) See Alfreda.
Elfie (nickname) See Alfreda, Elva, Elvira, Freda, Freddie, Freddy, Frieda.
Elfreda (nickname) See Alfreda.
Elfrieda (nickname) See Alfreda.
Elga (German) See Olga.
Eliana (Spanish, Hebrew) See Eleanor, Elise.
Elianora (variant) See Eleanor, Helen.
Elianore (variant) See Eleanor, Helen.
Elice (English) See Elyse.
Eliisa (Finnish) See Elizabeth.
Elin (variant) See Helen.
Elina (Finnish) See Helen.
Elinor (variant) See Elenore, Helen.
Elinora (variant) See Elenore, Helen.
Elisa (Italian, Spanish, Greek) See Elizabeth.
Elisabet (Scandinavian) See Elizabeth.
Elisabeth (English) See Elizabeth.
Elisabetta (Italian) See Elizabeth.

Elise "The Lord Is God" (feminine form of Elijah) or "The Truthful One" (variant form of Alice) or "Consecrated to God" (French form of Elizabeth) or "The Sweet, Blissful One" (variant form of Elyse).

Patron Saints: Elise can arise from Elijah, Elizabeth, Alice, or Elyse. This creates five dozen patrons.

The greatest is Elijah, a Jewish prophet who lived about 876 B.C. He reprimanded King Ahab because the king and his wife, Jezebel, had led Northern Israel into paganism. Later he held a contest on Mount Carmel between himself and the four hundred fifty prophets of Baal. He challenged them to make fire come down from heaven. They failed and he won the people back to the one true God. Then he had false prophets executed, which made Queen Jezebel angry. Thus Elijah had to hide in a cave while he waited for God to make his appearance in power. But God came to him only in silence and nothingness. It is the genius of Elijah that he found God even in this most unlikely place. Eventually the Lord instructed him to carry out several tasks, among them naming Elisha to succeed him as prophet.

Feast Dates: July 20 — St. Elijah.

Eliska (Czech, Slovakian) See Elizabeth.

Elissa (variant) See Alice, Elizabeth, Melissa, Lisa.

Eliz (Hungarian) See Elizabeth.

Eliza (Latvian, Slovenian, English, Hebrew) See Elizabeth.

Elizabet (Hebrew) See Elizabeth.

Elizabeta (Latvian, Slovenian) See Elizabeth.

Elizabeth "One Consecrated to God" (German, Dutch, Danish, English).

Patron Saints: There are at least two dozen Sts. Elizabeth. A well-known one is the mother of St. John the Baptist. The Bible tells how she and her husband, Zechariah, were old and childless and how an angel appeared to Zechariah telling him that Elizabeth would bear a son, who was to be named John (see Luke 1:7-13).

When Elizabeth was six months pregnant, her cousin Mary visited her. Elizabeth greeted Mary with: "And why is this granted me, that the mother of my Lord should come to me?" (Luke 1:43). As Mary had conceived Jesus within just a few hours of this greeting, this argues for the creation of a person (ensoulment) at the moment of conception and it becomes an argument against abortion.

Tradition adds that Elizabeth died when John was about seven years old. According to this same story, Mary and the Child Jesus mourned with John and then buried Elizabeth.

Feast Dates: November 5 — St. Elizabeth, Jewish Matriarch.

Elizabethdaughter (American double) See Elizabeth+Daughter.

Elizaveta (Russian, Bulgarian, Polish) See Elizabeth.

Elka (Polish) See Elizabeth.

Elke (German) See Adelaide, Alice.

Ella (nickname) See Elly, Cinderella, Eleanor, Helen, Joella.

Elladine (variant) See Eleanor, Helen.

Elle (nickname) See Elly, Eleanor, Ellen, Helen, Joella.

Ellen "The Light" (Czech form of Eleanor, Helen) or "The Beautiful Fairy Woman" (Old English).

Patron Saints: There is a Bl. Ella, a St. Elenara, and about a half-dozen Sts. Helen. St. Elenara, a single woman, died as a martyr in France in the 200s.

Feast Dates: May 1 — St. Elenara; February 1 — Bl. Ella (see Elly).

Ellena (variant) See Eleanor, Helen.

Ellene (variant) See Eleanor, Ellen, Helen.

Ellenor (English) See Eleanor, Helen.

Ellete (variant) See Ette, Helen.

Ellette (variant) See Elly+Ette, Helen.

Elli (German) See Elizabeth, Elly, Helen.

Ellice (German) See Elizabeth, Elise, Elly, Helen.

Ellie (nickname) See Eleanor, Ellen, Elly, Helen.

Ellis (English) See Elizabeth.

Ellise (English) See Elise, Elizabeth.

Elly "The Light" (English form of Eleanor, Helen) or "The Beautiful Fairy Woman" (Old English).

Patron Saints: There is a Bl. Ela and a St. Elli. St. Elli, a male, was a Welsh abbot and a disciple of St. Cadoc.

Feast Dates: January 23 — St. Elli.

Ellyn (English) See Eleanor, Ellen, Helen.

Ellyne (English) See Eleanor, Ellen, Helen.

Ellynn (English) See Eleanor, Ellen, Helen.

Elma "Amiable One" (Greek) or "God Protects" (German).

Patron Saints: Elma is the feminine form of Elmo. St. Elmo was a very popular saint in the Middle Ages. He was a bishop who died a martyr in 303. He suffered horrible tortures and made many converts. He is a patron of sailors, women in labor, seasickness, against cramps, stomachaches, and colic.

Feast Dates: June 2 — St. Elmo.

Elmira (English) See Almira.

Elmire (English) See Almira.

Elna (Czech, Swedish, Norwegian) See Eleanor, Helen.

Elnora (American double) See Eleanor/ Helen+Nora.

Elnore (variant) See Eleanor, Helen.

Eloisa (French) See Eloise, Louise.

Eloise "The Famous Warrior Woman" (French form of Louise).

Patron Saints: There is one St. Eloi, 588-660, who was a skilled metalworker. The king appointed him master of the mint in Paris, but he quit to become a priest. He was soon consecrated a bishop and worked to evangelize the area given to him. He is patron of coin collectors, garage and gas station workers, metalworkers, smiths, jewelers, jockeys, veterinarians, and horses.

It is helpful to know that Eloise is a form of Louise. There are a half-dozen Sts. Louise.

Feast Dates: December 1 — St. Eloi, also known as Elegius; March 15 — St. Louise de Marillac (see Louise).

Elona "The Beautiful One" (Hungarian) or "The Light" (Hungarian form of Helen).

Patron Saints: Elona is thought to be a form of Helen. And there are about a dozen Sts. Helen.

Feast Dates: August 18 — St. Helena (see Helen).

Elone (variant) See Elona, Helen.

Elora (variant) See Eleanor, Helen.

Elsa (Danish, German, Hebrew, Spanish) See Elizabeth, Elsie.

Elsbeth (Swiss, German) See Elizabeth.

Else (German, Dutch, Danish) See Elizabeth.

Elsey (variant) See Elizabeth.

Elsi (variant) See Elizabeth.

Elsie "The Noblewoman" (Old German) or "Consecrated to God" (English nickname for Elizabeth).

Patron Saints: While Elsie can be considered a name in its own right, most scholars accept it as an English nickname for Elizabeth. There are two dozen Sts. Elizabeth.

Feast Dates: November 5 — St. Elizabeth (see Elizabeth).

Elspeth (Scottish) See Elizabeth.

Elsy (variant) See Elizabeth, Elsie.

Eltha (English) See Althea.

Elthea (English) See Althea.

Elva "The Elfin One" (Old English) or "The Good One" (Old English) or "The Wise Counselor" (variant of Alfreda).

Patron Saints: There is at least one ancient saint with a very similar name. St. Alvera lived and died in ancient France. She is remembered for being both a virgin and a martyr.

Feast Dates: March 6 — St. Alvera.

Elvere (English) See Elvira.

Elvia (English, Spanish) See Elva.

Elvie (English) See Elva.

Elvina (Old English) See Elvira.

Elvira "She Who Excels [Elfin One]" (Spanish, Italian) or "The White [Blond] One" (Latin, from Albina).

Patron Saints: Elvira is a form of Albinia (Alban), and there are a half-dozen Sts. Alban. St. Albina was a young Christian maiden who died for Christ at Caesarea in 230 during the reign of Emperor Decius.

Feast Dates: December 16 — St. Albina; March 6 — St. Alvera (see Elva).

Elvire (French) See Elvira.

Elyce (variant) See Elyse.

Elyn (variant) See Eleanor, Helen.

Elysa (variant) See Elyse.

Elyse "The Sweet, Blissful One" (Latin) or "One Consecrated to God" (nickname for Elizabeth).

Patron Saints: If we accept the meaning of Elyse as "the blissful one," we are led to a few Sts. Gaudentia. *Gaudium* is the Latin word for "blissful, joyful." However, if Elyse is accepted as a variant form of Elizabeth, two dozen more patrons surface.

Feast Dates: August 30 — St. Gaudentia (see Bliss, Blythe); November 5 — St. Elizabeth, Matriarch (see Elizabeth).

Elysia (Latin) See Elyse.

Elyssa (English) See Elyse, Elizabeth.

Elysse (variant) See Elyse, Elizabeth.

Elza (Bulgarian, Czech, Hungarian) See Elizabeth.

Elzada (Portuguese-Spanish double) See El+Zada.

Elzara (African-American double) See El+Zara.

Elzbieta (Polish) See Elizabeth.

Elzena (African-American double) See El+Xenia.

Elzora (Portuguese-Spanish double) See El+Zara.

Elzsebet (Hungarian) See Elizabeth.

Em (nickname) See Amelia, Emma, Emily.

Ema (Spanish, Bulgarian, Lithuanian) See Amelia, Emma, Emily.

Emalee (Latin) See Amelia, Emily.

Emalia (variant) See Amelia, Emily.

Emelda (English) See Amelia, Emily.

Emelia (Latin) See Amelia, Emily.

Emelie (English) See Amelia, Emily.

Emelina (English) See Amelia, Emma, Emily.

Emeline (English) See Amelia, Emma, Emily.

Emelita (Spanish double) See Amelia/Emily+Ita.

Emelyne (variant) See Amelia, Emma, Emily.

Emera (English) See Amelia, Emily.

Emila (Latvian, Ukrainian) See Amelia, Emily.

Emilee (English) See Amelia, Emily.

Emilia (Spanish, Italian, German) See Amelia, Emily.

Emilie (French, Scandinavian) See Amelia, Emily.

Emilija (Russian, Lithuanian, Bulgarian) See Amelia, Emily.

Emiline (English) See Amelia, Emily.

Emilka (Czech, Bulgarian) See Amelia, Emily.

Emily "Flatterer" (Latin) or "The Whole One" (Old German).

Patron Saints: There are about two dozen Sts. Amelia, Aemilia, Aemiliana, Emilian, Emiliana, and Emma. These are all just different forms of Emily.

St. Emily de Rodat, 1787-1852, at age eighteen was teaching children at Maison Saint-Cyr. Then she joined three different religious orders but did not feel at home with them. By the time she was twenty-eight she decided to give her life to teaching poor children and with three lady friends formed her own short-lived religious order.

She tried again and eventually opened thirty-eight convents in France. She also expanded her services to include nursing the sick, poor, and aged, visiting prisoners and orphans, and ministering to wayward women. She died at the age of sixty-five.

Feast Dates: September 19 — St. Emily de Rodat.

Emlyn (English) See Amelia, Emily.

Emlynn (English) See Amelia, Emily.

Emlynne (variant) See Amelia, Emily.

Emma "The Whole One" (Italian, German) or "The Nurse" (German) or "The Flatterer" (Latin) or "The Precious Stone" (Latin, Italian).

Patron Saints: There are a couple of Sts. Emma and a St. Emmada. There are also about two dozen Sts. Amelia, Aemilia, Aemiliana, Emilian, Emiliana, and Emily. One St. Emma was the countess of Friesach-Zeltschach. After her husband died and her son was mur-dered by his enemies, she retired to a monastery. She also gave all her possessions to the Church. She died in 1045.

Feast Dates: June 17 — St. Emma.

Emmalee (American double) See Emily+Leigh.

Emmali (Iranian) See Amelia, Emily.

Emmaline (German, French) See Amelia, Emily.

Emmalyn (American double) See Amelia/Emily/Emma+Lynn.

Emmalyne (American double) See Amelia/Emily/Emma+Lynn.

Emmalynn (American double) See Amelia/Emily/Emma+Lynn.

Emmalynne (American double) See Amelia/Emily/Emma+Lynn.

Emmanuele (variant) See Emmanuella.

Emmanuella "God Is with Us" (Hebrew).

Patron Saints: One of the names given to Jesus was Emmanuel. Thus Jesus is the finest patron, but there are also over a dozen saints named Emmanuel.

Here is a story shared by four missionaries to South America. It starts with Father Ignacio de Azevedo, S.J., who in 1566 became very concerned about the lack of priests in Brazil. He set about recruiting priests and seminarians in Spain and Portugal, who sailed for Brazil on two different ships. In 1570, a short time after leaving the Canary Islands, Father Azevedo's group was captured by pirates under the command of Jacques Sourie, a former Catholic and a deadly enemy. Sourie immediately killed Father Azevedo. Then he stripped the priests naked and made them walk the plank. Among them were four Jesuit Scholastics with the first name Emmanuel: Bls. Álvares, Fernandes, Pacheco, and Rodrigues.

Feast Dates: January 19 — The Four South American Martyrs.

Emmeline (English) See Amelia, Emily, Emma.

Emmie (nickname) See Amelia, Emily, Emma.

Emmy (nickname) See Amelia, Emily, Emma.

Emmye (nickname) See Amelia, Emily, Emma.

Emogene (variant) See Imogene.

Emyle (variant) See Amelia, Emily.

Emylee (variant) See Amelia, Emily.

Encarnación (Spanish) See Incarnata.

Encina "One Who Dwells Near the Live Oaks" (Spanish).

Patron Saints: The Latin words *quercus* and *querneus* mean "oak." This leads to St. Querelinus, a holy Augustinian monk in Bruges who died in 1060.

Feast Dates: October 2 — St. Querelinus.

Endora "The One with+The Gift" (Greek double) See Dora.

Eneida (Hispanic-American) See Onida.

Engel (German) See Angela, Angelica.

Engracia (Spanish) See Grace.

Enid "The One of Pure Soul" (Old Welsh).

Patron Saints: One saint has a similar name, St. Ennodius, 473-521. He converted to Catholicism and became bishop of Pavia, Lombardy. In 514 the pope entrusted him with two delicate missions to Byzantium. He is chiefly remembered as a composer of Christian poems and hymns.

Feast Dates: July 17 — St. Ennodius.

Enola Meaning unknown (North American Indian) or "The Famous, Noble One" (American variant of Irish name Nolan).

Patron Saints: St. Felix of Nola served in the army for a while and then became a priest and an adviser as well as friend to St. Maximus, bishop of Nola.

When St. Maximus died in 250, the bishopric of Nola was offered to him, but he refused. When the next bishop also died, Felix was again invited to become bishop and this time he accepted. His long life was filled with holiness and charity. St. Felix died in 260.

Feast Dates: January 14 — St. Felix of Nola; January 15 — St. Maximus of Nola.

Enolia (African-American) See Enola.

Enrica (Italian) See Henrietta.

Enrichetta (Italian) See Henrietta.

Enrika (Greek) See Erica, Henrietta.

Enriqueta (Spanish) See Henrietta.

Ensa (African-American) See any "En" name+any "Sa" name (for example, Enola+Sabina).

Eolande (English) See Iolanthe, Viola, Violet, Yolanda.

Epatha "The One Who Is Open" (Aramaic).

Patron Saints: There is one St. Epaphras, a man most loved by St. Paul (Colossians 1:7). It seems that he served as bishop of Colossae and suffered martyrdom there.

Feast Dates: July 10 — St. Epaphras.

Epifanee (English) See Tiffany.

Epifani (English) See Tiffany.

Epiphana (variant) See Tiffany.

Epiphani (variant) See Tiffany.

Epiphania (variant) See Tiffany.

Epiphany (Greek) See Tiffany.

Eppie (English) See Euphemia.

Era (African-American) See Erica.

Eran (variant) See Erin.

Erasma (nickname) See Euphemia.

Erda (variant) See Eartha.

Ereline (English) See Earlene.

Erena (English) See Irene.

Erica "The Powerful One" (Scandinavian, Spanish).

Patron Saints: There are a few Sts. Eric. The best known St. Eric was king of Sweden for about ten years, around 1150 to 1160. He is noted for codifying all the ancient laws and spreading Catholicism in his kingdom. He built Old Uppsala, the first large church to be erected on Swedish land.

However, his zeal for Catholicism was not enough and his enemies revolted. Eric was at Mass when told that the enemy army was close. He said, "Let us finish the sacrifice, the rest of the Feast I shall keep elsewhere." After Mass he met his enemies and they killed him. He is patron of Sweden.

Feast Dates: May 18 — St. Eric IX of Sweden.

Ericha (variant) See Erica.

Ericka (Scandinavian) See Erica.

Erika (Scandinavian) See Erica.

Erin "The One from Ireland" (Irish Gaelic) or "The Peaceful One" (Irish Gaelic).

Patron Saints: One saint has Erin as a part of his name: St. Erinhard. He was from Normandy and he became prior of his monastery. He died in 739.

It is also helpful to know that Erin means "Ireland," and this leads to two priests: Bls. John and William Ireland. In addition, there are four saints officially appointed as patrons of Ireland (Erin). They are Sts. Columba, Kevin, Patrick, and Brigid. All can serve as patrons for a person named Erin.

Feast Dates: September 24 — St. Erinhard; February 1 — St. Brigid of Ireland (see Brigid).

Erina (variant) See Erin.

Erinn (variant) See Erin.

Erinna (variant) See Erin.

Erleen (English) See Earlene.

Erlene (English) See Earlene.

Erlina (English) See Earlene.

Erma "The Noblewoman" (short form of Hermione) or "The Whole One" (variant form of Irma).

Patron Saints: The name Erma comes from Hermione, and there is one St. Hermione. There are also about a dozen saints with similar names: Sts. Ermen, Ermin, Ermelindis, Ermenburga, and Ermenilda.

In the late 600s two saintly sisters named Sexburga and Etheldreda lived in England. Etheldreda became a religious superior. Sexburga married Ercombert, the king of Kent, and bore one daughter, Ermenilda.

Ermenilda married Wulfhere, king of the Mercians, and bore two saintly daughters. Moreover, her zeal for the faith so impressed her husband that he also worked to spread Catholicism in his kingdom. When her husband died in 675, Ermenilda and her children went to live with her mother. After the children were raised, Ermenilda became a religious sister. In time, Ermenilda, her aunt, and her daughter succeeded one another as superiors of their convent.

Feast Dates: February 13 — St. Ermenilda; September 4 — St. Hermione (see Hermione).

Ermina (variant) See Erma, Irma.

Erminia (variant) See Erma, Irma.

Erminie (variant) See Erma, Irma.

Erna "The Eagle" (Old English) or "The Earnest One" (nickname for Ernestine).

Patron Saints: There are about a half-dozen Sts. Ernan. Little is recorded about any of them. For example: St. Ernan of Tigh-Ernain is listed only as an "Irish saint."

Feast Dates: January 17 — St. Ernan.

Ernaline (variant) See Ernestine.

Ernesta (variant) See Ernestine.

Ernestina (variant) See Ernestine.

Ernestine "The Earnest One" (Old English).

Patron Saints: There is one known St. Ernest, about eight Sts. Ernan, and some fifteen Sts. Ernin. A St. Ernin O'Driunun is remembered only as an "Irish virgin."

Feast Dates: February 28 — St. Ernin O'Driunun.

Ersa (African-American) See Ursula.

Ertha (American) See Eartha.

Eryka (American) See Erica.

Erykah (American) See Erica.

Eryn (Irish) See Erin.

Esbeey (Hispanic-American double) See Essi (Esther)+Bee (Beatrice).

Esfir (Russian) See Esther.

Esma (variant) See Aimee.

Esme (variant) See Aimee.

Esperanza (Spanish) See Hope.

Essa (nickname) See Estelle, Esther.

Essi (nickname, Finnish) See Estelle, Esther.

Essie (nickname) See Estelle, Esther.

Essy (nickname) See Estelle, Esther.

Esta "The One from the East" (Italian) or "The Star" (variant form of Esther or Estelle).

Patron Saints: Esther and Estelle both provide patrons, and there is also St. Ethelburga of Essex (which means "East"). She became a religious sister after her husband died. She died in 735.

Feast Dates: September 8 — St. Ethelburga of Essex; December 20 — St. Esther (see Esther).

Estanislao (Spanish) See Stephanie.

Estefania (Spanish) See Stephanie.

Estel (variant) See Estelle.

Estela (Polish, Czech, Spanish) See Estelle.

Estell (variant) See Estelle.

Estella (Italian) See Estelle.

Estelle "The Star" (French).

Patron Saints: Estelle is the French form of Esther, and there is one St. Estella. St. Estella was converted to the Catholic faith in France and consecrated herself to God. A short time later she was baptized and then her brother had her tortured and killed.

Also, because Estelle means "star," the Blessed Virgin, Star of the Sea, may serve as a patron.

Feast Dates: May 11 — St. Estella; All Saturdays — The Blessed Virgin Mary, Star of the Sea (see Star).

Estephanie (Spanish) See Stephanie.

Ester (Spanish) See Esther.

Estera (Polish, Czech, Romanian) See Esther.

Esteri (Finnish) See Esther.

Esterina (Italian) See Esther.

Esther "The Star" (Hebrew).

Patron Saints: The Old Testament provides one St. Esther, who was a Jewish queen. In about 500 B.C., while in exile, Haman, an enemy of the Jewish people, devised a plan to kill all Jews. He persuaded the king to decree that on a given date all the people of the land could kill any Jew they wanted.

Esther discovered the plot and knew she had to help her people, but that might mean her own execution. Feeling all alone and overwhelmed, she prayed to God for help. Then she made a meal for the king and asked him to cancel his decree. He could not change the decree, but he could authorize the Jews to defend themselves. This they did — by attacking their enemies before their enemies attacked them, and they were victorious. Thus began the Jewish feast of independence called Purim.

Feast Dates: December 20 — St. Esther; All Saturdays — The Blessed Virgin Mary, Star of the Sea (see Star).

Estrela (Italian) See Estelle.

Estrelita (Spanish double) See Estelle+Ita.

Estrella (Spanish) See Estelle.

Eszter (Hungarian) See Esther.

Ethel "The Noble One" (Old English).

Patron Saints: There are about a half-dozen Sts. Ethelburga. There is also a St. Ethelreda, a St. Etheldritha, and a St. Ethelwitha. The last-mentioned was the daughter of Ethelred and Eadburg of Mercia. She was married to King Alfred. She had a convent for women built at Winchester and after the death of her husband she took up residence there and dedicated herself to a life of prayer.

Feast Dates: July 20 — St. Ethelwitha.

Ethelda (English) See Ethel.

Ethelinda (English) See Ethel.

Etheline (English) See Ethel.

Ethelle (English) See Ethel.

Ethyl (English) See Ethel.

Ethylin (English) See Ethel.

Etolia (African-American) See Estelle.

Etoria (African-American) See any "E" name+Victoria.

Etta "The Little One" (Old German diminutive).

Patron Saints: "Etta" is often added to the end of modern feminine names, such as Henrietta, Vonetta, and Antonetta. It is also often used as a nickname but rarely as a full name.

There is one St. Etto and he died in Ireland in 670. He served as a missionary bishop to medieval France and was a good friend of St. Fursey. Note that many saints were in contact with other saints.

Feast Dates: July 10 — St. Etto.

Ette "The Little One" (French diminutive).

Patron Saints: "Ette" is often added to the end of modern feminine names, such as Annette and Bernadette. It is also often used as a nickname but rarely as a full name. There is one St. Etto.

Feast Dates: July 10 — St. Etto (see Etta); April 16 — St. Lota (see Lottie).

Etti (nickname) See Etta, Ette, Lottie, Esther.

Ettie (nickname) See Etta, Ette, Lottie, Esther.

Etty (nickname) See Etta, Ette, Lottie, Esther.

Eubh (Scottish Gaelic) See Eve.

Eudora (Greek) See Dora.

Eufamia (nickname) See Euphemia.

Eufemia (Italian, Spanish) See Euphemia.

Eugenia "Well-Born One" (Greek, Italian, German, Spanish).

Patron Saints: There are about a dozen Sts. Eugenia and four dozen Sts. Eugene. One St. Eugenia lived at Utica in Spain in the 900s, during the time Muslims were in power. She was imprisoned with Pelagius, a ten-year-old boy, but remained firm in her faith. Eventually she was decapitated for her Christian principles.

Feast Dates: June 26 — St. Eugenia.

Eugenie (French) See Eugenia.

Eula "The One Who Speaks Beautifully" (Greek).

Patron Saints: There are about a half-dozen Sts. Eulalia. The most famous of them is St. Eulalia of Merida, a girl of twelve who openly showed a great love for Jesus during the persecutions of 304. To protect the girl, her mother hid her, but Eulalia would have none of it. During the night the twelve-year-old went back to Merida and presented herself to the judge, telling him that he was destroying souls by insisting that they worship idols or die.

The judge first flattered her, then tried to bribe her, but she persisted. His patience exhausted, he ordered torture. Her body was torn with hooks; then fire was applied to her wounds, which caused her hair to catch on fire and she died.

Feast Dates: December 10 — St. Eulalia of Merida.

Eulalee (variant) See Eula.

Eulalia (variant) See Eula.

Eulalie (variant) See Eula.

Eulania (African-American double) See Eula+Lane.

Eunice "The Happy, Victorious One" (Greek).

Patron Saints: There are several Sts. Eunice available, but little is known about any of them. One of them is remembered in the Bible as the mother of St. Timothy (see 2 Timothy 1:5). Another, with St. Terentius, was killed for her faith in ancient Africa. She was probably black.

Feast Dates: October 28 — St. Eunice.

Eunie (nickname) See Eunice.

Euny (nickname) See Eunice.

Euphemia "The Notable Speaker" (Greek, German) or "The One of Good Reputation" (Greek, Spanish).

Patron Saints: There are almost a dozen-and-half Sts. Euphemia. One is among the most popular saints venerated in the Eastern Catholic Church. This single woman was thrown to the beasts in ancient times.

Feast Dates: September 16 — St. Euphemia.

Euphemie (French) See Euphemia.

Eurcelyn (African-American variant double) See Ursuline, any "Eu" name+ Seline.

Eurena (African-American double) See any "Eu" name+René.

Eusebia Meaning unknown (Greek).

Patron Saints: There are a half-dozen Sts. Eusebia. One of them was the abbess of a monastery near Marseilles, France. When a Saracen army attacked the monastery in 732, all the nuns were tortured and had their noses cut off. Then they were murdered because they refused to give up their Catholic faith.

Feast Dates: October 11 — St. Eusebia; March 15 — Ven. Eusebio Kino, S.J. (see Arizona).

Eustacia "The Tranquil One" (Latin).

Patron Saints: There are about three dozen male Sts. Eustacius but not one female Eustacia. The nearest we can come is St. Eustadiola. She was a matron of a noble family in Bourges in the 600s. After the death of her husband, St. Eustadiola founded a convent, built many churches, and abstained from meat for seventy years.

Feast Dates: June 8 — St. Eustadiola.

Eva (German, Italian, Spanish, Portuguese) See Eve, Evangeline.

Evaleen (Irish) See Eve, Evelyn.

Evalene (Irish) See Eve, Evelyn.

Evalina (American) See Evelyn.

Evaline (variant) See Eve, Evelyn.

Evangelia (variant) See Eve.

Evangelina (variant) See Eve.

Evangeline "The Bearer of Good Tidings" (Greek).

Patron Saints: Catholic tradition gives some additional information about the four Gospel writers.

St. Matthew preached to the Hebrews for fifteen years. Then he moved to the south shore of the Caspian Sea, where he was martyred.

St. Mark may or may not have known Jesus. He ended his life as the bishop of Alexandria, Africa. He was dragged behind a cart through the streets of that city until he died.

St. Luke never personally met Jesus. A physician who painted a portrait of Christ, he remained single all his life and died (probably not martyred) at the age of seventy-four in Achaia.

St. John is usually thought to be the youngest Apostle. He was about four years younger than Jesus and died when he was a hundred years old. It is not certain if he died as a martyr or not.

Feast Dates: September 21, April 25, October 18, December 27 — The Four Evangelists.

Evanthia (African-American) See Eve+Thea.

Evashti (African-American) See Eve+Vashti.

Eve "The Mother of the Living" (Hebrew, English, French).

Patron Saints: There are about a dozen Sts. Eve and Eva. The most famous, of course, is the wife of Adam. A later St. Eva died for her faith with St. Felix in ancient Numidia. She was probably a black woman.

Feast Dates: August 30 — St. Eva; December 24 — Sts. Adam and Eve (see Eartha).

Eveleen (variant) See Eve, Evelyn.

Evelene (English) See Eve, Evelyn.

Evelin (English) See Eve, Evelyn.

Evelina (Spanish) See Eve, Evelyn.

Eveline (English) See Eve, Evelyn.

Evelis (Hebrew-French double) See Eve+Lisa.

Evelyn "The Mother of the Living+From the Stream [or The Beautiful One or The Light]" (Old English double).

Patron Saints: Evelyn can be a form of Eve and it can also be a combination of Eve and Lynn, Eve and Alana, or Eve and Lisa. This leads to about a dozen Sts. Eva and Eve, a few Sts. Lina, Alan, and Helen, and a dozen Sts. Elizabeth.

Feast Dates: December 24 — Sts. Adam and Eve (see Eartha); July 5 — St. Lina (see Lynn).

Evetta (Italian double) See Eve+Etta.

Evette (French double) See Eve+Ette.

Evey (variant) See Eve.

Evgenia (Russian) See Eugenia.

Evica (Bulgarian) See Eve.

Evie (variant) See Eve.

Evita (Spanish double) See Eve+Ita.

Evlin (English) See Evelyn.

Evline (English) See Evelyn.

Evon (variant) See Evonne.

Evona (African-American) See Evonne.

Evone (variant) See Evonne.

Evonia (variant) See Evonne.

Evonne "Mother of the Living" (Old French variant of Eve).

Patron Saints: There are about a dozen Sts. Eve and Eva. There is also one St. Evonius. Evonius was a holy, learned bishop in ancient France. His many very scholarly writings are all lost.

Feast Dates: May 19 — St. Evonius; December 24 — Sts. Adam and Eve (see Eartha).

Evonnie (variant) See Evonne.

Evora (African-American double) See Eve+Nora.

Evvie (variant) See Eve.

Evy (variant) See Eve.

Ewa (Polish) See Eve.

Eyde (nickname) See Edith.

Eydie (nickname) See Edith.

Ezzetta (African-American double) See Ezra+Zetta.

ℱ

Fabia "The Bran Grower" (Latin).

Patron Saints: St. Fabiola was a Roman matron who grew in spirituality under the guidance of St. Jerome. She gave most of her fortune to the poor. She founded a hospice and nursed the sick. She died in 400.

Feast Dates: December 27 — St. Fabiola.

Fabiana (Latin) See Fabia.

Fabiola (Spanish) See Fabia.

Fae (nickname) See Faith.

Faina (variant) See Fawn.

Faith "The Faithful One" (Middle English).

Patron Saints: There are three ancient Sts. Faith. One, a teenager, was arrested and brought before a pagan judge in about the year 250. First, he asked her name. She signed herself with the cross and answered, "My name is Faith and I will try to live as I have been named." He demanded she offer sacrifice to the pagan goddess Diana and she refused. Then he ordered that she be tied to a red-hot bed and executed.

Feast Dates: October 6 — St. Faith of Agen; August 1 — St. Faith (with Charity) (see Charity).

Fallon "Grandchild of the Ruler or Leader" (Irish Gaelic).

Patron Saints: There is a St. Fal, St. Lon, and a dozen Irish Sts. Fallon (Foillanna). One St. Foillanna is simply remembered as a medieval female "Irish saint."

St. Fal, the son of a Roman official, was captured by enemy soldiers and sold into slavery. After gaining his free-

dom he became a religious priest and, eventually, an abbot. He died in 540.

Feast Dates: March 3 — St. Foillanna; May 16 — St. Fal; December 5 — St. Lon (see Loni).

Fame (English) See Euphemia.

Fan (nickname) See Frances.

Fanchette (French double) See Frances+Ette.

Fanchon (French) See Frances.

Fancie (nickname) See Frances.

Fancy (nickname) See Frances.

Fanechka (variant) See Frances.

Fania (variant) See Frances.

Fanni (nickname) See Frances.

Fannie (nickname) See Frances.

Fanny (nickname) See Frances.

Fanya (variant) See Fawn.

Farica (English) See Freda, Frederica.

Farrah "The Beautiful Pleasant One" (Middle English) or "The Joyful One" (Arabic).

Patron Saints: There are a couple of ancient saints with similar names. St. Fara was born in Burgundy, France, in about 595, the daughter of a duke. Her refusal to marry caused some unhappiness at home. In fact, her father made her life miserable for a long time. At one point this undermined her health, but she slowly convinced him that she wanted to dedicate her life to God, and he finally built a convent for her. Because of her example, her brothers gave themselves to God and eventually became bishops. She died at the age of sixty-two.

Feast Dates: April 3 — St. Fara.

Farrand (variant) See Farrah.

Fatima "The Abstainer" (Arabic).

Patron Saints: An angel appeared to three children near Fátima, Portugal, several times in 1916 and taught them a prayer to the Blessed Trinity. Then from May 13, 1917, to October 13, 1917, the Blessed Virgin appeared six times, on the thirteenth day of each month, to ten-year-old Lucia dos Santos and her two younger cousins, Francisco and Jacinta, who were tending the family's sheep.

On September 13 the Lady asked that the Rosary be prayed. On October 13 she revealed that she was the "Lady of the Rosary" and asked for prayers and penance. A spinning, dancing, and falling sun seen by eighty thousand people accompanied this.

The message of Fátima can be summed up in the words of Mary: "I have come to exhort the faithful to change their lives, to avoid grieving our Lord by sin, and to pray the Rosary."

Feast Dates: October 13 — Our Lady of Fátima.

Fatimah (variant) See Fatima.
Fatique (African-American) See Fatima.
Fatma (variant) See Fatima.
Fatrice (African-American double) See any "F" name+Patrice.
Faun (variant) See Fawn.
Fawn "A Baby Deer" (Middle French).

Patron Saints: There are a few Sts. Fawn. The emperor Diocletian in about 304 ordered Christians to be killed everywhere, and at one point seven young ladies were put on trial for the crime of being Christian. St. Faina was one of them. She and her companions refused to renounce their faith in Jesus and were drowned. Stones were attached to their bodies so that they would be lost to the faithful. But this did not stop Theodotus, who made it his business to bury the Christian dead even though it was unlawful. Eventually he was arrested and executed.

Feast Dates: May 18 — St. Fawn, also known as Faina.

Fawna (French) See Fawn.
Fawnia (variant) See Fawn.
Fay (nickname) See Faith.
Faye (French) See Faith.
Fayre (variant) See Farrah.
Fayth (English) See Faith.
Faythe (English) See Faith.
Fearn (variant) See Fern.
Fearne (variant) See Fern.
Febe (Spanish) See Phoebe.
Febronia (Spanish) See February.
February "The Purified One" (Latin).

Patron Saints: There are several Sts. Febronia. One St. Febronia died in 304. She lived the life of a religious sister in a convent in Assyria. Her aunt, St. Bryene, was the superior. When persecution of Christians broke out, Febronia was arrested and offered marriage in return for denying Christ. This she refused to do and was tortured. This led to the conversion of the man that the government had tried to force upon her. In the end, she was beheaded.

Feast Dates: June 25 — St. Febronia.

Federica (Italian, Spanish) See Frederica.
Fedora (Slavic) See Theodora.
Feeby (African-American) See Phoebe.
Felia (Dutch) See Felicia, Felicitas.
Felica (Spanish) See Felicia.
Felicata (Russian) See Felicitas.
Felice (French) See Felicia, Felicitas.
Felicia "The Happy One" (Latin, Italian, Spanish) or "Lover of Green Foliage" (variation of Phyliss).

Patron Saints: There are a dozen Sts. Felicia, Feliciana, and Felicissima. St. Felicia of Meda, 1378-1444, was born in Italy. While still very young, she became an orphan. This had a lasting effect on her. She became very serious about life and at the young age of twelve promised God to remain chaste. At the age of twenty-two she became a Poor Clare nun and pursued a life of prayer and penance. It seems that the devil never ceased to tempt her and provided great trials, but she overcame them all. At the age of forty-seven she was elected abbess of her convent. She ruled for fourteen years.

Feast Dates: October 5 — Bl. Felicia of Meda; March 7 — St. Felicitas (see Felicitas).

Feliciana (Spanish) See Felicia, Felicitas.
Felicidad (Spanish) See Felicia, Felicitas.
Felicie (Dutch) See Felicia, Felicitas.
Felicija (Russian) See Felicia, Felicitas.
Felicitas "The Happy One" (Dutch, German, Scandinavian, Romanian).

Patron Saints: There are almost two dozen Sts. Felicitas. One St. Felicitas was a black slave who lived in Carthage and was studying to become a Catholic when arrested. Because of her belief in Catholic teachings, she and several companions were thrown into prison, tortured, and then beheaded in 202.

Feast Dates: March 7 — St. Felicitas; October 5 — Bl. Felicia of Meda (see Felicia).

Felicité (French) See Felicitas.
Felicity (English) See Felicia, Felicitas.
Feliksa (Polish, Greek) See Felicia, Felicitas.
Felipa (Spanish) See Philippa, Philippine.
Felise (French) See Felicia, Felicitas.
Felisha (English) See Felicia, Felicitas.
Felita (variant) See Felicia, Felicitas.
Feliza (Spanish) See Felicia, Felicitas.
Felizia (German, Spanish) See Felicia, Felicitas.
Ferdinanda (English) See Fernanda.
Ferdinande (French) See Fernanda.

Fern "The Fernlike One" (Old English) or "The Adventurous One" (nickname for Fernanda).

Patron Saints: While there are probably many Ferns in heaven, not one St. Fern can be found on the official Church lists. However, we can adopt a few saints for whom Fern would have been a nickname.

Feast Dates: May 30 — St. Fernando III (see Fernanda); September 10 — Bl. Isabel Fernandez (see Isabel).

Fernanda "The Adventurous One" (Old German).

Patron Saints: There are a few saints named Ferdinand. One of them, St. Fernando, 1198-1252, became king of Castile when he was eighteen. Two years later he married Beatrice, daughter of King Philip of Swabia, and they had ten children. Later in life, after being left a widower, he married again and his second wife gave him three more children. King Ferdinand was quick to forgive personal injury, but he was almost unbending in dispensing public justice. He was also a great champion of learning and he founded the University of Salamanca. During his reign he struggled to recover his country from the Moors. He fought the final battle that led to victory over the Moors. He died at the age of fifty-three.

Feast Dates: May 30 — St. Fernando III; September 10 — Bl. Isabel Fernandez (see Isabel).

Fernande (variant) See Fernanda.
Fernandina (English) See Fernanda.
Ferne (variant) See Fern.
Feodora (Slavic) See Theodora.
Fiala (Czech) See Viola, Violet, Yolanda.
Fialka (Czech) See Viola, Violet, Yolanda.
Fidelia (Latin) See Faith.
Fidelity (English) See Faith.

Fidella (Latin) See Faith.

Fifi (French) See Josephine.

Fifine (variant) See Josephine.

Filia "The Daughter" (Latin).

Patron Saints: The word "daughter" in Latin is *filia nata*. There is one St. Fillian. He preached the Gospel in Ireland during the time of St. Patrick.

Feast Dates: June 20 — St. Fillian.

Filida (Bulgarian, Polish) See Phyllis.

Filipa (Spanish) See Philippa, Philippine.

Filippa (Italian) See Philippa, Philippine.

Filis (Spanish) See Phyllis.

Filisa (Russian) See Phyllis.

Fillide (Italian) See Phyllis.

Filomela (Spanish double) See Philana+ Melody.

Filomena (Spanish) See Philomena.

Fina (Spanish) See Josephina.

Fio (nickname) See Flora, Florence, Florida.

Fiona "The Fair [White] One" (Irish Gaelic).

Patron Saints: There are a few Irish patrons, such as Sts. Fionnbhar (Finbar) and Fionntain. To these we add St. Fionnan. He was born in Ireland in the early 600s. Early in life he became a monk and later became a bishop. His diocese covered much of central England and his flock was scattered, half-civilized, and very unruly. He strenuously supported the Celtic traditions and opposed innovations that arose in southern England. His ten-year stewardship as bishop was very peaceful and he made many converts.

Feast Dates: February 17 — St. Fionnan, also known as Finan.

Fionna (Irish) See Fiona.

Fiora (Italian) See Flora.

Fiorella (Italian) See Flora.

Fiorenza (Italian) See Flora, Florence.

Flavia "The Blond One" (Latin) or "The Yellow-Haired One" (Latin).

Patron Saints: There are a half-dozen Sts. Flavia. One of them was martyred for the Catholic faith in ancient Rome and buried in the catacombs of St. Priscilla.

Feast Dates: June 29 — St. Flavia.

Flemmie (African-American) See Fleming.

Fleur (French) See Flora.

Fleurette (French double) See Flora+Ette.

Flo (nickname) See Flora, Florence, Florida.

Floora (variant) See Flora, Florida.

Flor (Spanish) See Flora, Florence, Florida.

Flora "The Flower" (Latin) or "The Blooming One" (Spanish).

Patron Saints: There are a half-dozen Sts. Flora. There is also a Bl. Richard Flower, an English martyr who was executed in 1588. Anyone given a "flower name" can also claim these saints as patrons.

St. Flora was born to a Muslim father and Christian mother in about 835 in Cordova, Spain, and was secretly raised a Catholic by her mother. In 850 the Moors in Cordova began persecuting Christians, and Flora's brother accused her of being Christian before a local judge. The magistrate had her brutally scourged and placed under the authority of this same brother, but she escaped and fled the city to her sister's home, where she hid for a while. Later, she returned to Cordova and publicly prayed in a Catholic church.

While in that church she met Mary, a teenage sister of a recently martyred deacon. Together they decided to give themselves up to the local authorities.

They were swiftly jailed and were beheaded.

Feast Dates: November 24 — St. Flora; May 4 — Bl. Richard Flower (see Lotus).

Florance (English) See Flora, Florence.

Florastine (African-American) See Flora, Florence.

Flore (French) See Flora, Florida.

Florella (variant) See Flora.

Florence "The Blooming One" (Latin).

Patron Saints: There are almost a dozen Sts. Florentia and Florentina. In about 600 three brothers in Spain dedicated themselves to the religious life. Because their parents were deceased, they shared in raising and educating their younger sister, who was named Florentina. Their good example led this sister to choose to become a Benedictine nun. All three brothers and the sister are officially recognized as saints.

Feast Dates: June 20 — St. Florentina, O.S.B.

Florencia (Spanish) See Florence, Flora.

Florene (African-American) See Flora.

Florenica (Spanish) See Florence, Flora.

Florentina (German) See Florence, Tine, Tyne.

Florenza (African-American) See Flora, Florence.

Florenze (variant) See Florence.

Floretta (variant double) See Flora+Etta.

Florette (French double) See Flora+Ette.

Flori (nickname) See Florence, Florida.

Floria (English) See Flora, Florence, Florida.

Florica (variant) See Flora.

Florida "The Flowery One" (Spanish).

Patron Saints: There is one St. Florida and a half-dozen Sts. Flora. St. Florida was a martyr in ancient Rome.

Feast Dates: August 29 — St. Florida; November 24 — St. Flora; June 20 — St. Florentina (see Florence).

Florie (nickname) See Flora.

Florina (Spanish) See Flora.

Florinda (English) See Flora, Florence, Florida.

Florine (English) See Florence.

Floris (English) See Flora, Florence.

Florka (variant) See Flora.

Florri (nickname) See Flora, Florence, Florida.

Florrie (nickname) See Flora, Florence, Florida.

Florry (nickname) See Flora, Florence, Florida.

Floss (nickname) See Florence.

Flossy (nickname) See Florence.

Flower (English) See Flora, Lotus.

Floy (nickname) See Florence.

Flozell (African-American double) See Flora+Zella.

Fonda "Affectionate One [or Foolish One]" (Middle English) or "The Profound One" (Spanish, Latin).

Patron Saints: The name Fonda in Latin is *amans*. This is the same root from which the name Amy arises.

Feast Dates: June 6 — St. Ama (see Aimee).

Fondea (variant) See Fonda.

Fondes (variant) See Fonda.

Fortuna "One with a Destiny" (Latin).

Patron Saints: There is one St. Fortuna and a half-dozen Sts. Fortunata. St. Fortuna, a black woman of Carthage, Africa, was imprisoned because she insisted on remaining Catholic. She died there in 250, of starvation.

Feast Dates: May 6 — St. Fortuna.

Fortunata (Spanish) See Fortuna.

Fortune (English) See Fortuna.

Fran (nickname) See Frances.

Frances "Free One" (Latin) or "One from France" (Latin).

Patron Saints: There are a half-dozen Sts. Frances. One of them, St. Frances Xavier Cabrini, lived from

1850 to 1917. As a child she dreamed of becoming a missionary to China. At the age of eighteen, after her parents died, she tried to become a religious but was refused because of poor health. However, a local priest approached her and asked her to take charge of an orphanage and she accepted. Soon she found seven helpers and in 1877 they all took vows as religious sisters.

In 1889 the pope asked her to take a group of her sisters to New York to aid the immigrants. In time, she opened orphanages, hospitals, and halfway houses in New York, Chicago, New Orleans, Seattle, and Denver. She also opened schools and other institutions in Costa Rica, Panama, Chile, and Brazil.

Nothing was easy. She faced constant opposition, even from bishops. She practically lived out of a suitcase, but she toiled and triumphed. She died suddenly at the age of sixty-seven, physically worn out. She was the first United States citizen to be canonized a saint.

Feast Dates: December 22 — St. Frances Xavier Cabrini.

Francesca (Italian) See Frances.

Franchette (French double) See Frances+Ette.

Franci (Hungarian) See Frances.

Francie (nickname) See Frances.

Francine (English, French) See Frances.

Francisca (Spanish) See Frances.

Franciska (Bulgarian, Danish, Hungarian) See Frances.

Franciszka (Polish) See Frances.

Françoise (French) See Frances.

Francy (nickname) See Frances.

Francyne (English) See Frances.

Frank (nickname) See Frances.

Franka (Russian, Norwegian) See Frances.

Frankie (nickname) See Frances.

Franky (nickname) See Frances.

Franni (nickname) See Frances.

Frannie (nickname) See Frances.

Franny (nickname) See Frances.

Fransina (Dutch) See Frances.

Frantiska (Czech, Greek) See Frances.

Franuse (Latvian) See Frances.

Franzi (German) See Frances.

Franzie (nickname) See Frances.

Franziska (German) See Frances.

Fraser (English) See Frasier.

Frasier "The Curly-Haired One" (Old English) or "The Strawberry" (Old French).

Patron Saints: There is no St. Frasier. However, knowing that Frasier can mean "curly-haired" leads to twelve Sts. Crispinus and Crispinianus and one St. Crispina. Their names also mean "curly-haired."

Feast Dates: December 5 — St. Crispina (see Crispina).

Fraze (nickname) See Frasier.

Frazier (English) See Frasier.

Fred (nickname) See Frasier, Freda, Frederica.

Freda "The Peaceful Ruler" (Old German) or "The Wise Counselor" (short form of Alfreda).

Patron Saints: Freda can be a short form of Alfreda, Frederica, and Winifred. There is one St. Alfrida. There is a greater saint, who is the wisest of counselors. She is the Blessed Virgin Mary.

Feast Dates: August 2 — St. Alfrida (see Alfreda); April 25 — Our Lady of Good Counsel (see Consuelo).

Freddi (nickname) See Freda, Frederica, Guinevere, Winifred.

Freddie (nickname) See Freda, Frederica, Guinevere, Winifred.

Freddy (nickname) See Freda, Frederica, Guinevere, Winifred.

Fredella (variant double) See Freda+Della.

Frederica "The Peaceful Ruler" (Old German).

Patron Saints: There are about a dozen Sts. Frederick. One of them was a native of Frisia and was ordained a priest. By 825 his piety and knowledge became well known, and he was elected bishop of Utrecht. As bishop, he worked hard to bring order and converts to his diocese. In time, he was drawn into a quarrel between the sons of the emperor (their father) and stepmother. This drew the wrath of the empress and she hired assassins to kill Frederick. They stabbed him to death on July 18, 838, just after he celebrated Mass.

Feast Dates: July 18 — St. Frederick of Utrecht.

Fredericka (variant) See Freda, Frederica.

Frederika (English) See Freda, Frederica.

Frederique (French) See Freda, Frederica.

Fredi (variant) See Freda, Frederica, Guinevere, Winifred.

Fredia (variant) See Freda, Frederica.

Fredonia (African-American double) See Freda+Dona.

Fredra (variant) See Freda, Frederica.

Fredrike (German) See Freda, Frederica.

Freetta (African-American) See Freda.

Frerika (English) See Frederica.

Frica (English short form) See Africa.

Frida (Spanish) See Freda, Frederica.

Friday "Born on the Goddess Frigg's Day" or "The Devoted Helper" (Old English).

Patron Saints: There is one group of citizens from ancient Alexandria, Egypt, who were actually martyred on Good Friday. In 332, on Good Friday, the apostate prefect ordered a great number of Catholics killed. His battalions of soldiers methodically descended upon the Catholic churches in Alexandria, where they found large groups of Catholics gathered in prayer. Without hesitation, they slaughtered everyone they could find and a great multitude of Christians died.

And then there is a St. Frigia, who was one of many single young ladies who accompanied St. Ursula on her journey and then died with her in about 360.

Feast Dates: March 21 — Good Friday Martyrs, Alexandria; October 21 — St. Frigia.

Frieda (variant) See Freda, Frederica.

Friede (variant) See Freda, Frederica.

Friederike (German) See Frederica.

Frika (English short form) See Africa.

Fritzi (German) See Frederica.

Fritzie (German) See Frederica.

Fritzy (German) See Frederica.

G

Gabbi "God Is My Strength" or "The Man of God" (English nickname for Gabriel).

Patron Saints: There is one Bl. Gabriela and about two dozen Sts. Gabriel. The greatest is the archangel Gabriel mentioned in the Book of Daniel and the Gospel of Luke. He is patron of childbirth, diplomats, messengers, postal workers, stamp collectors, telephone workers, television workers, and anyone involved in the communications industry.

Feast Dates: September 29 — St. Gabriel, Archangel; June 24 — Bl. Gabriela Henrica (see Gabriela).

Gabbie (nickname) See Gabbi, Gabriela.

Gabby (nickname) See Gabbi, Gabriela.

Gabe (nickname) See Gabbi, Gabriela.

Gabey (nickname) See Gabbi, Gabriela.

Gabi (nickname) See Gabbi, Gabriela.

Gabie (nickname) See Gabbi, Gabriela.

Gabor (variant) See Gabbi, Gabriela.

Gabra (Czech) See Gabbi, Gabriela.

Gabrail (variant) See Gabbi, Gabriela.

Gabriel (Hebrew) See Gabbi, Gabriela.

Gabriela "God Is My Strength" or "The Man of God" (English, Spanish, Portuguese, Polish).

Patron Saints: There is one Bl. Gabriela and more than two dozen Sts. Gabriel. Sister Gabriela Henrica of Jesus was one of fifteen Carmelite sisters who was arrested and executed by the French government during the Revolution in 1794.

Feast Dates: June 24 — Bl. Gabriela Henrica; September 29 — St. Gabriel, Archangel (see Gabbi).

Gabriele (German) See Gabbi, Gabriela.

Gabriella (English, Italian, Swedish) See Gabbi, Gabriela.

Gabrielle (French) See Gabbi, Gabriela.

Gabriellia (variant) See Gabbi, Gabriela.

Gabrila (variant) See Gabbi, Gabriela.

Gaby (French) See Gabbi, Gabriela.

Gabysia (Polish) See Gabbi, Gabriela.

Gae (nickname) See Abigail, Gaea, Gail, Gayle, Gay.

Gaea "The Earthy One" (Greek) or "The Bringer of Joy" (nickname for Abigail).

Patron Saints: Christian tradition does not provide a St. Gaea. But the Bible gives us an Abigail (see, for example, 1 Samuel 25:3, 14, 18, 23, 32, 36, 39-40; 2 Samuel 2:2; and 1 Chronicles 2:16-17).

Feast Dates: December 24 — Sts. Adam and Eve (see Eartha); November 1 — St. Abigail (see Abigail).

Gael (variant) See Abigail, Gail.

Gai (variant) See Gay.

Gaia (nickname) See Eartha.

Gail "The Lively One" (Old English) or "The Bringer of Joy" (nickname for Abigail).

Patron Saints: Christian tradition does not provide a St. Gail. But the Bible gives us an Abigail (see Scripture references under Gaea, above).

Feast Dates: November 1 — St. Abigail (see Abigail).

Gala (variant) See Abigail, Eartha, Gail, Galatea, Gaea.

Galatea "The Milky White One" (Greek, Spanish).

Patron Saints: There is one St. Galatia. She died for Jesus in Melitene, Armenia, in ancient times.

Feast Dates: April 19 — St. Galatia.

Galateia (variant) See Galatea.

Galatia (variant) See Galatea.

Gale "The One Who Sings" (Old Norse) or "The Bringer of Joy" (nickname for Abigail).

Patron Saints: Christian tradition does not provide a St. Gale. But the Bible gives us an Abigail (see Scripture references under Gaea, above).

Feast Dates: November 1 — St. Abigail (see Abigail).

Galetea (variant) See Galatea.

Galiana (Moorish double) See Helen+ Ana.

Galina (Russian) See Helen.

Gar (nickname) See Gardenia.

Gard (nickname) See Gardenia.

Gardenia "The Gardenia Flower" (Latin, Spanish).

Patron Saints: The gardenia, an aromatic flower, was named after the American botanist Alexander Garden. This leads to the English martyr Bl. Jermyn Gardiner. Other patrons can be found when one realizes that a gardener is "one who cares for a garden." The Catholic Church has officially appointed six saints to act as patrons of gardeners. They are Sts. Adam, Adelard, Dorothy, Fiacre, Gertrude of Nivelles, and Phocas.

Father Jermyn Gardiner, secretary to the bishop of Winchester, was executed in 1544 for refusing to take the Oath of Supremacy, recognizing the king of England as head of the Church.

Feast Dates: March 7 — Bl. Jermyn Gardiner; December 24 — Sts. Adam and Eve (see Eartha).

Gardie (nickname) See Gardenia.

Gardy (nickname) See Gardenia.

Garland (Middle English) See Rosario.

Garnat (variant) See Garnet.

Garnet "Like the Dark Red Gem" (Middle English).

Patron Saints: There is one Irish St. Garnat, a hermit, and an English martyr. The Englishman was Father Thomas Garnet, who was ordained in 1599 and then worked in England for five years as a diocesan priest before becoming a Jesuit. He was arrested as a suspect in the Gunpowder Plot of 1605. After seven months of imprisonment, he and forty-six other priests were exiled and warned not to return to England under threat of death. Despite the warning, Father Garnet returned, was arrested, convicted, and then hanged, drawn, and quartered.

Feast Dates: June 23 — St. Thomas Garnet, S.J.

Garnette (French) See Garnet.

Gasha (Russian) See Agatha.

Gavra (variant) See Gabbi, Gabriela.

Gavraila (Bulgarian) See Gabbi, Gabriela.

Gavraille (variant) See Gabbi, Gabriela.

Gavrina (Romanian) See Gabbi, Gabriela.

Gavrylo (variant) See Gabbi, Gabriela.

Gay "The Bright, Lively One" (Old French) or "The Joyful One" (Old French).

Patron Saints: There is an ancient saint named Gaiana, who served as the head of a community of virgins in Rome. When a persecution broke out, she fled with some of the women to Armenia, but they were still persecuted and martyred. However, their deaths led to the conversion of King Tiridat of Armenia.

Feast Dates: September 30 — St. Gay, also known as Gaiana.

Gaye (variant) See Abigail, Gail, Gale, Gay.

Gayel (variant) See Abigail, Gail, Gale, Gay.

Gayla (variant) See Abigail, Gail, Galatea, Gale, Gay.

Gayle (variant) See Abigail, Gail, Gale, Gay.

Gayleen (variant) See Abigail, Gail, Gale, Gay.

Gaylene (variant) See Abigail, Gail, Gale, Gay.

Gaylynn (African-American double) See Gay+Lynn.

Gaynelle (African-American double) See Gay+Nelly.

Gaynor (Spanish) See Guinevere.

Geena (nickname) See Eugenia, Georgene, Gina, Regina, Virginia.

Geertruida (Dutch) See Gertrude.

Geisha "The Elegant Companion" (Japanese).

Patron Saints: A great many of the martyred saints did not die alone. Family and friends often accompanied them. Often they are numbered, but the names of these valuable companions are not given.

Feast Dates: November 1 — All Saints (especially those not named, who died for Christ).

Gelina (nickname) See Angelina.

Geltruda (Italian) See Gertrude.

Gelya (Russian) See Angela, Angelica.

Gem (variant) See Gemini, Gemma.

Gemina (Greek) See Gemini.

Gemini "The Twin" (Greek).

Patron Saints: There is one St. Gemina. Gemina was probably a black woman who died for Jesus in Africa.

Feast Dates: April 20 — St. Gemina; July 3 — St. Thomas, Apostle (see Thomas).

Gemma "The Precious Stone" (Italian, Spanish).

Patron Saints: There are two known Sts. Gemma. One is patron of Goriano, Italy, She lived her early years as a simple shepherd. Her last forty-two years were lived as a recluse devoted to prayer. She died in 1249.

Feast Dates: May 12 — St. Gemma.

Gemma (variant) See Emma.

Gen (nickname) See Geneva, Genevieve, Jennifer.

Gena (nickname) See Eugenia, Georgene, Geneva, Genevieve, Gina, Regina, Virginia.

Gene (variant) See Jane, Jean.

Generosa "The Generous One" (Spanish).

Patron Saints: St. Generosa died a martyr in ancient Scilla.

Feast Dates: July 17 — St. Generosa.

Genesia "The Origin [Birth]" (Hebrew).

Patron Saints: At least two patrons can be found. One is St. Genesia, who was martyred in ancient Turin. The second is God, the Creator of all, who makes all things new.

Feast Dates: June 8 — St. Genesia; Holy Saturday — God the Creator and Re-Creator of All.

Genesis (English) See Genesia.

Geneva "The Gateway" (French) or "The White Wave" (short form of Genevieve) or "The Juniper Tree" (form of Juniper).

Patron Saints: Geneva may be a form of Geneva, Genevieve, or Juniper.

Feast Dates: January 3 — St. Genevieve (see Genevieve); July 1 — Bl. Junípero Serra (see Sierra).

Genevie (variant) See Genevieve.

Genevieve "The White Wave" (Old German) or "The White Phantom" (variant of Guinevere).

Patron Saints: There is one St. Genevieve, who lived between the years 422 and 500. At the age of fifteen she became a nun. When it became known that she had visions, many Parisians became hostile. However, she had a champion in the bishop of Auxerre, and the accuracy of her predictions helped change the ill feeling.

Later, when a foreign army occupied Paris, she organized food shipments to feed the hungry. She also successfully interceded with the conquering king to gain the release of many political prisoners. She died at the age of seventy-eight. After her death, those who visited her tomb reported many miracles.

Feast Dates: January 3 — St. Genevieve.

Genevra (Latin) See Geneva, Genevieve.

Geni (variant) See Genevieve, Guinevere, Jennifer.

Genia (nickname) See Eugenia.

Genice (American) See Janice.

Genilee (English double) See Jennifer+Leigh.

Genna (variant) See Genevieve, Guinevere, Jennifer.

Genni (variant) See Genevieve, Guinevere, Jennifer.

Gennie (nickname) See Genevieve, Guinevere, Jennifer.

Gennifer (English) See Genevieve, Guinevere, Jennifer.

Genny (nickname) See Genevieve, Guinevere, Jennifer.

Genora (African-American double) See Genevieve+Nora.

Genovaite (Lithuanian) See Genevieve.

Genovefa (Dutch, Russian) See Genevieve.

Genoveffa (Italian) See Genevieve.

Genovera (variant) See Genevieve.

Genoveva (Spanish, Swedish, German) See Genevieve.

Genowefa (Polish) See Genevieve.

Georgeanna (American double) See Georgene+Anna.

Georgena (variant) See Georgene.

Georgene "The Farmer" (English).

Patron Saints: Georgene is the feminine form of George. And there is one St. Georgene (also known as Gorgonia).

In about 350 a man named Gregory Nazianzen the Elder married a woman named Nonna. They had three children, two boys and a girl. One son became a priest and was eventually recognized as a Doctor of the Church. The other son became a medical doctor. The oldest child, a girl, was named Gorgonia.

Gorgonia married and bore three children. She had a happy marriage, was generous to all, and frequently fasted and prayed. Her confidence in God was great. Years later, in 374, she made her last day on earth a "Festival of Celebration." First, she held a party and then she died in the arms of her mother, St. Nonna. The whole family has been recognized as saints.

Feast Dates: December 9 — St. Georgene, also known as Gorgonia.

Georgetta (English double) See Georgene+Etta.

Georgette (French double) See Georgene+Ette.

Georgia (Italian, English, Greek) See Georgene.

Georgiana (English double) See Georgene+Ann.

Georgianna (Latin double) See Georgene+Ann.

Georgianne (variant double) See Georgene+Ann.

Georgie (nickname) See Georgene.

Georgienne (French) See Georgene.

Georgina (German, Dutch, Spanish) See Georgene.

Georgine (French) See Georgene.

Geralda (Czech, Dutch) See Geraldine.

Geraldina (Spanish, Portuguese, Italian) See Geraldine.

Geraldine "The Mighty Spear Warrior" (Old German).

Patron Saints: The Church provides a dozen Sts. Gerald and Gerard. St. Gerard Majella, 1726-1755, became a tailor's apprentice and lived with and supported his mother and three sisters. At the age of twenty-three he became a religious brother. Once he was falsely accused of a serious crime but refused to defend himself. He gave the problem to God. Many thought him to be crazy, but he was eventually exonerated.

His prayers were real conversations with God. Once, while deep in prayer, he was heard to protest to God, "You must let me go; I have work I must do." He also experienced levitation and bilocation; he could read the consciences of sinners and worked miracles. In his twenty-ninth year he died of consumption. He is patron of mothers, expectant mothers, and of the falsely accused.

Feast Dates: October 16 — St. Gerard Majella.

Geralyn (American double) See Geraldine+Lynn.

Gerda (Dutch, Spanish) See Gertrude.

Gerelda (African-American) See Geraldine.

Gerhardine (German) See Geraldine.

Geri (nickname) See Geraldine.

Gerianna (variant double) See Geraldine+ Anna.

Gerianne (variant double) See Geraldine+ Anne.

Germain (French) See Germaine.

Germaine "The One from Germany" (French).

Patron Saints: There are a few Sts. Germana. One of them lived from 1579 to 1602 and was born near Toulouse of very poor parents. She also suffered from scrofula and the neglect and harshness of her parents. Nevertheless, she tended the sheep, prayed, and practiced charity toward others. She died all alone on her bed of straw at the age of twenty-one.

There is also an English martyr who qualifies to be a patron: Bl. Jermyn Gardiner.

Feast Dates: June 15 — St. Germana; March 7 — Bl. Jermyn Gardiner (see Gardenia).

Germana (Latin) See Germaine.

Geronda (African-American double) See Geraldine+Rhonda.

Gerri (nickname) See Geraldine.

Gerrie (nickname) See Geraldine.

Gerrilee (double) See Geraldine+Leigh.

Gerry (nickname) See Geraldine.

Gerrylee (double) See Geraldine+Leigh.

Gert (nickname) See Gertrude.

Gerta (nickname) See Gertrude.

Gerti (nickname) See Gertrude.

Gertie (nickname) See Gertrude.

Gertraud (German) See Gertrude.

Gertrud (German, Scandinavian, Hungarian) See Gertrude.

Gertruda (variant) See Gertrude.

Gertrude "The Mighty Spear Warrior" (Old German).

Patron Saints: There are about a dozen Sts. Gertrude. One, called "The Great," was born in 1256. She was only five years old when she became the pupil of St. Mechtildis. She was an attractive girl and learned her lessons well. Upon reaching adulthood, she became a religious sister in the convent where she had been taught and raised. At the age of twenty-six she began to receive revelations from Jesus; she eventually wrote five books about her divine encounters. Today they are called *The Revelations of St. Gertrude.* She died at about age forty-five.

Feast Dates: November 16 — St. Gertrude the Great.

Gertrudis (Spanish) See Gertrude.

Gerty (nickname) See Gertrude.

Giacinta (variant) See Hyacinth.

Giada (Italian) See Jade.

Giandrea (Hispanic-American double) See Jane+Adrea.

Gianina (Italian, Spanish) See Jane.

Gianna (Italian) See Jane.

Gigi (nickname) See Gilbertine, Georgene, Virginia.

Gil (nickname) See Gilbertine.

Gilberta (variant) See Gilbertine.

Gilbertina (variant) See Gilbertine.

Gilbertine "Trusted One" (English) or "Hostage" (English).

Patron Saints: There is no female St. Gilbertine, but there are about a half-dozen Sts. Gilbert. St. Gilbert of Sempringham, 1083-1189, became a priest, worked as a teacher, and gave his inheritance to the poor. His prayer life and discipline were an inspiration for all. Soon he opened a convent for young women and then some houses for men. When old, he faced much controversy and physical pain. He died at the age of one hundred six. The Gilbertine religious order was the only order founded in England during the Middle ages and it died at the hands of King Henry VIII.

Feast Dates: February 4 — St. Gilbert of Sempringham.

Gilda "The One Covered with Gold" (Old English) or "The Sacrifice" (Old German, Spanish).

Patron Saints: There is one St. Gilda, one St. Gildas, and one St. Goldrophes, but they are all male. St. Gildas the Wise, 500-570, was the grandson of a saint. Born in Scotland, he traveled throughout the British Isles. Eventually he settled in England as a hermit, practicing a very severe discipline known as asceticism. He also studied very hard and wrote a book entitled *De Exicidio Britanniae.* It is filled with severe comments about the moral evils of his time. In revealing faults, he hoped to encourage people to repent of their sins and reform their lives. Gildas also had a firm knowledge of the Bible and near the end of his life a small group of followers gathered around him. He died when he was about seventy.

Feast Dates: January 29 — St. Gildas the Wise.

Gill (nickname) See Gilbertine, Gillian, Juliana, Julie.

Gilli (nickname) See Gilbertine, Gillian, Juliana, Julie.

Gillian "The Youthful One" (Latin form of Julie) or "The Downy-Haired One" (Latin).

Patron Saints: Gillian is from a medieval form of Juliana. There are more than two dozen Sts. Julia and Julie.

Feast Dates: April 8 — St. Julie Billiart (see Julie).

Gillie (nickname) See Gilbertine, Gillian, Juliana, Julie.

Gilly (nickname) See Gilbertine, Gillian, Juliana, Julie.

Gina "Well-Born One" (short form of Eugenia).

Patron Saints: Gina functions as a nickname for seven different names. They include Angelina, Eugenia, Ginger, Georgene, Luigina (or Louise), Regina, and Virginia. They provide many patrons.

Feast Dates: June 26 — St. Eugenia (see Eugenia); August 22 — The Blessed Virgin Mary, Queen of Heaven (see Queen).

Ginebra (Spanish) See Guinevere.

Ginevra (Italian) See Guinevere.

Ginger "Like a Spice" (Greek) or "The Virginal One" (English form of Virginia).

Patron Saints: The name Ginger comes from Virginia and means "virgin" or "maiden." This, of course, reminds Catholics of the doctrine that

Mary is the Virgin Mother of God. She is patron of virgins.

Most Christians believe that Mary was a virgin before she gave birth to Jesus because the Bible explicitly teaches it. This belief teaches that Jesus is God and his conception was a miracle worked by God.

Catholic, Orthodox, and some Protestant adherents also believe that Mary remained a virgin during the birth of Jesus because Scripture hints at it (see Matthew 1:23). This is simply a way to teach Jesus came to defeat original sin.

Finally, Catholic and Orthodox believers are convinced that Mary remained a virgin after the birth of Jesus. This is a way of saying Mary remained perfectly faithful (always saying "yes") to God. It required no miracle, just God's grace and Mary's cooperation. Mary is our example and guide.

Feast Dates: January 1 — The Blessed Virgin Mary, Mother of God.

Ginni (nickname) See Ginger, Virginia.

Ginnie (nickname) See Ginger, Virginia.

Ginnifer (variant) See Genevieve, Guinevere, Jennifer.

Ginnis (nickname) See Ginger, Virginia.

Ginny (nickname) See Ginger, Virginia.

Giorsal (Scottish) See Grace.

Giovanna (Italian) See Jane.

Giralda (Italian) See Geraldine.

Gisela (Dutch, English, Finnish, Italian, Spanish) See Giselle.

Gisella (English, Italian, French, Spanish) See Giselle.

Giselle "The Pledge" (Old German) or "The Hostage" (Old German) or "The Queen" (Spanish).

Patron Saints: There is one known St. Giselle and two Sts. Gisela (or Gisella). One St. Gisela is simply remembered as a "holy virgin" who died in 1277.

Feast Dates: February 8 — St. Gisela.

Gita (Polish) See Margaret.

Gitana "The Female Wanderer [Gypsy]" (Spanish).

Patron Saints: Gitana has the same meaning as Wendelin. This leads to a fine patron.

Feast Dates: October 21 — St. Wendelin (see Wendelin).

Gitta (German, Hungarian) See Brigid.

Giuditta (Italian) See Judith.

Giulia (Italian) See Julie.

Giulietta (Italian) See Julie.

Giuseppina (Italian) See Josephine.

Giustina (Italian) See Justina.

Gizela (Polish) See Giselle.

Glad (nickname) See Gladys.

Gladdie (nickname) See Gladys.

Gladdy (nickname) See Gladys.

Gladeece (variant) See Gladys.

Gladis (Spanish) See Gladys.

Gladys "The Lame One" (Welsh).

Patron Saints: There is one St. Gladys (also known as Gwladys). Moreover, knowing that Gladys is the Welsh form of Claudia leads to three more patrons. St. Gladys married St. Gwynllyw (better known as Gundleus), a Welsh chieftain, and gave birth to ten children, all of whom became saints. She was also instrumental in converting her husband to Catholicism and leading him to sainthood. She died in 500.

Feast Dates: March 29 — St. Gladys; August 7 — St. Claudia (see Claudia).

Glen (variant) See Glenna.

Glenda (Old Welsh, Spanish) See Glenna.

Glenine (variant) See Glenna.

Glenis (variant) See Glenna.

Glenn (variant) See Glenna.

Glenna "The Clean, Pure One" (Welsh) or "From the Valley" (English).

Patron Saints: The name's meaning leads to a great patron. Psalm 23:4 records, "Even though I walk through the valley of the shadow of death"; and Catholic tradition gives us the Hail Holy Queen, which includes the line "To you we send up our sighs, mourning and weeping in this valley of tears."

Feast Dates: Sept. 15 — Mother of Sorrows (see Dolores); January 29 — St. Dallan Forgaill (see Dale).

Glennie (nickname) See Glenna.

Glennis (English) See Glenna.

Glorea (Latin) See Gloria.

Glori (variant) See Gloria.

Gloria "The Glorious One" (Latin, Spanish).

Patron Saints: Two ancient saints are named Gloria. One is remembered for being a martyr in ancient Laodicea. Furthermore, if one remembers that *gloria* refers to "the heavenly glory of God," the seraphim can be adopted as patrons, for it is their job to unceasingly give glory to God.

Feast Dates: July 22 — St. Gloria, also known as Gloriosa; September 29 and October 2 — The Holy Seraphim (see Amber).

Gloriana (Spanish double) See Gloria+Ana.

Glorina (Spanish double) See Gloria+Ana.

Glory (English) See Gloria.

Glyn (English) See Glenna.

Glynice (African-American) See Glenna.

Glynis (English) See Glenna.

Glynnis (English) See Glenna.

Glynys (English) See Glenna.

Golda (English) See Gilda.

Goldie (nickname) See Gilda.

Gosia (Polish) See Margaret.

Grace "Gift" (English) or "Grace-Filled One" (English).

Patron Saints: The Latin word for "grace" is *gratia*, and there are about a half-dozen Sts. Engratia, Grata, Grazia, and Gracia. One St. Grace was a single woman who lived at Saragossa in about 304. She was arrested and condemned to death for being a Christian. Some of the atrocities she suffered included cutting off one of her breasts and the damaging of her liver. Then she was sent back to prison to die of her wounds.

Feast Dates: March 13 — St. Grace.

Gracely (American double) See Grace+Leigh/Leah.

Gracia (Spanish) See Grace.

Graciana (Spanish) See Grace.

Gracie (nickname) See Grace.

Graciela (Spanish, Bulgarian) See Grace.

Gracja (Polish) See Grace.

Grata (variant) See Grace.

Gratia (German, Dutch, Scandinavian) See Grace.

Gratiana (variant) See Grace.

Gratija (Greek, Russian) See Grace.

Gray (variant) See Grace.

Grayce (variant) See Grace.

Grazia (Italian) See Grace.

Graziella (Italian) See Grace.

Greer "The Watchful One" (Scottish).

Patron Saints: Greer is a feminine form of Gregory, and there are about eighty Sts. Gregory. St. Gregory the Wonderworker, 213-270, was born of royal pagan parents at Neocaesarea. He and his brother studied law, then at the age of twenty-five Gregory converted to Christianity. Two years later he was consecrated bishop of Neocaesarea. To attract converts he organized amusements and festivals in honor of the martyrs.

With the help of the Holy Spirit, he had great power over evil spirits and he had the ability to foretell future events. He is patron of those facing desperate situations and against floods and earthquakes.

Feast Dates: November 17 — St. Gregory, Wonderworker.

Greet (Dutch) See Gretchen, Margaret.

Gregoria (Latin) See Greer.

Greir (English) See Greer.

Greta (Swedish, Spanish) See Gretchen, Margaret.

Gretal (variant) See Gretchen, Margaret.

Gretchen "The Pearl" (German short form of Margaret).

Patron Saints: There are about two dozen Sts. Margaret. The earliest known St. Margaret was born a pagan at Antioch in Pisidia and converted to Christianity. Thrown out by her father she became a shepherdess. Then a young man became infatuated with her, but she turned him down, so he reported her to the government for being Christian. She was arrested, tortured, and imprisoned and beheaded in about the year 200.

Feast Dates: July 20 — St. Margaret of Antioch.

Grete (Danish, German) See Gretchen, Margaret.

Gretel (German) See Gretchen, Margaret.

Grethal (German) See Gretchen, Margaret.

Grethel (variant) See Gretchen, Margaret.

Gretna (variant) See Gretchen, Margaret.

Gretta (variant) See Gretchen, Margaret.

Griffin "The Dedicated Protector" (Middle English).

Patron Saints: A griffin is a mythological animal that comes from the ancient Minoans of Crete. It has the head, wings, and front legs and claws of an eagle while its body, hind quarters, legs, and claws are those of a lion. Because of the preying eagle and the ferociousness of the lion, the griffin in ancient times symbolized opposition to Christianity and attacks on the human soul.

However, in time, Christianity adopted and rehabilitated this creature. It began to see the griffin as a dedicated protector against evil, much like the gargoyles on church buildings. Soon Christians "baptized" the griffin to stand as a symbol of Jesus Christ, Lord and Savior. Remember, "Jesus" means "God Saves." Christ brought salvation to mankind as the "Man of Sorrows."

Feast Dates: Good Friday — Jesus the Protector.

Griffyn (variant) See Griffin.

Griselda "The Gray Woman Warrior" (Old German, English, Spanish).

Patron Saints: One saint is St. Grisold of Saxony. The other is Bl. Robert Grissold, a layman who was executed by the English government in 1604 because he gave shelter to priests.

Feast Dates: May 4 — Bl. Robert Grissold; April 30 — St. Ronan the Gray (see Zelda).

Griseldis (Dutch, German) See Griselda.

Grishilda (Dutch, German, English) See Griselda.

Grishilde (Dutch, German) See Griselda.

Grissel (nickname) See Griselda.

Grizel (nickname) See Griselda.

Grizelda (variant) See Griselda.

Guadalupe "My Image Will Crush the Serpent God" (Aztec-Spanish) or "River of Black Stones" (Arabic).

Patron Saints: On December 9, 1531, at dawn, Juan Diego, an Indian convert, was walking near a hill named Tepeyac, close to Mexico City. Out of the frosty mist nearby he heard a woman calling his name. To his surprise, he met a very beautiful Lady. She told him to go and tell the bishop to build a church where he was standing. Juan delivered the message, but the bishop did not believe his story.

December 12 found Juan on the same hill again and there met the Lady once again. Even though it was winter, there were roses growing nearby; she told Juan to pick the flowers, which he was to take to the bishop. Juan obeyed and filled his cloak with the roses. When he opened his cloak for the bishop, the roses fell out and on the cloak was a picture of the Lady, just as Juan had described. She appeared as an Indian. The bishop, astonished, finally believed him and had a church built on Tepeyac. The miraculous picture of Mary is still displayed above the main altar of this world-famous Marian shrine. The painting has not faded in the least during the nearly five hundred years it has been in existence nor has the rough fabric rotted. Our Lady of Guadalupe is known as "Patron of Mexico" and "Empress of the Americas."

Feast Dates: December 12 — The Blessed Virgin Mary, Our Lady of Guadalupe.

Guanita (Hispanic-American triple) See Jane+Ann+Ita.

Guendolen (variant) See Gwendolyn.

Guenevere (Cornish) See Guinevere.

Guenna (English) See Gwendolyn.

Guenora (Cornish) See Guinevere.

Guenore (Cornish) See Guinevere.

Guglielma (Italian) See Wilhelmina.

Guilla (Spanish) See Julia.

Guillelmina (Spanish) See Wilhelmina.

Guillelmine (French) See Wilhelmina.

Guillemette (French) See Wilhelmina.

Guillerma (Spanish) See Wilhelmina.

Guinevere "The White Wave" (Old Welsh) or "The White Phantom" (Old Welsh).

Patron Saints: There is one St. Guinevere, also known as St. Winifred. It seems a young chieftain fell in love with her, but she fled from him. He pursued her and, with great rage, beheaded her. Pious legend insists St. Beuno found her remains and restored her to life. Guinevere then became a nun and eventually an abbess of her convent until her death in 650. There is a blessed spring associated with her memory. For more than a thousand years, miracles have been reported at her spring, known as Holywell.

Feast Dates: November 3 — St. Guinevere, also known as Gwenfrewi or Winifred.

Guinna (variant) See Guinevere.

Gus (nickname) See Augusta.

Gussi (nickname) See Augusta.

Gussie (nickname) See Augusta.

Gussey (nickname) See Augusta.

Gusta (nickname) See Augusta.

Gusti (nickname) See Augusta.

Gustie (nickname) See Augusta.

Gusty (nickname) See Augusta.

Gvendolina (Czech) See Gwendolyn.

Gwen (nickname) See Gwendolyn.

Gwenda (English) See Gwendolyn.

Gwendalina (Polish) See Gwendolyn.

Gwendolen (English) See Gwendolyn.

Gwendolin (English) See Gwendolyn.

Gwendolina (variant) See Gwendolyn.

Gwendoline (French) See Gwendolyn.

Gwendolyn "The White-Haired One" (Old Welsh).

Patron Saints: There is a St. Gwendolyn, a St. Gwyddelan, a St. Gwynllyw (Gundleus), and a half-dozen others with similar names. One medieval St. Gwendolene is simply remembered as a "Welsh saint."

Feast Dates: October 18 — St. Gwendolene.

Gwenetta (German double) See Gwendolyn+Etta.

Gwenette (French double) See Gwendolyn+Ette.

Gwenni (nickname) See Gwendolyn.

Gwennie (nickname) See Gwendolyn.

Gwenny (nickname) See Gwendolyn.

Gwladys (Welsh) See Claudia, Gladys.

Gwyn (nickname) See Gwendolyn.

Gwyneth (American) See Gwendolyn.

Gwynyth (American) See Gwendolyn.

Gynell (African-American double) See Gwendolyn+Nelly.

Gynne (variant) See Gwendolyn.

Gypsy "The Wanderer" (Old English).

Patron Saints: There is no saint named Gypsy. However, there are some very popular female names, Wanda and Wendy, which mean "wanderer," the same as Wendelin. A gypsy is a "wanderer." Furthermore, it should not be forgotten that a St. Sara has been named patron of gypsies.

Feast Dates: May 24 — St. Sara (see Zara); October 21 — St. Wendelin (see Wendy).

H

Hada (Spanish) See Destiny.

Hadara "The One Adorned with Beauty" (Hebrew).

Patron Saints: The closest name is St. Hadra. He was an Egyptian monk of ancient days who raised the dead.

Feast Dates: January 28 — St. Hadra.

Haddie (nickname) See Hadara, Hadria, Hattie.

Hadessa (Hebrew) See Esther.

Hadria (variant) See Adrienne.

Haidie (Spanish) See Heidi.

Hailee (English) See Haley.

Haily (variant) See Haley.

Hajj (Arabic) See Wanda.

Haleigh (variant) See Haley.

Halette (variant double) See Haily/Haley+Ette.

Haley "From the Hay+Meadow" (Old English double) or "The Peace Heroine" (Scandinavian).

Patron Saints: Haley serves as a name in its own right and as a nickname for Mahala. Patrons can be found when one knows that Haley means "peace hero." Hero in Latin is *heros*, and there are Sts. Heros and Herosus. One St. Herosus was martyred for the faith in ancient Egypt.

Feast Dates: September 10 — St. Hero, also known as Herosus.

Hali (variant) See Halley, Mahala.

Halie (variant) See Haley, Mahala.

Halimeda (variant) See Halley.

Halina (Russian) See Helen.

Halle (variant) See Halley, Harrie, Holly.

Halley "Thinking of the Sea" (Greek) or "The Peace Heroine" (variant form of Haley).

Patron Saints: Halley serves as a nickname for Harriet and is a full name in its own right, which means "thinking of the sea." This leads to four saints who have been named patrons of sailors. They are Sts. Brendan, Michael, Cuthbert, and the Blessed Virgin Mary, Star of the Sea.

Feast Dates: All Saturdays — The Blessed Virgin Mary, Star of the Sea (see Star); September 10 — St. Hero (see Halley).

Halli (variant) See Halley, Harriet.

Hallie (variant) See Halley, Harriet.

Hallique (African-American) See Halley.

Hally (variant) See Halley, Harriet.

Haly (variant) See Haley.

Hana (German, English) See Hannah.

Hanka (Frisian) See Jane.

Hanna (English) See Hannah.

Hannah "The God-Graced One" (Hebrew form of Ann).

Patron Saints: the Bible presents a St. Hannah. The second Book of Samuel tells us that Hannah, who lived in about 1100 B.C., was one of two wives of Elkanah. She had no children. On a visit to the Lord's Tent she prayed for a son. God heard her prayer and blessed her with a son, Samuel. He would become a great prophet in ancient Israel. It is also good to know that Anna and Anne are forms of Hannah. There are several Sts. Anna and Anne.

Feast Dates: December 9 — St. Hannah; July 26 — St. Anne (see Ann).

Hanne (Scandinavian, German) See Hannah.

Hannele (German) See Hannah.

Hannelore (German, Italian) See Hannah+Laura.

Hanni (Hebrew) See Ann.

Hannie (English) See Ann, Hannah.

Hanny (English) See Ann, Hannah.

Happi (English) See Happy.

Happie (English) See Happy.

Happy "The Cheerful One" (English).

Patron Saints: There are a dozen Sts. Hilaria whose name means "cheerful one." Furthermore, all the saints in heaven are happy and can also be adopted as patrons.

Feast Dates: December 3 — St. Hilaria (see Hilary); November 1 — All Saints (see Crystal).

Harmonia (English) See Harmony.

Harmonie (English) See Harmony.

Harmony "The Harmonious One" (Latin) or "The Bringer of Concord" (Latin).

Patron Saints: There is one St. Harmon, 378-448. He became governor of a part of ancient Gaul. In 418, at the age of forty, he became bishop of Auxerre and often dealt with the Church in Britain. In fact, he had the privilege of leading the victorious British army in thanksgiving when they conquered the Saxons. He died when he was seventy.

More patrons can be found when one remembers that another Latin word for harmony is *concordia*.

Feast Dates: July 31 — St. Harmon; February 22 — St. Concordia (see Concordia).

Harri (English) See Harriet.

Harrie (English) See Harriet.

Harriet "The Mistress of the Home" (Old French).

Patron Saints: Harriet is a feminine form of Henry, and there are two dozen Sts. Henry. There is also an American saint-in-the-making named Henriette.

Feast Dates: November 17 — SG Henriette De Lille (see Henriette); June 24 — Bl. Gabriela Henrica (see Gabriela).

Harrietta (Old German double) See Harriet+Etta, Henrietta.

Harriette (French double) See Harriet+Ette, Henrietta.

Harriot (French) See Harriet, Henrietta.

Harriott (French double) See Harriet+Lottie, Henrietta.

Hatti (nickname) See Harriet, Henrietta.

Hattie (nickname) See Harriet, Henrietta.

Hatty (nickname) See Harriet, Henrietta.

Haylee (English) See Haley.

Hayley (English) See Haley.

Hazel "From the Hazelnut Tree" (Old English) or "One Who Commands Authority" (Old English).

Patron Saints: There is one saint with a very similar name. St. Hazeka gave herself to a life of prayer as a Cistercian recluse in Thuringia. She died in 1261.

Feast Dates: January 26 — Bl. Hazeka.

Hazell (variant) See Hazel.

Hazelle (variant) See Hazel.

Heath (nickname) See Heather.

Heather "The Wild Flower" (Middle English).

Patron Saints: There is one Bl. Henry Heath. He was executed by the British government in 1643 because he insisted upon functioning as a diocesan Catholic priest in anti-Catholic England.

Feast Dates: May 4 — Bl. Henry Heath.

Heda (English) See Hedwig.

Hedda (German) See Hedwig.

Hedi (nickname) See Hedwig.

Hedvige (French) See Hedwig.

Hedwig "From the Strife [Fight]" (Old German).

Patron Saints: There is one St. Hedwig and two Sts. Hedda. St.

Hedwig of Bavaria, 1174-1243, became the duchess of Silesia, having married the duke of Silesia. She bore him six children and then both she and her husband took solemn vows to abstain from sexual relations. Hedwig brought many missionaries to Germany. She also founded a nunnery, and after her husband died she lived there as a religious sister.

Feast Dates: October 15 — St. Hedwig.

Hedwiga (English) See Hedwig.

Hedy (Slavic) See Hedwig.

Heida (German) See Ada, Adelaide.

Heidi (variant) See Ada, Adelaide.

Heidie (variant) See Ada, Adelaide.

Heidy (variant) See Ada, Adelaide.

Hela (Czech) See Helen.

Helaina (variant) See Helen.

Helaine (Latin) See Helen.

HeleenAlouAlynn (American triple) See Helen+Louise+Lynn.

Helen "The Light" (English).

Patron Saints: There are several Sts. Helen and Helena. The greatest of them is St. Helena of Constantinople, 250-330, born an innkeeper's daughter, raised a pagan, and married to an emperor. She bore him a son and divorced him. Converting to Catholicism late in life, she worked twice as hard to make up for lost time. She had great wealth and power and used it to help the poor, build churches, and rediscover sacred places. She had Calvary and the tomb of Christ uncovered in Jerusalem and she found the true cross of Christ.

Feast Dates: August 18 — St. Helena of Constantinople.

Helena (Latin) See Helen.

Helene (French) See Helen.

Helenka (Czech) See Helen.

Helga "The Holy One" (German form of Olga).

Patron Saints: Because Helga means "holy one," many patrons are available.

Feast Dates: March 13 — St. Sancia (see Sancia); January 21 — St. Wynnin of Holywood (see Wynne).

Helka (variant) See Helen.

Helli (nickname) See Helen.

Helma (German) See Wilhelmina.

Helmine (German) See Wilhelmina.

Heloise (French) See Eloise, Louise.

Helsa (variant) See Elizabeth.

Helyn (variant) See Helen.

Hendrika (Dutch) See Henrietta.

Henka (variant) See Henrietta.

Henna (nickname) See Henrietta.

Henrica (variant) See Henrietta.

Henrie (nickname) See Henrietta.

Henriene (African-American) See Henrietta.

Henrieta (variant) See Henrietta.

Henriete (variant) See Henrietta.

Henrietta "Little+Mistress of the Home" (French double).

Patron Saints: SG Henriette De Lille, 1813-1862, was born into one of the oldest free black families in New Orleans, Louisiana. She was well-educated in French literature, music, dance, poise, fashion, the social graces, medicine, and nursing. At the age of eleven, she met Sister St. Marthe Fontier, a French nun. This sister's charity toward blacks and the education she provided greatly impressed her. Henriette became involved in this ministry and soon founded a religious order.

Feast Dates: November 17 — SG Henriette De Lille; June 24 — Bl. Gabriela Henrica (see Gabriela).

Henriette (French-German) See Henrietta.

Henrika (Swedish) See Henrietta.

Henr'ta (African-American) See Henrietta.

Henryetta (variant) See Henrietta.

Hermelinda (Spanish double) See Hermione+Linda.

Hermia (variant) See Hermione.

Hermina (Spanish) See Hermione.

Herminia (variant) See Hermione.

Hermione "From the Earth" (Greek).

Patron Saints: There is at least one St. Hermione. She was a daughter of St. Philip the Deacon, who is mentioned in the Acts of the Apostles. She was learned in medicine and dedicated her life to serving the sick for the sake of Jesus Christ. Under the reigns of the emperors Trajan and Adrian she was imprisoned for being a Catholic. Hermione, however, had the good fortune of eventually being released in 117.

Feast Dates: September 4 — St. Hermione.

Hermonica (African-American double) See Hermione+Monica.

Hermosa "The Beautiful One" (Spanish).

Patron Saints: There is no St. Hermosa, but knowing the name means "beautiful" leads to a patron.

Feast Dates: September 10 — SG Frances Allen (see Alana).

Herrita (African-American) See Harriet.

Herta (nickname) See Eartha.

Hertha (nickname) See Eartha.

Hester (Dutch) See Esther.

Hesther (English) See Esther.

Hestia (Persian) See Star.

Hetti (nickname) See Esther, Henrietta.

Hettie (nickname) See Esther, Henrietta.

Hetty (nickname) See Esther, Henrietta.

Hiawatha "The One Who Makes Rivers" (Iroquois).

Patron Saints: Although Hiawatha is a male name, it would probably lend itself to a modern feminine use. The best patron is God, the Creator.

Feast Dates: Holy Saturday — God the Creator and Re-Creator.

Hida (Spanish) See Hilda.

Hilaree (variant) See Hilary.

Hilaria (Spanish, Danish, Portuguese, Hungarian) See Hilary.

Hilarie (French) See Hilary.

Hilary "The Cheerful One" (Greek).

Patron Saints: There are a half-dozen Sts. Hilaria and almost forty Sts. Hilarius. Hilaria, a Roman saint, was married to Claudius and had two sons, Jason and Maurus. Claudius was an army tribune and when it was discovered that seventy of his men were Christians, they were immediately arrested and condemned to be beheaded. Claudius converted to Catholicism because of the fine example given by these Catholic soldiers. Soon he and his two sons were arrested and condemned to die with the soldiers. Hilaria saw her whole family perish, buried their bodies, and then was put in prison where she died.

Feast Dates: December 3 — St. Hilaria and Family.

Hild (English) See Hilda, Hildegarde.

Hilda "The Warrior Woman" (Old German).

Patron Saints: There is one St. Hilda, at least two Sts. Hildegarde, and three Sts. Hildagund. St. Hilda, 614-680, was baptized at the age of thirteen. Wanting to become a nun, she was sent to a monastery near Paris where her sister was living. Sometime later, the bishop of Lindisfarne, England, sent for Hilda and made her abbess of a monastery in England.

Feast Dates: November 17 — St. Hilda of Whitby; September 17 — St. Hildegarde (see Hildegarde).

Hildagard (variant) See Hildegarde.

Hildagarda (Spanish) See Hildegarde.

Hilde (Norwegian, German) See Hilda, Hildegarde.

Hildegarde "From the Fortress" (Old German).

Patron Saints: There are two Sts. Hildegarde and three Sts. Hildegund. St. Hildegarde of Germany, 1098-1179, at eight years of age, was given into the care of Bl. Jutta, a recluse. As an adult, Hildegarde founded a Benedictine monastery and became its abbess. While of fragile health, she had a strong mind and much energy, and was learned in poetry, herbal medicine, music, politics, natural history, and psychological disorders. She carried on an extensive correspondence with kings, popes, emperors, bishops, and abbots, often warning of disasters, lamenting the laxity of the clergy, and speaking of God as "The Living Light." She was also blessed with visions from God, performed miracles, and died at the age of eighty-one.

Feast Dates: September 17 — St. Hildegarde; November 17 — St. Hilda of Whitby (see Hilda).

Hildie (English) See Hilda, Hildegarde.

Hildy (English) See Hilda, Hildegarde.

Hillaree (English) See Hilary.

Hillari (variant) See Hilary.

Hillarie (variant) See Hilary.

Hillary (variant) See Hilary.

Hillery (variant) See Hilary.

Holda (variant) See Hulda.

Holde (variant) See Hulda.

Holi (variant) See Holly, Hulda.

Holland "From the Empty [Low] Lands" (Middle English).

Patron Saints: St. Willibrord, a Benedictine abbot in the 700s, is patron of the Netherlands (Holland).

Feast Dates: November 7 — St. Willibrord.

Holle (variant) See Holly, Hulda.

Hollee (variant) See Holly.

Holley (variant) See Holly.

Holli (variant) See Holly.

Hollie (variant) See Holly.

Holly "From the Holly Tree" (Old English) or "The Holy One" (Latin).

Patron Saints: Holly makes one think of Christmas. And there are about a dozen Sts. Noël, Natividad, and Natalie who can serve as patrons. Furthermore, if Holly is accepted as a form of "holy," then saints such as Sts. Sancia and Wynnin of Holywood become important. Also, Christian art associates holly with the passion of Christ, and this leads to Jesus the Suffering Servant.

Finally, there is one English saint surnamed Holiday. Between 1535 and 1681, hundreds of Catholics, especially priests, were hanged, drawn, and quartered by the British government, simply because they were Catholic. Father Richard Holiday, a diocesan priest, was killed in 1590.

Feast Dates: May 4 — Bl. Richard Holiday; March 13 — St. Sancia (see Sancia).

Hollyann (English double) See Holly+Ann.

Hollyn (English double) See Holly+Ann.

Holy (variant) See Holly.

Honbria (variant) See Honey.

Honee (variant) See Honey.

Honey "The Sweet One" (Old English) or "The Honorable One" (nickname for Honoria).

Patron Saints: Through the ages, Honey has often served as a term of endearment, meaning "sweet one." The Latin word *dulcissimus* means "most sweet," and there is a St. Dulcissima as well as a St. Dulcissimus. Also, in Greek the word for "honey" is *mella*, and there are two Sts. Mella. Honey, which can serve as a form of Honora, leads to a few Sts. Honoria and Honorata.

Feast Dates: November 6 — St. Honoria (see Honoria); April 25 — St. Mella (see Melissa).

Honi (variant) See Honey.

Honie (variant) See Honey.

Honna (nickname) See Hannah, Honoria.

Honor (variant) See Honoria.

Honora (Irish) See Honoria.

Honoria "The Honorable One" (Latin).

Patron Saints: There are a few Sts. Honoria and Honorata. One St. Honoria was the daughter of an ancient Catholic British king. According to the custom of the day, she was given in marriage to the son of an Irish chieftain. However, she and her husband decided to live a celibate marriage. Eventually they moved to Brittany, where they became hermits.

Feast Dates: November 6 — St. Honoria.

Honorine (variant) See Honoria.

Hope "The Hopeful One" (Old English).

Patron Saints: There are a couple of Sts. Hope. Remember, "hope" in Greek is *elpis*. St. Elpidius was a court official in the Roman court of Constantius, 337-361. However, when the next emperor was enthroned, he fell into disfavor because that emperor was Julian the Apostate who renewed persecution of Catholics. Elpidius was dragged by wild horses and then burned at the stake.

Feast Dates: November 15 — St. Hope, also known as Elpidius; August 1 — St. Hope and Sisters (see Carita).

Hortense "The Gardener" (Latin).

Patron Saints: There are at least three saints with this name, but they are all males. One St. Hortense embraced a martyr's death in ancient Alexandria, Egypt.

Feast Dates: May 19 — St. Hortensius.

Hosanna (Greek) See Osanna.

Hosannah (Hebrew) See Osanna.

Hotensia (German, Dutch, Danish, English) See Hortense.

Hotenzie (Dutch) See Hortense.

Hulda "Gracious, Beloved One" (Old German, Hebrew).

Patron Saints: The Jewish prophetess Hulda is mentioned in 2 Kings 22:14f. She was the wife of Shallum. King Josiah consulted her when he discovered the Book of Deuteronomy while having the Jewish Temple repaired and rebuilt. She died in about 620 B.C.

Feast Dates: April 10 — St. Hulda.

Huldah (Hebrew) See Hulda.

Huldie (nickname) See Hulda.

Huldyh (variant) See Hulda.

Huma "Like the Mist Rising from the Fire" (Spanish).

Patron Saints: Isaiah states that "the foundations of the thresholds shook at the voice of him who called, and the house was filled with smoke" (6:4). The Book of Revelation pictures Jesus offering the prayers of the saints, like smoke rising from burning incense. Thus the best patron is Jesus Christ the Eternal High Priest. Also, the smoke and prayers point to all the saints of God as patrons.

Feast Dates: November 1 — All Saints; Feast of Christ the King — Eternal High Priest.

Hyacinth "The Blue Larkspur Flower" (Greek) or "The Color Purple" (Greek).

Patron Saints: There are a few Sts. Hyacintha who will serve very well. St. Hyacintha de Mariscotti, 1585-1640, was very vain as a youth. Her lover married her sister, and this drove her to join the Third Order of Franciscans. Then she became very ill, which brought about her full conversion. She devoted her life to the continual practice of penance, which led to the conversion of many sinners. She founded a community of women dedicated to nursing the sick and aged. She died at the age of fifty-five.

Feast Dates: January 30 — St. Hyacintha de Mariscotti.

Hyacintha (English) See Hyacinth.

Hyacinthe (French) See Hyacinth.

Hyacinthia (English) See Hyacinth.

Hyacinthie (German) See Hyacinth.

I

Ianatha (African-American) See Iolanthe.

Ianthe (Greek) See Iolanthe.

Ib (nickname) See Isobel.

Ibana (Spanish) See Jane.

Ibbie (nickname) See Isobel.

Ibby (nickname) See Isobel.

Ice "The Quality Of" (English suffix sometimes written as Nice; favored by African-Americans).

Patron Saints: A saint's name usually precedes this suffix.

Feast Dates: Depends on the saint presented.

Ida "The Prosperous One" (Old English) or "The Industrious One" (Old German).

Patron Saints: There are about a dozen Sts. Ida. St. Ida of Herzfeld was raised in the royal court and the emperor gave her in marriage to a nobleman. They had one son, but her husband soon died. Ida then redoubled her dedication to prayer and self-denial and used her revenues to help the poor. Ida had a novel way to daily remind herself of her duty to the poor. She had her stone coffin filled daily with the distribution to the needy. Her final years were filled with constant illness and pain. She died in 825.

Feast Dates: September 4 — St. Ida of Herzfeld.

Idalette (African-American double) See Ida+Ette.

Idalia (variant) See Adela, Ida.

Idalina (variant) See Adela, Ida.

Idaline (variant) See Adela, Ida.

Idalla (variant) See Adela, Ida.

Idata (African-American) See Ida.

Idda (German) See Ida.

Idde (French, Danish) See Ida.

Iddia (German) See Ida.

Ide (variant) See Ida.

Idealis (African-American) See Ida.

Ideashia (African-American double) See Ida+Isha.

Idelia (Spanish) See Adela, Ida.

Idella (variant) See Adela, Ida.

Idelle (variant) See Adela, Ida.

Idena (African-American) See Iduna.

Idette (French) See Ida.

Idina (African-American) See Iduna.

Idis (variant) See Ida.

Idonia (African-American) See Iduna.

Iduna "The Loving One" (Old Norse).

Patron Saints: A patron with a similar name is St. Idunet. He was a hermit who lived in Brittany in the 400s.

Feast Dates: Fifth Sunday After Easter — St. Idunet.

Iesha (African-American) See Aisha, Isha.

Ietta (African-American double) See any "I" name+Etta.

Ieva (Latvian, Lithuanian) See Eve.

Ignacia (variant) See Ignatia.

Ignatia "The Ardent, Fiery One" (Latin).

Patron Saints: There are about twenty Sts. Ignatius. Thus it is good to know that there is an American saint-in-the-making named Ignatia. She was born Della Gavin in Ireland in 1889. When she was eight years old, her family emigrated to Cleveland, Ohio. At the age of twenty-five, she joined the Sisters of Charity, taught music, and cared for orphans. Three years later she developed stomach ulcers and stopped teaching. Assigned to St. Thomas Hospital in Akron, she met Drs. Robert

Smith and William Wilson, founders of Alcoholics Anonymous, and made a major contribution to that program. Sister Ignatia insisted on approaching alcoholics as ill and had to deal with opposition from many people, including the clergy. She is credited with helping alcoholics appeal for help to a "Higher Power." Without her, AA would probably have never developed into what it is now.

It is also good to know that Ignatia and Seraphina mean the same thing. There are several Sts. Seraphina.

Feast Dates: April 1 — SG Sister Ignatia of Cleveland, C.S.A.; March 12 — St. Seraphina (see Seraphina).

Ignatzia (variant) See Ignatia.

Iida (Finnish) See Ida.

Ijada (variant) See Jade.

Ikella (African-American double) See any "I" name+Kelly.

Ilana "The Big Tree" (Hebrew).

Patron Saints: There is one saint, St. Ilan. He was both a bishop and a martyr in ancient Wales.

Feast Dates: November 1 — St. Ilan.

Ilaria (Russian, Italian) See Hilary.

Ileana (Romanian, Spanish) See Helen.

Ileane (English) See Aileen, Eileen, Helen.

Ileen (English) See Aileen, Eileen, Helen.

Ilene (English) See Aileen, Eileen, Helen.

Ilia (American) See Elly, Leah.

Ilise (variant) See Elyse.

Ilka (variant) See Elona, Helen.

Ilona (Hungarian, Spanish) See Elona, Helen.

Ilonka (variant) See Elona, Helen.

Ilsa (German) See Aileen, Elizabeth, Elsa, Elsie.

Ilse (German) See Else, Elizabeth.

Ilysa (variant) See Alice, Elizabeth, Elsa, Elsie, Elyse.

Ilyse (variant) See Elizabeth, Else, Elsie, Elyse.

Ilyssa (variant) See Alice, Elsa.

Ilze (Latvian) See Elizabeth, Else.

Imelda "From the Great Battle" (German-Spanish).

Patron Saints: There is one known Bl. Imelda. She was born into the noble Lambertini family in Bologna, Italy. As a child she entered the local Dominican nunnery. She had great reverence for the Holy Eucharist and died on her First Communion day after receiving the sacrament in 1333 at the age of thirteen.

Feast Dates: May 12 — Bl. Imelda Lambertini.

Immanuella (variant) See Emmanuella.

Imogen (variant) See Imogene.

Imogene "The Image" (French, Latin).

Patron Saints: There is a patron and she is none other than the Blessed Virgin. "Our Lady of Imoge" was the title attached to an ancient statue or picture that was honored at Imoge, France. The feast of the Nativity of Mary was adopted as the feast day for Our Lady of Imoge.

Feast Dates: September 8 — Our Lady of Imoge.

Imogine (English) See Imogene.

Imojean (variant) See Imogene.

Ina, Ine "The Female One [Mother]" (Scottish feminine suffix used with masculine names).

Patron Saints: "Ina" or "Ine" is often added to the end of modern masculine names: Caroline, Carolina, etc. Ina, by itself, is often used as a nickname for Agnes.

Feast Dates: January 21 — St. Agnes (see Agnes).

Inabel (African-American double) See Ina+Belle.

Incarnación (Spanish variant) See Incarnata.

Incarnata "One with a Human Form" (Latin).

Patron Saints: Incarnata means the "enfleshment of God" in Jesus Christ. There are also a couple of female Sts. Incarnata. One is an American, the Bl. Marie Guyart, 1599-1672. She was born in France and at the age of seven had a dream of Jesus in which he asked her, "Will you be mine?" She said, "Yes!"

She always wanted to be a nun but obeyed her parents and married Claude Martin, a merchant. At eighteen years of age, she gave birth to a son, at which time her husband died. She took over the carting business, gave herself to prayer, and gained deep insights in the Sacred Heart of Jesus and the Eucharist.

Then she became a nun and took the name Incarnata. Not long after that she became depressed and found relief by going to Canada as a missionary. There she faced much hardship but always managed to show great love for the Indian people. One of her students was St. Marie Marguerite d'Youville. She died at the age of seventy-three.

Feast Dates: April 30 — Bl. Marie of the Incarnation.

Inda (African-American) See India.

Indee (variant) See Indiana.

India "From the River Country" (Latin, Greek).

Patron Saints: There is a group of unnamed martyrs from India whom the Catholic Church has never forgotten. The Indian martyrs were killed by order of King Abenner in ancient times.

One can also adopt St. Thomas the Apostle, who is patron of India.

Feast Dates: August 3 — The Holy Martyrs of India; July 3 — St. Thomas the Apostle (see Thomasina).

Indiana "From the Indian Country" (Latin).

Patron Saints: Probably the finest patron available is the first North American Indian saint.

Feast Dates: April 17 — Bl. Kateri Tekakwitha (see Kateri).

Indie (variant) See Indiana.

Indira (variant) See India.

Indra (variant) See India.

Indy (variant) See Indiana.

Ineatha (African-American double) See any "In" name+Eartha.

Ines (Portuguese) See Agnes.

Inesita (Spanish double) See Inez+Etta.

Inessa (variant) See Agnes.

Inetha (African-American double) See any "In" name+Eartha.

Inez (Spanish) See Agnes.

Inga (Swedish) See Ingrid.

Ingaberg (variant) See Ingrid.

Inge (Danish, German) See Ingrid.

Inger (Swedish) See Ingrid.

Ingrid "The Hero's Daughter" (Scandinavian, Spanish).

Patron Saints: Patrons can be found for Ingrid if one is reminded that Ingrid means "daughter of a hero." Hero in Latin is *heros*. In German it is *heldrad*.

St. Heldrad spent much of his early life as a wanderer. Finally, in 837, he became a Benedictine monk in the diocese of Susa. This was quite a commitment because Benedictines take a vow to stay in one place for a lifetime. Seven years later he became abbot and he served in this post until his death in 874.

Feast Dates: March 13 — St. Heldrad, O.S.B.; September 10 — St. Hero (see Haley).

Ingunna (variant) See Ingrid.

Iniga (Latin) See Ignatia.

Iola "The Violet-Colored Cloud at Dawn" (Greek).

Patron Saints: One saint has a similar name. St. Iolana is remembered as an ancient "French martyr."

Feast Dates: January 17 — St. Iolana.

Iolana (variant) See Iola.

Iolanda (English) See Viola, Violet, Yolanda.

Iolande (English) See Viola, Violet, Yolanda.

Iolanthe (English, Lithuanian) See Iola, Viola, Violet, Yolanda.

Iole (variant) See Iola.

Ioma (African-American) See Iona.

Iona "From the Island Monastery" (Celtic) or "The Violet-Colored Flower" (Greek).

Patron Saints: There is at least one St. Ionius. He was one of the companions of St. Denis, who preached the Gospel in France. He was eventually imprisoned for the Gospel and was beheaded in 275.

Moreover, "Iona" also leads to the famous medieval monastery of Iona, founded off the coast of Scotland by St. Columba. It produced many saints, all of whom can be adopted as patrons. Also, Iona may be a form of "violet," which leads to St. Vio.

Feast Dates: August 15 — St. Ionius; June 15 — St. Vio (see Violet).

Ione (variant) See Iona.

Ionia (variant) See Iona.

Ionnella (American double) See Iona+ Nellie.

Ira (Serbo-Croatian) See Irene.

Irais (Spanish) See Iris.

Irena (English, Polish) See Irene.

Irene "The Peaceful One" (Greek).

Patron Saints: There are about two dozen Sts. Irene. One of them, at fourteen years of age and still a pagan, was called upon to perform an act of courage. She saw St. Porphyrius become the object of fury by a pagan mob. Unable

to condone such violence, she rescued him. Later she received instruction in the faith from him and was baptized. A short time after her baptism, while still only a teen in 490, she died.

Feast Dates: February 26 — St. Irene.

Irenea (Spanish) See Iris.

Irina (English, Russian, Romanian) See Irene.

Iris "A Rainbow" (Greek) or "Messenger of the Gods" (Greek).

Patron Saints: There are two Sts. Iriase as well as a St. Irias who lived in Alexandria, Egypt, in 310. Her uncle was the great Egyptian prefect of Antioch, St. Basilides. When she was only ten years old, a persecution of Christians was begun by Emperor Diocletian. She was arrested for being Christian with almost four thousand others. She refused to deny Jesus and was beheaded with the other prisoners.

In Christian art, the iris flower is symbolic of the sorrow suffered by the Blessed Virgin.

Feast Dates: September 22 — St. Irias; September 15 — Our Lady of Sorrows (see Dolores).

Irisa (Romanian) See Iris.

Irita (Spanish double) See Iris+Ita.

Irlene (American double) See Irene+ Eileen.

Irma "The Noblewoman" (Old German) or "The One of the Earth" (nickname for Hermione).

Patron Saints: There is a St. Imina and a St. Irmingard. Irmina was born in 662 to King Dagobert of Austria. She was betrothed to a young prince named Herman. However, skulduggery was afoot. Another man loved her and lured Herman to a cliff, pushed him over the edge, and killed him. Irmina was deeply hurt and asked her father to allow her to become a nun. He bought a convent for her and she also supported the missionary work of St. Willibrord. In 698 she gave him a manor house. She died in 708.

It is also good to note that Irma is a variant of Hermina This leads to St. Hermione as patron.

Feast Dates: December 24 — St. Irmina; September 4 — St. Hermione (see Hermione).

Irmina (Polish, Lithuanian, Italian) See Irma.

Isa (Danish, German, Spanish) See Isabel, Isadora, Luisa.

Isabeau (French) See Isabel.

Isabel "Consecrated to God" (Spanish form of Elizabeth).

Patron Saints: There are about a half-dozen Sts. Isabel. One was a Spanish widow in Japan in 1622. She was condemned for giving shelter to a missionary priest, Father Charles Spinola, who had baptized her son, Ignatius. Father Charles, seeing Isabel had been gathered into his group of martyrs, inquired after her son. She held him up and said, "Here he is. I brought him with me to die for Christ before he is old enough to sin against him." The priest blessed both the mother and the child. Then Isabel hugged and encouraged her son. The little boy, who was only four years old, watched as his mother was beheaded. Then he loosed his collar to bare his neck for the sword and was also executed.

One should know also that Isabel is a Spanish form of Elizabeth. This provides two dozen more patrons.

Feast Dates: September 10 — Bl. Isabel Fernandez; November 5 — St. Elizabeth, Matriarch (see Elizabeth).

Isabella (Italian-French-Spanish double) See Elizabeth, Isabel+Bella.

Isabellita (Italian-Spanish-Swedish double) See Elizabeth, Isabel+Ita.

Isadora "The Gift+Of Isis" (Latin-Spanish double).

Patron Saints: There are a couple of ancient Sts. Isadora. One of them was a nun at Tabennisi Monastery in ancient Egypt. She was often ridiculed but bore the trials patiently. When St. Pitirm recognized her holiness and made it known, she was embarrassed and fled into the desert to seek solitude. There she died in 365.

Feast Dates: May 1 — St. Isadora.

Isbel (Scottish) See Isabel.

Iseabail (Scottish Gaelic) See Isabel.

Isetta (African-American double) See Isa+Etta.

Isha "The Female One" (Hebrew) or "She Is Alive and Well" (African-American form of Aisha).

Patron Saints: Isha is very popular as a name or part of a name for modern African-American girls. However, few Americans know that Isha is the Hebrew name Adam gave to Eve when he said that "she shall be called Woman" (Genesis 2:23). In doing this, Adam actually gave Eve a feminine form of his own name, Ish, which means "the male one." This is the Bible's way of teaching the equality of the sexes.

Feast Dates: December 24 — Sts. Adam and Eve (see Eartha).

Ishbel (Scottish) See Isabel.

Isibeal (Irish Gaelic) See Isabel.

Isidora (variant) See Isadora.

Isletta (African-American double) See Isabel+Leticia.

Isobel (Scottish) See Isabel.

Isolda (Italian, Spanish) See Isolde.

Isolde "The Beautiful One" (Old Welsh) or "The Ice Rules" (Old German).

Patron Saints: Isolde is the heroine of an ancient tragic Celtic love tale. Its plot is similar to Shakespeare's *Romeo and Juliet*. The only way a patron can be found for Isolde is by finding a name that has the same meaning as Isolde, which is "beautiful one."

Feast Dates: April 14 — St. Jacinta (see Jacinta); September 10 — SG Frances Allen of Montreal (see Alana).

Isolina (Spanish) See Isolde.

Isotta (Italian) See Isolde.

Issi (nickname) See Isabel.

Issie (Polish, Hungarian) See Isabel.

Issy (Polish, Bulgarian) See Isabel.

Ita "The Thirsty One" (Irish) or "The Little One" (Spanish diminutive suffix used with feminine names).

Patron Saints: There is one St. Ita, an Irish noblewoman, 480-569. She became a religious sister in spite of much family opposition. Often called the "St. Brigid of Munster," she is patron of Killeedy, Limerick.

Also, "Ita" is frequently added to the end of modern feminine names, such as Anita, Danita, and Conchita. It is also often used as a complete name.

Feast Dates: January 15 — St. Ita.

Itha (variant) See Ita.

Itu (variant) See Ita.

Iva (Slavic) See Ivana.

Ivana "God Is Gracious" (Russian form of Jane).

Patron Saints: Ivana is the Russian feminine form of John. St. Ivan was from Dalmatia and lived the life of a hermit for forty-two years in Bohemia. He was murdered in the 900s by peasants who lived in that area.

Feast Dates: June 24 — St. Ivan.

Ivannetta (French double) See Ivana+Etta.

Ivanona (variant) See Ivana.

Ivelisse (Hispanic-American double) See Ivette+Lisa.

Ivett (variant) See Ivette, Yvette.

Ivetta (variant double) See Ivette+Etta.

Ivette "The Mother of the Living+Little One" (French double) or "Like a Yew Tree" (French).

Patron Saints: There is a St. Ivetta. She was born in about 1150, married, and gave birth to two children. At age eighteen, she became a widow. Then she devoted herself to caring for lepers in the hospice of Huy in Belgium. In her old age she became a recluse in a local convent and devoted herself to prayer. She died at the age of seventy-eight and was noted for her miracles.

Furthermore, knowing that Ivette comes from Eve leads to a half-dozen Sts. Eve.

Feast Dates: January 13 — St. Ivetta; December 24 — Sts. Adam and Eve (see Eartha).

Ivie (variant) See Ivy.

Ivonne (Spanish) See Yvette, Yvonne.

Ivonnia (variant) See Yvette, Yvonne.

Ivonnie (French) See Yvette, Yvonne.

Ivory "The Creamy White One" (Latin).

Patron Saints: There are a handful of Sts. Ivory, which in Latin is *abor*. One St. Ivory was a bishop and a martyr in ancient Persia in about 200.

Feast Dates: November 13 — St. Ivory, also known as Ebora.

Ivy "Like an Ivy Vine" (Old English).

Patron Saints: There is a St. Ives and a St. Ivo. St. Ivo, 1253-1303, was a lawyer and later a judge. He protected orphans, defended the poor, administered justice with great kindness, and could not be bribed.

In 1284, at the age of thirty-one, he was ordained a priest. Three years later he resigned his legal practice and devoted himself entirely to his parishioners. He tended the poor, sick, and beggars, often giving them the clothes off his own back. During Lent he disciplined himself by fasting on bread and water and using a straw mat for a bed and a stone for his pillow. He is patron of judges, lawyers, and notaries.

Feast Dates: May 19 — St. Ivo Hélory.

Izabela (African-American double) See Isa+Bella.

Izadora (African-American double) See Isa+Dora.

Izell (African-American double) See Izabela+Elle.

Izetta (African-American double) See Izabela+Etta.

Izzie (Spanish) See Izabela, Izadora.

Izzy (Spanish) See Izabela, Izadora.

J

Ja "Yes" (German).

Patron Saints: Modern Hispanic-Americans seem to favor the "Ja" sound and prefix it to many names. It can also be recognized as a short form of any name beginning with those letters.

Jacenta (variant) See Hyacinth, Jacinta.

Jacey (nickname) See Hyacinth, Jacinta.

Jaci (American) See Hyacinth, Jacinta.

Jacie (American) See Hyacinth, Jacinta.

Jacinda (Greek, Spanish) See Hyacinth, Jacinta.

Jacinna (variant) See Hyacinth, Jacinta.

Jacinta "The Hyacinth Flower" (Spanish) or "The Wearer of Purple" (Portuguese) or "The Beautiful One" (Spanish).

Patron Saints: Jacinta is a form of Hyacinth, and there are almost two dozen Sts. Hyacinth. One of them is Bl. Jacinta Marto, 1910-1920, a Portuguese child saint.

Her life was uneventful until May 13, 1917. Then between May and October of 1917 she was privileged to experience six apparitions of the Blessed Virgin at Fátima, and the apparitions attracted almost one hundred thousand people. Jacinta had to face a hostile police and a skeptical clergy, but her testimony and the "Miracle of the Sun" convinced many doubters.

The apparitions made Jacinta very concerned about "poor sinners." She was often found praying for them and was willing to sacrifice for them. Her greatest sacrifice was dying alone from influenza. Just before she was to die, she was anointed and confessed her sins. Then she asked that the priest hurry and bring her Communion, but he did not feel it was urgent and delayed. She was only ten years old.

Feast Dates: April 14 — Bl. Jacinta Marto.

Jacinth (variant) See Hyacinth, Jacinta.

Jacintha (English) See Hyacinth, Jacinta.

Jacinthe (French, Spanish) See Hyacinth, Jacinta.

Jackee (nickname) See Jacoba, Jacqueline.

Jackelyn (English) See Jacqueline.

Jacki (nickname) See Jacoba, Jacqueline.

Jackie (nickname) See Jacoba, Jacqueline.

Jacklin (English) See Jacqueline.

Jackline (English) See Jacqueline.

Jacklyn (American double) See Jacki+ Lynn.

Jacklynn (American double) See Jacki+ Lynn.

Jackquel (French) See Jacqueline.

Jackqueline (French) See Jacqueline.

Jacky (nickname) See Jacoba, Jacqueline.

Jaclin (variant) See Jacqueline.

Jaclyn (English) See Jacqueline, Jocelyn.

Jacoba "The Supplanter" (Spanish, Dutch).

Patron Saints: There is at least one patron with a similar name: Bl. Jacobina of Pisa. She lived in about 1310 to 1370 and married Pietro Cascina. After becoming a widow, she became a religious sister and then superior of her convent. She died at the age of sixty.

Feast Dates: November 1 — Bl. Jacobina of Pisa; July 25 — St. James the Elder (see Jacqueline).

Jacobina (variant) See Jacoba, Jacqueline.

Jacobine (variant) See Jacoba, Jacqueline.

Jacobyn (English) See Jacoba, Jacqueline.

Jacque (French) See Jacqueline.

Jacquelin (French) See Jacqueline.

Jacqueline "The Supplanter" (French) or "May God Protect Her" (Hebrew).

Patron Saints: Knowing that Jacqueline is a feminine form of Jacob or James leads us to many patrons. The greatest of them is St. James the Elder, an Apostle of Jesus. The most recent was a child aged two. A native of Japan, Bl. James Guengoro was the son of Bls. Thomas and Mary Guengoro. The preschool child was crucified with his parents in Japan in 1620.

Feast Dates: August 18 — Bl. James Guengoro.

Jacquelyn (English) See Jacqueline.

Jacquelynn (variant) See Jacqueline.

Jacquenetta (English double) See Jacqueline+Etta.

Jacquenette (French double) See Jacqueline+Ette.

Jacquetta (variant double) See Jacqueline+Etta.

Jacquette (French double) See Jacqueline+Ette.

Jacqui (French) See Jacqueline.

Jacqulin (American) See Jacqueline.

Jacy (nickname) See Hyacinth, Jacinta.

Jacynthe (Spanish) See Hyacinth, Jacinta.

Jada (Spanish) See Jade.

Jade "The Gem That Cures" (Spanish).

Patron Saints: There is a St. Jader. He was the bishop of Midila in Africa in ancient times and died a martyr. He was probably a black man.

The ancients' value for jade leads to more patrons. It seems that many thought of it as "the gem that cures." Many pagans believed jade had a special connection with life and placed a piece of it in the mouth of the deceased in order to ensure life beyond the grave. Its green color connected it to life.

Bible scholars think that its presence on the Jewish high priest's breastplate may have served as a symbol of justice. Its presence among the twelve gems that make up the walls of heavenly Jerusalem speak of justice, security, and eternal life. Those that possess these gifts are the saints in paradise.

Feast Dates: September 10 — St. Jader; November 1 — Eternal Life of All Saints.

Jaden (Spanish) See Jade.

Jadyn (Spanish) See Jade.

Jae (French, Latin) See Jacqueline, Jaye.

Jaeleen (English) See Jaye.

Jaelyn (American double) See Jaye+Lynn.

Jaeson (English double) See Jaye+Son.

Jahaida (Hispanic-American double) See Jade/Jahna+Aida.

Jahna (American) See Jane.

Jaid (American) See Jade.

Jailene (Hispanic-American double) See Ja+Aileen.

Jaime "The Beloved One" (modern variant of Aime) or "The Supplanter" (form of James).

Patron Saints: Jaime finds its root in either Amata, which means "beloved," or James, which means "the supplanter." There are about a half-dozen Sts. Ama and Amata and a dozen Sts. Amator and Amatus. To these there can be added a couple dozen Sts. James.

Feast Dates: June 6 — St. Ama (see Aime); July 25 — Bl. James Guengoro (see Jacqueline).

Jaimie (English) See Jaime.

Jaine (variant) See Jane.

Jai-Vine "The Celebration+Of the Divine" (Basque+Middle English in an African-American usage).

Patron Saints: The whole name is meant to rhyme with "divine." Also, when both parts are taken together, they mean "celebration of the divine." For Catholics this means the Mass. This makes Jesus in Communion the patron.

Feast Dates: Holy Thursday — The Eucharistic Real Presence of Jesus' Birthday.

Jakobina (Swedish, Hungarian) See Jacoba, Jacqueline.

Jakobine (German) See Jacoba, Jacqueline.

Jaleesa (African-American double) See Jane+Lisa.

Jalena (African-American double) See Jane+Lena.

Jalia (African-American double) See Jane+Leah.

Jalisa (African-American double) See Jane+Lisa.

Jamaica "From the Land of Forest and Water" (South American Indian).

Patron Saints: Two saints easily qualify as patrons: St. Silvia, from the Latin *silva* for "forest," and St. Maris, from the Latin *mare* for "sea."

Feast Dates: November 3 — St. Silvia (see Sylvia); July 19 — St. Maris (see Maris).

Jamaria (African-American double) See Jae+Maria.

Jamee (French) See Jaime.

Jamell (Arabic) See Jamil.

Jamella (African-American) See Jamil.

Jamesha (African-American double) See Jaime+Sha.

Jami (variant) See Jaime.

Jamie (variant) See Jaime.

Jamil (Arabic) See Alana.

Jamilah (Arabic) See Jamil.

Jamilet (Hispanic-American) See Jamil.

Jamilla (African-American) See Jamil.

Jamille (Arabic) See Jamil.

Jamonica (African-American double) See Jaime+Monica.

Jan (nickname) See Jane, Janice, January.

Jana (Czech) See Jane.

Janae (English) See Jane.

Janalyn (American double) See Jane+Lynn.

Janan (Arabic) See Cora.

Janaya (variant) See Jane.

Jandina (Spanish) See Alexandra.

Jandy (variant) See Jane.

Jane "God Is Gracious" (English).

Patron Saints: There are about two dozen Sts. Jane and another half-dozen saints named Joan. One patron, Bl. Jane of Aza, was born in a castle in Old Castile, Spain. She married Felix de Guzman, a warden of the small town of Calaruegaand, with whom she had four children. Her youngest was St. Dominic. Her eldest, Antony, was ordained a priest and gave all his possessions to the sick and poor. Another son, Bl. Mannes, chose to follow Dominic. Her daughter's two children also followed their Uncle Dominic.

Before she gave birth to Dominic, Jane dreamed that she had a dog in her womb. It broke away from her, and with a torch in its mouth, set the world on fire. Thus the Dominicans, founded by her son, are called the "Watchdogs of God." Bl. Jane died in 1190.

Feast Dates: August 8 — Bl. Jane of Aza; May 30 — St. Joan of Arc (see Joan).

Janean (variant) See Jane.

Janeane (variant) See Jane.

Janece (African-American) See Jane.

Janeczka (variant) See Jane.

Janeen (English) See Jane.

Janel (African-American) See Jane.

Janela (African-American) See Jane.

Janelia (African-American) See Jane.

Janella (African-American double) See Jane+Ellen.

Janelle (Polish-French-Latvian double) See Jane, Jane+Ellen.

Janene (variant) See Jane.

Janessa (variant double) See Jane+Essa.

Janet (Polish, Latvian, English) See Jane.

Janeta (variant) See Jane.

Janetta (English double) See Jane+Etta.

Janette (English double) See Jane+Ette.

Janeva (English) See Genevieve, Geneva.

Janey (nickname) See Jane.

Jani (nickname) See Jane.

Jania (variant) See Jane.

Janice (Polish, Latvian, English) See Jane.

Janie (English) See Jane.

Janifer (variant) See Genevieve, Guinevere, Jena, Jennifer.

Janina (Polish, Latvian, English) See Jane.

Janine (Hungarian) See Jane.

Janis (English) See Jane.

Janita (African-American double) See Jane+Anita.

Janith (variant) See Jane.

Janka (Hungarian) See Jane.

Janna (Hebrew) See Johana.

Janne (Norwegian) See Jane.

Jannelle (African-American double) See Jane+Elle.

Jannette (variant double) See Jane+Ette.

Jannike (Norwegian) See Jane.

Jannon (African-American) See Jane.

January "Born During the Month of the Two-Faced God" (Middle English).
Patron Saints: There are at least a dozen Sts. Januaria. Most were martyrs. One of them gave her life with St. Felix in ancient Africa. She was probably a black woman.
Feast Dates: January 5 — St. Januaria.

Jany (variant) See Jane.

Janyne (variant) See Jane.

Jaquana (African-American double) See Jacqueline+Ana.

Jaquelin (variant) See Jacqueline.

Jaquelina (Spanish) See Jacqueline.

Jaquenetta (variant double) See Jacqueline+Etta.

Jaquenette (variant double) See Jacqueline+Ette.

Jaquith (variant) See Jacqueline.

JaraLee (African-American double) See Jared+Leigh.

Jardena "The Garden" (French, Spanish) or "The Descending One" (Hebrew form of Jordan).
Patron Saints: If accepted either as a form of Jordan or Eden, a few dozen patrons appear.
Feast Dates: August 31 — St. Eden, also known as Aidan or Aedan.

Jarena (African-American) See Jared.

JaShanda (African-American double) See Ja+Shawna.

Jasmarie (African-American double) See Jasmine+Marie.

Jasmin (Persian) See Jasmine.

Jasmina (variant) See Jasmine.

Jasmine "The Jasmine Flower" (Persian).
Patron Saints: It helps to know that jasmine is a flower. Its white color and beautiful scent led Christian artists to use it as a symbol for the grace and amiability of the Blessed Virgin Mary.
Feast Dates: All Saturdays — The Blessed Virgin Mary, Gentle Woman (see Alma); November 24 — St. Flora (see Flora).

Jatara (African-American double) See Jane+Tara.

Javiera (Spanish) See Xaviera.

Javina (Hispanic-American) See Xaviera.

Jay (English) See Jaye.

Jaycee (English double) See any "J" name+any "C" name.

Jayda (Spanish) See Jade.

Jayde (Spanish) See Jade.

Jayden (Spanish) See Jade.

Jaye "The Blue Jay" (Middle Latin) or "The Healer" (short feminine form of Jason).
Patron Saints: Jaye finds its source in two names. When it is accepted as a feminine form of Jason, a handful of patrons appear. The most famous is the Jason mentioned in Acts 17:5-9. He was

a prominent member of Thessalonica and a convert to Christianity. After St. Paul arrived there, the Jews became jealous and soon a mob went to Jason's home, intending to bring Paul and Silas before a group of enemies. When they could not find them, they dragged Jason and some others before the crowd and accused Jason of aiding the troublemakers. Jason paid a fine for Sts. Paul and Silas and they left. Ancient Christian tradition claims that Jason later worked with St. Paul and identifies him as the Jason mentioned in Romans 16:21. He eventually became a bishop and a martyr.

Feast Dates: July 12 — St. Jason.

Jaylaan (African-American) See Jaye.

Jayleen (English) See Jaye.

Jaylene (English) See Jaye.

Jayme (English) See Jaime.

Jaymee (English) See Jaime.

Jaymie (variant) See Jaime.

Jayne (English) See Jane.

Jaynell (variant) See Jane.

Jayson (English) See Jaye.

Jazma (variant) See Jasmine.

Jazmin (Persian, Spanish) See Jasmine.

Jazmine (Persian) See Jasmine.

Jazmyn (Persian) See Jasmine.

Jazz (nickname) See Jasmine.

Jazzmin (Persian) See Jasmine.

Jazzmine (Persian) See Jasmine.

Jazzmyn (Persian) See Jasmine.

Jean "God Is Gracious" (French form of Jane).

Patron Saints: There are two dozen Sts. Jane and Jean. One, SG Jean Donovan, 1953-1980, is a saint-in-the-making. Born in Connecticut, she received an excellent education, graduating from Western Reserve University in 1975. She was also an active member of the Legion of Mary and worked with youth.

When an opportunity arose to serve as a lay missionary in El Salvador for the Catholic diocese of Cleveland, she jumped at the chance despite the fact that El Salvador was a dangerous place because of the civil war raging there. At the mission, she did bookkeeping and dietician jobs. In 1980 she drove to the airport with Sister Dorothy Kazel to meet two Maryknoll sisters. On the return trip, all four were murdered. She was only twenty-seven years of age.

Feast Dates: December 2 — SG Jean Donovan.

Jeana (Scottish) See Jane, Jean.

Jeane (French) See Jane, Jean.

Jeanean (Scottish) See Jane, Jean.

Jeaneen (Scottish) See Jane, Jean.

Jeanene (variant) See Jane, Jean.

Jeanette (French double) See Jane/Jean+Ette.

Jeanie (variant) See Jane, Jean.

Jeanine (Scottish) See Jane, Jean.

Jeanne (French) See Jane, Jean.

Jeanneen (variant) See Jane, Jean.

Jeannelle (variant double) See Jane/Jean+Elle.

Jeannette (French double) See Jane/Jean+Ette.

Jeannica (variant) See Jane, Jean.

Jeannie (nickname) See Jane, Jean.

Jeannine (French) See Jane, Jean.

Jeanyn (variant) See Jane, Jean.

Jeanyne (variant) See Jane, Jean.

Jelena (Croatian, Slovenian, Russian) See Helen.

Jelisa (African-American double) See Jean+Lisa.

Jem (variant) See Gemma, Jemima.

Jemie (Hebrew) See Jemima.

Jemima "The Little Dove" (Hebrew).

Patron Saints: There is no saint with this name. However, there are saints with similar names — for example, Sts. Jemata and Mimus. St. Jemata was one of the missionaries who traveled to Abyssinia in 479.

Feast Dates: October 25 — St. Jemata; October 31 — St. Mimus (see Mimi); March 5 — St. Palomartus (see Paloma).

Jemimah (variant) See Jemima.

Jemma (variant) See Gemma.

Jemmie (variant) See Jemima.

Jemmy (variant) See Jemima.

Jen (variant) See Genevieve, Guinevere, Jennifer.

Jena "A Small Bird" (Arabic).

Patron Saints: If Jena is accepted as a nickname for Genevieve and Guinevere, then Sts. Genevieve and Guinevere can be adopted. If Jena means a "small bird," then Bl. James Bird becomes a patron.

Feast Dates: March 25 — Bl. James Bird (see Bird); January 3 — Genevieve (see Genevieve).

Jenalee (American double) See Jennifer+Leigh.

Jenda (variant) See Jane.

Jenee (American double) See Jennifer+Renée.

Jenelle (American double) See Jennie+Neala.

Jenessa (American double) See Jena+Essa.

Jenette (variant double) See Jane+Ette.

Jeni (variant) See Genevieve, Guinevere.

Jenica (Romanian) See Jane.

Jenice (variant) See Jane, Jennifer.

Jenifer (variant) See Genevieve, Guinevere, Jennifer.

Jeniffer (variant) See Genevieve, Guinevere, Jennifer.

Jenilee (American double) See Jennifer+Leigh.

Jenilee (English double) See Jenifer+Leigh.

Jenisha (African-American double) See Jenny+Isha.

Jenissa (American double) See Jenifer+Nissa.

Jenn (nickname) See Genevieve, Guinevere, Jena, Jennifer.

Jenna (variant) See Genevieve, Guinevere, Jena, Jennifer.

Jennee (nickname) See Genevieve, Guinevere, Jane, Jena, Jennifer.

Jenneen (variant) See Jane, Jean.

Jennet (variant) See Jane.

Jennette (English double) See Jane+Ette.

Jenni (nickname) See Genevieve, Guinevere, Jane, Jena, Jennifer.

Jennica (nickname) See Genevieve, Guinevere, Jena, Jennifer.

Jennie (nickname) See Genevieve, Guinevere, Jane, Jena, Jennifer.

Jennifer "The White Wave" (English form of Genevieve) or "The White Phantom" (English form of Guinevere).

Patron Saints: Jennifer finds its roots and patron saints in Genevieve and Guinevere.

Feast Dates: January 3 — St. Genevieve (see Genevieve); November 3 — St. Guinevere (see Guinevere).

Jennilee (American double) See Jenny+Leigh.

Jennilyn (American double) See Jenny+Lynn.

Jennine (variant) See Jane, Jean.

Jenny (nickname) See Genevieve, Guinevere, Jane, Jena, Jennifer.

Jennyn (variant) See Jane, Jean.

Jennyne (variant) See Jane, Jean.

Jenovefa (Czech, Greek) See Genevieve, Guinevere.

Jensine (Danish) See Jane.

Jenylee (American double) See Jenifer+Leigh.

Jeralee (American double) See Geraldine+Leigh.

Jere (variant) See Geraldine.

Jeri (variant) See Jerrilee.

Jerlyn (African-American double) See Geraldine+Lynn.

Jermyn (variant) See Germaine.

Jerri (variant) See Geraldine.

Jerrie (variant) See Geraldine.

Jerrilee (African-American double) See Geraldine+Leigh.

Jerrine (variant) See Geraldine.

Jerry (variant) See Geraldine.

Jerrylee (American double) See Geraldine+Leigh.

Jesenia (Hispanic-American) See Yesenia.

Jesica (variant) See Jessica.

Jess (nickname) See Jane, Jasmine, Jessica.

Jessalin (American double) See Jessica+Lynn.

Jessalyn (American double) See Jessica+Lynn.

Jessamine (English double) See Jessica+Jasmine.

Jessamyn (English double) See Jessica+Jasmine.

Jesseca (variant) See Jessica.

Jessee (variant) See Jessica.

Jesselin (American double) See Jessica+Lynn.

Jessenia (Hispanic-American) See Yesenia.

Jessica "The Wealthy One" (Hebrew) or "God Is Gracious" (Hebrew, Spanish).

Patron Saints: The name Jessica was invented by Shakespeare for a character in *The Merchant of Venice.* Its masculine root, Jesse, leads us to a couple of Sts. Jesse. One is found in the Bible and the other is given to us by Christian tradition. The Bible tells us that Jesse was the grandson of Ruth and Boaz and the father of King David. He was a prominent citizen and leader in Bethlehem in about 1100 B.C. He was married and had eight sons. He entertained the prophet Samuel and discovered that his last son, David, would someday be the king of Israel and Judah.

In David's time, the term "son of Jesse" was spoken with a sneer to indicate that David came from humble (nonroyal) origins. In time, the title was exalted to mean "the expected Messiah."

Feast Dates: December 24 — St. Jesse, Patriarch.

Jessie (variant) See Jane, Jasmine, Jessica.

Jessika (variant) See Jessica.

Jessy (nickname) See Jessica.

Jessye (variant) See Jessica.

Jestine (African-American) See Justine.

Jésua (Spanish) See Jesus.

Jet (variant) See Jetta.

Jett (variant) See Jetta.

Jetta "The Black Gemstone" (Middle English).

Patron Saints: Jet means "black" and thousands of Catholic saints are black. One was St. Benedict the Black, 1522-1585. He was born a slave but was soon set free. All his life he was taunted because of his dark skin. One day he was being taunted when a nobleman passed by. The nobleman was so impressed by Benedict's patience and kindness that he publicly reprimanded the persecutors. Then he invited Benedict to join him and become a Franciscan. Benedict became a cook and he did everything so well that his fellow brothers said they "saw angels helping him in the kitchen." In 1578 the members of this friary elected him superior even though he was not a priest nor could he read. However, he prayed and practiced penance and observed seven Lents every year. He is patron of African-Americans.

Feast Dates: April 4 — St. Benedict the Black; August 7 — St. Ebona (see Ebony).

Jette (variant) See Jetta.

Jewel "The Precious Gem" (Old French) or "The Mother of the Living" (Lithuanian form of Eve).

Patron Saints: There are three patrons of jewelers: Sts. Agatha, Dunstan, and Elroy. Also, if one accepts Jewel as a Lithuanian form of Eve, then we have a few Sts. Eve.

The Bible leads to more patrons than can be counted. Their identity is heralded in the Old Testament: "I will greatly rejoice in the Lord, . . . for he has clothed me with the garments of salvation, . . . [and] as a bride adorns herself with her jewels" (Isaiah 61:10). The Book of Revelation (21:10ff) pictures heaven like a great walled city. Its walls are built of twelve courses of precious jewels and its twelve gates are made of twelve pearls. This image tells us that the heavenly Jerusalem is pure, peaceful, and precious. It is the city of the saved.

Thus to talk about the jewels of the heavenly city leads directly to its saintly inhabitants, for the saints are God's most precious treasures. And they make fine patrons for a person named Jewel.

Feast Dates: November 1 — All Saints; December 24 — Sts. Adam and Eve (see Eartha).

Jewele (variant) See Jewel.

Jewelie (variant) See Jewel.

Jewell (French) See Jewel.

Jewelli (variant) See Jewel.

Jewellie (variant) See Jewel.

Jil (nickname) See Gillian, Juliana, Julie.

Jili (nickname) See Gillian, Juliana, Julie.

Jilie (nickname) See Gillian, Juliana, Julie.

Jill (nickname) See Gillian, Juliana, Julie.

Jillana (variant) See Juliana.

Jilli (nickname) See Gillian, Juliana, Julie.

Jillian (nickname) See Gillian, Juliana, Julie.

Jillie (nickname) See Gillian, Juliana, Julie.

Jilly (nickname) See Gillian, Juliana, Julie.

Jimeka (variant) See Jacqueline.

Jimelle (African-American double) See Jimmy+Elle.

Jimina (Spanish) See Simeon.

Jinni (nickname) See Ginger, Virginia.

Jinnie (nickname) See Ginger, Virginia.

Jinny (nickname) See Jane, Jenny, Ginger, Virginia.

Jitka (Czech) See Judith.

Jo (nickname) See Joanna, Jody, Joelle, Jolie, Josephine.

Joan "God Is Gracious" (Portuguese, Lithuanian, English form of Jane, Joanna).

Patron Saints: There are about two dozen Sts. Joan and Jane. The most famous is St. Joan of Arc, 1412-1431, born of peasant parents, and was known as La Pucelle, or the Maid of Orléans. She never learned to read or write but could sew and spin very well. However, political unrest filled her early years. Then at age fourteen she experienced a voice speaking to her in a blaze of blue light. Soon it became apparent that various saints were speaking to her and slowly revealing her mission to save France. When she first told others, they laughed. Then she set out, in male clothing, to see the king. The king and his council were impressed and an army was given to her. After winning the crown for France, she was betrayed to the enemy. They convicted her of witchcraft and burned her at the stake. She was only nineteen years old. She is now the patron of France and of the Wacs (from WAC, or Women's Army Corps) and the Navy WAVES (the acronym for Women Accepted for Volunteer Emergency Service).

Feast Dates: May 30 — St. Joan of Arc; March 24 — St. Joanna (see Joanna).

Joana (Portuguese, Lithuanian) See Jane, Joan, Joanna.

Joane (variant) See Jane, Joan, Joanna.

Joanelyn (variant double) See Jane, Joan+Lynn.

Joani (nickname) See Jane, Joan, Joanna.

Joanie (nickname) See Jane, Joan, Joanna.

Joann (Czech, Slovakian) See Jane, Joan, Joanna.

JoAnn (English double) See Jane, Joanna, Jane+Ann.

Joanna "God Is Gracious+The God-Graced One" (Czech-Slovakian+Hebrew).

> *Patron Saints:* Joanna is the Hebrew form of Jane. There are two known Sts. Joanna and about two dozen Sts. Joan and Jane. The most famous is St. Joan of Arc. Furthermore, some like to think that Joanna is constructed out of Jane plus Ann. This provides us with a couple dozen Sts. Ann to choose for patrons.
>
> The St. Joanna (Jane) presented here was the wife of Chuza, the procurator of Herod Antipas, who was tetrarch of Galilee. She was healed by Jesus and became his devoted follower. She also went to the tomb of Jesus on Easter Sunday morning and found it empty. Because of her, Herod and his government officials were well aware of Jesus, but this knowledge was not enough to convert them.
>
> *Feast Dates:* March 24 — St. Joanna; May 30 — St. Joan of Arc (see Joan).

Joanne (Czech, Slovakian) See Jane, Joan, Joanna.

JoAnne (English double) See Jane, Joan, Joanna, Jane+Ann.

Joany (nickname) See Jane, Joan, Joanna.

Joaquína "The Lord Will Judge" (Spanish).

> *Patron Saints:* There is one Spanish saint with this name. Joaquína, 1783-1854, obediently married Don Teodore de Mas at the age of sixteen. His family often made trouble for her because

they thought he married beneath his station. More sadness followed when two of her eight children died and then her husband left her a widow at the age of thirty-three.

She mourned for several years and then joined the Third Order of St. Francis. She wore the order's habit and worked at several charities. Some thought she was crazy, but not her pastor. He asked her to found a religious order, which she did. In 1835, at the age of fifty-two, she was arrested, dragged through the streets, and thrown into prison. Upon release she fled the country. Ten years later she suffered a number of strokes that took away her ability to speak. After several more years of suffering, she died in 1854.

> *Feast Dates:* May 22 — St. Joaquína de Mas y de Vedruna.

JoBe (nickname) See Jobina.

Jobeth (American double) See Jo+Beth.

Jobey (nickname) See Jobina.

Jobi (nickname) See Jobina.

Jobie (nickname) See Jobina.

Jobina "The Persecuted One" (Hebrew).

> *Patron Saints:* Jobina is a feminine form of Job, and there are a half-dozen Sts. Job. St. Job of Potshajew gave his life to God as a monk at Ugornitsh in Galicia. Near the end of his life he served as abbot of Dubensk Monastery. He died in 1651.
>
> *Feast Dates:* August 8 — St. Job of Potshajew.

Jobye (variant) See Jobina.

Jobyna (variant) See Jobina.

Jocelyn "The Playful One" (Latin) or "From the Goths" (French) or "The Beautiful One" (Spanish).

> *Patron Saints:* Jocelyn may be a modern English variant of Justine or an American variant of Jacqueline. This provides two dozen Sts. Justin, a dozen

Sts. Justina, and a dozen Sts. James. Furthermore, if Jocelyn is a combination of Josephina and Lynn, then we gain another two dozen patrons.

Finally, accepting Jocelyn as a name in its own right leads to one St. Joscelin, who is remembered for living a very holy life in ancient Trèves.

Feast Dates: August 6 — St. Joscelin; September 26 — St. Justina (see Justina).

Jod (nickname) See Jane, Joan, Joanna, Josephine, Judith.

Jodee (nickname) See Jane, Joan, Joanna, Josephine, Judith.

Jodelle (African-American double) See Jody+Elle.

Jodi (nickname) See Jane, Joan, Joanna, Josephine, Judith.

Jodiann (American double) See Jodi+Ann.

Jodie (nickname) See Jane, Joan, Joanna, Josephine, Judith.

Jodoca (English) See Joy.

Jody "He Shall Add" (short form of Joseph) or "God Is Gracious" (short form of Jane, Joan, Joanna) or "The Praised One" (variant of Judith).

Patron Saints: Some think that Jody is a form of Josepha or Josephine, which leads to over sixty saints. Others think Jody is a form of Jane, Joan, and John, and there are over four hundred twenty-five of these saints. Still others accept it as a form of Judith, and this provides a handful of Sts. Judith.

Christian tradition also provides us with one saint with a very similar name. St. Jodocus, 591-669, was the son of Hoel III of Brittany and was raised in the monastery of St. Maelmon. After his father died, his brother inherited the throne but soon wished to pass it to Jodocus. However, Jodocus did not want it, so he fled Brittany with twelve friends. Soon he was ordained to the priesthood. Then he went to live in the desert of Brabic. He spent the rest of his life in peace and at prayer. He died at the age of seventy-eight.

Feast Dates: December 13 — St. Jodocus, also known as Judoce or Josse.

Joeann (double) See Jane, Joanna, Joan/Josepha+Ann.

Joeanna (double) See Jane, Joanna, Joan/Josepha+Ann.

Joeanne (double) See Jane, Joanna, Joan/Josepha+Ann.

Joela (variant) See Joelle.

Joell (variant) See Joelle.

Joella (variant) See Joelle.

Joelle "The Lord Is Willing" (Hebrew-American double).

Patron Saints: Some would like to accept Joelle as a combination of Josepha and Elly. This would provide over sixty Sts. Joseph and another dozen Sts. Josepha and Josephine. However, other scholars insist that Joelle is simply a feminine form of Joel. There is at least one St. Joel.

Joel is one of the twelve minor prophets of the Old Testament and is known as the "Preacher of Repentance." Born in about 360 B.C., he was one of the last of the prophets. He interpreted a plague to be part of the judgment of God and promised a new outpouring of God's "spirit" on Israel. With this statement, he brings the Jews closest to introducing the Holy Spirit as a separate Person of God.

St. Peter quotes Joel in Acts to prove that Jesus was the fulfillment of all God's promises.

Feast Dates: July 13 — St. Joel, Jewish Prophet.

Joellen (American double) See Joelle, Joelle+Ellen.

Joelly (variant) See Joelle.

Joely (variant) See Joelle.
Joelynn (variant double) See Joella+Lynn.
Joette (variant double) See any "Jo" name+Ette.
Joey (variant) See Josephine.
Johana (Czech, Slovakian) See Jane.
Johanna (German double) See Jane/ Joanna/Jane+Ann.
Johannah (Hebrew double) See Jane/ Joanna/Jane+Ann.
Johanne (Norwegian) See Jane.
Johnalee (English double) See Jane+ Leigh.
Johnelle (African-American double) See Jane+Elle.
Johnetta (African-American double) See Jane+Etta.
Johnette (Danish) See Jane.
Johnise (African-American) See Jane.
Johnna (Danish) See Jane.
Johnnee (nickname) See Jane.
Johnnie (nickname) See Jane.
Johnny (nickname) See Jane.
Johnsie (African-American) See Jane.
Joi (English) See Joy.
Joice (English) See Joy.
Joie (English) See Joy.
Jola (variant) See Jolie.
Jolanda (variant) See Yolanda.
Jolee (variant) See Jolie.
Joleen "This One Shall Increase" (American nickname for Josephine).

> *Patron Saints:* There are two Sts. Jolenta. Because Joleen is a feminine variant of "Joseph," some want to adopt St. Joseph, the husband of Mary and stepfather of Jesus, as patron.
>
> St. Jolenta, 1235-1299, was the daughter of King Bela IV of Hungary. She married Boleslav VI, king of Poland, but he died young. Then she became a Poor Clare religious sister and died at the age of sixty-four.
>
> *Feast Dates:* June 15 — St. Jolenta; March 19 — St. Joseph (see Norma).

Jolene (variant) See Jolie.
Jolenta (variant) See Jolie.
Joletta (English) See Julie.
Joli (variant) See Jolie.
Jolie "The Pretty One" (French).

> *Patron Saints:* There are two ancient saints with this name. One is St. Jolus and the other is St. Jola. The latter was martyred in the ancient African pentapolis known as Cyrene.
>
> *Feast Dates:* May 22 — St. Jola; September 20 — Ven. Mother Mary Theresa Dudzik, O.S.F. (see Josephine).

Joline (variant) See Jolie.
Joly (variant) See Jolie.
Jolyn (variant) See Jolie.
Jonell (African-American double) See Jane+Elle.
Jonesha (African-American double) See Jo+Isha/Sha.
Joni (nickname) See Jane, Joan.
Jonie (nickname) See Jane, Joan.
Jonise (African-American) See Jane, Joan.
Jonna (Danish) See Jane, Joan.
Jonnee (nickname) See Jane, Joan.
Jonnie (Serbian) See Jane, Joan.
Jonny (nickname) See Jane, Joan.
Jony (Serbian) See Jane, Joan.
Jordain (variant) See Jordan.
Jordan "The Descending One" (Hebrew).

> *Patron Saints:* There are about six Sts. Jordan and they are all males. Among them is Bl. Jordan of Pisa, 1250-1311, who was appointed the "Official Teacher of Theology" in Florence. He knew the breviary, the missal, most of the Bible with its marginal notes, the second part of the *Summa*, and many other writings — by heart. He became the best preacher of his time, often preaching five times a day. His preaching helped give birth to the modern Italian language because he insisted on using the Tuscan dialect in his talks.

He pointed out that before St. Dominic only bishops announced the Word of God. This was considered the privilege of their office. Priests, monks, and hermits were expected to preach through the example of their lives. But after Jordan, clerics were expected to preach. He died at about sixty years of age.

Feast Dates: March 6 — Bl. Jordan of Pisa.

Jordana (double) See Jordan+Ann.

Jordanka (Czech) See Jordan.

Jordanna (English double) See Jordan+Ann.

Jordanne (English double) See Jordan+Ann.

Jorey (nickname) See Jordan.

Jorge (Spanish) See Georgene.

Jori (Hebrew) See Jordan.

Joriann (American double) See Jordan+Ann.

Jorie (Hebrew) See Jordan.

Jorgina (Spanish) See Georgia.

Jorja (American) See Georgia.

Jorrie (nickname) See Jordan.

Jorry (nickname) See Jordan.

Josaphina (variant) See Josephine.

Josaphine (variant) See Josephine.

Joscelyn (English) See Jocelyn.

Jose (variant) See Josephine.

Josean (Hispanic-American double) See Jose+Ana.

Josefa (Spanish) See Josephine.

Josefina (Spanish) See Josephine.

Josefine (variant) See Josephine.

Josie (English) See Josephine.

Josepha (German) See Josephine.

Josephina (Portuguese) See Josephine.

Josephine "This One Shall Increase" (French).

Patron Saints: The greatest patron for anyone named Josephine (or variants of it) is St. Joseph, the husband of Mary. However, it is also important to recognize female saints named after St. Joseph. Among their number is an American saint-in-the-making. She is Ven. Mother Mary Theresa Dudzik, 1860-1918, born Josaphine Dudzik in Poland. Because of harsh German domination of Poland, many Poles emigrated to the United States. Thus in 1881 Josaphine's family moved to Chicago, Illinois. After her father died, Josaphine helped support the family by working as a seamstress. She also began helping the poor, often housing them in her own home.

Soon she founded a religious order to help the homeless and orphans and took the name Mary Theresa. She spent her own money to acquire land and buildings and was then ousted from office. She spent her time doing household chores. In 1910 she again served briefly as superior and was again the victim of in-fighting among the sisters of her community. She spent the last eight years of her life caring for the garden, the laundry, and sewing room. She died at age fifty-eight years in Chicago.

Feast Dates: September 20 — Ven. Mother Mary Theresa Dudzik, O.S.F.

Josetta (English double) See Josephine+Etta.

Josette (French double) See Josephine+Ette.

Josey (variant) See Josephine.

Josi (variant) See Josephine.

Josie (variant) See Josephine.

Josy (variant) See Josephine.

Josypa (Ukrainian) See Josephine.

Jourdan (English) See Jordan.

Jourdyn (English) See Jordan.

Jovanie (English) See Jane.

Jovanka (Serbian) See Jane.

JoVette (American double) See Josephine+Yvette.

Jovita (Latin) See Joy, Hilaria.

Joy "The Joyful One" (Latin).

Patron Saints: The Latin word for joy is *gaudium* and the Italian is *felicita*. This leads to many patrons.

Feast Dates: August 30 — St. Gaudentia (see Bliss, Blythe); March 7 — St. Felicitas (see Felicitas).

Joya (English) See Joy.

Joyan (English double) See Joy+Ann.

Joyann (English double) See Joy+Ann.

Joyce (English, Spanish) See Joy.

Joycelyn (American double) See Joyce+Lynn.

Joye (English) See Joy.

Joyita (Spanish double) See Joy+Ita.

Joyous (English) See Joy.

Jozefa (Polish) See Josephine.

Juana (Spanish) See Jane.

Juandalyn (Spanish) See Juanita.

Juanita "God Is Gracious" (Spanish form of Jane).

Patron Saints: Juanita (the diminutive of Jane in English) is the feminine Spanish form of Juan (or John). There are about two dozen Sts. Jane. Among them is St. Juanita Teresita, 1900-1920, born in Santiago, Chile. She was a very religious child and received First Communion at the age of ten. When she was fourteen, she read the story of St. Thérèse of the Child Jesus, entitled *The Story of a Soul*, and vowed to become a spouse of Jesus. In early 1919 she entered the Carmelite convent. Her letters home are filled with happiness. But in March of 1920 she told her confessor that she would die within a month and she did at the age of nineteen, just eleven months after entering the convent.

Feast Dates: July 13 — St. Juanita, also known as Teresa of Jesus.

Jude (English) See Judith.

Judee (English) See Judith.

Judi (English) See Judith.

Judia (African-American) See Judith.

Judie (English) See Judith.

Judit (Spanish, Swedish) See Judith.

Judith "The Praised One" or "Jewish Woman" (Hebrew).

Patron Saints: The Bible provides one St. Judith and Catholic tradition provides two more. The St. Judith who died in 1070 was the daughter of an English king. She married King Bertric of the West Saxons, but her husband soon died. She dealt with her grief by making a pilgrimage to Jerusalem, accompanied by her cousin Salome. While on pilgrimage she felt called to become a nun and a hermit. This she did.

Feast Dates: June 29 — St. Judith.

Juditha (English) See Judith.

Judy (English) See Judith.

Judyann (American double) See Judy+Ann.

Judye (English) See Judith.

Juel (variant) See Jewel.

Juleane (English double) See Juliana, Julie+Ann.

Julee (variant) See Juliana, Julie.

Julene (variant) See Juliana, Julie.

Julet (African-American double) See Julie+Ette.

Juli (nickname) See Juliana, Julie.

Julia (Spanish) See Juliana, Julie.

Juliana "Youthful One+Graceful One" (Spanish double).

Patron Saints: There are more than two dozen Sts. Julia and Juliana and many more Sts. Anne. Julian (or Juliana) of Norwich is a mystery. Not even her real name is known. She got her present name from the small one-room cell (shack) attached to the cathedral Church of St. Julian of Norwich, England, where she lived.

She lived the life of a single person dedicated to prayer, poverty, and chastity. She had visions and spent twenty years meditating and writing about them. They are printed in *Revelations of Divine Love* and tell of the love of God, the incarnation, redemption, sin, and divine consolation. For example, this is what she wrote about the soul: "I understood that the human soul is made from nothing. It is made, not out of anything preexisting. For the making of man's soul, God took nothing at all. He simply made it." And about sin she wrote: "Sin has to happen, but all shall be well. All shall be well, and all manner of things shall be well." Living from about 1342 to around 1413, she died at the about the age of seventy-one.

Feast Dates: May 13 — St. Julian of Norwich.

Juliane (variant double) See Juliana, Julie+Ann.

Juliann (variant double) See Juliana, Julie+Ann.

Julianne (variant double) See Juliana, Julie+Ann.

Julie "Youthful One" (French, German, English, Latin).

Patron Saints: There are more than two dozen Sts. Julia and Julie. Included among them is St. Julie Billiart, 1751-1816. The sixth child of a poor shopkeeper in France, Mary Rose Julie Billiart liked to play "school" as a child. She also was so prayerful that the priest gave her First Communion and also confirmed her at the age of nine years.

As a young adult during the French Revolution, she offered her home as a hiding place for priests. After the Revolution had destroyed the schools, she gradually gathered together a group of women dedicated to quality education. From this group came the Sisters of Notre Dame.

As a child she was also robbed, and this brought on a paralysis caused by fright, which lasted twenty years. Julie often suffered from poor health and was she unable to walk or speak. Only in 1804 did she experience a healing. After this she increased her work. She said, "The good God has given me back my legs; surely He intended that I should use them." She died at age sixty-five.

Feast Dates: April 8 — St. Julie Billiart.

Julienne (variant double) See Juliana, Julie+Ann.

Juliet (Spanish) See Julie.

Julieta (Spanish) See Julie+Etta.

Julietta (Italian double) See Julie+Etta.

Juliette (French double) See Julie+Ette.

Julina (English) See Juliana, Julie.

Juline (English) See Juliana, Julie.

Julisa (variant) See Julie.

Julissa (variant double) See Julie+Lisa.

Julita (Spanish double) See Julie+Ita.

July "Born in Jupiter's Month" or "The Youthful One" (variant form of Julie).

Patron Saints: There are a few ancient saints named after Jupiter, or Jove. Christian tradition reports that Jovita was an ardent lay preacher of the Gospel in ancient Lombardy. This last activity got him into trouble and he was beheaded during the reign of the Roman emperor Hadrian.

Feast Dates: February 15 — St. Jovita; April 8 — St. Julie Billiart (see Julie).

Jumaris (African-American double) See June+Maris.

June "The One Born in June" (Latin).

Patron Saints: There are about a half-dozen Sts. Junias and Junelle. A St. Junias is mentioned by St. Paul in Romans 16:7. He calls this Junias an "Apostle." The problem is that Junias was a name used by both males and females in ancient times, and in about 400 St. John Chrysostom identified

Junias as the wife of St. Andronicus, also mentioned in Romans. As a married couple they seem to have served as local Catholic leaders. Another ancient tradition insists that this Junias wrote the Epistle to the Hebrews. Another tradition credits this to St. Apollos. It seems Junias and Andronicus were martyred.

Feast Dates: May 17 — St. Junias.

Junella (African-American double) See June+Ella.

Junelle (African-American double) See June+Elle.

Junette (American double) See June+Ette.

Junia (Latin) See June.

Juniata (Spanish) See June.

Junine (English) See June.

Junita (Spanish) See John.

Justa (variant) See Justina.

Justina (Italian, Spanish) See Justine.

Justine "The Just One" (Latin).

Patron Saints: There are two dozen Sts. Justin and almost a dozen Sts. Justina. The story of St. Justina, who was martyred in 305, begins with a man called Cyprian the Magician. He was a pagan, well versed in the black arts,

and had no inhibitions about using his powers to seduce women.

It seems that Justina caught the attention of a young man who hired Cyprian to work a love spell. But the magician himself fell in love with her and began harassing her. She prayed to the Blessed Virgin for help. Cyprian, feeling he was losing, threatened to quit serving the devil if he did not fix things and the devil began attacking Cyprian. The magician turned to God, converted to Christianity, and eventually became a bishop. Justina was so impressed by the power of God to change hearts that she dedicated herself to the service of the poor. Sometime later both Cyprian and Justina were executed.

Feast Dates: September 26 — St. Justina.

Justyn (English) See Justine.

Justyna (English) See Justine.

Justyne (English double) See Justine+Tyne.

Jusztina (variant) See Justina.

Jutta (German, Finnish) See Judith.

Jyssica (English) See Jessica.

𝒦

Kaapo (nickname) See Gabbi, Gabriela.

Kaate (variant) See Katherine.

Kacey (American double) See Casey, Casimira, any "K" name+any "C" name.

Kachina "The Sacred Dancer" (North American Indian).

Patron Saints: There is no saint with a name that even remotely resembles Kachina, thus we must turn to the name's meaning, "sacred dancer." The Latin word for sacred is *sanctus* or *sancia*. Moreover, there is a saint who has been appointed as patron of dancers: St. Vitus.

Feast Dates: March 13 — St. Sancia (see Sancia); June 15 — St. Vitus (see Vita).

Kacia (nickname) See Acacia.

Kacie (nickname) See Acacia, Casey, Casimira, any "K" name+any "C" name.

Kacy (nickname) See Casey, Casimira, any "K" name+any "C" name.

Kadedra (African-American double) See Kady+Deidre.

Kadee (American double) See any "K" name+any "D" name.

Kadesha (African-American double) See Kady+Aisha/Isha.

Kadie (nickname) See Katie.

Kadijah "The Prophet's Wife" (African) or "The Trustworthy [Faithful] One" (Arabic).

Patron Saints: There are a few saints whose name reflects "trustworthy."

Feast Dates: October 6 — St. Faith of Agen; August 1 — St. Faith (with Charity) (see Charity).

Kady (American double) See any "K" name+any "D" name.

Kaela "The Sweetheart" (Arabic) or "The Beloved One" (Arabic) or "The Pure One+From the Meadow" (short form of Katherine+Leigh).

Patron Saints: There is one St. Kali. And the fact that Kalila means "beloved" leads to a few more patrons.

Feast Dates: May 24 — St. Kali, also known as Sarah (see Zara); March 1 — St. David (see Davita).

Kaelee (Arabic-American double) See Katherine, Kay+Leigh.

Kaeleigh (Arabic-American double) See Katherine, Kay+Leigh.

Kaelin (Arabic, variant double) See Cailin, Katherine, Kay+Lynn, Kaela.

Kaelyn (Irish-Arabic, variant double) See Cailin, Katherine, Kay+Lynn, Kaela.

Kaelynn (American double) See Cailin, Katherine, Kay+Lynn, Kaela.

Kai "From the Sea" (Hawaiian) or "The Pure One" (short form of Katherine, Kay).

Patron Saints: There are a great many Sts. Katherine and at least one St. Katharine.

Feast Dates: March 3 — St. Katharine Drexel (see Katherine); April 17 — Bl. Kateri Tekakwitha (see Kateri).

Kaia (Estonian) See Katherine, Kay.

Kaila (Arabic-English double) See Katherine, Kay+Leigh, Kaela.

Kailee (Arabic-English double) See Katherine, Kay+Leigh, Kaela, Kalila.

Kaileela (Arabic-English double) See Katherine, Kay+Leigh, Kaela, Kalila.

Kailey (Arabic-English double) See Katherine, Kay+Leigh, Kaela, Kalila.

Kailida (Spanish) See Adora.

Kailin (Irish-English double) See Cailin, Katherine, Kay+Lynn, Kaela.

Kaily (Arabic-English double) See Katherine, Kay+Leigh, Kaela.

Kailynn (English double) See Cailin, Katherine, Kay+Lynn, Kaela.

Kaitlin (Irish) See Caitlin.

Kaitlyn (Arabic-English double) See Katherine, Kay+Lynn.

Kaitlynn (English double) See Katherine, Kay+Lynn.

Kaja (variant) See Katherine, Kay.

Kakalina (variant) See Katherine.

Kakisha (African-American) See Keisha.

Kala (African-American, Hindu) See Jett.

Kalandra (variant) See Calandra.

Kalani " Chieftain" (Hawaiian) or "The Sky" (Hawaiian).

Patron Saints: Ken means "royalty" or "chief." St. Kendeus suffered martyrdom in ancient Nicomedia.

Feast Dates: January 20 — St. Kendeus.

Kaleena (variant) See Kalinda.

Kalen (African-American double) See Kay+Lynn.

Kaley (Arabic, variant double) See Katherine, Kay+Leigh, Kaela.

Kali (Arabic, variant double) See Calandra, Calida, Callista, Katherine, Kay+Leigh, Kaela, Kalila.

Kalie (Arabic, variant double) See Calandra, Calida, Callista, Katherine, Kay+Leigh, Kaela, Kalila.

Kalil (Arabic variant) See Kalila.

Kalila "The Girlfriend" (Arabic) or "The Beloved One" (Arabic) or "The Pure One+From the Meadow" (short forms of Katherine+Leigh).

Patron Saints: There is one St. Kali. And the fact that Kalila means "beloved" leads to a few more patrons.

Feast Dates: May 24 — St. Kali, also known as Sarah (see Zara); March 1 — St. David (see Davita).

Kalin (Irish-Arabic double) See Cailin, Katherine, Kay+Lynn.

Kalina (variant) See Cailin, Kalinda.

Kalinda "The Sun" (Sanskrit).

Patron Saints: There are two saints who will have to be patrons here: Sts. Callinica and Berlindis.

Callinica was a servant of a rich woman named Basilissa. Together they nursed Christians in prisons until they themselves were arrested. Then they embraced martyrdom. Both were beheaded. Two other women, Matidia and Drusilla, the sister and daughter of Emperor Trajan, were executed with them.

Feast Dates: March 22 — St. Callinica; February 3 — St. Berlindis (see Linda).

Kalindi (variant) See Kalinda.

Kalisa (African-American double) See Kalani/Kalila/Kalinda+Lisa.

Kalisha (African-American double) See Kalani/Kalila/Kalinda+Aisha.

Kalista (variant) See Callista.

Kalli (Arabic, variant double) See Calandra, Calida, Callista, Katherine, Kay+Leigh, Kaela, Kalila.

Kallie (Arabic, variant double) See Calandra, Calida, Callista, Katherine, Kay+Leigh, Kaela, Kalila, Kelly.

Kally (Arabic, variant double) See Calandra, Calida, Callista, Katherine, Kay+Leigh, Kaela, Kalila.

Kalyn (Arabic double) See Katherine, Kay+Lynn, Kaela, Kalila.

Kalynn (Arabic double) See Katherine, Kay+Lynn, Kaela.

Kamali "The Guiding Spirit" (Zimbabwean).

Patron Saints: This name leads to the guardian angels.

Feast Dates: October 2 — Guardian Angels (see Angela).

Kamea (Hawaiian) See Andrea.

Kami (variant) See Camilla.

Kamia (variant) See Andrea, Camilla.

Kamie (nickname) See Andrea, Camilla.

Kamila (Slavic) See Camilla.

Kamilah (variant) See Camilla.

Kamilia (variant) See Camilla.

Kamiliah (variant) See Camilla.

Kamran (American) See Cameron.

Kamryn (American) See Cameron.

Kamy (variant) See Camilla.

Kandace (English) See Candace.

Kandee (nickname) See Candace.

Kandi (American) See Candace.

Kandice (English) See Candace.

Kandida (variant) See Candace.

Kandie (nickname) See Candace.

Kandis (English) See Candace.

Kandy (nickname) See Candace.

Kanesha "The Handsome+Woman" (African-American double).

Patron Saints: Kanesha is often spelled Kenisha. The first half of the name is considered a form of Kenneth. St. Kenneth lived the life of a monk, later becoming an abbot. He moved to different monasteries many times and he met many saints. He died in 599.

The second half of the name finds its root in *isha*, which is the Hebrew word for "female."

Feast Dates: October 11 — St. Kenneth; December 24 — Sts. Adam and Eve (see Isha).

Kaniesha (African-American) See Kanesha.

Kanika (African-American double) See Kay+Nicole.

Kanini "The Little One" (Hispanic-American). See Niña.

Kanisha (African-American) See Kanesha.

Kara (Greek, Danish) See Katherine.

Kara (Polish, Russian) See Carissa, Carla, Carol, Caroline.

Kare (nickname) See Charity.

Karee (variant) See Carey, Charity, Katherine.

Karel (variant) See Carla, Carol, Caroline.

Karelle (American) See Carla, Carol, Caroline.

Karen (Danish) See Caren, Katherine, Karina.

Karena (Scandinavian) See Caren, Katherine, Karina.

Kari (Norwegian, Danish) See Carey, Charity, Katherine, Karina.

Kariane (American double) See Kari+ Anne.

Karie (variant) See Carey, Katherine, Karina.

Karilynn (American double) See Kari+ Lynn.

Karin (Swedish) See Caren, Katherine.

Karina "The Witty One" (Greek) or "The Dear One" (Italian) or "The Pure One" (Swedish, Russian form of Karen).

Patron Saints: St. Carina gave her life for Jesus at Rome during the Roman persecutions.

Feast Dates: November 7 — St. Carina.

Karine (Russian) See Caren, Katherine.

Karisa (variant) See Carissa.

Karissa (variant) See Carissa.

Karizma (American) See Charisma.

Karita (nickname) See Charity.

Karla (variant) See Carla, Carol, Caroline.

Karlee (American) See Carla, Carol, Caroline.

Karleen (English) See Carla, Carol, Caroline.

Karlen (variant) See Carla, Carol, Caroline.

Karlene (English) See Carla, Carol, Caroline.

Karley (English) See Carla, Carol, Caroline.

Karli (variant) See Carla, Carol, Caroline.

Karlie (variant) See Carla, Carol, Caroline.

Karline (English) See Carla, Carol, Caroline.

Karlita (Spanish double) See Carla/Carol/Caroline+Ita.

Karlotta (Irish double) See Carla/Charlotte+Lottie.

Karlotte (German double) See Carla/Charlotte+Lottie.

Karly (variant) See Carla, Carol, Caroline.

Karma "One's Actions Determines One's Fate" (Hindu) or "From the Garden" (short form of Carmella).

Patron Saints: Most Christians agree that the greatest teacher of righteous living is Jesus. He taught the "Golden Rule," based on the two greatest commandments, which state: "You shall love the Lord your God with all your heart, and with all your soul, and with all your mind, and with all your strength" and "You shall love your neighbor as yourself" (Mark 12:30-31). And Jesus told us to be compassionate: to "the measure you give will be the measure you get, and still more will be given you" (Mark 4:24). And the Blessed Virgin Mary adds, "Do whatever he [Jesus] tells you" (John 2:5). The Blessed Virgin also bears the title of Our Lady of Mount Carmel, a title that sounds similar to "Karma."

Feast Dates: Sundays — Jesus the Teacher of Righteousness; July 16 — Our Lady of Mount Carmel (see Carmella); April 25 — Our Lady of Good Counsel (see Consuelo).

Karmel (Polish) See Carmella.

Karmela (Polish) See Carmella.

Karol (variant) See Carla, Carol, Caroline.

Karole (variant) See Carla, Carol, Caroline.

Karolina (Polish, Russian) See Carla, Carol, Caroline.

Karoline (German) See Carla, Carol, Caroline.

Karra (English) See Katherine.

Karree (English) See Carey, Caroline, Katherine.

Karrie (English) See Carey, Caroline, Katherine.

Karry (English) See Carey, Caroline, Katherine.

Karrye (English) See Carey, Caroline, Katherine.

Kary (English) See Carey, Caroline, Katherine.

Karylin (variant double) See Katherine+Lynn.

Karylyn (American double) See Katherine+Lynn.

Karylynn (American double) See Katherine+Lynn.

Karymya (Hispanic-American) See Carissa+Mia.

Karyn (variant) See Caren, Katherine.

Kasey (variant) See Acacia, Casey.

Kasia (Polish) See Acacia, Casey, Katherine.

Kasie (nickname) See Acacia, Casey, Cassandra, Katherine.

Kass (nickname) See Cassandra, Katherine.

Kassandra (Greek) See Cassandra.

Kassi (nickname) See Cassandra, Katherine.

Kassia (Slavic) See Katherine.

Kassidy (Irish) See Cassidy.

Kassie (nickname) See Cassandra, Katherine.

Kat (nickname) See Katherine.

Kata (Croatian, Hungarian) See Katherine.

Katalin (Hungarian) See Katherine+Lynn.

Katalina (variant) See Katherine.

Katalyn (English double) See Katherine+Lynn.

Katarazyna (Polish) See Katherine.

Katarina (German, Scandinavian) See Katherine.

Kate (nickname) See Katherine.

Katee (nickname) See Katherine.

Katelin (Irish-English double) See Caitlin, Katherine+Lynn.

Katelyn (English double) See Katherine+Lynn.

Katelyna (English double) See Katherine+Lynn.

Katelynn (English double) See Katherine+Lynn.

Kateri "The Pure One" (Dutch).

Patron Saints: Kateri Tekakwitha, known as the "Lily of the Mohawks," lived in upper New York from 1656 to 1680. The daughter of an Algonquin Indian woman who had been captured by the Iroquois, she was orphaned when a smallpox epidemic swept her village and killed her family. She was badly pock-marked the rest of her life and her eyesight was also impaired by the disease.

In 1676, at the age of twenty, she converted to Catholicism because of the teachings of a Jesuit missionary, Father Jacques de Lamberville. Her conversion cost her rejection, abuse, and ostracism. Then on Christmas Day of 1677, she made her First Communion. Two years later she took a vow of chastity and dedicated herself to Jesus. She died the following year at the age of twenty-four.

Feast Dates: April 17 — Bl. Kateri Tekakwitha.

Katerina (Czech, Russian, Bulgarian) See Katherine.

Katerine (variant) See Katherine.

Katerna (variant) See Katherine.

Katey (nickname) See Katherine.

Kath (nickname) See Katherine.

Katha (nickname) See Katherine.

Katharina (German, Estonian) See Katherine.

Katharine (English) See Katherine.

Kathe (German) See Katherine.

Kathee (nickname) See Katherine.

Katherine "The Pure One" (English).

Patron Saints: St. Katharine Drexel, 1858-1955, was born of a wealthy Philadelphia, Pennsylvania, banker. Even though her mother died just five weeks after she was born, her childhood was happy and carefree. She had all the comforts that money could buy and she traveled widely throughout Europe. When Katharine was only fourteen years old, she began to feel a special devotion to the Eucharist. Soon after her stepmother and father died, she and her sister inherited a large sum of money, with estimates ranging between fourteen million and twenty million dollars.

But their parents had provided a strong example of charity and the sisters began to donate money. They also became aware of the needs of the blacks and Indians in North America. In 1891, at the age of thirty-three, Katherine organized a religious order of sisters at the suggestion of Pope Leo XIII. She called her community the Sisters of the Blessed Sacrament for Indians and Colored People. Over the next several years Mother Katharine opened schools and in 1915 she founded Xavier University in Louisiana to educate blacks. In time, she spent some twelve million dollars on these endeavors. She died at the age of ninety-six after spending the last twenty years of her life in prayer and reflection at the community's motherhouse not far from Philadelphia.

Feast Dates: March 3 — St. Katharine Drexel.

Kathi (nickname) See Katherine.

Kathie (nickname) See Katherine.

Kathleen (Irish) See Katherine.

Kathleena (Irish) See Katherine.
Kathlene (Irish) See Katherine.
Katheryn (English) See Katherine.
Kathline (Irish) See Katherine.
Kathryn (English) See Katherine.
Kathryne (English) See Katherine.
Kathy (nickname) See Katherine.
Kathye (nickname) See Katherine.
Kati (nickname) See Katherine.
Katia (African-American) See Katherine.
Katie (nickname) See Katherine.
Katina (Modern Greek, Bulgarian) See Katherine.
Katine (variant) See Katherine.
Katinka (Russian, Slavic) See Katherine.
Katrea (African-American) See Katherine.
Katri (Finnish) See Katherine.
Katriane (Russian) See Katherine.
Katrien (Dutch) See Katherine.
Katrina (Latvian, German, Czech, Scottish) See Katherine.
Katrine (Norwegian, Danish, Scottish) See Katherine.
Katrinka (variant) See Katherine.
Katrya (Ukrainian) See Katherine.
Katti (nickname) See Katherine.
Kattie (nickname) See Katherine.
Katty (nickname) See Katherine.
Katuscha (variant) See Katherine.
Katushka (variant) See Katherine.
Katuska (Czech) See Katherine.
Katya (Russian) See Katherine.
KaVon (African-American double) See Kay+Vanna.
Kay "The Pure One" (short form of Katherine).
  Patron Saints: There is one St. Kayne. She lived in ancient Cainsham and dedicated her virginity to God.
  Feast Dates: October 8 — St. Kayne; April 17 — Bl. Kateri Tekakwitha (see Kateri).
Kaycee (nickname) See Acacia, Casey.
Kaycie (English) See Acacia, Casey.

Kaye (English) See Katherine, Kay.
Kayla (Arabic-English double) See Kaela, Katherine/Kay+Leigh.
Kaylee (Arabic-English double) See Kaela, Kalila, Kay+Leigh.
Kayley (Arabic-English double) See Kaela, Kalila, Katherine/Kay+Leigh.
Kayli (Arabic-English double) See Kaela, Kalila, Kay+Leigh.
Kaylil (Arabic) See Kalila.
Kaylila (Arabic) See Kalila.
Kaylin (Irish-Arabic-English double) See Cailin, Kaela, Kalila, Katherine/Kay+Lynn.
Kaylyn (English double) See Kaela, Kalila, Katherine/Kay+Lynn.
Kaylynn (English double) See Kaela, Kalila, Katherine/Kay+Lynn.
Kayne (English) See Katherine, Kay.
Kebby (Danish) See Kibby.
Keely "The Ship Keel+At the Meadow" (Old English double).
  Patron Saints: St. Cele was a holy medieval Irish bishop.
  Feast Dates: March 3 — St. Cele Crist.
Keeya (African-American) See Kiah.
Keisha "The Handsome+The Woman" (African-American double from Hebrew).
  Patron Saints: Keisha seems to be constructed out of Ke and Isha. Ke is probably from Kendra. It also helps to know that in the Book of Genesis Adam gives the name Isha to Eve, which means "the woman."
  Feast Dates: December 24 — Sts. Adam and Eve (see Eartha, Isha); October 29 — St. Kennera (see Kendra).
Keishla (African-American triple) See "Ke" name+Isha+any "La" name.
Kelcey (English) See Kelsey.
Kelci (English) See Kelsey.
Kelcie (English) See Kelsey.
Kelcy (English) See Kelsey.

Keli (American-Irish) See Kelly.

Kelisie (English) See Kelsey.

Kellen (variant) See Kelly.

Kelley (Irish) See Kelly.

Kelli (American-Irish) See Kelly.

Kellia (American-Irish) See Kelly.

Kellie (American-Irish) See Kelly.

Kellina (variant) See Kelly.

Kelly "The Warrior Woman" (Irish Gaelic) or "The Churchgoer" (Irish Gaelic).

Patron Saints: The half-dozen Sts. Kelly are all male and they spelled their names as Ceallach. One St. Kelly was an Irish saint who lived in the 600s. He became a monk at the Iona monastery. Later, he was appointed bishop of Litchfield. In 656 he retired to Iona, where he died.

Feast Dates: February 14 — St. Kelly, also known as Ceallach.

Kelsey "From the Ship Island" (Scandinavian) or "One with a Dry Neck" (Cornish).

Patron Saints: There are a few ancient saints who have names that are very similar, including Sts. Celsa, Celsinus, and Celsus. St. Celsa was from medieval Flanders and was the niece of St. Berlindis. She is remembered for remaining single and giving her life to prayer and charity.

Feast Dates: February 14 — Celsa.

Kelsi (variant) See Kelsey.

Kelsie (variant) See Kelsey.

Kelsy (variant) See Kelsey.

Kemba (Swahili) See Faith.

Kenan "The Enduring One" (Irish) or "The White-Haired One" (Old German).

Patron Saints: All four known Sts. Kenan are male. One of them was a holy abbot of Plou-Kernaw Parish in Brittany. It is remembered that he gave the sacraments to the dying St. Jova. Kenan died in 550.

Feast Dates: February 25 — St. Kenan, also known as Cienan.

Kenda "The Child of Pure Water" (English) or "The One with Magical Power" (North American Indian).

Patron Saints: St. Kendeus died a martyr in Nicomedia.

Feast Dates: January 20 — St. Kendeus; November 1 — St. Kendelion (see Kenya).

Kendra "The Knowledgeable One" (Old English) or "The Handsome One" (feminine form of Kenneth).

Patron Saints: Many regard Kendra as a feminine form of Kenneth or as a variant of Kenda. This leads to St. Kennera, whose name is the female form of Kenneth. She served God by living a life of prayer and solitude in medieval Scotland. And there are a few saints with very similar names, including St. Kendelion, Kendeus, and Cendeus.

Also recognizing that Kendra means "knowledgeable" leads to the patron of scholars, St. Bridget of Sweden. She might be pressed into service as a patron.

Feast Dates: October 29 — St. Kennera; November 1 — St. Kendelion (see Kenya).

Kendre (Irish) See Kendra.

Kenen (Irish) See Kenan.

Kenisha (African-American) See Kanesha, Kendra.

Kenna (Irish) See McKenna, Kenan, Kendra.

Kennan (Irish) See Kenan.

Kennera (Irish) See Kenya.

Kennon (Irish) See Kenan.

Kenon (Irish) See Kenan.

Kenya "The White Mountain" (African) or "The Handsome One" (Irish) or "The Animal Horn" (Hebrew).

Patron Saints: Some parents think Kenya is a feminine form of Kenneth and use it as such. This leads to St. Kennera, whose name is the female form of Kenneth. St. Kendelion is another possibility. She married Arthfael, the son of the king of Gwent. She is remembered for her piety and prayer life. *Feast Dates:* November 1 — St. Kendelion; October 29 — St. Kennera (see Kendra).

Keri (Irish) See Carey, Kerry.

Keriann (English double) See Kerry+ Ann.

Kerianne (English double) See Kerry+ Ann.

Kerie (Irish) See Carey, Kerry.

Kerie (nickname) See Kerry.

Kernisha (African-American double) See Kanesha.

Kerri (nickname) See Carey, Kerry.

Kerry "The Black Haired One" (Irish Gaelic) or "The Little Strong One" (vague connection to Caroline).
Patron Saints: Kerry in Gaelic is "Ciarda," and there is one St. Ciaran (or Kiara, also known as Kerry). She died in Cork, Ireland, in 680, and is remembered for founding a couple of monasteries. Also, some like to make a connection to "Caroline" or "Carla." Seeing Caroline is the feminine form of Charles may lead to many more patrons. *Feast Dates:* October 16 — St. Kiara, also known as Kerry; August 17 — Bl. Carolomann (see Carla).

Kerryn (variant) See Katherine.

Kerstin (Swedish) See Christine.

Kesa (African-American) See Kizzy.

Kesabi (African-American double) See Kesia/Kessiah/Keziah+Sabina.

Keshia (African-American) See Kanesha.

Kesia (African-American) See Kizzy.

Keslie (variant) See Kelsey.

Kesly (variant) See Kelsey.

Kessiah (African-American) See Kizzy.

Kette (nickname) See Katherine.

Ketterle (German) See Katherine.

Ketti (nickname) See Katherine.

Kettie (nickname) See Katherine.

Ketty (nickname) See Katherine.

Keyah (African-American) See Kiah.

Keziah (African-American) See Kizzy.

Khadijah (Arabic, African) See Kadijah.

Khandi (American) See Candace.

Ki (nickname) See Kiah, Kiki.

Kia (African-American) See Kiah.

Kiah "The Season's Beginning" (African).
Patron Saints: A saint with a similar name, St. Ciwa, served as nurse to St. Kieran in medieval Wales. *Feast Dates:* February 8 — St. Ciwa, also known as Kiwa.

Kial (variant) See Kyla.

Kiana (American double) See Kiah/ Kiara+Ana.

Kiara (Irish) See Kerry.

Kibbie (Danish) See Kibby.

Kibby "From the Market+Town" (Danish double).
Patron Saints: St. Cybi was a holy abbot who founded a monastery in Wales in the 500s. *Feast Dates:* November 8 — St. Cybi.

Kice "The Blind One" (nickname).
Patron Saints: Kice can be a shortened form of Kicely, which came from Cicely, which in turn came from Ceciley, which arose out of Cecilia. *Feast Dates:* November 22 — St. Cecilia (see Cecilia).

Kiel (variant) See Kyla.

Kiele (variant) See Kyla.

Kielene (variant) See Kyla.

Kiera (Irish) See Kerry.

Kierestin (variant) See Christine, Kiersten.

Kierra (Irish) See Kerry.

Kierstan (variant) See Christine, Kiersten.

Kierste (variant) See Kiersten.

Kierstee (variant) See Kiersten.

Kiersten "Anointed One" (Scandinavian form of Christine).

Patron Saints: Kiersten is a form of Christine, and there are about a dozen Sts. Christine.

Feast Dates: July 24 — St. Christina the Astonishing (see Christine).

Kiersti (variant) See Kiersten.

Kierstie (variant) See Kiersten.

Kiersty (variant) See Kiersten.

Kika (Spanish) See Kiki.

Kiki "Castor Plant" (Egyptian) or "Mistress of the Home" (short form of Henrietta; also Spanish suffix).

Patron Saints: Kiki is a nickname for Henrietta and is also the feminine form of Castor, which leads to a dozen Sts. Castor and one Bl. Castora Gabrielli. When Castora grew up, she married, had children, and joined the Third Order of St. Francis. After her husband died, she gave herself to the service of the poor, to prayer, and to sacrifice. She died in 1391 at Sant' Angelo in Vado.

Also note that because the castor plant was valued for its medicinal qualities, it might be possible to adopt as the patrons of druggists the following: Sts. Cosmas, Damian, Emilian, and Raphael.

Feast Dates: June 14 — Bl. Castora Gabrielli; September 29 — St. Raphael (see Raphaela).

Kikilia (Russian) See Cecilia.

Kiley (nickname) See Kyla.

Kilian (English) See Killian.

Killian "The Little Warlike One" (Irish Gaelic) or "From the Church by the Pool" (Scottish Gaelic).

Patron Saints: There are a half-dozen Sts. Kilian and Killian. One was a priest in Ireland in the late 600s. He and two friends decided to become missionaries and went to Rome to get permission to pursue this vocation.

While there, Kilian was consecrated a bishop. Full of zeal, the trio went to Franconia in the spring of 689 to make converts. Later, in July, they were murdered by the wife of one of their converts. She was angry at Kilian because he had asked her husband to part company with her because of a previous marriage.

Feast Dates: July 8 — St. Kilian and Companions.

Killie (nickname) See Killian.

Killy (nickname) See Killian.

Kim (nickname) See Kimberly.

Kimba (African-American) See Kemba, Kimberly.

Kimberlee (English) See Kimberly.

Kimberley (English) See Kimberly.

Kimberli (English) See Kimberly.

Kimberly "From Royal Fortress Meadow" (Old English) or "The Chief Ruler" (Old English short form of Kimball).

Patron Saints: There is one St. Kimberly, but she died in 725 and spelled her name Cyneburga. She was a nun and the virgin daughter of the king of Wessex.

There is also a Korean Catholic saint named Agatha Kim A-gi, 1783-1839. She was born into a pagan family and was married to a very superstitious man. She converted to Catholicism in the face of strong opposition from her husband. Soon she was arrested, imprisoned, tortured, and beheaded.

Feast Dates: August 31 — St. Kimberly; September 20 — St. Agatha Kim A-gi.

Kimberlyn (English double) See Kimberly+Lynn.

Kimbra (variant) See Kimberly.

Kimmi (nickname) See Kimberly.

Kimmie (nickname) See Kimberly.

Kimmy (nickname) See Kimberly.

Kinna (variant) See Kendra.

Kiomayra (Hispanic-American) See Xiomayra.

Kiona "From the Brown Hills" (North American Indian).

Patron Saints: There are several saints that can be called upon to be patrons here. They include Cionia, Cionius, Ciwa, and Ona.

St. Cionia was martyred in ancient Constantinople.

Feast Dates: July 3 — St. Cionia; May 4 — Bl. Richard Hill (see Kipp).

Kip (variant) See Kipp.

Kipp "From the Pointed Hill" (Old English).

Patron Saints: There is no St. Kipp, but there is a saint whose name is derived from Kipp. He is Bl. Richard Hill, who was arrested for being a Catholic priest. He was tried, convicted, and executed in 1590.

Feast Dates: May 4 — Bl. Richard Hill.

Kippie (nickname) See Kipp.

Kippy (nickname) See Kipp.

Kirbee (variant) See Kirby.

Kirbi (variant) See Kirby.

Kirbie (variant) See Kirby.

Kirby "From the Church Village" (Old English).

Patron Saints: In 1580 Father Luke Kirby, a convert to Catholicism and a diocesan priest, went to England and was arrested immediately upon landing and imprisoned for two years. Then he was taken to the Tower of London and placed in the "Scavenger's Daughter," an iron-hoop torture device shaped like a ball. He was placed inside and squeezed until blood came from his nose, hands, and feet. Then he was hanged.

It is also good to know that Kirby, Kirk, and Kilian all mean "church." Thus one can also adopt Bl. Richard Kirkman and St. Killian as patrons.

Feast Dates: May 30 — St. Luke Kirby; July 8 — St. Killian (see Killian).

Kiri "The Sun" (Persian) or "The Female Ruler" (Persian).

Patron Saints: Kiri is a feminine form of Cyrus, and there are about a dozen Sts. Cyrus. One of them was a Christian physician at Canopus, Egypt. When persecution broke out, he fled into the Egypto-Arabian desert. While there he met a catechumen named John. Together, in 312, they went to Alexandria to comfort some imprisoned Christians. They were soon arrested and executed.

The Bible presents us with another Cyrus. He was the pagan emperor who set the Jewish people free from exile in Babylon. In Isaiah 44:28 God calls Cyrus "my shepherd" because he did God's will so well.

Feast Dates: November 1 — St. Cyrus, Holy Persian Emperor; January 31 — Sts. Cyrus and John.

Kirstee (nickname) See Christine, Kiersten.

Kirsten (Danish) See Christine, Kiersten.

Kirsteni (variant) See Christine, Kiersten.

Kirsti (nickname) See Christine, Kiersten.

Kirstie (Scandinavian) See Christine, Kiersten.

Kirstin (Scottish, Scandinavian) See Christine, Kiersten.

Kirsty (nickname) See Christine, Kiersten.

Kirstyn (Greek) See Christine, Kiersten.

Kisha (African-American) See Keisha.

Kishia (African-American) See Keisha.

Kissa (African-American) See Kizzy.

Kissee (African-American) See Kizzy.

Kissia (African-American) See Kizzy.

Kissiah (African-American) See Kizzy.

Kissie (African-American) See Kizzy.

Kit (nickname) See Katherine.

Kitti (nickname) See Katherine.

Kittie (nickname) See Katherine.
Kitty (nickname) See Katherine.
Kizzi (African-American) See Kizzy.
Kizzie (African-American) See Kizzy.
Kizzy "The Favorite One" (Ugandan) or "From the Cassia Tree" (from the Hebrew word Keziah).

Patron Saints: The martyrs of Uganda provide a St. Kizito, 1877-1886. He was one of twenty-two men and boys executed by the king of Uganda when they refused to submit to the king's illicit sexual advances.

Being only nine years old, Kizito was the youngest of the martyrs. A short time before being thrown into prison Kizito had asked to be baptized, but the missionaries did not think he knew enough and denied him. However, with martyrdom imminent, St. Charles Lwanga baptized him in prison the night before the execution. It is not known what Christian name little Kizito took. But it does not matter because his baptism and martyrdom made "Kizito" a Christian name.

Feast Dates: June 3 — St. Kizito.
Klara (Slavic, German, Baltic) See Clare.
Klare (Danish) See Clare.
Klarika (variant) See Claudia.
Klarissa (variant) See Claudia.
Klarrisa (variant) See Claudia.
Klementine (German) See Clementine.
Kodi (American) See Cody.
Kodie (American) See Cody.
Kody (American) See Cody.
Koko (American) See Coco, Kora.
Konstance (Latin) See Constance.
Konstancia (Russian) See Constance.
Konstanze (German) See Constance.
Kora (Greek) See Cora.
Koraina (Hispanic-American) See Cora.
Koral (English) See Coral.
Kordula (American) See Cordelia.

Korella (variant) See Coral.
Koren (variant) See Cora.
Korena (variant) See Cora.
Koressa (English double) See Corissa+Essa.
Koretta (English double) See Cora+Etta.
Korette (American double) See Cora+Ette.
Korey (nickname) See Cora, Coral.
Kori (American) See Cora.
Korie (nickname) See Cora.
Korin (variant) See Katherine.
Korina (Greek) See Cora.
Korinna (American) See Cora.
Korinne (American) See Cora.
Korisa (American) See Corissa.
Korissa (American) See Corissa.
Korra (American) See Cora.
Korri (nickname) See Cora.
Korrie (nickname) See Cora.
Korrine (American) See Cora.
Korry (American) See Cora.
Kortney (American) See Courtney.
Kortnie (American) See Courtney.
Kory (nickname) See Cora, Coral.
Kotryna (Lithuanian) See Katherine.
Kourtney (variant) See Courtney.
Kricket (American) See Cricket.
Kriestan (variant) See Christine, Kiersten.
Kriesten (variant) See Christine, Kiersten.
Krin (German) See Katherine.
Kris (variant) See Christiana, Christine, Christy.
Krissie (nickname, variant) See Christine, Christy.
Krissten (variant) See Christiana, Christine, Kiersten.
Krissy (variant) See Christine, Christy.
Krista (American, German, Czech, Estonian) See Christine, Christy, Crystal.
Kristabel (French double) See Christine+Belle.
Kristabelle (French-American double) See Christine+Belle.

Kristal (American) See Christine, Crystal.

Kristan (American) See Christiana, Christine.

Kristee (nickname) See Christine, Christy, Crystal.

Kristel (Latin) See Christine, Crystal.

Kristen (Norwegian) See Christiana, Christine.

Kristi (nickname) See Christine, Christy, Crystal.

Kristie (nickname) See Christine, Christy, Crystal.

Kristin (Norwegian) See Christiana, Christine.

Kristina (Czech, Swedish, Lithuanian) See Christiana, Christine.

Kristine (Latvian) See Christiana, Christine.

Kristle (American) See Christine, Crystal.

Kristmelly (Hispanic-American double) See Christine+Melanie.

Krisztina (Hungarian) See Christine, Crystal.

Krystabel (American double) See Christa+Belle.

Krystabelle (American double) See Christa+Belle.

Krystal (American) See Christine, Crystal.

Krystalie (nickname) See Christine, Christy, Crystal.

Krystalle (American) See Christine, Crystal.

Krystee (nickname) See Christine, Christy, Crystal.

Krystel (Latin) See Christine, Christy, Crystal.

Krysti (nickname) See Christine, Christy, Crystal.

Krystie (nickname) See Christine, Christy, Crystal.

Krystin (Greek) See Christy, Christine.

Krystina (variant) See Christiana, Christine.

Krystle (variant) See Christine, Crystal.

Krysty (nickname) See Christine, Christy, Crystal.

Krystyn (American) See Christiana, Christine.

Krystyna (Polish) See Christiana, Christine.

Kwanza "The First Harvest" (African-American) or "The Firstborn" (African-American).

Patron Saints: The fact that *kwanza* means "firstborn" leads to the finest patron anyone can have. St. Paul teaches that Jesus is "the first-born of all creation" (Colossians 1:15).

Feast Dates: All Sundays — Jesus the Firstborn of All Creation (see Winona); June 9 — St. Prima (see Prima).

Kwasi "Born on Sunday" (African).

Patron Saints: St. Sunday is from Campagna, Italy. In 304 she was arrested, tortured, and finally put to death by decapitation.

Feast Dates: July 6 — St. Sunday.

Kyla "The Graceful One" (Irish Gaelic) or "The Handsome One" (Irish) or "From the Woods" (Scottish Gaelic).

Patron Saints: St. Kyle (also known as Kenocha) was a Scottish nun who died in 1007. It also helps to know that Kyle can mean "the handsome one." This is the same meaning as Kenneth (also known as Canice).

Kenneth was an abbot. First, he attached himself to St. Cadoc in Wales, then he became a disciple of St. Mobhi and then St. Finnian in Ireland. Later, he lived with St. Columba at the monastery of Iona and went with him to convert King Brude. He died in 599. He is patron of Kilkenny.

Feast Dates: March 25 — St. Kyle; October 11 — St. Kenneth.

Kyle (variant) See Kyla.
Kylee (American double) See Kyla+Leigh.
Kyleen (variant) See Kyla.
Kylen (variant) See Kyla.
Kylene (variant) See Kyla.
Kyley (American double) See Kyla+Leigh.
Kylie (nickname) See Kyla.

Kylila (Arabic) See Kalila.
Kylyn (American double) See Kyla+ Lynn.
Kym (English) See Kimberly.
Kynthia (American) See Cynthia, Hyacinth.
Kyra (Greek) See Lady, Martha.

La "The" (French, Spanish, Italian feminine article).

Patron Saints: The French feminine article *la* (which is also a feminine personal pronoun for "she") is much preferred by modern African-American families when building female names, and sometimes for male names. Some examples are LaBlanche, Ladora, LaJune, Lafay, LaToya, and Lakeisha. In the late 1990s African-Americans began to replace "La" with "Sha," which was their own invention. Still later they began substituting both with "Na."

Feast Dates: A patron can usually be found for the name that follows "La" (see Sha, Na).

Labhaoise (Irish) See Louise.

Lacee (variant) See Lacey, Larissa.

Lacey "From the Lascius Estate" (Norman French) or "The Cheerful One" (nickname for Larissa).

Patron Saints: There are two English martyrs with the name of Lacey. The first, William Lacey, was a married man from Yorkshire who converted to Catholicism. Because of this, he and his family were persecuted for fourteen years. After his wife died from these hardships, William traveled to France and was ordained a priest. He returned to England as a missionary and was hanged, drawn, and quartered in 1582.

The second, Brian Lacey, was a layman who was executed by the British government in 1591 simply because he insisted upon being a practicing Catholic.

Feast Dates: August 22 — Bl. William Lacey of Horton; December 10 — Bl. Brian Lacey.

Laci (Latin) See Lacey, Larissa.

Lacie (Latin) See Lacey, Larissa.

Lacrecia (variant) See Leticia.

Lacy (Greek) See Lacey, Larissa.

Ladee (English) See Lady.

Ladie (variant) See Lady.

Ladiedra (African-American double) See La+Deidre.

Ladina (African-American double) See La+Dina/Lady+Ina.

Ladonna (African-American double) See La+Donna.

Lady "The Well-Bred Woman" (Middle English) or "The Wife" (English).

Patron Saints: There are about twenty Sts. Lady. However, in ancient Rome they were called *matrona*, the Latin word for "lady." One St. Lady worked as a servant in the home of a rich Jewish woman at Thessalonica in Roman times. When it was discovered that she was a Christian, her mistress turned her over to government authorities who beat her to death with a stick in 304.

Also keep in mind that the name Martha means "lady," and there are two dozen Sts. Martha.

Feast Dates: March 15 — St. Lady, also known as Matrona; July 29 — St. Martha (see Martha).

Laetitia (Italian) See Leticia.

LaFalice (African-American double) See La+Felicia.

Lafiette "From the Beech Tree Grove" (African-American form of Lafayette).

Patron Saints: There are three ancient Sts. Fay (also known as Faith). One, a teenager, was brought before a pagan judge in about 250. First, he asked her name. She signed herself with the cross and answered, "My name is Faith and I will try to live as I have been named." He ordered her tied to a red-hot bed and killed.

Feast Dates: October 6 — St. Faith of Agen; July 10 — St. Etto, also known as Hetto (see Ette).

Lainey (nickname) See Elaine, Helen.

LaJuan (African-American double) See La+Juan.

LaJune (African-American double) See La+June.

Lakayla (African-American double) See La+Kayla.

Lakeesha (African-American double) See La+Keisha/Leticia.

Lakeisha (African-American double) See La+Keisha/Leticia.

Lakeya (African-American double) See La+Kiah.

Lakendra (African-American double) See La+Kendra.

Lakenya (African-American double) See La+Kenya.

Lakisha (African-American double) See La+Keisha/Leticia.

Lakishia (African-American double) See La+Keisha/Leticia.

Lakota (North American Indian) See Dakota.

Lali (Spanish) See Lulani.

Lalita "The Talkative One (Greek) or "The Charming Candid One" (Sanskrit).

Patron Saints: Lalita means about the same thing as Eula, and there is a St. Eulalia.

Feast Dates: December 10 — St. Eulalia of Merida (see Eula).

Lallie (English) See Eula, Lalita.

Lamonica (African-American double) See La+Monica.

Lana "The Bright, Fair One" (Irish Gaelic) or "The Light, Airy One" (Hawaiian) or "The Light" (variant form of Helen through Aileen) or "From the Narrow Road" (variant of Lane).

Patron Saints: Lana can be a variant form of Alana, Helen, or Lane. This leads to many patrons.

Feast Dates: September 12 — SG Frances Allen (see Alana); August 18 — St. Helena (see Helen).

Lanae (variant) See Alana, Lana.

Lanah (African-American) See Alana, Lana.

Landa (Basque) See Mary.

Landra (German, Spanish) See Consuelo.

Lane "From the Narrow Road or Way" (Middle English).

Patron Saints: Three saints can qualify as patrons. The first is St. Frances Lanel, 1745-1798. She was a member of the Ursuline community in France during the French Revolution. She insisted on teaching the children their religion, which was contrary to the Revolution. She was guillotined at age fifty-three.

The second is Bl. William Way of Devon, who was ordained a Catholic priest in 1586 and then sent to England. He was executed in 1588 for being a Catholic priest.

But the finest patron of them all is Jesus Christ, who is the Way, the Truth, and the Light.

Feast Dates: June 26 — St. Frances Lanel; September 23 — Bl. William Way of Devon.

Lanetta (American double) See Lynn+Etta.

Lanette (American double) See Lynn+Ette.

Laney (nickname) See Lane, Leilani.

Lani (nickname) See Lane, Lanisha, Leilani.

Lanie (nickname) See Elaine, Helen, Lane, Lanisha, Leilani.

Lanieash (African-American) See Lane, Lanisha.

Lanisha "From the Narrow Way+The Female" (English form of Lane+Hebrew form of Isha).

Patron Saints: Lanisha is a combination of Lane and Isha, which means "the female from the narrow way." This leads to a number of patrons.

Feast Dates: June 26 — St. Lanel (see Lane); December 24 — Sts. Adam and Eve (see Isha).

Lanita (Spanish) See Lane.

Lanna (variant) See Alana, Lana.

Lanni (nickname) See Lana, Lane.

Lanny (nickname) See Lana, Lane.

Laportia (African-American double) See La+Portia.

Laqueena (African-American double) See La+Queen.

Laquetha (African-American double) See La+Queta.

Laquiana (African-American triple) See La+Kiah+Na.

Lara (Russian) See Larissa, Laura.

Laraine "The Seabird [Gull]" (Latin) or "From the Place of the Warrior" (Old German).

Patron Saints: A candidate for patron is St. Margaret of Lorraine, 1463-1521. She was the daughter of Duke Ferri of Lorraine and married Duke René of Alençon at the age of twenty-five. Four years later she was a widow with three small children. She occupied herself by managing the ducal estate and practicing a life of prayer. After her children had grown, she moved to a convent and cared for the sick. Sometime later, she and a group of friends founded a Poor Clare convent and she became a religious sister.

Feast Dates: November 6 — St. Margaret of Lorraine.

Larane (variant) See Laraine.

LaReina "The+Queen" (Spanish).

Patron Saints: The Blessed Virgin makes the finest patron.

Feast Dates: August 22 — The Blessed Virgin Mary, Queen of Heaven (see Queen).

Lareina (variant) See LaReina.

Larena (variant) See LaReina.

Lari (variant) See Laura.

Larissa "The Laughing Cheerful One" (Greek).

Patron Saints: Two saints with a very similar name can be pressed into service. One St. Lassar is remembered for being a holy single lady who lived at Cill-Arcalgach in Westmeath. The second St. Lassar was a holy Irish nun who followed Sts. Finan and Kiernan in the 500s.

Feast Dates: August 20 — St. Lassar; March 29 — St. Lassar.

Lark "The Skylark" (Middle English).

Patron Saints: There is an English martyr with a name similar to this. In 1544 Bl. John Larke was executed for treason by the British government because he insisted upon serving his people as a Catholic priest.

Feast Dates: March 7 — Bl. John Larke of Chelsea.

Larke (variant) See Lark.

LaRoux "The+Redheaded One" (French).

Patron Saints: Ann Joseph Leroux, 1747-1794, became a religious sister during the French Revolution. When the government closed her convent, she and the other sisters fled to safety. However, in 1794 they returned and were immediately arrested and jailed. They were charged with the unlawful return and reopening of a convent. Eventually they were found guilty and sentenced to death.

Feast Dates: October 23 — St. Josephine Leroux.

Larra (variant) See Larissa.

Larsina (Norwegian) See Laura, Lauren.

Laryssa (variant) See Larissa.

Lashawna (African-American double) See La+Shawna.

Latanya (African-American double) See La+Tanya.

Latasha (African-American) See La+Tasha.

Latasha (English) See Leticia.

Latashia (variant) See Leticia.

Lateefah "The Gentle, Pleasant One" (North African) or "The Comedian" (Arabic).

Patron Saints: Africa means "pleasant one," and there is a St. Genesius who is patron of comedians.

Feast Dates: August 26 — St. Genesius (see Thalia); August 5 — St. Afra (see Africa).

Latia (variant) See Leticia.

Latifa (African-American) See Lateefah.

Latiffah (African-American) See Lateefah.

Latisha (variant) See Leticia, Patricia.

Latonia (African-American double) See La+Tonya.

Latoria (African-American double) See La+Victoria.

LaToya (African-American double) See La+Toya.

Latoye (African-American double) See La+Toya.

Latoyia (African-American double) See La+Toya.

Latreece (African-American) See Leticia, Patricia.

Latreese (African-American) See Leticia, Patricia.

Latreshia (African-American) See Leticia, Patricia.

Latrice (African-American) See Leticia, Patricia.

Latricia (African-American) See Leticia, Patricia.

Laura "The One Crowned with Laurel Leaves" (Latin).

Patron Saints: There are two Sts. Laura and about a half-dozen female saints with names like Laurentia, Laurina, and Lauriana. Another patron is the Blessed Virgin, under the title of Our Lady of Loretto.

Laura Vicuña, 1891-1904, was the daughter of an upper-class father in Chile, but he died when Laura was only three years old. Soon her mother became a live-in mistress for a rich man, Señor Mora, who supported both the mother and child in return for sexual favors.

This situation began to bother Laura when she was eight, so she was sent away to a Catholic school, where she prayed for her mother. Then Señor Mora began making drunken advances toward Laura when she was home. When she refused him, he canceled her tuition. At the age of twelve, she offered her life for her mother's conversion. The rich man kicked and whipped her so hard she died from the injuries. Laura's mother returned to the practice of the faith after Laura's death at the age of thirteen.

Feast Dates: January 29 — SG Laura Vicuña.

Lauraine (African-American) See Laura, Laurentia.

Laural (variant) See Laura, Laurentia.

Lauralee (American double) See Laura+Leigh.

Lauranell (African-American double) See Laura+Nelly.

Laure (French) See Laura.

Laureana (Spanish double) See Laura+Ana.

Laureen (French) See Laura, Lauren.

Laurel (Latin) See Laura, Laurentia.

Laurella (variant double) See Laura/Laurentia+Ella.

Laurelle (variant double) See Laura/Laurentia+Elle.

Lauren "The One Crowned with Laurel Leaves" (English).

Patron Saints: Lauren is an alternate form of Laura. A religious priest by the name of Loran made his home in County Mayo, Ireland, and was a disciple of St. Patrick.

Feast Dates: August 30 — St. Loran.

Laurena (variant) See Laura, Laurel, Laurentia.

Laurence (French) See Laura, Lauren, Laurentia.

Laurencia (Spanish) See Laurentia.

Laurene (variant) See Laura, Lauren, Laurentia.

Laurentia "The One Crowned with Laurel Leaves" (Latin).

Patron Saints: There are several Sts. Laurentia. One of them died for the Catholic faith in ancient Rome.

Feast Dates: May 21 — St. Laurentia.

Laurette (French double) See Laura+Ette.

Lauri (English) See Laura, Laurentia.

Laurice (Czech, Greek) See Laura.

Laurie (English) See Laura, Laurentia.

Laurina (Spanish, Italian) See Laura, Lauren.

Lauryn (English) See Lauren.

Laveda (African-American) See Lavinia.

Lavena (Latin) See Lavinia.

Laverine (variant) See Laverne.

Laverna (variant) See Laverne.

Laverne "The+Springlike One" (Latin) or "From the Alder Tree Grove" (French).

Patron Saints: A patron can be found in the meaning of the word "springlike." Spring is the time when nature wakens to new life. It is the season when Easter is celebrated. For this reason the Spanish called Easter "Florida," or the "Feast of Flowers." Catholicism often uses "spring" and "garden" images to speak of the miracle of new life in Christ. Thus Jesus is the "Tree of Eternal Life" growing in Paradise.

The "garden" is symbolic of his mother, Mary, in her motherhood. Mary has long been recognized as the "Paradise Planted by God," "Ever Green and Fruitful," "God's Eden," "The Unplowed Field of Heaven's Bread," "A Garden Enclosed," the "Forth-Bringer of God," and the "Springtime of New Life."

Feast Dates: January 1 — The Blessed Virgin Mary, Garden of God; April 30 — St. Adjutor of Vernon (see Verne).

LaVerne (variant) See Laverne.

Lavina (Latin) See Lavinia.

Lavine (variant) See Lavinia.

Lavinia "Purified One" (Latin) or "The Wife" (Spanish).

Patron Saints: There is one ancient saint with a very similar name who can be adopted. St. Laventius was one of a group of martyrs who died in ancient Cappadocia.

Feast Dates: July 12 — St. Laventius.

Lavinie (variant) See Lavinia.

Lavista (Spanish) See La+Vista.

Lavonia (African-American double) See La+Yvonne.

Lavra (Czech, Greek) See Laura.

Lawanda (African-American double) See La+Wanda.

Layla (Hebrew, Arabic) See Leila, Lila, Lilith.

Layne (English) See Lane.

Layney (nickname) See Elaine, Helen.

Le "The [or To or Him]" (French) or "The [or Her or You or Them or To Her or To You]" (Italian) or "The Weary One" (short form of Leah) or "From the Meadow" (short form of Leigh).

Patron Saints: "Le" in French and Italian can be used as a definite article, personal pronoun, etc., and is used in many African-American names for both males and females. In its own right "Le" serves as a short form of Leah and Leigh.

Feast Dates: December 24 — St. Leah (see Leah); August 30 — Bl. Richard Leigh (see Leigh).

Lea (variant) See Leah.

Leah "The Weary One" (Hebrew).

Patron Saints: There are two known Sts. Leah. One is provided by the Bible and the other by Christian tradition. And there is one English martyr surnamed Leigh.

The biblical Leah lived in about 1700 B.C. The Jewish patriarch Jacob worked six years for Laban in order to marry Rachel and was tricked into marrying Leah. Only later did he gain Rachel for his own. Leah was rather plain and less favored by Jacob. However, God blessed her and allowed her to give birth to six of Jacob's twelve sons (Reuben, Simeon, Levi, Judah, Issachar, Zebulun) and a daughter, Dinah.

Feast Dates: December 24 — St. Leah; August 30 — Bl. Richard Leigh (see Leigh).

Lean (Irish Gaelic) See Helen.

Leana (variant double) See Juliana, Leandra, Leanne, Julie/Leah/Leigh+ Ann.

Leandora (Greek) See Leandra.

Leandra "Like a Lioness" (Latin).

Patron Saints: This name leads to a handful of Sts. Leander. One of them, upon reaching adulthood, became a Benedictine monk and in 579 was elected to be bishop of Seville, then fled into exile.

He returned to Spain just in time to be sent into exile again, this time for one year. Upon his second return, he held Synods to reform the Spanish liturgy and insist that the Nicene Creed be recited at Mass. He was also a gifted orator, and one of his great victories was the conversion of the Spanish Visigoths to the Catholic Church. He brought them into the Church through the sheer force of his logic.

Feast Dates: February 27 — St. Leander.

Leane (variant double) See Juliana Leandra, Leanne, Julie/Leah/Leigh+ Ann.

Leann (variant double) See Juliana, Leandra, Leanne, Julie/Leah/Leigh+ Ann.

Leanna (variant double) See Juliana, Leandra, Leanne, Julie/Leah/Leigh+ Ann.

Leanne "Like a Lioness" (English).

Patron Saints: Leanne can be a nickname for Leandra and Juliana. Furthermore, Leanne can be a combination of two names: Lee plus Ann. This leads to one Bl. Leigh and about two dozen Sts. Ann. Finally, there is one St. Lean who is simply remembered as an "Irish saint."

Feast Dates: June 5 — St. Lean; August 30 — Bl. Leigh (see Leigh); July 26 — St. Anne (see Ann).

Leanor (Spanish) See Eleanor, Helen.

Leanora (Greek) See Eleanor, Helen.

Leanore (Greek) See Eleanor, Helen.

Lecia (nickname) See Felicia, Leticia.

Leda (Greek, Spanish) See Lady.

Lee (nickname) See Leah, Leigh.

Leeann (variant double) See Juliana, Leandra, Leanne, Leah/Leigh+Ann.

Leeanna (variant double) See Juliana, Leandra, Leanne, Leah/Leigh+Ann.

Leeanne (variant double) See Juliana, Leandra, Leanne, Leah/Leigh+Ann.

Leela (variant) See Leila, Leilani.

Leena (variant) See Eleanor, Helen.
Leesa (variant) See Elizabeth, Lisa.
Leeza (variant) See Elizabeth, Lisa.
Lehannah (African-American double) See Le+Hannah.
Leia (variant) See Leah, Leigh, Leila.
Leigh "From the Meadow" (Old English).

Patron Saints: There is an English martyr who can serve as a patron. Bl. Richard Leigh, 1561-1588, traveled to Rheims, France, and Rome, Italy, to study for the Catholic priesthood. After ordination in Rome in 1586 he was sent to the English missions. He traveled under the alias of "Bart." However, he was soon caught and banished from the country and he immediately returned and was convicted of being a Catholic priest. He was hanged, drawn, and quartered at Tyburn at the age of twenty-seven.

Feast Dates: August 30 — Bl. Richard Leigh.
Leigha (variant) See Leigh.
Leighanna (English double) See Leanne, Leah/Leigh+Ann.
Leighanne (English double) See Leanne, Leah/Leigh+Ann.
Leila "One as Dark as Night" (Arabic, Hebrew).

Patron Saints: There is a saint whose name sounds almost like Leila. Lelia was the daughter of Sedna and a niece of Bloid, king of Thomond. She lived in Limerick in Ireland and is remembered for dedicating her single life to God in the mid-600s.

Feast Dates: August 11 — St. Lelia.
Leilah (variant) See Leila, Leilani.
Leilani "The Flower+The Heavenly One" (Hawaiian double).

Patron Saints: There are three saints with similar-sounding names who can be pressed into service. They are Sts. Lie, Lelia, and Lanel. Furthermore, the few Sts. Flora whose name means "flower" and Sts. Celestina whose name means "heaven" can also be pressed into service.

Feast Dates: May 17 — St. Lie (see Lorelei); June 26 — St. Frances Lanel (see Lane); August 11 — St. Lelia (see Leila); May 19 — St. Celeste (see Celeste); November 24 — St. Flora (see Flora).
Leisha (variant) See Alicia, Leticia.
Leishia (variant) See Leticia.
Lela (variant) See Leila.
Lelah (variant) See Leila.
Leli (Swiss) See Magdalen.
Lelia (Greek, Spanish) See Eula, Leila.
Lemona (African-American double) See Le+Mona.
Lena (nickname) See Adelaide, Alena, Cathlene, Eleanora, Helena, Leilani, Magdalena, Marlena.
Lene (nickname) See Arleen, Cathlene, Kathleen, Madlin, Magdalene, Marleen, Nyleen.
Lenette (variant double) See La+Ette, Lynnette.
Lenka (Slavic) See Helen.
Lenna (nickname) See Madeline.
Lenor (variant) See Eleanor, Helen.
Lenora (Spanish, Portuguese) See Eleanor, Helen, Leonore.
Lenore (variant) See Eleanor, Helen.
Lenuta (Romanian) See Helen.
Leoine (variant) See Leona.
Leola (African-American double) See Leona+La.
Leona "Like a Lion" (French, Spanish).

Patron Saints: There are six saints whose names are variations of Leona. One is St. Leonella. She was the grandmother of a set of triplets who are also recognized as saints. In her old age Leonella embraced martyrdom. She was beheaded at Cappadocia in Asia Minor. Her courage and dedication led to the conversion of a pagan named Junilla. They share the same feast day.

Feast Dates: March 15 — St. Leonella.

Leonarda "The One Brave as a Lioness" (German).

Patron Saints: Leonarda is the feminine form of Leonard, and there are a dozen Sts. Leonard. One of them served as a holy abbot in France in the sixth century.

Feast Dates: December 30 — St. Leonard.

Leone (Lithuanian) See Leona.

Leonella (Italian double) See Leandra, Leona+Ella.

Leonelle (Russian, Ukrainian) See Leandra, Leona.

Leonia (English) See Leona.

Leonie (French) See Leona.

Leonne (French) See Leona.

Leonne (variant) See Leandra.

Leonor (Spanish, Portuguese) See Eleanor, Helen, Leonore.

Leonora (Italian) See Eleanor, Helen, Leonore.

Leonore "The Light" (English).

Patron Saints: Leonore is a variant of Helen, which leads to many Sts. Helen for patrons. Furthermore, there is one known St. Leonore. He is sometimes known as St. Lunaire.

Feast Dates: July 1 — St. Lunaire (see Monday); August 18 — St. Helena (see Helen).

Leontine "The Lionlike One" (Latin).

Patron Saints: There are a half-dozen saints with this name. Leontine was a citizen of Carthage, Africa, and was probably a black woman. Because she refused to renounce her Catholic faith, she was tortured during the reign of the Arian heretic king Huneric. However, she gained release from prison and died later.

Feast Dates: December 6 — St. Leontine.

Leontyne (Latin) See Leontine.

Leora (Greek) See Eleanor, Helen, Leanore.

Leroux (variant) See LaRoux.

LeSheryl (African-American double) See Le+Sheryl.

Lesley (variant) See Leslie.

Lesli (variant) See Leslie.

Leslie "The Gray Fortress Dweller" (Scottish Gaelic) or "The One Who Leases" (Teutonic).

Patron Saints: The ancient spelling of Leslie is Lios-laith, and one ancient saint has a name that has a spelling that is similar. She is St. Lioba, an Anglo-Saxon nun and relative of St. Boniface. She seems to have corresponded with kings Pepin and Charlemagne of France. She became a hermit near the end of her life. Also note that the meaning of the phrase "gray fortress" leads to a far more powerful patron.

Feast Dates: All Sundays — Jesus, Our Fortress (see Shayla); September 26 — St. Lioba.

Lesly (Scottish) See Leslie.

Lesya (nickname) See Alexandra.

Leta (variant) See Lady, Leticia.

Lethia (variant) See Leticia.

Leticia "The Joyful One" (Spanish, English) or "The Joys of Mary" (Latin).

Patron Saints: There are a few ancient Sts. Leticia, but in Roman times they spelled their names as Laetus and Laetissima. St. Leticia was martyred in ancient Nicomedia.

Feast Dates: April 27 — St. Leticia, also known as Laetissima.

Letisha (variant) See Leticia.

Letizia (Italian) See Leticia.

Letreece (variant) See Leticia.

Letrice (variant) See Leticia.

Lett (nickname) See Leticia.

Letta (nickname) See Leticia.
Letti (nickname) See Leticia.
Lettice (Polish) See Leticia.
Lettie (nickname) See Leticia.
Letty (nickname) See Leticia.
Letycja (Polish) See Leticia.
Levana "The Rising Sun" (Latin).
> *Patron Saints:* There is one St. Levan who was a medieval Irish priest with some writing ability.
> *Feast Dates:* August 9 — St. Levan.
Levisa (African-American double) See Le+Visa.
Levita (African-American double) See Le+Vita.
Levona "The Spicy One" (Hebrew).
> *Patron Saints:* The word for "spice" in Latin is *condimentum*. Therefore, an English priest known as St. Condetus can be adopted. He preached the Gospel in France and then became a hermit. He died in 651.
> *Feast Dates:* February 28 — St. Condetus.
Lewanna "The Beaming White Moon" (Hebrew).
> *Patron Saints:* There is a saint with a similar-sounding name. St. Lewina was martyred by pagan Saxon invaders in medieval England.
> *Feast Dates:* July 24 — St. Lewina.
Lewina (English) See Lewanna.
Lexie (nickname) See Alexis.
Lexis (nickname) See Alexis.
Leya (Spanish) See Faith.
Leyia (variant) See Leila.
Lezlie (American) See Leslie.
Lhizz (American) See Liz.
Lia (Spanish) See Leah.
Liaha (variant) See Leah.
Lian (variant double) See Juliana, Leandra, Leanne, Julie/Leah/Leigh+ Ann.
Liana (American) See Lian.
Liana (Hispanic-American double) See Lia+Ana.

Liana (Romanian) See Lillian.
Liane (variant double) See Lian.
Liann (variant double) See Lian.
Lianna (variant double) See Lian.
Lianne (variant double) See Lian.
Lib (nickname) See Elizabeth.
Libbey (nickname) See Elizabeth.
Libbi (nickname) See Elizabeth.
Libbie (nickname) See Elizabeth.
Libby (nickname) See Elizabeth.
Liberty "The Free One" (Latin).
> *Patron Saints:* There are two Sts. Liberty (also known as Libertus). One of them was killed by the pagan Norsemen before a church altar. He was trying to flee a pagan invasion in medieval times.
> *Feast Dates:* July 14 — St. Liberty.
Licha (Spanish) See Alice.
Lici (Spanish) See Alice.
Licia (Spanish) See Lucia.
Lida (variant) See Lady, Leticia, Merry.
Liddi (Spanish, Polish, Italian) See Lydia.
Liddy (nickname) See Lydia.
Lidia (Spanish, Polish, Italian) See Lydia.
Lidija (Russian) See Lydia.
Liela (variant) See Leila.
Liese (German) See Alice, Elizabeth, Lisa.
Liesel (German) See Alice, Elizabeth, Lisa.
Lieta (African-American double) See Lisa+Etta.
Ligia (Spanish) See Melody.
Lil (nickname) See Lillian.
Lila "The Gentle One" (short form of Delilah) or "Creature of the Night" (short form of Lilith) or "The Lilac" (Persian).
> *Patron Saints:* There are a few saints who can be adopted.
> *Feast Dates:* August 11 — St. Lelia (see Lelia); March 2 — St. Lily (see Lillian).
Lilac (variant) See Lelia, Lillian.
Lili (German) See Lillian.

Lilia (Italian, Portuguese, Spanish, Slavic) See Lillian.

Lilian (variant) See Lillian.

Liliana (Italian, Spanish, Slavic) See Lillian.

Lilianne (French double) See Lily+Anne.

Lilias (Scottish) See Lillian.

Lilibeth (African-American double) See Lily+Beth.

Lilija (African-American) See Lillian.

Liliosa (Spanish) See Lillian.

Lilith "Creature of the Night" (Arabic, Hebrew).

Patron Saints: There are a couple of saints who can be adopted as patrons.

Feast Dates: March 2 — St. Lily (see Lillian).

Liliya (American) See Lillian.

Lilla (variant) See Lillian.

Lilli (German) See Lillian.

Lillian "A Lily Flower" (Latin).

Patron Saints: There is one St. Liliosa and one St. Lily. St. Liliosa died a martyr in Cordova, Spain. A male St. Lily was known as the "Servant of David." He was one of the favorite disciples of St. David of Wales.

In addition, the few Sts. Susan can be pressed into service because Susan means "lily." And finally, it helps to know that Lillian is a variant form of Elizabeth in Scandinavia.

Feast Dates: July 27 — St. Liliosa; March 2 — St. Lily.

Lillie (nickname) See Lillian.

Lilly (English) See Lillian.

Lily (Old English) See Lillian.

Lilyan (English) See Lillian.

Lilybet (Cornish) See Elizabeth.

Limari (Hispanic-American double) See Lilia+María.

Lin (nickname) See Belinda, Linda, Lindsay, Lynn.

Lina "The Little One" (English-Latin diminutive suffix for names ending in "Lina") or "From the Pool Below the Waterfall" (variant of Lynn) or "From the Stream" (Old English).

Patron Saints: Besides serving as a diminutive suffix, Lina also serves as a nickname and a proper name by itself. It helps to know that Lina is a Ukrainian form of Helen. Also, there is a St. Lina, who is remembered for being a virgin in ancient Andresey.

Feast Dates: July 5 — St. Lina; November 8 — St. Newlyna (see Lynn).

Lind (nickname) See Belinda, Linda, Lindsay.

Linda "Pretty One" (Spanish) or "Mild One" (German).

Patron Saints: There are a few saints that have Linda as part of their names. They are Sts. Berlindis, Harlindis, and Relindis. There is also a St. Lindru, a virgin who lived in Partois.

St. Berlindis was born at Meerbeke, the daughter of Odolard, the duke of Lothringia and Nona. Her father disinherited her because she refused to drink from the same glass he had drunk from. She had good reason to act in such a manner because her father was a leper. In time, she entered a convent at Moorsel. She later became a hermit. She died in 702.

Feast Dates: February 3 — St. Berlindis; September 22 — St. Lindru.

Lindi (variant) See Belinda, Linda.

Lindie (variant) See Belinda, Linda.

Lindsay "From Linden Tree Island" (Old English) or "From Lincoln's Island" (Old English).

Patron Saints: There is a St. Ethelwin, bishop of Lindsey in the 700s, who was a devoted friend of St. Egbert.

It also helps to know that Lindsey arises out of Lincoln, and this makes two more saints available. They are Bl. Roger

Dickenson of Lincoln and St. Hugh of Lincoln. St. Hugh, 1140-1200, established the first Carthusian charterhouse (similar to a monastery) in England. He also served as bishop of Lincoln. He was very kind to the Jews. He always befriended and defended them.

Feast Dates: May 3 — St. Ethelwin of Lindsey; November 17 — St. Hugh of Lincoln.

Lindsey (English) See Lindsay.

Lindsie (English) See Lindsay.

Lindsy (English) See Lindsay.

Lindy (Spanish) See Belinda, Linda.

Line "The Little One" (English diminutive suffix for names ending in "Line") or "From the Pool Below the Waterfall" (variant of Lynn) or "From the Stream" (Old English).

Patron Saints: Besides serving as a diminutive suffix, Line also serves as a nickname or as a proper name by itself. There is one saint with this name. St. Anne Line grew up in a Protestant family and was disowned when she converted and married a Catholic. In time, her husband, Roger, was arrested because of his religion. In order to escape execution, he went to Flanders, Belgium, and died there in 1594. After her husband fled, Anne spent her time hiding fugitive Catholic priests in her home. She was arrested for doing this in 1601, was tried, found guilty, and sent to the gallows.

Feast Dates: February 27 — St. Anne Line; November 8 — St. Newlyna (see Lynn).

Linell (variant) See Lynn.

Linet (variant) See Lynn.

Linetta (American double) See Lynn+Etta.

Linette (French double) See Lynn+Ette.

Linn (variant) See Lynn, Madeline.

Linne (variant) See Lynn.

Linnea "From the Lime Tree" (Old Norse) or "From the Pond" (Gaelic variant of Lynn).

Patron Saints: Saints named Lina, Line, Lynn, and Lynna may be adopted here as patrons.

Feast Dates: February 27 — St. Anne Line (see Line).

Linnell (variant double) See Lynn+Elle.

Linnet (English double) See Lynn+Ette.

Linzy (American) See Lindsay.

Liona (variant) See Leona.

Lionia (variant) See Leona.

Lira (variant) See Elvira.

Lis (Scandinavian) See Elizabeth.

Lisa "Consecrated to God" (Italian, Scandinavian form of Elizabeth) or "Honeybee" (nickname for Melissa).

Patron Saints: Lisa is recognized as a variant of Elizabeth. This leads to two dozen Sts. Elizabeth.

Feast Dates: November 5 — St. Elizabeth (see Elizabeth).

Lisabeth (Swedish) See Elizabeth.

Lisandra (variant) See Lysandra, Melisandra.

Lisbet (Swedish) See Elizabeth.

Lisbeth (French) See Elizabeth.

Lise (French) See Elizabeth, Lisa.

Liselotte (variant double) See Lisa+Ette/Lottie.

Liseta (Spanish) See Elizabeth.

Lisetta (variant double) See Elizabeth, Lisa+Etta.

Lisette (Hispanic-American double) See Lisa+Ette.

Lisha (nickname) See Alice.

Lissa (nickname) See Alice, Elizabeth, Larissa, Melissa.

Lissandra (Hispanic-American double) See Lisa+Sandra.

Lissette (French double) See Elizabeth+Ette.

Lissi (nickname) See Allison, Elyse, Elizabeth.

Lissie (nickname) See Allison, Elyse, Elizabeth.

Lissy (nickname) See Allison, Elyse, Elizabeth.

Lita (Spanish suffix) See Ita.

Liusaidh (Scottish Gaelic) See Lucy.

Livana (Hebrew) See Lewanna.

Livia (Spanish) See Olivia.

Livvi (nickname) See Olivia.

Livvie (nickname) See Olivia.

Livvy (nickname) See Olivia.

Liz (nickname) See Elizabeth, Lisa.

Liza (English) See Elizabeth, Lisa.

Lizabeth (French) See Elizabeth.

Lizbeth (English) See Elizabeth.

Lizette (Hispanic-American double) See Lisa+Ette.

Lizzie (nickname) See Elizabeth, Lisa.

Lizzy (nickname) See Elizabeth, Lisa.

Llesenia (Hispanic-American) See Yesenia.

Llessna (Hispanic-American) See Elizabeth.

Llora (Hispanic-American) See Laura, Lora.

Lluvia (Hispanic-American) See Love.

Lois (English) See Louise.

Loise (English) See Louise.

Lola "The Woman Warrior" (Spanish for Louise) or "The Sorrowful One" (Spanish for Dolores).

Patron Saints: Scholars identify the source of Lola as Dolores or Louise. If one chooses Dolores, then one is led directly to the Blessed Virgin, Mother of Sorrows. If one chooses Louise, then a few more patrons surface. It is also helpful to know that there is one St. Lollia. She was the sister of Sts. Urbanus and Proba. Because of her Catholic faith she was tortured and then beheaded during the reign of the Roman emperor Maximinus.

Feast Dates: June 23 — St. Lollia; March 15 — St. Louise de Marillac (see Louise).

Loleta (Spanish double) See Louise/ Dolores+Ita.

Lolita (Spanish double) See Louise/ Dolores+Ita.

Loll (variant) See Lola.

Lollia (variant) See Lola.

Loma "The One from the Ridge" (Spanish).

Patron Saints: A nephew of St. Patrick, St. Loman was the first bishop of Trim, Ireland.

Feast Dates: February 17 — St. Loman.

Lon (nickname) See Apollonia, Lona, Loni.

Lona "The Solitary One" (Old English) or "The Giver of Life [Sun]" (nickname for Apollonia).

Patron Saints: One patron can be found in St. Lon. Another can be found in St. Sola. Remember, *solus* is the Latin word for "solitary."

St. Sola was an Anglo-Saxon priest who became a disciple of St. Boniface. He spent much time in prayer, leading the life of a hermit at the Fulda monastery. When difficult times came, he and a few other companions fled the area and founded a new monastery at Solhofen. He died in 794.

Feast Dates: December 3 — St. Sola; December 5 — St. Lon (see Loni).

Loni "The Solitary One" (Middle English) or "The Giver of Life [Sun]" (short form of Apollonia) or "The Laurel Leaves" (short form of Laurentia) or "Like a Lion" (short form of Leontia).

Patron Saints: Loni, besides being a name in its own right, can also serve as a nickname for Apollonia, Laurentia, Leona, and Leontia. There is at least one patron for each name. And there is one St. Lon. He was from Cillgobhra in medieval Ireland and is simply remembered as an "Irish saint."

Feast Dates: June 24 — St. Lon; May 21 — St. Laurentia (see Laurentia); March 15 — St. Leonella (see Leona).

Lonna (nickname) See Apollonia, Lona, Loni.

Lonnee (nickname) See Apollonia, Lona.

Lonnetta (African-American double) See Apollonia/Lona/Loni+Etta.

Lonnee (nickname) See Apollonia, Lona.

Lonni (nickname) See Apollonia, Lona, Loni.

Lonnie (nickname) See Apollonia, Lona, Loni.

Lonny (nickname) See Apollonia, Lona, Loni.

Lonteshia (African-American double) See Apollonia/Lona/Loni+Tishia.

Lonzella (African-American double) See Apollonia/Lona/Loni+Zella.

Lonzetta (African-American double) See Apollonia/Lona/Loni+Zetta.

Loola (nickname) See Tallulah.

Lora (German) See Laura, Lauren, Loretta.

Lorain (variant) See Laraine.

Loraine (variant) See Laraine.

Loralee (variant) See Lorelei.

Loralie (variant) See Lorelei.

Loralyn (variant) See Lorelei.

Lorea (variant) See Laura, Loretta.

Lorean (variant double) See Laraine, Loreann/Laura/Leonore/Loretta+Ann.

Loreann (variant double) See Laraine, Lorean/Laura/Leonore/Loretta+Ann.

Loreanne (variant double) See Laraine, Lorean/Laura/Leonore/Loretta+Ann.

Loree (nickname) See Laura, Lauren.

Loreen (variant) See Laura, Lauren.

Lorel (variant) See Laurentia.

Lorelei "The Alluring One" (German) or "The One Crowned with Laurel Leaves" (variant form of Laura).

Patron Saints: There is a St. Laura and a St. Lie. Furthermore, as "Lore" can be a shortened form of Lenore, St. Leonore can, in a pinch, fill in as a patron.

St. Lie was born in Savina, France. As a boy, he dedicated himself to chastity for Jesus. Apparently, his relatives disapproved of his commitment and killed him because of it. He was only a boy at the time of his death in 1169.

Feast Dates: May 17 — St. Lie, also known as Laetus; January 29 — St. Laura (see Laura); December 6 — St. Lenore (see Lenore).

Loren (Spanish, Italian, English) See Laura, Lauren.

Lorena (Spanish, Italian) See Laura, Lauren.

Lorene (Spanish, Italian) See Laura, Lauren.

Lorenza (Spanish, Italian) See Laura, Lauren, Laurentia.

Loreta (Spanish) See Loretta.

Loretta "The One Crowned with Laurel Leaves+The Little One" (English double).

Patron Saints: There are two Sts. Laura and a few Sts. Laurentia, Laurina, and Lauriana who can serve as patrons. But the best patron is the Blessed Virgin Mary, under the title of "Our Lady of Loreto." According to Catholic tradition, the home of the Holy Family in Nazareth was moved through the air by angels in 1291 to Tersato, a place in Italy owned by a nobleman named Loreta. It seems that God, knowing that destruction was to be unleashed soon upon Palestine, ordered his angels to remove Jesus' Nazareth home to safety.

Investigations conducted soon after the appearance of the house in Loreto showed that its dimensions and construction were identical to that of a home in Nazareth that had mysteriously disappeared. Catholic tradition knows no mention of this house before 1315. In that year it was officially recognized as the Church of St. Mary of Loreto (Mother of Grace). Slowly a few prayers said in honor of Mary gained popularity at this shrine-house. By 1400 the prayers were known as the Litany of Loreto. In 1586 the house was made a cathedral, and in 1929 it was made a basilica.

Feast Dates: January 1 — The Blessed Virgin Mary, Our Lady of Loreto, Mother of Mercy. Under this title, the Blessed Virgin is patron of aviators, flyers, home builders, and lamp makers.

Lorette (English) See Laura.

Lorey (nickname) See Laraine, Laura, Laurentia, Loretta.

Lori (nickname) See Laraine, Laura, Laurentia, Lorelei, Loretta.

Loriann (American double) See Laraine/Laura/Laurentia/Lorean/Leonore/Loretta+Ann.

Lorie (nickname) See Laraine, Laura, Laurentia, Loretta.

Lorilee (variant double) See Laura+Leigh.

Lorilyn (variant double) See Laura+Lynn.

Lorinda (Spanish) See Laura.

Lorine (Portuguese) See Laraine, Laura, Lauren.

Lorita (Spanish double) See Laura+Ita.

Lorna (English) See Laura, Lauren.

Lorne (English) See Laura, Lauren.

Lornella (African-American double) See Lorne+Nella.

Lorraine (variant) See Laraine.

Lorrayne (variant) See Laraine.

Lorri (nickname) See Laraine, Laura, Lauren, Loretta.

Lorrie (nickname) See Laraine, Laura, Lauren, Loretta.

Lorrin (variant) See Laura, Lauren.

Lorry (nickname) See Laraine, Laura, Lauren, Loretta.

Lota (variant) See Carla, Charlotte, Lottie.

Lotta (variant) See Carla, Charlotte, Lottie.

Lotte (variant) See Carla, Charlotte, Lottie.

Lotti (variant) See Carla, Charlotte, Lottie.

Lottie "The Little One" (French).

Patron Saints: Lottie seems to be a form of "Etta." This leads to St. Etto as a patron. However, it also must not be forgotten that there is a St. Lota. She gave her life for Jesus, along with her friends Sts. Callistus and Charisius. She was thrown into the sea and drowned in ancient times.

Feast Dates: April 16 — St. Lota; July 10 — St. Etto (see Etta).

Lotty (variant) See Carla, Charlotte, Lottie.

Lotus "Lotus Flower" (Greek) or "Lily of Egypt" (Greek).

Patron Saints: Knowing that a "lotus" is a flower leads to St. Flora and Bl. Richard Flower. After the defeat of the Spanish Armada in 1588, the English anti-Catholic laws were enforced with a vengeance. This led to the arrest of Richard Lloyd, a layman. His treasonable crime was helping a Catholic priest. For this he was executed in 1588.

Also note that if one defines lotus as a "river lily," then St. Lily can be adopted as a patron.

Feast Dates: May 4 — Bl. Richard Lloyd, also known as Flower; March 2 — St. Lily (see Lily).

Lou (nickname) See Louise, Tallulah.

Louane (English double) See Luan, Louise+Ann.

Louann (English double) See Luan, Louise+Ann.

Louanna (English double) See Luan, Louise+Ann.

Louanne (English double) See Luan, Louise+Ann.

Louella (variant) See Louise.

Louetta (English double) See Louise+Coletta/Etta.

Louisa (English) See Louise.

Louise "The Woman Warrior Heroine" (Old German).

Patron Saints: There are a half-dozen Sts. Louise. St. Louise de Marillac, 1591-1660, was born in France. From an early age she wanted to be a nun but was turned down because of poor health. Thus at the age of twenty-two she married Antoine le Gras, an official of the queen. Twelve years later he died and Louise met St. Vincent de Paul. She devoted the rest of her life to working with him caring for the sick, poor, and neglected. She also founded the Sisters of Charity of St. Vincent de Paul. At the age of forty-three, she took her vows as a religious. The order grew very quickly. She died at the age of sixty-nine and is considered the patron of social workers.

Feast Dates: March 15 — St. Louise de Marillac.

Louisette (French double) See Louise+Ette.

Loula (nickname) See Tallulah.

Lourane (African-American double) See Louise+Lorraine.

Lourdes (Spanish) See Bernadette.

Lourenca (Portuguese) See Laura, Lauren, Laurentia.

Lourencia (variant) See Laura, Lauren, Laurentia.

Loutitia (variant) See Leticia.

Love (English) See Charity.

Lovey (American) See Charity.

Lovie (American) See Charity.

Lovisa (variant) See Louise.

Loyce (English) See Louise.

Lozetta (African-American double) See Louise+Zetta.

Lu (nickname) See Louise, Luan, Lucy, Lucille, Lucinda, Tallulah.

Luan "The Woman Warrior Heroine+The God-Graced One" (English double).

Patron Saints: Luan is a combination of Louise and Ann, and there is a St. Luan. He was a disciple of St. Comgal and founded more than one hundred twenty monasteries in Ireland and Scotland. He died in 622.

Feast Dates: August 4 — St. Luan; August 30 — St. Anne (see Ann).

Luana (English double) See Luan, Louise+Ann.

Luane (English double) See Luan, Louise+Ann.

Luann (English double) See Luan, Louise+Ann.

Luanna (English double) See Luan, Louise+Ann.

Luanne (English double) See Luan, Louise+Ann.

Luanni (English double) See Luan, Louise+Ann.

Luberta (African-American double) See Louise+Alberta.

Luca (Hungarian) See Lucy.

Luce (French) See Lucy.

Lucella (Spanish double) See Lucy+Cecilia.

Lucera (Spanish) See Lucy.

Lucetta (Spanish, Italian, Portuguese, Scandinavian double) See Lucy+Etta.

Lucette (Spanish, Italian, Portuguese, Scandinavian double) See Lucy+Ette.

Luci (nickname) See Lucille, Lucinda, Lucy.

Lucia (Spanish, Italian, Portuguese, Scandinavian) See Lucy.

Luciana (variant double) See Lucy+Ana.

Lucianne (variant double) See Lucy+ Anne.

Lucie (Dutch, French, Czech, German) See Lucille, Lucinda, Lucy.

Lucienne (French) See Lucy.

Lucila (Spanish) See Lucille, Lucy.

Lucile (French) See Lucy.

Lucilla (Spanish) See Lucille, Lucy.

Lucille "The Bringer of Light" (diminutive of Lucy).

Patron Saints: There are three known Sts. Lucille and about a half-dozen Sts. Lucillianus and Lucillus. St. Lucille and twenty-two companions were martyred in about 258 and buried along the Ostian Way in Italy.

Feast Dates: July 29 — St. Lucille, also known as Lucilla.

Lucina (Spanish) See Lucy.

Lucinda "The Bringer of Light" (Spanish form of Lucy).

Patron Saints: There are about a half-dozen Sts. Lucina. One of them was a wife and mother. She was martyred for her faith in Jesus in ancient times.

Feast Dates: June 30 — St. Lucina.

Lucine (variant) See Lucy.

Lucita (Spanish double) See Lucy+Ita.

Lucja (Polish) See Lucy.

Luckee (variant) See Lucinda, Lucky.

Lucki (nickname) See Lucinda, Lucky.

Luckie (nickname) See Lucinda, Lucky.

Lucky "The Fortunate One" (Middle English) or "The Bringer of Light" (nickname for Lucinda).

Patron Saints: The Latin word for "fortune" is *fortuna*, and there are a great many saints with this name. However, it should also be remembered that there is one more saint available who has an even better name. He is Bl. Lucker, who was of Alemannic descent.

Feast Dates: November 1 — Bl. Lucker.

Lucretia "The Liberator of Men" (Greek).

Patron Saints: There are two Sts. Lucretia. One died a martyr in ancient Spain.

Feast Dates: November 23 — St. Lucretia.

Lucy "The Bringer of Light" (English).

Patron Saints: There are at least six Sts. Lucy, a half-dozen Sts. Lucina, and dozens of Sts. Lucius.

St. Lucy of Syracuse, probably a Sicilian, was raised in the Catholic faith. When she became a teenager, her mother pressed her to marry a young pagan man. Only then did Lucy tell her mother of her secret vow to remain single. Her mother relented. However, this made the young man very angry. He denounced Lucy as a Christian before the governor and she was condemned to be killed by the sword. Her eyes were put out before her death in 304.

St. Lucy is patron of those with eye problems, of gondoliers, glaziers, and lamplighters and can be called upon against dysentery, hemorrhage, and throat disease.

Feast Dates: December 13 — St. Lucy.

Ludell (African-American double) See Louise+Adela.

Ludella (African-American double) See Louise+Adela.

Ludelle (African-American double) See Louise+Adele.

Ludessa (African-American double) See Louise+Agnesa/Vanessa.

Ludina (African-American double) See Louise+Dinah.

Ludovica (variant) See Louise.

Ludovika (German) See Louise.

Ludwiga (English) See Louise.

Ludwika (variant) See Louise.

Luellen (African-American double) See Louise+Ellen.

Luetta (African-American double) See Louise+Etta.

Luette (African-American double) See Louise+Ette.

Lugenia (African-American double) See Louise+Regina.

Luighseach (Irish) See Lucy.

Luigina (Italian) See Louise.

Luisa (Italian, Spanish) See Louise.

Luise (German) See Louise.

Lukija (Greek, Ukrainian) See Lucy.

Lulani "The Apex of the Heavens" (Hawaiian).

    Patron Saints: Sts. Lullus and Lanel will fit the bill. St. Lullus worked with St. Boniface in the 700s in the conversion of Germany.

    Feast Dates: October 16 — St. Lullus; June 26 — St. Frances Lanel (see Lane).

Luleta (variant) See Louise.

Lulita (variant) See Louise.

Lulu (nickname) See Louise.

Luminosa (Spanish) See Candelaria.

Luna "The Moon" (Latin).

    Patron Saints: There are three saints with variations of this name: Sts. Lunitanus, Lunaire, and Lunecharia. Lunecharia is remembered as a holy single lady who served God in Ireland in medieval times.

    More patrons can be found when it is realized that the names Celine and Cynthia also mean "moon."

    Feast Dates: June 7 — St. Lunecharia; July 1 — St. Lunaire (see Monday).

Lunete (variant double) See Luna+Ette.

Lunetta (African-American double) See Luna+Etta.

Lunette (variant double) See Luna+Ette.

Lupe (Spanish) See Guadalupe.

Lupita (Spanish double) See Guadalupe+Ita.

Lura (variant) See Laura, Lorelei.

Lurdez (Hispanic-American) See Lourdes.

Lurette (variant) See Lorelei+Ette.

Lurleen (American) See Lorelei.

Lurlei (American) See Lorelei.

Lurlene (American) See Lorelei.

Lurline (American) See Lorelei.

Lusa (variant) See Elizabeth.

Luwana (American double) See Luan, Louise+Ann.

Luwanna (American double) See Luan, Louise+Ann.

Luz (Spanish) See Lucy.

Luzia (Portuguese) See Lucy.

Lyda (French) See Lydia.

Lydia "The One from Lydia" (Greek).

    Patron Saints: The Bible provides us with one St. Lydia. And Catholic tradition provides a second.

    St. Lydia was the first European convert made by St. Paul at Philippi (see Acts 16:11-15). St. Paul preached Jesus, and the Lord opened Lydia's heart to pay attention to what Paul was saying. She invited Paul to stay at her home, where he baptized her and her household.

    This is one of almost a dozen stories in the Book of Acts that speaks of baptism as the primary way to become a member of the Church.

    Feast Dates: August 3 — St. Lydia.

Lydie (French) See Lydia.

Lyn (nickname) See Lindsay, Lynn.

Lyna (nickname) See Lynn.

Lynda (Spanish) See Belinda, Linda.

Lyndel (English) See Lynn.

Lyndi (Spanish) See Belinda, Linda.

Lyndie (English) See Belinda, Linda.

Lynea (variant) See Linnea.

Lynelle (nickname) See Lynn.

Lynetta (English double) See Lynn+Etta.

Lynette (English double) See Lynn+Ette.

Lynn "From the Pool Below the Waterfall" (Old English) or "From the Stream" (Old English).

Patron Saints: Lynn, as a nickname for Evelyne, Marilyn, Lyndsay, Madeline, and Magdala, provides a few patrons. As a name in its own right (including variants), Lynn gives us a few more patrons. One is St. Newlyna, a single woman. In medieval times she traveled from England to Brittany and was eventually martyred.

Feast Dates: November 8 — St. Newlyna; July 5 — St. Lina (see Lina); February 27 — St. Anne Line (see Line).

Lynna (nickname) See Lynn.

Lynne (English) See Lindsay, Madeline.

Lynnea (variant) See Linnea.

Lynnell (English double) See Lynn+Elle.

Lynnelle (English double) See Lynn+Elle.

Lynnett (English double) See Lynn+Ette.

Lynnetta (English double) See Lynn+Etta.

Lynnette (English double) See Lynn+Ette.

Lynsey (American) See Lindsay.

Lynzie (American) See Lindsay.

Lysa (nickname) See Alice, Elizabeth, Lisa.

Lysandra "The Liberator of Men" (Greek).

Patron Saints: There is a St. Lei and a St. Sandila.

Feast Dates: May 17 — St. Lie (see Lorelei); September 3 — St. Sandila (see Sandra).

Lyssa (nickname) See Alice, Elizabeth, Lisa.

Lyzola (African-American double) See Elizabeth+Ola.

Maara (Finnish) See Martha, Mary.

Maarva (Estonian) See Martha.

Mab (nickname) See Mabel.

Mab "The Joyful One" (Irish) or "The Baby" (Welsh) or "The Lovable One" (short form of Mabel).

Patron Saints: A half-dozen saints are available.

Feast Dates: November 1 — St. Mabel; August 30 — St. Gaudentia (see Bliss).

Mabe (nickname) See Mabel.

Mabel "The Lovable One" (Latin) or "The Beautiful One" (French).

Patron Saints: Linguists trace the origin of the name Mabel to Amabel and Amabilis. And there are two Sts. Amabilis. There is also a St. Mabel, a single young lady who lived in medieval Wales.

Moreover, the French *ma belle*, meaning "beautiful one," leads directly to the Blessed Virgin Mary. Christian authors through the ages have sung of her great beauty, which extends into the depth of her soul. The ancient *Akathist Hymn* speaks of Mary as a "star that goes before the sun." The *Ave Regina Coelorum* in 1100 calls her the "Loveliest in Heaven." The *Litany of Mary,* of 1982, calls her the "Fount of Beauty."

Feast Dates: November 1 — St. Mabel; All Saturdays — The Blessed Virgin Mary, The Lovely One.

Mabelia (African-American) See Mabel.

Mabelle (French) See Mabel.

Macayla (American) See Michaela.

Mace (nickname) See Macy.

Macenna (variant) See McKenna.

Maceo (Spanish) See Macy.

Macey (variant) See Macy.

Machaela (Hebrew) See Michaela.

Maci (variant) See Maisie.

Mackena (variant) See McKenna, Kennera.

Mackenna (American) See McKenna, Kennera.

MacKenzie (Irish) See McKenna, Kennera.

Mackenzie "Son of+Handsome One" (Scottish Gaelic).

Patron Saints: Patrons can be found by adopting saints with similar names. Thus it is helpful to know that *mac* means "son of." And there are about a hundred saints with names that begin with "Mc" or "Mac." One was St. Macra, a Catholic maiden in Rheims who suffered torture and death in 287 because others hated her faith. Also, *ken* means "chief," and there is one St. Kendeus. He was a martyr who died for the faith in ancient Nicomedia.

Feast Dates: January 6 — St. Macra; January 20 — St. Kendeus; October 29 — St. Kennera (see Kenya).

Macy "From Matthew's Estate" (Old French).

Patron Saints: Any of the two dozen Sts. Matthew can serve as patron.

Feast Dates: September 21 — St. Matthew the Apostle.

Mada (nickname) See Madeline, Magdalen.

Madailein (Irish Gaelic) See Madeline.

Madalena (Italian, Portuguese) See Madeline, Magdalena.

Madalene (Italian) See Madeline.

Madaline (English) See Madeline.

Madalyn (Greek) See Madeline.

Maddalena (Italian, English) See Magdalena, Madeline.

Madallyne (English) See Madeline.

Maddee (nickname) See Madison, Madonna.

Maddi (nickname) See Madeline, Madison, Madonna.

Maddie (nickname) See Madeline, Madison, Madonna.

Maddy (nickname) See Madeline, Madison, Madonna.

Madel (Norwegian) See Madeline.

Madelaine (French) See Madeline.

Madeleine (French) See Madeline.

Madelena (Dutch) See Madeline.

Madelene (variant) See Madeline.

Madelina (Dutch) See Madeline.

Madeline "The Magnificent One" (Greek) or "The One from Magdala" (English).

Patron Saints: Madeline is an English form of Magdalen, and there are over two dozen Sts. Magdalen. There are also a couple of Sts. Madeleine. St. Madeleine Barat, 1779-1864, was born in Burgundy just in time to rebuild the education system after the Reign of Terror.

Her brother challenged her by asking, "Can you be satisfied with mediocrity when heroism is within your grasp?" Thus at the age of twenty-one she and two friends consecrated themselves to Jesus and dedicated themselves, first and foremost, to the education and welfare of girls. Madeleine insisted on both physical and moral education. By the time of her death, she had founded ninety-two convents in twelve countries.

Feast Dates: May 25 — St. Madeleine Sophie Barat.

Madella (English) See Madeline, Magdalena.

Madelle (African-American double) See any "Ma" name+Adelle.

Madelle (English) See Madeline, Magdalena.

Madelon (French) See Madeline.

Madena (African-American) See Madonna.

Madesta (African-American double) See Madonna+Esther.

Madge (Greek) See Madeline, Magdalena, Margaret.

Madi (German) See Madeline.

Madison "Son of Maud" (Middle English) or "The Son of+Matthew" (Middle English double).

Patron Saints: Madison was a boy's name until 1984 when Disney used it as a name for a mermaid character in *Splash*. There is no St. Madison, but patrons can be found in two saints who have very similar names, both in pronunciation and in meaning. Sts. Maden and Sontius have names that mean "powerful soldier" and "son." For centuries St. Maden (also known as Madern) has been remembered by the residents of Cornwall, England, where he lived as a hermit in 545. Healings still take place at a well on this site known as St. Madern's Well.

Feast Dates: May 17 — St. Maden; November 17 — St. Sontius (see Sonny).

Madisyn (American) See Madison.

Madlen (German) See Madeline.

Madlin (variant) See Madeline.

Madlyn (English) See Madeline.

Madonna "My+Lady" (Latin).

Patron Saints: The greatest patron for Madonna is the Blessed Virgin Mary. However, it is also helpful to know that Martha means "lady," which leads to another dozen patrons.

Feast Dates: July 29 — St. Martha of Bethany (see Martha); January 1 — The Blessed Virgin Mary, Mother of God (see Queen).

Madora (African-American double) See any "Ma" name+Dora.

Madra (variant) See Mama.

Madre (Spanish) See Mama.

Madrona (Spanish) See Mama.

Mady (German) See Madeline, Maida.

Madzia (Polish) See Madeline.

Mae "Great One" (Latin) or "Springtime Goddess" (Greek).

Patron Saints: Mae means "great." In Latin the word "great" is *magnus*, and there are two dozen Sts. Magnus. Moreover, May also refers to Maia, the "goddess of springtime."

Feast Dates: May 6 — St. Mae (see Magnolia).

Maecile (African-American double) See any "Ma" name+Cecile.

Maegan (Irish) See Megan.

Maelyn (African-American double) See Mae+Lynn.

Maeve (variant) See Mauve.

Mag (nickname) See Magdalena, Magnolia, Margaret.

Magalina (African-American) See Magdalena.

Magaly (Spanish) See Magdalena.

Magd (German) See Maida.

Magda (Spanish) See Madeline, Magdalena.

Magdala (English) See Madeline, Magdalena.

Magdalen (Spanish) See Madeline, Magdalena.

Magdalena "The Magnificent One" (Spanish) or "The One from Magdala" (Spanish).

Patron Saints: There are about a dozen Sts. Magdalen and a few more Sts. Mary Magdalen. The most famous one, St. Mary from Magdala, is the classic example of the repentant sinner. Jesus said of her, "Her sins, which are many, are forgiven, for she loved much" (Luke 7:47). Tradition identifies her as Mary of Bethany, who anointed Christ's feet in Simon's house. Jesus cast seven devils out of her and she traveled with Jesus and ministered to his needs. She was a witness of the crucifixion and, after the resurrection, she discovered the empty tomb. Then she was the first one chosen to announce the good news of Christ's resurrection.

Catholic tradition insists that, after the resurrection, Mary accompanied John and the Blessed Virgin to Ephesus. There, she helped care for Jesus' mother. A less reliable tradition claims she went to France to preach the Gospel with Martha and Lazarus. She is patron of contemplatives, fallen women, glove makers, hairdressers, and perfumers.

Feast Dates: July 22 — St. Mary Magdalen.

Magdalene (German) See Magdalena.

Magdalina (Russian) See Madeline.

Magdalini (Greek) See Madeline.

Magdoina (Hungarian) See Madeline.

Magena (Hebrew) See Melody.

Maggie (nickname) See Magdalena, Magnolia, Margaret.

Maggy (nickname) See Magdalena, Magnolia, Margaret.

Magli (Danish) See Madeline.

Magnolia "The Magnolia Flower" (Latin).

Patron Saints: Her patrons are Sts. Magna, Lea, and Nola (Magna plus Lea, Magna plus Nola). St. Magna is simply remembered as "a virgin" who lived for Jesus in ancient Ancyra, Turkey.

Feast Dates: May 6 — St. Magna; December 24 — St. Leah (see Leah); November 15 — St. Felix of Nola (see Nola).

Magra (variant) See Magdalen, Margaret.

Mahala "The Tender One" (Hebrew, English) or "The Harp Player" (Hebrew) or "The Fat One" (Arabic).

Patron Saints: The use of music and musical instruments such as harps, lyres, cymbals, and trumpets to worship God was inherited by Catholicism from Jewish Temple liturgy. Also, during much of history the only significant relief from labor available to the average peasant was the diversion offered by music. Music was a way to celebrate and came to be associated with heavenly bliss. This led artists to picture angels and saints playing musical instruments in heaven. This was only natural because the Bible itself presents us with images of angels singing and blowing trumpets.

Furthermore, the 144,000 in the New Testament, symbolizing all the saints, are pictured being present during the playing of harps before God (see Revelation 14:1-3). The harps are symbolic of prayer. The prayer-filled voice of all the people of God are "like the sound of harpers playing on their harps" (Revelation 14:2).

Feast Dates: September 29 and October 2 — The Holy Seraphim (see Amber); November 1 — Family of All Saints.

Mahalah (Hebrew) See Mahala.

Mahelia (African-American) See Mahala.

Mahoganee (American) See Mahogany.

Mahogani (American) See Mahogany.

Mahogany "The Reddish-Brown One" (Spanish) or "The Rich, Strong One" (Spanish).

Patron Saints: It helps to know that the word "mahogany" means the "reddish brown one." This leads directly to St. Rufina, whose name means the "reddish one," and to Bl. William Browne. Bl. Browne was a layman from Northamptonshire, England. He insisted on practicing his Catholic faith and was arrested by British government authorities. He was executed at Ripon in 1605.

Feast Dates: September 5 — Bl. William Browne; August 31 — St. Rufina (see Rufina).

Maia (Greek, Spanish) See Maya, Mama, Maxine.

Maible (Irish) See Mabel.

Maida "The Maiden" (Old English).

Patron Saints: There is one St. Maidos. He served God as the abbot of Clonmore, which he founded.

Feast Dates: April 11 — St. Maidos.

Maidel (variant) See Madeline, Maida.

Maiga (variant) See Margaret.

Maighdlin (Irish) See Magdalena.

Main (variant) See Mayne.

Maine (variant) See Mayne.

Maire (Irish Gaelic) See Mary.

Mairead (Irish, Scottish Gaelic) See Margaret.

Mairghread (variant) See Margaret.

Mairi (Scottish Gaelic) See Mary.

Maisie "The Pearl" (Scottish form of Margaret).

Patron Saints: There are over two dozen Sts. Margaret, and there is one St. Maisse. She is simply remembered as an "Irish virgin."

Feast Dates: August 21 — St. Maisse; October 8 — St. Pearl, also known as Pelagia (see Pearl).

Maita (Spanish) See Maida.

Maitilde (Irish) See Matilda.

Maizee (variant) See Maisie.

Maizie (variant) See Maisie.

Maizy (variant) See Maisie.

Maj (Swedish) See Margaret.

Makalonca (Slovenian) See Madeline.

Mal (nickname) See Mallory, Malvina.

Mala (variant) See Madeline.

Malanie (variant) See Melanie.

Malena (variant) See Madeline.

Malerie (variant) See Mallory.

Malgorzata (Polish) See Margaret.

Malika (Hebrew) See Queen.

Malin (Swedish) See Madeline.

Malina (Swedish) See Madeline.

Malinda (American) See Melinda.

Malinde (American) See Melinda.

Maline (variant) See Madeline.

Malissa (American) See Melissa.

Malka (Hebrew) See Queen.

Malkin (French) See Mary.

Mallissa (African-American) See Melissa.

Mallo (variant) See Mauve.

Mallori (variant) See Mallory.

Mallorie (English) See Mallory.

Mallory "The Unhappy One" (Old French) or "The Army Counselor" (French) or "The Armored Knight" (Old German).

Patron Saints: This name was masculine until recently. There are a few male saints with very similar names, such as St. Malo, who was a member of the famous ancient Theban Legion of the Roman army. In about 287 Emperor Maximian marched against an enemy with his army. One unit of it, the Theban Legion, was composed entirely of Christians.

Just before battle, Maximian required all members of the army to sacrifice to the gods, praying for success. The Theban Legion refused. Executions were threatened, but the soldiers still refused. Maximian then ordered that every tenth man be killed. This was done several times. Then he threatened death for all. The soldiers declared they were soldiers loyal to the emperor but could not worship false gods.

Maximian ordered the legion be cut to pieces. The butchering commenced and the legionnaires offered no resistance. With their weapons in their hands, they allowed themselves to be martyred for Christ. In all, about six thousand died for Jesus. Malo is patron of the diocese of Nevers, France.

Feast Dates: October 10 — St. Malo.

Mallow (English) See Mauve.

Malorie (English) See Mallory.

Malory (English) See Mallory.

Malva (variant) See Malvina, Mauve, Melba.

Malvie (variant) See Malvina.

Malvina "The Smooth-Browed One" (Scottish) or "The Sweet Friend" (Irish Gaelic).

Patron Saints: There is one female saint with a very similar name. St. Malina gave her life for Jesus at Tarsus in Roman times.

Feast Dates: April 28 — St. Malina.

Mama "The Mother" (English).

Patron Saints: There are actually three Sts. Mama and a half-dozen Sts. Mamas. One of the Sts. Mama celebrates her feast with a St. Papa. Both were martyrs in ancient times.

Feast Dates: October 1 — St. Mama and St. Papa; January 1 — The Blessed Virgin Mary, Mother of God (see Mary).

Mame (nickname) See Mary.

Mamie (nickname) See Mary.

Manda (Spanish) See Amanda.

Mandi (nickname) See Amanda, Melinda.

Mandie (nickname) See Amanda, Melinda.

Mandita (Spanish double) See Amanda+Ita.

Mandy (nickname) See Amanda, Melinda.

Manetta (variant double) See Mary+Etta.

Manette (French double) See Mary+Ette.

Manica (Slovenian) See Mary.

Manni (nickname) See Emmanuella.

Mannie (nickname) See Emmanuella.

Manny (nickname) See Emmanuella.

Manon (French) See Mary.

Manuela (Spanish) See Emmanuella.

Manuelle (nickname) See Emmanuella.

Manya (Russian) See Mary.

Maquisha (African-American double) See Marcia, Marcille, Margaret+Sha.

Mar (nickname) See Martha, Mary.

Mara (variant) See Damara, Mary.

Marabel (variant double) See Mary+Belle.

Marah (English) See Mara, Mary.

Maralina (English) See Mara, Mary.

Maraline (French) See Mara, Mary.

Maranda (variant) See Miranda.

Maraya (variant) See Mariah.

Marca (variant) See Marcia.

Marcail (Scottish) See Margaret.

Marcee (English) See Marcia, Marcille.

Marcela (Spanish) See Marcille.

Marcelene (English) See Marcille.

Marcelia (variant) See Marcille.

Marcelina (Spanish) See Marcille.

Marcelle (variant) See Marcia, Marcille.

Marcellena (variant) See Marcille.

Marcellina (variant) See Marcille.

Marcelline (variant) See Marcille.

Marcenia (variant) See Marcille.

Marcey (nickname) See Marcia, Marcille.

March "The Month of the God Mars" (Middle English) or "The Warlike One" (form of Marcia, Marcille).

Patron Saints: March is a shortened and familiar form of Marcia and Marcella.

Feast Dates: January 20 — St. Marcia (see Marcia); January 31 — St. Marcella (see Marcille).

Marchelle (variant) See March, Marcia, Marcille.

Marcheta (variant) See March, Marcia.

Marchita (variant) See March, Marcia.

Marcia (Spanish) See Marcia, Marcille.

Marcia "The Warlike One" (Latin).

Patron Saints: There are at least a dozen Sts. Marcia and another half-dozen Sts. Marciana. Unfortunately, very little is known about any of them.

For example, all we know about one of the Sts. Marcia is that she died a martyr in ancient Alexandria, Egypt.

Feast Dates: January 20 — St. Marcia; January 31 — St. Marcella (see Marcille).

Marcial (Spanish) See Marcia, Marcille.

Marciana (Spanish double) See Marcia+Ana.

Marcie (nickname) See March, Marcia, Marcille.

Marcile (variant) See Marcia.

Marcille "The Warlike One" (English).

Patron Saints: One of about a half-dozen Sts. Marcella was a noble Roman lady who became a widow after only seven months of marriage. She then dedicated her single life to the service of the Church, fasting, and prayer. This impressed many women and soon many small religiouslike communities were formed in Rome. In time, her home became the first convent in Rome. When the Goths plundered Rome in 410, they tortured her for hidden treasure, but she had none to give. She had long ago spent it all on the poor.

Feast Dates: January 31 — St. Marcella; January 20 — St. Marcia (see Marcia).

Marcy (variant) See March, Marcia, Marcille.

Mare (nickname) See Mary.

Mareesha (African-American double) See Maressa/Marie+Sha/Shana.

Marella (French) See Mary.

Marelle (French) See Mary.

Maren (Dutch variant) See Marina, Mary.

Marena (English) See Marina.

Maressa (variant) See Maris, Marissa.

Maret (Danish) See Margaret.

Marete (Norwegian) See Margaret.

Maretta (English double) See Mary+Etta.

Marette (French double) See Mary+Ette.

Marfa (Russian) See Martha.
Marga (Swedish) See Margaret.
Margalo (Swedish) See Margaret.
Margara (Spanish) See Margaret.
Margaret "The Pearl" (English).

Patron Saints: Of the more than two dozen Sts. Margaret, one is a Canadian American named Marguerite Bourgeoys, 1620-1700, who was born in France.

When the governor of Canada came to her town looking for help, she volunteered. In Montreal she kept house for the governor and then opened a school for children. She soon included all children, both those of the settlers and those belonging to the Indians. She constantly faced troubles and difficulties, which included learning the Iroquois language, embracing poverty, enduring the cold, making three round-trip crossings of the Atlantic, and braving long winter overland journeys. When she tried to found an order of non-contemplative nuns dedicated to teaching, she encountered opposition from both secular and religious authorities. Eventually the Sisters of Notre Dame de Montreal congregation was born; it was given ecclesiastical approval just two short years before Marguerite died.

Feast Dates: January 19 — Bl. Marguerite Bourgeoys; December 23 — St. Marie Marguerite d'Youville (see Marguerite).

Margareta (Swedish) See Margaret.
Margarete (Danish, German) See Margaret.
Margareth (variant) See Margaret.
Margaretha (Dutch) See Margaret.
Margarethe (German) See Margaret.
Margaretta (Portuguese) See Margaret.
Margarette (Portuguese) See Margaret.
Margarida (Portuguese) See Margaret.
Margarita (Lithuanian, Spanish) See Margaret.

Margarite (Spanish) See Margaret.
Marge (nickname) See Margaret.
Margeaux (French) See Margaret.
Margella (African-American double) See Margery+Ella.
Margerie (French) See Margaret.
Margery (English) See Margaret.
Marget (variant) See Margaret.
Margette (variant) See Margaret.
Magherita (Italian double) See Margaret+Ita.
Margie (variant) See Margaret.
Margit (Hungarian, Norwegian) See Margaret.
Margo (variant) See Margaret.
Margola (French) See Margaret.
Margory (variant) See Margaret.
Margot (French) See Margaret.
Margret (Dutch) See Margaret.
Margrethe (Dutch) See Margaret.
Margriet (Dutch) See Margaret.
Marguerita (Spanish double) See Margaret+Ita.
Marguerite "The Pearl" (French).

Patron Saints: St. Marie Marguerite d'Youville, 1701-1771, was born in Varennes, which is on the outskirts of Montreal in Quebec, Canada. After her father died, she spent most of her time helping her mother care for her siblings.

In time, a marriage was arranged for her, to a wealthy, handsome young man, but he spent most of his time bribing the Indians with liquor and he lost most of his money to gambling. In addition, her first few children died as infants and then her husband died, leaving her with debts. She and her two sons opened a sewing supplies shop and eventually paid off the debts.

She began helping criminals and the destitute. Then she started taking the poor into her home and other ladies joined her. From this group the Grey

Nuns community was founded. They received the name "Grey" not only from the color of their habits but also from a play on words, for *gris* not only meant "gray" but "tipsy" as well, which referred to the drunks that came to their convent for help.

Feast Dates: December 23 — St. Marie Marguerite d'Youville.

Marguerta (Spanish) See Margaret.

Margy (nickname) See Margaret.

Mari (Spanish) See Mara, María.

Maria (Italian, Latin) See Mary.

María (Spanish) See Mary.

Mariah "The Bitter One" (Hebrew form of Maria).

Patron Saints: Mariah can be considered a variant of Maria, and there are over a hundred Sts. Mary. There is also one St. Mara. He was a holy bishop who lived in Syria in the 400s.

Feast Dates: January 25 — St. Mara; September 8 — The Birth of Mary (see Mary).

Mariam (French) See Mary.

Marian (Latin) See Mary.

Mariana (Latin double) See Mary+Ana.

Mariane (Latin double) See Mary+Ann.

Marianna (Latin double) See Mary+Ann.

Marianne "The Bitter One+God-Graced One" (French double).

Patron Saints: Marianne is a combination of two names: Mary plus Ann. There are a half-dozen Sts. Marianne. One is an American. Barbara Cope, 1838-1918, was born in Heppenheim, Germany, and was only two years old when her parents emigrated to the United States and settled in Utica, New York. At the age of twenty-four she entered a convent and took the name Marianne. She was assigned to teach in a school in Syracuse, New York. Her administrative talent and her ability to work with people led to her being made

a superior of St. Joseph Hospital in Syracuse.

Then in 1883, when she was forty-five years old, she and a few other religious sisters answered a call for help from a hospital in Honolulu. There she met Father Damien and set up a home for boys and one for girls. She revolutionized life on Molokai, bringing cleanliness and pride.

Feast Dates: August 9 — SG Marianne Cope, O.S.F.

Maribel (French double) See Mary+Belle.

Maribelle (French double) See Mary+Belle.

Maribeth (English double) See Mary+Bethany/Elizabeth.

Marica (French) See Mary.

Marice (Italian) See Mary.

Maridel (English) See Mary.

Marie (French) See Mariah, Mary.

Mariel (Italian) See Mary.

Mariele (variant) See Mary.

Mariella (Italian) See Mary.

Marielle (German) See Mary.

Mariellen (English double) See Mary+Ellen.

Marietta (Spanish double) See Marie+Etta.

Mariette (French double) See Marie+Ette.

Marieve (African-American double) See Marie+Eve.

Marifa (Spanish) See Mary.

Marijane (English double) See Mary+Jane.

Marijo (English double) See Mary+Josepha.

Marika (Spanish) See Mary.

Marikate (English double) See Mary+Katherine.

Marilee (American double) See Marleen, Mary+Helen/Leigh/Magdalen.

Mariliana (Hispanic-American triple) See Mari+Lia+Ana.

Marilin (English double) See Mary+ Lynn.

Marilla (German) See Mary.

Marilou (English double) See Mary+ Louise.

Marilu (English double) See Mary+ Louise.

Mariluz (Spanish double) See Mary+Luz.

Marilyn (English double) See Mary+ Lynn.

Marin (variant) See Mary.

Marina "The One from the Sea" (Latin).

Patron Saints: There are over a dozen Sts. Marina. One has a very unusual story. It seems that in ancient times, after Marina's mother died, her father entered a monastery in Alexandria, Egypt. He took Marina along with him, disguised as a boy. In time, she grew up and became a monk herself, no one in the monastery guessing her real sex.

Then she was falsely accused of fathering an illegitimate child. She bore the false accusation in silence and was expelled from the monastery. Only after doing much penance was she readmitted.

Feast Dates: July 17 — St. Marina.

Marinka (Spanish) See Mary.

Marinna (English) See Marina, Maris.

Marion (Spanish) See Marian, Mary.

Maripat (English double) See Mary+ Patricia.

Mariquilla (Spanish) See Mary.

Mariquita (Spanish) See Margaret, Mary.

Marirose (English double) See Mary+ Rose.

Mariruth (English double) See Mary+ Ruth.

Maris "The Wife" (short form of Damara, Mavis) or "The One from the Sea" (Latin).

Patron Saints: There are three known Sts. Maris and seven more Sts. Mares. One St. Maris was a follower of St. Addai in the Middle East. He built a church and a monastery at Nisbis and preached the Gospel in a great many places. As bishop, he founded the patriarchal see of Koke. He is honored as the "Apostle of Assyria and Babylonia." He died in 891.

Feast Dates: July 19 — St. Maris.

Marisa (Spanish double) See María+ Luisa.

Mariska (Spanish) See Mary.

Marisol (Spanish double) See María+ Solana.

Marissa (Latin) See Maris.

Marita "The Little+Bitter One" (Spanish double).

Patron Saints: There is one ancient St. Marita and more than a hundred Sts. Mary. St. Marita died for Jesus in ancient Egypt. She may have been a black woman.

Feast Dates: March 15 — St. Marita.

Maritere (Spanish double) See María+ Thérèse.

Maritina (Spanish) See Martha.

Maritsa (variant) See Mary.

Marja (French) See Mary.

Marjarita (Slavic) See Margaret.

Marje (variant) See Margaret, Mary.

Marjeta (Slavic) See Margaret.

Marji (English) See Margaret.

Marjie (English) See Margaret.

Marjo (American double) See Mary+Jo.

Marjorie (Scottish) See Margaret.

Marjory (English) See Margaret.

Marjy (English) See Margaret.

Marketa (Czech) See Margaret.

Marketta (Finnish) See Margaret.

Markita (Czech) See Marcia, Margaret.

Marla (English) See Marleen, Mary.

Marlane (variant double) See Marleen, Mary+Helen/Leigh/Magdalen.

Marleah (variant) See Madeline.

Marlee (English double) See Marleen, Mary+Helen/Leigh.

Marleen "The Bitter One+The Light" (variant double or Mary+Helen) or "From the Meadow" (variant of Leigh) or "The Magnificent One" (variant of Magdalen through Madeline).

Patron Saints: Marleen is a combination of many names: Mary and Helen, Mary and Leigh, even Mary plus Magdalen; and this brings up some two hundred patrons.

A relatively recent saint is Annetta Bentivoglio, 1834-1905, who at the age of thirty-one became a Poor Clare religious sister and took the name Mary Maddalena. Ten years later she responded to a request to found a contemplative monastery in the United States. Her attempts to set up a house in New York, Philadelphia, and New Orleans all failed. In Cleveland, Ohio, things began to change for the better. This was followed by Omaha and Evansville, Indiana. She died in Indiana and her body has never decayed.

Feast Dates: August 18 — Bl. Mary Maddalena Bentivoglio.

Marlena (English) See Marleen.

Marlene (English) See Marleen.

Marley (English) See Marleen.

Marline (English) See Marleen.

Marlo (English) See Mary.

Marlyn (Hebrew) See Marilyn.

Marna (English) See Marina, Marleen.

Marne (nickname) See Marina, Marleen.

Marni (nickname) See Marina, Marleen.

Marnia (variant) See Mary.

Marnie (nickname) See Marina, Marleen.

Marny (nickname) See Marina, Marleen.

Marquetta (African-American) See Marcia, Marcille, Margaret.

Marquita (Spanish) See Marcia.

Marris (English) See Maris.

Marrissa (English) See Maris.

Marsaili (Scottish Gaelic) See Margaret.

Marsha (English) See Marcia.

Marsi (Estonian) See Marcia.

Marsiella (variant) See March, Marcia, Marcille.

Mart (nickname) See Martha, Martina.

Marta (English, Hungarian, Italian, Norwegian, Swedish) See Martha, Martina, Mary.

Martella (French, German) See Martha.

Martelle (English) See Martha.

Martha "The Lady" (Aramaic).

Patron Saints: There are almost two dozen Sts. Martha. The best remembered is St. Martha of Bethany, the sister of Mary and Lazarus. The Gospel of John says that "Jesus loved Martha and her sister and Lazarus" (John 11:5). In fact, when Lazarus died, Jesus wept.

It was to Martha that Jesus proclaimed, "I am the resurrection and the life" (John 11:25). He did this just before he raised Lazarus from the dead. Christian tradition relates that after the resurrection of Jesus, the enemies of Martha, Mary, and Lazarus placed them in a leaky boat and set them adrift to die. However, God caused the boat to land in France, at the mouth of the Rhône River. Martha assisted her brother, now a bishop. Of the three, Martha was the last to die. She is patron of cooks, dieticians, domestic servants, housekeepers, housewives, innkeepers, servants, and waitresses.

Feast Dates: July 29 — St. Martha of Bethany.

Marthe (French, German) See Martha.

Marthena (Finnish) See Martha.

Marthenia (African-American double) See Martha+Athena.

Marthine (Finnish) See Martha.

Marthini (Finnish) See Martha.

Marti (nickname) See Martha, Martina.

Martie (nickname) See Martha, Martina.

Martina "The Lady" (variant of Martha) or "The Warlike One" (feminine form of Martin).

Patron Saints: There is one St. Martina. She died in Rome in 228, a victim of the persecution of Emperor Alexander Severus. She was beheaded and is now patron of nursing mothers and of Rome.

Feast Dates: January 30 — St. Martina.

Martine (English) See Martha, Martina.

Martita (Finnish) See Martha, Martina.

Martta (Finnish) See Martha.

Martyanne (English double) See Martha+Ann.

Martynne (English double) See Martha+Ann.

Maruca (Spanish) See Miriam.

Marva "The Miraculous One" (Old French).

Patron Saints: There are two ways to surface patrons of Marva. Both are based on the name's meaning, "a miracle" (which is what many other names mean, including Milagros). The first way is to adopt saints whom the Church has officially described as "wonderworkers." They include Sts. Cyril the Wonderworker, Luke the Wonderworker, and Stephen the Wonderworker.

A second way is to adopt as patron the greatest Wonder or Miracle Worker of them all: Jesus the Christ, who worked all kinds of miracles. For example, he demonstrated his power over nature by walking on the water.

He also showed he had the power to heal those who were physically sick by restoring sight to the blind, hearing to the deaf, and wholeness to lepers.

He displayed his power over evil spirits by driving out devils. He even had the power to defeat death. All his miracles were performed to lead people to place faith in him so as to receive deeper healings. These consisted of the forgiveness of sin and the reception of eternal life.

Feast Dates: All Sundays — Jesus the Wonder or Miracle Worker.

Marvel (English) See Marva.

Marvela (English) See Marva.

Marvella (English) See Marva.

Marvelle (English) See Marva.

Mary "The Bitter One" (Hebrew).

Patron Saints: There are over a hundred Sts. Mary, but the finest patron is the Mother of God. The Bible tells us that Mary conceived the Son of God, gave birth to him, fled with him and Joseph into Egypt, found her son in the Temple, asked him for help at Cana, and stayed with him during his crucifixion and death on the cross.

Christian tradition adds that Mary was the daughter of Anna and Joachim, was born in about 15 B.C., was placed in the care of the Temple priests who chose Joseph for her, and moved to Nazareth.

Tradition also tells us that one day, when she was about fourteen or fifteen, she was sewing a purple garment and decided to take a break to go to the town well for some water. Then an angel appeared to her and told her she would become the "Mother of God." She accepted God's will (see Luke 1:38). Mary supposedly lived to be between sixty-three and seventy-two years of age.

Feast Dates: January 1 — The Blessed Virgin Mary, Mother of God.

Marya (French, Slavic) See Mary.

Maryal (French) See Mary.

Maryane (English double) See Mary+Ann.

Maryanna (English double) See Mary+Ann.

Maryanne (English double) See Mary+
Ann.

Marybel (English double) See Mary+
Belle.

Marybelle (English double) See Mary+
Belle.

Marybeth (English double) See Mary+
Bethany/Elizabeth.

Maryellen (English double) See Mary+
Ellen.

Maryjane (English double) See Mary+
Jane.

Maryjo (English double) See Mary+
Josepha.

Marykate (English double) See Mary+
Katherine.

Marylee (English double) See Mary+
Leigh.

Marylin (English double) See Mary+
Lynn.

Marylou (English double) See Mary+
Louise.

Marylu (English double) See Mary+
Louise.

Marylyn (English double) See Mary+
Lynn.

Marypat (English double) See Mary+
Patricia.

Maryrose (English double) See Mary+
Rose.

Maryruth (English double) See Mary+
Ruth.

Marys (English) See Maris, Mary+Son.

Marysa (French) See Mary.

Maryse (African-American) See Mary.

Marzetta (African-American double) See
Mary+Zetta.

Marzia (Italian) See Marcia.

Masha (Russian) See Mary.

Mat (nickname) See Martha, Matilda.

Mata (nickname) See Martha.

Matelda (Italian) See Matilda.

Matelle (variant) See Matilda.

Mater (Latin) See Mama.

Mathea (variant) See Matthew.

Mathia (variant) See Matthew.

Mathilda (variant) See Matilda.

Mathilde (German, French) See Matilda.

Matilda "The Strong Battle Woman"
(Old German).

Patron Saints: There are a half-
dozen Sts. Matilda. The best-known
St. Matilda, 895-968, was the daughter of Count Dietrich in Denmark. At
the age of fourteen she was married
to Henry, the son of the duke of
Saxony. At forty-one she became a
widow and filled her life with charitable works. Her sons, who took control of the government, severely criticized her for suspected extravagance
with royal funds used for charities. In
the face of these accusations, she resigned her inheritance and retired to
her country home. She forgave her
sons and spent most of her final days
at the convent of Nordhausen, which
she had built.

Feast Dates: March 14 — St.
Matilda; May 31 — St. Maud (see
Maud).

Matilde (Spanish) See Matilda.

Matoka (African-American double) See
Martha/Mattea/Matilda+Okay.

Matrona (Latin) See Lady.

Mattea "The Gift of God" (Hebrew).

Patron Saints: This name leads to two
dozen Sts. Matthew. The best-known
is St. Matthew the Apostle, who was
stoned to death at Hieropolis. He is the
patron of tax collectors and bankers.

Feast Dates: September 21 — St.
Matthew the Apostle; September 21
— St. Matthew (see Evangeline).

Matthea (variant) See Mattea.

Matthia (variant) See Mattea.

Matti (nickname) See Martha, Matilda.

Mattie (nickname) See Martha, Matilda.

Mattline (African-American) See
Madeline.

Mattwilda (African-American double) See Martha/Mattea/Matilda+Wilda.

Matty (variant) See Martha, Matilda.

Matusha (Spanish) See Matilda.

Matuxa (Spanish) See Matilda.

Maud "From Magdala" (nickname for Madeline or Magdalen) or "The Strong Battle Woman" (variant of Matilda).

Patron Saints: Over two dozen Sts. Magdalen and a couple of Sts. Madeleine exist. There is also one St. Maud. Born in 1125, she served as the abbess of her community, led reforms of convent practices, and possessed the gift of miracles.

Feast Dates: May 31 — St. Maud.

Maude (English) See Madeline, Matilda.

Maudlin (variant) See Madeline.

Maura (Irish) See Mary, Maureen.

Maureen "The Little Bitter One" (Irish form of Mary) or "The Dark One" (Old French).

Patron Saints: There are almost a dozen Sts. Maura. One St. Maura was a daughter of King Ella of Northumberland. With her brother and sister, Sts. Brigid and Espian, and eight sons, she made a pilgrimage to Rome and Jerusalem. On the trip home, they were killed by robbers in 866.

Feast Dates: February 13 — St. Maura.

Maurene (Irish) See Mary, Maureen.

Maurine (variant) See Mary, Maureen.

Maurise (variant) See Mary, Maureen.

Maurisha (African-American double) See Maureen+Isha.

Maurita (variant) See Mary, Maureen.

Maurizia (variant) See Mary, Maureen.

Mauve "The Mallow Flower" (French).

Patron Saints: There is one known St. Mauve who was a bishop. He was born at Verdun, France, and became a monk before serving as bishop of Verdun for forty years. He is remem-bered for solving the financial problems of his diocese. He died in 776.

Feast Dates: October 5 — St. Mauve, also known as Magdalveus; November 24 — St. Flora (see Flora).

Mava (variant) See Mary.

Maven (Hispanic-American double) See Mavis+Savannah.

Mavis (nickname) See Damara.

Max (nickname) See Maxine.

Maxi (nickname) See Maxine.

Maxie (nickname) See Maxine.

Maxima (variant) See Maxine.

Maxine "The Great One" (Latin).

Patron Saints: There are about twenty Sts. Maxima and Maxine. One St. Maxine was a citizen of Carthage in Africa. In 304, when persecution of Christians broke out in Carthage, she was arrested and put on trial, but she refused to deny Jesus. The judge sentenced her to be torn apart by the beasts in the arena, but the animals would not touch her. She was then beheaded.

Feast Dates: July 30 — St. Maxine, also known as Maxima.

Maxy (nickname) See Maxine, Maya, May.

May (Irish) See Mae, Mary.

Maya "The Wet-Nurse [Mother]" (Greek) or "The Great One" (Greek, Spanish) or "May" (Latin).

Patron Saints: A few patron saints are available.

Feast Dates: July 30 — St. Maxine (see Maxine); May 6 — St. Mae (see Mae).

Mayb (nickname) See Mabel.

Maybelle (English double) See May+Belle.

Maychelle (African-American double) See May+Shelly.

Mayda (variant) See Maida.

Mayde (variant) See Maida.

Maydelle (African-American double) See May+Della.

Maydena (variant) See Maida.

Maydia (African-American) See Maida.

Maye (English) See Mae, Margaret.

Mayn (variant) See Mayne.

Mayne "The Great One" (Old French).
Patron Saints: Mayne means the same thing as the Latin word *magnus*, and there are about three dozen Sts. Magnus. There is also one English martyr, St. Cuthbert Mayne, 1544-1577, who was ordained a Protestant minister at the age of nineteen. Later, while studying at Oxford, he met St. Edmund Campion, who urged him to become Catholic. He traveled to France, converted to Catholicism, and was ordained a Catholic priest. In 1575 he returned to England and became an estate steward to Francis Tregain of Golden, but he was soon arrested for being a Catholic priest. This led to his being hanged, drawn, and quartered.
Feast Dates: November 29 — St. Cuthbert Mayne.

Maynelle (African-American double) See May+Nelly.

Mayola (African-American double) See May+Ola.

Mayra (Hispanic-American double) See Maya+Myra.

Mazella (African-American double) See May+Zella.

McKenna (Irish) See Kenan, Kennera.

McKenzie (variant) See Mackenzie, Kennera.

Meadhbh (Irish) See Margaret.

Meagan (English) See Megan.

Meagen (English) See Megan.

Meaghan (English) See Megan.

Meara (Irish) See Merry.

Meayghan (English) See Megan.

Mechelle (African-American) See Michelle.

Medgaris (Hispanic-American double) See Madge+Edgar.

Medora (Greek double) See Mama+Dora.

Meg (nickname) See Margaret.

Megan "The Great One" (Irish Gaelic form of Meigan) or "The Pearl" (Welsh form of Margaret).
Patron Saints: As an Irish name in its own right, Meigan means "great one." And there is at least one known St. Meigan and he is remembered for being a holy monk who lived at Cor Beuno in Carnarvon, Wales.

In addition, some scholars insist that other spellings of Megan can be accepted as familiar forms of Margaret. This leads to two dozen Sts. Margaret.
Feast Dates: November 1 — St. Meigan.

Meggi (Dutch) See Margaret.

Meggie (nickname) See Margaret.

Meggy (nickname) See Margaret.

Meghan (English) See Margaret.

Mei (variant) See Mae.

Meigan (English) See Megan.

Meisha (African-American) See Moesha, Aisha, Isha.

Mel (variant) See Melantha, Melba, Melina, Melinda, Melisandra, Melissa, Melody, Melvina.

Mela (variant) See Melantha, Melba, Melina, Melinda, Melisandra, Melissa, Melody, Melvina.

Melain (Greek, Polish) See Melanie.

Melaina (Greek, Polish) See Melanie.

Melaine (Greek, Polish) See Melanie.

Melaini (English) See Melanie.

Melania (Greek, Polish) See Melanie.

Melanie "Dark-Clothed One" (Greek) or "Black One"(Greek).
Patron Saints: There are two Sts. Melanie, who are grandmother and granddaughter. The older St. Melanie was widowed at the age of twenty-two.

Being a socially high-placed matron, she then decided to make a pilgrimage to the Holy Land. When in Jerusalem, she founded a convent for fifty nuns and led a very austere life. In 402, after thirty-one years in Palestine, she returned to Rome.

Feast Dates: June 8 — St. Melanie the Elder, also known as Melania.

Melantha "The Dark+The Flower" (Greek) or "The Dark-Clothed One" (variant of Melanie).

Patron Saints: Melantha is constructed from two words: *melan*, meaning "dark," and *anthos*, meaning "flower." The two known Sts. Melanie (as well as a couple of Sts. Mella) can also serve as patrons.

St. Mella was a saint of ancient Ireland who married and became a mother. Two of her children, Cannech and Tigernach, are also recognized as canonized saints. Later in life, she entered the Doire-Melle convent and served for many years as an abbess. She died in the year 800.

Feast Dates: March 31 — St. Mella.

Melany (English) See Melanie.

Melba "The Soft, Slender One" (Greek) or "Mallow Flower" (Latin) or "Wealthy One" (Spanish).

Patron Saints: Knowing that Melba can mean "mallow flower" leads to St. Mauve.

Feast Dates: October 5 — St. Mauve (see Mauve).

Melda (nickname) See Imelda.

Meleda (African-American) See Melody.

Meledia (African-American) See Melody.

Melesa (variant) See Melissa.

Melessa (Spanish, Polish) See Melissa.

Melia (African-American) See Melanie.

Melicent (variant) See Melissa, Millicent.

Melina "The Yellow-Colored One" (Latin).

Patron Saints: As the Latin word for "the yellow-colored one," Melina can be a full name in its own right. It can also be seen as a combination of Melanie and Linda. Finally, it can be considered a nickname for Carmella, Magdala, and Melissa.

Feast Dates: June 8 — St. Melanie the Elder (see Melanie); March 31 — St. Mella (see Melantha).

Melinda (Greek-Spanish double) See Melissa, Melody+Linda.

Melisa (Spanish, Polish) See Melissa.

Melisande (French double) See Melisandra, Melissa/Millicent+Sandra.

Melisandra "Honeybee or Industrious One+Helper of Humanity" (Greek double).

Patron Saints: Melisande seems to be a combination of Melissa or Millicent and Sandra. Sandra, of course, is accepted as a short form of Alexandra or Cassandra. This leads to two Sts. Melanie, one each of Sts. Alexandra, Milisa, Milia, and Sandro.

Feast Dates: June 8 — St. Melanie (see Melanie); June 1 — St. Melosa (see Melissa).

Melise (French) See Melissa.

Melisenda (Spanish combination) See Melisandra, Melissa/Millicent+Sandra.

Melisent (English) See Melissa.

Melissa "The Honeybee" (Greek).

Patron Saints: There are a few saints who have names that are very similar to Melissa. They include Sts. Melosa, Melusina, Mella, and Isa. St. Melosa is remembered as a martyr who died in ancient Thessalonica.

Also knowing that *melissa* in Greek means "honeybee" leads to two more saints. They are Sts. Bernard and Modomnoc. They are patrons of honeybees.

Feast Dates: June 1 — St. Melosa; March 31 — St. Mella (see Melantha).

Melisse (French) See Melissa.

Melita (Spanish) See Carmelita.

Melitta (English) See Melissa.

Mella (variant) See Melantha, Melba, Melanie, Melina, Melinda, Melisandra, Melissa, Melody, Melvina.

Melleta (variant) See Melissa.

Melli (English) See Amelia, Melanie, Melissa.

Mellicent (variant) See Melissa.

Mellie (English) See Amelia, Melanie, Melissa.

Mellisa (variant) See Melissa.

Melly (English) See Amelia, Melanie, Melissa.

Melodie (variant) See Melody.

Melody "The One Like Beautiful Music" (Greek).

Patron Saints: There are a few saints that can serve as patrons for Melody. One is called St. Romanus the Melodist. Born in Emesa, Syria, and of Jewish ancestry, he was the greatest of the Byzantine liturgical priest-poets. He died in 540 after writing some one thousand hymns. Only about eighty have survived to our time.

Two more men are called "hymnographers" (or "melodists"). Another candidate for patron is St. Cecilia, who is recognized as patron of music.

Feast Dates: October 1 — St. Romanus the Melodist; November 22 — St. Cecilia (see Cecilia).

Melloney (English) See Melanie.

Meloni (English) See Melanie.

Melonie (English) See Melanie.

Melony (English) See Melanie.

Melora (American double) See Melanie/Melissa/Melody+Lora.

Melosa (Spanish) See Melissa.

Melva (Irish) See Melba, Melvina.

Melvena (Irish) See Melvina.

Melvina "The Polished Chieftain" (Irish) or "The Sweet Lady" (Spanish.

Patron Saints: Mela is a nickname for Melvin, and this leads to a couple of Sts. Mella. One of them was a prayerful person in medieval Londonderry, Ireland.

Feast Dates: March 19 — St. Mella.

Melzetta (African-American double) See Melissa+Zetta.

Melzore (African-American double) See Melissa+Zorah.

Mema (Spanish) See Emily.

Mena (variant) See Mina.

Mendora (African-American double) See any "Me" name+Dora.

Menora (African-American double) See any "Me" name+Nora.

Merced (variant) See Mercy, Mercedes.

Mercedes "The Compassionate One" (Spanish) or "The Payment [Reward]" (Latin).

Patron Saints: Mercedes derives from the Spanish *merced* (which means "mercy") and leads directly to the Blessed Virgin, the "Mother of Mercy." She was given this title simply because she gave birth to Jesus, who is Divine Mercy. The use of the title "Mother of Mercy" dates to the third century and appears in many Catholic prayers. St. Thomas Aquinas explained, "When the Virgin conceived the Eternal Word in her womb she obtained half of God's Kingdom and became the 'Queen of Mercy.' Her Son remained the 'King of Justice.'"

Catholic tradition suggests that Mary, with God's permission, gave the title to herself in a vision to St. Bridget. She is supposed to have said, "I am the Mother of Mercy. There are no sinners on earth who are so unfortunate as to be beyond my mercy. None are so abandoned that they cannot return to God if they invoke my aid. I am compassionate toward all and eager to help sinners." Jesus has shared an important part of his ministry with his Mother. We can rely on her maternal love.

Feast Dates: All Saturdays — The Blessed Virgin Mary, Mother of Mercy.

Mercedez (variant) See Mercedes.

Mercee (variant) See Mercedes.

Merci (French) See Mercedes.

Mercia "From the Kingdom of Mercia" (Old English).

Patron Saints: The ancient kingdom of Mercia in England has given us many saints. One is St. Edburga of Mercia. A daughter of King Penda, she became a nun at Aylesbury in the 600s.

Feast Dates: July 18 — St. Edburga of Mercia.

Mercie (variant) See Mercedes.

Mercy (English) See Mercedes.

Meredee (variant) See Meredith.

Meredith "The Guardian from the Sea" (Welsh).

Patron Saints: Two Sts. Meriadec can serve as patrons for Meredith. One of the Sts. Meredith was born in Wales in the early 600s. He was ordained a priest by St. Hingueten, the bishop of Vannes, and lived much of his priestly life as a hermit. Then in 666 he was elected bishop of Vannes. He is patron of those suffering from deafness.

Feast Dates: June 7 — St. Meredith, also known as Meriadec.

Meredithe (variant) See Meredith.

Merete (Dutch) See Margaret.

Merial (variant) See Muriel.

Meribeth (English double) See Merry+ Bethany/Elizabeth.

Meridel (English) See Mary.

Meridia "The One Born at Midday" (Latin).

Patron Saints: There is one St. Meridia. She was a martyr for Jesus in Umbria during the reign of Diocletian.

Feast Dates: May 26 — St. Meridia.

Meridie (variant) See Meredith.

Meridith (English) See Meredith.

Meriel (Irish) See Maris.

Merila (variant) See Muriel.

Merilla (variant) See Muriel.

Merisa (Hispanic-American) See Marissa.

Merissa (English) See Maris.

Merl (variant) See Meryl.

Merla (variant) See Meryl.

Merle (variant) See Meryl.

Merlina (variant) See Meryl.

Merline (variant) See Meryl.

Merna (variant) See Myrna.

Merola (variant) See Meryl.

Merribeth (variant double) See Merry+ Bethany/Elizabeth.

Merrie (English) See Merry, Meredith.

Merrielle (variant) See Merry.

Merril (variant) See Merry, Meryl, Muriel.

Merrile (variant) See Merry.

Merrilee (English double) See Merry+ Leigh.

Merrili (variant) See Mary.

Merrill (variant double) See Muriel, Meryl, Mary+Lynn.

Merrily (variant) See Merry.

Merry "The Happy One" (Middle English) or "The Guardian from the Sea" (nickname for Meredith).

Patron Saints: Some patron candidates are Sts. Merry, Merryn, and Mederic. St. Merry (also known as Mederic) was born into nobility, received a fine education, became a monk, and later an abbot. Slowly his reputation for holiness and miracles grew and the monastery was swamped with pilgrims. Eventually growing tired of all this activity, he retired to a hermit's cell that he had built himself. Years later, he moved near Paris and lived as a recluse. He died in 700.

Feast Dates: August 29 — St. Merry, also known as Mederic.

Mersey (variant) See Mercedes.

Mertlce (variant) See Myrtle.

Mertle (variant) See Myrtle.

Meryl "The Thrush [or Blackbird or Crow]" (French-Latin).

Patron Saints: This name leads to one male and one female St. Merle. The female St. Merle died a martyr's death in ancient Antioch. Another patron can be found when one realizes that Merle means "blackbird" or "crow" — for example, Bl. Alexander Crow.

Feast Dates: November 30 — St. Merle, also known as Merula; May 4 — Bl. Alexander Crow (see Raven).

Messalina (Latin double) See Messina+Lina/Ina.

Messina "The Middle Child" (Latin).

Patron Saints: Seventy-nine martyrs died for the faith in ancient Messina.

Feast Dates: February 21 — The Seventy-nine Martyrs of Messina.

Meta (Norwegian) See Margaret.

Metra (variant) See Demetria.

Metria (variant) See Demetria.

Mia "Mine Own" (Swedish form of Maria) or "She Who Is Like God" (American form of Michaela).

Patron Saints: Mia is usually accepted as a form of Michaela. There are over five dozen male and female Sts. Michael. One is St. Mianach McFailbhe, who is simply remembered as an "Irish saint."

Feast Dates: July 18 — St. Mianach.

Micaela (Hebrew) See Michaela, Michaelina.

Michaela "She Who Is Like God" (Italian).

Patron Saints: There are about fifty male Sts. Michael and a few female saints. One female, St. Mary-Michaela Dermaisiéres, was born in Madrid,

Spain, in 1809, and was the countess of Sorbalán. She founded a religious order to serve the poor and died at the age of fifty-one.

Feast Dates: August 26 — St. Mary-Michaela Dermaisiéres; June 19 — Bl. Michelina Metelli (see Michaelina).

Michaele (Italian) See Michaela, Michaelina.

Michaelea (variant) See Michaela, Michaelina.

Michaelia (variant) See Michaelina.

Michaelina "She Who Is Like God" (German).

Patron Saints: Michelina, 1300-1356, was born into a wealthy family in Italy. At the age of twelve, she was married to the duke of Malatesta. A worldly woman, she had one son. Nine years later tragedy struck when her husband and son died. She grieved for fourteen years and sought answers to life and death. At the age of thirty-five she converted to Catholicism because of a very pious woman friend.

Her relatives were not impressed. First they treated her as a fool and then they imprisoned her. After being released from prison, she gave all her possessions to the poor and dedicated herself to a life of sacrifice, discipline, and prayer. She died when she was fifty-six years old.

Feast Dates: June 19 — Bl. Michelina Metelli.

Michaella (Italian) See Michaela, Michaelina.

Michala (Hebrew) See Michaela, Michaelina.

Michel (French) See Michaela, Michaelina.

Michele (French) See Michaela, Michaelina.

Micheline (French) See Michaela, Michaelina.

Michell (variant) See Michaela, Michaelina.

Michelle (French) See Michaela, Michaelina.

Michica "My Girl" (Spanish) or "Beautiful" (Japanese).

   Patron Saints: "My girl" leads to Niña and "beautiful" leads to Alana. These names lead to a number of patron saints, including St. Helena.

   Feast Dates: August 18 — St. Helena (see Helen).

Micki (nickname) See Michaela, Michaelina.

Mickie (nickname) See Michaela, Michaelina.

Micky (nickname) See Michaela, Michaelina.

Midges (nickname) See Michaela, Michaelina.

Migalia (Hispanic-American) See Michaela.

Miguela (Spanish) See Michaela, Michaelina.

Miguelita (Spanish) See Michaela, Michaelina.

Mikaela (English) See Michaela, Michaelina.

Mikelina (Russian) See Michaela, Michaeline.

Mikeline (variant) See Michaela, Michaelina.

Miki (nickname) See Michaela, Michaelina.

Mil (nickname) See Amelia, Camilla, Emily, Melissa, Mildred, Millicent.

Mila (Serbian, Croatian, Czech) See Amelia, Emily.

Milagras (variant) See Marva.

Milagron (variant) See Marva.

Milagros (Spanish) See Marva.

Mildred "The Gentle Counselor" (Old English).

   Patron Saints: There is one St. Mildred. There are also Sts. Milia and Mildgitha. St. Mildred was born in about 700, the second daughter of Prince Merowald of Mercia, England. Because of political unrest, she was sent to France, where she received her education. While there, she was courted by an ardent suitor whom she eventually rejected. Years later she had to flee to her mother's convent. In time, she decided to enter religious life. When her mother resigned as abbess, Mildred was elected. She proved to be a fine and able administrator and had great concern for the poor and the afflicted.

   Feast Dates: July 13 — St. Mildred; January 25 — St. Milia (see Millie).

Mildrid (variant) See Mildred.

Milena (Spanish) See Magdalen.

Milia (German) See Millicent, Mildred.

Milicent (variant) See Melissa.

Milisent (variant) See Millicent.

Milisia (variant) See Millicent.

Milissent (variant) See Melissa, Millicent.

Milka (Slavic) See Amelia, Emily.

Milli (nickname) See Amelia, Camilla, Emily, Melissa, Mildred, Millicent.

Millicent "The Industrious Worker" (Old German) or "The Honeybee" (variant form of Melissa).

   Patron Saints: There are two saints who bear variations of this name. One is St. Milisa, who died for Jesus in ancient Nicomedia. The other is St. Milia.

   Feast Dates: March 16 — St. Milisa; January 25 — St. Milia (see Millie).

Millie "Industrious One" (nickname for Amelia, Emily, Millicent) or "Honeybee" (nickname for Melissa) or "The Gentle Counselor" (nickname for Mildred) or "The Young Church Server" (nickname for Camilla).

   Patron Saints: Millie can be a shortened form of Camille, Emily, Melissa, Millicent, and Mildred. There are patrons for all of these names. There is also one St. Milia, who is remembered for being a holy virgin in ancient Lisbon, Portugal.

Feast Dates: January 25 — St. Milia.

Millisent (English) See Melissa.

Milly (nickname) See Amelia, Camilla, Emily, Melissa, Mildred, Millicent.

Milzie (variant) See Millicent.

Mima (nickname) See Jemima.

Mimi "The Bitter One" (French for Mary, Miriam) or "The Industrious One" (short form of Emily) or "The Dove" (nickname for Jemima).

Patron Saints: Mimi is a shortened form of either Mary, Miriam, or Emily. Each name leads to a number of patron saints. There is also one St. Mimus. He and forty-nine companions were martyred for their belief in the Catholic faith in ancient Africa. Most of them were probably black.

Feast Dates: October 31 — St. Mimus; July 1 — St. Miriam (see Miriam).

Min (nickname) See Mina, Mindy, Minerva, Minnie, Myna.

Min (Scottish) See Mary.

Mina "The Tender, Affectionate One" (Old German).

Patron Saints: There is one male saint with this name who lived in the 900s. St. Mina was born in ancient Sammanud in Egypt. He grew up and married but embraced a celibate life with his wife. After she died, he moved into the desert to live as a monk. Later he was consecrated bishop and was known for the gift of miracles.

Feast Dates: November 3 — St. Mina.

Minda (Indian) See Mindy.

Mindee (variant) See Mindy, Melinda.

Mindi (variant) See Melinda, Mindy.

Mindie (variant) See Melinda, Mindy.

Mindy "The Knowledgeable One" (variant of Minda) or "The Tender, Affectionate One" (nickname for Minna) or "The Sweet, Beautiful One" (variant form of Melinda).

Patron Saints: Mindy can be a shortened form of Minda, Minna, and Melinda. Each of these names leads to at least one patron. St. Mindina died a martyr's death in ancient Africa. She may have been black.

Feast Dates: May 26 — St. Mindina; November 3 — St. Mina (see Minda).

Mineola (African-American double) See Minni+Ola.

Minerva "The Wise One" (Greek, Spanish).

Patron Saints: Three ancient saints can be patrons: Sts. Minervinus, Minervius, and Minervus. A St. Minervinus died for Jesus in ancient Catania. St. Minervius died for Catholicism in the 300s in Lyons.

Feast Dates: December 31 — St. Minervinus; December 31 — St. Minervius.

Minetta (English double) See Minni+Etta.

Minetta (variant) See Mary, Mina, Minerva.

Minette (French double) See Minni+Ette.

Minette (variant) See Mary, Mina, Minerva.

Minna (nickname) See Gemini, Mary, Minnie, Minerva, Wilhelmina.

Minnee (nickname) See Gemini, Mary, Minna, Minnie, Minerva, Wilhelmina.

Minni (nickname) See Gemini, Mary, Minna, Minnie, Minerva, Wilhelmina.

Minnie "The Tender One" (Old German).

Patron Saints: Minnie, as a name in its own right, leads to a St. Minia, a virgin who was a martyred in ancient times. She is still honored in the Latin Cathedral of Smyrna.

Minnie can also serve as a nickname for Minerva, Wilhelmina, and Gemini, which lead to more patrons.

Feast Dates: Third Sunday of November — St. Minia.

Minny (nickname) See Gemini, Mary, Minna, Minnie, Minerva, Wilhelmina.

Minta (variant) See Minni.

Mira "The Wonderful One" (Latin, Spanish).

Patron Saints: There is a Bl. Miro. He was born at Tagamen. He became a monk with the Canons Regular of St. Augustine. He died in 1161. He is patron against headaches and toothaches.

Besides being a name in its own right, Mira can also be a nickname for Myra, Miranda, and Mary.

Feast Dates: September 12 — Bl. Miro.

Mirabel (variant double) See Mira+Belle.

Mirabella (Latin double) See Mira+Bella.

Mirabelle (French double) See Mira+Belle.

Miracle (English) See Marva.

Miranda "The Admirable One" (Spanish) or "The Strange One" (Latin).

Patron Saints: There is one St. Miranda, but he is a male. There is also a Bl. Miro.

In the 500s St. Portianus of Miranda was born a slave. Reaching adulthood, he became a monk. Later he became the abbot of the monastery of Miranda in the Auvergne. At one point in his life he fearlessly traveled to Austrasia to obtain the release of Auvergnate prisoners.

Feast Dates: November 24 — St. Portianus of Miranda; September 12 — Bl. Miro (see Mira).

Mireillei (Hebrew) See Mira.

Mirella (variant) See Mira, Miranda.

Mirelle (variant) See Mira, Miranda.

Miren (Basque) See Mary.

Miriam "The Bitter One" (Hebrew, original form of Mary) or "The Pearl" (variant form of Margaret).

Patron Saints: The Old Testament provides a St. Miriam, who was the older sister of Moses and Aaron and lived in about 1250 B.C. She was probably the sister who kept watch over the baby Moses when he was placed in the basket in the bulrushes. During the Exodus, she filled an important role, serving as a prophetess, teaching God's will. In fact, her song of victory at the Red Sea, in Exodus 15, is one of the oldest pieces of literature preserved in the Bible.

At one point, she overstepped her authority and challenged Moses. As a result, she became a leper for a short time, but Moses' prayer restored her to full health. It was her name that was given to the "Mother of God."

Feast Dates: July 1 — St. Miriam.

Mirian "The Bitter One" (variant form of Mary).

Patron Saints: This male saint, 265-342, was the king of Georgia. St. Mirian and his wife, Nana, seem to have been very wise rulers. When a slave girl, St. Christina (also known as Nino), cured a little baby in Jesus' name, they immediately took note. In a short time they converted to Christianity and invited missionaries into their country. He died at the age of seventy-seven.

Feast Dates: August 6 — St. Mirian.

Mirilla (Hebrew) See Mira.

Mirna (Spanish) See Myrna.

Mirra (variant) See Miranda.

Miryam (variant) See Miriam.

Mirza (Spanish) See Martha.

Misha (Israeli, Russian) See Melissa, Michaela.

Missi (nickname) See Melissa, Millicent.

Missie (nickname) See Melissa, Millicent.

Missy (nickname) See Melissa, Millicent.

Misti (Spanish) See Misty.

Misty "The One Covered by Fog [Mist]" (Middle English).

> *Patron Saints:* Mist or fog is really a low-lying cloud, and there is a St. Cloud who was heir to the throne of France. When his two brothers were killed because of politics, Cloud hid in a monastery. In time, he began living a life of prayer, became a disciple of St. Severinus, and spread the teachings of Jesus. He died in 560.
>
> *Feast Dates:* September 7 — St. Cloud.

Mitria (Greek) See Demetria.

Mitrina (variant) See Demetria.

Mitsey (variant) See Miriam.

Mitsi (variant) See Miriam.

Mitsie (variant) See Mary, Miriam.

Mitzi (German) See Mary, Miriam.

Mitzie (American) See Mary, Miriam.

Mitzy (American) See Miriam.

Modelia (African-American double) See any "Mo" name+Adella.

Modelle (African-American double) See any "Mo" name+Adella.

Modesta (Latin) See Modesty.

Modestia (Latin) See Modesty.

Modestine (English) See Modesty.

Modesty "The Modest One" (Latin).

> *Patron Saints:* The Latin word for "modesty" is *modestia*, and there are two Sts. Modesta. One of them lived in Roman times and gave her life as a martyr for Jesus in ancient Nicomedia.
>
> *Feast Dates:* March 13 — St. Modesta.

Moesha "The One Taken from the Water+The Female" (African-American double).

> *Patron Saints:* Moesha is a double word composed of Monica and Isha or Moses and Isha. St. Moses was the most important person in the entire Old Testament. He was the Jewish prophet and lawgiver. Through him the Jewish nation was born and the Ten Commandments were given to the world. *Isha* in Hebrew means "female" and was the name Adam gave Eve.
>
> *Feast Dates:* September 1 — St. Moses; December 24 — Sts. Adam and Eve (see Isha).

Moibeal (Scottish) See Mabel.

Moina (variant) See Myrna.

Moira (Irish) See Mary, Maureen.

Moire (Scottish Gaelic) See Mary.

Moll (nickname) See Mary.

Mollee (nickname) See Mary.

Molli (nickname) See Mary.

Mollie (nickname) See Mary.

Molly (nickname) See Mary.

Mom (nickname) See Mama.

Mona "Single One" (Greek) or "Born on the Moon Goddess's Day" (Middle English) or "Noblewoman" (Spanish).

> *Patron Saints:* Monas, a variant of Mona, can also be accepted as a form of Monica, which leads to many patrons or can be considered a complete name in its own right. And there is a St. Monas. She was a black lady from Africa who died a martyr in ancient times.
>
> *Feast Dates:* February 26 — St. Monas; August 27 — St. Monica (see Monica).

Monah (variant) See Mona.

Monas (variant) See Mona.

Monca (Irish) See Monica.

Monday "Born on the Moon Goddess's Day" (Middle English).

> *Patron Saints:* The fact that Monday means "moon day" helps find a patron. *Luna* is Latin for "moon" and the name Diana means "moon goddess." These lead to about a dozen saints.

St. Lunaire, 509-570, was the son of King Hoel I of Brittany and his mother was St. Pompeo. He and his brother, St. Tugdual, were educated by St. Illtyd. The brothers were then ordained priests by St. Dyfrig of Caerleon. Later, Lunaire became a bishop and founded a monastery in Brittany. He died at sixty-one years of age.

Feast Dates: July 1 — St. Lunaire, also known as St. Leonore; June 7 — St. Lunecharia (see Luna).

Monetta (English double) See Mona+ Etta.

Monica "The Wise Counselor" (Latin) or "The Lover of the Sun" (Spanish).

Patron Saints: There are two known Sts. Monica. The greatest is St. Monica, 332-387, probably a black woman and the mother of St. Augustine who lived near Carthage. One story tells us that she was a teen alcoholic. When she hit bottom she converted to Catholicism. Then she was given in marriage to a pagan with a violent temper. After many years of good example and prayer, Monica finally won over her husband to Christ. Two years after he died, Monica was deeply hurt when she learned that Augustine had embraced the Manichean heresy. She decided to do something about it and she began storming heaven with her prayers and tears. It took nine years, but Augustine finally converted to Catholicism. One year later she died at the age of fifty-five. She is patron of married women, mothers, and those who persevere in prayer.

Feast Dates: August 27 — St. Monica.

Monika (German, Polish) See Monica.

Monique (French) See Monica.

Monisha (African-American double) See Monica+Aisha/Isha.

Monna (variant) See Mona.

Montana "From the Mountain" (Spanish).

Patron Saints: There are two known Sts. Montana and a dozen Sts. Montanus. One St. Montana was a religious sister who eventually became the abbess of the Ferrières convent near Orléans in the 700s.

Feast Dates: October 3 — St. Montana.

Moon (English) See Luna.

Mora (Irish) See Mary, Maurene.

Morag (Scottish) See Sarah.

Moraima (Hispanic-American double) See Mora+Aime.

Moreen (Irish) See Mary, Maureen.

Morena "The Brown-Haired One" (Spanish) or "The Bitter One" (Irish form of Maureen, Mary).

Patron Saints: There is one saint-in-the-making with this name. SG Sister Moreno, 1885-1936, was a schoolteacher and a local superior for her religious order. She was devoted to helping the poor. In 1936 the sisters had to flee from Spain because the Red army had begun a severe persecution of religious. Sister Carmen and Sister Amparo Carbonell remained behind to stay with a seriously ill nun in the hospital. Soon after the release of the sick sister, all were arrested by army authorities. The sick nun was released, but the other two were taken to the local stadium, where they were beaten and shot in the head.

Feast Dates: September 6 — SG Carmen Moreno, F.M.A.

Moria (Irish) See Mary, Maurene.

Moriah "God Is My Teacher" (Hebrew).

Patron Saints: Two great saints qualify to serve a person named Moriah. The first is Jesus Christ, the Teacher. The second is Our Lady of Good Counsel.

Feast Dates: April 25 — Our Lady of Good Counsel (see Consuelo).

Morine (Irish) See Mary, Maurene.

Morgan (English) See Morgana.

Morgana "From the Seashore" (Welsh, Breton).

Patron Saints: It helps to know that Pelagia is a Breton form of Morgana. And there are almost a dozen Sts. Pelagia from which to choose. One of these was a committed fifteen-year-old Catholic who lived with her mother in the early part of the fourth century. As the soldiers approached her home to arrest her and her mother, the two jumped from the roof into the Orontes River. In their struggle to escape, they drowned.

Also note that one of the nieces or nephews of St. Patrick was named St. Morgornon.

Feast Dates: June 9 — St. Pelagia of Antioch, also known as Morgana.

Morganica (variant) See Morgana.

Morganne (English double) See Morgan+Ann.

Morgen (English) See Morgana.

Morgen (variant) See Morgana.

Morissa (English) See Maris.

Morna (variant) See Myrna.

Mosella "The One Drawn from the Water" (Hebrew).

Patron Saints: Mosella is a feminine form of Moses, and there are about a dozen Sts. Moses.

Feast Dates: September 1 — St. Moses (see Moesha).

Moselle (English) See Mosella.

Mosetta (African-American double) See Mosella+Etta.

Mother (English) See Mama.

Moya (Irish) See Mary.

Moyna (variant) See Mona, Myrna.

Mozella (English) See Mosella.

Mozelle (English) See Mosella.

Mozetta (African-American double) See Mosella+Etta.

Muffee (American) See Muffin.

Muffi (American) See Muffin.

Muffie (American) See Muffin.

Muffin "A Soft Bread" (Old French).

Patron Saints: Because a muffin is a "type of bread," we can turn to four saints who are patrons of bakers: Sts. Elizabeth of Hungary, Honoratus, Meingold, and Nicholas of Myra. To them we can add one great patron.

The Gospel of John 6:30-71 provides Catholics with the foundation for the belief in the "Real Presence." The Jews asked Jesus what kind of work he did. Jesus' response was that he was the "bread of life." When the Jews reacted in disgust, Jesus told them that his flesh was real food and his blood was real drink. He insisted several times that they must eat his flesh and drink his blood. Jesus did not back down from this teaching even though many of his disciples quit following him at this time. Among them was Judas Iscariot. Catholic theology further insists that the Jesus that comes to us in Holy Communion is the risen Jesus. While the Mass remembers the passion and death of Jesus, it is not a participation in killing him again. Jesus died once for all, some two thousand years ago. What the Mass is, to put it in its proper context, is a celebration of intimate union with God. This, of course, is the primary meaning of "sacrifice."

Feast Dates: Corpus Christi — Jesus the Bread of Life.

Muffy (American) See Muffin.

Muire (Gaelic) See Mary.

Muireall (Irish) See Muriel.

Muirell (variant) See Mary, Muriel.

Muirgheal (Irish) See Mary, Muriel.

Muriel "The Sea-Bright One" (Irish Gaelic) or "The Bitter One" (variant of Mary).

Patron Saints: There is one St. Muriel. She is remembered as a "Scottish virgin." Because Muriel is also considered a form of Mary, over a hundred Sts. Mary are available.

Feast Dates: November 1 — St. Muriel.

Mya (variant) See Mia.

Mychal (American) See Michaela, Michaelina.

Myesha (Hispanic-American double) See Myra+Isha.

Myna (variant) See Minerva, Mina.

Myndy (American) See Mindy.

Myra "A Fragrant Ointment" (Latin) or "The Wonderful One" (variant of Mira).

Patron Saints: Myra is the feminine form of Myron. There are almost a half-dozen Sts. Myron. In addition, some think Myra is a form of Mary or Miranda, and this leads to more patrons. To all of these, one must add St. Nicholas, bishop of Myra, 280-350, who used the great wealth he inherited to help the poor. The story is told how he helped the three daughters of a bankrupt local citizen. They each needed a dowry for marriage and Nicholas provided it — on three separate occasions. Under the cover of darkness, he delivered bags of money to their home. From this story was born Santa Claus.

He is patron of bakers, bootblacks, brewers, children, coopers (barrel-makers), dockworkers, fishermen, merchants, pawnbrokers, perfumers, prisoners, sailors, spinsters, and travelers; also of bridges, Greece, Russia, Sicily, and Switzerland.

Feast Dates: December 6 — St. Nicholas of Myra.

Myranda (Latin) See Miranda.

Myriam (American) See Miriam.

Myrilla (variant) See Mira, Miranda.

Myrle (variant) See Meryl.

Myrlene (variant) See Meryl.

Myrlie (African-American) See Meryl.

Myrline (variant) See Meryl.

Myrna "The Polite, Gentle One" (Irish Gaelic) or "The Beloved" (Irish) or "The Bitter One" (variant of Mary).

Patron Saints: This name leads to a St. Myra and a few other saints with similar names: Sts. Murina, Murenna, and Mirax. Furthermore, if Myrna is accepted as a form of Mary, then over a hundred Sts. Mary are available. A St. Murna is simply remembered as an "Irish saint" from medieval times.

Feast Dates: May 21 — St. Murna.

Myrt (nickname) See Myrtle.

Myrta (English) See Myrtle.

Myrtaline (African-American) See Myrtle.

Myrtia (variant) See Myrtle.

Myrtice (variant) See Myrtle.

Myrtie (variant) See Myrtle.

Myrtis (African-American) See Myrtle.

Myrtle "Like a Myrtle Tree" (Greek).

Patron Saints: The Bible teaches that Esther is an alternate form of Myrtle. This leads to St. Esther as a patron. There is also a St. Murrita. She was a black woman who was executed for belief in Catholicism in ancient Carthage.

Feast Dates: July 13 — St. Murrita; December 20 — St. Esther (see Esther).

N

Na "No" (Scottish).

Patron Saints: After "La" and "Sha" the "Na" sound is preferred by African-Americans as a name prefix. The patron saint is usually found in the name attached to these prefixes.

Naa'ila (Arabic) See Victoria.

Nada (nickname) See Nadine.

Nadean (variant) See Natalie.

Nadene (variant) See Natalie.

Nadia (Spanish) See Esperanza, Hope.

Nadina (Spanish) See Nadia.

Nadine "The Hopeful One" (French, Slavic) or "The Gift" (modern feminine form of Nathan).

Patron Saints: It is helpful to know that Nadine means "hope," and there are a few Sts. Hope. Furthermore, some scholars insist that Nadine is a feminine form of Nathan.

Feast Dates: November 15 — St. Hope, also known as Elpidius; August 24 — St. Nathaniel (see Nathania).

Nadiya (variant) See Natalie.

Nady (variant) See Natalie.

Nadya (variant) See Natalie.

Na'eema (Arabic) See Joy.

Naesha (Hispanic-American double) See Na'eema+Sha.

Nahla (African-American) See Na+La.

Naida (African-American) See Na+Aida.

Najah (African-American) See Najam, Najat.

Najam (Arabic) See Star.

Najat (North African) See Opal.

Najee (Arabic) See Star.

NaKeisha (African-American double) See Na+Keisha.

NaKeshia (African-American double) See Na+Keisha.

Na'il (African-American) See Naa'ila.

Nan (nickname) See Ann, Hannah, Nancy.

Nana (Spanish) See Ann, Hannah, Nancy.

Nancee (nickname) See Ann, Hannah, Nancy.

Nancey (nickname) See Ann, Hannah, Nancy.

Nanci (nickname) See Ann, Hannah, Nancy.

Nancie (nickname) See Ann, Hannah, Nancy.

Nancy "The God-Graced One" (English form of Ann) or "The Lamb" (nickname for Agnes).

Patron Saints: St. Nana, 270-340, can be a patron of Nancy. Nana and her husband, Mirian, were the pagan queen and king of ancient Georgia. One day they heard about a healing miracle brought about through the prayers to Jesus by a slave girl named Nino. Eventually Nana and her husband became Christians, and this led to the conversion of their entire nation.

Also note that Nancy is a form of Ann, which makes available two dozen Sts. Ann or Anne for patrons.

Feast Dates: August 6 — St. Nana; July 26 — St. Anne (see Ann).

Nanete (variant) See Ann, Hannah, Nancy.

Nanetta (English double) See Ann, Hannah/Nancy+Etta.

Nanette (French double) See Ann, Hannah/Nancy+Ette.

Nani (nickname) See Ann, Hannah, Nancy.

Nanice (variant) See Ann, Hannah, Nancy.

Nanie (nickname) See Ann, Hannah, Nancy.

Nanni (nickname) See Ann, Hannah, Nancy.

Nannie (nickname) See Ann, Hannah, Nancy.

Nanny (nickname) See Ann, Hannah, Nancy.

Nanon (variant) See Ann, Hannah, Nancy.

Nansi (nickname) See Nancy.

Nansie (nickname) See Nancy.

Naoma (English) See Naomi.

Naomi "The Pleasant One" (Hebrew).

Patron Saints: One must turn to the Bible to find a holy Naomi. She lived in about 1100 B.C. in Bethlehem and was married to an Israelite named Elimelech, with whom she had two sons. A famine came upon the land and the family fled to Moab, where her husband died. Her sons grew up, married pagan women, and died. There were no grandchildren. Naomi decided to return to live near her kin in Bethlehem. She suggested that her pagan former daughters-in-law, Orpah and Ruth, return to their own people. Orpah did so.

However, Ruth refused, declaring, "For where you go, I will go, and where you lodge, I will lodge; your people shall be my people, and your God my God" (Ruth 1:16).

Naomi arranged for Ruth to be married to a cousin and all her debts to be paid. Eventually a son was born to Ruth. These women became the ancestors, not only of King David, but also of Jesus.

Feast Dates: November 1 — The Holy Naomi.

Nara (Greek) See Hillary.

Narda (Spanish) See Joy.

Na'Sheeman (African-American) See Na'eema.

Nasia (nickname) See Athanasia.

Nasstka (Polish) See Anastasia.

Nastasia (nickname) See Anastasia.

Nastasja (nickname) See Anastasia.

Nastassia (nickname) See Anastasia.

Nastya (Russian) See Anastasia.

Nat (nickname) See Natalie.

Nata (nickname) See Natalie, Nathania.

Natacha (Spanish) See Natalie.

Natala (Polish, Portuguese, Spanish) See Natalie.

Natalee (variant double) See Natalie+ Leigh/Leah.

Natalia (Polish, Portuguese, Spanish) See Natalie.

Natalie "The One Born on Christmas" (Latin).

Patron Saints: There are about a half-dozen Sts. Natalia, Natalie, Natalis, and Natalena. In 304 St. Natalia, a Christian, had married Adrian, a pagan officer at the imperial court of Nicomedia when a persecution broke out. One day Adrian saw twenty-three Christians being brutalized, and this ill-treatment moved him to proclaim himself a Christian. He was immediately imprisoned.

His young bride, Natalia, came to the prison, encouraged him, and asked her Christian friends to instruct him in the faith. A week later Adrian refused to offer sacrifice to the idols, was scourged, and returned to prison. The emperor, hearing that some women were ministering to the wounded in prison, forbade it. At this, Natalia cut her hair, put on men's clothes, and bribed her way into prison to be near her husband and nurse everyone. When the Christians were sentenced to have their limbs broken and cut off, Natalia remained at her husband's side. She died not long after Adrian, who has also been canonized. He is patron of butchers, prison guards, and soldiers.

Feast Dates: September 8 — St. Natalie.

Natalina (Russian) See Natalie.

Natalya (Russian) See Natalie.

Natasha (Russian) See Natalie.

Nathalia (French) See Natalie.

Nathalie (French) See Natalie.

Nathaly (Hispanic-American) See Natalie.

Nathania "The Gift" (Hebrew).

Patron Saints: There are a few Sts. Nathalan and Nathanel. One gave himself to a life of prayer and solitude for twenty-seven years in the Egyptian desert. He died in 375.

Feast Dates: November 27 — St. Nathaniel.

Natheen (English) See Nathania.

Nathene (English) See Nathania.

Natividad "The One Born on Christmas" (Spanish).

Patron Saints: St. María Natividad Venegas is the first native Mexican female saint. Born in 1868, she entered the convent at the age of fifteen. She is remembered for her devotion to the Blessed Sacrament and to the Sacred Hearts of Jesus and the Virgin Mary.

She also took special care of the religious sisters who joined her. She showed great respect for the pope and bishops, prayed for priests, and took care of the sick and poor. She died in 1959 at the age of ninety.

Feast Dates: July 30 — St. María Natividad Venegas.

Natka (variant) See Natalie.

Natti (nickname) See Natalie.

Nattie (nickname) See Natalie.

Natty (nickname) See Natalie.

Nawanna (African-American double) See Na+Wanda.

Neala "The Champion" (Celtic) or "The Yellow-Colored One" (nickname for Cornelia).

Patron Saints: Neala could be accepted as a feminine form of Neal or Neil. There is one St. Nielchus and he was the bishop of ancient Ardagh.

Feast Dates: February 6 — St. Nielchus; September 26 — St. Nilus of Rossano (see Nyleen).

Nebula (Latin) See Misty.

Necha (Spanish) See Agnes.

Neda "The One Born on Sunday" (Slavic) or "The Wealthy Guardian" (short feminine form of Edward).

Patron Saints: If one accepts Neda as meaning "born on Sunday," then Jesus Christ becomes the principal patron. However, if one accepts the name as a feminine form of Edward and means "wealthy guardian," then two dozen Sts. Edward qualify.

Feast Dates: July 6 — St. Dominica (see Sunday); August 21 — St. Dominica (see Dominica).

Nedda (nickname) See Neda.

Nedi (nickname) See Neda.

Nedra (African-American) See Neda.

Neela (English) See Cornelia.

Nefera (African-American) See Nefertari, Nefertiti.

Nefertari Meaning unknown (Egyptian).

Patron Saints: Nefertari was the wife of the Egyptian king Tutankhamen. During the Christian era, one St. Neffrei became a priest and, with his brothers, preached the Gospel in Spain.

Feast Dates: November 1 — St. Neffrei.

Nefertia (African-American) See Nefertari, Nefertiti.

Nefertiti Meaning unknown (Egyptian).

Patron Saints: Nefertiti was the wife of the Egyptian king Akhenaton, who introduced monotheism to ancient Egypt. Scholars present strong arguments to prove that Nefertiti was a Jewish woman and possibly responsible for the king's espousal of belief in one God. In more recent times two Sts. Neffyd have emerged. One was a medieval Welsh woman who was married to a saint and had many saintly children.

Feast Dates: November 1 — St. Neffyd.

Neile (variant) See Neala.

Neilla (variant) See Neala.

Neille (variant) See Neala.

NeKishia (African-American) See Na+Keisha.

Nekita "The Unconquerable One" (American form of the Russian name Nikita).

Patron Saints: There are about two dozen Sts. Nikita. One is a Syrian saint known as "The Wonderworker." In ancient times Nikita was spelled Nicetas.

Feast Dates: August 4 — St. Nikita, also known as Nicetas.

Nela (variant) See Cornelia.

Nelda (variant) See Cornelia, Eleanor.

Nelia (Spanish) See Cornelia.

Nelie (English) See Cornelia.

Nelieke (variant) See Cornelia.

Nelina (variant) See Cornelia.

Nelita (Spanish double) See Cornelia+Ita.

Nell (variant) See Cornelia, Eleanor, Helen, Neala, Olivia, Parnella, Prunella.

Nella (variant) See Nell.

Nellee (variant) See Nell.

Nelli (variant) See Nell.

Nellie (nickname) See Nell.

Nelly (nickname) See Nell.

Nelsida (Hispanic-American double) See Nelia+Ida.

Nemi (variant) See Naomi.

Nenah (Hispanic-American) See Niña.

Neneca (Spanish) See Emily.

Neona "The New Moon" (Greek).

Patron Saints: There are two ancient saints with similar names. One St.

Neonilla was the sister of Claudius, Asterius, and Neon. She was martyred by being drowned at Aegae, Cilicia, in 285.

Feast Dates: October 29 — St. Neonilla.

Nera "The Nymph from the Water" (Greek).

Patron Saints: There is at least one St. Nera. When she refused to marry, her mother had her locked in a prison. It is said that she often had grand visions of our Lord and the saints while incarcerated. After her release, she placed herself under the guidance of Bl. Ambrose Sansedoni and gave herself to prayer.

Feast Dates: December 25 — Bl. Nera Tolomei.

Nereida (Spanish) See Nera.

Nerine (Greek) See Nera.

Nerisse (Greek) See Nera.

Nesha (Spanish) See Agnes.

Nessa (nickname) See Agnesa, Vanessa.

Nessie (nickname) See Agnesa, Vanessa.

Nessy (nickname) See Agnesa, Vanessa.

Nesta (nickname) See Agnes.

Netta (nickname) See Antonia, Jane.

Netti (nickname) See Ann, Annette, Antonia, Hannah, Henrietta, Nancy, Nanette, Natalie.

Nettie (nickname) See Netti.

Netty (nickname) See Netti.

Neva (Spanish) See Nevada.

Nevada "That Snowed Upon" (Spanish).

Patron Saints: Nevada, which means "that snowed upon," this leads to the Blessed Virgin Mary under the title of "Our Lady of the Snows." This is the name of the third patriarchal basilica located within the walls of Rome (after St. Peter and St. John Lateran). It is known as St. Mary Major (Santa Maria Maggiore or the Great St. Mary's). It was the first church in Rome and in the entire Western Church to be dedicated to the honor of our Lady.

Pope Sixtus III ordered it erected on the Esquiline Hill shortly after the Council of Ephesus had declared Mary the "Mother of God" in 431.

This ancient church has also been known as "St. Mary at the Crib." This is because it was believed to house a relic from the manger at Bethlehem. Another treasured possession now found in the church is an icon of "Our Lady, Health of the Roman People." It is thought to have been painted by St. Luke.

An ancient pious legend recalls that Mary appeared to a Roman patrician named John, asking to have a church built in her honor. In the middle of a hot summer, miraculous snow fell on the Esquiline Hill, and John immediately funded the building project. Thus, its name.

Feast Dates: August 5 — The Blessed Virgin Mary, Our Lady of the Snows.

Neve (Spanish) See Nevada.

Neysa (nickname) See Agnes.

Nezka (Slovenian) See Agnes.

Ni "The Daughter of" (Irish).

Patron Saints: Just as "O" in Irish indicates "son of," "Ni" indicates "daughter of." It is sometimes used in African-American names. Any Irish female saint such as St. Niadh of Luighne, Meath, Ireland, can be a patron of someone with a "Ni" in her name.

Feast Dates: June 5 — St. Niadh.

Nichol (variant) See Nichole.

Nichola (English) See Nichole.

Nichole "The Victorious One" (Greek).

Patron Saints: There is one known St. Nichole and she served God as abbess of Almenenches.

Also remember that "Nichole" and "Collette" both come from "Nicholas" and that makes a St. Collette and fifty Sts. Nicholas available for patrons.

Feast Dates: November 1 — St. Nichole; March 6 — St. Collette (see Colette); December 6 — St. Nicholas of Myra (see Myra).

Nicholle (French) See Nichole.

Nicki (nickname) See Nichole.

Nickie (nickname) See Nichole.

Nicky (nickname) See Nichole.

Nicol (English) See Nichole.

Nicola (English) See Nichole.

Nicole (variant) See Nichole.

Nicolea (variant) See Nichole.

Nicolette (French) See Nichole.

Nicoli (variant) See Nichole.

Nicolina (Greek, English) See Nichole.

Nicoline (English) See Nichole.

Nicolle (French) See Nichole.

Nida (Spanish) See Nidia.

Nidan (Scottish) See Nidia.

Nidia "The Nest" (Spanish).

Patron Saints: St. Nidan served as a holy priest in medieval Scotland. He died in 610.

Feast Dates: November 3 — St. Nidan.

Niela (variant) See Neala.

Niesha (African-American) See Nisaa', Nyssa.

Nijah "The Saved One" (Arabic).

Patron Saints: St. Nidger was bishop of Augsburg in the 800s. See also Nijeri.

Feast Dates: October 9 — St. Nidger.

Nijeri "The Warrior's Daughter" (West African).

Patron Saints: St. Nidger will have to do duty here.

Feast Dates: October 9 — St. Nidger.

Nike (nickname) See Nichole.

Nikki (nickname) See Nichole.

Nikkie (nickname) See Nichole.

Nikolia (variant) See Nichole.

Nimia "The Over-Zealous One" (Latin).

Patron Saints: St. Nimmia died a martyr in ancient Augsburg.

Feast Dates: August 12 — St. Nimmia.

Niña "The Girl" (Spanish).

Nina "The God-Graced One" (Hebrew short form of Hannah).

Patron Saints: Nina (or Niña) can be a complete name in its own right, and there is a St. Nino and a St. Ninnius. The latter served God as a medieval holy bishop.

Furthermore, the Spanish name Niña can serve as a nickname for Antonia and Anna, and this reveals more patrons.

Feast Dates: August 5 — St. Ninnius; December 15 — St. Nino (see Christiana).

Ninette "The Little One+The Girl" (French double) or "The God-Graced One" (form of Ann, Nancy).

Patron Saints: There is one St. Nino and a St. Ninnita. St. Ninnita died for Jesus in ancient Nivedunum.

Feast Dates: June 4 — St. Ninnita; July 10 — St. Etto (see Etta).

Ninita (Spanish double) See Niña+Ita.

Ninnia (variant) See Niña.

Ninnita (Spanish double) See Niña+Ita.

Nino Meaning unknown (see Christiana).

Ninon (Spanish) See Ann, Nancy, Niña.

Ninoshka (Slavic) See Ann, Nancy, Nina.

Nisaa' (Arabic) See Andrea.

Nisha "The Night" (Hindu).

Patron Saints: A St. Nisia was martyred in ancient Africa.

Feast Dates: June 28 — St. Nisia.

Nissa (Greek) See Nyssa.

Nita (Spanish suffix) See Hannah, any name ending in "Ita."

Nixi (nickname) See Bernice.

Noami (English) See Naomi.

Noël "The One Born at Christmas" (French).

Patron Saints: There is an American St. Noël, and it helps to know that the name Noël is the French form of the Latin word *natalia*, meaning "birth" or "birthday." One can find about a half-dozen Sts. Natalia, Natalie, Natalis, and Natalena.

One of them is St. Natalia, the wife of St. Aurelius, who converted from Islam near Cordova in the 800s. She was beheaded for abandoning the Muslim religion.

Feast Dates: July 27 — St. Natalia; September 8 — St. Natalie (see Natalie).

Noelani "The Beautiful One from Heaven" (Hawaiian).

Patron Saints: There are a half-dozen Sts. Noël and Natalie.

Feast Dates: July 27 — St. Natalia; June 26 — St. Lanel (see Lane).

Noell (variant) See Noël.

Noella (variant) See Natalie, Noël.

Noelle (English) See Natalie, Noël.

Noellyn (variant) See Noël.

Noelyn (variant) See Noël.

Noemi (Hebrew) See Naomi.

Noesha (Hispanic-American double) See Noël+Shaba.

Nohely (Hispanic-American) See Noël.

Nola "The Small Bell" (Latin) or "The Famous, Noble One" (Irish Gaelic) or "Like an Olive Tree" (Irish form of Olivia) or "The One from Magdala" (short form of Magdalena).

Patron Saints: Some think Nola is the Irish form of Olivia. Furthermore, the town of Nola in Campania, southern Italy, is noted for turning out a great number of saints.

St. Felix of Nola served in the army and then became a priest and an adviser to St. Maximus, bishop of Nola. During the persecution of Christians by the emperor Decius, 249-251, Felix was arrested and thrown into a dungeon. But he was freed by an angel.

Then St. Maximus died and the bishopric of Nola was offered to St. Felix, which he accepted. His very long life was filled with holiness and charity.
Feast Dates: November 15 — St. Felix of Nola; January 15 — St. Maximus of Nola.

Nolana (English variation of Olivia) See Nola.

Noleta "The Unwilling One" (Latin).
Patron Saints: The ancient martyrs of Nola are the best candidates for patron.
Feast Dates: November 14 — St. Felix of Nola (see Nola); January 15 — St. Maximus of Nola (see Nola).

Noletta (variant) See Noleta.

Nolia (English) See Noleta.

Nolle (nickname) See Magdalena, Olivia.

Nolli (nickname) See Magdalena, Olivia.

Nollie (nickname) See Magdalena, Olivia.

Nolly (nickname) See Magdalena, Olivia.

Nona "The Ninth Daughter" (Latin).
Patron Saints: There are about a half-dozen Sts. Nona. One, whose name is spelled Nonna, was the wife of St. Gregory of Nazianzus the Elder and was a deaconess of the Church of Nazianzus. She was also the mother of St. Gregory of Nazianzus the Younger and St. Gorgonia. She made many prayers and sacrifices during her life and has become a model of the brave, virtuous, and noble woman. She died in 374.
Feast Dates: August 5 — St. Nonna.

Nonah (variant) See Nona.

Noni (nickname) See Nona.

Nonie (nickname) See Nona.

Nonna (variant) See Nona, Norma.

Nonnah (variant) See Nona, Norma.

Nora "The Light" (short form of Eleanor, Leonora) or "The Honorable One" (short form of Honora).

Patron Saints: Considering the various sources of the name, there are about a dozen Sts. Honora, Honorata, and Honoria, one known St. Leonore, two Bls. Eleanora, and one St. Elenara. And knowing Eleanor is a variant of Helen, there are more than a dozen Sts. Helen from which to choose.
Feast Dates: November 6 — St. Honora (see Honoria); August 18 — St. Helena (see Helen).

Norah (variant) See Helen, Honoria, Leonore, Nora.

Noralma (Spanish double) See Nora+Alma.

Noreen (Irish) See Nora, Norma.

Norella (Scandinavian) See Noël.

Norene (Irish) See Nora, Norma.

Nori (nickname) See Eleanor, Honoria, Leonore, Nora, Norma.

Norie (nickname) See Eleanor, Honoria, Leonore, Nora, Norma.

Norina (variant) See Nora, Norma.

Norine (variant) See Nora, Norma.

Norita (variant) See Nora, Norma.

Norma "The Carpenter's Square" (Spanish) or "The Exact Pattern" (Latin).
Patron Saints: In Latin, *norma* means a "carpenter's square." This allows four Catholic Church-appointed patrons of carpenters to serve as patrons of Norma: Sts. Joseph (husband of Mary), Eulogius of Cordova, Thomas the Apostle, and Wolfgang.

St. Eulogius was a priest in Cordova in the 800s. At this time the Muslims ruled Spain. St. Eulogius was repeatedly jailed because of his faith. Appointed archbishop of Toledo, he was beheaded by Muslim authorities before he could be consecrated. His "crime" was protecting a young female convert.
Feast Dates: March 11 — St. Eulogius.

Norri (nickname) See Eleanor, Leonore, Honoria.

Norrie (nickname) See Eleanor, Leonore, Honoria.

Norry (nickname) See Eleanor, Leonore, Honoria.

Nory (nickname) See Eleanor, Honoria, Leonore, Nora, Norma.

Norzelle (African-American double) See Nora+Zella.

Nova (Latin) See Novia.

Novella (Latin) See Novia, Natalie.

Novellia (variant) See Natalie, Noël.

November "Born in the Ninth Month" (Latin).

Patron Saints: A saint with a similar name may be adopted. She is St. Novella, from *novem*, the Latin for "nine."

Feast Dates: April 12 — St. Novella (see Novia).

Novia "The New One" (Latin) or "The Sweetheart" (Spanish).

Patron Saints: St. Novella died for her faith in ancient Capua, Italy.

Feast Dates: April 12 — St. Novella.

Nuela (Spanish) See Amelia.

Nydia (Latin) See Nidia.

Nyeema (African-American) See Na'eema.

Nykesha (African-American double) See any "Ny" name+Keisha.

Nyleen "The Champion" (American).

Patron Saints: Nyleen is a feminine form of Niles or Neil, and there are a half-dozen Sts. Nilus and one St. Nielchus. Among them is St. Niles, 910-1004. He was born into a Greek family at Calabria and was baptized "Nicholas." As a youth and a young adult, he was rather lukewarm, religiously. It seems he was living with a young lady for a while and had a child outside of marriage.

However, when he was about thirty years old, both his female companion and his child died. He himself almost died of sorrow and serious illness. These tragedies forced him to examine his life and he decided to turn to God. A short time later he entered a monastery of monks of the Byzantine rite. In time, he became an abbot and his reputation for knowledge and sanctity grew.

Feast Dates: September 26 — St. Nilus of Rossano; February 6 — St. Nielchus (see Neala).

Nylena (variant) See Nyleen.

Nylene (variant) See Nyleen.

Nyssa "The Beginning" (Greek) or "The Friendly Elf" (Scandinavian).

Patron Saints: St. Nisia embraced martyrdom in ancient Africa. She was probably a black woman.

Feast Dates: June 28 — St. Nisia.

O

O' "Descendant of" (Irish prefix used with surnames).

Octavia "The Eighth Daughter" (Latin, Spanish).

Patron Saints: There is one known St. Octavia and a half-dozen Sts. Octavius. One St. Octavia died for Jesus, with a number of friends in ancient Antioch.

Feast Dates: April 15 — St. Octavia.

Octavie (French) See Octavia.

October "Born in the Eighth Month" (Old English).

Patron Saints: St. October was one of the forty-seven martyrs of ancient Lyons.

Feast Dates: June 2 — St. October.

Oda (nickname) See Odele.

Odalys (Hispanic-American) See Odele, Odelia.

Odel (variant) See Odele, Odelia.

Odele "Like a Melody [or a Song]" (Greek).

Patron Saints: There are a half-dozen Sts. Oda, one St. Odelger, and two Sts. Odilo. One St. Oda was the sister of Sts. Eucharius, Elophius, Libaria, Susanna, Menna, and Gontrud and was martyred in ancient Toul.

Another St. Oda was the daughter of a medieval Scottish king. She was cured of blindness at the tomb of St. Lambert. She died in 726.

Feast Dates: February 16 — St. Oda; November 27 — St. Oda.

Odelete (Greek double) See Odele+Ette.

Odelette (English double) See Odelia+Ette.

Odelette (Greek double) See Odele+Ette.

Odelia "The Little Wealthy One" (Old Anglo-French, Spanish) or "I Will Praise God" (Hebrew).

Patron Saints: This name leads to a half-dozen Sts. Odilia and Odilo. One St. Odilia, 660-720, was the daughter of a Frankish lord. She was born blind, so her father wanted to leave her to die of exposure; but her mother gave the baby to a peasant woman who, in turn, gave her to a convent. At the age of twelve Odilia was finally baptized a Christian and her baptism healed her of her blindness.

Word of this miracle reached her brother and he petitioned his father for his sister's return, but the father had him killed. Then the father repented, received the girl home, fawned over her, and insisted that she marry. She refused and fled the castle, and her father tried to kill her. He again repented and built two convents for her. She is patron of Alsace, of the blind, and against blindness.

Feast Dates: December 13 — St. Odilia.

Odelinda (Greek double) See Odelia+Linda.

Odell (English) See Odele, Odelia.

Odilia (Spanish) See Odelia.

Ofelia (Greek) See Ophelia.

Ofilia (Greek, Spanish) See Ophelia.

Ofra (Jewish) See Oprah.

Oksana (Slavic) See Osanna.

Ola "The Holy One" (Norwegian variant of Olga) or "The Defender of Men" (German form of Olesia).

Patron Saints: St. Olcese served God as a bishop in medieval Switzerland.

Feast Dates: November 1 — St. Olcese; June 11 — St. Olga (see Olga).

Olalee (African-American double) See Ola+Leigh.

Olalla (Spanish) See Eulalia.

Ole (African-American) See Ola.

Olena "The Light" (Russian form of the Greek for "light").

Patron Saints: There is one St. Elena, one St. Elenara, and about eighteen Sts. Helena.

Feast Dates: June 18 — St. Elena (see Elena); May 25 — Bl. Eleonora (see Eleanor).

Oletha (African-American) See Aletha.

Olga "The Holy One" (Old Norse, Spanish) or "Like an Olive Tree" (English form of Olivia).

Patron Saints: There is one very famous St. Olga, 883-969. She became the wife of Igor I, the duke of Kiev. She was his faithful wife for forty-two years, until he was assassinated. She became the regent of the country. At the age of seventy-five, she traveled to Constantinople to visit the court of Emperor Constantine Porphyrogenitus and converted to Catholicism. The Greek emperor served as her godfather. She tried to establish Catholicism in Russia but failed. Her son remained a pagan, but when she died he honored her request and gave her a Christian funeral. She is Russia's first canonized saint.

Feast Dates: July 11 — St. Olga.

Oliana "Like the Oleander Flower" (Polynesian).

Patron Saints: St. Olivia, whose nickname is Oli, can be adopted, as can Sts. Olla and Ann. St. Olla was a holy virgin in France in the eleventh century.

Feast Dates: October 9 — St. Olla; July 26 — St. Ann (see Ann).

Olimpa (Italian, Portuguese) See Olympia.

Olimpia (Spanish) See Olympia.

Olinda "The Fragrant [Pretty] One" (Latin) or "The Protector of Property" (Spanish).

Patron Saints: There is a St. Lindru and a St. Berlindis.

Feast Dates: February 3 — St. Berlindis (see Linda); September 22 — St. Lindru (see Linda).

Olive (English) See Olga, Olivia.

Olivette (French double) See Olga, Olivia+Ette.

Olivia "Like an Olive Tree" (English, Spanish).

Patron Saints: There are about a dozen Sts. Oliva, Oliveria, and Olga. In the 800s a St. Olive was born at Palermo. When she was only thirteen years old, she was carried off to Tunis by Saracen invaders. For a short time she was allowed to live in a cave near Tunis. But trouble grew when she converted some Muslims to Christianity. She was immediately brought back to Tunis, locked in a dungeon, scourged, racked, and beheaded.

Feast Dates: June 10 — St. Olive.

Olli (nickname) See Olivia.

Ollie (nickname) See Olivia.

Olly (nickname) See Olivia.

Olva (English) See Olga, Olivia.

Olympe (French) See Olympia.

Olympia "The One from Heaven" (Greek).

Patron Saints: There is one St. Olympias, 386-408. She grew up in ancient Constantinople and married the prefect of the city. At one point their large fortune was confiscated by the government because she was a Christian. However, after the death of her husband her money was returned to her. With it, she helped the poor and founded a convent. Because she sided with St. John Chrysostom in a local controversy, she was sent into exile and died at the age of twenty-two.

Feast Dates: December 17 — St. Olympias.

Olympie (Czech) See Olympia.

Oma "The Female Commander" (Arabic) or "The Grandmother" (German).

Patron Saints: There is one St. Omer. He lived from 597 to 670. When his mother died, both he and his father became religious monks. Eventually he was elected bishop of Therouanne. Evangelization of local pagans became his primary objective.

Feast Dates: September 9 — St. Omer.

Omaire (Hispanic-American form of Irish Gaelic) See O'+Maire.

Omaly (Hispanic-American form of Irish Gaelic) See O'Malley.

O'Malley "The Descendant+From the Edge of the Hill" (Irish Gaelic double).

Patron Saints: The original spelling of Malley is Mala, and there is a St. Malaleel mentioned in the Book of Genesis. He was the fifth of the pre-flood patriarchs.

Feast Dates: April 2 — St. Malaleel (see Mary).

Omayrah (Hispanic-American form of Irish Gaelic) See O'+Mary.

Omelia (African-American) See Amelia.

Omera (African-American) See Oma.

Omizell (African-American double) See Amelia+Zella.

Ona "The First One" (form of Una) or "The Lamb" (variant form of Agnes).

Patron Saints: Besides being a name in its own right, Ona also serves as a nickname for Agnes and Guinevere and as a Lithuanian form of Ann.

Feast Dates: February 26 — St. Monas (see Una); January 21 — St. Agnes (see Agnes).

Onda (African-American) See Andrea through Ondrea.

Ondrea (African-American) See Andrea.

Oneida (North American Indian) See Désirée.

Onella (African-American double) See Ona+Elle.

Onetha (African-American double) See Ona+Etta.

Onetta (African-American double) See Agnes through Ona+Etta.

Onia (African-American) See Ona.

Onida (North American Indian) See Désirée.

OnieLee (African-American double) See Ona+Leigh.

Onora (Latin) See Honora.

Oona (variant) See Guinevere, Ona, Una, Winifred.

Oonagh (variant) See Ona, Una.

Opal "The Safe One" (Sanskrit).

Patron Saints: There is a St. Opio, who can be adopted as a patron. Many ancient pagan cultures regarded opal as a defense against the "evil eye." Others believed that a warrior wearing opal would be made invisible and spared from danger in battle. Taken together, these references lead to the heavenly city of Jerusalem. By describing heaven in terms of gold and precious stones, the Bible speaks of a precious, trusting, and harmonious family. This family has found ultimate safety and security with God.

Feast Dates: November 1 — All Saints; October 12 — St. Opio (see Ophelia).

Opalina (English) See Opal.

Opaline (English) See Opal.

Opel (variant) See Opal.

Ophelia "The One Who Helps [Needs Help]" (Middle English) or "The Serpent" (Greek).

Patron Saints: There is no known St. Ophelia. However, St. Opio can be adopted. He was a priest in France and is remembered for his great prayerfulness. St. Gideon of Ophra can also be adopted.

Feast Dates: October 12 — St. Opio; September 1 — St. Gideon of Ophrah (see Oprah).

Ophelie (French) See Ophelia.

Ophrah (variant) See Oprah.

Oprah "A Fawn" (Hebrew) or "A Forelock" (Hebrew) or "The One Who Helps" (English form of Ophelia).

Patron Saints: The Bible provides a patron. He is St. Gideon of Ophrah, born in about 1150 B.C. When the oppression of Israel became great, God called him to lead an army against the pagans. He objected, pointing out that he was the most insignificant person in Manasseh. But God reassured him that he would be Gideon's strength and Gideon relented.

Gideon then raised an army of thousands of men, but God pared it down to three hundred. Gideon, with faith in God, won the decisive battle and ruled as a judge over Israel for forty years.

Feast Dates: September 1 — St. Gideon of Ophrah.

Ora "From the Shore" (Old English) or "The Golden One" (Spanish) or "The One Who Prays" (Latin).

Patron Saints: See Aurelia, Aurora, Ora, Oriana, Oriola, and Zona for many patron saints.

Feast Dates: September 25 — St. Aurelia (see Aurelia).

Orabel (variant double) See Ora+Bella.

Orabelle (variant double) See Ora+Belle.

Orala (English, Latin) See Aurelia, Ora, Orialie.

Oralee (variant) See Aurelia.

Oralia (Latin) See Aurelia, Ora, Oralie.

Oralie "From the Divine Mouth" (Latin) or "The Golden [Dawn] One" (French form of Aurelia).

Patron Saints: The fact that *orela* means "spoken from the divine (golden) mouth" leads to St. John Chrysostom,

349-407. He was born a pagan in Antioch. At the age of nineteen, he converted to Catholicism, entered a monastery, lived the life of a hermit, was ordained a priest, and became a great preacher in Antioch. In 398 he became bishop of Constantinople. He was exiled twice, in spite of objections by the pope, and died in exile. He was given the surname Chrysostom (the Greek word for "golden-mouthed") after he died. He is a Doctor and Father of the Church and patron of church orators.

Feast Dates: September 13 — St. John Chrysostom.

Oralis (English) See Aurelia, Ora, Oralie.

Orana (variant) See Aurelia, Ora.

Orel (variant) See Aurelia.

Orelee (variant) See Aurelia.

Orelia (English) See Aurelia.

Orelle (variant) See Aurelia.

Oriana "The Golden One" (Irish) or "Dawn" (Old English).

Patron Saints: The fact that *oriana* means "dawn" leads to several patrons. *Aurora* also means "dawn" and Rori is a short form of Aurora and leads to St. Roricius. Both St. Roricius, 430-507, and his wife dedicated themselves to works of charity, especially ransoming captives. After his wife died, he was elected bishop.

Also, Oriana can mean "golden," and this leads to a few Sts. Aurelia.

Feast Dates: July 21 — St. Roricius; September 25 — St. Aurelia (see Aurelia).

Oriane (French) See Oriana.

Oriel (English) See Ora, Oriola.

Orielda (English) See Ora, Oriola.

Oriola "The [Golden] Fair-Haired One" (Latin).

Patron Saints: There is one St. Joseph Oriol, 1650-1702, of Barcelona. He was ordained a priest and became a doctor of theology. He is also remembered for living on just bread and water for twenty-two years and making many converts. It is also good to know that Oriola means about the same thing as Albina.

Feast Dates: March 23 — St. Joseph Oriol; March 4 — St. Albina (see Albina).

Oriole (English) See Ora, Oriela.

Oriella (English) See Ora, Oriola.

Orlanda (Italian) See Rolanda.

Orlena (English) See Ora, Oriola.

Orlene (English) See Ora, Oriola.

Orpah (variant) See Oprah.

Orsa (nickname) See Ursula.

Orsel (Dutch) See Ursula.

Orsola (Italian) See Ursula.

Ortensia (Italian) See Hortense.

Osanna "Praise the Lord" (Latin).

Patron Saints: There is one St. Osanna. Nothing more is remembered about him.

Feast Dates: June 18 — St. Osanna.

Osie "The Bone" (African-American).

Patron Saints: Ossius is Latin for "bone." St. Ossien is remembered simply as an "Irish saint."

Feast Dates: May 3 — St. Ossien.

OsieOla (African-American double) See Osie+Ola.

Otha (variant) See Odelia.

Othilia (variant) See Odelia.

Ottavia (Italian) See Octavie.

Ottilia (variant) See Odelia.

Oxanna (Slavic) See Osanna.

Oz (nickname) See Ozora, Zorah.

Ozney (African-American double) See Ozora+Ny.

Ozora "The Strength of God" (Hebrew).

Patron Saints: There is one saint with the similar name of Osorius. He was a holy bishop of Coimbra.

Feast Dates: January 26 — St. Osorius.

$\mathcal{P}$

Paca (Spanish) See Frances.

Padget (French) See Paige.

Page (Greek) See Paige.

Paige "The Child" (American) or "The Young [Helpful] Assistant" (American).

Patron Saints: Two English martyrs with the surname of Page can serve as fine patrons.

Bl. Antony Page, 1571-1593, studied at Douai, France, and was ordained a diocesan priest in 1591. He was hanged, drawn, and quartered in 1593 for being a Catholic priest. He was only twenty-two years old.

A short time later, in 1602, Bl. Francis Page met his death at Tyburn, a place of execution not far from Newgate Prison. Father Page was born into a Protestant family in England and converted to Catholicism. He was ordained a secular priest in 1600 at Douai in France. While in prison, awaiting execution in 1602, he became a Jesuit.

Feast Dates: May 4 — Bl. Antony Page; April 20 — Bl. Francis Page, S.J.

Palma "Born on Palm Sunday" (Latin) or "Like a Palm Tree" (Latin, Spanish).

Patron Saints: There are two Sts. Palmatius and one St. Palmus. St. Palmus died for Jesus in ancient Alexandria, Egypt. He may have been a black man.

Feast Dates: May 18 — St. Palmus.

Palmira (Spanish) See Palma.

Palmyra (variant) See Palma.

Paloma "The Dove" (Spanish).

Patron Saints: There is one St. Palomartus. He gave his life for the Catholic faith in ancient Antioch.

Feast Dates: March 5 — St. Palomartus.

Palometa (English) See Paloma.

Palomita (English) See Paloma.

Pam (nickname) See Pamela.

Pamela "The All+Honeylike [Sweet] One" (Greek double) or "The Singer" (Spanish).

Patron Saints: There is a saint with a similar name. St. Pambo was a disciple of the great St. Anthony, the founder of desert monasticism. He died in 390.

Patrons can also be found when one discovers that Pamela finds its source in two Greek words: *pan*, meaning "all," and *mela*, meaning "honey" or "sweet." This leads to Sts. Panacea, Mela, and Melosa. One is also led to St. Dulcissima, whose name means "most sweet."

Feast Dates: July 18 — St. Pambo; May 11 — St. Panacea (see Panacea); April 25 — St. Mella (see Melantha).

Pamelina (English) See Pamela.

Pamella (English) See Pamela.

Pammi (nickname) See Pamela.

Pammie (nickname) See Pamela.

Pammy (nickname) See Pamela.

Pan (nickname) See Panacea, Pansy.

Panacea "All-Healing One" (Latin).

Patron Saints: There is at least one St. Panacea, 1378 -1383. She was only five years old when her grandmother killed her because she was praying. It seems her grandmother had a hatred of religion.

Feast Dates: May 11 — St. Panacea.

Pancha (Spanish) See Frances.

Panchita (Spanish double) See Pancha+Ita.

Panda (nickname) See Pandora.

Pandi (nickname) See Pandora.

Pandie (nickname) See Pandora.

Pandora "The All+Gifted One" (Greek double, Spanish).

Patron Saints: Pandora comes from *pan*, meaning "all," and *dora*, meaning "gift." There is one saint with a similar name. St. Pandwyna was born into a noble Irish family. Later in life she became a nun at Cambridgeshire. She died in the year 904.

Feast Dates: August 26 — St. Pandwyna; May 1 — St. Isidora (see Isadora).

Pandoura (variant) See Pandora.

Pandy (nickname) See Pandora.

Panni (nickname) See Panacea.

Pannie (nickname) See Panacea.

Panny (nickname) See Panacea.

Pansie (nickname) See Pansy.

Pansy "The Thoughtful One" (French) or "The Fragrant One" (Greek).

Patron Saints: In Christian art the pansy is used to symbolize meditation. And we remember that Mary "pondered," meditated on the mystery of her being chosen to bear the Christ. Also, there is one female St. Pansemne and one male St. Pansius available.

St. Pansemne was a prostitute but was eventually converted to Jesus by St. Theophanes. Thereupon, she embraced a life of penance and prayer in ancient Antioch. She died in 369.

St. Pansius was one of thirty-seven Egyptians martyred for preaching about Jesus.

Feast Dates: June 10 — St. Pansemne; January 18 — St. Pansius.

Panzy (variant) See Pansy.

Paola (Italian) See Paula.

Paolina (Italian) See Pauline.

Paquita (Spanish) See Frances.

Paris "The Lovers" (French).

Patron Saints: There is at least one saint named Paris. He was born in Athens, Greece. After he converted to Jesus, he traveled to Italy. Eventually he became bishop of Tiano. He died in 333.

Feast Dates: August 5 — St. Paris.

Parnella (Old French) See Petronella.

Pascale (French) See Easter.

Pat (nickname) See Martha, Patience, Patricia.

Patience "The Enduring One" (English).

Patron Saints: There are two known Sts. Patiens and one St. Patientia. One of them was the wife of St. Orentius and mother of the deacon-martyr St. Vincent.

Feast Dates: May 1 — St. Patience, also known as Patientia.

Patrice (French) See Patricia.

Patricia "The Noblewoman" (Latin).

Patron Saints: There are at least three Sts. Patricia. Among them is one born in Constantinople in the early 600s into the imperial household of the emperor Constant I, 641-665. Not wishing to marry, she used a ploy common to her time and requested permission to make a pilgrimage to Rome. Once there, she made her vows as a nun. Upon learning of her parents' deaths, she returned to Constantinople to take charge of the estate she inherited and promptly distributed its wealth among the poor.

Feast Dates: August 25 — St. Patricia.

Patrizia (Italian) See Patricia.

Patsey (nickname) See Patricia.

Patsy (nickname) See Patricia.

Patti (nickname) See Martha, Patricia.

Pattie (nickname) See Martha, Patricia.

Patty (nickname) See Martha, Patricia.

Paula "The Little One" (Latin).

Patron Saints: There are almost a dozen Sts. Paula. St. Paula, 347-404, was born in Rome of a noble family, married, and had five children. Many thought she had an ideal marriage until her husband died. She then began to seek solace in prayer and filled her time by helping the poor. In 382 she had the joy of meeting St. Jerome. But she also had the heartbreak of burying a daughter in 384.

Then she traveled with Jerome to the Holy Land. Settling in Bethlehem she built a hospice, a monastery, and a convent. She died at the age of fifty-seven. She is patron of widows.

Feast Dates: January 26 — St. Paula; February 20 — St. Paula the Bearded (see Chiquita).

Paule (French) See Paula.

Pauletta (English double) See Paula+Etta.

Paulette (French double) See Paula+Ette.

Pauli (nickname) See Paula.

Paulie (nickname) See Paula.

Paulina (Italian) See Pauline.

Paulina (French, Spanish) See Paula.

Pauline "The Little One" (English, French).

Patron Saints: There are about a dozen Sts. Pauline and Paulina. One St. Paulina was a German princess. After her husband died, she founded a monastery. She died in 1107.

Feast Dates: March 14 — St. Paulina; January 26 — St. Paula (see Paula).

Paulita (Spanish double) See Paula+Ita.

Pauly (nickname) See Paula.

Pavia (Russian, Czech, Bulgarian) See Paula.

Payton (Irish) See Patricia.

Peace "The Tranquil One" (Latin).

Patron Saints: There is one known St. Pacianus. He married early and later became a priest and then a bishop. He is remembered as being a great Catholic writer in defense of the faith. He wrote the famous line "My name is Christian, and my surname is Catholic." He died in 390. He is a Church Father.

Feast Dates: March 9 — St. Pacianus.

Peaches "The Persian Apple" (Middle English).

Patron Saints: Medieval art leads to a patron. When an artist depicted the Madonna and Child Jesus, an apple was inappropriate because it symbolized sin. Therefore, the artist substituted a peach. The peach, or "Persian apple," was a positive symbol meaning "a virtuous heart and tongue." Thus the Madonna and Child Jesus make perfect patrons.

Feast Dates: January 1 — The Blessed Virgin Mary, Mother of God (see Mary).

Pearl "The Pearl" (Latin).

Patron Saints: There is one known St. Pearl who lived in about 400. That was her stage name, her real name being Pelagia. She was a glamorous singer-dancer-stripper in ancient Antioch. One day Bishop Nonnus of Edessa saw her act and exclaimed, "This woman teaches us bishops a lesson. She takes more time to care for her beauty and dancing than we do to care for our flocks."

Pearl heard his sermon and was moved to repent of her sins. She then gave a large donation to the Church and went on pilgrimage to the Holy Land, dressed as a male monk to avoid being troubled by others. In time, she became known as the "beardless monk" and is now patron of actresses.

Also, because Pearl is a familiar English form of Margaret, two dozen Sts. Margaret are available.

Feast Dates: October 8 — St. Pearl, also known as Pelagia; January 19 — St. Marguerite Bourgeoys (see Margaret).

Pearla (Italian) See Pearl.
Pearlie (Latin) See Pearl.
Pearline (French) See Pearl.
Peg (nickname) See Peggy, Margaret.
Pega (nickname) See Peggy, Margaret.
Pegeen (nickname) See Peggy, Margaret.
Peggee (nickname) See Peggy, Margaret.
Peggi (nickname) See Peggy, Margaret.
Peggie (nickname) See Peggy, Margaret.
Peggy "The Pearl" (English nickname for Margaret).
   Patron Saints: There is a St. Pega. She was the sister of St. Guthlac. She lived as a recluse, giving herself to prayer. She died on pilgrimage to Rome in 719.
   Feast Dates: January 8 — St. Pega; December 23 — St. Marie Marguerite d'Youville (see Marguerite).
Pela (Polish) See Penelope.
Pen (nickname) See Penelope.
Penelopa (Slavic) See Penelope.
Penelope "The Weaver" (Greek) or "The Duck" (Greek).
   Patron Saints: One ancient saint, St. Irene, was nicknamed Penelope. She is an ancient Byzantine convert. After becoming a Christian, she converted her parents. Her making of converts caught the attention of the local governor. He had her beheaded in the year 100.
   Feast Dates: May 5 — St. Irene, also known as Penelope.
Penina (English) See Penelope.
Penine (French) See Penelope.
Penni (nickname) See Penelope.
Pennie (nickname) See Penelope.
Penny (nickname) See Penelope.
Pensee (French) See Pansy.
Peonia (nickname) See Peony.
Peony "The God of Healing" or "Peony Flower" (Latin).
   Patron Saints: There is one St. Peon. He gave his life for Jesus in ancient times.
   Feast Dates: June 1 — St. Peon.
Pep (nickname) See Pepper.

Pepe (Spanish) See Josephine.
Pepi (Spanish) See Josephine.
Pepita (Spanish) See Josephine+Ita.
Pepper "Like a Hot Spice" (Sanskrit).
   Patron Saints: In Greek, pepper is spelled *piperi*, and there is a St. Piperio. He is an ancient saint who lived in Alexandria, Egypt. Probably a black man, he died a martyr's death because of his faith in Jesus.
   Feast Dates: March 11 — St. Piperio.
Peppi (nickname) See Josephine, Pepper.
Perla (Spanish) See Pearl.
Perpetua "The Enduring One" (Greek, Spanish).
   Patron Saints: There are over a half-dozen Sts. Perpetua. One of the most famous of them is the wife of St. Peter. It was her mother that Jesus cured one day while visiting in Capernaum. It is also probable that she played the hostess for Jesus on many occasions during his ministry.
   Later, when Peter began preaching the Gospel, it seems that Perpetua and her daughter often accompanied him. This probably created a lot of work for her because her daughter, Petronilla, was partially paralyzed. Ancient records also insist that Perpetua died a martyr's death in Rome about two years before her husband. As she was being led off to execution, Peter encouraged her to remain faithful.
   Feast Dates: November 4 — St. Perpetua.
Perri (nickname) See Pearl.
Perrie (nickname) See Pearl.
Perrine (French) See Petrina.
Perry (nickname) See Pearl.
Pet (nickname) See Perpetua, Petrina, Petronella, Petula, Petunia.
PetaGay (African-American double) See Petrina+Gay.

Petra (Latin) See Petrina, Petronella.

Petrina "Like a Rock" (Latin).

Patron Saints: There is one known St. Petra and two Sts. Petronia. One of the Sts. Petronia was a Greek woman who was put to death because of her faith.

Feast Dates: September 29 — St. Petronia.

Petrona (variant) See Petrina.

Petronella "The Little Rock" (English).

Patron Saints: There are about a half-dozen Sts. Petronella. The most famous of them is the crippled daughter of St. Peter. Some Christians wondered why Peter healed so many people but not his daughter. Peter healed her temporally with the Sign of the Cross to prove the power was there and then taught that it was for her salvation that God allowed her to be crippled. It was only after many years and near the end of Peter's ministry that God allowed a permanent healing of Petronella. Flaccus, a nobleman, asked for her hand in marriage, but she refused him, explaining that she wished to devote her time to prayer. She died three days later. She is patron of France, of treaties between the pope and the Frankish emperors, and against ague.

Feast Dates: May 31 — St. Petronilla.

Petronia (English) See Petrina.

Petronila (Spanish) See Petrina, Petronella.

Petronille (German) See Petrina, Petronella.

Petua (nickname) See Perpetua.

Petula "The Petulant One" (Latin) or "The Impatient One" (Latin) or "The Seeker" (Latin).

Patron Saints: Two patrons can be found if we separate the name into two parts. The first patron, St. Petra, was a black woman who was martyred in ancient Carthage in Africa. A patron for the second half of the name can be found in St. Tulia. She was the daughter of St. Eucherius of Lyons and a sister of St. Consortia of Manosque. She died in 430.

Feast Dates: February 16 — St. Petra; October 5 — St. Tulia.

Petunia "The Petunia Flower" (North American Indian).

Patron Saints: There is one saint with a similar name: St. Petrunia. She was martyred in ancient times. Also, because a petunia is a flower, St. Flora can also serve as patron.

Feast Dates: September 29 — St. Petrunia; November 24 — St. Flora (see Flora).

Peyton (Irish) See Patricia.

Phaedra (variant) See Phedra.

Phaidra (variant) See Phedra.

Phebe (English) See Phoebe.

Phedra "The Bright One" (Greek).

Patron Saints: There is one known St. Phaedrus. He died a martyr for his belief in Jesus.

Feast Dates: November 29 — St. Phaedrus.

Phil (nickname) See Philana, Philantha, Philippa, Philippine, Philomena, Philothea, Phyllis.

Phila (nickname) See Philana, Philantha.

Philana "The Loving One" (Greek).

Patron Saints: There is one saint with a similar name.

Feast Dates: December 4 — St. Phileas (see Phyllis).

Philantha "The Lover+Of Flowers" (Greek double).

Patron Saints: There is one ancient St. Philanthus. He was martyred in ancient Pontus.

Feast Dates: August 18 — St. Philanthus.

Phileas (variant) See Phyllis.

Philein (variant) See Philana.

Philene (variant) See Philana.

Philida (variant) See Philana.

Philie (nickname) See Philippa, Philippine, Philomena.

Philina (variant) See Philana.

Philine (variant) See Philana.

Philippa "The Lover of Horses" (Greek).

Patron Saints: There are a couple of Sts. Philippa. One was Bl. Philippa Mareri, who was from a noble family in Abruzzi. She founded a community of nuns and died in 1236.

Feast Dates: February 16 — Bl. Philippa Mareri.

Philippina (variant) See Philippine.

Philippine "The Lover of Horses" (French).

Patron Saints: There are a couple of Sts. Philippine. St. Philippine Rose Duchesne was born in 1769. At the age of seventeen she announced that she was going to be a nun. However, the French Revolution delayed the dream. Only in 1801 did she acquire a convent.

In 1806 she made it clear that she wanted to go to the New World to teach the Native Americans. But her request was not granted for twelve years. Finally, when she was forty-nine years old, she was able to go to St. Louis, Missouri, and then only to care for the settlers' children. She seemed to suffer frustration at every turn.

Some twenty years later, at the age of seventy, she was finally able to go to the Indians. Unfortunately, she could not learn the language, so she spent her time in prayer. The Indians were impressed by the "Woman Who Always Prays," the name they gave her, and many converts were made. She died at the age of eighty-three.

Feast Dates: November 18 — St. Philippine Rose Duchesne.

Philis (variant) See Phyllis.

Philli (variant) See Philippa, Philippine, Philomena, Philothea.

Phillie (variant) See Philippa, Philippine, Philomena, Philothea.

Phillis (variant) See Phyllis.

Philly (variant) See Philippa, Philippine, Philomena, Philothea.

Phillys (variant) See Phyllis.

Philomena "The Loving Song" (Greek).

Patron Saints: There is one great St. Philomena and a few others who are lesser known. Nothing is known about the "great" St. Philomena other than that she was a young girl who suffered martyrdom for Jesus' sake. After her death in ancient times she was forgotten until 1802. In that year a tomb was discovered in the catacomb of St. Priscilla, outside of Rome. With the bones there was a broken stone tablet that bore the inscription *Filumena Pax Tecum*, Latin for "Philomena, Peace Be With You."

Then in 1835 a crippled Bl. Pauline Jaricot visited Pope Gregory XVI who, seeing her condition, expressed concern that she would soon die. Pauline told him she was going to go to the shrine of St. Philomena to ask for a cure. The pope said he would open an investigation into Philomena's sainthood if Pauline was cured. During Benediction at the shrine Pauline was completely healed and the Holy Father cleared the way for Philomena's canonization.

Feast Dates: August 10 — St. Philomena.

Philothea "The Lover of God" (Greek).

Patron Saints: There are at least two known Sts. Philothea. One of them was born in Ternova, Bulgaria, in 1030. When she came of age, it was arranged that she marry, but her proposed husband was a drunkard and she had no intention of entering such a union.

Thus she fled her parents' home and the "road" became her home. Only after her mother died did she feel free to return home, but her father turned her into a slave in her own house. He abused her and, in 1060, he killed her. She is patron of the mentally ill.

Feast Dates: December 7 — St. Philothea.

Phily (nickname) See Philippa, Philippine, Philomena.

Phoebe "The Shining One" (Greek).

Patron Saints: There is one known St. Phoebe. When St. Paul was near Corinth in Greece, he wrote a letter to the Romans, introducing himself and announcing his planned future visit. He sent his letter-of-intent with Phoebe, who was visiting Rome. Thus St. Paul introduces Phoebe to the church and calls her a deaconess (see Romans 16). It seems she was appointed to that office perhaps to attend to female catechumens who were often baptized totally unclothed.

Feast Dates: September 3 — St. Phoebe.

Phylicia (variant) See Felicia, Felicitas.

Phylida (variant) See Phyllis.

Phyllis "Lover of Green Foliage" (Greek).

Patron Saints: There is one ancient saint with a variation of this name: St. Phileas. He served God as a bishop during the persecutions of Emperor Diocletian. He was imprisoned and executed in 304. Furthermore, because most people mistakenly think that Phyllis is the feminine form of Philip, the many Sts. Philip and Philippa can be adopted as patrons.

Feast Dates: December 4 — St. Phileas.

Phyllys (American) See Phyllis.

Pi (nickname) See Pia, Piper.

Pia "The Pious One" (Latin, Spanish).

Patron Saints: There is one St. Piala and one St. Pia. St. Pia was a native of ancient Africa. She was probably a black woman who gave her life as a martyr for Jesus.

Feast Dates: January 19 — St. Pia.

Picabo "Now I See You, Now I Don't" (American).

Patron Saints: "Peek-a-Boo" is a child's game of hiding and surprise discovery that mirrors perfectly the theme of the Gospel of St. Mark. Three times Mark reveals that Jesus is the divine Son of God. However, each time it is hidden in the fleshy envelope of Christ's humanity. He urges the reader to find the divine in the midst of the human, warning all not to look for God only in power and wonders. Rather, God is most powerfully present in suffering and death. Thus St. Longinus the Centurion declares upon viewing the newly dead body of Jesus, "Truly this man was the Son of God!" (Mark 15:39).

Feast Dates: April 25 — St. Mark the Evangelist; March 15 — St. Longinus the Centurion.

Piedad (Spanish) See Pia.

Pierette (French double) See Etta, Petrina, Pierre+Ette.

Pietra (Italian) See Petrina.

Pilar "The Pillar" (Spanish).

Patron Saints: The word *pilar* means "pillar." It honors a Spanish shrine dedicated to the Blessed Virgin Mary called Nuestra Señora de Pilar ("Our Lady of the Pillar"). The Church of Nuestra Señora de Pilar is believed to have had its beginnings in a chapel built by St. James the Great, an Apostle of Jesus. Pious legend insists that James ordered the chapel built in honor of the Blessed Virgin in the year 40, even before Mary had died.

It seems that one January day while James was at prayer near the banks of the Ebro River in Saragossa, Mary, carried by angels, came to James and asked that a church be built in her honor. Then the angels presented James with a miraculous picture of Mary and a marble pillar made by them, which was to be its throne. Mary asked James for prayers and promised her help through the ages. The marble column was to symbolize the "pillar of cloud" that led and protected ancient Israelites through the wilderness.

James immediately ordered a chapel built and the picture enthroned. And this great treasure of the Church has, for centuries, been enthroned upon that same marble pillar. Thousands of pilgrims have expressed their piety there and numerous miracles have occurred there.

Feast Dates: January 1 — Our Lady of the Pillar.

Pinkie (nickname) See Rose.

Pinky (nickname) See Rose.

Piper "The Pipe Player" (Old English).

Patron Saints: There are two saints with a very similar names: Sts. Piperio and Pipio. St. Pipio served as a deacon in the diocese of Dijon in ancient France.

An additional patron can be discovered by considering the meaning of the name. "Piper" in Latin is *tibicen*, and there is one saint with a similar name: St. Tibba.

Feast Dates: October 2 — St. Pipio; March 11 — St. Piperio (see Pepper).

Pipere (variant) See Piper.

Pippa (nickname) See Philippa, Philippine.

Pippi (nickname) See Philippa, Philippine.

Pippie (nickname) See Philippa, Philippine.

Pippy (nickname) See Philippa, Philippine.

Pirkko (Finnish) See Brigid.

Piroska (Hungarian) See Priscilla.

Pita (Spanish) See Guadalupe.

Pixley (English double) See Pixy+Leigh/Leah.

Pixy "The Gentle, Helpful Spirit" (Middle English).

Patron Saints: To a Christian, the finest "gentle helpful spirits" are the guardian angels.

Feast Dates: October 2 — The Holy Guardian Angels.

Placida "The Gentle, Peaceful One" (Latin).

Patron Saints: There is one St. Placidina and one St. Placidia. St. Placidia lived a very austere life. She was given the gift of miracles. She died in 460.

Feast Dates: October 11 — St. Placidia.

Pol (nickname) See Apollonia, Mary, Polly.

Pola (Slavic) See Paula.

Polli (nickname) See Apollonia, Mary, Polly.

Pollie (nickname) See Apollonia, Mary, Polly.

Pollon (nickname) See Apollonia.

Pollona (nickname) See Apollonia.

Pollonia (nickname) See Apollonia.

Polly "The Bitter One" (English nickname for Mary, Molly) or "Little One" (English nickname for Paula) or "The Sunlight" (nickname for Apollonia).

Patron Saints: The name Polly is accepted by moderns as a nickname for Apollonia, Mary, Molly, or Paula. This makes over a hundred patrons available. Polly can also be found as part of the names of over three dozen other saints. The best known is St. Polycarp, an ancient, holy bishop-martyr. There is also one ancient female saint, St. Polyxena, who was a native of Spain in the first century A.D. She dedicated her single life to the service of God and became a disciple of the Apostles. She was joined in this dedication by her friends Rebecca and Xantippe.

Feast Dates: September 23 — St. Polyxena; January 1 — The Blessed Virgin Mary, Mother of God (see Mary).

Pollyanna (English double) See Polly+Anna.

Pomona "The Fruitful One" (Latin, Spanish).

Patron Saints: There is one ancient saint with a very similar name. St. Poma was the holy sister of St. Memmius, the bishop of Châlons-sur-Marne in medieval times.

Feast Dates: June 27 — St. Poma.

Porsche (German) See Portia.

Porsha (Latin) See Portia.

Portia "The Pig Farmer" (Latin) or "An Offering" (Latin) or "A Safe Port [Gate]" (Middle English).

Patron Saints: There are two male saints who bear variants of the name: Sts. Portianus and Portus. St. Portus was probably a black man who lived in ancient Africa and died a martyr's death for Jesus.

Also, because Portia can mean "gate," one can adopt St. Peter, who is often pictured in charge of the gates of heaven.

Feast Dates: March 31 — St. Portus; November 24 — St. Portianus of Miranda (see Miranda).

Prane (Lithuanian) See Frances.

Pretty (English) See Linda.

PrettyLee (African-American double) See Pretty+Leigh.

Pretty (English) See Linda.

Prima "The Firstborn Daughter" (Latin).

Patron Saints: There are almost a half-dozen Sts. Prima. All are martyrs.

One was a black woman who was executed at Carthage in 304.

Feast Dates: February 9 — St. Prima; All Sundays — Jesus the Firstborn of All Creation (see Winona).

Primavera (Italian, Spanish) See Easter, Laverne, Spring.

Princess "The Female of Royal Rank" (French).

Patron Saints: There are about a half-dozen Sts. Princess. However, they would have written their names as *mulier regia,* Latin for "royal lady." The ancient town of Regia contributed a church full of martyrs in 459. The Christians were celebrating Easter services when suddenly they faced and embraced execution. The Arian heretic king Genseric had ordered their execution. The massacre began with a prearranged signal. When the lector began intoning the *Alleluia,* he was shot through the neck with an arrow.

It is also helpful to know that the name Sarah also means "princess." There are a few Sts. Sarah.

Feast Dates: April 5 — Holy Martyrs of Regia; August 19 — St. Sarah (see Sarah).

Princetta (African-American double) See Princess+Etta.

Pris (nickname) See Priscilla.

Prisca (variant) See Priscilla.

Priscilla "From Ancient Times" (Latin).

Patron Saints: There are almost a half-dozen Sts. Priscilla. One Priscilla was the wife of Manius Acilius Glabrio, a Roman senator and convert to Christianity. He was condemned and executed on charges of sedition and impiety. Priscilla was also the mother of St. Pudens, who served as a Roman senator. St. Peter the Apostle used her villa as his headquarters when he was in Rome. She spent her fortune on helping the poor and imprisoned and gave her property for a cemetery. She is patron of widows.

Feast Dates: January 16 — St. Priscilla.

Prissie (nickname) See Priscilla.

Prissy (nickname) See Priscilla.

Priya (Hindu) See Davita.

Pru (nickname) See Prudence, Prunella.

Prudenca (variant) See Prudence.

Prudence "The Foresighted Intelligent One" (Latin).

Patron Saints: There are about a dozen Sts. Prudens, Prudentia, and Prudentius. A Bl. Prudence, who died in 1492, was a member of the noble Casatori family of Milan in Italy. She joined the Hermitesses of St. Augustine. She served as the superior of her convent for thirty-seven years. She had a talent for settling disputes. No one took any special notice of her until after she died and miracles were reported.

Feast Dates: May 5 — Bl. Prudence.

Prudencia (Spanish) See Prudence.

Prudy (Latin) See Prudence.

Prue (nickname) See Prudence, Prunella.

Prunella "The Color of Plums" (French) or "Like a Plum Tree" (Latin).

Patron Saints: One ancient saint with a similar name qualifies as a patron. St. Punica was martyred in ancient Africa and was probably a black woman.

Feast Dates: January 3 — St. Punica.

Psyche "The Soul" (Greek) or "The Spirit" (Greek).

Patron Saints: In our modern times, when we often talk about having good mental health, we often speak of a healthy psyche. Thus St. Dymphna, the patron of good mental health, makes the perfect patron.

Feast Dates: May 15 — St. Dymphna.

Pulcheria "The Physically Beautiful and Attractive One" (Middle English).

Patron Saints: There is one St. Pulcheria, 399-453, who was a Byzantine princess and regent. She held fast to the true faith and was an opponent of the Nestorian and Monophysite heresies. Pulcheria carried on an extensive correspondence with Pope Leo I and took an active interest in the Councils of Ephesus and Chalcedon. She also built three churches in Constantinople and was recognized, in her own time, as "Guardian of the Faith and Maker of Peace." She died at the age of fifty-four.

Feast Dates: September 10 — St. Pulcheria.

Purificación "The Pure, Sinless One" (Spanish).

Patron Saints: This name leads directly to the Blessed Virgin under the title of the Immaculate Conception.

Feast Dates: December 8 — Immaculate Conception (see Concepción).

Purity "The Pure One" (Middle English).

Patron Saints: A saint with a similar name is St. Purilius, who served as a bishop in Switzerland in the 400s. Furthermore, any St. Catherine can also serve as patron because Catherine means "pure one."

Feast Dates: June 9 — St. Purilius; April 17 — Bl. Kateri Tekakwitha (see Kateri).

2

Qua (African-American) See Quadeen.

Quadeen (Arabic) See Valerie, Audrey.

Quan (African-American) See Quanah.

Quanah "The Fragrant One" (North American Indian).

Patron Saints: Myra also means "fragrant." This leads to a well-known patron.

Feast Dates: December 6 — St. Nicholas of Myra (see Myra).

Quaneesha (African-American) See Quanesha.

Quanesha "Born on Monday" (African-American double).

Patron Saints: Quanesha is a combination of Qua and Tanisha or Qua and Kanisha. Tanisha is from the Nigerian for "born on Monday." With this in mind we can find a St. Lunecharia to act as patron. However, if one accepts Kanisha, then it is important to know that it is often spelled Kenisha and is considered a form of Kenneth. There is only one known St. Kenneth.

It is also probable that Quanesha is a combination of Quan and Aisha or Quan and Isha. This leads to more patrons.

Feast Dates: June 7 — St. Lunecharia (see Luna); October 11 — St. Kenneth (see Kenisha).

Quaneshia (African-American) See Quanesha.

Quarta "The Fourth Daughter" (Latin).

Patron Saints: There is at least one St. Quartus. He was a disciple of the Apostles and is mentioned by St. Paul in Romans 16:23.

Feast Dates: November 3 — St. Quartus.

Queen "The Female Ruler" (Old English).

Patron Saints: The Latin word for "queen" is *regina*, and there are a half-dozen Sts. Regina. However, one of the finest patrons is the Blessed Virgin Mary under the title of "Queen of Heaven and Earth."

St. Paul, in 2 Timothy 2:12, counsels, " If we endure, we shall also reign with him [Christ]." And the Book of Revelation pictures the saints in heaven seated upon thrones, reigning in glory. Thus it seems that the Bible uses the image of "kingly or queenly reign" as a way of speaking about eternal life. We must keep in mind, therefore, that to declare Mary "Queen of Heaven" recognizes that she has received salvation through the grace of Jesus, her son. The Catholic Church has continuously declared Mary to be "Queen of Heaven and Earth" from the ancient *Akathist Hymn* of 532 to the *Litany of Mary's Queenship* in 1981.

Feast Dates: August 22 — The Blessed Virgin Mary, Queen; July 6 — St. Regina (see Regina).

Queenetta (Old English double) See Queen+Etta.

Queenie (variant) See Queen.

Quenna (English) See Queen.

Quenni (variant) See Queen.

Quennie (Old English) See Queen.

Quentilla (variant) See Quinta.

Quentina (variant) See Queen, Quinta.

Querida "The Beloved One" (Spanish).

Patron Saints: Knowing that *querida* means "beloved" leads us to Davita, which means the same thing.

Feast Dates: March 1 — St. David (see Davita); June 6 — St. Ama (see Aimee).

Queta "The Mistress of the Home" (Spanish).

Patron Saints: Queta is the Spanish nickname for Henrica or Henrietta.

Feast Dates: November 17 — SG Henriette De Lille (see Henrietta).

Quiana "The One Who Feels Soft Like Silk" (American).

Patron Saints: The Latin word for "soft" is *mollis*. St. Molibba was a bishop in seventh-century Ireland.

Feast Dates: January 8 — St. Molibba.

Quieta "The Quiet One" (Latin).

Patron Saints: There is one St. Quieta and one St. Quietus. St. Quieta was the wife of the Roman senator St. Hilarius and the mother of St. John de Reome. They lived in the fifth century.

Feast Dates: August 28 — St. Quieta.

Quina (nickname) See Joaquína.

Quinesha (African-American double) See Quanesha, Quinn+Aisha/Isha.

Quinn "The Queen" (Old English).

Patron Saints: The most important patron is the Blessed Virgin, Queen of Heaven and Earth.

Finally, there is one Irish woman now being considered for canonization. She is Bl. Edel Quinn, 1907-1944. She wanted to become a contemplative nun, but poor health prevented her. Thus at the age of twenty she dedicated herself to the work of the Legion of Mary in Dublin.

Everything she did was marked by a childlike trust in God. Her devotion to Mary was also constant. She would often say, "Mary loves us because we are Christ's gift to her." Edel was always happy.

In 1936, at twenty-nine years of age, she became an envoy for the Legion, with the goal of establishing this organization in Africa. Struggling against constant ill health, she met every challenge with unwavering faith and courage. She established hundreds of Legion branches and died in Nairobi at the age of thirty-seven.

Feast Dates: May 12 — Bl. Edel Quinn; August 22 — The Blessed Virgin Mary, Queen of Heaven (see Queen).

Quinta "The Fifth Daughter" (Latin).

Patron Saints: There are two known Sts. Quinta and three Sts. Quintillia. One St. Quinta refused to renounce her faith in about 249. She was dragged through the streets of Alexandria and stoned to death.

Feast Dates: February 8 — St. Quinta.

Quintessa "The Essence" (Latin).

Patron Saints: Three Sts. Quintilla can be adopted. One of them died a martyr's death in ancient Sorrento.

Feast Dates: March 19 — St. Quintilla.

Quintie (variant) See Quinta, Quintessa.

Quintina (variant) See Quinta.

Quo Vadis "Where Are You Going?" (Latin).

Patron Saints: Catholic tradition tells how St. Peter fled Rome in the year 64 when he heard his life was in peril. As he left Rome, he met Jesus entering the city and he asked the Lord: "Where are you going?" Jesus replied, "To be crucified." Peter realized it was his time to die for Christ. So he returned to Rome and was arrested and crucified.

Feast Dates: St. Peter, Apostle — June 29.

Qwanisha (African-American double) See Quanesha.

R

Rachael (Hebrew) See Rachel.

Rachel "The Lamb" (Hebrew).

Patron Saints: Catholic tradition provides a St. Rachildis, and the Bible provides the great saintly Rachel, the wife of Jacob, who lived in about 1799 to 1600 B.C. Having become the wife of Jacob, she looked forward to wedded bliss, but this was not to be because she was barren. In the meantime, her older sister, Leah, bore Jacob child after child.

In the end, however, God allowed Rachel to give birth to two sons. Both proved to be the favorites of Jacob. The first was Joseph and the other was Benjamin. But even the two sons born to her brought her pain. The older son, Joseph, was sold into slavery in Egypt by his brothers. These brothers then reported that he had been killed by a wild animal. This broke the hearts of both Jacob and Rachel.

The birth of her second son brought even more sorrow for Jacob. This is because Rachel died in giving birth and was buried in ancient Bethlehem. Her tomb can be found there even in modern times.

Feast Dates: November 1 — Rachel, Jewish Matriarch; November 23 — St. Rachildis (see Raquel).

Rachele (Italian) See Rachel.

Rachell (variant) See Rachel.

Rachelle (Hungarian, German, French) See Rachel.

Racquel (French) See Rachel.

Rae (nickname) See Rachel.

Raelyn (African-American double) See Rachel+Lynn.

Rafa (variant) See Raphaela.

Rafaela (Spanish) See Raphaela.

Rafaella (Italian) See Raphaela.

Rafaellia (variant) See Raphaela.

Ragen (variant) See Regan, Regina.

Ragine (French) See Regina.

Rahal (variant) See Rachel.

Rahel (German) See Rachel.

Raimonda (Italian) See Ramona.

Rain (African-American) See Regina.

Raina (English) See Regina.

Raine (Latin) See Rani, Regina.

Raisa (Russian) See Rose.

Raissa "The One Who Thinks" (French) or "The One Who Believes" (French).

Patron Saints: St. Rasius died a martyr in the Roman persecutions.

Feast Dates: November 5 — St. Rasius.

Rajmunda (Polish, Hungarian) See Ramona.

Ramona "The Wise Protector" (Spanish) or "The Doe+The Single One" (Old English double).

Patron Saints: If Ramona is accepted as a feminine form of Raymond, then one is led to a half-dozen Sts. Raymond. If, however, it is viewed as a form of Mona, then one St. Monas can be pressed into service.

Raymond (or Ramón), 1175-1275, was born in Peñafort Castle in Catalonia. In 1214, at the age of thirty-nine, he was appointed archdeacon of Barcelona. Eight years later he became a Dominican and then he served as a professor for six years. He filled his life with prayer, preaching, instructing, hearing confessions, and converting heretics and nonbelievers.

Then the pope ordered him to collect and codify all the official papers that were issued during the past one hundred years. This became the standard Church law until 1917. He is patron of canonists, lawyers, law schools, and medical records librarians.

Feast Dates: January 7 — St. Raymond of Peñafort, O.P.; February 26 — St. Monas (see Mona).

Ramonda (English) See Ramona.

Ramonde (English) See Ramona.

Rana (nickname) See Rani.

Randa (nickname) See Miranda, Randi.

Randee (nickname) See Miranda, Randi.

Randi "The Shield Wolf" (Old English) or "The Admirable One" (English form of Miranda).

Patron Saints: Randi is recognized as a feminine form of Randal or Randolph. And there is one St. Randoald. He was martyred in ancient Grandval for his belief in Jesus.

It is also helpful to know that Randi is recognized as a short form of Miranda.

Feast Dates: February 21 — St. Randoald; November 24 — St. Portianus of Miranda.

Randie (nickname) See Miranda, Randi.

Randy (nickname) See Miranda, Randi.

Ranee (variant) See Rani.

Rani "The Female Ruler [Queen]" (Hindu).

Patron Saints: Rani means "queen" in Sanskrit, which leads directly to the Blessed Virgin.

Feast Dates: August 22 — The Blessed Virgin Mary, Queen of Heaven (see Queen).

Rania (variant) See Rani.

Ranice (variant) See Rani.

Ranna (nickname) See Roseanna, Rowena, Veronica.

Raoghnailt (Scottish) See Raphaela.

Rapha (variant) See Raphaela.

Raphaela "The One Healed by God" (Hebrew).

Patron Saints: Although there seem to be no saints named Raphaela, Catholic tradition does provide us with a Benedictine monk named St. Raphael, an archangel called St. Raphael, and a St. Raphaildis. The last mentioned is a medieval martyr who was killed with her infant son in East Flanders in about 652.

Feast Dates: November 12 — St. Raphaildis.

Raphaelle (French) See Raphaela.

Raquel "The Lamb" (Spanish form of Rachel).

Patron Saints: Catholic tradition supplies one saint, St. Rachildis, O.S.B. She was a religious hermit and lived in a walled-up cell near that of St. Wiborada and under the direction of the abbot of St. Gall in Switzerland. She died in 946.

The Bible supplies another holy woman with this name. Further, because Rachel means "lamb," which is *agnus* in Latin, this leads to St. Agnes.

Feast Dates: November 23 — St. Rachildis, O.S.B.; November 1 — St. Rachel (see Rachel).

Ra'Quel (African-American) See Rachel.

Ra'Shawnda (African-American double) See any "Ra" name+Shawna.

Rasia (Greek) See Rose.

Raven "The Blackbird" (Old English) or "The Crow" (Old English).

Patron Saints: There is no St. Raven, but there is an English martyr surnamed Crow. Because a raven is really a "crow," Bl. Alexander Crow can be adopted as a patron. During the reign of Queen Elizabeth I, Father Alexander Crow was arrested for being a Catholic priest. He was tried, convicted, and executed in 1586.

Feast Dates: May 4 — Bl. Alexander Crow.

Ray (nickname) See Raphaela.

Raye (nickname) See Raphaela.

Rayevelyn (African-American double) See Raye+Evelyn.

Raymonde (French) See Ramona.

Rayna (variant) See Rani.

Rayne (African-American) See Regina.

Raynell (English) See Rani.

Raynoma (African-American) See Ramona.

Rea (variant) See Rhea.

Reagan (Irish) See Regan, Regina.

Reagen (Irish) See Regan, Regina.

Reatha (African-American) See Aretha.

Reba (English) See Rebecca.

Rebeca (Spanish) See Rebecca.

Rebecah (English) See Rebecca.

Rebecca "The Bound [Yoked] One" (Hebrew) or "The Heifer" (Hebrew).

Patron Saints: The Old Testament provides one saint and Christian tradition provides two more. One was St. Rebecca, who became the mother of five saints: Sts. Agatho, Ammon, Ammonius, Peter, and John. Rebecca also embraced a martyr's death in ancient Shabra. She must have been quite a woman to have all five of her children officially recognized as saints.

Feast Dates: November 4 — St. Rebecca.

Rebeccah (Spanish) See Rebecca.

Rebeka (English, Swedish) See Rebecca.

Rebekah (English) See Rebecca.

Rebekka (German) See Rebecca.

Redempta "The Redeemed One" (Latin).

Patron Saints: There are a few Sts. Redempta, including one who, with two of her friends, practiced a life of austere solitude and prayer near St. Mary Major in medieval Rome. St. Redempta died in 580.

Feast Dates: July 23 — St. Redempta.

Redolia (African-American double) See any "Re" name+Dolores.

Redonia (African-American double) See any "Re" name+Donna.

Ree (English) See Riva.

Reeba (English) See Rebecca.

Reena (Greek) See Irene, Serena.

Reeta (Estonian) See Rita.

Reeva (English) See Riva.

Reevabel (English) See Riva.

Regan "Little Queen" or "The Little Royal One" (English).

Patron Saints: One ancient saint who can serve as a patron is St. Regan. Regan served the Church as a deacon in ancient times. He was martyred for the faith in Omer.

It also helps to know that, when used for a female, another connection can be made with Regina.

Feast Dates: May 25 — St. Regan, also known as Regenar; July 1 — St. Regina (see Regina).

Regen (variant) See Regan, Regina.

Regina "The Female Ruler [Queen]" (Latin, Spanish).

Patron Saints: There are a half-dozen saints named Regina, but none are well known. One of them is a virgin and martyr who died for the faith in about 386. Another is St. Regina, countess of Ostrevent.

Furthermore, when one realizes that *regina* is the Latin word for "queen," a very powerful patron emerges. She is none other than the Blessed Virgin Mary, Queen of Heaven and Earth.

Feast Dates: September 7 — St. Regina; July 1 — St. Regina (see

Countess); August 22 — The Blessed Virgin Mary, Queen of Heaven (see Queen).

Regine (French) See Regan, Regina.

Rehema "The Second-Born" (Kiswahili) or "The Compassionate One" (Swahili).

Patron Saints: There are no known saints named Rehema. However, the Latin word for "second-born" is *secunda*, which leads to about a dozen Sts. Secunda. One of them died a martyr in ancient Rome.

Feast Dates: July 10 — St. Secunda.

Reietta (African-American double) See any "Re" name+Etta.

Reina (Spanish) See Regina.

Reine (French) See Regan, Regina.

Reinette (Irish) See Regina+Ette.

Rellestine (African-American double) See Rilla+Stina.

Rema (African-American) See Rehema, Rhema.

Rena (nickname) See Irene, Katherine, Renata, René, Rowena, Serena.

Renae (nickname) See Renata, René.

Renata "The One Born Again" (Latin, Spanish).

Patron Saints: There are two Sts. Renatus. One of them was a bishop who died in 422. Toward the end of his life he embraced a solitary life of prayer.

Feast Dates: October 6 — St. Renatus.

Renate (German) See René.

Renaye (African-American) See René.

René "The One Born Again" (French form of Renata) or "The Peaceful One" (French form of Irene).

Patron Saints: There are two Sts. Renatus (also known as René), six Sts. Raynier, and one American St. René.

St. René served as the bishop of Angers in medieval times. To find a female patron, one must pursue an alter-

nate course. Some scholars suggest that René can be identified as a short French form of Irene. This leads to about two dozen Sts. Irene.

Feast Dates: November 12 — St. René, also known as Renatus; February 26 — St. Irene (see Irene).

Renée (Latin, French) See René.

Renetta (African-American double) See any "Re" name+Etta.

Renia (African-American) See Irene, René, Rowena.

Renie (nickname) See Irene.

Renita (African-American double) See any "Re" name+Nikita.

Renni (nickname) See Renata, René.

Rennie (nickname) See Renata. René.

Renny (nickname) See Renata, René.

Reola (African-American double) See any "Re" name+Ola.

Resi (German) See Teresa, Thérèse.

Reta (variant) See Rita.

Retha (nickname) See Aretha.

Retta (nickname) See Loretta or (African-American) Reta or any "R" name+Etta.

Reva (English) See Rebecca.

Revekka (Russian) See Rebecca.

Reyna (Irish Gaelic) See Regan, Regina.

Rhea "From the Stream" (Greek) or "A Poppy" (Latin).

Patron Saints: Two ancient saints with very similar names may serve: Sts. Rheanus and Rhais. St. Rheanus served as an abbot in Wales during ancient times.

To find more patrons, the meaning of the name must be considered. In Latin, *rhea* means "poppy." The red color of the poppy reminded Christian artists of the passion of Jesus. Thus the suffering Jesus may be adopted as a patron.

Feast Dates: March 8 — St. Rheanus; Good Friday — The Suffering Christ.

Rheanna (Greek double) See Rhea+Anna.

Rheba (English) See Rebecca.

Rhema "The All-Powerful Word" (Greek) or "The Compassionate One" (African-American form of Rehema).

Patron Saints: Near the end of the twentieth century a small group of American Fundamentalist Christians began founding Rhema churches. *Rhema* is a Greek word used by St. Paul in his Epistles to talk about the power of the Word of God. His listeners misinterpreted this to mean that anyone sick or hurt could experience immediate cures if they simply "name it and claim it." Just speak of the cure as if one already had experienced it and the power of the "Word" would make it so. While this conclusion is faulty, the recognition of Jesus as the all-powerful redeeming Word of God is absolutely true. For Scripture, the Word and Jesus Christ are all one. For a Catholic, Christ is encountered in the Liturgy of the Word at every Mass.

Feast Dates: All Sundays — Jesus Christ the Word of God.

Rheta (variant) See Rita.

Rho (nickname) See Rhoda, Rose.

Rhoda "The Rose Flower" (Greek).

Patron Saints: There is one St. Rodena and one St. Rhodana. About St. Rhodana all that is known is that she died a martyr in ancient Lyons. And because Rhoda is a form of "Rose," six Sts. Rose are available.

Feast Dates: June 2 — St. Rhodana; August 23 — St. Rose of Lima (see Rose).

Rhodia (English) See Rhoda, Rose.

Rhodie (nickname) See Rhoda, Rose.

Rhodon (variant) See Rhoda, Rose.

Rhody (Greek) See Rhoda, Rose.

Rhona "Powerful One" (Scandinavian) or "The Rough Island" (Scandinavian).

Patron Saints: Rhona is the feminine form of Ronald, which in turn is a form of Reginald. There is one St. Ronald and about a half-dozen Sts. Reginald.

St. Ronald lived in the twelfth century. He was the earl of Orkney. This means he was a chieftain and a warrior prince. Because of a vow he had made, he had the Cathedral of St. Magnus built at Kirkwall. He was murdered by rebels in 1158. After his death, many miracles were attributed to him.

Feast Dates: August 20 — St. Ronald, Earl of Orkney.

Rhonda "Grand One" (Welsh) or " Good Lance" (Welsh).

Patron Saints: A patron can be found when one knows that Rhonda means "grand." This leads to Bl. John Grande, 1546-1600, who was born in Carmona in Andalusia, Spain. As a young man, he was employed in the linen business, but he soon tired of it and looked for something better.

This led him to become a hermit at Marcena. Thus he made a pun of his name. His Spanish surname was Grande, which means "great," and he used to tell everyone that he was "Juan Grande Pecador." Translated from the Spanish it means "John the Great Sinner." He gave much of his time to charity, hospital work, and visiting the imprisoned. Finally, it is helpful to know that the Latin word for "great" or "grand" is *magnus*. This leads to Sts. Magina and Magnentia. St. Magina gave her life as a martyr in ancient Africa.

Feast Dates: June 3 — Bl. John Grande; December 3 — St. Magina.

Rhondalynn (American double) See Rhonda+Lynn.

Ria (nickname) See Victoria.

Ria "From the Flowing River" (Spanish).

Patron Saints: Flumen is Latin for "river," and there is a St. River, a martyr in ancient Rome.

Feast Dates: May 28 — St. River, also known as Fluminus.

Riane "The Vassal Ruler" (English feminine form of Ryan).

Patron Saints: Riane can be a variant form of Briana or Breanna, and this leads to some patrons. It is also helpful to know that Riane can be a form of Ryan, which means the same thing as the Latin word *regulus* (or "vassal ruler"). There are a few Sts. Regula and Regulus.

Regula and her brother, St. Felix, fled to Switzerland in the 200s when St. Maurice and the Theban Legion were massacred because of the faith. Eventually they were found and executed.

Feast Dates: September 11 — St. Regula; August 30 — St. Bryenna (see Breanna).

Rica "The Rich One" (Spanish) or "Dear" (Spanish).

Patron Saints: The Latin word for rich is *dives*, and there is a St. Divus. He was a priest who died for the faith in Roman Caesarea in Cappadocia.

Feast Dates: July 11 — St. Divus.

Ricarda (Old German) See Richella.

Richardine (African-American) See Richella.

Richel (variant) See Richella.

Richela (variant) See Richella.

Richella "Powerful Ruler" (English feminine form of Richard).

Patron Saints: Richella is nothing more than a feminine form of Richard, and there are at least two dozen Sts. Richard. The one St. Richella was a virgin who served God in medieval Ireland.

Feast Dates: May 19 — St. Richella.

Richelle (French) See Richella.

Richette (African-American double) See Richella+Ette.

Richidine (African-American double) See Richella+Ine.

Ricki (nickname) See Africa, Erica, Frederica.

Rickie (nickname) See Africa, Erica, Frederica.

Ricky (nickname) See Africa, Erica, Frederica.

Rika (nickname) See Africa, Erica.

Rikki (nickname) See Erica, Frederica.

Rilla (Low German) See Bourne, Brook.

Rillaestine (African-American double) See Rilla+any name ending in "Stine."

Rillette (variant double) See Rilla+Ette.

Rillie (nickname) See Rilla.

Rina "The Peaceful One" (nickname for Irene) or "The Ruler [Queen]" (English short form of Regina) or "The Pure One" (English, Norwegian, Italian forms of Katherine).

Patron Saints: Rina can be a short form of Regina, Irene, or Katherine. This leads to two dozen patrons.

Feast Dates: February 23 — St. Irene (see Irene); March 3 — St. Katharine Drexel (see Katherine).

Rine (African-American) See Regina.

Riognach (variant) See Regina.

Riona (Irish) See Regina.

Risa "The One Who Laughs" (Latin).

Patron Saints: There is one saint with a similar name. St. Risiba was a martyr for Jesus in ancient Terracina. However, if one explores the meaning of the Latin word *risa*, which is "laughter," over fifty more patrons can be found. For example: Isaac means "he laughs" in Hebrew. The Sts. Isaac range from the biblical patriarch Isaac to a relatively recent missionary to the Native Americans, St. Isaac Jogues, S.J.

Feast Dates: November 1 — St. Risiba.

Rise (variant) See Risa.

Rita "The Pearl" (English, Spanish nickname for Margaret).

Patron Saints: Rita is from Margarita. There are two dozen Sts. Margaret and one St. Rita, 1381-1457, whose parents insisted that she marry. Unfortunately, the man she married was dissolute and violent and she became a battered wife for eighteen years. Her life was filled with tears and prayers, but she lived to see her husband repent just before he was murdered. During that dark time of her life, she watched her two sons fall under his evil influence. After her husband died, they vowed and plotted revenge. She prayed this might be stopped and both young men died of an illness before they could carry out their plans.

Now a widow and alone, she tried to join a religious order but was repeatedly refused. Finally accepted at the age of forty-two, she filled her life with obedience to her superior, prayer for the unfaithful, charity to her sister religious, and doing sacrifices. She often achieved ecstasy in prayer and, when fifty years old, she received part of the stigmata, the crown-of-thorns wounds.

During her final years she suffered from a wasting disease. She died at the age of seventy-six. Nearing death during the winter, she asked for a rose from her garden, and one was there for her. She is considered the patron of desperate situations, healing wounds, loneliness, and those suffering from tumors.

Feast Dates: May 22 — St. Rita of Cascia; October 16 — St. Margaret Alacoque (see Margaret).

Riva "From the Riverbank" (French) or "The Bound One" (English short form of Rebecca).

Patron Saints: If one accepts the name to mean "from the riverbank," then St. Rivanone can serve as a patron. She was a poor woman and the wife of a minstrel. She was the mother of the great St. Harvey (Hervé), who was born blind. Poverty and her son's blindness were great trials for her. She died in 535.

If, however, one identifies the name as a form of Rebecca, then a few Sts. Rebecca qualify as patrons.

Feast Dates: June 19 — St. Rivanone; November 1 — St. Rebecca (see Rebecca).

Rivabel (English double) See Riva+Belle.

Rivalee (English double) See Riva+Leigh/Leah.

Rivi (English) See Riva.

Rivka (Modern Hebrew) See Rebecca, Riva.

Rivy (English) See Riva.

Roa (variant) See Rowena.

Roana (variant) See Rhona.

Roanna (variant) See Ann, Rose, Roseanne.

Roanne (variant) See Ann, Rose, Roseanne.

Robbi (nickname) See Roberta, Robin.

Robbie (nickname) See Roberta, Robin.

Robby (nickname) See Roberta, Robin.

Robbyn (variant) See Roberta, Robin.

Robena (variant) See Roberta, Robin.

Robenia (variant) See Roberta, Robin.

Roberta "The Bright [Famous] One" (Old English).

Patron Saints: There are a dozen Sts. Robert. The most famous is St. Robert Bellarmine, 1542-1621. He became a Jesuit priest and, even though he was very short and had to stand on a stool when doing public speaking, he was very effective.

However, a health breakdown forced him to slow down, but he never quit. For eleven years he was involved with books and teaching as the leading mind of his age. He revised the Vulgate Bible and wrote a couple of catechisms. In time, he became a theologian to the pope, the archbishop of Capua, a cardinal, and a friend of Galileo. He is patron of catechists and canonists and a Doctor of the Church.

Feast Dates: September 13 — St. Robert Bellarmine.

Roberte (French) See Roberta.

Robertina (Dutch) See Roberta.

Robin "The Bright [Famous] One" (Old English).

Patron Saints: The name Robin is generally accepted as a form of Robert, and there are about a dozen Sts. Robert. There are also two Bls. Robinson.

Bl. Christopher Robinson was executed by the British government in 1597 because he insisted on ministering to the Catholics in England. Bl. John Robinson was born in York, England, during the time of the English persecutions. He married, but after his wife died he went to France to be ordained a priest. After ordination in 1585 he went back to England. He was arrested and executed in 1588.

Feast Dates: May 4 — Bl. Christopher Robinson; October 1 — Bl. John Robinson.

Robina (English, French) See Roberta, Robin.

Robine (French) See Roberta, Robin.

Robinet (English double) See Roberta, Robin+Ette.

Robinett (English double) See Roberta, Robin+Ette.

Robinette (English double) See Roberta, Robin+Ette.

Robinia (German) See Roberta, Robin.

Robyn (variant) See Roberta, Robin.

Robynette (English double) See Roberta, Robin+Ette.

Roch (variant) See Rochelle.

Rochell (variant) See Rochelle.

Rochella (English) See Rochelle.

Rochelle "From the Little Rock" (French).

Patron Saints: The best candidate for patron is St. Peter the Apostle, whose name was changed from Simon to Peter (or "Rock") by Jesus. There is also an English martyr, Bl. John Rochester, as well as a St. Rock (or Roche).

This latter patron, St. Rock, was probably a native of Montpellier, France. In about 1348 he traveled to Italy, where a pestilence was raging. He gave himself to nursing the sick and dying at a hospital in Rome. It is said that Rock cured a great many sick, simply by making the Sign of the Cross over them. Later he returned to Montpellier, but he was arrested for being a vagrant and a foreign spy. After five years in jail he died of neglect. Miracles were reported after his death. He is patron of cattle, dog lovers, invalids, prisoners, those suffering cholera, and against contagious diseases, skin diseases, and the plague.

Feast Dates: August 16 — St. Rock.

Rochette (English) See Rochelle.

Rod (variant) See Rhoda, Rose.

Rodelle (African-American double) See Rhoda/Rose+Della.

Rodi (English) See Rhoda, Rose.

Rodie (variant) See Rhoda, Rose.

Rodina (variant) See Rhoda, Rose+Ina.

Roe (variant) See Rowena.

Rois (Irish) See Rose.

Rolanda "From the Famous Land" (Old German).

Patron Saints: There is one St. Rolande and a half-dozen Sts. Roland. St. Rolande was the daughter of a Gallic king who insisted that she marry an Irish prince in about 700. However, she had dedicated herself to live a single life for Christ, so she fled to Cologne but died en route. She is patron against colic.

Feast Dates: May 13 — St. Rolande.

Rolande (French) See Rolanda.

Roma "From the Eternal City" (Latin).

Patron Saints: There are a half-dozen ancient saints named Romana. One of them was a convert and part of a party of twelve young ladies who accompanied St. Denis to Gaul. She suffered martyrdom in 303.

Feast Dates: October 3 — St. Romana.

Romaine (variant) See Roma.

Romana (variant) See Roma.

Romelle (variant) See Roma.

Romie (variant) See Roma.

Romilda (variant) See Roma.

Romina (variant) See Mina, Roma.

Romonda (variant) See Ramona.

Romy (variant) See Roma.

Rona (variant) See Rhona.

Ronalda (variant) See Rhona.

Ronda (variant) See Rhoda, Rhonda, Rose.

Ronee (variant) See Rhona, Roseanne, Rowena, Veronica.

Roneet (variant) See Rhona/Roseanne/Rowena/Veronica+Ette.

Ronetta (variant) See Rhona/Roseanne/Rowena/Veronica+Etta.

Roni (variant) See Rhona, Roseanne, Rowena, Veronica.

Ronica (variant) See Veronica.

Ronna (variant) See Veronica.

Ronni (variant) See Rhona, Roseanne, Rowena, Veronica.

Ronnica (variant) See Veronica.

Ronnie (variant) See Rhona, Roseanne, Rowena, Veronica.

Ronny (variant) See Rhona, Roseanne, Rowena, Veronica.

Roquesila (African-American double) See Rochelle+Priscilla.

Rora (variant) See Aurora, Oriana, Zona.

Rori (variant) See Aurora, Oriana, Zona.

Rorie (variant) See Aurora, Oriana, Zona.

Rory (variant) See Aurora, Oriana, Zona.

Ros (variant) See Rosabel, Rosalie, Rosalind, Rosamond, Rose.

Rosa (Italian, Spanish, Danish, Dutch, Swedish) See Rosabel, Rosalie, Rosalind, Rosamond, Rose.

Rosabel (variant double) See Rose+Belle.

Rosabela (Dutch, Italian, Latin, Spanish, Swedish, French) See Rose+Belle.

Rosabele (English double) See Rose+Belle.

Rosabella (English double) See Rose+Belle.

Rosabelle (English double) See Rose+Belle.

Rosalba (Spanish double) See Rose+Albina.

Rosalee (English double) See Rose+Leigh.

Rosaleen (English double) See Rosalie/Rose/Rosalind+Line.

Rosalene (English double) See Rosalie/Rose/Rosalind+Line.

Rosalia (English, Italian, Spanish) See Rosalie, Rose.

Rosalie "The Rose Flower" (English, French).

Patron Saints: There is at least one St. Rosalia and about a half-dozen Sts. Rose. St. Rosalia was born of a noble family in Sicily. However, upon growing up, she embraced the life of a hermit and lived in a cave near Palermo. In 1624 her body was brought into Palermo and devotions were offered to help stop a plague. She died in about 1166 and is patron against pestilence and earthquakes.

Feast Dates: September 4 — St. Rosalia.

Rosalin (variant) See Rose, Rosalind.

Rosalina (Swiss) See Rose, Rosalind.

Rosalind "Like a Rose Flower+The Pretty One" (double).

Patron Saints: There are a half-dozen Sts. Rose, and noticing that Rosalind is a combination of Rose and Linda or Rose and Lynn leads to another half-dozen Sts. Lina and the like.

St. Rosalina, 1288-1329, was born at Château d'Arx, Provence, of the house of Villeneuve. At the young age of twelve she entered the Carthusian religious order. In time, she became the prioress. It seems that she had the gift of miracles and exercised power over demons. She died at the age of forty-one.

Feast Dates: October 16 — St. Rosalina; August 23 — St. Rose of Lima (see Rose); July 5 — St. Lina (see Lynn).

Rosalinda (Spanish double) See Rosalind, Rose+Linda.

Rosalinde (English double) See Rosalind, Rose+Linda.

Rosaline (Swiss) See Rose, Rosalind.

Rosalyn (Swiss) See Rose, Rosalind.

Rosalynd (English double) See Rosalind, Rose+Linda.

Rosann (English double) See Rose+Ann.

Rosanna (English double) See Rose+Ann.

Rosanne (English double) See Rose+Ann.

Rosamond "The Famous Guardian" (Old German) or "The Rose of the World" (Modern Latin).

Patron Saints: There is one known St. Rosamunda. She is remembered for producing one saint for the family of God. He was her son, St. Adjutor of Vernon.

Feast Dates: April 30 — St. Rosamunda.

Rosamonda (variant) See Rosamond.

Rosamonde (English, French) See Rosamond.

Rosamund (English) See Rosamond.

Rosamunda (Spanish) See Rosamond.

Rosamunde (variant) See Rosamond.

Rosana (Spanish double) See Rose+Ana.

Rosaria (variant) See Rosario.

Rosario "She Who Prays the Rosary" (Spanish, Italian) or "The Garland of Flowers" (Latin).

Patron Saints: Counting one's prayers on beads is a very old practice, found in many different cultures and religions. In the Catholic Church the practice dates to the 100s with the Jesus Prayer, which was prayed on each bead. The use of the rosary can be traced to about 1200. At that time it became the custom to recite anywhere from fifty to one hundred fifty Our Fathers. This prayer was introduced to help the illiterate pray.

In the 1400s the Rosary devotion, preached by the Dominican Alan de la Roche, was essentially the same as that prayed today. In 1573 the pope established the feast of the Holy Rosary. It celebrated the victory of Christian forces over the Muslims at Lepanto in 1571.

Feast Dates: October 7 — Our Lady of the Holy Rosary.

Rosaura (Spanish double) See Rose+Aura.

Rose "A Rose Flower" (English) or "Pink Color" (Latin).

Patron Saints: There are a half-dozen Sts. Rose. St. Rose of Lima, 1586-1617, was the first person born in the New World to be declared a saint. She was born in Lima, Peru, and christened Isabel, but she is remembered by Rose, her confirmation name.

In order to help her parents, she worked in the garden all day and did needlework at night. She also chose to live in a hut behind her parents' home so she could devote more time to prayer. This led to ridicule and misunderstanding. She also experienced great temptations by the devil and deep desolation, but her love of Jesus and the time spent before the Blessed Sacrament eased her pain.

Feast Dates: August 23 — St. Rose of Lima.

Roseann (English double) See Rose+Ann.

Roseanna (English double) See Rose+Ann.

Roseanne (English double) See Rose+Ann.

Rosel (Swiss) See Rosalind, Rose.

Roselane (variant double) See Rose+Lani.

Roselani (Hawaiian double) See Rose+Lani.

Roselie (Lithuanian) See Rosalind.

Roselin (variant) See Rosalind.

Roseline (variant) See Rosalind, Roselani.

Rosella (Italian) See Rosalind, Rose, Rosalie.

Roselle (Italian) See Rosalind, Rose.

Rosemaria (English double) See Rose+Maria/Mary.

Rosemarie (English double) See Rose+Marie/Mary.

Rosemary (English double) See Rose+Mary.

Rosena (Italian) See Rose.

Rosenda (Spanish) See Rose.

Rosetta (Italian double) See Rose+Etta.

Rosette (Italian-French-English double) See Rose+Ette.

Roshawna (African-American double) See Rose+Shawna.

Roshelle (variant) See Rochelle.

Rosi (nickname) See Rosalie, Rosalind, Rose.

Rosie (nickname) See Rose, Rosina.

Rosina (Italian) See Rose, Rosalind, Rowena.

Rosina "Like a Rose Flower" (English).

Patron Saints: There are a half-dozen Sts. Rose and one St. Rosina. Little is known about St. Rosina.

Feast Dates: March 11 — St. Rosina; August 23 — St. Rose of Lima (see Rose).

Rosine (Spanish) See Rose, Rosina.

Rosita (Spanish double) See Rose+Ita.

Roslyn (variant) See Rosalind, Rose.

Rosy (nickname) See Rosalie, Rosalind, Rose, Rosina.

Roux (French) See LaRoux.

Row (nickname) See Rowena.

Rowe (variant) See Rowena.

Rowena "The Famous+Friend" (English double) or "The Famous+Fair One" (Old English double) or "The White One" (Celtic).

Patron Saints: Rowena may be a combination of Roa and Wynne. There is no known St. Rowena, but there is a St. Roa and a Bl. Bartholomew Roe. There are also a half-dozen saints with variations of Wynne.

Bl. Bartholomew Roe was raised a Protestant in Suffolk, England, and became a Catholic as an adult in 1612. Then he fled England and became a Benedictine, was ordained, and returned to England. He labored in the English missions from 1615 to 1642, when he was arrested by the government.

On his way to execution he was accompanied by an eighty-year-old priest who was terrified of the coming tortures. He calmed his fears. Then upon arriving at the place of execution he worked to reconcile a couple of criminals who were also awaiting execution.

Feast Dates: January 21 — Bl. Bartholomew Roe; January 21 — St. Wynnin of Holywood (see Wynne).

Rox (nickname) See Rochelle, Roxanne.

Roxana (Spanish double) See Rochelle+Ann.

Roxane (English double) See Rochelle+Ann.

Roxann (English double) See Rochelle+Ann.

Roxanna (English double) See Rochelle+Ann.

Roxanne (English double) See Rochelle+ Ann.

Roxene (English double) See Rochelle+ Ann.

Roxi (nickname) See Rochelle, Roxanne.

Roxie (nickname) See Rochelle, Roxanne.

Roxine (English) See Rochelle, Roxanne.

Roxy (Persian) See Rochelle, Roxanne.

Roz (nickname) See Rosalie, Rosalind, Rosamond, Rose, Roseanne.

Rozalie (Lithuanian) See Rosalie.

Rozalin (variant) See Rose, Rosalind.

Rozalyn (variant) See Rose, Rosalind.

Rozamond (Dutch) See Rosamond.

Rozann (English double) See Rose+Ann.

Rozanna (English double) See Rose+ Anna.

Rozanne (English double) See Rose+ Ann.

Rozeann (English double) See Rose+ Ann.

Rozeanna (English double) See Rose+ Anna.

Rozeanne (English double) See Rose+ Ann.

Rozele (Lithuanian) See Rosalie, Rose.

Rozella (English double) See Rose+Ella.

Rozelle (English double) See Rosalie/ Rosalind/Rosamond/Rose/Roseanne+Elle.

Rozie (nickname) See Rosalie, Rosalind, Rose, Rosina.

Rozina (variant) See Rosalie, Rosalind, Rose, Rosina.

Rozy (nickname) See Rosalie, Rosalind, Rose, Rosina.

Rubena (variant) See Ruby.

Rubetta (variant) See Ruby.

Rubi (Spanish) See Ruby.

Rubia (English) See Ruby.

Rubina (English) See Ruby.

Ruby "The Ruby Gem" (Old French) or "The Red Stone" (Latin).

Patron Saints: There is only one saint with a similar name. She is St. Rubra, a black woman who suffered martyrdom with a great number of companions somewhere near ancient Carthage.

For many ancients, the red ruby seemed to imprison a glowing spark of fire. Pagans thought it could be used to warm corpses and guard homes. It was also thought to protect gardens and livestock from destructive storms. Crushed rubies were thought to bring healing and even to stop the advance of death. The ruby was a wonderful mystery to them.

In the New Testament, a rubylike gem, carnelian, is found in the walls of Jerusalem (see Revelation 21:20). It was a reminder of divine purity and also speaks of all the people of God, that is, all saints.

Feast Dates: January 17 — St. Rubra; November 1 — All Saints (see Jewel).

Rubye (variant) See Ruby.

Rue (nickname) See Ruth.

Rufina "The Red-Haired One" (Latin).

Patron Saints: There are a half-dozen Sts. Rufina from which to choose. One died a martyr's death in 262. She is also remembered for giving the world her son, St. Mamas, to whom she gave birth while being held in prison because of her faith. She was executed a short time after she gave birth. About twelve years later, St. Mamas followed her example and died as a martyr.

Feast Dates: August 31 — St. Rufina.

Ruperta (German, Spanish) See Roberta.

Rupertta (German) See Roberta.

Rupetta (German) See Roberta.

Rut (Spanish, Polish, Scandinavian) See Ruth.

Ruth "The Compassionate, Beautiful Friend" (Hebrew).

Patron Saints: Christian tradition fails to provide a St. Ruth. However, the Bible does not disappoint. It presents the great ancient matriarch Ruth. Born to pagan parents, she married a Jewish man. Ten years later, he died, leaving Ruth a widow. Her mother-in-law, Naomi, urged her to return to her own people.

But she declared, "For where you go, I will go, and where you lodge, I will lodge; your people shall be my people, and your God my God" (Ruth 1:16). She returned to Israel with Naomi and presented herself to Boaz, the next relative eligible to marry her. Boaz accepted Ruth as his wife. A short time later Ruth conceived and bore a son. In this way she became the great-grandmother of King David and an ancestor of Jesus Christ.

Feast Dates: November 1 — Holy Ruth.

Ruthann (English double) See Ruth+Ann.

Ruthanna (Hebrew double) See Ruth+Anna.

Ruthanne (Hebrew double) See Ruth+Ann.

Rut (Spanish, Polish, Scandinavian) See Ruth.

Ruthe (nickname) See Ruth, Ruthann.

Ruthi (nickname) See Ruth, Ruthann.

Ruthie (nickname) See Ruth, Ruthann.

Ruthy (nickname) See Ruth, Ruthann.

Ryan (variant) See Riane.

Ryann (variant) See Riane.

Ryanna (English double) See Riane+Anna.

Ryanne (English double) See Riane+Ann.

Ryta (English) See Margaret.

S

Saara (Finnish, Estonian) See Sarah.

Saarje (Dutch) See Sarah.

Saba (variant) See Sabina, Sava, Sheba.

Sabaloo (African-American double) See Saba/Sabina+Louise.

Sabana (Spanish) See Savannah.

Sabas (Greek) See Sava, Sheba.

Sabina "From the Sabine Country" (Latin, Spanish) or "From the Plain" (variant of Sabana).

Patron Saints: There are a few Sts. Sabina. One was the widow of Herod Metallarius, a nobleman who lived near Umbria. She converted to the faith because of the witness given by her servant St. Serapia. She was arrested and martyred in 275. She is patron of housewives and against hemorrhages.

Feast Dates: August 29 — St. Sabina; Month of May — The Blessed Virgin Mary, Rose of Sharon (see Sharon).

Sabine (French, German, Dutch) See Sabina.

Sabra "From the Thorny Cactus" (Hebrew) or "The Resting One" (Hebrew).

Patron Saints: There is one St. Sabra. He was a boy from Modiat, the capital of Turabdin in ancient Mesopotamia. He suffered martyrdom because he would not turn his back on Jesus.

Feast Dates: June 3 — St. Sabra.

Sabrina "Boundary Line" (Latin) or "Princess" (Spanish).

Patron Saints: Some consider Sabrina to be a modern form of Sabina. This leads to a handful of patrons. One St. Sabina was a widow who came from a noble family in ancient Lodi. She faced the persecution of Christians under the Roman emperor Maximian.

She made it her ministry to visit the Christians in prison and buried their bodies after execution. Her life was filled with prayer and sacrifice. She died in 311.

Feast Dates: January 30 — St. Sabina.

Sacajawea "The Bird Woman" (North American Indian).

Patron Saints: Sacajawea is famous in North American history, having accompanied the Lewis and Clark expedition. Her name leads to two patrons.

Feast Dates: March 25 — Bl. James Bird; December 24 — Sts. Adam and Eve (see Isha).

Sacha (Russian) See Sasha.

Sachi (Japanese) See Benedicta, Fortuna.

Sadella (English) See Sarah.

Sadhbh (Irish) See Sophie.

Sadie (English) See Sarah.

Sadye (English) See Sarah.

Safira (variant) See Sapphire.

Sage "The Very Wise One" (Latin) or "The Sage Herb" (English form of Salvia).

Patron Saints: St. Matthew tells us that the Magi, the wise men from the East, offered homage to Jesus shortly after his birth and they presented him with gifts of gold, frankincense, and myrrh. The gifts reveal who Jesus is. Gold indicates he is a king. Frankincense points to his priesthood and divinity. Myrrh tells us that Jesus is united to us in our sin and suffering.

Feast Dates: January 6 — The Three Holy Magi.

Sahara (African-American) See Shahara, Zahara.

Sahara "The Wilderness" (Arabic).

Patron Saints: The Spanish names Sabina and Savannah can also mean "wilderness." This leads to St. Sabina.

Feast Dates: August 29 — St. Sabina.

Sahbba (Irish) See Sophie.

Saidhbhin (Irish) See Sabina.

Sal (nickname) See Sarah.

Salaidh (Scottish) See Sarah.

Salama (Arabic) See Salome.

Salena (variant) See Salina.

Salenia (variant) See Salina.

Salilyn (English double) See Sally+Lynn.

Salima (Arabic) See Salome.

Salina "From the Salty Place" (Latin).

Patron Saints: There are a few saints with similar names. They include one St. Saldia, two Sts. Sallita, and one St. Salona. The last, St. Salona, is remembered for giving her life as a martyr in ancient times.

Furthermore, Bl. Robert Salt was a Cistercian religious brother and one of the first martyrs to die for the faith during the reign of King Henry VIII. The king had him slowly starved to death in 1537.

Feast Dates: May 20 — St. Salona; June 6 — Bl. Robert Salt, M.O. Cart.

Salinda (African-American double) See Salina+Linda.

Salli (nickname) See Sarah.

Sallie (nickname) See Sarah.

Sally (nickname) See Sarah.

Saloma (Polish) See Salome.

Salome "The Peaceful One" (Hebrew, French).

Patron Saints: There are almost a half-dozen Sts. Salome and Salomea. St. Salome of Perojavra served God as the wife of Reff, king of Georgia. Reff was the son of St. Mirian, who welcomed Catholicism into his country.

Feast Dates: January 15 — St. Salome of Perojavra.

Salomea (Polish) See Salome.

Salomi (Turkish) See Salome.

Salomie (variant) See Salome.

Salona (African-American) See Salome.

Salvia "The Sage Herb" (Latin) or "The Saved" (Spanish).

Patron Saints: There are about a dozen Sts. Salvius. One died a martyr in ancient Spain.

Feast Dates: January 13 — St. Salvius.

Salvina (English) See Salvia.

Sam (nickname) See Samantha, Samara, Samuela.

Samala (Hebrew) See Samuela.

Samanta (Hispanic-American) See Samantha.

Samantha "One Who Listens+Flower" (Hebrew double).

Patron Saints: The first part of Samantha is recognized as a feminine form of Samuel, and Christian tradition provides us with about a half-dozen Sts. Samuel. The Bible adds the great prophet Samuel. The second part of the name comes from *anthos,* which means "flower." It leads to one St. Antha and a half-dozen Sts. Anthusa.

Feast Dates: August 20 — St. Samuel; December 12 — St. Antha.

Samanthee (variant) See Samantha.

Samanthie (variant) See Samantha.

Samanthy (variant) See Samantha.

Samara "Guarded by God" (Hebrew) or "City" (Spanish).

Patron Saints: The 1,480 ancient martyrs of Samaria are patrons enough.

Feast Dates: June 22 — The 1,480 Martyrs of Samaria.

Samaria (Latin) See Samara.

Samella (English double) See Samantha/Samara/Samuela+Ella.

Samelle (English double) See Samantha/ Samara/Samuela+Elle.

Sametta (variant double) See Samantha/ Samara/Samuela+Etta.

Sami (nickname) See Samantha, Samara, Samuela.

Sammi (nickname) See Samantha, Samara, Samuela.

Sammie (nickname) See Samantha, Samara, Samuela.

Samuela "The One Who Listens" (Hebrew).

Patron Saints: While there is no St. Samuela, there are a number of Sts. Samuel.

Samuel, 1100-1020 B.C., was the last of the judges and the first of the prophets of Israel. He was the product of his mother's prayer in her old age. When he was three years old, his parents gave him to the high priest, and the Lord called him by name and appointed him to be a prophet. He founded the first prophetical school, then became a Jewish judge. Many years later, when he was old, he anointed Saul and then later David to be king.

Feast Dates: August 20 — St. Samuel.

Samuella (English double) See Samuela+ Ella.

Samuelle (French double) See Samuela+ Elle.

Sancha (Spanish) See Sancia.

Sanchia (Spanish) See Sancia.

Sancia "The Holy One" (Latin, Spanish).

Patron Saints: There are a few Sts. Sancia, Sancta, and Sanctina. One St. Sancia, 1180-1229, was the daughter of King Sancho I of Portugal. At the age of forty-three she became a Cistercian religious and helped bring the first Franciscans and Dominicans into Portugal. She died a short six years later.

Feast Dates: March 13 — St. Sancia.

Sancta (Latin) See Sancia.

Sande (nickname) See Sandy.

Sandi (nickname) See Sandy.

Sandie (nickname) See Sandy.

Sandor (Hungarian) See Sandy.

Sandra "Helper of Humanity" (nickname for Alexandra) or "One Not Believed" (nickname for Cassandra) or "The Liberator of Men" (nickname for Lysandra) or "Honeybee or Helper of Humanity" (nickname for Melisandra).

Patron Saints: There is one St. Sandila who was martyred by the Muslims in Cordova, Spain, in 855.

Feast Dates: September 3 — St. Sandila, also known as Sandalus; March 20 — St. Alexandra (see Alexandra).

Sandrica (African-American double) See Sandy+Rica.

Sandy (nickname) See Alexandra, Cassandra, Lysandra, Melisandra, Sandra.

Sanna (Finnish) See Susan.

Santana (Spanish) See Sancia.

Sante (Spanish) See Sancia.

Santina (Italian) See Sancia.

Saphira (English) See Sapphire.

Sapphira (Hebrew) See Sapphire.

Sapphire "The Blue Gemstone" (Greek).

Patron Saints: For many ancient pagans, the blue sapphire was believed to attract divine favor. Jewish tradition suggested that the Ten Commandments were inscribed upon sapphire tablets, which were a sign of God's love. The New Testament Book of Revelation (21:19) mentions the sapphire in the walls of the heavenly city of Jerusalem. This leads us to a wonderful discovery. It is the Bible's way of describing eternal life and divine favor. It teaches that all the saints are united in one family.

Feast Dates: November 1 — All Saints.

Saphronia (African-American) See Sophie.

Sara (English, French, German, Italian, Spanish) See Sarah.

Sarah "The Princess" (Hebrew).

Patron Saints: Catholic tradition provides three Sts. Sarah, and the Bible adds one more. The Bible Sarah is the wife of Abraham and lived in about 1700 B.C. She joined her husband in his conversion to the true God and followed him from Ur and Haran into the desert of Canaan.

Like Abraham, she was specially chosen by God to fulfill an essential part of the divine plan. Thus when Sarah was ninety years old she laughed when she heard the angels say she was to become a mother. Her laughter became her son, Isaac. The name Isaac means "laughter." Her life teaches that an encounter with God will eventually end in laughter. She died at the age of one hundred twenty-seven.

Feast Dates: August 19 — St. Sarah.

Saralee (English double) See Sarah+Leigh/Leah.

Saralynn (English double) See Sarah+Lynn.

Saree (nickname) See Sari.

Sarella (African-American double) See Sarah+Ella.

Sarene (English) See Sarah.

Saretta (variant double) See Sarah+Etta.

Sarette (French double) See Sarah+Ette.

Sari "The Bitter, Contentious One" (Hebrew) or "The Princess" (Hungarian form of Sarah).

Patron Saints: Sari was the name of Abraham's wife before God changed it to Sarah.

Feast Dates: August 19 — St. Sarah (see Sarah).

Sarina (Dutch) See Sarah, Sari, Serena.

Sarine (English) See Sarah, Sari, Serena.

Sarita (Spanish double) See Sarah, Sari+Ita.

Saritia (Spanish double) See Sarah, Sari+Ita.

Sarra (Russian) See Sarah.

Sascha (variant) See Sasha.

Sasha "Helper of Humanity" (short form of Alexandra) or "Born on Christmas" (short form of Natalie).

Patron Saints: Sasha is the short Russian form of Alexandra and Natalie.

Feast Dates: March 20 — St. Alexandra (see Alexandra); September 8 — St. Natalie (see Natalie).

Sashenka (variant) See Sasha.

Sassa (Swedish) See Sarah.

Satara (African-American double) See Sarah+Tara.

Saturday "Born on Saturn's Day" (Middle English).

Patron Saints: There are a handful of Sts. Saturnina. One St. Saturnina was a single young woman who came from Germany into the area of Arras. She met her death defending herself against a rape attack.

Another patron, the Blessed Virgin Mary, becomes available once one becomes aware of the Catholic custom of honoring Mary on Saturdays. She is honored on Saturdays because it is a way of remembering that on that first Holy Saturday Mary was the only living human on the earth who placed faith in her martyred son, Jesus. In effect, she was the whole Catholic Church for one day.

Feast Dates: June 4 — St. Saturnina; All Saturdays — The Blessed Virgin Mary, Mother of the Church.

Saundra (variant) See Cassandra, Sandra.

Sava "The Old One" (Slavic) or "From the Open Plain" (nickname for Savanna).

Patron Saints: There are about a dozen Sts. Sava, all males. One St. Sava, 439-532, was a Cappadocian who fled as a youth to Palestine and led the life of a hermit. Eventually he founded the Mar Saba monastery, which is still in operation. He strongly opposed the heresies prevalent in his day. He is revered as one of the founders of Eastern monasticism. He died at the age of ninety-three.

Feast Dates: December 5 — St. Sava.

Savana (variant) See Savanna.

Savanna "The Barren Place" (Spanish) or "From the Open Plain" (Old Spanish).

Patron Saints: With a little stretching, the dozen Sts. Sabina (or Savina) can be adopted as patrons.

A greater patron can be found if one pursues the meaning of the Old Spanish *sabana*, which means "an open plain." This patron is none other than the Blessed Virgin under the title of "Rose of Sharon" (since *sharon* means "from the fertile plain").

Feast Dates: Month of May — The Blessed Virgin Mary, Rose of Sharon (see Sharon); August 29 — St. Sabina (see Sabina).

Savannah (English) See Savanna.

Savilla (African-American double) See any "Sa" name+Villa.

Savina (English) See Sabina.

Savory "The Pleasant One" (Middle English) or "The Morally Agreeable One" (Middle English).

Patron Saints: The names Africa and Naomi mean the same thing as Savory.

Feast Dates: August 5 — St. Afra.

Savrina (variant) See Sabrina.

Savyna (Ukrainian) See Sabina.

Scarlet (variant) See Scarlett.

Scarlett "The Bright Red One" (Middle English).

Patron Saints: Many saints have Red as part of their names.

Feast Dates: October 23 — St. Josephine Leroux (see LaRoux); August 31 — St. Rufina (see Rufina).

Scholastica "The Learned One" (Latin).

Patron Saints: There are a half-dozen Sts. Scholastica. One of them lived from 480 to 543, and was an abbess of the Benedictine religious order and a sister of St. Benedict. She gave her life to prayer.

Feast Dates: February 10 — St. Scholastica.

Schura (Russian) See Susan.

Schuyler (Dutch) See Skye.

Schyler (Dutch) See Skye.

Scylla (African-American double) See Skye+Ella.

Seana (Irish American) See Jane.

Seanna (Irish-American) See Jane.

Searlait (Irish) See Carla, Charlotte.

Season "A Favorable Time For" (Middle English).

Patron Saints: The name Season leads to one great patron. He is St. Francis of Assisi. He has been officially appointed as patron of ecology by the Catholic Church. The Blessed Virgin may also qualify as a patron.

Feast Dates: October 4 — St. Francis of Assisi (see Kiah); All Saturdays — The Blessed Virgin Mary, Garden of God (see Laverne).

Seba (nickname) See Eusebia, Sebia.

Sebana (African-American) See Savanna.

Sebastia (Greek) See Sebastiana.

Sebastiana "The Venerated Majestic One" (English).

Patron Saints: There are a number of saints who can serve as patrons. They include Sts. Sebastia and Sebastiana.

St. Sebastia died for her faith in Jesus in ancient Sirmium.

Feast Dates: July 4 — St. Sebastia.

Sebbi (nickname) See Eusebia, Sebastiana, Sebia.

Sebea (variant) See Eusebia, Sebastiana, Sebia.

Sebi (nickname) See Eusebia, Sebastiana, Sebia.

Sebia "Like Tallow" (Latin) or "The Venerated Majestic One" (nickname for Sebastiana).

Patron Saints: Sebia may be a name in its own right or it may be a shortened form of Eusebia, Sebbi, Seboa, Sebastiana, Sebastia, Eusebia, and Theosebia. This leads to a plethora of patron saints.

St. Theosebia was the wife of St. Gregory of Nyssa and served as a deaconess in their church. St. Gregory of Nazianzen praises her in one of his sermons.

Feast Dates: January 10 — St. Theosebia; October 11 — St. Eusebia (see Eusebia).

Seboa (variant) See Sebastiana.

Sebra (African-American) See any "Se" name+Debra.

Secunda "The Second Daughter" (Latin).

Patron Saints: There are over a dozen Sts. Secunda. All of them died martyrs' deaths. One St. Secunda was a single woman who gave her life for her belief in Jesus and his Church in ancient Rome.

Feast Dates: July 10 — St. Secunda.

Sedalia (African-American double) See any "Se" name+Dahlia.

Sedna "The Goddess of Food" (Eskimo).

Patron Saints: There are a half-dozen Sts. Sedna. One was bishop of Ossory in 570.

Feast Dates: March 10 — St. Sedna of Ossory.

Sedonia (African-American double) See any "Se" name+Donna.

Sefira (variant) See Sapphire.

Sefora (Spanish) See Eve.

Segunda (Spanish) See Secunda.

Seila (English) See Sheila.

Sela (English) See Selena.

Selda (nickname) See Griselda, Zelda.

Selema (African-American) See Selena.

Selena "The Moonlike One [or Moonlight]" (Greek) or "The Heavenly One" (Latin).

Patron Saints: There is one St. Celerina and one St. Celinia.

Feast Dates: October 21 — St. Celinia (see Celinia); November 16 — SsG Elba and Celine Ramos (see Elba).

Selene (English) See Selena.

Selenia (Spanish) See Selena.

Selestina (variant) See Celeste.

Selia (variant) See Selena.

Selie (variant) See Selena.

Selima "The Peaceful One" (Hebrew, Turkish).

Patron Saints: There is one saint with a very similar name who can be adopted as patron.

Feast Dates: October 21 — St. Celinia (see Celinia).

Selina (Greek) See Selena.

Selinda (variant) See Selena.

Seline (French) See Selena.

Selma "The Divinely Protected One" (Latin, Spanish) or "The Peaceful One" (German, Scandinavian).

Patron Saints: Selma is a short form of Anselma, and there are a half-dozen Sts. Anselm. The great St. Anselm of Canterbury, 1033-1109, had a father who was a violent spendthrift. His father's harshness drove him from the family home after his mother died. After three years of wandering, he attached himself to Lanfranc of Pavia and followed him into the Benedictine monastery at Bec. He was ordained a priest in 1063, at the age of thirty. Years later he became the abbot. In 1089 he went to Chester, England, to restore a monastery and was named to be bishop of Canterbury. Anselm was a man of great learning and settled many disputes. He also had a great influence in reforming the liturgy. He is a Doctor of the Church.

Feast Dates: April 21 — St. Anselm of Canterbury.

Sema (African-American) See Samantha, Selma.

Semeka (African-American double) See Samantha+Tamika.

Sena (variant) See Selena.

Senalda (Spanish) See Signe.

Sennetta (African-American double) See Señora+Etta.

Sennie (African-American) See Señora.

Señora (Spanish) See Lady.

Seonaid (Scottish) See Jane.

Seosaimhin (Irish Gaelic) See Josephine.

Sephira (variant) See Sapphire.

September "The One Born in the Seventh Month" (Middle English).

Patron Saints: There is a whole group of martyrs known as the September Martyrs, numbering one hundred ninety-one. They were executed because of their faith during the French Revolution in 1792. First they were imprisoned by the legislative assembly for refusing to take the French oath supporting the civil constitution. Then they were killed by a mob.

Feast Dates: September 2 — Blessed Martyrs of September.

Septima "The Seventh Daughter" (Latin).

Patron Saints: There are at least three Sts. Septimia. One of them died for Jesus in ancient Tuburbum.

Feast Dates: July 30 — St. Septimia.

Septimia (variant) See Septima.

Sera (variant) See Sierra.

Serafina (Hebrew) See Seraphina.

Seraphina "The Burning, Ardent One" (Hebrew).

Patron Saints: Patrons can be found in the angelic seraphim and a few Sts. Seraphina.

One St. Seraphina was born of poor parents in Italy. Her father died and she and her mother were reduced to great poverty. She was a pretty child who loved to help the poor by sharing her food.

Then she fell victim to a series of illnesses that left her totally paralyzed and deformed. For six years, she had only a plank of wood for a bed and rats often bit her. Then her devoted mother died and she was left destitute. But she suffered patiently, knowing that in her own flesh she was completing "what is lacking in Christ's afflictions for the sake of his body, that is, the church" (Colossians 1:24). She was only a teen at the time of her death in 1253.

Feast Dates: March 12 — St. Seraphina; September 29 and October 2 — The Holy Seraphim (see Amber).

Serefina (variant) See Seraphina.

Serena "The Fair, Bright, Calm One" (Latin, Spanish).

Patron Saints: There are three known Sts. Serena. One St. Serena was a single woman who lived in ancient Spoleto when she was arrested by government authorities because she was a Christian. She was tortured to try to make her renounce Jesus. She died during torture in 291.

Feast Dates: January 20 — St. Serena.

Serene (English) See Serena.

Serenity (English) See Serena.

Serephine (variant) See Seraphina.

Serilda (African-American double) See Sierra+Hilda/Wilda.

Serita (Spanish double) See Sierra+Ita.

Serra (variant) See Sierra.

Seville (Spanish) See Sibyl.

Sevilla (Spanish) See Sibyl.

Sha "She or The" (African-American feminine suffix or prefix).

Patron Saints: In the late 1990s "Sha" replaced "La" as the sound of choice for African-American female names. "Sha" can also be treated as a shortened form of Shana, Shane, Shawna, and Shannon.

Feast Dates: August 8 — Bl. Jane of Aza (see Shana); March 17 — St. Patrick McSannon (see Shannon).

Shaakira (Arabic) See Gratia.

Shaba (Spanish) See Rose.

Shae (Irish) See Shayla, Shea.

Shafeequa "The Compassionate One" (Arabic).

Patron Saints: The Blessed Virgin, under the title of "Our Lady of Compassion," has been honored in Mexico City since 1595.

Feast Dates: Any Marian Feast — Our Lady of Compassion.

Shahara (Arabic) See Luna.

Shaheena (Arabic) See Eustacia, Placida.

Shahna (variant) See Shana.

Shaifa (African-American) See Shafeequa.

Shaina "The Beautiful One" (Hebrew).

Patron Saints: Although recently adopted by African-American parents, Shaina is actually an ancient Hebrew name. Many modern people think it is just another form of Seana, Shane, Shawna, or Jane.

Feast Dates: August 8 — Bl. Jane of Aza (see Jane).

Shaine (variant) See Shaina.

Shainise (variant) See Shanice, Shana+Ice.

Shaka (African-American) See Chaka.

Shakari (African-American) See Shaakira, Gratia.

Shakeda (Arabic) See Pulcheria, Mabel.

Shakra (African-American) See Chakra.

Shakyia (Hebrew) See Dawn.

Shaleah (African-American double) See Sha+Leah.

Shalesse (African-American double) See Sha+Lisa.

Shalona (African-American double) See Sha+Lona.

Shalyn (African-American double) See Sha+Lynn.

Shameka (African-American double) See Sha+Tamika.

Shameeka "The Beautiful One" (Hindu) or "God Is Gracious+The Female" (African-American double).

Patron Saints: Shameeka can be accepted as a Hindu name or as a modern combination of Shawna and Tamika.

Feast Dates: August 8 — Bl. Jane of Aza (see Jane).

Shameena (variant) See Shameeka.

Shana "The Small Wise One" (Irish variant of Shannon) or "God Is Gracious" (Irish variant of Seana) or "The Beautiful One" (modern variant of Shaina).

Patron Saints: Shana can come from Shaina, Shanahan, Shawna, Seana, Jan, John, or Joan. These lead to over five hundred Sts. John and a few dozen Sts. Joan and Jane.

Feast Dates: August 8 — Bl. Jane of Aza (see Jane); March 17 — St. Patrick McSannon (see Shannon).

Shanae (African-American) See Shana.

Shanay (African-American) See Shana.

Shanaye (African-American) See Shana.

Shandra (American) See Chandra.

Shandy (English) See Shannon.

Shane (English) See Shannon.

Shanequa (African-American double) See Sha, Shane/Shanice+Tamika/Qua.

Shaneequa (African-American double)
See Sha, Shane/Shanice+Tamika/Qua.
Shaneice (African-American double) See
Shanice, Shana+Ice.
Shanel (American) See Chanelle.
Shanelle (American) See Chanelle.
Shani (American) See Shania, Shannon.
Shania "On My Way" (North American
Indian).

Patron Saints: All one has to remember is that Jesus is "the way, and the truth, and the life" (John 14:6) and a patron appears.

Feast Dates: All Sundays — Jesus the Way (see Delta).
Shanice (variant) See Shana.
Shanice "The Small Wise One" (African-American form of Shannon) or "The Beautiful One" (African-American form of Shaina) or "God Is Gracious" (African-American form of Shawna).

Patron Saints: Shanice is a recent African-American creation. The first part, Shan, may come from Shannon, Shaina, or Seana. The ending, Ice, is an English suffix meaning "the quality of."

Feast Dates: March 17 — St. Patrick McSannon (see Shannon); August 8 — St. Jane of Aza (see Jane).
Shanie (variant) See Shana, Shanice.
Shaniece (variant) See Shana, Shanice.
Shaniesha (African-American double) See Sha+Niesha.
Shanika (African-American double) See Shanice+Tamika.
Shanikwua (African-American double) See Shane/Shanice+Tamika/Qua.
Shaniqua (African-American double) See Shane/Shanice+Tamika/Qua.
Shanise (African-American) See Shanice.
Shanna (variant) See Shana, Shannon.
Shannen (Irish) See Shannon.
Shannon "The Small Wise One" (Irish).

Patron Saints: There is one Irishman with a similar name. St. Patrick McSannon was the nephew of the great St. Patrick. He was ordained a priest and later he was consecrated a bishop. He helped his uncle convert Ireland to the Catholic faith in the 400s.

To find more patrons one must search for names that match Shannon's meaning, which is "wise one." This search leads to the Italian and Roman names Sts. Prudentia and Sapientia.

Feast Dates: March 17 — St. Patricia (see Patricia).
Shanon (English) See Shannon.
Shantae (French) See Chantal.
Shantal (American) See Chantal.
Shantel (American) See Chantal.
Shantelle (American) See Chantal.
Shaquanda (African-American triple) See Sha+Quanah+Wanda.
Shaqueita (African-American double) See Sha+Quieta.
Shara (nickname) See Charlene, Sarah, Sharon.
Sharai (nickname) See Sarah, Sharon.
Shareena (African-American double) See Sharon+Rena.
Shari (nickname) See Charlene, Sharon.
Sharie (nickname) See Charlene, Sharon.
Sharima (African-American) See Charlene, Sharon.
Sharina (African-American) See Charlene, Sharon.
Sharita (Spanish double) See Charlene/Sharon+Ita.
Sharla (nickname) See Charlene, Charlotte, Sharon.
Sharleen (English) See Charlene, Charlotte.
Sharlene (English) See Charlene, Charlotte.
Sharlette (variant double) See Charlene/Charlotte+Ette.

Sharline (English) See Charlene, Charlotte.

Sharlonda (African-American double) See Charlotte+Linda.

Sharmain (English) See Charmaine.

Sharmin (English) See Charmaine.

Sharoka (African-American double) See Sharon+Tamika.

Sharon "From the Fertile Plain" (Hebrew) or "The Princess" (English form of Sarah) or "The Beloved One" (English form of Cherise).

Patron Saints: Patron saints can be found by making two connections. The first is knowing that Sharon is an English form of Sarah and of Cherise. This leads us to many patrons. The second is the discovery that the Blessed Virgin is reverenced by Catholics as the "Rose of Sharon."

There is a great plain in Israel along the Mediterranean coast between Mount Carmel on the north and Joppa on the south, about forty-five miles long by twelve miles wide. The Jews called it *sharon,* that is, "the plain." Both Testaments mention it. It is recognized as a place of fertile vegetation, a fine place for pasture.

The Song of Songs speaks of a "flower" or "rose" of Sharon, which is similar to the hibiscus. Because the "garden of flowers" is a poetic way for God to speak about his beloved, the "flower of Sharon" (defined as the "lily of the valley") becomes a symbol of God's spouse at her finest and purest.

This, or course, applies most completely to the Blessed Virgin. In the *Litany of the Blessed Virgin,* approved in 1587, she is called the "Mystical Rose." She is recognized as the "Garden" from whom the God-Man sprang forth. As the "Flower (Rose)," she is a most faithful spouse of God.

Feast Dates: Month of May — The Blessed Virgin Mary, Rose of Sharon.

Sharona (nickname) See Sharon.

Sharwyn (African-American double) See Sarah/Sharon+Wynn.

Sharyl (variant) See Charlene, Charlotte.

Shauna (Irish-American) See Jane, Shaina, Shannon.

Shauntel (African-American double) See Shauna+Chantal.

Shauntice (Hindu) See Salima.

Shavon (Irish-American) See Jane.

Shawna (Irish-American) See Jane, Shaina, Shannon.

Shawnee (Irish-American) See Jane, Shaina, Shannon.

Shay (variant) See Shayla.

Shayla "From the Fairy Fort" (Irish Gaelic).

Patron Saints: Shayla can be recognized as a variant form of both Shea and Sheila. It can also be regarded as a complete name that means "fairy fort." Just remember Psalms 18:2, which says, "The Lord is my rock, and my fortress, and my deliverer, . . . my stronghold." This means that the Father is a sturdy defense against evil.

Furthermore, Jesus shares the job of being our sturdy refuge, for Isaiah 33:16 tells us, "He will dwell on the heights; his place of defense will be the fortresses of rocks." This passage shows that Jesus would be a strong and protective king. Acts 4:11 adds, "This is the stone which was rejected by you the builders, but which has become the head of the corner." Thus Jesus as the "Cornerstone" becomes our sure guarantee of salvation. He is the "Rock of Our Salvation."

Feast Dates: Thirty-fourth Sunday of the Year — Jesus, Our Fortress.

Shaylyn (Irish-Old English) See Shayla, Lynn.

257

Shaylynn (Irish-Old English) See Shayla, Lynn.

Shayna (English) See Shana, Shaina.

Shayne (English) See Shana, Shaina.

Shea (Irish) See Shayla.

Sheba "The Daughter of an Oath" (Hebrew).

> *Patron Saints:* An alternate spelling of Sheba is Saba. There are about thirty Sts. Sabas. One St. Sabas served as an officer in the Roman army. When it was discovered that he was a Christian, he was executed in 272. Seventy other soldiers were executed with him for the same reason.
>
> *Feast Dates:* April 24 — St. Sabas.

Sheela (African-American) See Sheila.

Sheelagh (Irish) See Sheila.

Sheelah (English) See Sheila.

Sheena (Irish) See Jane, Seana.

Sheeree (nickname) See Sharon, Sherry.

Sheereen (Arabic) See Africa, Lateefah, Shereen.

Sheesha (Hindu) See Shesha.

Sheila "The Blind One" (Irish form of Cecilia) or "From Sabine Country" (Irish form of Sabina).

> *Patron Saints:* Sheila is an Irish form of Cecilia. It is also accepted as a form of Sabina.
>
> *Feast Dates:* November 22 — St. Cecilia (see Cecilia); August 29 — St. Sabina (see Sabina).

Sheilah (English) See Sheila.

Shel (nickname) See Rochelle, Sheila, Shelby, Shelley.

Shela (nickname) See Sheila.

Shelagh (nickname) See Sheila.

Shelbee (American) See Shelby.

Shelbi (American) See Shelby.

Shelbie (American) See Shelby.

Shelby "From the Ledge+Estate" (Old English double).

> *Patron Saints:* Shelby is accepted as an alternate form of Shelley. And there

is one English martyr with the similar name of Shelley.

> *Feast Dates:* August 30 — Bl. Edward Shelley (see Shelley).

Shelia (English, Danish) See Sheila.

Shell (nickname) See Michelle, Rachel, Rochelle, Shelby, Shelley.

Shelldonia (African-American double) See Michelle/Rachel/Rochelle/Shelby/Shelley+Dona/Madonna.

Shellee (nickname) See Michelle, Rachel, Rochelle, Shelby, Shelley.

Shelleen (African-American) See Michelle, Rachel, Rochelle, Shelby.

Shelley "From the Meadow+On the Ledge" (Old English double) or "The Blind One" (nickname for Sheila).

> *Patron Saints:* Shelley can be identified as a familiar form of Michelle, Rachel, Rochelle, and Shelby. Each name provides patrons. There is also an English martyr surnamed Shelley. He lived during the persecution of Catholics in England that lasted for almost two hundred years.
>
> During the reign of Queen Elizabeth I, new laws were passed that made it treason, punishable by death, to be a Catholic priest, to house a Catholic priest, to attend Catholic Mass, or to celebrate the sacraments. Edward Shelley, an English gentleman, was arrested because he did just that. He was tried and executed in 1588.
>
> *Feast Dates:* August 30 — Bl. Edward Shelley.

Shelli (nickname) See Michelle, Rachel, Rochelle, Sheila, Shelby, Shelley.

Shellie (nickname) See Michelle, Rachel, Rochelle, Sheila, Shelby, Shelley.

Shelly (nickname) See Michelle, Rachel, Rochelle, Sheila, Shelby, Shelley.

Shelsy (American) See Chelsea.

Shemeka (African-American double) See any "She" name+Tamika.

Shena (Irish) See Jane.

Shenikwa (African-American double) See Shena/Seana+Kwanza/Kwasi.

Sher (American) See Cherise, Sharon, Sherry, Shirley.

Sheree (nickname) See Charlene, Charlotte, Cherise, Sharon, Sherry, Shirley.

Shereen (American) See Cherise, Sharon, Sherry.

Sherelle (English) See Shirley.

Sheri (nickname) See Charlene, Sharon, Sherry, Shirley.

Sherica (African-American) See Sherika.

Sherie (nickname) See Charlene, Cherise, Sharon, Sherry, Shirley.

Sherika "The One from the East" (Arabic) or "The Princess+Female" (African-American double).

Patron Saints: Sherika can stand as an Arabic name in its own right or be an African-American combination of Sharon and Tamika.

Feast Dates: All Saturdays — The Blessed Virgin Mary, Rose of Sharon (see Sharon); September 8 — St. Ethelburga of Essex (see Esta).

Sherill (variant) See Shirley.

Sherilyn (nickname) See Lynn, Sharon, Sherry, Shirley.

Sherita (Spanish double) See Cherise/Sarah/Sharon+Ita.

Sherline (English) See Shirley.

Sherri (nickname) See Charlene, Charlotte, Cherise, Sharon, Sherry, Shirley.

Sherrie (nickname) See Charlene, Charlotte, Cherise, Sharon, Sherry, Shirley.

Sherry "Like a Fine Wine" (English) or "The Fertile Plain" (nickname for Sharon).

Patron Saints: Sherry can be a nickname for Cherie, Charlotte, Cher, Sarah, Sharon, and Shirley. Each name leads to a number of patrons. But when a connection is made to wine, a different patron surfaces.

Bl. Matt Talbot was born in Ireland in 1856 and at the age of twelve got his first job. He also began coming home drunk. He drank steadily harder until he ended up, at the age of twenty-eight, begging in the streets. One day he collapsed outside a church, at which time he decided to take "the pledge" (that is, the pledge to quit drinking).

He recovered with God's help, went to confession often, attended Mass regularly, and made evening visits to the Blessed Sacrament. He received Communion daily, and read the religious classics and the Bible. He gave up tobacco and added acts of self-denial to gain mastery over his body.

Then he turned his attention to helping others. His extra money went to help neighbors in distress. During his last two years, his health failed and Matt found himself the object of charity. In 1925 he died of heart failure while on his way to attend Mass. He was sixty-nine years old. He is considered the patron of alcoholics.

Feast Dates: June 7 — Bl. Matt Talbot; All Saturdays — The Blessed Virgin Mary, Rose of Sharon (see Sharon).

Sherye (nickname) See Charlene, Charlotte, Cherise, Sharon, Sherry, Sheila.

Sheryl (English) See Charlene, Charlotte, Cherise, Shirley.

Shesha "The Large Sequins on an Indian Woman's Sari" (Hindu) or "The Blind One+God Is Gracious" (African-American double) or "The Blind+Princess" (African-American double).

Patron Saints: Shesha can either be a Hindu name or an African-American combination of Sheila (Cecilia) and Shawna or Sheila and Sharon.

Feast Dates: November 22 — St. Cecilia (see Cecilia).

Shevin (African-American double) See Sha+Yvonne.

Shevonne (African-American double) See Sha+Yvonne.

Sheyla (Hispanic-American) See Sheila.

Sheyleigh (African-American double) See Shirley+Leigh.

Shianne (variant) See Cheyenne.

Shir (nickname) See Shirley.

Shireen (African-American) See Shirley.

Shirl (American) See Shirley.

Shirlee (variant) See Seana.

Shirleen (English) See Shirley.

Shirlene (English) See Shirley.

Shirley "From the Bright Meadow" (Old English) or "The Beloved One" (variant of Cherise).

Patron Saints: It helps to know that the name Shirley is a combination of two words. The first is the Old English *scir*, which means "bright." This leads to St. Scire, who came from Kill-Sgire, which is now known as Kilskyre, Meath, Ireland. She is remembered as being the sister of St. Corcaira Caoin. She lived during the 500s and is remembered for dedicating her single life to God.

The second part of Shirley is *lea* or *leigh*, which means "meadow." This leads to another saint, an English martyr named Bl. Richard Leigh.

Feast Dates: March 24 — St. Scire; August 30 — Bl. Richard Leigh (see Leigh).

Shirlie (English) See Shirley.

Shirline (variant) See Shirley.

Shivan (Irish-American) See Joan.

Shontel (variant) See Chantal.

Shonté (variant) See Chantal.

Shontell (variant) See Chantal.

Shontelle (variant) See Chantal.

Shoshana (Hebrew) See Susan.

Shoshi (Israeli) See Susan.

Shyann (variant) See Cheyenne.

Shyanne (American) See Cheyenne.

Shyniece (African-American) See Shanice.

Sian (Welsh) See Jane.

Sib (nickname) See Sibyl.

Sibbi (nickname) See Sibyl.

Sibeal (Irish) See Sibyl.

Sibel (English) See Sibyl.

Sibella (Italian) See Sibyl.

Sibelle (Italian) See Sibyl.

Sibil (English) See Sibyl.

Sibilla (variant) See Sibyl.

Sibille (variant) See Sibyl.

Sibley (variant) See Sibyl.

Sibyl "The Prophetess" (Greek).

Patron Saints: There are at least three Sts. Sybil. One is Bl. Sibyllina Biscossi, 1287-1367, who is recognized as the patron of maids and servants. Soon after birth she became an orphan. By the time she was twelve, she had lost her eyesight.

A short time later she joined the Third Order of St. Dominic and began to live in a cell connected to a local Dominican church. There, she embraced a life of penance and prayer. In return for her dedication, God performed many miracles through her. She died at the age of eighty.

Feast Dates: March 23 — Bl. Sibyllina Biscossi.

Sibylia (Dutch, Swedish) See Sibyl.

Sibyll (English) See Sibyl.

Sibylla (Polish See Sibyl.

Sibylle (French) See Sibyl.

Sibyllina (Italian) See Sibyl.

Sidney (English) See Sydney.

Sidra "She Belongs to the Stars" (Latin).

Patron Saints: Although there are no saints named Sidra, the Latin word for "star," *sidus*, could lead one to a number of saints whose names have a similar sound. Among them are at least one St. Sidonia and a dozen Sts. Sidonius, one of whom died a martyr's death in ancient days.

Feast Dates: October 1 — St. Sidonia.

Sidsel (Danish) See Cecilia.

Sierra "From the Saw-Toothed Mountain Range" (Spanish).

Patron Saints: Two saints with very similar names can serve as patrons. One is St. Sierius, a medieval hermit. The other is a North American, Bl. Junípero Serra, 1713-1784. Born in Majorca, he became a Franciscan and at twenty-five years of age he was ordained a priest. He longed to go to the New World to teach the Indians, but it was not until he was thirty-seven that he finally got to Mexico City. Then for the next ten years he worked with the poor and Indians near Mexico City.

Only at the age of fifty-six did he get a chance to go to California. He immediately founded the Mission of San Diego, his first. For the next thirteen years Father Serra walked thousands of miles, all over California, despite an ulcerated leg. His life was one long martyrdom of labor, loneliness, and sacrifice; but he taught the Indians, provided the sacrament, and is credited with twenty-one missions (although twelve of them were built after his death). He died at the age of seventy-one.

Feast Dates: July 1 — Bl. Junípero Serra, O.F.M.

Signe "The Sign" (Latin) or "The Senior Tenant" (short form of Sigourney).

Patron Saints: St. John of the Cross, 1542-1591, is one of many choices. He is remembered for his mystical writings. He is a Doctor of the Church.

Feast Dates: December 14 — St. John of the Cross.

Sigourney "The Senior Tenant" (French) or "The Victorious Conqueror" (English).

Patron Saints: One saint with a similar name can be adopted as patron. Sigolena was born in France into a wealthy family and eventually married a nobleman. After her husband died, she became a deaconess. Later, she was elected to serve as abbess of a local monastery. She died in 769.

Feast Dates: July 24 — St. Sigolena.

Sigrid "The Beautiful, Victorious Counselor" (Scandinavian).

Patron Saints: St. Sigrada was the mother of a saint. She was forced into exile because of her Catholic faith.

Feast Dates: August 8 — St. Sigrada.

Sila (nickname) See Priscilla.

Sile (Irish) See Cecilia, Julie.

Sileas (Scottish Gaelic) See Cecilia, Julie.

Silla (nickname) See Priscilla.

Silva (Bulgarian) See Sylvia.

Silvana (Latin, Spanish) See Sylvia.

Silvanna (Latin) See Sylvannah.

Silvannah (Latin) See Sylvannah.

Silvia (Italian, Spanish) See Sylvia.

Silvie (French) See Sylvia.

Simia (African-American) See Simone.

Simona (variant) See Simone.

Simone "The One Who Hears" (Hebrew).

Patron Saints: There are at least thirty saints who bear the name of Simon and another fifty named Simeon. One of the greatest is St. Simon the Apostle. Another well-known Simon is St. Simon of Cyrene, who helped Jesus carry his cross. Tradition relates that Simon of Cyrene was killed by the sword in ancient Chios.

Feast Dates: November 1 — St. Simon of Cyrene.

Simonette (variant) See Simone.

Simonia (variant) See Simone.

Simonne (variant) See Simone.

Simplicia "The Uncomplicated One."

Patron Saints: There is at least one St. Simplicia. She was a martyr in ancient times.

Feast Dates: April 12 — St. Simplicia.

Sina (Irish Gaelic) See Seana, Jane.

Sinclair (French double) See Sancia+Clare.

Sindee (American) See Cynthia, Hyacinth.

Sine (Irish Gaelic) See Seana, Jane.

Sinead (Irish Gaelic) See Jane.

Sineta (African-American double) See Sine+Etta.

Siobhan (Irish Gaelic) See Jane, Joan, Judith.

Sirena "The Sweet Singing Mermaid" (Greek, Spanish) or "The Enchanter" (Greek, Spanish).

Patron Saints: This name leads to two Sts. Sirina. St. Sirina, who died for the Catholic faith, was the mother of two children, Behnam and Sarah, who also were put to death for becoming Catholics. They were murdered by their father, King Sanherib, in 331.

Feast Dates: February 8 — St. Sirina.

Sirina (variant) See Sirena.

Sisile (variant) See Cecilia.

Sisly (African-American) See Cecilia.

Sissel (Norwegian) See Cecilia.

Sissie (variant) See Cecilia.

Sissieretta (African-American double) See Sissie+Retta.

Sissy (variant) See Cecilia.

Siubhan (Gaelic) See Jane, Joan, Judith.

Siusaidh (Scottish) See Susan.

Siusan (Scottish) See Susan.

Sivan (Irish-American) See Siwan, Jane, Joan.

Siwan (Irish-American) See Jane, Joan.

Sky (variant) See Skye.

Skye "The Teacher" (Dutch) or "The Sheltering One" (Dutch).

Patron Saints: Skye can mean "teacher" and the Catholic Church has appointed five patrons of teachers: Sts. Cassian of Imola, Catherine of Alexandria, Gregory the Great, John Baptist de la Salle, and Ursula.

Feast Dates: November 28 — St. Catherine Labouré (see Catherine); October 21 — St. Ursula (see Ursula).

Skyla (Dutch) See Skye.

Skylar (Dutch) See Skye.

Skyler (Dutch) See Skye.

Snowflake "Like a Grain of Soft White Crystallized Water" (Middle English).

Patron Saints: Bl. Peter Snow was executed in England in 1598 because he insisted upon being a Catholic.

Feast Dates: May 4 — Bl. Peter Snow.

Sofia (Italian, Spanish) See Sophie.

Soficita (Spanish double) See Sophie+Ita.

Sofie (French, Danish, Dutch) See Sophie.

Sofronia (Spanish) See Sophie.

Sojourner "The One Who Stayed a Short Time" (Middle English).

Patron Saints: A sojourner is a pilgrim or traveler. In Latin this is *viator*, and there is one St. Viatrix. She was killed during the Roman persecutions of 304.

Feast Dates: July 29 — St. Viatrix.

Solana "The Sunshine" (Spanish).

Patron Saints: There is one ancient saint with a similar name: St. Solina. She was born of pagan parents in ancient Gascony and, as an adult, she converted to Catholicism. Then she refused to marry and fled to Chartes but was found. Her parents had her beheaded in 290.

Feast Dates: October 17 — St. Solina.

Soledad "The One Who Lives in Solitude" (Spanish).

Patron Saints: Father Miguel Martínez Sanz, a pastor in Madrid, Spain, wanted to found a religious order of sisters to nurse the sick at home and in the hospital. Bibiana Torres Acosta, 1826-1887, shared his deep concern for the poor and, with six companions, soon founded the Sisters Servants of Mary. She took the name of Sister María Soledad. Her community ran into a number of difficulties and she was ousted as superior general. In time, she was reinstalled as their head.

She dedicated her life to the sick even though she was small, frail, revolted by diseases, and terrified of dead bodies. Slowly she overcame her fears and encouraged her sisters to "serve God with enthusiasm." She died of pneumonia at the age of sixty.

Feast Dates: October 11 — St. María Soledad Torres Acosta, S.M.

Soleil (variant) See Sunny.

Solene (English) See Solana.

Solenne (English) See Solana.

Solina (English) See Solana.

Solivia (Hispanic-American double) See Solana+Olivia.

Somer (English) See Summer.

Sommer (variant) See Summer.

Son (nickname) See Sonny, Sophie.

Sondra (variant) See Alexandra, Cassandra, Sandra.

Sonia (Spanish, Danish, Slavic) See Sonny, Sophie.

Sonja (Slavic, Scandinavian) See Sonny, Sophie.

Sonnee (nickname) See Sonny, Sophie.

Sonni (nickname) See Sonny, Sophie.

Sonnie (nickname) See Sonny, Sophie.

Sonny "The Son" (Middle English) or "The Bright, Cheerful One" (English form of Sophie).

Patron Saints: It seems strange to name a girl Sonny. However, in the modern American Catholic culture, Sonny is a play on words such as "Sunny." After all, Jesus, the "Son of God," is the "Sun in our lives."

Another patron can be found in St. Sontius, who died a martyr for Jesus in ancient Italy. In addition, some scholars point out that Sonny can also serve as a familiar form of Sonya (or Sophie). Finally, any saint with a name that means "bright" or "cheerful" can be adopted. These include, among others, St. Scire. (The Old English word *scir* means "bright.")

Feast Dates: August 6 — Jesus Christ the Son of God; November 17 — St. Sontius.

Sonya (Slavic, Scandinavian) See Sophie.

Sophenia (African-American) See Sophie.

Sophey (variant) See Sophie.

Sophi (variant) See Sophie.

Sophia (Greek) See Sophie.

Sophie "The Wise One" (French).

Patron Saints: There are over a dozen Sts. Sophia. One of them was the mother of three daughters, whose names were Pistis, Elpis, and Agape (that is, Faith, Hope, and Charity). They were arrested in about 130 and brought before a pagan judge and condemned to death for the crime of being Christians. At the time of their deaths, Faith was twelve years old, Hope was ten, and Charity, nine.

The oldest, Faith, was scourged, then thrown into boiling pitch, taken out alive, and beheaded. Hope and Charity escaped the scourging, but not being dipped in the boiling pitch, and they were also beheaded. Their mother watched, prayed, and suffered through this barbarous activity. Then she also was killed.

Feast Dates: September 30 — St. Sophia.

Sophronia (variant) See Sophie.

Sophy (English) See Sophie.

Sorcha (Irish) See Sarah.

Sorcha (Scottish) See Clare.

Sosana (Romanian) See Susan.

Sosanna (Irish) See Susan.

Spring "The Time of New Life" (Old English).

Patron Saints: A patron can be found in the meaning of the name, "the time nature wakes to new life." It is the season when Easter is celebrated. Thus Jesus becomes the first patron of anyone named after this time of new life. Also, because the Blessed Virgin gave birth to Jesus, who is this New Life, she also can serve as a patron.

Feast Dates: All Saturdays — The Blessed Virgin Mary, Garden of God (see Laverne).

Stace (American) See Anastasia, Eustacia.

Stacee (American) See Anastasia, Eustacia.

Stacey (American) See Anastasia, Eustacia.

Staci (American) See Anastasia, Eustacia.

Stacia (variant) See Anastasia, Eustacia.

Stacie (variant, nickname) See Anastasia, Eustacia.

Star "The Heavenly Guiding Light" (Old English).

Patron Saints: There are two saints whose names mean "Star": Sts. Esther and Estella. And there are also two mightier patrons who could be referred to as Sts. Starr. One is Jesus the Rising Morning Star; the other is the Blessed Virgin, Star of the Sea.

Stars are used by the sailors to navigate. Catholic writers from the most ancient times have always spoken of the Church as the "Ark" or "Bark of Peter." It is like a ship on a turbulent sea, the sea being the world and its inhabitants' destination being the heavenly Jerusalem. However, the trip is fraught with dangers that can cause the passengers (God's people) and the sailors (clergy) to often become seasick (sin). But the journey is guaranteed to be successful if one only steers the proper course and Mary is the star or guide. Remember that at the wedding of Cana she said, "Do whatever he [Jesus] tells you" (John 2:5). Mary is patron of sailors, navigators, yachtsmen, travelers, and all forms of transportation. Thus, the saying "To Jesus through Mary."

Feast Dates: All Saturdays — The Blessed Virgin Mary, Star of the Sea.

Starr (English) See Star.

Stef (nickname) See Stephanie.

Stefa (nickname) See Stephanie.

Stefani (variant) See Stephanie.

Stefania (Polish, Swedish, Italian) See Stephanie.

Stefanida (Russian) See Stephanie.

Stefanie (Dutch) See Stephanie.

Stefanny (Dutch) See Stephanie.

Steffane (variant) See Stephanie.

Steffee (nickname) See Stephanie.

Steffi (nickname) See Stephanie.

Steffie (nickname) See Stephanie.

Steffy (nickname) See Stephanie.

Stella (nickname) See Estelle.

Stepana (Czech) See Stephanie.

Stepha (English) See Stephanie.

Stephana (Italian) See Stephanie.

Stephani (variant) See Stephanie.

Stephania (Serbian) See Stephanie.

Stephanie "The Crowned One" (German).

Patron Saints: There are about a hundred Sts. Stephan, but only one St. Stephania and two Sts. Stephana. St. Stephana, 1457-1530, was born at Orzinovi in the diocese of Brescia. At the early age of fifteen, she joined the

Dominican religious order. Much later she became the foundress and first abbess of the St. Paolo monastery near Soncino. She is remembered for her great charity toward the poor and her great devotion to the Blessed Sacrament. She died at the age of seventy-three.

Feast Dates: January 2 — Bl. Stephana de Quinzanis.

Stephannie (variant) See Stephanie.
Stephanos (Greek) See Stephanie.
Stephenie (Greek) See Stephanie.
Stephi (nickname) See Stephanie.
Stephie (nickname) See Stephanie.
Stephine (variant) See Stephanie.
Stesha (variant) See Stephanie.
Stevana (English) See Stephanie.
Stevanka (Serbian) See Stephanie.
Stevena (French) See Stephanie.
Stevie (nickname) See Stephanie.
Stina (Swedish, Norwegian) See Christiana, Christine.
Stockard "The Hardy Tree Stump" (Old English).

Patron Saints: Probably the most eligible saint available for adoption is St. Simon Stock. He is remembered for receiving the apparition of Our Lady of Mount Carmel.

Feast Dates: July 16 — Our Lady of Mount Carmel (see Carmella).

Storm "The Stormy One" (Middle English).

Patron Saints: While there is no saint named Storm, there are two who have been named patrons of storms. One of them, Agrippina, was publicly stripped, scourged, and then executed in 262 by order of the Roman emperor Valerian because she refused to deny Christ. She is the patron against demons, leprosy, and storms.

Feast Dates: June 23 — St. Agrippina; December 4 — St. Barbara (see Barbara).

Stormee (American) See Storm.
Stormi (American) See Storm.
Stormie (English) See Storm.
Stormy (English) See Storm.
Sudie (nickname) See Susan.
Sue (nickname) See Susan.
Suehelie (Hispanic-American double) See Susana+Helen.
Suela (Spanish) See Consuelo.
Suelita (Spanish double) See Consuelo.
Sugar "The Sweet One" (Middle English).

Patron Saints: There is an English martyr named Sugar. John Sugar was executed by the English government because he insisted on functioning, in 1604, as a diocesan priest in England.

Feast Date: May 4 — Bl. John Sugar; September 16 — St. Dulcissima (see Delcine).

Sukey (Hawaiian) See Susan.
Suki (Hawaiian) See Susan.
Sukie (nickname) See Susan.
Sula (nickname) See Ursula.
Sumer (variant) See Summer.
Summer "Born in the Summertime" (Middle English).

Patron Saints: There is one saint, Bl. Thomas Somers, who will serve nicely. He often went by the name of Wilson and was born at Skelsmergh, Westmorland, England. Early in life he worked as a schoolmaster. In time, he traveled to Douai, France, was ordained a priest, and immediately returned to England to serve the Church. In 1610 he was arrested by English civil authorities and condemned to death because he insisted on working as a Catholic priest. He was hanged at Tyburn.

Feast Dates: December 10 — Bl. Thomas Somers.

Sunday "Born on the Sun's Day" (Middle English) or "The Lord's Day" (English form of Dominique).

Patron Saints: There is one St. Sunday from Campagna, Italy. When the Roman emperor Diocletian was persecuting Christians in 304, she was arrested, tortured, and finally beheaded.

It should also be noted that Sunday in Spanish is *domingo* and *domínica.* There are a half-dozen Sts. Dominica.

Feast Dates: July 6 — St. Sunday; August 21 — St. Dominica (see Dominica).

Sunnee (American) See Sunny.

Sunnie (American) See Sunny.

Sunny "The Bright One" (English) or "The Wise One" (nickname for Sophie).

Patron Saints: There is one saint who has a very similar name. St. Suniman, an abbot, was killed with his monks by invading pagan Danes in 870.

Also, some scholars point out that Sunny can serve as a familiar form of Sonja or Sophie. However, the best patron is Jesus himself. The New Testament teaches, "And the city has no need of sun or moon to shine upon it, for the glory of God is its light, and its lamp is the Lamb" (Revelation 21:23). Matthew 17:2 compares the glory of Jesus with the sun. The Church celebrates the "Lighting of the Light of Christ" on Holy Saturday.

Feast Dates: February 15 — St. Suniman; Holy Saturday — Jesus, Light of the World.

Sunray (African-American) See Sunny.

Sunshine (English) See Sunny.

Susa (Italian, German) See Susan.

Susan "The Graceful Lily" (English).

Patron Saints: There are a dozen-and-a-half Sts. Susanna. One of them was a daughter of a Catholic priest. Beautiful and well-educated, she caught the eye of Emperor Diocletian, who wanted her to be the wife of his son-in-law. He sent her pagan uncle to her to plead his case, but Susanna refused, saying that she was a "bride of Christ." Her uncle was so impressed with her dedication to Christ that he and his family converted and were baptized. The emperor sent others and they too were converted to Jesus. This greatly upset the emperor and he had everyone arrested. All were convicted of being Christians and were executed.

Feast Dates: August 11 — St. Susanna.

Susana (Spanish, Portuguese) See Susan.

Susanetta (English double) See Susan+Etta.

Susann (variant) See Susan.

Susanna (Italian, Russian) See Susan, Zsa Zsa.

Susannah (German) See Susan.

Susanne (variant) See Susan.

Suse (German) See Susan.

Susetta (Italian double) See Susan+Etta.

Susette (French double) See Susan+Ette.

Susi (nickname) See Susan.

Susie (nickname) See Susan.

Susy (nickname) See Susan.

Suvena (African-American double) See Sunny+Venus.

Suzana (Romanian, Bulgarian, Croatian) See Susan.

Suzanna (French) See Susan.

Suzannah (French) See Susan.

Suzanne (French) See Susan.

Suzen (American) See Susan.

Suzene (African-American) See Susan.

Suzette (French double) See Susan+Ette.

Suzi (nickname) See Susan.

Suzie (nickname) See Susan.

Suzon (French) See Susan.

Suzy (nickname) See Susan.

Suzzy (nickname) See Susan.

Svetlana "The Bright Light" (Russian).

Patron Saints: The name Roberta means "bright" and Helen means "light." This leads to many patrons.

Feast Dates: September 13 — St. Robert Bellarmine (see Roberta); August 18 — St. Helena (see Helen).

Swoosie (American) See Susan.

Sybil (Greek) See Sibyl.

Sybila (Greek) See Sibyl.

Sybile (Greek) See Sibyl.

Sydel (English) See Sydney.

Sydelle (English) See Sydney.

Sydney "From the City of St. Denis [Goddess Queen]" (Old French).

Patron Saints: It is helpful to know that Sydney is a form of Denis or Denise. Furthermore, Denise is a form of Dionysia, and there are six Sts. Dionysia.

Feast Dates: December 12 — St. Dionysia (see Denise); December 6 — St. Dionysia (see Dione).

Sylva (French) See Sylvia.

Sylvania (Latin) See Sylvannah.

Sylvanna (American double) See Sylvia+Vanna.

Sylvannah "From the Forest+From the Plain" (Latin double) or "The Graceful One" (Hebrew).

Patron Saints: This name is a combination of Sylvia and Savannah. Remember, Savannah means "plain" and the Hebrew word for this is *sharon.*

Feast Dates: November 3 — St. Silvia (see Sylvia); Month of May — The Blessed Virgin Mary, Rose of Sharon (see Sharon).

Sylvia "From the Forest" (Latin).

Patron Saints: There are a dozen Sts. Silvius, but there seems to be only one St. Silvia. She had the good fortune to be the mother of St. Gregory the Great, the pope who ruled the Catholic Church in about 590. Surrounded by saints during her entire life, she had her son elected to the papacy. She died in 592 and is patron of Sicily in Messina and of the Camaldolite religious order.

Feast Dates: November 3 — St. Silvia.

Sylvie (French) See Sylvia.

Sylwia (Polish) See Sylvia.

Symora (African-American double) See any "Sy" name+Mora.

Synesta (African-American) See Synestra.

Synestra "From the Left Hand" (African-American form of Sinestra).

Patron Saints: The Latin word for "left" is *sinister.* St. Synesius was a lector who was martyred in ancient Rome.

Feast Dates: December 12 — St. Synesius.

T

Taaj (Arabic) See Stephanie.

Tabatha (Aramaic) See Tabitha.

Tabbi (nickname) See Tabitha.

Tabbie (nickname) See Tabitha.

Tabbita (nickname) See Tabitha.

Tabbitha (nickname) See Tabitha.

Tabby (nickname) See Tabitha.

Tabina "The Follower of Muhammad" (Arabic).

Patron Saints: When a follower of Muhammad is baptized she becomes a follower of Christ, a Christian.

Feast Dates: December 15 — St. Christiana, also known as Nino.

Tabitha "Like a Gazelle" (Aramaic) or "The Child of Grace" (Greek, Spanish).

Patron Saints: There is only one St. Tabitha (or Dorcas, in Greek). She lived in Joppa during the time of Jesus. She did good deeds and almsgiving and then she died. Lydda, her friend, knew St. Peter was near and asked him for help. Peter immediately went to Joppa, where he saw many crying. Peter sent them all out of the room, knelt down, and prayed. Then he ordered Tabitha to get up. She did and he gave her back to her family and friends. As a result of this miracle, many came to believe in the teachings of Jesus.

Feast Dates: October 25 — St. Tabitha.

Tacey (English) See Tacita.

Tacita (Latin) See Quieta.

Taff (nickname) See Taffy.

Taffee (variant) See Taffy.

Taffey (variant) See Taffy.

Taffi (variant) See Taffy.

Taffie (variant) See Taffy.

Taffy "The Beloved One" (Welsh nickname for Davita).

Patron Saints: It helps to know that Taffy is a Welsh nickname for Davita.

Feast Dates: December 6 — St. Davita (see Davita); June 6 — St. Ama (see Aimee).

Tahnya (African-American) See Tanya.

Tailer (variant) See Taylor.

Tailor (variant) See Taylor.

Taj (African-American) See Taaj.

Tajama (African-American) See Taaj.

Talesia "The Beautiful Water" (North American Indian).

Patron Saints: In ancient times St. Talida lived the life of a holy nun in an Egyptian convent for eighty years.

Feast Dates: St. Talida — January 5.

Talia "The Gentle Dew from Heaven" (Hebrew, Spanish) or "Born on Christmas Day" (nickname for Natalie).

Patron Saints: There is one St. Talia. In 421 St. Talia was just a toddler, aged two, when he was killed because of hatred for the faith in Byblos, Syria.

Also, because some think Talia is a short form of Natalia, a few Sts. Natalie become available.

Feast Dates: August 8 — St. Talia; September 8 — St. Natalie (see Natalie).

Talisa (English) See Tallis.

Talitha (Aramaic) See Cailin, Colleen, Maida.

Talli (nickname) See Talia, Tallis, Tallulah.

Tallia (variant) See Talia, Tallis.

Tallie (nickname) See Talia, Tallulah.

Tallis "From the Forest" (French-English).

Patron Saints: Bl. John Forest became the confessor of Queen Catherine of Aragon. He soon found himself in opposition to King Henry VIII because he opposed the royal divorce. Further, he refused to recognize Henry as the head of the Church. As a result, the king had a particular hatred for Father Forest. He had him burned at the stake in 1538.

Feast Dates: May 22 — Bl. John Forest, O.F.M.

Tallou (nickname) See Tallulah.

Tallulah "From the Leaping Water" (North American Indian).

Patron Saints: One ancient saint with a similar name can be pressed into service. St. Talona gave her life for the Catholic faith in ancient Burchata.

Feast Dates: November 20 — St. Talona.

Tally (nickname) See Talia, Tallulah.

Talya (variant) See Talia.

Talyah (variant) See Talia.

Tam (nickname) See Tamara, Tamika.

Tamala (African-Hispanic-American double) See Tamar+Pamela.

Tamanisha "Palm Tree+Female" (African-American double).

Patron Saints: This name seems to be a combination of Tamara and Isha. It could also be based on Nisha, which is a Hindu name that means "night."

Feast Dates: November 1 — Holy Tamar; June 28 — St. Nisia.

Tamar (English) See Tamara.

Tamara "The Palm Tree" (Hebrew, Spanish) or "The Perfect One" (Hebrew, when written as Tammy).

Patron Saints: The Bible speaks of three female Tamars. The best known is the wife of Judah's two elder sons, who died childless. Because Judah would not give her to his third son as required by law, she deceived Judah, had sexual relations with him, and bore him two sons (see Genesis 38:6ff). The

Gospel of Matthew lists her as an ancestor of Jesus. There is also a St. Tammarus, an ancient African bishop.

Feast Dates: November 1 — Holy Tamar; October 15 — St. Tammarus.

Tamarah (variant) See Tamara.

Tamarla (African-American double) See Tamara+Marla.

Tameka (African-American) See Tamika.

Tamena (African-American) See Tamara.

Tamera (Hebrew) See Tamara.

Tami (nickname) See Tamara, Tamika, Thomasina.

Tamia (nickname) See Tamara, Tamika, Thomasina.

Tamicka (African-American) See Tamika.

Tamika "A Female Person" (African-American adaptation).

Patron Saints: Tamika is an African-American adaptation of the Japanese word *tamiko,* which simply means "a female person." In Hebrew this is rendered *isha.* The Bible identifies the first Isha as Eve. Another Christian connection can be made to Tamara, through the mutually shared nickname Tammy.

Feast Dates: December 25 — Sts. Adam and Eve (see Isha); October 15 — St. Tammarus (see Tamara).

Tamiko (Japanese) See Tamika.

Tamma (nickname) See Tamara.

Tammi (nickname) See Tamara, Tamika, Thomasina.

Tammie (nickname) See Tamara, Tamika, Thomasina.

Tammy (nickname) See Tamara, Tamika, Thomasina.

Tamra (Hebrew) See Tamara.

Tamyene (African-American) See Tamara.

Tana "The One from Denmark" (variant of Dana).

Patron Saints: Tana can be an alternate form of Dane or a nickname for

Antonia and Titania. All these names lead to patrons. Among them is St. Tanea. She lived in ancient Scotland in the Middle Ages and is specially remembered for dedicating her single lifestyle to the service of Jesus and his Church.

Feast Dates: July 18 — St. Tanea; February 28 — St. Antonia (see Antonia); January 12 — St. Tatiana (see Tatiana).

Tancha (Hispanic-American double) See Tania+Chalina.

Tandee (nickname) See Tandy.

Tandi (nickname) See Tandy.

Tandie (variant) See Tandy.

Tandra (African-American double) See Tandy+Sandra.

Tandy "The Immortal One" (Greek) or "The Tenacious One" (Latin) or "The Team" (English).

Patron Saints: The title "Immortal One" leads a Christian directly to the Triune Godhead.

Feast Dates: Trinity Sunday — Bl. Trinity (see Trinidad).

Taneea (African-American) See Tanya.

Taneisha (African-American) See Tanisha.

Tanema (African-American double) See Tanya+Ema.

Tanesha (African-American) See Tanisha.

Taneshia (African-American) See Tanisha.

Tanessia (African-American) See Tanisha.

Tangi (African-American double) See any "Tan" name+Angie.

Tangia (African-American double) See any "Tan" name+Angela.

Tanhya (variant) See Tanya, Titania.

Tania (Spanish) See Tanya, Tawny, Titania.

Tanie (nickname) See Tawny.

Taniesha (African-American) See Tanisha.

Taniesha (variant) See Tanisha.

Tanika (African-American) See Tania.

Tanisha "Born on the Moon Goddess's Day" (Nigerian-African-American).

Patron Saints: Tanisha is an African-American adaptation of the Nigerian word *tani*, which means "moon goddess day." "Moon" in Latin is *luna*, and this leads to St. Lunecharia. Furthermore, Diana also means "moon goddess."

Feast Dates: June 7 — St. Lunecharia (see Luna); June 9 — Bl. Diana d'Andalo (see Diana).

Tanishia (African-American) See Tanisha.

Tanja (African-American) See Tanya.

Tanni (nickname) See Tawny.

Tannie (nickname) See Tawny.

Tanny (nickname) See Tawny.

Tansy "The Immortal One" (Greek) or "The Tenacious [Persistent] One" (Latin).

Patron Saints: There is a St. Perseveranda. She lived in Spain in the 700s and was known for her piety.

Feast Dates: June 26 — St. Perseveranda.

Tanya Meaning unknown (Slavic) or "The Giant One" (short form of Titania) or "From Denmark" (variant of Dana).

Patron Saints: Some think Tanya is a form of Tatiana. This leads us to three Sts. Tatiana.

Feast Dates: January 12 — St. Tatiana (see Tatiana).

Tara "From the Rocky Point [Tower]" (Irish Gaelic, Spanish).

Patron Saints: Tara is from *taran*, which means "rocky pinnacle," and there are many saints who can serve as a patron for the name Rock. The finest candidate is St. Peter the Apostle, whom Jesus named "Rock."

After St. Peter, the second greatest is St. Rock, a Frenchman who lived from about 1350 to 1380.

Feast Dates: August 16 — St. Rock (see Rochelle).

Taran (Irish) See Tara.

Tarasia (Spanish) See Queen.

Tareyn (Irish) See Tara.

Tarra (Irish) See Tara.

Tarrah (Irish) See Tara.

Tarryn (Irish) See Tara.

Taryn (Irish) See Tara.

Feast Dates: January 12 — St. Tatiana.

Tasha "Born on Christmas Day" (Russian nickname for Natasha) or "The Resurrected One" (English nickname for Anastasia).

Patron Saints: Tasha is a short form of Natasha, which means "birthday," and Anastasia, which means "resurrected one." This leads to a half-dozen Sts. Natalie and about a dozen Sts. Anastasia.

Feast Dates: September 8 — St. Natalie (see Natalie); December 25 — St. Anastasia (see Anastasia).

Tashara (African-American double) See Tasha+Sharon.

Tashica (African-American double) See Tasha+Tamika.

Tasia (Spanish) See Anastasia.

Tate (English) See Tatum.

Tatiana "The Fairy Queen" (Russian).

Patron Saints: There is a St. Tatia and three Sts. Tatiana. One of the Sts. Tatiana served the ancient Roman Church as a deaconess. She was beheaded with her father in 225.

Tatta (variant) See Tatum.

Tatum "She Who Brings Cheer" (Modern English).

Patron Saints: There are two Sts. Tatta, two Sts. Tatwin, and a St. Tatuna. One St. Tatta gave her life for Jesus in Damascus in ancient times.

It also helps to know that Tatum means "cheer bringer." The Latin word for "cheerful" is *hilarious*, which leads to about forty Sts. Hilary.

Feast Dates: September 25 — St. Tatta; December 3 — St. Hilaria (see Hilaria).

Tauja (African-American) See Taaj.

Tavia (nickname) See Octavia.

Tavon (African-American double) See Tara+Yvonne.

Tavy (nickname) See Octavia.

Tawana (African-American double) See any "Ta" name+Wanda.

Tawnee (variant) See Tawny.

Tawni (English) See Tawny.

Tawnie (nickname) See Tawny.

Tawny "The Tan One" (Middle English) or "Giant One" (nickname for Titania) or "Little One" (Romany).

Patron Saints: There is one known saint who bears the name Tawny. However, almost no information has survived the ages about Sawyl the Tawny. We do know, though, that his grandfather, Meurig, was one of the four kings who bore the legendary magic sword Excalibur before it became the possession of King Arthur of the Round Table fame.

Feast Dates: January 15 — St. Sawyl Feljin the Tawny.

Tawnya (African-American) See Tanya, Tawny, Titania.

Tawsha (African-American) See Tasha.

Taycha (Hispanic-American double) See Taylor+Chalina.

Tayler (variant) See Taylor.

Taylor "The One Who Sews" (Old French).

Patron Saints: There is one English martyr surnamed Taylor. He is Bl. Hugh Taylor, who was arrested in 1585 in England for being a Catholic priest. He was tried, convicted, and executed by being hanged, drawn, and quartered in 1585.

And knowing that Taylor means "tailor" leads to five more saints who have been named patrons of tailors. They are Sts. Boniface of Crediton, Homobonus, Martin of Tours, Quentin, and Ursula.

Feast Dates: May 4 — Bl. Hugh Taylor; October 21 — St. Ursula (see Ursula).

Tea (nickname) See Teresa, Thea, Tia.

Teacake (African-American) See Muffin.

Techa (Spanish) See Summer.

Tecla (Greek) See Thecla.

Tecora (African-American double) See Tecla+Cora.

Ted (nickname) See Theodora.

Tedda (nickname) See Theodora.

Teddi (nickname) See Theodora.

Teddie (nickname) See Theodora.

Teddy (nickname) See Theodora.

Tedessa (African-American double) See Theodora+Essie.

Tedi (nickname) See Theodora.

Tedra (nickname) See Theodora.

Teena (variant) See Augustina, Celestine, Christine, Katrina, Martina.

Tega (English) See Tegan.

Tegan "Young Female Deer" (Irish Gaelic) or "The Pearl" (African-American form of Megan).

Patron Saints: There is one St. Tega, one St. Tegal, and one St. Tegan. St. Tegan is remembered for being a rather good pupil of St. Fiace of Sletty. He was from medieval Wicklow, Ireland. Some think Tegan is an African-American variant of Megan. This leads to even more patrons.

Feast Dates: September 9 — St. Tegan; November 1 — St. Meigan (see Megan).

Tegfan (variant) See Tegan.

Tegfar (variant) See Tegan.

Tehais (variant) See Thaïs.

Tekawitha (North American Indian) See Kateri.

Telissa (African-American double) See any "Te" name+Lisa.

Tempest "The Stormy One" (Middle English, Middle French).

Patron Saints: A tempest is a storm and two saints have been named patron of storms.

Feast Dates: December 4 — St. Barbara (see Barbara); June 23 — St. Agrippina (see Storm).

Templa "The Sanctuary [Church]" (Latin).

Patron Saints: There is one saint who came from Eccleston, which means the same as "temple." John Finch, a farmer, was executed in 1584 because he reconciled with the Catholic Church and let priests sleep in his home.

Feast Dates: April 20 — Bl. John Finch of Eccleston.

Teneisha (African-American) See Tanisha.

Tenesha (African-American) See Tanisha.

Tenisha (African-American) See Tanisha.

Tennille (Hispanic-African-American double) See any "Te" name+Neil.

Tenny (Middle English) See Denise.

Teodora (Czech, Italian, Spanish) See Theodora.

Teodosia (Spanish) See Theodora.

Teophila (Polish-Spanish double) See Theophilia, Theo+Phila.

Tera (Lithuanian) See Tara, Teresa, Teresita, Thérèse.

Terae (African-American) See Terry.

Terchie (variant) See Tertia.

Terdema (African-American double) See Teresa+Demetria.

Tere (Spanish) See Teresa.

Teresa "The Reaper" (Italian).

Patron Saints: There are about a dozen saints named Teresa. One is Teresa Cepeda y de Ahumada, 1515-1582, better known as St. Teresa of Ávila. She was born in Old Castile, Spain, and as a teen was vain and sentimental. But moved by the *Letters of St. Jerome* when she was twenty years of age, she entered the Carmelite convent.

At the age of forty, after reading the writings of St. Augustine, she embraced serious prayer and dedicated herself to reform. Seven years later, she founded her own "reformed convent."

All this time she enjoyed visions from God. A person of sound common sense and good humor, she described her mystical experiences in books entitled *The Life, The Way of Perfection,* and *Interior Castles.* They are regarded as spiritual classics. She is patron of aviators, those suffering headaches, and of Spain. She is also the first woman to be recognized as a Doctor of the Church.

Feast Dates: October 15 — St. Teresa of Ávila, O.C.D.; October 1 — St. Thérèse of Lisieux, O. Carm. (see Thérèse).

Terese (Lithuanian) See Teresa, Thérèse.
Teresia (Swedish) See Teresa, Thérèse.
Teresina (Italian) See Teresa, Thérèse.
Teresita "The Reaper+The Little One" (Spanish double).

Patron Saints: There are about a dozen saints that bear the name Teresita in one of its many forms.

Feast Dates: July 13 — St. Juanita Teresita (see Juanita).

Teressa (Hungarian) See Teresa, Thérèse.
Teretha (African-American) See Teresa, Thérèse.
Terez (Hungarian) See Teresa, Thérèse.

Tereza (Romanian, Portuguese) See Teresa, Thérèse.
Terezia (Hungarian) See Teresa, Thérèse.
Terezie (Czech) See Teresa, Thérèse.
Teri (nickname) See Teresa, Teresita, Thérèse.
Terica (African-American double) See Tera/Tere/Teri+Rica.
Terika (African-American double) See Teri+Erika.
Terilyn (English double) See Teresa/Teresita/Thérèse+Lynn.
Terita (African-American double) See Teri+Rita.
Terka (Bulgarian) See Tara.
Terra (Latin) See Tierra.
Terri (nickname) See Teresa, Teresita, Thérèse.
Terrica (African-American double) See Terry+Erica.
Terrie (nickname) See Teresa, Teresita, Thérèse.
Terry (nickname) See Teresa, Teresita, Thérèse.
Terrye (nickname) See Teresa, Teresita, Thérèse.
Tertia "The Third Daughter" (Latin).

Patron Saints: There are a half-dozen Sts. Tertius. One of them was a follower of St. Paul the Apostle and became the second bishop of Iconium. He also helped St. Paul write the Epistle to the Romans.

Feast Dates: November 10 — St. Tertius.

Tess (nickname) See Quintessa, Teresa, Thérèse.
Tessa (nickname) See Quintessa, Teresa, Thérèse.
Tessi (nickname) See Quintessa, Teresa, Thérèse.
Tessie (nickname) See Quintessa, Teresa, Thérèse.
Tessy (nickname) See Quintessa, Teresa, Thérèse.

Teté (Spanish) See Teresa.

Texanna (African-American double) See Texas+Anna.

Tezenia (Hispanic-American double) See Terese+Zenia.

Thaïs Meaning unknown (Greek).

Patron Saints: St. Thaïs was a holy penitent who lived in the 300s. She often prayed, "O God, who created me, have mercy on me." A modern opera has been written about her.

Feast Dates: October 8 — St. Thaïs.

Thalia "The One in Bloom" (Greek) or "The Gentle Dew from Heaven" (variant of Talia).

Patron Saints: In Greek mythology, Thalia was the Muse of Comedy. St. Genesius was an actor in ancient Rome who converted to Catholicism and was martyred in 303. He is patron of comedians.

Feast Dates: August 25 — St. Genesius; August 8 — St. Talia (see Talia).

Thanaira (Hispanic-American triple) See any "Th" name+Ana+Ira.

Thandeka "The One Beloved by God" (African).

Patron Saints: St. Davita, whose name means "the beloved one," may be pressed into service. St. Thanus who died a martyr in ancient Egypt, might also be put to work, as well as St. Decima (see December).

Feast Dates: December 6 — St. Davita; February 17 — St. Thanus.

Thandie (African-American) See Thandeka, Sandy, Candie.

Thea "The Goddess" (Greek) or "The Gift of God" (Greek).

Patron Saints: There is at least one St. Thea. She and her friend St. Meuris were martyred at Gaza, Palestine, in 307. Finally, Thea is recognized as a short form of Althea, Philothea,

Theasha, and Theodora, and this leads to even more patrons.

Feast Dates: December 19 — St. Thea; May 14 — Bl. Theodore Guerin (see Theodora).

Theasha (Hispanic-American double) See Thea+Sha.

Thecla "The Divinely Famous One" (Greek).

Patron Saints: There are a very few Sts. Thecla. One of them was a Benedictine nun who set out for a missionary journey under St. Lioba. St. Boniface named her the first abbess of Ochsenfurt and then of Kitzingen on the Main. She died in 790.

Feast Dates: October 15 — St. Thecla.

Theda (English) See Theodora.

Theeasha (African-American double) See any "Th" name+Aisha/Isha.

Thekla (variant) See Thecla, Theodora.

Thelma "The Well-Wisher" (Greek, Spanish) or "A Nursling" (Greek, Spanish).

Patron Saints: Thelma can mean "a nursling," which in turn can mean a "sick person" or "one who needs the care of a nurse." This leads directly to St. Camillus de Lellis. He is officially recognized by the Catholic Church, among other things, as the patron of the sick.

St. Camillus, 1550-1614, was born in Italy to a mother who was almost sixty years of age at the time of his birth. Growing to a height of more than six-and-a-half feet, Camillus joined the Venetian army at the age of seventeen as a mercenary and fought against the Turks. He was wounded in the leg and the wound eventually became an infection that would flare up periodically. He was discharged from his military duties and returned to his home, where he became addicted to gambling and lost heavily. By 1574, at the age of twenty-four, he had lost everything and he began to beg. He had hit bottom.

Soon he began to devote himself to the sick at the hospital where he had been a patient. In time, he rose to the office of superintendent and, becoming much bothered by the laxity of the hired help, he began recruiting men who wished to serve purely out of love for their fellowmen. Following the advice of his confessor, St. Philip Neri, he started his own religious order to help the sick. He is patron of hospitals, nurses, the sick, and against gambling.

Feast Dates: July 14 — St. Camillus de Lellis.

Thena (nickname) See Athena.

Theo (nickname) See Theodora.

Theodora "The Gift of God" (Greek).

Patron Saints: There are a handful of Sts. Theodora from which to choose. One is a naturalized American, Anne-Thérèse Guerin, 1798-1856. She was born in Brittany in northwest France and was dedicated to the Blessed Virgin Mary by her mother. When she was twenty-five, her mother allowed her to enter a new religious order dedicated to works of charity. She took the name Theodore. A year later she was placed in charge of children in the worst section of the city of Rennes.

In 1839 the bishop of the newly established diocese of Vincennes, Indiana, came to her town looking for religious sisters. Sister Theodore was put in charge of the American mission. Over the next sixteen years she struggled to build a religious community and to provide excellent education for Catholic children in Indiana. Worn out by her labors, she died at the age of fifty-eight.

Feast Dates: May 14 — Bl. Mother Theodore Guerin; April 28 — St. Theodora (see Dora).

Theodosia (variant) See Theodora.

Theola "A Heavenly Odor" (Greek, popular with African-Americans).

Patron Saints: St. Theolus was martyred for the Catholic faith in ancient Greek city of Nicopolis.

Feast Dates: July 10 — St. Theolus.

Theophilia "The Lover+Of God" (Greek double).

Patron Saints: There are two saints named Theophila and one named Theophilia. St. Theophilia was a single woman who died a martyr in ancient times.

Feast Dates: February 6 — St. Theophilia.

Theophilla (Greek double) See Theophilia, Theo+Phila.

Theresa (variant) See Teresa, Thérèse.

Thérèse "The Reaper" (French).

Patron Saints: There are about a dozen saints who bear the name Thérèse in one of its many forms. The best known are St. Teresa of Ávila and St. Thérèse of Lisieux.

Marie Françoise Thérèse Martin, 1873-1897, was raised at Lisieux. At the age of fifteen she was allowed to enter a convent. Nothing extraordinary happened while she was a nun, but she caught the attention of others simply because she was perfect in her simplicity, obedience, humility, and charity. She always gave good example. Commanded by her superior to write her memoirs, she tells of her "little way" in *The Story of a Soul*, which became a spiritual classic. Her "little way" included enduring tuberculosis.

Her love for others and her desire to lead them to Jesus was unceasing. She wrote, "I count on not being idle in heaven. I long to work, even there, for the Church and souls. The Lord will work wonders for me that will surpass my desire." She died of tuberculosis at the age of twenty-four. She is patron of France, those suffering from tuberculosis, and of the Catholic foreign missions.

Feast Dates: October 1 — St. Thérèse of Lisieux, O. Carm.; October 15 — St. Teresa of Ávila (see Teresa).

Theresia (German) See Teresa, Thérèse.

Thessia (African-American double) See any "Th" name+Essie.

Thoma (variant) See Thomasina.

Thomasa (Greek) See Thomasina.

Thomasena (Greek) See Thomasina.

Thomasin (variant) See Thomasina.

Thomasina "The Little Twin" (Latin, Greek).

Patron Saints: There are two female Sts. Thomais. One of them was martyred in 476. Her father-in-law, blinded by lust, tried to seduce her. Failing this, he killed her.

Feast Dates: April 14 — St. Thomais.

Thomasine (English) See Thomasina.

Thora "The Thunderer" (Scandinavian).

Patron Saints: One female, St. Thorette, will serve very well. She lived in the 1100s and spent most of her time performing the duties of a shepherdess in France. During her last years she spent her life in solitude and prayer.

Feast Dates: May 1 — St. Thorette.

Thordia (variant) See Thora.

Thordis (variant) See Thora.

Thorette (English-French double) See Thora+Etta.

Thulie (African-American) See Tulie.

Thursday "Born on Thor's Day" (Middle English).

Patron Saints: Thursday is "Thor's Day," and there is a St. Thorette. But there is a better patron available. One

might ask, "What is the most important Thursday of the year for a Christian?" The answer would be, "Holy Thursday." For it was on Holy Thursday that Jesus instituted the sacrament of the Eucharist.

Holy Communion is God's food, which gives us strength to make our pilgrim journey to heaven. That is certainly "far to go," as the modern anonymous poem speaks of Thursday's child. Thus Jesus Christ, the Holy Eucharist, is the finest of patron for anyone named Thursday.

Feast Dates: May 1 — St. Thorette (see Thora); Holy Thursday — Jesus the Holy Eucharist (see Muffin).

Tia "The Princess" (Greek, Egyptian) or "God's Gift" (nickname for Theodora) or "Aunt" (Spanish).

Patron Saints: There is a St. Tianus, who died a martyr in ancient Rome, and because Tia can be considered a variant of Theodora, two dozen Sts. Theodora qualify.

Further, because the name also has the same meaning as Sarah, many Sts. Sarah can qualify.

Finally, because Tia can also mean "aunt," any female saint who had a niece and/or nephew can be adopted as a patron.

Feast Dates: February 15 — St. Tianus; August 19 — St. Sarah (see Sarah).

Tiana (Latin-Spanish double) See Tatiana, Tia+Ana.

Tiandre (African-American double) See Tia+Andrea.

Tiara "A Woman's Jeweled Crown" (Latin, Spanish).

Patron Saints: Knowing that a tiara is "a crown of a queen or princess" leads to a patron. She is the Blessed Virgin Mary, the "Queen of Heaven."

Feast Dates: August 22 — The Blessed Virgin Mary, Queen of Heaven (see Queen).

Tiarra (Latin) See Tiara.

Ticia (nickname) See Leticia, Patricia.

Tiena (nickname) See Valentina.

Tiennette (French) See Valentina+Ette.

Tierra "The Earth" (Spanish).
  Patron Saints: Tierra means "earth," and this leads directly St. Earthongota.
  Feast Dates: February 26 — St. Earthongota (see Eartha).

Tierney "The Grandchild of the Lordly" (Irish Gaelic).
  Patron Saints: One Irish saint is available. St. Terenan McLaisir served as bishop of Armagh in 610.
  Feast Dates: September 2 — St. Terenan McLaisir.

Tifany (Latin) See Tiffany.

Tiff (nickname) See Tiffany.

Tiffanee (American) See Tiffany.

Tiffani (American) See Tiffany.

Tiffanie (American) See Tiffany.

Tiffany "The One Who Reveals God" (French, English, Greek).
  Patron Saints: Tiffany is a modern form of Epiphany. And there is one St. Epiphana and one St. Epiphania. In about 300 St. Epiphana was tortured for being a Christian and then executed.
  Feast Dates: May 12 — St. Epiphana.

Tiffi (nickname) See Tiffany.

Tiffie (nickname) See Tiffany.

Tiffy (nickname) See Tiffany.

Tilda (nickname) See Clotilda, Matilda.

Tildi (nickname) See Clotilda, Matilda.

Tildie (nickname) See Clotilda, Matilda.

Tildy (nickname) See Clotilda, Matilda.

Tiler (English) See Tyler.

Tillie (nickname) See Clotilda, Matilda.

Tilly (nickname) See Clotilda, Matilda.

Tim (variant) See Timothea.

Tima (variant) See Selena, Timothea.

Timi (variant) See Timothea.

Timia (variant) See Selena.

Timias (variant) See Timothea.

Timmi (variant) See Timothea.

Timmie (variant) See Timothea.

Timmy (variant) See Timothea.

Timotea (Spanish) See Timothea.

Timothea "She Who Honors God" (Greek).
  Patron Saints: There are over fifty male Sts. Timothy and a St. Athanasia of Timia. To them can be added one ancient St. Timias. She was martyred with Sts. Maurus, Attus, Genosa, and Sodalis in ancient Antioch.
  Feast Dates: April 27 — St. Timias; August 14 — St. Athanasia of Timia (see Athanasia).

Tina (nickname) See Augustina, Christina, Celestina, Martina, Valentina.

Tina (English) See Catherine, Katherine.

Tine (nickname) See Christine, Celestine, Clementine, Leontine, Tyne.

Tini (English) See Trini, Trinidad.

Tinisha (variant) See Tanisha.

Tiny (nickname) See Christine, Celestine, Clementine, Leontine, Tyne.

Tiona (variant) See Dione.

Tione (American) See Dione.

Tiphani (Latin) See Tiffany.

Tiphanie (Latin) See Tiffany.

Tiphany (Latin) See Tiffany.

Tipper "The Water Carrier" (Irish).
  Patron Saints: The closest name we have is St. Tipasius. He was a converted Roman soldier who retired to the desert in Africa to pray. He was martyred in 304.
  Feast Dates: January 11 — St. Tipasius.

Tirza "The Pleasant One" (Hebrew).
  Patron Saints: Tirzah is listed as the fifth daughter of Hepher of the tribe of Manasseh in Numbers 26:33.
  Feast Dates: November 1 — Holy Tirzah.

Tish (nickname) See Leticia, Patricia.

Tisha (nickname) See Leticia, Patricia.

Tishia (nickname) See Leticia, Patricia.

Tita (nickname, Spanish) See Titania, Pearl, Loretta.

Titania "The Giant One" (Greek).

Patron Saints: While there is no St. Titania, there are a half-dozen Sts. Titianus. One of them embraced martyrdom for Jesus' sake in ancient Sardinia.

Feast Dates: May 27 — St. Titianus; July 18 — St. Tanea (see Tana).

Titia (nickname) See Leticia, Patricia.

T'Keyah (African-American) See T+Kiah.

Tobe (variant) See Toby.

Tobey (variant) See Toby.

Tobi (variant) See Toby.

Toby "God Is Good" (Hebrew).

Patron Saints: There are a few Sts. Toby. One died a martyr in ancient Sebaste.

Feast Dates: November 2 — St. Toby.

Tobye (English) See Toby.

Toinette (nickname) See Antonia.

Toireasa (Irish Gaelic) See Teresa, Thérèse.

Tomasina (English) See Thomasina.

Tomasine (English) See Thomasina.

Tomika (African-American) See Tamika.

Tona (Spanish) See Antonia.

Toni (nickname) See Antonia.

Tonia (nickname) See Antonia.

Tonie (nickname) See Antonia.

Tonja (African-American) See Tanya.

Tony (nickname) See Antonia.

Tonya (variant) See Antonia, Tanya.

Tonye (nickname) See Antonia.

Topanga "From Where the Two Rivers Meet" (North American Indian).

Patron Saints: In Latin, "two rivers" is loosely translated *duo flumen*. This leads to Sts. Duonius and Flumen. St. Duonius was a medieval Irish saint. St.

Fluminus died a martyr's death in ancient Rome.

Feast Dates: May 29 — St. Duonius; May 28 — St. Fluminus (see River).

Tori (Spanish) See Victoria.

Totti (nickname) See Charlotte.

Tova (Hebrew) See Toby.

Tove (variant) See Toby.

Toya "The Plaything" (African-American) or "The Victorious One" (Spanish form of Victoria).

Patron Saints: La is simply the French feminine article for "the" (although it is also the feminine personal pronoun for "she"). And a "toy" in modern American English is simply "a plaything." This leads to St. Nicholas of Myra, the giver of toys to good children on Christmas.

But a better patron appears when one discovers that Toya in Mexico is a nickname for Victoria. There are at least two dozen Sts. Victoria. One of them was executed by the Muslims at Cordova in about 800 because she insisted on remaining a Christian.

Feast Dates: November 17 — St. Victoria; December 6 — St. Nicholas of Myra (see Myra).

Tracey (Greek) See Teresa, Thérèse, Tracy.

Traci (Latin) See Teresa, Thérèse, Tracy.

Tracie (English) See Teresa, Thérèse, Tracy.

Tracy "The Fighter" (Irish Gaelic) or "The Reaper" (Basque nickname for Thérèse).

Patron Saints: One saint bears the Latin form of this name, St. Thracia. She was the daughter of the Roman emperor Hadrian. After she had converted to Christianity, her father had her burned alive.

Feast Dates: November 14 — St. Thracia; October 15 — St. Teresa of Ávila, O.C.D.

Treasie (African-American) See Tracy.

Treat (nickname) See Teresa, Teresita, Thérèse.

Treena (variant) See Catherine, Katherine.

Trella (Spanish) See Estelle.

Tresa (variant) See Teresa, Teresita, Thérèse.

Trescha (Greek) See Teresa, Teresita, Thérèse.

Trese (nickname) See Teresa, Teresita, Thérèse.

Tressa (Greek) See Teresa, Teresita, Thérèse.

Treva "The Prudent, Discreet One" (Irish Gaelic female form of Trevor).

Patron Saints: There is one St. Trevor. He was born into a noble Roman family in northern France. He became a monk, but he soon left the monastery and embraced the life of a hermit. He died in 550.

Feast Dates: January 16 — St. Trevor, also known as Treverius.

Trexa (Basque) See Teresa, Thérèse.

Trey "The Third-Born" (Middle English).

Patron Saints: There is one St. Trey. She was a convert of St. Patrick and dedicated her single life to prayer and solitude in the 450s.

Feast Dates: August 3 — St. Trey, also known as Trea.

Tria (Latin) See Trey.

Tricia (nickname) See Leticia, Patricia.

Triduana "Three Days Long" (Spanish).

Patron Saints: There is one saint with this name. St. Triduana was a holy Benedictine abbess who accompanied the relics of St. Andrew to Scotland in medieval times and founded an abbey there. She is patron against diseases of the eyes.

Feast Dates: October 8 — St. Triduana; The Sacred Triduum — Jesus the Redeemer.

Trina (nickname) See Catrina, Demetria, Kateri, Katrina, Petrina, Trini.

Trine (Danish) See Katherine.

Trini "Threefold One" (Spanish nickname for Trinidad).

Patron Saints: There are a couple of eligible saints named Sts. Trinio and Trian. St. Trinio, a native of Wales in about 470, became a monk at the Bardsey monastery. St. Trian was a disciple of St. Patrick around the year 450 and served as bishop of Croebheach in Ireland.

Feast Dates: June 29 — St. Trinio; March 23 — St. Trian.

Trinia (variant) See Trini, Trinidad.

Trinidad "The Threefold One" (Spanish).

Patron Saints: Trinidad is the Spanish form of "trinity." Thus the Blessed Trinity is the first and finest patron. The Old Testament reveals the Father, while the Son is strongly hinted at in the literary figure of Lady Wisdom. References in Genesis and Joel hint at the Holy Spirit.

Only in the New Testament is the Trinity fully revealed. The Gospel of Matthew (28:19) commands that baptisms be done in the "name of the Father and of the Son and of the Holy Spirit." Matthew, Mark, and Luke also make it clear that the Father and Son are God. The Gospel of John reveals the Godhood of the Holy Spirit.

Eventually the Catholic Church coined the word "Trinity" to speak of this Bible truth. Of all doctrines, that of the Trinity is the most important Christian belief. For without the Trinity there would have been no Jesus Christ. Nor could anyone explain the existence of love and need for relationship or charity.

One can also adopt Bl. Elizabeth of the Trinity, O.C.D., 1880-1906, and a few others.

Feast Dates: Sunday After Pentecost — Trinity Sunday.

Trinity (English) See Trinidad.

Trinka (variant) See Catherine, Katherine.

Tris (Latin) See Trista.

Trisha (nickname) See Leticia, Patricia.

Trishia (nickname) See Leticia, Patricia.

Trissa (nickname) See Beatrice, Patricia.

Trissy (nickname) See Beatrice.

Trista "Sorrowful One" (Latin) or "Melancholy One" (Latin).

Patron Saints: There is no St. Trista. But the name means "sorrowful" or "melancholy," and this leads to two patrons. One is Jesus the Man of Sorrows. The other is the Blessed Virgin, the Mother of Sorrows.

Feast Dates: September 15 — Mary, Mother of Sorrows (see Dolores).

Trix (nickname) See Beatrice.

Trixi (nickname) See Beatrice.

Trixie (nickname) See Beatrice.

Trixy (nickname) See Beatrice.

Truda (nickname) See Gertrude, Tudy.

Trudee (nickname) See Gertrude, Tudy.

Trudel (Dutch) See Gertrude, Tudy.

Trudi (German) See Gertrude, Tudy.

Trudie (nickname) See Gertrude, Tudy.

Trudy (German) See Gertrude, Tudy.

Truemilla (African-American double) See Trudie+Milly.

Truzella (African-American double) See Trudie+Zella.

Tryna (variant) See Catherine, Kateri, Katherine.

Tudee (nickname) See Gertrude, Tudy.

Tudi (nickname) See Gertrude, Tudy.

Tudie (nickname) See Gertrude, Tudy.

Tudy "The Strong One" (English nickname for Gertrude).

Patron Saints: There are two Sts. Tudy and a St. Tuda. St. Tudy served God as a disciple of St. Winwaloe and as an abbot and a hermit in medieval Brittany.

It also helps to know that Tudy is a familiar form of Gertrude, which leads to a few more saints.

Feast Dates: May 9 — St. Tudy; November 16 — St. Gertrude the Great (see Gertrude).

Tuesday "Born on Tiwes [Mars] Day" (Middle English).

Patron Saints: An anonymous modern poem describes Tuesday's child as "full of grace." This leads one directly to the Immaculate Conception.

Feast Dates: December 8 — The Blessed Virgin Mary, Immaculate Conception (see Concepción).

Tula (nickname) See Gertrudis, Petula.

Tulia (Irish) See Petula.

Tulie (nickname) See Petula.

Twila (variant) See Twyla.

Twyla "The Star" (Louisiana Cajun from the French word *étoile*) or "That Double Woven" (Middle English).

Patron Saints: Knowing that "Twyla" comes from *étoile* leads to a St. Estella, whose name means "star." This leads to a St. Esther and the Blessed Virgin Mary, Star of the Sea.

Feast Dates: May 11 — St. Estella (see Estelle); December 20 — St. Esther (see Esther); All Saturdays — Mary, Star of the Sea (see Star).

Ty (nickname) See Tybie, Tye, Tyffany, Tyler, Tyna, Tyne, Tyra.

Tyanna (African-American double) See Ty+Anna.

Tybi (variant) See Toby.

Tybie (variant) See Toby.

Tyby (variant) See Toby.

Tye (nickname) See Tyler.

Tyeisha (African-American double) See Ty+Aisha/Isha.

Tyffany (variant) See Tiffany.

Tyler "The Tile Maker" (Old English) or "The Roofer" (Old English).

Patron Saints: It helps to know that Tyler means "tile maker or layer." Originally, a tile maker was a mason who worked in stone and/or ceramics. There are four saints named patrons of masons: Sts. Louis of France, Reinhold, Stephen, and Thomas. There is also St. Peter the Apostle, patron of stoneworkers, and a Bl. John Mason who may be added to them all.

Bl. John Mason was born in Kendal, Westmorland, England, in the mid-1500s. A layman, he was arrested and condemned to death for attending Mass and helping Catholic priests. He was executed with three diocesan priests and another layman in 1591.

Also, the two Bl. Taylors may be pressed into service. If in the past the Catholic Church allowed St. Brice to serve as a patron for a person named Bruce, then surely the two Bl. Taylors may be called upon to act as patrons for anyone named Tyler.

Feast Dates: December 10 — Bl. John Mason of Kendal.

Tyna (variant) See Celestina, Christina.

Tyne "Like the Flowing River" (Old English) or "The Anointed One" (nickname for Christine).

Patron Saints: There is one St. Tyne. But he spelled his name Tyneio. St. Tyneio was one of the sons of Seithenin Frenin of Wales. At one point in his life, the raging sea, possibly a tidal wave, completely destroyed his inherited property. Then he became a monk in Bangor.

Two other saints with similar names may also be adopted as patrons. They are Sts. Tynog and Tinidor. All of these saints called the British Isles their home. Tyne can also be a short form of Leontyne.

Feast Dates: June 5 — St. Tyneio; December 6 — St. Leontine (see Leontine).

Tynn (English) See Leontine, Tyne.

Tynne (English) See Leontine, Tyne.

Tyra "The One Like Thor" (Latin, Spanish) or "The Hard Rock" (Latin, Spanish).

Patron Saints: A patron with a similar name is St. Tyria. She died for her faith in Jesus in ancient Alexandria and may have been a black woman. Also, there are a half-dozen Sts. Rock.

Feast Dates: April 6 — St. Tyria.

Tyria (English) See Tyra.

Tyrica (Hispanic-American double) See Tyra+Rica.

𝒰

U Sixth-to-the-last letter of the alphabet (English).

Patron Saints: African-Americans seem to favor names with the letter "U" as a prefix. The name attached to this prefix usually leads to a patron saint.

Udele "The Wealthy One" (Old English).

Patron Saints: St. Udelina was one of the companions of St. Ursula when she traveled to Rome.

Feast Dates: October 19 — St. Udelina.

Udella (English) See Udele.

Udo (West African) See Salome.

Uhuru (Swahili) See Liberty.

Ulla (German, Latin) See Ursula.

Ulebelle (African-American double) See Ursula+Belle.

Uloise (African-American double) See U+Eloise.

Ulrica (African-American double) See Ulla+Rica.

Ulyssandra (African-American double) See Ulysses+Sandra.

Ulyssese (African-American double) See Ulysses+Essie.

Umayah (Hispanic-American double) See Una+Maya.

Una "The First One" (Latin).

Patron Saints: Una, as a complete name in its own right, means, "one" or "unity," which leads to St. Monas. It can also serve as a nickname for Agnes and Winifred.

Feast Dates: January 21 — St. Agnes (see Agnes); February 26 — St. Monas (see Mona).

Unice (French, English) See Eunice, Una.

Unique "The One and Only" (French) or "One of a Kind" (French form of *uno*).

Patron Saints: The name's meaning leads to St. Monas.

Feast Dates: February 26 — St. Monas (see Mona).

Unis (nickname) See Eunice, Una.

Unit (English) See Una.

Unita (Latin) See Una, Mona.

Unity "One" (English) or "United One" (English form of *uno*).

Patron Saints: The name's meaning leads to St. Monas.

Feast Dates: February 26 — St. Monas (see Mona).

Upsla (variant) See Opal.

Ura (Greek) See Urania.

Urana (Greek) See Urania.

Urania "The Heavenly One" (Greek, Spanish).

Patron Saints: There is one St. Urania. She lived in ancient Egypt and was also martyred there.

Feast Days: November 7 — St. Urania.

Ursa (nickname) See Ursula.

Ursala (Greek) See Ursula.

Ursel (Dutch, German) See Ursula.

Ursie (nickname) See Ursula.

Urska (Croatian, Slovenian) See Ursula.

Ursley (Spanish) See Ursula.

Ursola (English) See Ursula.

Ursula "The Female Bear" (Latin, Spanish).

Patron Saints: There is one St. Ursulina and one St. Ursula. Much of what is remembered about Ursula is preserved by pious legend. It seems that Ursula was the daughter of King Deonotus of Britain. He wanted her to marry a pagan prince, but she refused. She wished to remain single and dedicate her single life to Jesus. Thus she postponed the marriage for three years and traveled with some companions to Rome on a pilgrimage. On the return trip home she and her companions were taken captive by a pagan chieftain who also wanted to marry her. She again refused and she and all of her companions were killed. She is patron of orphans, schoolgirls, tailors, teachers, and universities. She can also be invoked against the plague.

Feast Dates: October 21 — St. Ursula.

Ursule (French) See Ursula.

Ursulina (Spanish) See Ursula.

Ursuline (English) See Ursula.

Ursy (nickname) See Ursula.

Uschi (German) See Ursula.

Utah "From the Hills [Mountains]" (English form of North American Indian word).

Patron Saints: St. Utto founded a monastery and became an abbot in Bavaria in the twelfth century. At least two patrons qualify.

Feast Days: October 3 — St. Utto; October 3 — St. Montana (see Montana).

Uzee (African-American) See Suzy.

$\mathcal{V}$

Val (nickname) See Valentina, Valerie.

Valaida (African-American double) See Val+Aida.

Valaree (English) See Valerie.

Valaria (variant) See Valerie.

Valaria (Italian, Spanish) See Valerie.

Valarianna (Spanish double) See Valerie+Anna.

Valarie (variant) Valerie.

Valda "The Heroine" (Spanish).
 Patron Saints: "Hero" in Latin is *heros*, and there are a few Sts. Hero and Herosus. A St. Herosus was martyred for the faith in ancient Egypt.
 Feast Dates: September 10 — St. Hero, also known as Herosus.

Vale (nickname) See Valentina.

Valeda (English) See Valentina, Valerie.

Valedia (African-American) See Valentina, Valerie.

Valeira (African-American) See Valentina, Valerie.

Valencia (Spanish) See Valentina.

Valenda (African-American) See Valentina, Valerie.

Valene (variant) See Valentina.

Valenka (variant) See Helen.

Valentia (English) See Valentina.

Valentina "The Strong, Healthy One" (Latin, Spanish).
 Patron Saints: There are three Sts. Valentina. One was martyred in ancient Rome; another died for Jesus in Caesarea. Nothing is known about the third one.
 Feast Dates: July 15 — St. Valentina; July 30 — St. Valentina.

Valentine (English) See Valentina.

Valera (Russian) See Valerie.

Valeri (Latin) See Valerie.

Valeria (variant) See Valerie.

Valeriane (French double) See Valerie+Anne.

Valerie "The Strong One" (Old French).
 Patron Saints: There are about a dozen Sts. Valeria from which to choose. One of them was the mother of Sts. Gervase and Protase. She was married to St. Vitalis, a soldier in Ravenna, part of the ancient Roman Empire, sometime between 160 and 180. When the physician St. Ursicinus wavered while faced with the prospect of dying for Jesus, Vitalis was there to encourage him to remain faithful.
 This encouragement became known to the governor. He ordered that Vitalis be tortured on the rack and then be burned alive. This condemnation made the pagans in the area very bold. They also attacked Valeria and beat her. She died of her wounds three days later.
 Feast Dates: April 28 — St. Valeria.

Valery (Latin) See Valerie.

Valerye (English) See Valerie.

Valida (English) See Valentina.

Valina (variant) See Valentina.

Valinda (African-American double) See Valerie+Linda.

Valisha (African-American double) See Valerie+Isha.

Valja (Estonian) See Valentina.

Vallatina (Dutch) See Valentina.

Valli (nickname) See Valentina, Valerie.

Vallie (nickname) See Valentina, Valerie.

Vally (nickname) See Valentina, Valerie.

Valma (nickname) See Wilhelmina.

Valonia (African-American double) See Valerie+Ona.

Valora (German) See Valerie.

Valoree (English) See Valerie.

Valorie (variant) See Valerie.

Valry (variant) See Valerie.

Valzora (African-American double) See Valerie+Zorah.

Van (nickname) See Vanessa.

Vana (nickname) See Savanna.

Vanda (German) See Wanda.

Vanesa (Dutch double) See Van+Essa.

Vanessa "Origin of+The Star" (Dutch double).

Patron Saints: "Vanessa" was coined in 1713 from Van plus Essa. Essa is a short form of Esther. There are many saints who can be adopted as patrons. They include Sts. Vanna, Van, Vandalet, Vando, Vandrille, and Vaningus.

One of them, St. Vanna, was born at Carnajola near Orvieto, some fifty miles north of Rome. She joined the Order of St. Dominic and is remembered for her great prayerfulness and piety. She died in 1306.

Feast Dates: July 23 — St. Vanna.

Vanetta (Dutch-German double) See Vanessa+Etta.

Vangie (nickname) See Evangeline.

Vangy (nickname) See Evangeline.

Vania (Russian) See Jane, Vanessa.

Vanna (nickname) See Savanna.

Vanni (nickname) See Vanessa.

Vannie (nickname) See Vanessa.

Vanny (nickname) See Vanessa.

Vanora (Scottish) See Guinevere.

Vanya (Russian) See Jane.

Varenka (Russian) See Barbara.

Varu (Estonian) See Barbara.

Varvara (Russian) See Barbara.

Varya (Russian) See Barbara.

Vashti "The Thread of Life Beautiful" (Persian).

Patron Saints: Vashti means the same thing as Alana and Alana provides a patron.

Feast Dates: September 10 — SG Frances Allen of Montreal.

Vaun (Welsh) See Vonetta.

Veatrice (African-American) See Beatrice.

Veatriks (variant) See Beatrice.

Veda "The Wise One" (Sanskrit) or "The Beloved One" (short feminine form of David).

Patron Saints: Veda is a Sanskrit name that means "wise one." This leads to about a dozen Sts. Sophie.

Feast Dates: September 30 — St. Sophie (see Sophia); March 1 — St. Davita (see Davita).

Vedette (English double) See Veda+Ette.

Vedis (English) See Veda.

Velda (variant) See Veda.

Veleda (variant) See Veda.

Velma "The Resolute Defender" (German, Swedish form of Wilhelmina).

Patron Saints: Velma is a short form of Wilhelmina, which is the feminine form of William. There is no St. Wilhelmina, but there are about fifty Sts. William. Also, Sts. Wilfrida and Wiltrudis can be adopted.

St. Wiltrudis was a duchess, the wife of Duke Berthold of Bavaria. She was well known for her embroidery craft. After becoming a widow she founded the Bergen monastery, near Neubrug on the Danube. Then she was elected its first abbess. She died in 947.

Feast Dates: January 6 — St. Wiltrudis, O.S.B.

Velora (English) See Valentina.

Velvet "Like a Smooth Cloth" (Middle English).

Patron Saints: Simply ask, "What kind of people do you associate with the wearing of velvet?" The answer is: "The rich and the royal." The word "royal" leads directly to Jesus Christ the King. And immediately one thinks of the newly scourged Jesus draped in a fine scarlet military cloak and being presented to the populace. It is clear that Jesus can be considered the patron of velvet.

Feast Dates: Thirty-fourth Sunday of the Year — Christ the King (see Acacia); Good Friday — Jesus the Suffering Servant (see Rhea).

Velvina (variant) See Velvet.

Velvor (variant) See Velvet.

Venice (English) See Venitia.

Venita (English) See Venetia, Venus.

Venite (variant) See Venus.

Venitia "The One Who Gains Permission" (Latin) or "The One Who Comes and Goes" (Latin).

Patron Saints: There is one St. Venusta who lived in ancient times.

Feast Dates: March 19 — St. Venusta (see Venus).

Venus "The Pleasing, Beautiful One" (Latin).

Patron Saints: There is one ancient St. Venusta. She was probably a black woman and was martyred for the faith in Roman times.

Feast Dates: March 19 — St. Venusta.

Venusta (English) See Venus.

Vera "The Truthful One" (Latin, Spanish) or "The Defender" (Old German) or "The Faith" (Russian) or "The True Image" (modern nickname for Veronica) or "The Springlike One" (alternate form of Vera).

Patron Saints: There is one St. Vera and one St. Verana. St. Vera and her companion St. Supporina are honored in Clermont, France. They are remembered for dedicating their single lifestyles to God.

St. Verana was one of the many single young women who traveled to Rome, making a pilgrimage with St. Ursula. On the trip home she was taken captive by a pagan chieftain and murdered.

Feast Dates: January 24 — St. Vera; October 6 — St. Verana.

Veradis (variant) See Vera.

Verana (variant) See Vera, Verena.

Verda (English, Spanish) See Laverne, Vera, Verena, Verne.

Verdad (Spanish) See Vera.

Verdelle (English) See Vera/Verena/Verne+Della.

Vere (English) See Vera, Verena.

Verena "The Defender" (Old German, Latin).

Patron Saints: Four Sts. Verena and one St. Verenus are available. St. Verena was a native of ancient Thebes in Upper Egypt. She was probably a black woman. At one point in her life she decided to make a pilgrimage to Switzerland to visit the tombs of the Theban Martyrs. Then she took up residence in a cave and occupied herself by doing works of piety and charity. Later, she traveled to other towns in Switzerland. Everywhere she went she taught the people by her good example. She died in peace in her little hut.

Feast Dates: September 1 — St. Verena.

Verene (English, French) See Vera, Verena.

Vergie (African-American) See Virginia.

Verina (English) See Vera, Verena.

Verine (English) See Vera, Verena.

Verity "The Truthful One" (Latin) See Vera.

Patron Saints: There is one St. Verissimus. He was beheaded with his sisters in witness of the Christian faith in 304.

Feast Dates: October 1 — St. Verissimus; January 24 — St. Vera.

Verla (English) See Vera.

Verlee (nickname) See Beverly.

Verley (nickname) See Beverly.

Verlie (nickname) See Beverly.

Verlina (African-American) See Beverly.

Vermona (African-American double) See any "Ver" name+Mona.

Verna (Spanish) See Laverne, Spring, Verne.

Vernall (English) See Laverne, Verne.

Vernarda (Modern Greek) See Bernadette, Bernadine.

Verne "The Springlike One" (English).

Patron Saints: There is one male saint who bears a variant of the name Verne. St. Adjutor was the lord of Vernon and served as a knight fighting against the Saracens in the Middle East. After seventeen years of service, he was captured by the enemy and imprisoned. Upon regaining his freedom he became a monk and then lived as a hermit. He died in 1131 and is a patron against the danger of drowning.

Also, the meaning of the word "springlike" leads to two greater patrons. Spring is the time nature births new life. Thus Jesus becomes a first choice for a patron. A second choice is the Blessed Virgin because she gave birth to Jesus.

Feast Dates: April 30 — St. Adjutor of Vernon; January 1 — The Blessed Virgin Mary, Mother of God (see Mary).

Vernessa (African-American double) See Laverne/Verne+Essie.

Verneta (variant) See Laverne, Verne.

Vernetta (African-American double) See Laverne/Verne+Etta.

Vernice (African-American double) See Laverne/Verne+Ice.

Vernis (variant) See Laverne, Verne.

Vernita (variant) See Laverne, Verne.

Vernola (African-American double) See Laverne, Verne+Ola.

Vernonia (African-American) See Laverne, Verne.

Veronica "The True+Image [Picture]" (Latin-Greek double).

Patron Saints: There are at least three Sts. Veronica. The most important is the one who wiped Jesus' face with her veil as he walked to Calvary. This Veronica is also known as St. Bernice. She is described in the Bible as "a woman who had had a flow of blood for twelve years" (Mark 5:25). Catholic tradition identifies her as Veronica, the woman who pushed through the crowds to wipe the face of Jesus while he was carrying his cross. Whether this really happened is uncertain.

It seems that the name Veronica is a combination of the Latin *vero* and the Greek *icon*, meaning "true picture," that is, the image of Christ's face on the veil. Thus the name of the image was transferred to its bearer, and Bernice became Veronica.

Christian tradition adds that Bernice eventually married Zacchaeus, the tax collector who climbed the sycamore tree to see Jesus. Earlier (again according to a pious legend), he had been a servant of the Holy Family in Nazareth.

After the resurrection of Jesus, a persecution broke out against Christians in Palestine. Bernice traveled with her husband to Gaul (France). There, her husband was known as Amator or Amadour and they spent their time doing missionary work. After Bernice died, at about the age of forty-five in the year 50, Zacchaeus became a hermit.

Feast Dates: July 12 — St. Veronica.

Veronika (Latin) See Bernice, Veronica.

Veronike (variant) See Bernice, Veronica.

Veronique (French) See Bernice, Veronica.

Vertille (African-American double) See any "Ver" name+Tillie.

Vesta "The Goddess of the Hearth" (Latin, Spanish).

Patron Saints: There is one St. Vestina. She was a martyr for the faith in ancient Scilla.

Feast Dates: July 17 — St. Vestina.

Vestina (Latin) See Vesta.

Veta (Slavic) See Elizabeth.

Vi (nickname) See Venus, Vincentia, Viola, Vivian.

Via "The Way" (Latin).

Patron Saints: St. Viatrix died a martyr in Rome in 304. She made it her business to bury dead Catholics, which was against the law. She was soon strangled to death.

Feast Dates: July 29 — St. Viatrix; All Sundays — Jesus the Way (see Delta).

Viana (African-American) See Via.

Vianca (variant) See Bianca.

Vianka (variant) See Bianca.

Viatrix (variant) See Beatrice.

Vica (Hungarian) See Eve.

Vicki (nickname) See Victoria.

Vickie (nickname) See Victoria.

Vicky (nickname) See Victoria.

Victoire (French) See Victoria.

Victoria "The Conqueror" (Latin).

Patron Saints: There are about two dozen Sts. Victoria and over one hundred thirty Sts. Victor. One St. Victoria was a young maiden in ancient Rome engaged to a man named Eugenius. Her sister, a Roman woman named Anatolia, had dedicated her single lifestyle to Jesus, and this led her to break her engagement to Aurelius. Aurelius then begged Victoria to plead his case with Anatolia. This Victoria did.

However, Anatolia presented her convictions so strongly that she won Victoria over to her point of view. In fact, she so convinced her that Victoria also decided to dedicate her single life to the service of Jesus. This led her to cancel her engagement to Eugenius.

Eugenius and Aurelius were both pagans and could not accept the actions of their prospective wives. Therefore, each made his girlfriend a prisoner on his large estate. First, they starved the young women, hoping to gain their submission. Finally, they denounced the women as Christians to the local authorities. Both were put to death by the sword at the request of their former suitors.

Feast Dates: December 23 — St. Victoria.

Victoriana (Spanish) See Victoria.

Victorina (Spanish) See Victoria.

Victorine (English) See Victoria.

Vida "The Beloved One" (short feminine form of David).

Patron Saints: Vida is a short form of Davita, and this leads to St. Davita.

Feast Dates: December 6 — St. Davita (see Davita).

Videlle (African-American double) See Vida+Della.

Vidonia (African-American double) See Vida+Donna.

Vijole (Lithuanian) See Viola, Violet.

Vik (nickname) See Victoria.

Vikki (nickname) See Victoria.

Vikkie (nickname) See Victoria.

Vikky (nickname) See Victoria.

Vikte (Lithuanian) See Victoria.

Viktoria (German, Swedish, Italian) See Victoria.

Vilhelmina (Swedish) See Wilhelmina.

Villa "From the Country Estate [Village]" (Italian).

Patron Saints: There is a St. Villanus, a St. Villicus, and a Bl. Villana.

Feast Dates: February 28 (29) — Bl. Villana de' Botti (see Wilhelmina}.

Villana (Italian double) See Villa+Ana.

Villangela (American double) See Villa+Angela.

Villete (French) See Villa.

Vilma (English, Estonian) See Velma, Wilhelmina, Willow.

Vin (nickname) See Alvina, Davina, Lavinia, Melvina, Venus.

Viña "From the Vineyard" (Spanish).

Patron Saints: The Blessed Virgin has been honored since 1484 as Our Lady of the Vineyard in Dettelbach, Germany. Also, Vina (without the tilde over the "n") can be a short form of Alvina, Davina, Lavinia, Melvina, and Venus.

Feast Dates: September 15 — Our Lady of the Vineyard; July 12 — St. Laventius (see Lavinia).

Vincentia "The Conquering One" (Latin).

Patron Saints: There is at least one St. Vincentia, one St. Vinciana, and over two dozen Sts. Vincent. St. Vincentia gave her life for Jesus in ancient Antioch.

Feast Dates: November 16 — St. Vincentia.

Vinete (English double) See Vincentia+Ette.

Viñita (Spanish) See Viña.

Vinlaria (African-American double) See Alvina/Vincentia+Lara/Larissa/Laura.

Vinnee (nickname) See Vinny.

Vinnette (French) See Winifred.

Vinni (nickname) See Vinny.

Vinnie (nickname) See Vinny.

Vinny (nickname) See Alvina, Lavinia, Venus, Vincentia.

Viola "The Violet Flower" (French, Spanish).

Patron Saints: The Latin word *viola* means "violet flower." There is one St. Viola. She is remembered for being an ancient martyr who died at Verona. There is one St. Vio and a half-dozen Sts. Flora, whose name means "flower."

Feast Dates: May 3 — St. Viola; June 15 — St. Vio (see Violet).

Violante (Spanish) See Viola, Violet.

Viole (variant) See Viola, Violet.

Violeea (African-American double) See Viola/Violet+Lisa.

Violet "The Violet Flower" (English form of Viola).

Patron Saints: There is a St. Viola, a St. Vio, a St. Flora, and a St. Yolanda (whose name also means "the violet flower"). We know that St. Vio was an Irish bishop who lived as a hermit in Brittany in the 500s.

Feast Dates: June 15 — St. Vio; May 3 — St. Viola (see Viola).

Violeta (Spanish double) See Viola/Violet+Etta.

Violete (Italian double) See Viola/Violet+Ette.

Violetta (German double) See Viola/Violet+Etta.

Violette (French double) See Viola/Violet+Ette.

Viorica (Romanian) See Viola, Violet.

Vira (nickname) See Elvira.

Virga (Estonian) See Virginia.

Virgie (English) See Virginia.

Virgin (English) See Virginia.

Virginia "The Virginal One" (Latin, Italian, German).

Patron Saints: There is one known St. Virginia. She was a shepherdess in medieval France.

Virginia, meaning "virgin" and/or "maiden," reminds Catholics of the doctrine that Mary, the Mother of God, remained "ever-virgin." For a Catholic, this means that Mary was a virgin — before, during, and after the birth of Jesus.

Feast Dates: January 7 — St. Virginia; January 1 — The Blessed Virgin Mary, Mother of God (see Ginger).

Virginie (Dutch, French) See Virginia.

Virgy (English) See Virginia.

Viridia (Spanish) See Chloris.

Virin (variant) See Laverne, Verne.

Virita (nickname) See Elvira.

Virna (variant) See Laverne, Verne.

Virtula (African-American double) See any "Ver" name+Tula.

Visa "The One Who Sees" (Latin).
Patron Saints: St. Visa served God as an abbot and bishop in Egypt in the 300s. There is also a female St. Vissia.
Feast Dates: July 30 — St. Visa; April 12 — St. Vissia (see Vista).

Vista "The Sight to See" (Latin).
Patron Saints: One saint has a similar name. St. Vissia, a single woman, died a martyr in ancient Rome.
Feast Dates: April 12 — St. Vissia.

Vita "Life [or The Living One]" (Latin) or "The Beloved One" (short form of Davita).
Patron Saints: There are about a dozen saints named Vitus. The best known St. Vitus lived in about 300. When he was about twelve, he converted to Christianity without his parents knowing. He quickly became a great inspiration for conversions and was noticed by the local Roman governor. He had Vitus arrested, but Vitus escaped and returned to Rome, where he exorcised the son of Emperor Diocletian. He was then accused of sorcery and was condemned to death. First he was racked until his limbs were dislocated and then he died of his wounds. He was about fourteen at the time of his death. He is patron of actors, comedians, dancers, and Sicily, as well as against epilepsy, oversleeping, nervous disorders, muscular motor disease, rheumatic chorea (St. Vitus's dance), snakebites, storms, and wild animals.
Feast Dates: June 15 — St. Vitus; January 22 — St. Avitus (see Aviva).

Vitia (variant) See Davita, Vida, Vita.

Vitoria (Spanish, Portuguese) See Victoria.

Viv (nickname) See Vivian.

Vivia (nickname) See Vivian.

Vivian "The Fully Alive One" (Latin).
Patron Saints: There is one St. Viviana and four Sts. Vivianus. There is also one St. Vivina. St. Vivian (also known as Viviana) died a martyr in ancient Rome.
Feast Dates: December 2 — St. Viviana.

Viviana (Italian, English, Spanish) See Vivian.

Viviane (variant) See Vivian.

Vivianna (English double) See Vivian+Anna.

Vivianne (English double) See Vivian+Anne.

Vivica (African-American double) See Vivian+any "Ca" name.

Vivien (English) See Vivian.

Vivienne (French double) See Vivian+Anne.

Vivyan (English) See Vivian.

Vivyanne (English double) See Vivian+Anne.

Von (nickname) See Veronica, Vonetta, Yvonne.

Vonetta "The Small+Little One" (English double).
Patron Saints: Vonetta is constructed out of two names: Vaun (or Vaughn) and Etta. This leads to two patrons.
St. Vaun served as bishop of Verdun from 500 to 525. He was so highly thought of that sometime later a Benedictine monastery was dedicated in his honor.
Feast Dates: November 9 — St. Vaun; July 10 — St. Etto (see Etta).

Vonni (nickname) See Veronica, Vonetta, Yvonne.

Vonnie (nickname) See Veronica, Vonetta, Yvonne.

Vonny (French) See Veronica, Vonetta, Yvonne.

Vrijida (Modern Greek) See Brigid.

Vynetta (African-American double) See Vincentia+Etta.

W

Wacila (African-American double) See any "Wa" name+any name ending in "Cilla."

Wadd (Arabic) See Davita.

Wadih (African-American) See Wadd.

WaKeisha (African-American) See Lakeisha, Leticia.

Walker "The Fuller [or The Thickener of Cloth]" (Old English).

Patron Saints: It helps to know that *walker* means "the fuller" or "the thickener of cloth." Four patrons have been appointed to this job: Sts. James the Younger, Homobonus, Athanasius the Fuller, and Paul the Hermit.

St. Paul, 229-342, a native of Egypt, became an orphan at the age of fifteen. He inherited great wealth, but he feared his brother-in-law would betray him to the government for being a Christian in order to get all the money. Thus he fled to the desert and learned to love solitude. He died at the age of one hundred thirteen.

Feast Dates: January 15 — St. Paul the Hermit.

Walli (German, nickname) See Valerie, Wallis.

Wallie (nickname) See Valerie, Wallis.

Wallis "The One from Wales" (Old English).

Patron Saints: Wallis means "Welshman." Therefore, the officially appointed patron of Wales, St. David, can serve as patron for Wallis. St. David settled in Wales with a group of followers and embraced manual labor and vegetarianism. Soon he became a bishop and took a strong stand against the heresies attacking the Catholic Church. He ruled his diocese until he was well into his sixties, dying in the year 589.

Feast Dates: March 1 — St. David, also known as Dewi.

Wanda "The Wanderer" (Old German, Spanish) or "The Shepherdess" (Slavic).

Patron Saints: St. Wando and the great St. Wendelin can both be pressed into service.

St. Wando was born in France and became a priest and then the abbot of Frontanelle Abbey. At one point in his life he was falsely accused of a crime and exiled from the monastery. Eventually he was proved innocent. As his life drew to a close he became blind. He died in 756.

Feast Dates: April 17 — St. Wando, O.S.B.; October 21 — St. Wendelin (see Wendy).

Wandie (nickname) See Wanda.

Wandis (English) See Wanda.

Wandra (Slavic, German) See Wanda.

Wandy (nickname) See Wanda.

Waneda (Spanish, German) See Juanita, Wanda.

Waneta "The One Who Rushes On" (North American Indian) or "God Is Gracious" (Spanish).

Patron Saints: As an alternate form of the Spanish "Juanita," one is led to hundreds of Sts. Jane, Joan, John, and Joanne.

Wanita (Spanish) See Juanita.

Wanza (African-American) See Wanda.

Wednesday "Born on Woden's Day" (Old English).

Patron Saints: A modern poem, which describes Wednesday's child as "full of woe," leads to a fine patron. She is the Blessed Virgin Mary, the Mother of Sorrows.

Surprisingly another, even greater, patron is possible. He is Jesus Christ himself, for an ancient Catholic tradition insists he was born on Wednesday.

Feast Dates: December 25 — Jesus' Birth; September 15 — Mother of Sorrows (see Dolores).

Wenda (English) See Gwendolyn, Wanda, Wendy.

Wendelin (English) See Wanda, Wendy.

Wendi (nickname) See Gwendolyn, Wanda, Wendy.

Wendie (nickname) See Gwendolyn, Wanda, Wendy.

Wendiline (English) See Gwendolyn, Wanda, Wendy.

Wendy "The Wanderer" (Old English form of Gwendolyn).

Patron Saints: The closest name that comes to Wendy is St. Wendelin, 554-607. He was born in Ireland, the son of a Scottish king. He loved to read the Psalms, so his father sent him away, and Wendelin became a wanderer, or pilgrim. Eventually he arrived in the valley of Bliess and became a shepherd. His holiness was noticed by some monks, and in the 590s they elected him to be their superior. He served as abbot for this order until his death.

Only after his death was any notice taken of him. This occurred because of the miracles that began to happen for those who visited his burial place. He is now patron of peasants, shepherds, and swineherds, and against sickness in cattle.

Feast Dates: October 21 — St. Wendelin; April 17 — St. Wando, O.S.B. (see Wanda).

Wendye (nickname) See Gwendolyn, Wanda, Wendy.

Wenona (English) See Winona.

Wenonah (English) See Winona.

Wes (nickname) See Wesley.

Wesley "From the West+From the Meadow" (Old English double).

Patron Saints: There is no St. Wesley, but there is a St. Swithun of Wessex. The word *wessex* means "west." The second part of the name, *ley* (or *leigh*), means "meadow." This leads to Bl. Richard Leigh.

Born in England, St. Swithun spent his boyhood in Winchester Abbey. Upon reaching adulthood, he was ordained a priest and became chaplain to Egber, king of the West Saxons, and tutor to the young prince. Later he became bishop of Wessex.

Feast Dates: July 2 — St. Swithun of Wessex; August 30 — Bl. Richard Leigh (see Leigh).

Westina (English double) See West+Tina.

Westleigh (English double) See West+Leigh/Leah.

Westley (English double) See West+Leigh/Leah.

Whit (nickname) See Whitney.

Whitey (nickname) See Whitney.

Whitney "The White-Haired One+From the Island" (Old English double).

Patron Saints: Originally a male name, it has increasingly been used for girls in the late twentieth century. Whitney comes from two words: *wit*, which means "white," and *ney*, which means "island." There are at least two saints named Wita and Nwy.

St. Wita was a pious laywoman in ancient Dorsetshire, England, and is often called St. Candida or St. Gwen. St. Nwy was a priest in Wales in ancient times. He is the patron of a chapel in Wales.

Feast Dates: June 1 — St. Wita; November 1 — St. Nwy.

Whitni (American) See Whitney.

Whitnie (American) See Whitney.

Whittany (American) See Whitney.

Whoopi "The One Involved in Excited Talk and Commotion" (Old English).

Patron Saints: The Latin word for "commotion" is *commotio*. A St. Commodus died a martyr in ancient Ostia.

Feast Dates: August 24 — St. Commodus.

Wil (nickname) See Wilhelmina, Willow.

Wilda (Old English) See Forest, Willow, Wilhelmina.

Wileen (English) See Wilhelmina.

Wilene (English) See Wilhelmina.

Wilfrida "The Friend+Of Peace" (Spanish double).

Patron Saints: St. Wilfrida was abbess of Wilton in the Middle Ages.

Feast Dates: September 9 — St. Wilfrida.

Wilhelma (German) See Wilhelmina.

Wilhelmena (Dutch) See Wilhelmina.

Wilhelmina "The Resolute Defender+Affectionate One" (Old German double).

Patron Saints: Wilhelmina is the feminine form of William. There is no St. Wilhelmina, but there are about fifty Sts. William. In addition, Sts. Wilfrida, Wiltrudis, Mina, and Villana (or Willana) can be adopted.

Bl. Villana, 1303-1360, was the daughter of a Florentine patrician. Being wealthy, she married and then led a worldly life. But after her husband died she became a member of the Third Order of St. Dominic and led a life of discipline and doing charitable works.

Feast Dates: February 28 (29) — Bl. Villana de' Botti; November 3 — St. Minna (see Mina).

Wilhelmine (German) See Wilhelmina.

Will (nickname) See Wilhelmina, Willow.

Willa (English) See Velma, Wilhelmina, Willow.

Willabella (German double) See Wilhelmina+Bella.

Willamena (Dutch) See Wilhelmina.

Willamene (variant) See Wilhelmina.

Willamina (Dutch) See Wilhelmina.

Willamine (Dutch) See Wilhelmina.

Willanny (Hispanic-American double) See any "Will" name+Annie.

Willetta (English double) See Wilhelmina+Etta.

Willette (English double) See Wilhelmina+Ette.

Willi (nickname) See Wilhelmina, Willow.

Willie (nickname) See Wilhelmina, Willow.

Willola (African-American double) See Willow/Wilhelmina+Ola.

Willow "From the Willow Tree" (American) or "The Free One" (Middle English).

Patron Saints: There is one St. Willow. A native of Ireland, Willow lived his life in Cornwall. After a life of prayer and solitude, he embraced a martyr's death at Llaneglos, near Fowey, by Melynus Kynrede.

Feast Dates: June 3 — St. Willow.

Willy (nickname) See Wilhelmina, Willow.

Wilma (German) See Wilhelmina.

Wilmetta (German double) See Wilma+Etta.

Wilmette (German double) See Wilma+Ette.

Wilona "The Desired One" (Old English).

Patron Saints: Wilona has the same meaning as Désirée and here we find a patron.

Feast Dates: September 8 — Bl. Jacques Désiré Laval (see Désirée).

Wilone (English) See Wilona.

Wilzetta (African-American double) See Wilhelmina/Willow+Zetta.

Win (nickname) See Guinevere, Gwendolyn, Wilhelmina, Winifred, Winona, Wynn.

Windy (nickname) See Wendy.

Winifred "The White Wave [Phantom]" (English form of Guinevere) or "The Peaceful Friend" (Old German).

Patron Saints: There is one St. Winifred (also known as Guinevere).

Feast Dates: November 3 — St. Winifred (see Guinevere); January 21 — St. Wynnin.

Winna (nickname) See Win.

Winne (nickname) See Win.

Winnee (nickname) See Win.

Winnie (nickname) See Win.

Winny (nickname) See Win.

Winona "The Firstborn Daughter" (North American Indian).

Patron Saints: The closest name to Winona is St. Winnow, an ancient English abbot. He lived in Ireland in the 500s. But a better patron can be found through the name's meaning. *Winona* means "firstborn daughter," which leads to Jesus, "the first-born of all creation" (Colossians 1:15). Being the firstborn of God the Father means the Son was begotten from all eternity. Then when the Son of God was born into the world, he was the firstborn of Mary (see Luke 2:7). The firstborn son, according to Jewish law, had special rights. He was the special possession of God and the apple-of-one's-eye to his parents.

Feast Dates: May 31 — St. Winnow; All Sundays — Jesus the Firstborn of All Creation.

Winonah (English) See Winona.

Winter "Born in the Cold Season" (Old English).

Patron Saints: The Catholic Church has appointed two saints as patrons for cold weather. The patron of frost is St. Urban of Langres and the patron of cold and against exposure and snowstorms is St. Valerian.

St. Valerian served for many years as the bishop of Tunis, Africa, in the mid-400s. When he was eighty years old, the heretic king of the Vandals, Hunneric, ordered him to turn over all Church treasures to the government. Valerian refused, and the king made him an exile in his own city. He was evicted from his home and forced to wander the streets. No one was allowed to feed, shelter, or care for him. He died of exposure one winter night.

Feast Dates: December 15 — St. Valerian.

Wioletta (Polish) See Viola, Violet.

Witney (variant) See Whitney.

Witni (variant) See Whitney.

Witnie (variant) See Whitney.

Witny (variant) See Whitney.

Wonderful "The Wonderful One" (Old English).

Patron Saints: One of the Latin words for "wonderful" is *mirus*, and there is a St. Mirus. He gave everything he had to the poor and lived a hermit's life devoted to prayer. He died in about 1035.

Feast Dates: May 10 — St. Mirus.

Wylena (African-American double) See any "Wy" name+Lena.

Wylma (American) See Wilhelmina.

Wylona (African-American double) See any "Wy" name+Lon.

Wynn (Welsh) See Gwendolyn, Winifred, Wynn.

Wynne "The Fair White One" (Welsh) or "The White Wave" (Welsh short form of Winifred or Gwendolyn).

Patron Saints: There are about a half-dozen ancient saints with very similar names who can serve as patrons. They include Sts. Wynnin (a holy Scottish bishop and patron of Kilwinning Abbey in Scotland), Winin, Winnian, and Winifred.

Feast Dates: January 21 — St. Wynnin of Holywood; November 3 — St. Winifred (see Guinevere).

Wynonna (variant) See Winona.

Wyomia (English) See Wyoming, Winona.

Wyoming "From the Great Plains" (North American Indian).

Patron Saints: Two saints are available. Together their names mean "great plain."

Feast Dates: July 30 — St. Maxine, also known as Maxima; Month of May — The Blessed Virgin Mary, Rose of Sharon (see Sharon).

Wytisha (African-American double) See Wyoming+Leticia.

X

Xandra (Greek) See Sandra.

Xavia (nickname) See Xaviera.

Xaviera "The New House Owner" (Spanish) or "The Bright One" (Spanish).

Patron Saints: There are about a half-dozen saints who have Xavier as part of their names. But the greatest of them is St. Francis Xavier, 1506-1552. Another saint bearing the name is St. Frances Xavier Cabrini, the first American citizen to be canonized.

Feast Dates: December 22 — St. Frances Xavier Cabrini (see Frances).

Xeenia (African-American) See Xenia.

Xena (English) See Xenia.

Xene (English) See Xenia.

Xenia "The Hospitable One" or "The Guest" (Greek).

Patron Saints: There are two Sts. Xenia. One of them, a single woman, lived in the fifth century. The only daughter of a Roman senator and his wife in Constantinople, she was named Eusebia. Raised in the Christian faith, she decided to remain single. However, her decision was not acceptable to her parents. Seeing no solution, she fled to Cyprus with two of her maids. Later, she went to Alex-

andria, Egypt, and became a nun and a deaconess.

Feast Dates: January 24 — St. Xenia, also known as Eusebia.

Xenon (English) See Zenon.

Xermona (African-American double) See Zere+Mona.

Xernona (African-American double) See Zere+Nona.

Xiména (Spanish) See Simone.

Xiomana (Hispanic-American double) See Xylia+Manda.

Xiomara "From the Glorious, Beautiful+ Forest" (Hispanic-American double).

Patron Saints: Xiomara is built from two words. The first part, *xio*, is a form of Xilia, Xylia, or Silvia and means "forest." The second half of the name is *mara*, which is a form of Amara and means "gloriously beautiful."

Feast Dates: November 3 — St. Silvia (see Sylvia); November 8 — St. Amaranthus (see Amara).

Xiomayra (Hispanic-American double) See Xylia+Maya.

Xuxu (Portuguese) See Susan.

Xylecia (African-American double) See Xylia+Lecia.

Xylene (English) See Sylvia, Xylia.

Xylia (Greek) See Sylvia.

𝒴

Y Second-to-the-last letter of the alphabet (English).

Ya "Yes" (Common English).

Patron Saints: Hispanic-Americans seem to have a high regard for Y, Ya, and Ye as prefixes to their names. The name attached to this prefix usually leads to a patron saint.

Yadira (Hispanic-American triple) See Ya+Adi+Ira.

Yahaira "Altar of+Peaceful One" (Hispanic-American triple) or "The Flower" (Hispanic-American use of African word) or "The Bitter One" (Hispanic-American).

Patron Saints: Yahaira can be constructed from Ya plus Ara plus Ira or from Y plus Zahara or from Ya plus Maira.

Feast Dates: March 13 — St. Araba (see Aracelis); February 26 — St. Irene (see Irene).

Yalina (Russian) See Helen.

Yamelia (Hispanic-American double) See Y+Amelia.

Yamilet (Hispanic-American triple) See Y+Amile+T.

Yamilex (Hispanic-American triple) See Y+Amile+X.

Yamiley (Hispanic-American double) See Y+Amile.

Yaminah "The Affectionate One" (Hispanic-American triple) or "The Correct, Proper One" (Swahili).

Patron Saints: Yamina may arise from Ya plus Mina plus H. This would lead to St. Mina.

Feast Dates: November 3 — St. Mina (see Mina).

Yana (Slavic) See Jana.

Yanice (Hispanic-American double) See Y+Janice.

Yanira (Hispanic-American triple) See Y+Ann+Ira.

Yarelis (Hispanic-American double) See Y+Aracelis.

Yarie (Hispanic-American triple) See Y+Areta.

Yarimilka "The Merchant+Hardworking" (Hispanic-American double of the Slavic name Yarmilla).

Patron Saints: The word *yarmilla* means "merchant" and *ilka* means "hardworking." St. Nicholas of Myra is the patron of merchants.

Feast Dates: December 6 — St. Nicholas of Myra.

Yaritea (Hispanic-American triple) See Y+Areta+Tea.

Yaritza "The Truth+Laughter" (Hispanic-American triple).

Patron Saints: Yaritza can be constructed from Y plus Areta plus Itzak.

Feast Dates: July 27 — St. Arethas (see Aretha); October 19 — St. Isaac Jogues, S.J. (see Isaac).

Yarmilla (Slavic) See Yarimilka.

Yasaman (variant) See Jasmine.

Yashira "From Ash Trees+In Peace" (Hispanic-American triple).

Patron Saints: Yashira can be constructed from Y plus Ash plus Ira. Also, Ash is a short form of Ashley.

Feast Dates: April 7 — Bl. Ralph Ashley, S.J. (see Ashley); February 26 — St. Irene (see Irene).

Yasiman (Hindu) See Jasmine.

Yasmeen (Persian) See Jasmine.

Yasmin (Persian) See Jasmine.

Yasmine (Persian) See Jasmine.

Yazira "The Precious, Beautiful+Peaceful One" (Hispanic-American triple).

Patron Saints: Yazira can be constructed from Y plus Azi plus Ira. The Azi part is a short form of Azisa.

Feast Dates: November 19 — St. Azi; February 26 — St. Irene (see Irene).

Yecenia (Spanish) See Yesenia.

Yehudit (Israeli) See Judith.

Yekaterina (Russian) See Katherine.

Yelena (Russian) See Helen.

Yelitza "The Light+Laughter" (Hispanic-American double).

Patron Saints: Yelitza can be constructed from Yelena and Itzak. Yelena is the Russian form of Helen, while Itzak is the Polish form of Isaac.

Feast Dates: August 18 — St. Helena (see Helen); October 19 — St. Isaac Jogues, S.J.

Yelizaveta (Russian) See Elizabeth.

Yenaira "The Pure Lamb+The Peaceful One" (Hispanic-American double).

Patron Saints: Yenaira can be constructed from Ynes plus Ira or Ynes plus Maira.

Feast Dates: January 21 — St. Ynes (see Agnes); February 26 — St. Irene (see Irene).

Yesenia "The Flower" (Arabic).

Patron Saints: In the 1980s a serial character with this name became very popular on Hispanic-American television. Soon a great many Hispanic children were so named even though the name is Arabic. Two patrons can be found. One is Bl. Richard Flowers; the other is any one of a dozen Sts. Arsenio.

St. Arsenio the Great was a Roman deacon whom Emperor Theodosius ordered to Constantinople in 383 to tutor his children. Ten years later he abandoned this thankless task and became a hermit in the Egyptian desert of Skete. He died in 449.

Feast Dates: July 19 — St. Arsenio the Great; May 4 — Bl. Richard Flowers (see Lotus).

Yesica (Hebrew) See Jessica.

Yesnelia (Hispanic-American double) See Yesenia+Nelia.

Yessenia (Hispanic-American) See Yesenia.

Yetta (nickname) See Henrietta.

Yettie (nickname) See Henrietta.

Yetty (nickname) See Henrietta.

Yevette (variant) See Ivette, Yvette, Yvonne.

Yezenia (Hispanic-American) See Yesenia.

Ynes (Spanish) See Agnes.

Ynesita (Spanish double) See Agnes+Ita.

Ynez (Spanish) See Agnes.

Yoko "The Positive Woman" (Japanese).

Patron Saints: Knowing that the name means "positive woman" leads to the greatest female patron. For did not the "yes" of the Blessed Virgin reverse the "no" of Eve? Thus with one positive statement — "Let it be to me according to your word" (Luke 1:38) —God-become-man was made possible.

Feast Dates: March 25 — The Annunciation of the Blessed Virgin Mary (see Annunciata).

Yolana (Greek) See Iola, Yolanda.

Yolanda "The Violet Flower" (Greek, Italian).

Patron Saints: One saint whose name is similar to Yolanda is St. Yolendis. She was an ancient Roman woman who accompanied her friend St. Benedicta to martyrdom.

And because *yolanda* means "violet," one can also call upon Sts. Vio and Viola.

Feast Dates: December 17 — St. Yolendis; May 3 — St. Viola (see

Viola); June 15 — St. Vio (see Violet).

Yolande (French) See Yolanda, Viola, Violet.

Yolandis (variant) See Iola, Yolanda.

Yolane (variant) See Yolanda, Viola, Violet.

Yolanta (variant) See Yolanda.

Yolanthe (variant) See Yolanda.

Yoli (Spanish) See Yolanda.

Yolunda (African-American) See Yolanda.

Yonah (African-American double) See Y+Jonah.

Yosenia (Spanish) See Yesenia.

Ysabel (Spanish) See Elizabeth, Isabel.

Yseult (variant) See Isolde.

Ysonda (variant) See Isolde.

Ytha (variant) See Ita.

Ytu (variant) See Ita.

Yuana (Spanish) See Juana.

Yudella (English) See Udele.

Yudita (Russian) See Judith.

Yulia (Russian) See Julia.

Yuliana (Spanish) See Juliana.

Yulissa (Hispanic-American double) See Julia+Lisa.

Yvette "The Hero with the Yew Bow" (French).

Patron Saints: There is one Bl. Yvette, who was a wife and mother. Later in life she became a recluse and gave herself to prayer. She died in 1228.

It should also be noted that both Yvette and Yvonne have the same meaning, "hero with a yew bow." There is a Bl. Yvoine and a St. Evonius. Some authorities also think both these names may have their origin in Eve. This opens the door to adopting as patron one of the few Sts. Eve.

Feast Dates: January 13 — Bl. Yvette; August 30 — St. Eva (see Eve).

Yvonna (variant) See Yvonne.

Yvonne "The Archer" (Old French) or "Hero with the Yew Bow" (French).

Patron Saints: There is one Bl. Yvoine. He embraced the life of a hermit and dedicated his life to doing penance for sinners. There is also one St. Evonius. Also, because some scholars think that the name may have its roots in the name Eve, the few Sts. Eve can be claimed as patrons.

Feast Dates: June 15 — Bl. Yvoine; December 24 — Sts. Adam and Eve (see Eartha).

Z

Z Last letter of the alphabet (English).

Patron Saints: Hispanic-Americans seem to favor the letter "Z" as the beginning letter for many of their names. The letter "Zee" is the final letter in the Roman alphabet. It is called *omega* in the Greek alphabet. Thus it can be used to identify the Divine Creator, who is the end of all that is.

Feast Dates: Trinity Sunday — God the Father, Creator of All.

Zada (Arabic) See Lucky.

Zadee (variant) See Sarah.

Zahara "A Flower" (African).

Patron Saints: There is no St. Zahara. But Zaharah means "flower," and there are a half-dozen Sts. Flora.

Feast Dates: November 24 — St. Flora (see Flora).

Zaira (Spanish) See Zahara.

Zakelina (Czech) See Jacqueline.

Zamira "The Queen" (Hispanic-American form of the West-African name Amira).

Patron Saints: Zamira is a compound of Z and Amira. Its meaning, "queen," leads to the Blessed Virgin.

Feast Dates: August 22 — The Blessed Virgin Mary, Queen of Heaven (see Queen).

Zandra (nickname) See Alexandra, Cassandra, Sandra.

Zaneta (Spanish) See Jane.

Zanna (Polish) See Jane.

Zara "Princess" (Arabic) or "The Bright Dawn" (Hebrew).

Patron Saints: Some scholars identify Zara as a form of Sarah, and Catholic tradition provides three Sts. Sarah. The Bible adds one more. Others suggest that Zara might be a form of Zorah, which means "dawn."

According to tradition, the St. Sara mentioned in the Bible was married, a mother, and a servant of the three Marys: St. Mary, wife of Cleophas; St. Mary Salome, the mother of James; and St. Mary Magdalen. According to tradtition, all three sailed with Martha and Lazarus to Marseilles after the resurrection of Jesus. It seems that Sara was a very strong, swarthy woman of Indian ancestry. She is patron of gypsies.

Feast Dates: May 24 — St. Sara, also known as Kali; August 19 — St. Sarah (see Sarah).

Zarah (variant) See Sarah, Zara, Zora.

Zari (nickname) See Sarah, Zara, Zora.

Zaria (variant) See Sarah, Zara, Zora.

Zarita (Spanish double) See Sarah+Ita.

Zaviera (Spanish) See Xavier.

Zavrina (variant) See Sabrina.

Zeda "The Lord Is Righteous" (Hebrew).

Patron Saints: Zeda is a short feminine form of Zedekiah. Only one saint can be found with a similar name. Bl. Zdislava belonged to a noble Bohemian family, got married, and had four children. However, her charity to the poor caused difficulties between her and her husband. She died in 1252.

Feast Dates: January 1 — St. Zdislava.

Zeena (African-American) See Xenia.

Zeenya (American) See Xenia.

Zefyma (English) See Breezy.

Zelda "The Gray Battle Maiden" (English short form of Griselda).

Patron Saints: There is no St. Zelda or Griselda. But the fact that both names mean "gray woman" or "gray battle maiden" leads to a few patrons. The first is an ancient saint known as St. Ronan the Gray, who was from Liath-Ros, Louth, Ireland. Then there are two more saints who have Gray as part of their names. Their common name, Grisold, means "gray moor." Finally, there is one ancient saint with a very similar name. He is St. Granus.

Feast Dates: April 30 — St. Ronan the Gray; May 4 — Bl. Robert Grissold (see Griselda); December 30 — St. Grisold (see Gray).

Zelie (variant) See Selena.

Zella (African-American double) See Z+Ella.

Zellena (African-American double) See Z+Ellena.

Zelma (German, African-American) See Selma.

Zena (English) See Xenia.

Zenia (English) See Xenia.

Zenobia "The Sign" (Greek).

Patron Saints: St. Zenobia died a martyr in ancient Aegae.

Feast Dates: October 30 — St. Zenobia.

Zenon "The Stranger" (Greek).

Patron Saints: There are over fifty Sts. Zeno. One died a martyr in ancient Nicomedia.

Feast Dates: April 20 — St. Zenon.

Zenoquia (African-American double) See Zenon+Qua.

Zeola (African-American double) See Z+Ola.

Zephylia (African-American double) See Zephyma+Phyllis/Filia.

Zephyma (Greek) See Breezy.

Zere (English) See Zora.

Zerlina (Spanish-Italian double) See Zere+Linda.

Zerlinda (Spanish-Italian double) See Zere+Linda.

Zeta (English) See Rose, Zetta, Zita.

Zetta "The Olive" (Hebrew).

Patron Saints: There are three Sts. Zetus. One, a black man, died a martyr in ancient Africa.

Feast Dates: November 22 — Zetus; June 10 — St. Olive (see Olivia).

Zilvia (English) See Sylvia.

Zina "The Name" (African) or "The Hospitable One" (Greek variant of Xenia).

Patron Saints: There are at least two Sts. Zina. One is remembered as a holy Abyssinian woman. The other woman lived a holy life in ancient Syria.

Feast Dates: October 21 and November 22 — both Sts. Zina.

Zita "The Little One" (Z+Spanish diminutive Ita) or "Like a Rose Flower" (English nickname for Rose) or "The Reaper" (nickname for Teresa).

Patron Saints: Among the saints there is one St. Zita, 1218-1278. She was born at Monsagrati, near Lucca, Italy. At the age of twelve, she entered the service of the Fratinelli family as a servant. A very simple woman, she remained at this job until her death. It was not an easy assignment, for she was often maltreated by her employers and her fellow servants. It seems she constantly cared for the poor who visited her master's house. She is patron of housemaids and domestic servants and finding lost keys.

Feast Dates: April 27 — St. Zita; August 23 — St. Rose of Lima (see Rose).

Zitella (American double) See Zita+Ella, Ellen.

Zoa (variant) See Zoe.

Zoe "The Living One" (Greek) or "The Mother of the Living" (Greek for Eve).

Patron Saints: There are two Sts. Zoe. Both died as martyrs for the Christian faith. There is also a St. Zoerard and a St. Zoilus. Also, it is good to know that St. Catherine Labouré was originally named Zoe.

In ancient times Zoe and her husband, Hesperus, were Christian slaves. However, they were only lukewarm Christians. Their two sons, in contrast, were very devout. When their master decided that every slave in his household must take part in pagan household worship, the sons refused and were cruelly tortured while their parents watched. Hesperus and Zoe were so moved by the example of their sons that they decided to remain steadfast in the faith. Zoe was then hanged from a tree by her hair. Later, the whole family was roasted to death — together.

Feast Dates: May 2 — St. Zoe; December 24 — Sts. Adam and Eve (see Isha).

Zoey (nickname) See Zoe.

Zofia (Polish) See Sophie.

Zoila (Spanish) See Vita, Zoe.

Zola (Italian) See Eartha.

Zona "A Girdle" (Latin) or "From the Place of Few Springs" (nickname for Arizona).

Patron Saints: There is one St. Zonus. He was a bishop who died for the faith in ancient Alexandria. He was accompanied by two deacons.

Feast Dates: February 12 — St. Zonus; March 15 — Ven. Eusebio Kino, S.J. (see Arizona).

Zondra (nickname) See Alexandra, Cassandra, Sandy.

Zone (English) See Zona.

Zora "From the Dawn [Sunrise]" (Slavic) or "The Sunrise" (variant of Aurora).

Patron Saints: The fact that *zora* means "dawn" helps. It is also helpful to know that Rori is a familiar form of Zora. This leads to two Sts. Roricius.

Feast Dates: July 21 — St. Roricius (see Oriana).

Zorah (Hebrew) See Aurora, Sarah, Zara, Zora.

Zorana (variant) See Aurora, Zora.

Zoriely "The [Golden] Fair-Haired One" (Hispanic-American triple).

Patron Saints: Zoriely is created out of Z plus Oriel plus Y. One saint qualifies as a patron.

Feast Dates: March 23 — St. Joseph Oriol (see Oriola).

Zorina (Slavic) See Aurora, Zora.

Zorine (English) See Aurora, Zora.

Zosel (German) See Susan.

Zosia (Polish) See Sophie.

Zsa Zsa "The Lily" (Hungarian form of Susan).

Patron Saints: Zsa Zsa is a Hungarian form of Susan. About eighteen Sts. Susan and Susanna are known. Two more are mentioned in the Bible, one in each Testament. The following is the story of Susanna, who probably lived in about 500 B.C., and is told in Chapter 13 of the Book of Daniel.

It seems the prophet Daniel came to the defense of a beautiful young married woman who was falsely accused of adultery. The two corrupt Jewish elders, who had lusted for Susanna, had her tried and condemned to death because she would not give in to their sinful advances. The purpose of the story is to teach that sometimes one must face death rather than sin against God. Also, God hears the prayers of the oppressed and fights for them. He hears the cry of the poor and powerless.

Feast Dates: August 11 and November 1 — both Sts. Susanna (see Susan).

Zura (African-American) See Zorah.

Zurehida "God Is My Foundation [Rock]+Woman Warrior" (Hispanic-American double of Hebrew-German).

Patron Saints: The first part of the name can come from either Ze'ura,

Zuriel, or Zuri. St. Ze'ura was an ancient Syrian saint who lived on top of a pillar. To him can be added Sts. Hilda and Hidulf. St. Hidulf was a priest and the prayerful count of Hainaut in the 700s.

Feast Dates: November 17 — St. Ze'ura; June 23 — St. Hidulf.

Zurehima "God Is My Foundation [Rock]+The Living One" (Hispanic-American double of Hebrew-German).

Patron Saints: The first part of the name can come from either Ze'hura, Zuri, or Zuriel and is coupled with the Hebrew name Hyman. One saint with a variant of this name is St. Himes, an Armenian. He opposed the persecution of Emperor Diocletian. For his trouble he was beheaded in about the year 100.

Feast Dates: November 17 — St. Ze'ura (see Zurehida); August 14 — St. Himes.

Zuri "The Good-Looking One" (Swahili).

Patron Saints: Kendra is the female form of Kenneth and can mean "good-looking."

Feast Dates: November 1 — St. Kendelion (see Kendra).

Zuriel "God Is My Foundation [Rock]" (Hebrew).

Patron Saints: Christian tradition teaches that St. Zuriel is the chief angel of the order of principalities. He is the healer of stupidity in human beings.

Feast Dates: September 29 — The Holy Archangels (see Angela); October 2 — The Holy Guardian Angels.

Zusa (Czech, Polish) See Susan.

Zuzanna (Polish) See Susan.

Zuzi (Swiss) See Susan.

Zuzu (variant) See Susan.

Zylvia (variant) See Sylvia.

Zynia (English) See Zina.

Zytka (Polish) See Rose.

Male Names
A-Z

A

Aadam (Arabic) See Adam.

Aarao (Portuguese) See Aaron.

Aaro (Finnish) See Aaron.

Aaron "The Exalted One" (Hebrew) or "The Enlightened, Shining One" (Hebrew.

Patron Saints: There are a half-dozen Christian Sts. Aaron, and the Bible adds one more. Aaron was the older brother of Moses and his helper in freeing the Israelites from slavery in Egypt in about 1200 B.C. He served as Moses' mouthpiece and shared duties with Moses.

Like Moses, Aaron also failed. When pressed by the people to make a golden calf, he did so. Further, he unjustly criticized his brother and was strongly reprimanded by God. But in spite of his mistakes, God chose him to be the founder of the Jewish priesthood and to be the first high priest.

Feast Dates: July 1 — St. Aaron.

Aaronas (Latvian) See Aaron.

Ab (nickname) See Abbot, Abdul, Abner.

Abba (Hebrew) See Abbot, Abraham, Daddy, Father, Papa.

Abbey (nickname) See Abbot.

Abbie (nickname) See Abbot.

Abbot "The Father" (Hebrew).

Patron Saints: Any of the hundreds of religious abbots can be adopted. In addition, there is one layman who converted to Catholicism and was hanged for it by the English government in 1597.

Feast Dates: July 4 — Bl. Henry Abbott.

Abbott (variant) See Abbot.

Abby (variant) See Abbot.

Abdel (variant) See Abbot.

Abdias (Greek) See Obadiah.

Abdon (Spanish) See Abdul.

Abdul "The Servant" (Arabic) or "The Son of" (Arabic).

Patron Saints: Westerners recognized Abdul as a Muslim name. While it is used by many believers in Islam, it is not strictly Muslim. It is, rather, an Arabic name, and many Arabs were Christian long before the rise of Islam, and they remain so today. Thus finding a patron is very easy.

Abdul means "servant of God," and Catholics immediately think of Jesus the "Servant of Man." The Jewish prophet Isaiah introduced the concept of the "suffering servant" who suffers and dies to bring salvation to others. Isaiah presented it to explain Israel's God-given vocation. In time, the concept was applied to the long-awaited Messiah, Jesus Christ. For Jesus said, "The Son of Man also came not to be served but to serve" (Mark 10:45). All Christians are to follow Jesus' example.

Feast Dates: Good Friday — Jesus the Suffering Servant.

Abdullah (Arabic double) See Abdul+Ali.

Abe (nickname) See Abel, Abraham, Abram.

Abel "The Breath" (Hebrew) or "The Meadow" (Assyrian).

Patron Saints: There are about a half-dozen Christian Sts. Abel, and the Bible adds the best one. Chapter 4 of Genesis records the major portion of what is known about Abel. He was a teenage shepherd who offered the best of his flock to God and his sacrifices were acceptable. His older brother, Cain, a farmer, was jealous of him. This led Cain to murder Abel. With his brother dead, Cain thought God would have to accept his mediocre offerings.

The lessons: 1. Always give God your best. 2. No one can manipulate God. 3. Each person is his brother's keeper. 4. All are tempted but need not sin. 5. If one sins, one must face the justice of God. Jewish tradition pictures Abel judging souls at the gates of heaven.

Feast Dates: January 2 — St. Abel.

Abie (nickname) See Abraham, Abram.

Abner "The Father of Light" (Hebrew).

Patron Saints: There is no St. Abner. However, Aba is a short form, and there are at least two Sts. Aba. One was a priest who was martyred for Christ in ancient Kaskhar.

Feast Dates: May 16 — St. Aba.

Abraham "The Father of a Multitude" (Hebrew).

Patron Saints: There are about three dozen Christian Sts. Abraham, and the greatest of them is the Old Testament's Abraham. He was born a pagan in the Middle East in about 1800 B.C. and whose name (until God changed it) was Abram. At the age of seventy-five, he became aware of the one true God (see Genesis 12) and moved to Canaan as God commanded. Later, God promised to give Abraham a son (see Genesis 15). In due time, Sarai, who was renamed Sarah by God, gave birth to Isaac (see Genesis 21).

When Abraham's son Isaac was born, it was considered a miracle, since Abraham was a hundred years of age and his wife was eighty-seven at the time. A short time later God tested Abraham by asking him to sacrifice his son and then did not allow it to happen. In this way God taught that he did not want human sacrifices (see Genesis 22).

If Abraham had not converted to the worship of Yahweh, there would never have been either the Jewish or the Catholic religions. This only goes to show how important each and every one of us is, no matter how powerless, unimportant, or insignificant we feel.

Feast Dates: October 9 — St. Abraham, Patriarch.

Abrahamo (Italian) See Abraham.

Abrahán (Spanish) See Abraham.

Abram "The Hollow Root" (Hebrew) or "The Father of Many" (Hebrew nickname for Abraham).

Patron Saints: This was Abraham's name before God changed it. Note that because Abraham put faith in God he ceased being a "hollow root" and became the "father of a multitude."

Feast Dates: October 9 — St. Abraham (see Abraham).

Abramo (Italian) See Abraham, Abram.

Abrán (Spanish) See Abraham.

Absalom (Hebrew) See Axel.

Ace "The United One" (Latin) or "The Best One" (Latin).

Patron Saints: A few ancient saints have Ace as part of their names, including Sts. Acesius, Acestus, and Aceneus. St. Acestus knew St. Paul the Apostle. When St. Paul was beheaded in Rome in about 64, his death actually caused the conversion of three soldiers present at the execution. Acestus was one. All three soldiers were beheaded immediately after St. Paul was killed.

Feast Dates: July 2 — St. Acestus.

Acevedo Meaning unknown (Hispanic-American).

Patron Saints: Bl. Ignacio de Azevedo, S.J., in 1566, became very concerned about the lack of priests in Brazil. Thus he recruited a number of priests and seminarians in Spain and Portugal, some seventy of them, to go with him to Brazil. They left for the New World on two separate vessels.

In 1570, a short time after leaving the Canary Islands, Father Azevedo's group was captured by pirates under the command of Jacques Sourie, a former Catholic and a deadly enemy. Sourie immediately killed Father Azevedo. Then he stripped the other priests naked and made them walk the plank.

Feast Dates: January 19 — The Brazilian Martyrs.

Acey (nickname) See Ace.

Achill (Hungarian) See Achilles.

Achille (Italian) See Achilles.

Achilles Meaning unknown (Greek).

Patron Saints: There are about twelve Sts. Achillas and Achilles. One St. Achillas headed a catechetical school in Alexandria, Egypt. In 311 he was appointed to be the patriarch of Alexandria. While he did many good things, he did make one mistake. He ordained a man by the name of Arius. This man developed heretical teachings that spread throughout the entire Christian world and threatened the very existence of the Catholic Church. Achillas totally rejected this new and wrong doctrine.

Feast Dates: November 7 — St. Achillas.

Achilleus (Greek) See Achilles.

Achmed "Most Praised One" (Arabic form of Muhammad).

Patron Saints: St. Achmed was an architect who converted to Christianity after witnessing a miracle. A short time later he was murdered in Con-stantinople by his Muslim friends. The year was 1682.

Feast Dates: December 24 — St. Achmed.

Acie (nickname) See Ace.

Acton "From the Town+Near the Oaks" (Old English double).

Patron Saints: There is an English martyr who fills the bill, Bl. Thomas Holford. He used the aliases "Acton" and "Brude" when working in the Catholic underground as a missionary in England. Born at Acton in Cheshire, and raised a Protestant, he became a schoolmaster in Herefordshire and then converted to Catholicism. Going to Rheims in France, he was ordained in 1583 and immediately returned to England. Five years later he was caught by the authorities and hanged at Clerkenwell.

Feast Dates: August 28 — Bl. Thomas Holford, also known as Acton.

Ad (nickname) See Adam, Adlai, Adolf.

Adalbert (nickname) See Adelbert.

Adao (Portuguese) See Adam.

Adam "The Man of the Red Earth" (Hebrew).

Patron Saints: There are a half-dozen Catholic Sts. Adam. To them, the Bible adds the greatest St. Adam. Practically every Christian and Jew knows how Adam and Eve lost paradise because of their disobedience.

Ancient Jewish tradition adds that they settled in a cave and had many more children. They faced continual temptations by the devil and slowly learned that the devil was their worst enemy. And they also learned that prayer and sacrifice (self-discipline) were their finest weapons against him. They lived long lives of repentance, hardship, pain, and prayer before dying. And God, in his mercy, forgave them. Adam and Eve are considered patrons of gardeners.

Feast Dates: December 24 — Sts. Adam and Eve.

Adamo (Italian) See Adam.

Adams "The Son of+Adam" (Old English double).

Patron Saints: Bl. John Adams was executed by the English government in 1586 for being a Catholic.

Feast Dates: May 4 — Bl. John Adams.

Adamson (Old English double) See Adams, Adam+Son.

Adán (Spanish) See Adam.

Adarius (African-American double) See Adam+ Darius.

Addie (nickname) See Adam, Adlai.

Addison (Old English double) See Adams, Adam+Son.

Addy (nickname) See Adam, Adlai.

Ade (nickname) See Adrian.

Adelbert "The Noble Brilliant One" (Dutch, German).

Patron Saints: There are a dozen Sts. Aldelbert. Also, when one realizes that Adelbert is the German or Dutch form of Albert, two dozen more Sts. Albert become available. When St. Adelbert, the Apostle to the Slavs, was only a twenty-six-year-old subdeacon, he was elected to serve as bishop of Prague. He spent most of his time preaching and ministering to the poor, but there was little fruit. Eventually he went to Rome and then he went on a missionary journey. When the pagans of central Europe killed him in 997, he was only forty-one.

Feast Dates: April 23 — St. Adelbert of Prague; November 15 — St. Albert the Great (see Albert).

Adelberto (Spanish) See Albert.

Adham (Arabic) See Blackie.

Adhamh (Irish, Scottish) See Adam.

Adlai "Yahweh Is Just" or "My Ornament" (Hebrew).

Patron Saints: There are a few saints with similar names, including St. Adleidis of medieval times. She was the mother of St. Grata of Bergamo. After her husband died, she performed charitable works and founded a convent.

Feast Dates: June 17 — St. Adleidis.

Adley (nickname) See Adlai.

Adolf "The Noble Hero" (Old German) or "The Noble Wolf" (Old German).

Patron Saints: There are a handful of Sts. Adolph (or Adolf). St. Adolf of Tecklenburg, 1185-1224, entered a local Cistercian monastery. In 1216, at the age of thirty-one, he was elected bishop of Osnabruck. His virtue and self-discipline made a deep impression on his people. He was always involved in charitable activities and was known as the "almoner of the poor." He died at the age of thirty-nine.

Feast Dates: February 11 — St. Adolf of Tecklenburg.

Adolfo (Spanish) See Adolf.

Adolph (English) See Adolf.

Adolphe (French) See Adolf.

Adolpho (variant) See Adolf.

Adolphus (Latin) See Adolf.

Adonis (Greek) See Kenneth.

Adrian "The Dark Rich One" (English, Spanish) or "The One from the Adriatic" (English).

Patron Saints: There are about three dozen saints named Adrianus. One of them was a disciple of St. Landoald in Flanders in 667. One day, just as he was returning home after a day of collecting alms for the poor, he was murdered by robbers.

Feast Dates: March 19 — St. Adrian.

Adriano (Italian, Spanish) See Adrian.

Adrianus (Latin) See Adrian.

Adrien (French) See Adrian.

Adrein (French) See Adrian.

Adry (nickname) See Adrian.

Aedan (Irish) See Aidan.

Aemilius (variant) See Emil.

Affonso (Portuguese) See Alphonse.

Afonso (Portuguese) See Alphonse.

Agostin (variant) See Augustine.

Agostinho (Portuguese) See Augustine.

Agostino (Italian) See Augustine.

Aguistin (Irish) See Augustine.

Agustín (Spanish) See Augustine.

Ahil (nickname) See Achilles.

Ahmed (Arabic) See Achmed, Muhammad.

Aidan "From the Warm Home" (Irish Gaelic) or "The Fiery One" (Irish Gaelic) or "From Paradise" (From Eden).

   Patron Saints: There are at least two dozen Sts. Aidan (or Aedhan). Very little is known about most of them. For example, St. Aidan McCuamsie is simply listed as an "Irish saint."

   Feast Dates: May 2 — St. Aidan, also known as Aedhan.

Ailbert (Scottish) See Albert.

Ailfrid (Irish) See Alfred.

Aindreas (Irish, Scottish) See Andrew.

Airel (Israeli) See Ariel.

Airleas (variant) See Arlen, Earl.

Akhylliy (Ukrainian) See Achilles.

Akilles (Norwegian) See Achilles.

Akim (variant) See Joachim.

Akoni (Hawaiian) See Anthony.

Al "On the" or "To the" (French prefix).

   Patron Saints: Standing alone, "Al" serves as a nickname for a great many male names. They include Adelbert, Alan, Alastair, Alban, Albert, Alden, Aldous, Aldrich, Alexander, Alexis, Alfred, Algernon, Aloysius, Alphonse, Alvin, and Elvis.

   Feast Dates: See individual names of patron saints.

Alain (French) See Alan.

Alaire (French) See Hilary.

Alamanzo (African-American) See Alonso, Alphonso.

Alan "The Handsome One" (Irish Gaelic) or "The Peaceful One" (Irish Gaelic).

   Patron Saints: There are about a half-dozen saints with the name of Alan or Alain. One St. Alan was the son of Emyr Llydaw, an Armorican (or Breton) chief. He had fled to Wales with his father and family. Later, in about 537, he was killed, probably by the pagan Saxons.

   Feast Dates: November 1 — St. Alan.

Alano (Spanish) See Alan.

Alanus (Latin) See Alan.

Alasdair (Scottish Gaelic) See Alexander.

Alaster (English, Scottish) See Alexander.

Alastair (Scottish Gaelic) See Alexander.

Alister (English) See Alexander.

Alastor (Greek) See Alexander.

Alban "The Fair Blond One" or "The Dawn of the Day" (English, Irish).

   Patron Saints: There are about a half-dozen Sts. Alban. One was a pagan in England during the persecution of Emperor Diocletian. He gave shelter to a priest, and this priest converted him to Christianity. When the government learned about the hidden priest and sent soldiers to capture him, Alban, seeing soldiers coming, put on the priest's cloak and presented himself as the priest. He was arrested, scourged, and beheaded. The year was 100, and Alban became the first martyr in Britain. He is patron of refugees.

   Feast Dates: June 20 — St. Alban.

Albano (Spanish) See Alban.

Alben (variant) See Alban.

Alberik (Swedish) See Aubrey.

Albert "The Noble Brilliant One" (Old English).

   Patron Saints: There are at least two dozen Sts. Albert. The best known is

St. Albert the Great, 1206-1280, a scholar who lived in Swabia. He served as a university teacher and his range of knowledge was unequalled. He wrote thirty-eight books covering topics as diverse as Bible study, theology, sermons, and philosophy. At that time, philosophy was considered the best of the disciplines, since it included logic, metaphysics, mathematics, ethics, and physical science. This last included physics, geography, astronomy, mineralogy, alchemy (chemistry), biology, botany, and animal physiology. Through personal observations and logical arguments he refuted much misinformation. He is now a Doctor of the Church and patron of medical technologists, science students, and scientists.

Feast Dates: November 15 — St. Albert the Great, O.P.

Alberto (Portuguese, Spanish, Italian) See Albert.

Albertok (Polish) See Albert.

Albertukas (Latvian) See Albert.

Albie (nickname) See Alban, Albert.

Albinus (Latin) See Alban.

Albrecht (German) See Albert.

Alby (nickname) See Alban.

Alden "The Wise Old Protector" (Old English) or "From the Old Town" (variant of Elton).

Patron Saints: There are several Sts. Aldo and Aldus. One Bl. Aldo was a count of Ostrevent and became the second abbot of a monastery built by his brother.

Feast Dates: May 31 — Bl. Aldo; January 10 — St. Aldous (see Aldous).

Aldin (variant) See Alden.

Aldis (variant) See Aldous.

Aldo (Spanish) See Alden, Aldous.

Aldon (variant) See Elton.

Aldos (variant) See Aldous.

Aldous "The Old Wise One" (Old German) or "From the Old House" (Old English).

Patron Saints: There are a few Sts. Aldo and Aldus. One St. Aldus lived the life of a hermit and gave himself entirely to prayer at Bobbio, Italy, in the 700s.

Feast Dates: January 10 — St. Aldous; May 31 — Bl. Aldo (see Alden).

Aldric (English) See Aldrich.

Aldrich "The Wise Old Ruler" (Old English).

Patron Saints: There are about a half-dozen Sts. Aldrich. St. Aldrich, 800-856, became a priest. Then Emperor Louis the Pious called him to serve in the royal court in Paris as the king's chaplain and confessor. At the age of thirty-two, he was chosen to be the bishop of Le Mans. There he devoted himself completely to helping the poor, providing public services, founding and building churches and monasteries, and promoting true religion. He died at the age of about fifty-six. He is the patron invoked against asthma.

Feast Dates: January 7 — St. Aldrich, also known as Aldric.

Aldridge (variant) See Aldrich.

Aldus (Modern Latin) See Alden, Aldous.

Aldwin (Old English double) See Aldo/Alden+Wynn.

Alec (nickname) See Alexander.

Alejandro (Spanish) See Alexander.

Alek (nickname) See Alexander.

Aleksander (Polish) See Alexander.

Aleksei (Russian) See Alexander.

Alen (variant) See Alan.

Alessandro (Italian) See Alexander.

Alex (nickname) See Alexander.

Alexander "The Helper of Mankind" (Greek).

Patron Saints: There are at least a hundred Sts. Alexander. A colorful one is St. Alexander the Charcoal Burner. He was born of a noble family but renounced his fortune to live life his own way. This resulted in his becoming a charcoal maker, which was a very dirty job. The people dismissed him as ignorant, but he was very pious and often studied his Bible while he worked.

When the local bishop died, St. Gregory the Wonderworker came to town to help elect a new bishop, but no one wanted the job. Eventually someone suggested they give it to Alexander and everyone laughed at the joke except Bishop Gregory. He called for Alexander, examined him, and advised the people to elect him. Alexander served as a wise and holy leader. Eventually he died the death of a martyr in 250 by being burned alive. He is patron of charcoal makers.

Feast Dates: August 11 — St. Alexander the Charcoal Burner.

Alexandr (Russian) See Alexander.

Alexandre (French) See Alexander.

Alexi (nickname) See Alexander.

Alexio (Portuguese) See Alexander.

Alexis (English) See Alexander.

Alf (nickname) See Alfred, Alphonse.

Alfa (Czech) See Alphonse.

Alfie (nickname) See Alfred, Alphonse.

Alfonsin (Spanish) See Alphonse.

Alfonso (Spanish, Italian, Swedish, English) See Alphonse.

Alfonsus (Latin) See Alphonse.

Alfonz (Slovakian) See Alphonse.

Alfonzo (German, English) See Alphonse.

Alfred "The Wise Counselor" (Old English) or "The All-Peaceful One" (Saxon).

Patron Saints: Few saints are named Alfred. One, Bl. Alfred Bessette, 1845-1937, is a Canadian American. Orphaned as the age of twelve, he was raised by relatives. Poor health prevented him from learning how to read until he was an adult. At the age of twenty-five, he became a religious and took the name André. For the next forty years he joyfully did menial tasks for his community.

His love for the Eucharist, his simplicity, his intense love of God, and his ability to speak of it passionately drew people to him, and they helped him to realize his dream of building the Oratory of St. Joseph, a church dedicated to the foster-father of Jesus. It was built on Mount Royale, near Montreal.

Feast Dates: January 6 — Bl. André (also known as Alfred) Bessette.

Alfredas (Lithuanian) See Alfred.

Alfredo (Spanish, Italian) See Alfred.

Alfredos (Greek) See Alfred.

Alfrid (variant) See Alfred.

Alfy (nickname) See Alfred.

Alger (variant) See Algernon.

Algernon "The Bearded One" (Old French) or "The Noble Spearman" (Old German).

Patron Saints: St. Alger was the holy abbot of a seventh-century monastery in France.

Feast Dates: April 11 — St. Alger.

Algie (nickname) See Algernon.

Algy (nickname) See Algernon.

Ali "The Lion of God" (Arabic) or "The Greatest, Highest One" (Arabic, Swahili).

Patron Saints: It helps to know that the name Ali means the "greatest." In Latin the word for this is *maximus*. There are over one hundred twenty-five Sts. Maximus and Maximinus. Because Ali can also mean "lion of God," one is led to St. Ariel. There are also a few Sts. Alipius. They have Ali as part of their names. One of them was a native of Tagaste in Africa and probably a black man. He was also a very close friend of St. Augustine. He even converted to Catholicism with Augustine and then accompanied him to Africa. He helped St. Augustine in all his many labors. Eventually, in 394, he was elected to serve as bishop of Tagaste. He died in 430.

Feast Dates: August 15 — St. Alipius; April 30 — St. Maximus (see Max).

Alic (nickname) See Alexander.

Alick (variant) See Alexander.

Alifonzo (German) See Alphonse.

Alisander (variant) See Alexander.

Alistair (variant) See Alexander.

Alistair (English) See Alexander.

Alister (English, Scottish) See Alexander.

Alix (nickname) See Alexander.

Allan (English) See Alan, Allen.

Allen (English) See Alan, Allan.

Allister (English) See Alexander.

Allistir (variant) See Alexander.

Allie (nickname) See Alan.

Aloin (French) See Alvin.

Alois (Latin) See Aloysius, Louis.

Aloisio (Spanish) See Louis.

Aloisius (Latin) See Aloysius, Louis, Luigi.

Alonso (German, English) See Alphonse.

Alonzo (Spanish) See Alphonse.

Aloys (French) See Aloysius, Louis, Luigi.

Aloysius (Spanish) See Louis, Luigi.

Alphons (German) See Alphonse.

Alphonse "The Noble Ready One" (Latin).

Patron Saints: There are more than a dozen Sts. Alphonse. One was a South American, part of a group of some forty priests and seminarians who sailed for Brazil in 1570. However, soon after leaving port they encountered five ships under the command of Jacques Sourie, a French pirate and former Catholic who was an enemy of the faith. He captured and boarded the priests' vessel and killed all but two priests. One of the executed missionaries was Bl. Alphonsus de Baena.

Feast Dates: July 15 — Bl. Alphonsus de Baena, S.J.

Alphonso (variant) See Alphonse.

Alpo (Finnish) See Albert.

Alroy (Spanish) See Roy.

Alsandair (Irish) See Alexander.

Alton "From the Old+Town" (Old English double) or "The Town+At the Head of the Stream" (Old English double).

Patron Saints: St. Alten McMaolan of Sligo, Ireland, will fill the bill nicely.

Feast Dates: January 11 — St. Alten McMaolan.

Aluin (French) See Alvin.

Aluino (Italian, Spanish) See Alvin.

Alv (nickname) See Alvin.

Alva (Spanish) See Alban.

Alvaro (Spanish) See Justin.

Alvan (English) See Alvin.

Alvertos (Greek) See Albert.

Alvin "The Noble+Friend" (Old English double) or "The Friend of All" (Old German).

Patron Saints: Alvin can be a variant of either Elvis or Alban. It can also serve as a name in its own right. There are a couple of Sts. Alvin (or variants of the name). One was St. Alveus, who was born in Gascogne and lived the life of a hermit near the end of the fifth century. Of course, if there is a connection of Alvin to Alban, then a few Sts. Alban become eligible to serve as patrons.

Feast Dates: September 11 — St. Alvin, also known as Alveus.

Alvino (Italian, Spanish) See Alvin.

Alvis (variant) See Elvis.

Alvy (nickname) See Alvin.

Alwin (German, English) See Alvin.

Alwyn (English) See Alvin.

Alyn (American) See Alan.

Amadee (French) See Amadeo.

Amadeo "The Lover of God" (Italian).

Patron Saints: There are about a half-dozen Sts. Amadeo. One Bl. Amadeus, 1435-1472, was the duke of Savoy. In 1451, at the age of sixteen, he married Yolanthe, the daughter of the king of France and soon succeeded to the kingship. When he began suffering epileptic seizures, he gave up his throne. Then some enemies imprisoned him. Set free a short time later by King Louis XI, his brother-in-law, he lived a life of poor health, dying at the age of thirty-seven.

Feast Dates: March 30 — Bl. Amadeus.

Amadeus (Latin) See Amadeo.

Amado (Spanish) See Amadeo.

Amal (Arabic) See Nathan.

Amalio (Hispanic-American) See Emil, Nathan.

Amand (variant) See Amando.

Amandis (variant) See Amando.

Amando "The One Worthy of Love" (Spanish).

Patron Saints: There are a dozen Sts. Amandus. St. Amand, 584-679, became a monk in France at twenty years of age. His father threatened to disinherit him unless he left the monastery. His cheerful reply to his father was, "Christ is my only inheritance." He was ordained a priest and then lived as a hermit for the next fifteen years.

Then he made a pilgrimage to Rome and was consecrated a missionary bishop. He devoted himself to converting the people who lived around Flanders and in Germany. He was occasionally beaten, but eventually large crowds of people came to him to be baptized. He died when he was about ninety-five. He is patron of brewers, innkeepers, and wine merchants.

Feast Dates: February 2 — St. Amand.

Amandus (Latin) See Amando.

Amar (Arabic) See Omar.

Amato (Spanish) See Amando.

Ambie (nickname) See Ambrose.

Amblaoibh (Irish) See Olaf.

Ambrogio (Italian) See Ambrose.

Ambroise (French) See Ambrose.

Ambros (Irish) See Ambrose.

Ambrose "The Divine Immortal One" (English).

Patron Saints: There are over a dozen Sts. Ambrose. The greatest St. Ambrose, 340-397, was the son of the prefect of Gaul. He studied Greek, poetry, oratory, and law. He pleaded cases before the Roman high court and became governor of Liguria before he was thirty-two years old.

Two years later, when the Arian bishop of Milan died, strife arose and Ambrose found himself keeping the peace. At a meeting held to elect a bishop, he was, much to his surprise, chosen bishop by acclamation. Since he was only a catechumen, he was reluctant to accept the position and tried to escape from Milan but was unsuccessful. He was then baptized, ordained, and consecrated. Dedicating himself to the Church, he proved to be a strong leader. He preached often and made converts, especially St. Augustine. He died at the age of fifty-seven. He is a Doctor of the Church and patron of beekeepers, wax chandlers (makers or sellers of wax), and orators, as well as of learning.

Feast Dates: December 7 — St. Ambrose.

Ambrosi (Italian) See Ambrose.

Ambrosio (Spanish) See Ambrose.

Ambrosius (German, Swedish, Dutch) See Ambrose.

Ambrotos (Greek) See Ambrose.

Ameer (variant) See Emir.

Amelio (Italian) See Emil.

America (Latin) See Emery.

Amerigo (Italian) See Emery.

Amery (variant) See Emery.

Amiah (Hispanic-American) See Amadeo, Amelio.

Amias (variant) See Amadeo.

Amile (Hispanic-American) See Emil.

Amir (variant) See Emir.

Amory (variant) See Emery.

Amos "The Burden Carrier" (Hebrew) or "God Is Just" (Hebrew).

Patron Saints: Christian tradition provides one St. Amo. The Bible speaks of Amos, the Jewish prophet who lived in about 750 B.C. God inspired him to make a trip to the shrine of Bethel in the northern kingdom of Israel and call the king and the people to repent of their sins of idolatry and correct their social injustice. He was the first Jewish prophet to speak of the "Day of the Lord," a time when God would separate the good from the bad. He was ignored and finally driven from the shrine. Returning home, he wrote down his prophecies in the Book of Amos. His enemies eventually murdered him.

Feast Dates: March 31 — St. Amos, Jewish Prophet.

Amyas (variant) See Amadeo.

Amyot (variant) See Amadeo.

Anaclete "The Summoned One" (Spanish).

Patron Saints: There are two Sts. Anacletus. One is a relatively recent Mexican martyr, Anaclete González Flores, 1890-1927, who was born in Tepatitlan, Mexico, of a middle-income family. He formed a lay society to promote Catholic teachings in a weekly Catholic newspaper, in an increasingly anti-Catholic Mexico.

Anaclete was arrested by the Mexican government because he refused to reveal the whereabouts of his archbishop. In jail he was stripped, hung by his thumbs, and whipped. Then his hands and feet were pierced with knives. In the midst of his torture he declared, "I have worked to defend Christ and his Church. You can kill me but you cannot kill the cause." His enemies bayoneted him and then shot him fourteen times. He left a widow and two young sons. He was about thirty-seven years of age.

Feast Dates: September 8 — SG Anaclete González Flores.

Anacletus (Latin) See Anaclete.

Anatole (Slavic) See Essex.

Ancell (variant) See Ansel, Anselm.

Andel (Czech) See Angel.

Ander (nickname) See Andrew, Leander.

Anders (Scandinavian double) See Leander, Andrew+Son.

Anderson "Son of+Manly One" (Middle English double).

Patron Saints: There is an English martyr, Bl. William Richardson, who often used the alias "Anderson" as he served the English Catholic underground at the turn of the seventeenth century. He was ordained a Catholic priest in 1594 and arrested in 1603. He was executed for the faith.

Feast Dates: February 17 — Bl. William Richardson, also known as Anderson.

Andie (nickname) See Andrew.

Andonios (Greek) See Anthony.

Andor (Hungarian) See Andrew.

Andrae (Irish) See Andrew.

André (French) See Andrew.

Andrea (Italian) See Andrew.

Andreas (Greek) See Andrew.

Andrei (Russian, Ukrainian) See Andrew.

Andrej (Slavic) See Andrew.

Andrejc (Slovenian) See Andrew.

Andrejko (Slovakian) See Andrew.

Andrés (Spanish) See Andrew.

Andrew "The Strong, Manly One" (English).

Patron Saints: Two dozen Sts. Andrew can be found. St. Andrew the Apostle is the greatest. Christian tradition testifies that after the resurrection of Jesus, Andrew traveled to Greece and then to the Middle East. There, he was tied to an X-shaped cross from which he preached for two days until he died. Another ancient tradition also insists that he was called upon to review the Gospel of John after it was written. He is considered the patron of Greece, Russia, Scotland, fishermen, sailors, single women, women wishing to conceive, and against gout and neck problems.

Feast Dates: November 30 — St. Andrew, Apostle; January 6 — Bl. André Bessette (see Alfred).

Andrique (Scottish) See Henry.

Andrius (Lithuanian) See Andrew.

Andrzej (Polish) See Andrew.

Andy (nickname) See Andrew, Anderson.

Andzs (Latvian) See Andrew.

Ange (nickname) See Angel.

Angel (variant) See Engelbert.

Angel "The Messenger" (Spanish, Cornish).

Patron Saints: All the angels make fine patrons, but a recent pope also qualifies. He is Bl. John XXIII (Angelo Roncalli), born in 1881 at Sotte il Monte, Italy, and served as apostolic nuncio to France from 1944 to 1953. He was made patriarch of Venice in 1953 and elected pope in 1958. He convened the Second Vatican Council in 1959 and died in 1963. This council ushered in a new era in the history of the Church. In 2000 he was declared "blessed" by Pope John Paul II.

Feast Dates: June 3 — Bl. John XXIII (also known as Angelo Roncalli), Pope; September 29 and October 2 — The Angels of God (see Harper).

Angell (English) See Angel.

Angelo (Italian) See Angel.

Angelyar (Russian) See Angel.

Angie (nickname) See Angel.

Angus "The Unique Choice" (Scottish Gaelic) or "The Uniquely Strong One" (Scottish Gaelic).

Patron Saints: There are at least two ancient Sts. Angus. One of them was the Irish abbot of Cluain-Edneach. Later consecrated a bishop, he compiled the very valuable Irish martyrology called the *Félire of Oengus.* He died in 824. Also, Enos is a variant of Angus, and this leads to a Bible saint, St. Enos.

Feast Dates: March 11 — St. Angus of Keld; March 1 — St. Enos, Patriarch (see Enos).

Angy (nickname) See Angel.

Angyal (Hungarian) See Angel.

Anibal (variant) See Hannibal.

Aniceto (Hispanic-American) See Anaclete.

Aniol (Polish) See Angel.

Anse (variant) See Ansel, Anselm.

Ansel "The Nobleman's Supporter" (Old French) or "The Divine Warrior" (variant form of Anselm).

Patron Saints: There are about a half-dozen Sts. Anselm from which to choose. There is also a St. Ansilio, a monk who lived at the great monastery of St. Pierre-de-Lagny in the 700s.

Feast Dates: October 11 — St. Ansilio; April 21 — St. Anselm of Canterbury (see Anselm).

Ansell (variant) See Ansel, Anselm.

Anselm (variant) See Elmo.

Anselm "The Divine Warrior" (Old German) or "The Divinely Protected One" (Old German).

Patron Saints: There are about a half-dozen Sts. Anselm. One is the great Doctor of the Church, St. Anselm, 1033-1109, born of a noble family in Lombardy. However, his father's harshness drove him from the family home after his mother died. He wandered for three years. Then he became a monk and a priest. At the age of forty-four he became an abbot and then the bishop of Canterbury. A man of great learning, Anselm was constantly involved in disputes. He worked hard to free the Church from the king, which aroused the king's ire, and he eventually went into exile. Returning to Canterbury he died at the age of seventy-six.

Feast Dates: April 21 — St. Anselm of Canterbury.

Anselmo (variant) See Anselm.

Anson "The Awesome One" (Old English) or "The Son+Of the God-Graced One" (Old English double).

Patron Saints: There is one saint who has Anson as part of his name. There are also three male Sts. Anno and about two dozen Sts. Ann who can be pressed into service. And do not forget the martyrs of Ansina.

St. Ansovinus was an Italian bishop who lived in the 800s. He is remembered for working many wonders such as filling a granary during a famine. He is now patron of harvests.

Feast Dates: March 13 — St. Ansovinus.

Antek (Polish) See Anthony.

Anthony "The Priceless One" (English).

Patron Saints: There are about eighty-five Sts. Anthony. One of them, St. Anthony of Padua, 1195-1231, was born in Portugal and baptized Fernando. He became a Franciscan in 1221, at which time he took the name Anthony. Filled with zeal, he traveled to Morocco to make converts but had to abandon his mission because of ill health. Upon returning to Italy he began preaching throughout the country, attracting huge crowds. One fact may help correct a wrong impression about the saints: he reportedly was a heavyset man, which proves saints are just like ordinary people. However, no statues of an overweight St. Anthony exist.

His connection to lost articles was made long after his death. Legend records that a novice had "borrowed" his prayer book without permission. He hastily returned it after having a "fearful apparition." St. Anthony is also recognized as a Doctor of the Church and patron of finding lost articles, of harvests, the poor, spinsters, Portugal, and against infertility.

Feast Dates: June 13 — St. Anthony of Padua.

Antin (variant) See Anthony.

Antjuan (Spanish) See Anthony.

Antoine (French) See Anthony.

Anton (Bulgarian, Czech, German, Norwegian, Romanian, Russian, Serbian, Slovenian, Swedish, Ukrainian) See Anthony.

Antone (French) See Anthony.

Antoni (variant) See Anthony.

Antonio (Spanish, Italian, Portuguese) See Anthony.

Antonius (Latin) See Anthony.

Antony (variant) See Anthony.

Antti (Finnish) See Andrew.

Antwan (Arabic) See Anthony.

Antwon (Arabic) See Anthony.

Anwar (Arabic) See Bert.

Anzhel (nickname) See Angel.

Aodh (Irish) See Hugh.

Aoidh (Scottish) See Hugh.

Apollo "The Manly One" (Greek).

Patron Saints: St. Apollo is mentioned several times in the Epistles. Raised in a Jewish household in Alexandria, he converted to Christianity and preached the Gospel in Greece. He later became the first bishop of Caesarea. Some scholars think he may have written the Letter to the Hebrews.

Feast Dates: December 8 — St. Apollo.

Apollos (variant) See Apollo.

Aquila "The Eagle" (Portuguese, Spanish).

Patron Saints: There are about three dozen Sts. Aquila and Aquilinus. One St. Aquila died a martyr's death in ancient Caesarea.

Feast Dates: April 23 — St. Aquila.

Ar (nickname) See Herman.

Araldo (Italian) See Harold.

Aralt (Irish) See Harold.

Arcángel (Hispanic-American) See Archangel.

Arch (nickname) See Archangel, Archibald.

Archaimbaud (French) See Archibald.

Archambault (French) See Archibald.

Archangel "The Divine Messenger" (Middle English, from the Greek *archangelos*).

Patron Saints: The Bible speaks of three archangels: Sts. Gabriel, Michael, and Raphael. Jewish tradition supplies four more names: Uriel, Raguel, Sereqael, and Haniel.

Feast Dates: September 29 — The Holy Archangels.

Archer (nickname) See Archibald.

Archibald "Very+Bold One" (Anglo-French-German double).

Patron Saints: Archibald is created from a combination of two words: *arch* means "very" or "most" and *bald* means "bold." There are a few ancient saints that bear one or the other of these two names, including Sts. Archus and Baldus. However, there is only one known ancient saint whose name combines both words.

St. Archibald came from the royal family of East Anglia (England) and was the brother of St. Ethelburg for whom he founded a convent. He also built an abbey for himself on an island in the middle of the Thames River, and he became its first abbot. In 675 he became the bishop of London. He was known for his holiness.

Feast Dates: November 14 — St. Archibald.

Archibaldo (Spanish) See Archibald.

Archimbald (German) See Archibald.

Archinold (variant) See Archibald.

Archy (nickname) See Archibald.

Arcy (variant) See Darcy.

Arel (Israeli) See Ariel.

Ari (variant) See Aaron.

Arial (variant) See Ariel.

Aric (German) See Eric.

Ariel "The Lion of God" (Hebrew, Israeli).

Patron Saints: In at least one translation of the Bible, specifically in Isaiah 33:7, the name Ariel refers to "brave men," which is the usual wording in other translations. Ariel is also one of the angels of God. Moreover, there is a holy human being with a similar-sounding name. He is St. Arialdus, a deacon who campaigned against simony. He was excommunicated by the simoniac archbishop of Milan and killed in 1066 by this bishop's henchmen.

Feast Dates: June 27 — St. Arialdus.

Arik (Israeli) See Ariel.

Arlan (variant) See Arlen.

Arlen "The Pledge" (Irish Gaelic) or "The Noble Chief" (variant of Earl).

Patron Saints: A patron can be found by investigating the name's meaning, "pledge." This leads to the French *gage*, and there are three Sts. Gagus. One of them was a black man. He died for the faith in ancient Africa.

Furthermore, if one accepts the popular opinion that Arlen is an Irish form of Earl, then one is led to Sts. Erlafrid and Erlembald. Moreover, saints who have held the royal title of "earl" also qualify.

Feast Dates: June 3 — St. Gagus; November 6 — St. Erlafrid (see Earl).

Arley (variant) See Harley.

Arlin (variant) See Arlen.

Arlo (Spanish) See Arlen.

Arm (nickname) See Herman.

Armand (French) See Herman.

Armando (Latin) See Herman.

Armant (Italian) See Herman.

Armin (Italian) See Herman.

Arminio (Italian) See Herman.

Armondo (Spanish) See Herman.

Arn (nickname) See Aaron, Arnold.

Arnaldo (Italian) See Arnold.

Arnaud (French) See Arnold.

Arne (Czech) See Arnold.

Arnie (nickname) See Aaron, Arnold.

Arnold "The One Strong as an Eagle" (Old German).

Patron Saints: There are about a half-dozen Sts. Arnold. One was of Greek ancestry, but he served in the royal court of Charlemagne. He was an accomplished musician. To reward him, the king gave him the Bürgelwald district of Jülich. Arnold, in turn, gave this land to the citizens in the surrounding villages for the benefit of the poor. He is considered the patron of musicians.

Feast Dates: July 8 — St. Arnold.

Arnoldo (Spanish) See Arnold.

Arnolds (Latvian) See Arnold.

Arnot (Hungarian) See Arnold.

Aron (Romanian) See Aaron.

Arrian (Scandinavian) See Adrian.

Arrigo (Italian) See Harry.

Arronn (Italian) See Aaron.

Arronne (Italian) See Aaron.

Arsenio "The Manly One" (Spanish).

Patron Saints: There are about a dozen Sts. Arsenius. One of them was born of Jewish parents and converted to Catholicism as an adult. He became the archbishop of Corfu and died in Corinth in 959.

Feast Dates: January 19 — St. Arsenio.

Arsenius (Latin) See Arsenio.

Arsinio (variant) See Arsenio.

Art (nickname) See Arthur.

Artair (Scottish Gaelic) See Arthur.

Artek (nickname) See Arthur.

Artemas (English) See Artemus.

Artemius (Latin) See Artemus.

Artemus "The Holy and Agreeable One" (Greek).

Patron Saints: There are about a dozen Sts. Artemius and one St. Artemas. St. Artemas was a disciple of St. Paul in the first century. He became the bishop of Lystra.

Feast Dates: October 30 — St. Artemas.

Arthur "The Noble One" (Welsh) or "The Man Who Is Strong Like a Bear" (Welsh).

Patron Saints: In 1640 the Puritans took control of the English parliament and sought to further reform the Anglican Church along Protestant lines. They were very hostile to the Catholic Church and sought the execution of many priests. It was during this time that Bl. Arthur Bell, 1590-1643, a Franciscan religious, was arrested for being a Catholic priest. He was tried, convicted, and executed in 1643.

Feast Dates: May 4 — Bl. Arthur Bell, O.F.M.

Arthuro (Bulgarian, Czech, German, Hungarian, Swedish, Portuguese) See Arthur.

Artie (nickname) See Arthur.

Artimus (variant) See Artemus.

Artur (Bulgarian, Czech, German, Hungarian, Portuguese, Swedish) See Arthur.

Arturo (Italian, Spanish) See Arthur.

Arturs (Russian) See Arthur.

Artus (French) See Arthur.

Arty (nickname) See Arthur.

Arvin "The Friend of the People" (Old German).

Patron Saints: There is one saint with a similar name. St. Arwan is patron of Montgomery, Wales.

Feast Dates: November 1 — St. Arwan.

Asa "The Physician" (Hebrew) or "The Falcon" (Yoruba African).

Patron Saints: Any Catholic physician, like St. Luke, could qualify as a patron. Moreover, there is a St. Asaph. He built a monastery in the 500s in South Wales. At one time he governed over a thousand monks.

Feast Dates: Sunday After May 1 — St. Asaph.

Asad (Arabic) See Leo.

Ase (variant) See Asa.

Ash (Old English) See Ashley.

Ashford (Old English double) See Ashley+Ford.

Ashleigh (Old English double) See Ashley+Leigh.

Ashley "From the Meadow+Ash Trees" (Old English double).

Patron Saints: Ashley is made from two Old English words, *ash* and *leigh.* The only saint named Ashley is an English martyr. He is Bl. Ralph Ashley, a Jesuit lay brother who acted as a ser-

vant to Father Edward Oldcorne in 1606 when both were convicted of treason. They were hanged, drawn, and quartered.

Feast Dates: April 7 — Bl. Ralph Ashley.

Ashlie (Old English double) See Ashley, Ash+Leigh.

Ashton (Old English double) See Ash+Town.

Asti (Swedish) See Augustine.

Attila "The Little Fatherly One" (Hungarian).

Patron Saints: There is at least one known St. Attila, 939-1009. He was born in Spain and founded a monastery. In 990 he was made bishop of Zamora. In 999, when the people were becoming excited by the popular expectation of the end of the world, he did public penance to help calm them. He also did a lot of preaching. He died at the age of seventy.

Feast Dates: October 5 — St. Attila, also known as Attilanus.

Aube (variant) See Aubrey.

Auberon (variant) See Aubrey.

Aubert (French) See Albert.

Aubin (French) See Alban.

Aubrey "The Elf Ruler" (Old French) or "The Blond Ruler" (Old French).

Patron Saints: There are about a dozen Sts. Alberic. Alberik is the Swedish form of Aubrey. One of these was a bishop of Utrecht in the late 700s. During his rule, all paganism was eradicated from his diocese.

Feast Dates: November 14 — St. Aubrey, also known as Alberic.

Aubrie (variant) See Aubrey.

Aubry (variant) See Aubrey.

Augie (nickname) See Augustine.

August (English) See Augustine.

Auguste (French) See Augustine.

Augustine "The Majestic Revered One" (English).

Patron Saints: The greatest of about a dozen Sts. Augustine is St. Augustine of Hippo, 354-430. Born in North Africa of a pagan Roman official and a Christian mother (St. Monica), he was probably a black man. He was taught Christian beliefs and had all the advantages of his upper class. However, he developed an interest in philosophy and Manichaean heresy, lived with his girlfriend, and fathered a child outside marriage.

Then he became interested in the sermons of St. Ambrose, whose influence, coupled with his mother's prayers, convinced him to embrace Christianity. Late in 387 he traveled back to Carthage in Africa, but his mother died on the way. Then he was elected bishop of Hippo and became the guiding light of northern Africa, writing book after book, refuting heresies. His thinking dominated Western Christian thought for almost a thousand years. He died at the age of seventy-six years and is regarded as a Doctor of the Church and patron of brewers, printers, and theologians.

Feast Dates: August 28 — St. Augustine of Hippo.

Augustus (Latin) See Augustine.

Augustyn (Polish) See Augustine.

Austen (English) See Augustine.

Austin (English) See Augustine.

Ave (nickname) See Avery.

Avellino (Hispanic-American double) See Evelino/Ave+Linus.

Averell (English) See Avery.

Averil (variant) See Avery.

Averill (French) See Avery.

Avery "The Elf Ruler" (Old English) or "From the Bird Display" (Middle English).

Patron Saints: Some think Avery is an alternate form of Everard, April, or Alfred, or that it can be a name in its own right. This leads to a variety of patrons.

One was St. Avery, a monk who lived in about 1000. He founded his own monastery in Bath, England. Later he became bishop of Canterbury and was taken hostage by the pagan Danes. However, he refused to allow a ransom to be collected from his diocese in spite of torture and imprisonment. The pagans eventually killed him with a battle-axe.

Feast Dates: April 19 — St. Avery, also known as Aelfeach; January 6 — Bl. André (see Alfred).

Avie (nickname) See Avery.

Avner (Hebrew) See Abner.

Avram (Hebrew) See Abraham, Abram.

Ax (nickname) See Axel.

Axe (nickname) See Axel.

Axel "Father of Peace" (Old German, Dutch form of Absalom).

Patron Saints: Christian tradition provides us with one St. Absalom and one St. Absalema. St. Absalom was a friend of St. Lucius, the bishop of Caesarea in Roman times. He died a martyr for the faith.

Feast Dates: March 22 — St. Absalom, also known as Axel.

Axl (variant) See Axel.

Axsel (variant) See Axel.

Aylmar (Latvian) See Elmer.

Aylmer (Latvian) See Elmer.

Aylwin (variant) See Alvin.

Aymer (Latvian) See Elmer.

Ayyoob (Arabic) See Job.

Aziz (Arabic) See Strong.

𝓑

Backstere (English) See Baxter.

Bail (variant) See Valle.

Bailey "From the Wood Clearing Where Berries Grow" (Old English) or "The Porter" (Old English) or "From Outside the Castle Wall" (Middle English) or "The Bailiff" (Old English).

Patron Saints: There is one St. Balay, who was a hermit at Ploermellac in Brittany in ancient times. Also knowing that *bailey* means "bailiff" in Old English leads to two more patrons. They are St. Catherine of Alexandria and St. Ives, both patrons of court personnel. And finally there is one North American who qualifies as a patron: St. Elizabeth Bayley Seton.

Feast Dates: July 12 — St. Balay; May 13 — St. Ivo Helory (see Yves).

Baillie (variant) See Bailey.

Baily (variant) See Bailey.

Baird "The Ballad Singer" (Irish Gaelic) or "The Poet" (Irish Gaelic).

Patron Saints: St. Coleman of Cloyne, a royal bard, lived in Munster, Ireland, in the 500s. He is called the "Sun-Bright Bard" because he had great poetic skill. In time, he became the royal bard of Cashel.

However, he did not embrace Christianity until he was about fifty years old. It seems that while St. Brendan was at Cashel the holy bones of St. Ailbhe were found, and Brendan would not allow them to be touched by non-Catholics. Coleman wanted to touch them. Thus he converted.

Another possible patron is St. Julian the Hospitaler, who is patron of traveling minstrels (or bards).

Feast Dates: November 24 — St. Coleman of Cloyne.

Baker (English) See Baxter.

Balay (variant) See Bailey.

Bald (nickname) See Baldwin.

Baldassare (Italian) See Balthasar.

Baldovino (Italian, Spanish) See Baldwin.

Balduin (German, Swedish, Danish) See Baldwin.

Baldwin "The Bold Friend" (Old German).

Patron Saints: There are a half-dozen Sts. Baldwin. One of them was an archdeacon who lived in about 600. He opposed some powerful religious leaders in his diocese on the issue of selling spiritual blessings. Thus he became the object of intense hatred. Eventually he was murdered by them.

Feast Dates: October 16 — St. Baldwin.

Bale (variant) See Valle.

Balta (Spanish) See Bartholomew.

Baltasar (German, Swedish) See Balthasar.

Balthasar "May the Lord Protect the King" (Greek, French).

Patron Saints: Balthasar was one of the three magi who brought gifts to the infant Jesus. After Jesus rose from the dead, Balthasar became a Christian bishop and converted his homeland.

Feast Dates: January 6 — St. Balthasar.

Balto (Scottish) See Walter.

Bar (nickname) See Baird, Barclay, Barlow, Barnum, Barret, Baruch.

Bar (Hebrew prefix meaning "Son of") See Bartholomew.

Barclay "From Birch Tree+Meadow" (Old English double).

Patron Saints: The last part of the name, *lay* (or *ley*, also *leigh*), means "meadow," and this leads to one patron.

Feast Dates: August 30 — Bl. Richard Leigh (see Leigh).

Barcley (English) See Barclay.

Bard (variant) See Baird, Barden, Barlow.

Barde (variant) See Baird, Barlow.

Barden "From the Barley+Valley" (Old English double).

Patron Saints: This name arises from two words: *bar*, meaning "barley," and *den*, meaning "valley." This leads to two patrons. St. Bardo was an abbot and then the archbishop of Mayence.

Feast Dates: June 10 — St. Bardo; August 28 — Bl. William Dean (see Dean).

Bardon (English) See Barden.

Barlow "From the Bare+Hill" (Old English double) or "From the Boar's+Hill" (Old English double).

Patron Saints: There is one English martyr with this name. St. Edward Barlow was baptized Catholic but raised Protestant. As an adult, he went to Douai in France to study for the Catholic priesthood. Then he became a Benedictine monk and was granted permission to go to the English missions. During the next twenty-four years he was arrested, imprisoned, and released four different times. The fifth time, in 1641, he was executed.

Feast Dates: September 10 — St. Edward Barlow, O.S.B.

Barn (nickname) See Barnett, Barney, Barnabas, Bernard.

Barna (Italian) See Barney, Barnabas.

Barnaba (Italian) See Barney, Barnabas.

Barnabas "Son of+Prophecy" (Hebrew-Greek double) or "Son of Consolation" (Hebrew-Greek double).

Patron Saints: Of the half-dozen Sts. Barnabas, the best known is St. Barnabas the Apostle. He was a Jew of the tribe of Levi, originally named Joseph, but the Apostles changed his name to Barnabas, which they interpreted to mean, "Man of Encouragement."

While not one of the original twelve Apostles, he is always called an "Apostle" because of the special call he received, with St. Paul, to deliver the decision of the Apostles at the Council of Jerusalem to the Gentile Christians. Barnabas shared much of Paul's ministry. He preached in Greece, Turkey, Rome, and Alexandria. And he may have written the Epistle to the Hebrews.

He was stoned to death sometime before the year 60. He is patron of weavers, harvests, and of Cyprus.

Feast Dates: June 11 — St. Barnabas, Apostle.

Barnabe (French) See Barnabas, Barney.

Barnaby (English) See Barnabas, Barney.

Barnard (French) See Bernard.

Barnebas (Spanish) See Barnabas, Barney.

Barnett "The Little+Nobleman" (Old English double).

Patron Saints: This name arises from the title Baron plus Ett. Any saint holding this title can serve as patron. Also, there are a few saints with very similar names: Sts. Barran, Barrin, and Barontius.

St. Barontius was a nobleman who left the royal court of King Thierry II and became a religious monk. It seems that a vision of heaven and hell was granted to him by God. This helped him decide to devote himself to a life of solitude. He died in 720.

Feast Dates: March 25 — St. Barontius.

Barney "The Son of Prophecy [Consolation]" (nickname for Barnabas) or "The

Nobleman" (nickname for Barnett) or "The One Brave as a Bear" (nickname for Bernard) or "From the Bear Town" (nickname for Barnum).

Patron Saints: Barney can serve as a nickname for Barnabas, Bernard, Barnett, and Barnum. There is one North American, Ven. Solanus Casey, 1870-1957, who can serve as a patron.

Ven. Solanus was one of sixteen children born in Wisconsin to Irish immigrant farmers. He helped support the family by working at various trades, including those of a handyman, a prison guard, a brickmaker, and a streetcar motorman. He even proposed marriage to a girlfriend but was opposed by her mother.

Then he entered the diocesan seminary but was asked to leave because of low grades. He was eventually accepted by the Capuchin seminary in Detroit and took the name Solanus. He struggled through his studies and was ordained in 1904 at the age of thirty-three, but because of his mediocre grades he was not allowed to preach or hear confessions. This positioned him for his life's work. Being a doorkeeper, he came into contact with all kinds of sick, poor, and troubled people. Soon he was ministering and praying for them and miracles were happening. He served in Wisconsin, New York, Michigan, and Indiana.

Feast Dates: January 6 — Ven. Solanus Casey, also known as Bernard "Barney" Casey, O.F.M. Cap.

Barnie (nickname) See Barney.

Barnum "From the Bear Town" (Swiss) or "From the Town+In the Woods" (Old English double).

Patron Saints: Barnum means about the same thing as Bernard, and there are three dozen Sts. Bernard.

Feast Dates: August 20 — St. Bernard (see Bernard).

Barny (nickname) See Barnabas, Barnett, Barney, Barnum, Bernard.

Baron (variant) See Barnett.

Barr (variant) See Baird, Barlow.

Barret "The One Mighty as a Bear" (Old German).

Patron Saints: Patrons are available because Barret means the same thing as Bernard.

Feast Dates: August 20 — St. Bernard (see Bernard).

Barrett (English) See Barret.

Barri (English) See Barry.

Barrie (English) See Barry.

Barris (English) See Barry.

Barron (variant) See Barnett.

Barry "Like a Pointed Spear" (Irish Gaelic) or "From the Barrier [Farm]" (Old French).

Patron Saints: Barry can be a nickname for Barnett and Baruch and as a full name in its own right. There are four Sts. Barry (also known as Finbar). The most famous was originally named Loan, but his teacher changed his name to Finbar, which means "shining hair." A native of Connaught, Ireland, and the illegitimate son of a metalworker and a royal lady, he became a priest, made a pilgrimage to Rome, founded a monastery, and built many churches in Ireland. He is also remembered for the many miracles he performed. It seems that he was notified of his elevation to bishop just before he died in 623. Pious legend insists that he was consecrated, not by an earthly bishop, but by Jesus himself. He is patron of Cork.

Feast Dates: September 25 — St. Barry, also known as Finbar.

Bart (nickname) See Bartholomew, Barton, Bartram.

Bartal (Hungarian) See Bartholomew.

Bartel (nickname) See Bartholomew.

Barth (nickname) See Bartholomew.

Barthel (German) See Bartholomew.

Barthelemy (French) See Bartholomew.

Bartholomaus (German) See Bartholomew.

Bartholome (French) See Bartholomew.

Bartholomew "Son of+The Farmer" (Greek-Hebrew double).

Patron Saints: Of the two dozen Sts. Bartholomew, the greatest is the Apostle. Many scholars point out that Bartholomew was not a proper name in Jesus' time. The Apostle's real name was probably Nathanael. His nickname was Bartholomew, that is, "Son of Talmei" or "Son of the Farmer."

The Bible tells us he was introduced to Jesus by Philip, an old friend. This teaches us that often Jesus does not call us directly, but rather through others in our lives. Christian tradition adds that Bartholomew preached the Gospel throughout the Middle East and provided his converts with a copy of the Gospel of Matthew. He was killed by King Astarges of Armenia because he had converted the king's brother. He is patron of Armenia, of cheesemakers, tanners, and plasterers, and against nervous tics.

Feast Dates: August 24 — St. Bartholomew, Apostle.

Bartie (nickname) See Bartholomew, Barton.

Bartley (Old English double) See Barden+Lee/Leigh.

Barto (Spanish) See Bartholomew.

Barto (variant) See Walter.

Bartoli (Spanish) See Bartholomew.

Bartollo (Italian) See Bartholomew.

Bartolo (Italian, Spanish) See Bartholomew.

Bartolomé (Spanish) See Bartholomew.

Bartolomeij (Czech) See Bartholomew.

Bartolomeo (Italian) See Bartholomew.

Bartolomeu (Portuguese) See Bartholomew.

Bartolomeus (Swedish, Dutch) See Bartholomew.

Barton "From the Barley+Town" (Old English double) or "He Owns the Farmstead" (Old English).

Patron Saints: There is one English martyr who can serve as patron.

Feast Dates: October 1 — Bl. Ralph Crockett of Barton-on-the-Hill (see Crockett).

Bartos (Czech) See Bartholomew.

Bartram (English) See Bertram.

Barty (nickname) See Bartholomew, Barton.

Baruch "The Blessed One" (Hebrew).

Patron Saints: The Latin for "the blessed one" is *beatus*, and Christian tradition gives a half-dozen Sts. Beatus. The name Benedict also means "blessed one." And there are two dozen Sts. Benedict. Finally, the Bible presents one Old Testament saint named Baruch. St. Baruch was a secretary of St. Jeremiah and he recorded what Jeremiah taught the people. Jewish tradition testifies that after Jerusalem fell, he went with Jeremiah into exile in Egypt. After Jeremiah was murdered, Baruch moved to Babylon in about 600 B.C. Some say that he returned to Jerusalem in 538 B.C., just before he died.

Feast Dates: September 28 — St. Baruch, Jewish Prophet; April 16 — St. Benedict Labre (see Benedict).

Bary (English) See Barry.

Bas (nickname) See Basil.

Base (nickname) See Basil.

Basil "The Kingly One" (Latin, English) or "The Magnificent One" (Latin, English).

Patron Saints: There are about three dozen Sts. Basil. This St. Basil, 329-

379, was born into a family of saints. His parents, grandmother, and three of his nine siblings have also been declared "saints."

Beginning at the age of eighteen he studied monasticism, spoke out against the Arian heresy, was ordained a priest, and gave his inheritance to the poor. From the age of thirty-seven onward he was elected archbishop, composed a liturgy, founded a hospital, wrote commentaries on the Bible, and insisted that the phrase "consubstantial with the Father" be added to the Nicene Creed. He worked to unite his fellow bishops and was one of the finest orators to have ever served the Church. He died at Caesarea at the age of fifty. He is recognized as a Doctor of the Church and patron of hospital administrators and of Russia.

Feast Dates: January 2 — St. Basil the Great.

Basile (French) See Basil.

Basileus (Dutch) See Basil.

Basilio (Spanish, Portuguese, Italian) See Basil.

Basilius (Swedish) See Basil.

Baste (Scandinavian) See Sebastian.

Bastian (variant) See Sebastian.

Bastien (French) See Sebastian.

Basto (Italian) See Sebastian.

Bat (nickname) See Bartholomew.

Baudelio (Spanish) See Baldwin.

Baudoin (French) See Baldwin.

Bax (nickname) See Baxter.

Baxie (nickname) See Baxter.

Baxter "The Baker of Bread" (Old English).

Patron Saints: The word *baxter* means "baker," and two saints have been appointed patrons of bakers. They are Sts. Elizabeth of Hungary and Nicholas of Myra. There is also an English martyr named Baker. Bl.

Charles Lewis, 1616-1679, often used the alias of "Charles Baker" when he ministered in the English Catholic underground. As an adult he converted to Catholicism, went to Rome, and became a Jesuit priest. Then he worked in Wales for thirty-one years. He was executed for being a Catholic priest.

Feast Dates: August 27 — Bl. Charles Lewis, also known as Charles Baker.

Baxy (nickname) See Baxter.

Bayley (variant) See Bailey.

Bazyli (Polish) See Basil.

Baz (nickname) See Basil.

Beach (nickname) See Beacher.

Beacher "The One+Lives by Beech Trees" (Old English double).

Patron Saints: Perhaps the closest name to this is Beccan, a name claimed by about a half-dozen saints. One of them was a blind holy man who lived in Dublin in medieval Ireland.

Feast Dates: February 26 — St. Beccan.

Beachy (nickname) See Beacher.

Beal (English) See Beauregard.

Beale (English) See Beauregard.

Bealle (English) See Beauregard.

Bear (nickname) See Bernard, Barret, Barnum, Orson.

Bearnard (Scottish) See Bernard.

Beathan (Scottish) See Benjamin.

Beau (nickname) See Beauregard.

Beaufort (English) See Beauregard.

Beauregard "The Handsome One" (French) or "The Beautiful Expression" (French).

Patron Saints: A number of patrons can be adopted. The little town of Beauvais, France, honors its patrons on January 15. Sts. Kenneth and Kyle, whose names mean "handsome one," can be pressed into service. Finally, there is one English martyr, St. Robert

Lawrence of Beauvale. Beauvale means "beautiful valley." Father Lawrence was the prior of the Carthusian charterhouse (monastery) when King Henry VIII began his persecution of the Catholic Church. He was part of the first group of martyrs to die for the Catholic faith in England in 1535.

Feast Dates: May 4 — St. Robert Lawrence of Beauvale; October 11 — St. Kenneth (see Kenneth).

Beauvais (French) See Bevis.

Bechtel (German) See Albert, Bertram.

Bede "The One Who Prays" (Middle English).

Patron Saints: The most famous is St. Bede the Venerable, O.S.B., a priest-scholar who lived in England from 673 to 735. Given into the care of the monks at a local abbey as a child, he stayed there his whole life, praying, writing, studying, reading, and teaching. One of his great works, *The Ecclesiastical History of the English People,* has earned for him the title of "Father of English History." He is now recognized as a Doctor of the Church.

Feast Dates: May 25 — St. Bede the Venerable.

Beech (nickname) See Beacher.

Beecher (English) See Beacher.

Beechy (nickname) See Beacher.

Beed (English) See Bede.

Beede (English) See Bede.

Bela (Hungarian) See Bert.

Belshazzar (Hebrew) See Balthasar.

Beltran (Spanish) See Bertram.

Ben (nickname) See Benedict, Benjamin, Benson, Bentley, Benton, Bernard.

Bendek (Polish) See Benedict.

Bendix (English) See Benedict.

Benedetto (Italian) See Benedict.

Benedick (English) See Benedict.

Benedict "The Blessed One" (Latin).

Patron Saints: There are about two dozen Sts. Benedict. A little-known one

is St. Benedict Labre, 1748-1783. He realized that serving God meant abandoning worldly goods. He sought entry into the Carthusian Order but was denied. Later, when accepted by the Cistericans, his health failed and he began making pilgrimages to the great shrines, walking and begging all the way. His twenty-sixth year found him living in the ruins of the Colosseum in Rome. People began to recognize that God worked miracles through him. Even as he got sicker, he still gave his food away to those he thought were more hungry than he was. He begged for others, even the children that taunted him. He died at thirty-five years of age and is considered the patron of beggars and of the homeless.

Feast Dates: April 16 — St. Benedict Labre.

Benedicto (Spanish) See Benedict.

Benedikt (Bulgarian, Czech, German) See Benedict.

Benediktas (Latvian) See Benedict.

Bengt (Swedish) See Benedict.

Beni (Spanish) See Benedict.

Beniamin (Polish) See Benjamin.

Beniamino (Italian) See Benjamin.

Beniek (Polish) See Benjamin.

Benitín (Spanish) See Benedict.

Benito (Italian, Spanish) See Benedict.

Benja (Spanish) See Benjamin.

Benjamin "The Son of the Right Hand" (Hebrew, French).

Patron Saints: There are about a dozen Sts. Benjamin. In the 400s a Persian bishop burned down the Temple of Fire, which was the chief place of pagan worship. This led to a forty-year persecution of Christians.

The most famous martyr of this persecution was a deacon named Benjamin, who was arrested, beaten, and imprisoned for a year. When the ambassador from the Christian emperor in Constantinople secured his release, promising that he would not preach his religion, Benjamin still preached. The king ordered that reeds be shoved under Benjamin's fingernails and be stuck in all the tender parts of his body. After undergoing this torture, Benjamin was impaled upon a stake, dying a slow and agonizing death in 421.

Feast Dates: March 31 — St. Benjamin.

Benjaminas (Lithuanian) See Benjamin.

Benjy (nickname) See Benjamin.

Benn (English) See Benedict, Benjamin, Benson, Bentley, Benton, Bernard.

Bennet (English) See Benedict.

Bennie (nickname) See Benn.

Benny (nickname) See Benn.

Benoît (French) See Benedict.

Benson (double) See Benedict/Benjamin+ Son.

Bent "From the Place of Bent Grass" (Old English).

Patron Saints: The original spelling of Bent is Beonet. St. Beoan was a single woman dedicated to God in medieval Ireland.

Feast Dates: February 1 — St. Bent, also known as Beoan.

Bentlee (Old English double) See Bent+ Lee/Leigh.

Bentley (Old English double) See Bent+ Lee/Leigh.

Benton (Old English double) See Bent+ Town.

Beppe (Italian) See Joseph.

Berg (German) See Bergen.

Bergen "The Mountain Dweller" (Scandinavian).

Patron Saints: St. Begga, the grandmother of Bl. Charlemagne, can be adopted. After the death of her husband, she founded a nunnery and became its abbess.

Feast Dates: December 17 — St. Begga.

Bergin (Scandinavian) See Bergen.

Bergren (Scandinavian) See Bergen.

Berk (variant) See Barclay, Burke.

Berke (English) See Burke.

Berkeley (variant) See Barclay.

Berkey (variant) See Barclay, Burke.

Berkley (variant) See Barclay.

Berky (variant) See Barclay, Burke.

Bern (nickname) See Bernard.

Bernabé (Spanish) See Barney, Barnabas.

Bernadel (Spanish) See Bernard.

Bernal (French) See Bernard.

Bernaldino (French) See Bernard.

Bernard "Brave as a Bear" (Old German).

Patron Saints: There are about three dozen Sts. Bernard from which to choose. St. Bernard of Clairvaux was born in a castle near Dijon, France. He had all the advantages that the world of the rich could provide, but all this gradually lost its appeal. At twenty-two years of age, he decided to become a Trappist.

Three years later his abbot ordered him to found a new monastery, the first of many. He became famous for his holiness and the miracles that occurred through his prayers. In time, his advice was sought by most of the leaders of Europe. He was a respected, moving force in Europe for forty years. He died at the age of sixty-three. He is recognized as a Doctor of the Church and patron of bees, beekeepers, wax chandlers (makers or sellers of wax), and candlemakers as well as patron of Gibraltar.

Feast Dates: August 20 — St. Bernard of Clairvaux.

Bernardin (French) See Bernard.

Bernardino (Italian, Spanish, Portuguese) See Bernard.

Bernardo (Italian, Spanish, Hungarian) See Bernard.

Bernarr (variant) See Bernard.

Bernat (Hungarian) See Bernard.

Berne (nickname) See Bernard.

Bernhard (German, Swedish) See Bernard.

Bernie (nickname) See Bernard.

Berny (nickname) See Bernard.

Bert "Bright, Shining One" (Old English variant of Burt).

Patron Saints: There is a St. Bert. He died a martyr's death in the Crimea in medieval times.

Furthermore, there are many names that have Bert (or a variation of it) as part of their names. Among them are Adelbert, Albert, Berthold, Bertram, Bertrand, Burt, Cuthbert, Delbert, Egbert, Engelbert, Filbert, Gilbert, Herbert, Hobart, and Philbert.

Feast Dates: March 26 — St. Bert, also known as Bertus; October 6 — St. Burt (see Burt).

Bertalan (Hungarian) See Bartholomew.

Berthold "The Brilliant Ruler" (Old German).

Patron Saints: There are a half-dozen Sts. Berthold, one of them being St. Berthold of Limoges, who studied theology in Paris, was ordained a priest, and went with the Crusaders on a campaign to the Middle East. In Antioch it was revealed to him that a siege was taking place because of the sins of the Christian soldiers. He immediately offered himself as a sacrifice for those sins and he promised that if the town was delivered he would devote the rest of his life to the service of the Blessed Virgin.

Jesus accepted his offering and Berthold called all to repentance. Some time later he formed a community of hermits. He died in 1195.

Feast Dates: March 29 — St. Berthold of Limoges.

Berthoud (French) See Berthold.

Bertie (nickname) See Bert.

Bertin (Spanish) See Bert.

Berto (Spanish) See Bert.

Bertold (English) See Berthold.

Bertoldi (Italian) See Berthold.

Bertoldo (Spanish) See Berthold.

Berton (variant) See Bertrand, Burton.

Bertram (English) See Bertrand.

Bertrand "The Brilliant Raven" (Old English) or "He Shall be Famous" (Old English).

Patron Saints: There are a half-dozen Sts. Bertrand. One St. Bertrand is simply remembered as the holy abbot of a Cistercian monastery in Toulouse in the 1100s.

Feast Dates: July 11 — St. Bertrand.

Bertrando (Italian) See Bertrand.

Bertrao (Portuguese) See Bertrand.

Berty (nickname) See Bert.

Beto (nickname) See Albert, Robert.

Betto (nickname) See Benedict.

Bevis "The Fair View" (Old French).

Patron Saints: Bevis finds its root in the French name Beauvais. One patron is available.

Feast Dates: May 4 — St. Robert Lawrence of Beauvale (see Beauregard).

Bhaltair (Scottish) See Walter.

Biagio (Italian) See Blaise.

Biartlaidh (Irish) See Bartholomew.

Bictar (Spanish variant) See Victor.

Bili (nickname) See William.

Bill (nickname) See William.

Billie (nickname) See William.

Billy (nickname) See William.

Bing "From Kettle-Shaped Hollow" (Old German) or "From the Grain Bin" (Dutch).

Patron Saints: A hollow is a "valley," and there are some saints whose names mean "valley."

Feast Dates: August 28 — Bl. William Dean (see Dean); May 21 — St. Vales (see Valle).

Bingham "From the Home+In the Valley" (English double) or "From the Grain Bin+In the Town" (Old English double).

Patron Saints: The word *bing* means "valley" and *ham* means "home." At least one saint can serve as patron.

Feast Dates: August 28 — Bl. William Dean (see Dean); April 30 — St. Hamo (see Hamilton).

Bink "The Dweller at the Slope" (English) or "The Victor" (variant of Vincent).

Patron Saints: St. Bina was executed in Egypt during the persecution of Emperor Diocletian.

Feast Dates: December 3 — St. Bina.

Binyamin (Hebrew) See Benjamin.

Birdie (nickname) See Bernard, Byrdie.

Birney "From the Hazelnut Trees" (Old English).

Patron Saints: The original English spelling for hazelnut is *brenuth*. This leads to a St. Brenach. He was a Celt layman who settled in Wales in the 400s and built a church.

Feast Dates: April 7 — St. Brenach.

Birnie (variant) See Birney.

Biron (variant) See Byron.

Bish (nickname) See Bishop.

Bishop "The One Who Oversees" (Old English).

Patron Saints: St. Toribio Alfonso de Mogrovejo, 1538-1606, a South American bishop-saint, has been named patron of bishops. Also known as St. Turibius of Lima, he is credited, according to one source, with conferring the sacrament of confirmation on St. Rose of Lima.

Peru was in a mess, due mostly to the excesses of the *conquistadores*. The Church's answer was to ordain and consecrate St. Turibius, a middle-aged layman who was chief judge of the Inquisition at Granada, Spain, and send him to Lima, Peru. Arriving in Peru, he was faced with eighteen thousand square miles of jungle and mountains, greedy Spanish landlords, murdering Spanish soldiers, and countless pagans. He learned the language of the Indians, baptized some half-million individuals, and put reins on the Spanish. He visited his parishes, opened seminaries, and had hospices built. Often when he enforced a reform, he would be met with, "But that is not our custom." And Turibius would reply, "Jesus did not say, 'I am the custom.' He said, 'I am the way.'" After twenty-five years of labor, Turibius died at the age of sixty-eight.

Feast Dates: March 23 — St. Turibius of Lima.

Bjarne (Danish, Norwegian) See Bernard.

Bjorn (Old Norse) See Bernard.

Bjorne (Swedish) See Bernard.

Blaan (English) See Blaine.

Black (English) See Blackie.

Blackie "The Black One" (Middle English).

Patron Saints: St. Moses the Black was a black Abyssinian slave with a vicious temperament. He soon became the leader of a group of robbers. Becoming a fugitive, he lived in hiding with the Christian hermits of Skete. In time, he was converted to the faith by them and became a priest. Before long he became known for his miracles. He was murdered by a Bedouin against whom he refused to defend himself.

Feast Dates: August 28 — St. Moses the Black; April 4 — St. Benedict the Black (see Jett).

Blade "The Prosperous and Glorified One" (Old English) or "The Knife Edge" (Middle English).

Patron Saints: St. Maurice, patron of knife sharpeners, can be adopted.

More appropriate is St. Blade, who was an early bishop on the Isle of Man.

Feast Dates: July 3 — St. Blade, also known as Bladus; September 22 — St. Maurice (see Maurice).

Blaine "The Thin One" (Irish Gaelic) or "The Yellow One" (Scottish Gaelic).

Patron Saints: There is a St. Blane, who can be recruited as patron. He was a missionary bishop in Scotland who died in 590. A missionary monk, he eventually became a bishop. He is remembered for the gift of miracles.

Feast Dates: August 10 — St. Blaine.

Blair (English) See Blaire.

Blaire "From the Plain [Battlefield]" (Scottish Gaelic).

Patron Saints: A great patron can be found by making a Bible connection. *Blaire* is Scottish for "plain." And the Hebrew word for it in the Bible is *sharon*. This refers to a great plain in Israel along the Mediterranean coast between Mount Carmel on the north and Joppa on the south (about forty-five miles long by twelve miles wide). It is considered a fertile place for farming and pasture.

The Song of Songs speaks of a "flower" or "rose" of Sharon, which is similar to the hibiscus. Because the "garden of flowers" is a poetic way for God to speak about his beloved, the "flower of Sharon" (defined as the "lily of the valley") becomes a symbol of God's spouse, the Blessed Virgin, at her finest and purest.

Feast Dates: Month of May — The Blessed Virgin Mary, Rose of Sharon.

Blaise "The Stammerer" (French).

Patron Saints: There are about a half-dozen saints named Blaise. The most famous is St. Blaise, in whose name throats are blessed every February 3. There is also a North American saint-in-the-making named Blas de Rodríguez, O.F.M. In 1595 several missions were opened in Florida as well as in Georgia among the Guale Indians, and for two years converts were made and the missions flourished. Then in 1597 Father Pedro de Corpa reprimanded a local chief because he had violated the laws on Christian marriage. The chief gathered a force of pagan Indians with the explicit intent of wiping out Catholicism and restoring paganism. They killed Father de Corpa in St. Augustine, Florida.

Then they went to Tupique, in what is now Georgia, and told Father Blas de Rodríguez that he had to die. He persuaded them to allow him to offer Mass first. After Mass he was made a prisoner for two days and then was killed with a hatchet blow as he knelt in the mission church. In all, four priests and one religious brother were murdered and four missions were closed.

Feast Dates: February 3 — St. Blaise, Bishop and Martyr; September 13 — SG Blas de Rodríguez and the Georgia Martyrs.

Blake "The Fair-Complected, Fair-Haired One" (Old English) or "The Pale [Black] One" (Old English).

Patron Saints: There is one saint surnamed Blake. He lived in England during the two-hundred-year English persecution of Catholics. During this time it was treason, punishable by death, to be a Catholic priest, to house a Catholic priest, to attend Catholic Mass, or to celebrate the sacraments. Bl. Alexander Blake, a layman, was arrested for giving shelter to a Catholic priest. He was tried, convicted, and executed in 1590.

Feast Dates: May 4 — Bl. Alexander Blake.

Blakey (nickname) See Blake.

Blane (English) See Blaine.

Blar (English) See Blaire.

Blas (Spanish) See Blaise.

Blase (English) See Blaise.

Blasien (German) See Blaise.

Blasius (Swedish) See Blaise.

Blayne (English) See Blaine.

Blayze (English) See Blaise.

Blaze (English) See Blaise.

Blu (English) See Blue.

Blue "The Blue One" (Middle English).

Patron Saints: There is one saint from ancient times, St. Blua, who is simply remembered as a "Coptic saint." Another possible patron would be the Blessed Virgin Mary, who is traditionally identified in Christian art by her blue veil. Blue used as a color in various holy articles signifies protection from evil.

Feast Dates: October 13 — St. Blua.

Bo (nickname) See Beauregard.

Bob (nickname) See Robert.

Boba (nickname) See Boris.

Bobbie (nickname) See Robert.

Bobby (nickname) See Robert.

Bodog (Hungarian) See Felix.

Bogart "The Strong-Bow One" (Old German).

Patron Saints: St. Bogoria, the duke of Rosstow, was the son of St. Vladimir the Great, of Russia, in about 1000. He worked hard to convert his people to Catholicism. His brother murdered him.

Feast Dates: July 24 — St. Bogoria.

Bonaventure "The Good Fortune" (Old German).

Patron Saints: St. Bonaventure, 1221-1274, was baptized John. St. Francis of Assisi gave him the name *bonaventura* when he cured the little boy. As an adult, he became a Franciscan and was one of the most learned men of his time. He is now recognized as a Doctor of the Church.

Feast Dates: July 15 — St. Bonaventure.

Bond "The Tiller of the Soil" (English, Icelandic).

Patron Saints: The word *bond* means "tiller of the soil" or "farmer," and the Catholic Church has named four saints patrons of farmers: Sts. Isidore, George, Sidwell, and Walstan.

There is also one ancient saint named St. Bond (also known as Baldus). He grew up in Spain and married. He accidentally killed his parents. In repentance, he made a pilgrimage to Jerusalem and embraced a life of great personal sacrifice and self-discipline. He died in 604.

Feast Dates: October 29 — St. Bond; April 23 — St. George (see George).

Bondie (nickname) See Bond.

Bondon (nickname) See Bond.

Bondy (nickname) See Bond.

Bone (nickname) See Boone.

Bonfilo (Spanish double) See Boone+Filius.

Boniface "The Good Friend" (Old German).

Patron Saints: St. Boniface, 680-754, whose baptismal name was Winfred, became a Benedictine monk and later a bishop. He is remembered as the "Apostle to Germany." He died a martyr at the age of seventy-four.

Feast Dates: June 4 — St. Boniface.

Bonifacio (Spanish) See Boniface.

Booker "The One Who Works with Books" (African-American).

Patron Saints: The Catholic Church has appointed St. Celestine V as patron of bookbinders and St. John of God as patron of booksellers. She has appointed three more saints — Catherine of Alexandria, Jerome, and Lawrence — to serve as patrons of librarians.

Feast Dates: August 10 — St. Lawrence (see Lawrence); September 30 — St. Jerome (see Jerome).

Boomer "One Who Makes a Loud Noise" (Middle English).

Patron Saints: In ancient days some pagan gods, such as Thor and Jupiter (Zeus), were associated with making "Boomers," or thunder noises. These facts lead to three patrons. First, there is a St. Thorlák Thórhallsson, possibly named after Thor. Second, there are Sts. James and John Zebedee, whom Jesus named the "Sons of Thunder." These were the men Jesus chose to announce the Gospel to the world.

Feast Dates: December 23 — St. Thorlák Thórhallsson (see Thor); July 25 — St. James the Elder (see James).

Boone "The Good One" (Latin).

Patron Saints: Since Boone is based on *bonus,* the Latin word for "good," there are a few Sts. Bonus available.

Feast Dates: August 1 — St. Bonus (see Osgood).

Boonie (nickname) See Boone.

Boony (nickname) See Boone.

Boot (nickname) See Booth.

Boote (nickname) See Boone.

Booth (nickname) See Boone.

Booth "From the Hut" (Middle English) or "The Herald" (Old Norse).

Patron Saints: In Latin the word for "hut" is *casa.* This leads to St. Casalius. He was a religious priest at Argyra in Sicily. He became abbot of his monastery. He died in about 800.

Feast Dates: March 2 — St. Casalius; September 29 — St. Gabriel, Archangel (see Scully).

Bord (nickname) See Borden.

Borden "From the Valley+Of the Boar" (Old English double).

Patron Saints: One saint can be found in the last part of this name. Den leads to Bl. William Dean.

Feast Dates: August 28 — Bl. William Dean (see Dean).

Bordie (nickname) See Borden.

Bordon (double) See Borden+Dean.

Bordy (nickname) See Borden.

Borenka (nickname) See Boris.

Boris "The Small One" (Tartar) or "From the Battle" (Russian).

Patron Saints: There are a handful of Sts. Boris. One of them was converted to the Catholic faith by St. Methodius in 866. He was the first Slavic ruler to become a Christian and worked to have all of Bulgaria divided into seven dioceses. Then after ruling Bulgaria for forty-five years, he resigned and became a religious brother. But when his son, Vladimir, began persecuting Christians, he again returned to power. He defeated his son, blinded him, and appointed a younger son to be king. He died in 906.

Feast Dates: May 2 — St. Boris.

Borisik (nickname) See Boris.

Borka (nickname) See Boris.

Borya (nickname) See Boris.

Borys (nickname) See Boris.

Borysko (nickname) See Boris.

Boston "St. Botolph's+Town" (Old English double) or "The Town+Near the Thicket" (Old English double).

Patron Saints: Boston arises from St. Botolph's Town, an English village that grew up around Ikenho Abbey. A St. Botolph founded Ikenho Abbey in the Lincolnshire marshlands. He died in 655.

Feast Dates: June 17 — St. Botolph; July 21 — St. Tondach (see Town).

Bourke (English) See Burke, Roarke.

Bourn (variant) See Bourne.

Bourne "From the Brook" (Old English) or "From the Boundary" (French).

Patron Saints: There are a couple of saints who have Bourne as part of their names. One is the Bl. Thomas Welbourne of Hutton Bushel in Yorkshire, England. He was a schoolmaster whom the English government hanged in 1605 because he tried to persuade people to convert to Catholicism.

Feast Dates: August 1 — Bl. Thomas Welbourne of Hutton.

Boutros (Arabic) See Peter.

Bow (nickname) See Bowen.

Bowen "The Blond One" (Irish Gaelic).

Patron Saints: Bowen means exactly the same as the name Alban. There are about a half-dozen Sts. Alban.

Feast Dates: June 20 — St. Alban (see Alban).

Bowie (nickname) See Bowen.

Boyd (Irish) See Bowen.

Boyde (variant) See Bowen.

Brad "The Broad [Wide] One" (Old English short form of Braden).

Patron Saints: There is one St. Bradan, an English saint who lived in 1000 on the Isle of Man.

Feast Dates: October 20 — St. Bradan.

Bradan (Old English double) See Brad+Dean.

Brade (nickname) See Brad.

Braden (nickname) See Brad+Dean.

Bradford (English double) See Brad+Ford.

Bradge "The Most Excellent One" (Old Norse).

Patron Saints: St. Bradge is simply remembered as an "Irish saint."

Feast Dates: July 21 — St. Bradge.

Bradie (variant double) See Brady, Brad+Lee/Leigh.

Bradlee (Old English double) See Brad+Lee/Leigh.

Bradley (Old English double) See Brad+Lee/Leigh.

Bradly (Old English double) See Brad+Lee/Leigh.

Bradney (Old English double) See Brad+Ny/Ney.

Brady "The Spirited One" (Irish Gaelic) or "From the Broad Island" (Old English).

Patron Saints: Two saints can serve as patrons for Brady. They are Sts. Bradan and Nwy.

Feast Dates: October 20 — St. Braden (see Brad); November 1 — St. Nwy (see Ny or Ney).

Bram (nickname, Dutch) See Abraham, Abram.

Bran (nickname) See Branch, Brand, Brandon, Brant, Brendon.

Branch "A Paw [Claw]" (Old French) or "The Limb of a Tree" (Spanish).

Patron Saints: In Spanish, "branch" is rendered *rama* or *ramo.* Thus Palm Sunday is called "Domingo de Ramos." On that day Jesus was proclaimed King by the people waving palm branches.

Feast Dates: Palm Sunday — Christ, King of Peace.

Brand "The Firebrand" (Old English) or "The Proud One" (variant form of Brant).

Patron Saints: Brand can be a variant of Brant and Brendan or a full name in its own right. Because the name Brand can mean "firebrand" or "torch," one is led to St. Zebedee's sons, James and John. Jesus described the brothers as "firebrands" who were suitable for setting the world on fire with the preaching of the Gospel.

Feast Dates: January 11 — St. Brandan; July 25 — St. James the Elder, also known as James of Zebedee (see James).

Branden (variant) See Brandon.

Brandon "From the Beacon Hill" (Old English) or "A Firebrand" (short form of Brandon).

Patron Saints: Brandon can be a variant of Brand, Brant, and Brendan; it can also be a full name in its own right. One ancient saint bears the name of Brandan. It seems that he was an Irishman who lived in the 400s. He traveled to Britain, where for the sake of the Gospel he suffered the opposition of the Pelagian heretics. Then he took refuge in the monastery of Gaul and eventually became its abbot.

Because Brand can also mean "firebrand" or "torch," one is led to the sons of St. Zebedee, James and John, whom Jesus identified as "firebrands" suitable for setting the world on fire with the preaching of the Gospel.

Feast Dates: January 11 — St. Brandan.

Brandy (nickname) See Brandon.

Brandyn (American) See Brandon.

Brannon (English) See Brandon.

Brant (nickname) See Brand, Brendan, Brandon.

Bravo "The Brave and Clever One" (Italian).

Patron Saints: There is one St. Bravius. He was a native of Bretagne (Brittany) in the 700s and served as an abbot for the Benedictine monastery of Manat.

And because *bravo* means "brave," and the Latin word for it is *fortis*, one is led to at least one Bl. Fortis.

Feast Dates: September 15 — St. Bravius, O.S.B.; March 13 — Bl. Fortis Gabrielli (see Riley).

Bravus (Latin) See Bravo.

Braxton "From the Bracca Boundary" (Old English).

Patron Saints: There is an English martyr with a very similar name. He is Bl. Christopher Buxton, who was born in Derbyshire. Being from a Catholic family, he was sent to Rheims and Rome for education. He was ordained a priest in 1586 and immediately sent to the English missions. In 1588 he was arrested, tried, and convicted of being a Catholic priest. He was then hanged, drawn, and quartered at Canterbury.

Feast Dates: October 1 — Bl. Christopher Buxton.

Braydan (variant double) See Brad+Dean.

Brayden (variant double) See Brad+Dean.

Braydon (variant double) See Brad+Dean.

Bredan (variant double) See Brad+Dean.

Breeze (nickname) See Zephyrin.

Breezy (nickname) See Zephyrin.

Bren (nickname) See Brendon, Brennan.

Brendan "The Little Raven" (Irish Gaelic) or "From the Crow's Hill" (Irish Gaelic) or "The Prince" (Irish Gaelic) or "Brave Young Man" (Irish Gaelic).

Patron Saints: There are about a half-dozen saints named Brendan. The best known is St. Brendan the Voyager, 484-577, born near Tralee, Kerry, Ireland. He was ordained a priest, and later a bishop, and founded a great many monasteries in Ireland. He is also is remembered for making many missionary journeys to England, Ireland, and Scotland. The stories about his voyages were very popular in the Middle Ages. Some modern scholars think that Brendan discovered Newfoundland in North America on one of his trips. He died at the age of ninety-three. He is patron of sailors and against ulcers.

Feast Dates: May 16 — St. Brendan the Voyager.

Brenden (variant) See Brendan.

Brendin (variant) See Brendan.

Brendis (variant) See Brendan.

Brendon (variant) See Brendan.

Brennan "Like a Tear" (Irish Gaelic) or "The Brave Man [Little Raven]" (variant of Brendan).

Patron Saints: Many scholars insist that Brennan is a form of Brendan, and there are about a half-dozen saints named Brendan. However, it might also be helpful to investigate the original spelling of this name. It is Bronain, and there is a St. Bron. He is remembered for being a disciple of St. Patrick in the 400s.

Feast Dates: June 8 — St. Bron; May 16 — St. Brendan the Voyager (see Brendan).

Brennen (variant) See Brendan, Brennan.

Brennon (variant) See Brendan, Brennan.

Brent "From the Steep Hill" (Celtic) or "From the Burnt Field" (Old English).

Patron Saints: Some think Brent is related to Brendan, which means "little raven." This would make the dozen Sts. Brendan patrons. Others point out that Brent, which means "steep hill," may be related to Brandon. This would make Bl. Richard Hill a primary candidate for patron.

Feast Dates: May 4 — Bl. Richard Hill (see Hill); May 16 — St. Brendan the Voyager (see Brendan).

Bret (variant) See Brett.

Breton (variant) See Brett.

Brett "From Britain [The Fair Tribe]" (Old French).

Patron Saints: The name Bret or Brett means "from Britain." Thus any saint from England can serve as a patron. Probably the best candidate is St. George, the patron of England. Also, there are a few saints with Britain as part of their names. For example, there is a Bl. John Bretton, who was arrested and executed in 1598 in England because he was caught helping the Catholic priests serve the people.

Feast Dates: May 4 — Bl. John Bretton; April 23 — St. George the Great.

Brevin (American double) See Brian/Brendan+Evan.

Brew (nickname) See Bruce.

Brewer (English) See Bruce.

Brewster (Old English) See Bruce.

Brian "The Strong One" (Celtic) or "The Virtuous One" (Irish).

Patron Saints: There are a half-dozen Sts. Brian, Bryan, and Briant. One of them is Bl. Brian Lacey. He was a Yorkshire layman who was tortured and then hanged by the British government in 1591 simply because he insisted upon being a practicing Catholic.

Feast Dates: December 10 — Bl. Brian Lacey; April 23 — Bl. Bryan Boroimha O'Kennedy (see Kennedy).

Briano (Italian) See Brian.

Briant (English) See Brian.

Brice "The Quick One" (Welsh) or "The Son of the Ardent One" (variant of Price).

Patron Saints: St. Brice was a proud, ambitious, and licentious priest and a disciple of St. Martin of Tours. A man who caused much trouble for twenty years, he became bishop of Tours when St. Martin died. After some hard times he repented and became a model bishop, much loved by his people.

Feast Dates: November 13 — St. Brice.

Bricio (Spanish) See Brice.

Brick "A Baked Clay Block" (Middle English).

Patron Saints: There are four saints whom we might call St. Brick. They spelled their names as Bricin, Brictius, and Briccius. One of them, St. Brictius, was bishop of Spoleto during the Roman era. When Christians became the target of persecution by Emperor

Diocletian, he was tortured but survived. He died in 325.

Also, the Catholic Church has named as patron of bricklayers St. Stephen the Deacon.

Feast Dates: July 11 — St. Brick, also known as Brictius; December 26 — St. Stephen (see Stephen).

Bridge "From the Road Built over a Stream" (Middle English).

Patron Saints: The name Bridge can be accepted as a short male form of Bridget, which allows one to choose from about a dozen-and-a-half Sts. Bridget. One is St. Bridget of Sweden, 1303-1373. A member of the Swedish royalty, she was married at the age of fifteen, bore eight children, and had a happy marriage for twenty-eight years. After her husband died, she founded a monastery and the Bridgettine religious order. In time, she became well known for the visions God granted her and which she wrote down.

Feast Dates: July 23 — St. Bridget of Sweden.

Bridger (English) See Bridge.

Bridges (variant) See Bridge.

Brien (variant) See Brian.

Brig (nickname) See Brigham.

Brigg (nickname) See Brigham.

Briggs (nickname) See Brigham.

Brigham "From the Cottage [Home]+ Near the Bridge" (Middle English double).

Patron Saints: There is one saint named Brigidan and about twenty Sts. Bridget and Brigid. St. Brigidan is remembered for being a holy Irish priest.

Feast Dates: February 22 — St. Brigidan; April 30 — St. Hamo (see Hamilton).

Brink (nickname) See Bink.

Brion (variant) See Brian.

Brit (variant) See Brett.

Briton (English) See Brett.

Britt (variant) See Brett.

Brock "Like a Badger" (Old English).

Patron Saints: One Welsh saint, St. Brocmail, served as king of Powys, Wales, in the 700s. Also, the Latin word for "badger" is *meles*, and there are a few Sts. Meleus.

Feast Dates: November 1 — St. Brocmail.

Brockie (nickname) See Brock.

Brocky (nickname) See Brock.

Brockley (double) See Brock+Lee/Leigh.

Brod (nickname) See Broderick.

Broddie (nickname) See Broderick.

Broddy (nickname) See Broderick.

Broderic (double) See Broderick, Brad+ Richard.

Broderick "From the Broad+Ridge" (Middle English double) or "The Famous Ruler" (Welsh).

Patron Saints: Broderick is made up of two words, *brod* and *ric*. This combination produces two different meanings. There are about a half-dozen saints eligible for patrons.

Feast Dates: October 20 — St. Bradan (see Brad); February — St. Richard (see Richard).

Brodie "From the Ditch" (Irish Celtic).

Patron Saints: In Celtic, the name Brodie is spelled Broth. This leads to St. Brothan who lived in Wales in the 600s.

Feast Dates: October 14 — St. Brothan, also known as Brodie.

Brody (variant) See Brodie.

Brok (variant) See Brock.

Bron (nickname) See Bronson.

Bronco "A Partially Trained Horse" (Spanish-American).

Patron Saints: St. Bronchan was a medieval Irish saint.

Feast Dates: September 30 — St. Bronchan; June 8 — St. Bron (see Brennan).

Bronnie (nickname) See Bronson.

Bronny (nickname) See Bronson.

Bronson "The Son of+Bron [The Dark-Skinned One]" (Old English double).

Patron Saints: Bronson is built from two words, *bron* and *son. Bron* means "dark" or "brown." And there is an ancient St. Bron, plus a Bl. William Browne. There are also about a dozen saints named Bruno, which is Italian for "dark" or "brown." Finally, there is a St. Sontius.

Feast Dates: June 8 — St. Bron (see Brennan); November 17 — St. Sontius (see Son).

Brook "From the Small Stream" (Middle English).

Patron Saints: The English name Brook means "a small stream." This is the same meaning as the name Bourne, and there is one Bl. Thomas Welbourne.

It is also good to know that the Spanish word for "brook" is *arroyo.* This leads to Bl. Joachim Royo, a Catholic religious missionary priest who was martyred in China in 1748. The local Chinese viceroy was a bitter enemy of Christianity and he had Father Royo, his bishop, and fellow priests arrested and put in chains and starved. They remained in prison a year and were then executed.

Feast Dates: May 27 — Bl. Joachim Royo, O.P.; August 1 — Bl. Thomas Welbourne (see Bourne).

Brooke (English) See Brook.

Brooks (Old English double) See Brook+Son.

Brose (nickname) See Ambrose.

Brown (English) See Browne.

Browne "The Dark One" (Middle English) or "The Dark-Reddish One" (Middle English).

Patron Saints: Bl. William Browne was an English layman. He was arrested when his affiliation to Catholicism became known. A native of Northamptonshire, he was condemned and executed in 1605.

Feast Dates: September 5 — Bl. William Browne.

Bru (nickname) See Bruno.

Bruce "From the Thicket" (Old French) or "A Brewer" (variant form of Brewster).

Patron Saints: Usually St. Brice is given as the patron for Bruce. But it should also not be forgotten that Bruce can mean "brewer." There are many saints that have been officially appointed as patrons of brewers. They include Sts. Amand, Arnulph, Augustine of Hippo, Boniface of Mainz (or Crediton), Nicholas, and Wenceslaus.

Feast Dates: November 13 — St. Brice (see Brice).

Brucie (nickname) See Bruce.

Bruhs (French) See Bruce.

Bruis (French) See Bruce.

Brun (nickname) See Bruno.

Bruni (nickname) See Bruno.

Bruno "The Dark-Skinned One" (Italian, Spanish).

Patron Saints: The name Bruno is an Italian form of "Browne." There are about a dozen Sts. Bruno. One of them was the duke of Saxony and fell in battle against the invading pagan Norsemen in 880.

Feast Dates: June 8 — St. Bruno.

Brunonas (Lithuanian) See Bruno.

Brunson (variant) See Bruno.

Bruny (nickname) See Bruno.

Bruys (Scottish) See Bruce.

Bryan (variant) See Brian.

Bryant (variant) See Brian.

Bryce (English) See Brice, Price.

Brydon (English) See Brett.

Bryn (variant) See Brendan, Brennan.

Bryndon (English) See Brendan, Brennan.

Bryon (variant) See Brian.

Bryton (English) See Brett.
Buadhach (Irish) See Victor.
Bubba (American) See Junior.
Bubba (German) See Ladd, Page.
Buck "The Stag Deer" (Dutch).

Patron Saints: There is a St. John Jones, a Catholic priest who worked in the English underground from 1592 to 1597 under the alias of John Buckley. He was arrested and executed.

The name Buckley means "from the stag's meadow," and this leads to two more patrons: Bl. William Hart and Bl. William Hartley.

Feast Dates: July 12 — St. John Jones, also known as John Buckley; October 5 — Bl. William Hartley (see Hartley).

Buckie (nickname) See Buck.
Buckley (English double) See Buck+Lee/Leigh.
Bucky (nickname) See Buck.
Bud (nickname) See Buddy.
Budd (English) See Buddy.
Budde (English) See Buddy.
Buddie (English) See Buddy.
Buddy "The Messenger" (Old English) or "The Brother and Friend" (Middle English).

Patron Saints: Knowing that *bud* means "brother" or "friend" leads to a dozen patrons. They are known as "The Twelve Holy Brothers." These twelve black men lived in Roman times, were natives of Carthage, and were arrested for being Christian. After being tortured, they were sent to Italy, chained together at their necks, and then executed. One ancient source insists they were brothers. Another insists they were simply friends.

Feast Dates: September 1 — The Twelve Holy Brothers.

Buenaventura (Spanish) See Bonaventure.

Bufford (variant) See Buford.
Buford "The River Crossing+Near the Castle" (Old English double).

Patron Saints: It is a great help to know that Buford comes from two words: *bu*, meaning "oxen," and *ford*, meaning "river crossing." This leads to two saints: St. Buo and Bl. Thomas Ford.

St. Buo was an Irishman who traveled to Iceland with St. Ernulph to convert pagans in the 800s.

Feast Dates: February 5 — St. Buo; May 28 — Bl. Thomas Ford (see Ford).

Buiron (variant) See Byron.
Bull "The Strong Farm Animal" (Middle English).

Patron Saints: There is one English martyr whose name contains the name Bull. Father Thomas Bullaker, a religious priest, was executed in England in 1542 because he insisted on being a Catholic priest.

Feast Dates: May 4 — Bl. Thomas Bullaker.

Burg (variant) See Burgess.
Burgess "The Citizen of a Town" (Old English).

Patron Saints: There is one St. Bergis. He was the founder of the abbey of St. Hubert in the diocese of Liège in France. He died in Belgium in 724.

Feast Dates: October 2 — St. Bergis.

Burk (English) See Burke.
Burke "The Dweller in the Fortress" (Old French).

Patron Saints: There are a half-dozen Sts. Burkhard. One was a parish priest in the 1300s in Switzerland.

Feast Dates: June 27 — St. Burkhard.

Burl "The Cup-Bearer" (Old English) or "The Home-Spun One" (variant of Burrell).

Patron Saints: There is one saint with a similar name. He is St. Burrus, a martyr in ancient Syria.

Feast Dates: October 12 — St. Burrus.

Burleigh "From the Meadow+Knotted Trees" (Old English double) or "From the Town+Near the Pasture" (Old English double).

Patron Saints: Burleigh is built from two names: Burl and Leigh. This leads to two patrons.

Feast Dates: October 12 — St. Burrus (see Burl); August 30 — Bl. Richard Leigh (see Lee or Leigh).

Burlie (nickname) See Burl.

Burley (English double) See Burleigh, Burl+Leigh.

Burn (variant) See Bourne, Rayburn.

Burnard (English) See Bernard.

Burne (variant) See Bourne, Rayburn.

Burney (English) See Birney.

Burny (variant) See Bourne, Rayburn.

Burr (variant) See Burgess.

Burrell (English) See Burl.

Burt "The Brilliant One" (variant of Bert).

Patron Saints: There is one St. Burt. He was a holy bishop at Vaison, France.

Feast Dates: October 6 — St. Burt, also known as Burtius; March 26 — St. Bert (see Bert).

Burtie (nickname) See Bert, Burt.

Burton "From the Fortified+Town" (Old English double) or "From the Town+ On the Hill" (Old English double).

Patron Saints: Burton is constructed from "burt" and "ton."

Feast Dates: October 6 — St. Burt, also known as Burtius (see Burt); July 21 — St. Tondach (see Town).

Burty (nickname) See Bert, Burt.

Busby "From the Town+In the Thicket" (Scottish double).

Patron Saints: There is a St. Bosa and a St. Bee. St. Bosa was a native of Northumbria and became the first bishop of York in 678. St. Bee was a beautiful Irish princess who gave herself to Christ from childhood. Reaching adulthood, she was forced to marry. Not wishing to do so, she sailed to a foreign land. Eventually she became the abbess of Egremont. She is remembered as patron of laborers.

Feast Dates: March 9 — St. Bosa; September 6 — St. Bee; July 21 — St. Tondach (see Town).

Buster "One Who Punches Through" (American).

Patron Saints: The name Buster in Latin is *punctum.* This leads to St. Punica, who was martyred in ancient Africa.

Feast Dates: January 3 — St. Punica.

Butch (nickname) See any name containing "Bert."

Buzz (nickname) See Busby.

By "From the Town, Village, or Farm" (Middle English).

Patron Saints: "By" is a suffix attached to many English male names and surnames. There is one saint who has a name similar to "town." He is St. Tondach and is remembered for being a holy bishop in medieval Ireland.

It might also be helpful to know that the Latin word for "farm" is *ager* or *agris.* There are two Sts. Agericus and one St. Ager.

St. Ager (also known as Field or Farm) died a martyr's death for Jesus in ancient Potenza.

Feast Dates: July 21 — St. Tondach; May 13 — St. Ager.

Byran (variant) See Byron.

Byrann (variant) See Byron.

Byrd (variant) See Byrdie.

Byrdie "The One Like a Bird" (Old English).

Patron Saints: One English martyr can be a patron. He is Bl. James Bird, an English layman who was hanged by the British government in 1593. He was only nineteen years old and a native of Winchester. He was executed because he had reconciled with the Catholic Church and had quit attending Protestant services.

Feast Dates: March 25 — Bl. James Bird.

Byrle (variant) See Burl.

Byrn (variant) See Bourne.

Byrom (variant) See Byron.

Byron "From the Cottage" (Old French).

Patron Saints: There is one medieval Irish saint with a similar name: St. Berran. There is also an English martyr who has a name that means about the same thing as Byron. *Cott* means "cottage," and the person whose name bears the closest resemblance is Bl. Thomas Cottam.

He was an Englishman who converted to Catholicism, went to France, was ordained a priest, and became a Jesuit. He returned to England, was arrested, and in 1580 was executed.

Feast Dates: July 11 — St. Berran; May 30 — Bl. Thomas Cottam, S.J.

C

Caelan (Scottish) See Nicholas.

Caesar "The Long-Haired One" (Latin, Swedish, Danish).

Patron Saints: There are over a dozen Sts. Caesarius. One was the younger brother of St. Gregory Nazianzen in the late 300s. He served as a physician in the court of Emperor Constantine. He converted to Christianity and was baptized shortly before his death.

Feast Dates: February 25 — St. Caesar.

Cai (Welsh) See Kai.

Cain "The One Possessed" (English).

Patron Saints: There are over a half-dozen Sts. Cain in medieval Ireland and Wales. One was St. Cain Comrac, the abbot-bishop of Louth. He died in 898.

Feast Dates: July 23 — St. Cain.

Caine (English) See Kane.

Caith (variant) See Keith.

Cal (nickname) See Caleb, Calvin.

Calaycay "From the Low Coral Reef Island+Near the Inlet" (Hispanic-American double).

Patron Saints: Two saints with a similar name can be pressed into service: Sts. Calanus and Cai. St. Calanus died a martyr in ancient Thessalonica with his friend St. Alexander.

Feast Dates: February 22 — St. Calanus; November 1 — St. Cai.

Calder "The Cold One" (Old English).

Patron Saints: St. Valerian served for many years as the bishop of Tunis, Africa, in the mid-400s. When he was eighty years old the heretic king of the Vandals, Hunneric, ordered him to turn over all Church treasure to the government. Valerian absolutely refused, and the king made him an exile in his own city. He was evicted from his home and forced to wander the streets. No one was allowed to feed, shelter, or care for him. He died one winter night and is now patron against exposure, snowstorms, and cold.

Feast Dates: December 15 — St. Valerian.

Caldwell "From Cold+Spring [Well]" (Old English double).

Patron Saints: Caldwell is composed of two parts: *cald*, meaning "cold," and *well*, meaning "spring" or "well." Bl. Roger Caldwallador was a diocesan priest who was executed in 1610 by English authorities.

Also, the Latin word for cold is *frigidus*. This leads to a St. Frigidian.

Feast Dates: November 18 — St. Frigidian (see Frost); May 4 — Bl. Roger Caldwallador.

Cale (nickname) See Caleb.

Caleb "The Bold One" (Hebrew) or "Like a Faithful Dog" (Hebrew).

Patron Saints: Christian tradition provides one St. Caleb, and the Bible presents two more. It seems that a Christian named Caleb ruled Abyssinia in the mid-500s. With the support of the Greeks, he overcame Dhu Nuwas, the Jewish king of the Homerites who had persecuted his people. Sometime later he resigned the throne in favor of his son and moved into a nearby cave as a hermit.

Feast Dates: October 27 — St. Caleb.

Calen (Scottish) See Caleb.

Calhoun "From the Narrow Forest" (Irish Gaelic) or "The Warrior" (Celtic).

Patron Saints: St. Callwen can serve as patron. A member of the saintly Welsh Brychan family, she dedicated herself to serving God.

Feast Dates: November 1 — St. Callwen.

Calicho (Spanish) See Carl, Charles.

Calo (Spanish) See Carl, Charles.

Calv (nickname) See Calvin.

Calvin "The Bald One" (Latin).

Patron Saints: There are a few saints with similar names. One of them, St. Callwen, was a native of Wales and a member of the famous Welsh Brychan family. She is remembered for embracing the single life and dedicating herself to the service of God and her fellowmen.

Feast Dates: November 1 — St. Callwen.

Calvino (Spanish, Italian) See Calvin.

Cam (Romany) See David.

Cam (nickname) See Cameron.

Camerino (Spanish) See Cameron.

Cameron "One with the Crooked Nose" (Scottish Gaelic).

Patron Saints: There is one St. Cameron. He died a martyr in ancient Cagliari in Italy. In addition, there are also 1,535 martyr-saints from Camerino in Italy. They have been recognized as Roman martyrs.

Feast Dates: August 21 — St. Cameron, also known as Camerinus; May 29 — Holy Martyrs of Camerino.

Camey (nickname) See Cameron.

Camillus (variant) See Kamil.

Cammy (nickname) See Cameron.

Canute (Scandinavian) See Knute.

Canuto (Spanish) See Knute.

Capable "The One Able to Handle" (Latin).

Patron Saints: One Latin word for "capable" is *capere*. There is no St. Capere, but we can call upon St. Caprasius to serve as patron. He and his companions lived on the Mediterranean island of Lérins, off the coast of ancient Gaul, devoting their lives to God in the manner of the Desert Fathers. St. Caprasius died in 430.

Feast Dates: June 1 — St. Caprasius, also known as Caprais.

Cardell (African-American double) See Carl+Darrell.

Care (nickname) See Carey.

Carey "The Castle Dweller" (Welsh).

Patron Saints: There is one English martyr named John Carey. He was an Irish layman who worked as a servant for Bl. Thomas Bosgrave, a wealthy Englishman. Carey, his employer, and a fellow servant, Bl. Patrick Salmon, were all hanged in 1594 because they insisted on giving shelter to Catholic priests.

Feast Dates: July 4 — Bl. John Carey.

Carl "The Strong, Manly One" (Italian, English, Swedish form of Charles) or "The Farmer" (Old German).

Patron Saints: The closest name to Carl is Bl. Carolomann, 707-754. Also known as Karlomann, he became king of Austrasia, Swabia, and Thuringia. As king, he was active in Church matters. He supported St. Boniface in Germany, founded abbeys, and tried to right the wrongs created by his father in regards to Church property. When he was about forty years old, a tragic slaughter of the Alemans led him to resign. He entered a Benedictine monastery and spent his time working in the kitchen and as a shepherd.

Feast Dates: August 17 — Bl. Carolomann.

Carleton (Old English double) See Carl, Carl+Town.

Carlino (Spanish) See Carl, Charles.

Carlito (Spanish double) See Carl/ Charles+Lito.

Carlo (Italian, Spanish) See Carl, Charles.

Carlos (Portuguese, Spanish) See Carl, Charles.

Carlton (Old English double) See Carl, Carl+Town.

Carlucho (Spanish) See Carl, Charles.

Carm (nickname) See Carmen.

Carmen "A Song" (Latin) or "Crimson Red" (Middle Latin) or "From the Garden" (Spanish form of Carmella).

Patron Saints: The fact that Carmen can mean "from the garden" leads to Adam and Eve, patrons of gardens. It also helps to know that in Middle Latin the name Carmen means "crimson red." This leads to a dozen Sts. Rufinus. Finally, knowing that Carmen can also mean "a song" surfaces Bl. Peter the Singer, St. Joseph the Hymn Writer, and St. Clement the Hymnographer. St. Clement was the abbot of the Studion monastery at Constantinople and, having a great devotion to the Blessed Virgin, wrote many hymns and canons in her honor. He also supported the use of icons as aids to worship.

Feast Dates: April 30 — St. Clement the Hymnographer; December 24 — Sts. Adam and Eve (see Adam).

Carnell (African-American double) See Cornell+Darnell.

Carol (Romanian) See Carl, Charles.

Carrol (variant) See Carl, Charles.

Carroll "The Champion" (Irish Gaelic) or "The Strong, Manly One" (English form of Charles).

Patron Saints: Carroll can be accepted as a variant of Charles, and there are a dozen Sts. Charles. Carroll can also mean "champion" in Irish Gaelic, and this leads to the English martyr

St. Edmund Campion. Campion is a French form of "champion."

Edmund Campion, 1540-1581, was born and raised Catholic in London. He became an Anglican and was educated at Oxford. Eventually he was reconciled with the Catholic Church, studied in France and Italy, joined the Jesuits in 1573, and was ordained. In 1580 he went to the English missions. He was so successful in making converts that his enemies called him "The Pope's Champion." Government agents hunted him down and jailed him. For three days he was locked in a room so small he could neither walk, stand, lie, or sit. Later, he was condemned for being a Catholic priest and was executed in 1581 at the age of forty-one. He is now known as the patron of printers.

Feast Dates: December 1 — St. Edmund Campion, S.J.; April 17 — Bl. Carolomann (see Carl).

Carson (double) See Charles/Carl+Son.

Carter "The Cart Driver" (Old English).

Patron Saints: There is an English martyr, Bl. William Carter. He was a layman who found himself arrested by government agents in 1584 because he helped Catholic priests and practiced his religion.

Feast Dates: May 4 — Bl. William Carter.

Cary (nickname) See Carey, Carl, Charles.

Caryl (variant) See Carl, Charles.

Casar (German) See Caesar.

Case (nickname) See Casey, Casimir.

Casey "The Watchful, Brave One" (Irish Gaelic) or "The Peacemaker" (nickname for Casimir).

Patron Saints: There is one North American, the Ven. Solanus Casey, who can serve as patron. However, if the name is accepted as a familiar form of the Polish Casimir, which means "peacemaker," then St. Casimer of Poland can serve as patron.

Feast Dates: January 6 — Ven. Solanus Casey (see Barney); March 4 — St. Casimir (see Casimir).

Cash (nickname) See Cassius.

Cashi (Spanish) See Casimir.

Casie (variant) See Casey.

Casimir "The Peacemaker" (Slavic).

Patron Saints: There is only one St. Casimir of Poland, 1458-1484. At the age of fifteen, he was called to become king of Hungary. He refused but then relented when pressured by his father. At his father's command he led an army to invade Hungary. Arriving at the Hungarian border he became aware that there was no need for a war and he refused to invade. This infuriated his father and he banished Casimir.

This made Casimir happy because he did not want anything to do with the royal court. He could often be found in prayer, either praying the rosary or meditating on the passion of Jesus. He also had a deep devotion to the Eucharist and to the Blessed Virgin.

After his brother became king of Poland, he was occasionally called upon to practice diplomacy. He died of consumption at the age of twenty-six. He is patron of Poland and Lithuania.

Feast Dates: March 4 — St. Casimir of Poland.

Casimiro (Spanish) See Casimir.

Caspar (variant) See Casper.

Casper "The Treasurer" (Persian) or "The Precious Stone" (English form of Jasper).

Patron Saints: There are about a dozen Sts. Casper. One of them, St. Caspar del Bufalo, 1786-1837, was ordained a priest at the age of twenty-two and soon found himself exiled when he and other members of the clergy refused to give up their allegiance

to the Holy See after Napoleon took over Rome. After Napoleon's fall, Caspar returned to Rome and began his ministry to the poor. Then he founded a society of secular priests to help in his work. These dedicated men eventually became known as the Congregation of the Precious Blood. St. Caspar died at the age of fifty-one.

Feast Dates: December 28 — St. Caspar del Bufalo; January 6 — St. Caspar (see Sage).

Cass (nickname) See Cassidy.

Cassidy "The Clever One" (Irish Gaelic).

Patron Saints: A St. Cassian might serve as patron, but knowing that Cassidy means "clever" or "ingenious" leads to more patrons. There are a half-dozen Sts. Ingenus and one St. Ingenuinus. The latter was the first bishop of Seben during the time of the controversy known as the "Three Chapters." This was a dispute among true Catholics, Nestorian heretics, and Monophysite heretics. Ingenuinus sided, first against, and then with, his metropolitan bishop. Finally, he supported the Holy Father. He was killed in 605.

Feast Dates: February 5 — St. Ingenuinus.

Cassie (nickname) See Cassidy.

Cassius "The Vain, Empty One" (Latin).

Patron Saints: There are about three dozen Sts. Cassius, Cassian, and Cassianus. In the 500s there was a St. Cassius, who was the bishop of Narni. He was a very pious man. One day, one of his priests told him that he would die at Rome on the feast of Sts. Peter and Paul. Thus for the next few years Cassius journeyed to Rome each year for that feast. The prophecy was fulfilled in the seventh year. He celebrated Mass, gave Communion to the people, and passed away very quietly.

Feast Dates: June 29 — St. Cassius.

Cassy (nickname) See Cassidy.

Cato "The Cautious One" (Latin) or "The Wise One" (Latin).

    Patron Saints: There is one St. Cato, a black man who died a martyr in ancient Africa.

    Feast Dates: December 28 — St. Cato.

Catulo (Spanish) See Cato.

Caz (nickname) See Cassius.

Cece (nickname) See Cecil.

Cecha (Spanish) See Jacob.

Ceche (Spanish) See Joseph.

Cecil "The Blind One" (Latin).

    Patron Saints: There are about a half-dozen Sts. Cecil. One of them was a disciple of the Apostles. St. Paul made him bishop of Granada. He died a martyr's death.

    There are also saints whom the Catholic Church has named as patrons of the blind. Among them are Sts. Odilia, Cosmas and Damian, Cury, Harvey, Leger, Raphael, Thomas the Apostle, and Thomas Becket.

    Feast Dates: March 1 — St. Cecil, also known as Caecilius.

Cecile (French) See Cecil.

Cecilio (Italian, Spanish) See Cecil.

Cecilius (Dutch) See Cecil.

Cedric "The War Chief" (Old English).

    Patron Saints: The names Cedric and Chad arise from the same root. Therefore, St. Chad (also known as Cedda) can serve as a patron for a person named Cedric.

    Feast Dates: March 2 — St. Chad, also known as Cedda (see Chad).

Ceejay (American double) See any "C" name+any "J" name.

Cenón (Spanish) See Zeus.

Cephas (Greek) See Peter, Rocky.

Ces (nickname) See Cecil.

César (French, Spanish) See Caesar.

Cesare (Italian) See Caesar.

Cesareo (Spanish) See Caesar.

Cezar (Slavic) See Caesar.

Chabalito (Italian) See Salvador.

Chacko (nickname) See Charles.

Chad "The Warlike One" (Old English) or "The Strong, Manly One" (variant of Charles).

    Patron Saints: There are about a half-dozen Sts. Chad. One was born in Northumbria, one of four brothers, all of whom became saints. Ordained a priest, eventually he traveled to Ireland, became an abbot, and then the bishop of York.

    For a short time there were some questions about the validity of his consecration, so the new archbishop of Canterbury traveled to York and judged Chad to be defectively consecrated. Chad humbly told him, "If you judge me not properly consecrated, I resign this responsibility. I have never thought myself worthy." The archbishop was so impressed with Chad's humility that he consecrated him properly and allowed him to retire to his monastery at Lastingham. He died in 672.

    Feast Dates: March 2 — St. Chad, also known as Cedda.

Chadbourne (English double) See Chad+ Bourne, Charles.

Chadd (variant) See Chad, Charles.

Chaddie (variant) See Chad, Charles.

Chaddy (nickname) See Chad, Charles.

Chadwick "From the Warrior's Town" (Old English) or "From the Strong Man's Town" (variant of Charles).

    Patron Saints: St. Chad will do nicely. Any of a number of Sts. Charles will also be helpful.

    Feast Dates: March 2 — St. Chad (see Chad); October 19 — St. Charles Garnier (see Charles).

Chago (Spanish) See Jacob.

Chai (nickname) See Chaim.

Chaim (Hebrew) See Hyman.

Chan (nickname) See Chance, Chandler, Channing, Juan.

Chance "The One with Good Fortune" (Middle English).

Patron Saints: One of the words for "chance" in Latin is *fortuna*, and there are about seventy-five saints with that name or a variant of it. Furthermore, there is one saint who has been appointed patron (or helper) in games of chance. She is St. Corona.

Feast Dates: June 18 — St. Fortunatus (see Lucky); May 14 — St. Ring, also known as Corona (see Ring).

Chandler "The Candlemaker" (Old French) or "The Ship Supply Merchant" (Middle English).

Patron Saints: St. Bernard of Clairvaux and St. Ambrose are both patrons of chandlers.

Feast Dates: August 20 — St. Bernard of Clairvaux, O. Cist. (see Bernard).

Chane (nickname) See Chandler.

Chango (Spanish) See Jacob.

Channing "The Church Dignitary [Canon]" (Old French) or "The Knowing One" (Old English).

Patron Saints: St. Robert Bellarmine has been officially appointed as patron of canonists. In addition, any sainted Catholic bishop or priest can served as patron.

Feast Dates: September 17 — St. Robert Bellarmine (see Robert).

Chanti (Spanish) See Jacob.

Charles "The Strong, Manly One" (English).

Patron Saints: St. Charles Garnier, 1605-1649, was born into a wealthy Parisian family. However, when he was nineteen years old, he turned his back on this life and entered the Jesuit novitiate. After ordination at the age of twenty-nine he volunteered to be a missionary in Canada.

Upon arriving in Canada in 1636, he spent thirteen years at a Huron mission. He was then sent to St. Jean in 1649, the year Fort St. Marie was abandoned. There the Iroquois attacked. As the Indians died he ministered to them despite the gunfire erupting around him.

He went down when he was shot through the chest and abdomen. Regaining consciousness, he attempted to help another fallen Indian and was immediately tomahawked by the enemy. He was only forty-four years old.

Feast Dates: October 19 — St. Charles Garnier, S.J.

Charleton (English double) See Carl, Charles+Town.

Charley (nickname) See Charles.

Charlie (nickname) See Charles.

Charlton (English double) See Carl, Charles+Town.

Charly (nickname) See Charles.

Charo "The Cowboy" (Spanish) or "The Strong, Manly One" (Spanish nickname for Charles).

Patron Saints: St. Sylvester and St. Charles Garnier qualify.

Feast Dates: December 31 — St. Sylvester (see Rangle); October 19 — St. Charles Garnier (see Charles).

Chas (nickname) See Charles.

Chase "The Hunter" (Old French).

Patron Saints: Knowing that *chase* means "hunter" leads to four patrons. Two are English martyrs, Bls. Thurston Hunt and Thomas Hunt. The other two are Sts. Hubert and Eustace, who are officially recognized as patrons of hunters.

Feast Dates: May 4 — Bl. Thomas Hunt (see Hunter); November 3 — St. Hubert (see Hubert).

Chauncey "The Chancellor" (Middle English) or "The Church Official" (Middle English).

Patron Saints: The best known saint who also served as lord chancellor is St. Thomas More, 1478-1535. The son of a lawyer and a judge, he studied law and was admitted to the bar in 1501. He soon became England's leading literary light of that time.

He steadily rose in rank during the reign of King Henry VIII, becoming lord chancellor in 1529. Then came the time when he was faced with the problem stemming from the king's divorce and subsequent remarriage in 1533. As a result of this situation, St. Thomas resigned his post and retired to his home in Chelsea.

But he was increasingly pressured to recognize the king as head of the Church. This he steadfastly refused to do. In 1534 the king had him arrested and imprisoned in the Tower of London. He was beheaded fifteen months later. Today he is patron of lawyers and civil servants.

Feast Dates: June 22 — St. Thomas More.

Chavez (Hispanic-American) See Salvador.

Chavo (nickname) See Salvador.

Chayse (Spanish) See Chase.

Chaz (nickname) See Charles.

Ché (Spanish) See Joseph, Buddy.

Cheche (Spanish) See Joseph.

Chenche (Spanish) See Vincent.

Chento (Irish Gaelic) See Vincent.

Chepe (Spanish) See Joseph.

Ches (nickname) See Chester.

Chester "From Fortified Camp [Walled Town]" (Old English).

Patron Saints: Bl. Robert Wilcox of Chester, England, was ordained a diocesan priest in 1585. The following year he returned to England and was murdered by the English government at the age of thirty.

Feast Dates: October 1 — St. Robert Wilcox of Chester; May 11 — Bl. John Rochester (see Rochester).

Chet (nickname) See Chester.

Chevalier (French) See Knight, Rider.

Cheviot (nickname) See Chevy.

Chevy "The Hunter's Cry" (English) or "The Knight" (French nickname for Chevalier).

Patron Saints: Knowing that the name Chevy means "to hunt" leads to four patrons. Two are English martyrs, Bls. Thurston and Thomas Hunt. The other two are Sts. Hubert and Eustace, patrons of hunters.

Feast Dates: May 4 — Bl. Thomas Hunt (see Hunter); May 4 — Bl. Thurston Hunt (see Thurston).

Chi (Spanish or Hebrew nickname) See Chiquito, Chaim.

Chic (nickname) See Charles.

Chico (Spanish, Portuguese) See Chiquito.

Chilo (Spanish) See Francis.

Chimone (Modern Hebrew) See Simon.

Chip "Small Piece of Rock" (nickname for Rocky) or "The Strong, Manly One" (nickname for Charles).

Patron Saints: If one recognizes that a chip is a "small piece of rock," then St. Peter the Rock, a few Sts. Rock, a St. Stone, and Jesus the Rock can all be considered patrons.

Moreover, if one accepts that "chip" is a nickname for Charles, then a half-dozen Sts. Charles surface.

Feast Dates: August 16 — St. Rock (see Rocky); October 19 — St. Charles Garnier (see Charles).

Chipito (Spanish) See Joseph.

Chiquito "The Little+Free One" (Spanish double).

Patron Saints: The word *chi* means "little one," while *quito* means "one who is free or exempt."

Paul is an ancient name found in the Bible that also means "little," and Francis is a name that means "free one."

Feast Dates: October 4 — St. Francis of Assisi; June 29 — St. Paul, Apostle.

Chombo (Italian) See Jerome.

Chomo (Italian) See Jerome.

Chrétien (French) See Christian.

Chrétienne (French) See Christian.

Chris (nickname) See Christian, Christopher.

Chrissy (nickname) See Christian, Christopher.

Christ (nickname) See Christian, Christopher.

Christian "The Anointed One" (English) or "The Follower of Christ" (English).

Patron Saints: There are about a half-dozen Sts. Christianus and two Sts. Christinus. One Christianus was the first bishop of Prussia and an abbot. In 1207 he served as an envoy from the pope to the duke of Prussia. Then in 1215 he was consecrated bishop of Prussia. In 1222 he returned to Prussia with some of the Crusaders and founded the Teutonic Knights. He died in 1245.

Feast Dates: December 4 — St. Christianus, O. Cist.

Christiano (Spanish, Italian) See Christian.

Christino (Portuguese) See Christian.

Christóbal (variant) See Christopher.

Christofora (variant) See Christopher.

Christoforus (variant) See Christopher.

Christoph (German) See Christopher.

Christophe (French) See Christopher.

Christopher "The Christ-Bearer" (English) or "The Anointed One" (English).

Patron Saints: There are two dozen Sts. Christopher. The best known is St. Christopher, the patron of bachelors,

bus drivers, ferryboat men, horsemen, police officers, skiers, travelers, truck drivers, and against nightmares, water peril, plague, sudden death, and violent storms. He lived in the fourth century in Palestine and was a giant of a man, reportedly about eight feet tall. Early on in life he decided he would serve only the strongest of kings.

One day he saw a Canaanite king make the Sign of the Cross when the devil was mentioned. He concluded that the devil was stronger and left to find him. Then he discovered that the devil feared the Cross. So he began searching for the "King of the Cross." In time, a child came to him at the place where he ferried people across the river and requested to be carried across. Christopher did so, but as he crossed, the child became unbearably heavy. Christopher asked the child who he was. The child identified himself as Jesus, King of the world, who bears its problems. This impressed Christopher and he became a Christian. Then he went about converting thousands and was eventually arrested, tortured, and killed with arrows by a pagan king.

Feast Dates: July 25 — St. Christopher the Giant.

Christophorus (German) See Christopher.

Christos (Greek) See Christian.

Christy (nickname) See Christian, Christopher.

Chucho (nickname) See Augustine, Jesus.

Chuck (nickname) See Charles.

Chuckie (nickname) See Charles.

Chucky (nickname) See Charles.

Chuminga (Spanish) See Dominic.

Chumo (Spanish) See Thomas.

Cianan (variant) See Keenan.

Cirilio (Portuguese) See Cyril.

Cirill (Hungarian) See Cyril.

Cirillo (Italian) See Cyril.

Cirilo (Spanish) See Cyril.

Ciro (Portuguese, Italian, Spanish) See Cyrus.

Cisco (Spanish, Portuguese) See Francis.

Claiborn (English double) See Clayborne, Clay+Bourne.

Claiborne (English double) See Clayborne, Clay+Bourne.

Clair (variant) See Clare, Clarence, Sinclair.

Claire (variant) See Clare, Clarence, Sinclair.

Clare "The Famous One" (short form of Clarence or Sinclair).

Patron Saints: There are about a dozen male Sts. Clare. Bl. Clare Voglia was the last male heir of the wealthy Voglia family. In 1342 he founded an Augustinian convent. He married, but his wife wanted to become a nun. He consented, and she entered the Augustinian convent he had founded. He spent the rest of his life working at the convent as a janitor and servant. He died in 1348.

Feast Dates: May 25 — Bl. Clare Voglia, also known as Claritus.

Clarence "The Famous One" (English form of Clare).

Patron Saints: There is one St. Clarence. He was the bishop of Vienne, France, and he died in 620.

Feast Dates: April 26 — St. Clarence.

Clark "The Scholar" (Old French) or "The Clergyman" (Old French).

Patron Saints: To find a patron one must turn to the name's meaning, which is "scholar." The Catholic Church has officially named three saints as patrons of scholars. They are Sts. Bede, Bridget of Sweden, and Thomas Aquinas.

Feast Dates: May 25 — St. Venerable Bede (see Bede); June 22 — St. Thomas Aquinas.

Clarke (variant) See Clark.

Claud (Latin) See Claude.

Claude "The Lame One" (French).

Patron Saints: There are more than three dozen Sts. Claudianus, Claudinus, and Claudius. One of them was the brother of Pope Gaius (or Caius). He was sent by the pagan Roman emperor to ask his niece to marry the emperor. But the girl refused, and the emperor had the entire family burned alive in 295.

Feast Dates: February 18 — St. Claudius.

Claudicio (Portuguese, Spanish, Italian) See Claude.

Claudino (Portuguese, Spanish, Italian) See Claude.

Claudio (Portuguese, Spanish, Italian) See Claude.

Claudiu (Romanian) See Claude.

Claudius (Dutch, English) See Claude.

Claudy (nickname) See Claude.

Claus (Celtic) See Nicholas.

Clay "The One from the Earth" (Old English).

Patron Saints: It helps to know that the name Clay means "earth." Adam means the same thing, and there are about a half-dozen Sts. Adam. There is also an English martyr, Bl. Richard Leigh, who used the alias Earth. In addition, there is one saint with a similar name, St. Clathaeus. He was the first bishop of Brescia and was beheaded for the faith in Milan in about the year 68.

Feast Dates: June 4 — St. Clathaeus; December 24 — Sts. Adam and Eve (see Adam).

Clayborn (English double) See Clayborne, Clay+Bourne.

Clayborne "Born+From Earth" (Old English double) or "From the Stream Near the Clay" (Old English double).

Patron Saints: The best patron would be St. Adam, who was literally "born from the Earth."

Feast Dates: December 24 — Sts. Adam and Eve (see Adam); August 1 — Bl. Thomas Welbourne (see Bourne).

Claybourne (English double) See Clayborne, Clay+Bourne.

Clayton (English double) See Clay+Town.

Cleavland (variant) See Cleveland.

Cleavon (English) See Cleveland.

Clem (nickname) See Clement.

Cleme (Spanish) See Clement.

Clemen (Spanish) See Clement.

Clemencio (Spanish) See Clement.

Clement "The Kind and Merciful One" (French).

Patron Saints: There are about three dozen Sts. Clement. One of them, St. Clement I, was a well-educated man who, in the 60s, received instructions, was baptized, and consecrated bishop by St. Peter the Apostle. In the year 92 he was elected pope. About four years later, a serious dispute arose in the Corinthian Church. John the Apostle was still alive at this time and was only two hundred miles from the problem; but the leaders of the Corinthian Church appealed to Clement, some two thousand miles away, to help them. Clement wrote a letter commanding obedience and repentance, and the Corinthians obeyed. Ancient churches (or dioceses) did not invite anyone outside their ecclesiastical jurisdictions to help them with their problems; neither did they tolerate such outsiders who tried to meddle in their internal affairs. Thus the intervention of the Roman Church is often noted as proof that ancient Christians recognized the authority of Rome. Clement died a martyr in 101.

He is patron of blacksmiths, farriers (blacksmiths who shoe horses), stonecutters, shoe tanners, and British lighthouses.

Feast Dates: November 23 — St. Clement, Pope.

Clemente (Spanish, Italian) See Clement.

Clementius (Dutch) See Clement.

Clemento (Spanish) See Clement.

Clennon (African-American) See Cleon.

Cleon (Greek) See Clare.

Cleon (variant) See Cleveland, Clive.

Cleophus "The One Who Gives a Speech" (Old English).

Patron Saints: St. Cleophus was a disciple of Christ to whom Jesus appeared on the way to Emmaus. His story is related in the Gospel of Luke.

Feast Dates: September 25 — St. Cleophus.

Cletis (Dutch) See Cletus.

Cleto (Spanish) See Cletus.

Cletus "The Summoned One" (Greek).

Patron Saints: There are a half-dozen Sts. Cletus. One of them became the third pope. He died a martyr.

Feast Dates: April 26 — St. Cletus, Pope; September 8 — SG Anaclete González Flores (see Anaclete).

Cleve (nickname) See Cleveland, Cliff.

Cleveland "From the Land+Of the Cliffs" (Old English double).

Patron Saints: A patron saint can be found once one realizes that Cleveland comes from two words: *cleve* means "cliff" and *land* means "land." Thus Cleve means the same as Clyde, and there is a St. Clyde (Clydno). There are also a few saints who have Land as part of their names, such as Lando.

Feast Dates: November 1 — St. Clyde (see Clyde); January 16 — St. Lando (see Land).

Clevey (nickname) See Cleveland.

Clevon (English-African-American double) See Cleveland, Cleve+Vaughn.

Cliff (variant) See Clifford, Clive.

Clifford "From the Cliff+At the River Crossing" (Old English double).

Patron Saints: The meaning of Clifford is helpful in finding a patron. A little research reveals that Montford means almost exactly the same as Clifford. There is an English martyr named Bl. Montford Scott.

Feast Dates: May 4 — Bl. Montford Scott (see Montford).

Cliffy (nickname) See Clifford.

Clift (English double) See Clive/Clifford+Town.

Clifton (English double) See Clifford+Town.

Clint "From the Cliff [Headland]" (Old English).

Patron Saints: It is helpful to know that Clint has about the same meaning as Clyde. This leads to St. Clyde.

There is also one saint with a similar name, St. Clinus, who can be adopted. He was born in Greece but traveled to Italy and entered the monastery of Monte Cassino. He was ordained and rose to the office of abbot. Then he became provost of a local parish in about 600.

Feast Dates: March 30 — St. Clinus, O.S.B.; November 1 — St. Clyde, also known as Clydno (see Clyde).

Clinton (English double) See Clint/Cliff+Town.

Clive (English) See Cleve, Cliff, Clyde.

Clodoveo (Spanish) See Louis.

Cloud "From the Mist" (Middle English).

Patron Saints: There is a St. Cloud who was heir to the throne of France. When his two brothers were killed because of politics, he hid in a monastery. In time, he began living a life of prayer, became a disciple of St. Severinus, and spread the teachings of Jesus. He died in 560.

Feast Dates: September 7 — St. Cloud.

Clovis (Latin) See Louis.

Cloyo (nickname) See Claude.

Clyde "From the Cliff [Headland]" (Scottish Gaelic) or "The Warm One" (Welsh).

Patron Saints: There is one St. Clyde. In his day he was known as Clydno and was the son of Cunwyd Cynwydion. He ruled in northern Britain and at one point he became a member of a religious order.

Feast Dates: November 1 — St. Clyde, also known as Clydno.

Clyve (English) See Cleve, Cliff, Clive.

Cnut (variant) See Knute.

Coal (variant) See Coleman.

Cob (nickname) See Jacob.

Cobb (nickname) See Jacob.

Cobbie (nickname) See Jacob.

Cobey (nickname) See Jacob.

Cobra "The Poisonous Serpent" (Portuguese).

Patron Saints: The Gospel of John teaches that Jesus took upon himself our sins and became the "serpent nailed to the tree." This reminds us of how Moses set up a staff with a serpent on it in order to bring life and health to those who had been bitten by desert serpents. In the same way Jesus redeemed us.

Feast Dates: Sacred Triduum — Jesus the Redeemer; September 4 — St. Moses, Jewish Deliverer.

Coby (Hebrew) See Jacob.

Cody "A Cushion" (Old English).

Patron Saints: There are two Sts. Cody. One St. Cody, 242-258, was a Greek who embraced martyrdom with a few friends at the age of sixteen. He seems to have been a Christian all of his life, which made his life very hard because Christians were persecuted in the Roman Empire during the 200s.

Feast Dates: March 10 — St. Cody, also known as Codratus.

Col (nickname) See Colby, Coleman, Colin, Colt, Colton, Columbus.

Cola (nickname) See Nicholas.

Colacho (English) See Colin.

Colacho (Celtic) See Nicholas.

Colan (English) See Colin.

Colas (Celtic) See Nicholas.

Colby "From the Black [Coal]+Place" (Old English double) or "The Supplanter" (variant of Jacob).

Patron Saints: Patrons can be found if one knows that the name Colby is formed from two words. *Col* means "black" or "coal," and *by* means "farm" or "place." Any saint with Cole as part of his name can serve as patron. The most popular "Cole" name is Coleman. There are over three hundred Sts. Coleman.

Feast Dates: November 24 — St. Coleman (see Baird); February 18 — St. Coleman (see Coleman).

Cole (Celtic) See Nicholas.

Cole (nickname) See Colby, Coleman, Colin, Colt, Colton, Columbus.

Coleman "The Follower of Nicholas" (Old English) or "The Little Dove" (Irish Gaelic).

Patron Saints: The fact that Coleman is a form of Nicholas leads to many patrons because there are more than three hundred Sts. Coleman and some fifty Sts. Nicholas from which to choose.

St. Coleman of Lindisfarne, 605-676, was born in Connaught, Ireland, and became a monk at the Iona monastery. When he was fifty-six, he became

bishop. In 664, after functioning as bishop for only three years, Coleman resigned his office and moved his monks from Scotland to Mayo in Ireland.

Feast Dates: February 18 — St. Coleman of Lindisfarne.

Colet (variant) See Nicholas.

Colin "The Young Strong Child" (Irish Gaelic) or "The Victorious People" (French-Greek of Nicholas).

Patron Saints: There are three Sts. Colin. One of them, who lived in the 600s, was a descendant of King Caradog. He became a knight and fought in many battles. However, when he got older, he decided to become a monk and entered the monastery of Glastonbury. Also, Colin can be regarded as a short form of Nicholas, and this leads to over fifty Sts. Nicholas.

Feast Dates: May 21 — St. Colin.

Collie (nickname) See Coleman.

Collin (variant) See Colin.

Colly (variant) See Colin.

Colman (English) See Colin.

Colt (English) See Colton.

Colton "From the Coal+Town" (Old English double).

Patron Saints: Knowing that Colton is made up of two words (*col*, meaning "coal," and *ton*, meaning "town") leads to many patrons. Also, any saint with Col as part of his or her name can serve as patron.

Feast Dates: February 18 — St. Coleman of Lindisfarne; July 21 — St. Tondach (see Town).

Colum (nickname) See Columbus.

Columba (variant) See Columbus.

Columbkill (Irish) See Columbus.

Columbus "The Dove" (Latin).

Patron Saints: There are over fifty saints who bear the names Colum, Columba, and Columbanus. One of them is St. Columba of Iona, 521-597, the greatest of the Scottish saints, although he was actually an Irishman whose parents were of royal lineage. He is also known as Columcille or Columbkill. Upon ordination in 551, according to one story, he founded a monastery at Derry. (Other sources credit him with several monasteries and a school.) Then he left Ireland, traveled to Scotland, and, with twelve companions, founded the great monastery at Iona, just off the coast. He served as abbot and traveled extensively for some thirty-four years, making many converts. He was an excellent speaker, scholar, poet, and statesman. He died at the age of seventy-six and is patron of Ireland and of poets.

Feast Dates: June 9 — St. Columba of Iona.

Columcille (Irish) See Columbus.

Combs (variant) See Columbus.

Con (nickname) See Conan, Connor, Conrad, Conway, Cornelius.

Conan "The Intelligent One" (Old English) or "The Exalted One" (Irish Gaelic).

Patron Saints: There are about a dozen Sts. Conan. One of them was a native of Ireland and a monk at the monastery of Iona. He also served for a while as a tutor to the three sons of King Eugene IV of Scotland. Then he served as the bishop of Sodor and of the Isle of Man. He died in 648.

Feast Dates: January 28 — St. Conan.

Conant (variant) See Conan.

Conn (nickname) See Con.

Conney (nickname) See Con.

Connie (nickname) See Con.

Connor "The Honest Wise Counselor" (Irish Gaelic) or "The Chief of the Men" (Celtic).

Patron Saints: There are a half-dozen Sts. Conon and Conrach. And

the name's meaning, "wise counselor," leads to a patron, since the definition also applies to the name Alfred.

Feast Dates: January 6 — Bl. Alfred Bessette (see Alfred).

Conny (nickname) See Con.

Conor (English) See Connor.

Conrad "The Bold Counselor" (Old German).

Patron Saints: There are at least a dozen-and-a-half Sts. Conrad. One was a nobleman of Piacenza who lived from 1290 to 1354. Once when he was hunting, he accidentally caused a great forest fire. No one suspected him, and a poor man was arrested and condemned to death. To save the innocent man, Conrad came forward and confessed his guilt and had to give up his entire fortune in order to make restitution.

At the approximate age of thirty-five he and his wife decided to part company and join religious orders. He became a hermit for the last thirty years of his life, dying at the age of sixty-four.

Feast Dates: February 19 — St. Conrad of Piacenza.

Conrado (Spanish) See Conrad.

Conway "The Hound of+The Plain" (Irish Gaelic double).

Patron Saints: Patron saints can be discovered once one realizes that the name Conway is formed from two words: *con*, meaning "hound," and *way*, meaning "way" or "plain."

There are two Sts. Conus and one English martyr named Bl. William Way. St. Conus joined the Benedictine Order at Diano in southern Italy.

Feast Dates: June 3 — St. Conus, O.S.B.; September 23 — Bl. William Way (see Wayland).

Coop (English) See Cooper.

Cooper "The Barrelmaker" (Old English).

Patron Saints: The Catholic Church has appointed Sts. Abdon, Nicholas, and Urba to be patrons of coopers (barrelmakers).

Feast Dates: April 12 — St. Urban of Langres (see Urban).

Corbet (English) See Corbin.

Corbett (English) See Corbin.

Corbie (nickname) See Corbin.

Corbin "The Raven" (Latin).

Patron Saints: There is one St. Corbin, 670-725. Also known as Corbinian, he lived as a hermit in a small shack near a chapel for fourteen years. His reputation for sanctity and miracles grew, and people began to besiege him from all sides. Thus he began to search for a new place where he could live in obscurity.

He traveled to Rome, but he found no peace and quiet there. Hearing of his arrival, the pope consecrated him a bishop and sent him to the Bavarian missions. He made many converts, but he also made enemies. It seems that the local duke was in a non-approved marriage. Corbin pointed this out, and the duke's wife conspired to kill him, forcing him to flee. Only after the death of his adversaries was he free to return to Bavaria.

Feast Dates: September 8 — St. Corbin.

Corby (nickname) See Corbin.

Cord (nickname) See Cordell.

Cordell "The Ropemaker" (Old French).

Patron Saints: Two saints, St. Cordius and Cordes, can be patrons. St. Cordius died a martyr in Roman times. And since Cord comes from Cordell, and the latter means "cord or ropemaker," one more patron can be found. She is St. Catherine of Alexandria and she is patron of ropemakers.

Feast Dates: February 17 — St. Cord, also known as Cordius; November 25 — St. Catherine of Alexandria (see Wheeler).

Cordero (Spanish) See Hamal.

Cordie (nickname) See Cordell.

Cordy (nickname) See Cordell.

Corey "From the Hollow [Valley]" (Irish Gaelic) or "From the Heart" (Latin).

Patron Saints: There is one ancient St. Corey. He was the prefect of Messina in Sicily. He converted to the faith in Roman times and was beheaded by order of the emperor Hadrian in about 135.

Moreover, if one realizes that *cor* is the Latin for "heart," a few more patrons appear, such as Sts. Cordius and Cordula. In addition, a most powerful patron appears: the Sacred Heart of Jesus.

From ancient times Catholics have been devoted to the love of God. This love took human form in Jesus. Thus in seeking to become one with the Sacred Heart of Jesus the believer seeks union with God. He also seeks to be loved and understood by a God-Man, by a heart that truly understands the human condition. Devotion to the Sacred Heart reached the height of popularity in the 1200s and 1300s.

Feast Dates: April 18 — St. Corey, also known as Corebus; Friday Following the Second Sunday After Pentecost — The Sacred Heart of Jesus.

Corie (English) See Corbin, Cordell, Corey.

Cornall (English) See Cornelius.

Cornel (English) See Cornelius.

Cornell (English) See Cornelius.

Cornelio (Spanish) See Cornelius.

Cornelius "The One with Horn-Colored Hair" (Latin).

Patron Saints: There are about two dozen Sts. Cornelius to choose from. During the persecution of the Roman emperor Decius, Pope St. Fabian was martyred. At first, no one wanted the pope's job, then a priest named Cornelius was finally elected, who knew very well that it would mean his death.

The first problem Cornelius had to face was how to handle those who had apostatized under torture. Some suggested leniency and others wanted strictness. Cornelius sided with the view of leniency. Then persecution intensified, and St. Cornelius was beheaded in 253. He had only been pope for about one year.

Feast Dates: September 16 — St. Cornelius, Pope.

Corney (English) See Cornelius.

Cornie (English) See Cornelius.

Corny (English) See Cornelius.

Cort (English) See Cortéz, Courtney, Harcourt.

Cort "The Short One" (Old Norse) or "The Bold One" (Old German).

Patron Saints: Besides being a name in its own right, Cort may also serve as a nickname for Conrad and Courtney. Thus many patrons are possible. It just depends on which name's meaning is picked.

Feast Dates: November 1 — Holy Martyrs (see Courtney).

Cortéz "The Court Dweller" (Spanish).

Patron Saints: Father Agustín Caloca Cortés, who was executed for the faith in Mexico on May 25, 1927, will make a fine patron saint.

Feast Dates: May 25 — St. Agustín Caloca Cortés.

Cortie (nickname) See Cort, Courtney, Harcourt.

Cortnay (English) See Courtney.

Corty (nickname) See Cortéz, Cort, Courtney, Harcourt.

Cory (nickname) See Corbin, Cordell, Korey.

Cos (nickname) See Cosmo.

Cosimo (variant) See Cosmo.

Cosmo "The Universe" (Greek) or "The Order and Harmony of Creation" (Greek).

Patron Saints: There are about two dozen Sts. Cosmas. The brothers Cosmas and Damian, medical physicians, belonged to a group of ancient saints known in the Eastern Church as the "Moneyless Ones." They practiced a trade without accepting any money for their services.

They were born in the late 200s in Arabia, studied medicine in Syria, met some Christians, and converted. Then in about 300 they were arrested and imprisoned. They were tortured but would not deny their faith. Finally, they were beheaded. They are now patrons of barbers, men's hairdressers, doctors, surgeons, dentists, druggists, and chemical workers.

Feast Dates: September 26 — Sts. Cosmas and Damian.

Cottrell (African-American double) See Colton+Terrell/Tyrell.

Coujoe "Born on Monday" (Ghana).

Patron Saints: In European culture, Monday means "moon day." *Luna* is Latin for "moon," and this leads to about a dozen saints. Among them is St. Lunaire, 509-570, the son of King Hoel I of Brittany. He and his brother, St. Tugdual, were educated by St. Illtyd, then the brothers were ordained priests by St. Dyfrig of Caerleon. Later St. Lunaire became a bishop and founded a monastery in Brittany. He died at the age of sixty-one.

Feast Dates: July 1 — St. Lunaire, also known as Leonore.

Court (nickname) See Courtney, Harcourt.

Courtenay (English) See Courtney.

Courtney "From the Law Court" (Old French).

Patron Saints: Throughout history Christians found the civil courts to be tools that often condemned them to death. Testimony that they were Christian provided the evidence that brought death.

For this reason, the Gospel of John uses "courtroom terms" throughout, such as: "testified," "witness," "judgment." It teaches that if one is condemned to be a "martyr" on earth for being a Christian, he or she will be found deserving of eternal life in heaven. This makes all the martyrs patron saints of Courtney.

Feast Dates: November 1 — All the Holy Martyrs.

Cowan (Irish) See Dean, Valle.

Cozmo (variant) See Cosmo.

Cragg (English) See Craig.

Craggie (nickname) See Craig.

Craggy (nickname) See Craig.

Craig "From the Rocky Eminence" (Irish Gaelic).

Patron Saints: A patron saint can be found once one realizes that Craig means "rocky eminence." The name Clyde means the same thing, and there is a St. Clyde.

Feast Dates: November 1 — St. Clyde (see Clyde).

Craigory (African-American double) See Craig+Gregory.

Cran (nickname) See Crandall.

Crandall "From the Crane's+Valley" (Old English double).

Patron Saints: The word *cran* means "crane bird," while *dall* means "valley." This leads to Bl. Bird, St. Dallan, and St. Gall. St. Gall is the official patron of birds. He was a religious brother and one of twelve disciples who followed St. Columba of Iona from Scotland to Switzerland in order to bring Christianity back to the European continent. He died in 627.

Feast Dates: October 16 — St. Gall; January 29 — St. Dallan (see Dale); March 25 — Bl. James Bird (see Bird).

Crandell (English) See Crandall.

Crane (English) See Crandall.

Craw (English) See Crawford.

Crawford "From the Crows+River Crossing" (Old English double).

Patron Saints: The two parts of this name lead to two saints who make the perfect patrons. They are Bls. Thomas Ford and Alexander Crow. In 1586 Father Alexander Crow was arrested for being a priest. He was condemned and immediately executed. His feast day is shared with eighty-four other English martyrs.

Feast Dates: May 4 — Bl. Alexander Crow; May 28 — Bl. Thomas Ford (see Ford).

Crispin "The Curly-Haired One" (Latin).

Patron Saints: There are twelve Sts. Crispinus and Crispinianus. Christian tradition tells of two martyrs who lived and died during the reign of the emperor Diocletian, 284-305. In order to avoid persecution, they fled to France and occupied themselves by learning the cobbler's trade.

Then they got caught in the middle of a military campaign. Emperor Maximian had them arrested and turned over to his enemy, the Christian-hating Rictivarus. Rictivarus tortured them with near-boiling and drowning. Finally, he beheaded them because of their faith. They are patrons of shoemakers, cobblers, harness makers, and tanners.

Feast Dates: October 25 — Sts. Crispinus and Crispinianus.

Crisanto (Spanish double) See Christopher+Santos.

Crisciano (Portuguese) See Christian.
Crisoforo (Spanish) See Christopher.
Cristian (Spanish, Romanian) See Christian.
Cristiano (Italian) See Christian.
Cristino (Spanish) See Christian.
Cristóbal (Spanish) See Christopher.
Cristofer (variant) See Christopher.
Cristoffer (Danish) See Christopher.
Cristoforo (Italian) See Christopher.
Cristoforos (Greek) See Christopher.
Cristovao (variant) See Christopher.
Crockett "The Crooked [Bent]+Little One" (Old English double).

> *Patron Saints:* There is an English martyr with this name. Bl. Ralph Crockett was born at Barton-on-the-Hill and was educated at Cambridge and Oxford. Then he became a schoolmaster in Norfolk and Suffolk. From there he went to Rheims in France to study for the Catholic priesthood. He was ordained in 1586 and went immediately to the English missions. Two years later he was arrested while engaging in missionary work and was imprisoned. This was followed by execution.
> *Feast Dates:* October 1 — Bl. Ralph Crockett of Barton-on-the-Hill.

Crow (English) See Crawford.
Cruz "The Cross" (Portuguese, Spanish).

> *Patron Saints:* St. John of the Cross, 1542-1591, is one of many choices. A Doctor of the Church, he is remembered for his mystical writings.
> *Feast Dates:* September 14 — Triumph of the Cross; December 14 — St. John of the Cross.

Crystek (Polish) See Christian.
Cuba Meaning unknown (Spanish, Caribbean Indian).

> *Patron Saints:* In 1510 the invading Spanish gave the chief of a Cuban Indian tribe a twelve-inch statue of Our Lady of Charity and then began a program of extermination of the natives. One hundred years later, in 1610, the statue was discovered floating in the sea by three boys who were in serious trouble because of a violent storm. By a miracle they survived. In 1916 Our Lady of Charity became patron of Cuba.
> *Feast Dates:* Any Saturday — Our Lady of Charity.

Cudjo (African-American) See Coujoe.
Cull (nickname) See Cullen.
Cullan (variant) See Cullen.
Cullen "The Handsome One" (Irish Gaelic).

> *Patron Saints:* There are a half-dozen Sts. Cullen. However, they spelled their names as Cuillen, Culan, and Cuilleann. One St. Cullen is remembered for being the prayerful bishop of Leamhegvill, Ireland.
> Also, because the name Cullen means "handsome," Sts. Kyle and Kenneth can be adopted as patrons. Their names also mean "handsome."
> *Feast Dates:* April 22 — St. Cullen, also known as Cuilleann; March 25 — St. Kyle of Fife (see Kyle).

Culley (nickname) See Cullen.
Cullin (variant) See Cullen.
Cully (nickname) See Cullen.
Curcio (Spanish) See Curtis.
Curclo (variant) See Curtis.
Curr (nickname) See Curran.
Curran "The Hero" (Irish Gaelic).

> *Patron Saints:* There are a few saints with similar names, including Sts. Curentus, Curitan, and Curnan. One St. Curentus suffered martyrdom in ancient Mauretania.
> Moreover, the fact that Curran means "hero" leads to other saints, such as Sts. Hero and Herolus.
> *Feast Dates:* March 18 — St. Curentus.

Currey (nickname) See Curran.

Currie (nickname) See Curran.

Currito (Spanish) See Francis.

Curro (Spanish) See Francis.

Curry (nickname) See Curran.

Curt (variant) See Conrad, Courtney, Curtis.

Curtice (variant) See Curtis.

Curtis "The Courteous One" (Old French).

Patron Saints: Curtis can serve as an alternate form of Courtney and Conrad or serve as a full name.

Feast Dates: February 19 — St. Conrad of Piazenza (see Conrad) November 1 — Holy Martyrs (see Courtney).

Curtiss (variant) See Curtis.

Cuthbert "The Famous, Brilliant One" (Old English).

Patron Saints: One English martyr qualifies for patron. Cuthbert Mayne, 1544-1577, was raised Protestant and ordained a Protestant minister at the age of nineteen. Later, while studying at Oxford, he met St. Edmund Campion and became Catholic. He was then ordained a priest in France.

Returning to England in 1575, he became an estate steward to Francis Tregain of Golden, but he was soon arrested for being a Catholic priest. This led to his conviction for treason. He was hanged, drawn, and quartered because he refused to recognize the queen of England as head of the Church.

Feast Dates: November 29 — St. Cuthbert Mayne.

Cy (nickname) See Cyril, Cyrus.

Cyprian "The One from Cypress" (Greek).

Patron Saints: There are almost two dozen Sts. Cyprian. One died a martyr in ancient Nicomedia.

Feast Dates: August 17 — St. Cyprian.

Cyrek (Czech) See Cyril.

Cyril "The Lordly One" (English).

Patron Saints: There are about fifty Sts. Cyril. The St. Cyril, 315-386, who is a Doctor of the Church, was a gentle man and a peacemaker. He was ordained a priest at the age of thirty. Five years later he became bishop of Jerusalem. Twice Cyril was deposed from his diocese. Then in 367 the emperor sent him into exile. He also had to deal with the failed attempt of Julian the Apostate to rebuild the Jewish Temple.

Through it all, Cyril remained faithful. He spent time writing his catechetical lectures on the divinity of Jesus and his "Real Presence" in Holy Communion. He was seventy-one years old at the time of his death.

Feast Dates: March 18 — St. Cyril of Jerusalem.

Cyrill (German) See Cyril.

Cyrille (French) See Cyril.

Cyrillus (Latin) See Cyril.

Cyrus "The One Like the Sun" (Persian).

Patron Saints: There are about a dozen Sts. Cyrus. One of the most famous is a St. Cyrus who embraced martyrdom with his friend John in 312. They belong to a group of ancient saints known as the "Moneyless Ones." Members of this group gave their services away without charge.

Cyrus was a Christian physician at Canopus, Egypt, and when persecution broke out, he fled into the Egypto-Arabian desert. While in his desert refuge, a catechumen named John attached himself to Cyrus. They became friends. In time, they traveled to Alexandria to comfort some imprisoned Christians. This led to their arrest, and they were swiftly condemned to death.

Feast Dates: January 31 — St. Cyrus.

𝒟

D' (French prefix) See De.

Da (Italian preposition) See De.

Daa'ood (Arabic) See David.

Dab (nickname) See Dabney.

Dabney "The One Who Touches Lightly+From the Island" (Old English double).

> *Patron Saints:* Sts. Dabius and Nwy are perfect patrons.
>
> *Feast Dates:* July 22 — St. Dabius; November 1 — St. Nwy (see Ny).

Dace (variant) See Dacey.

Dacey "The Southerner" (Irish Gaelic).

> *Patron Saints:* There are about a dozen Sts. Dacey. But they spelled their names Dacianus and Dacius. It was the custom in the ancient Roman army to elect a "Lord of Misrule" thirty days before the celebration of the Saturnalia. This soldier led the orgy and at the end was sacrificed to the pagan god Kronos.
>
> In 303 the Roman garrison in Bulgaria elected St. Dacey, and this created a problem for him. He had secretly become a Christian and did not want any part of this pagan celebration. Furthermore, he was caught in a dilemma. To lead the revels would mean his death and to reveal he was Christian would also mean death. He chose to reveal he was a Christian and thus die for a good cause rather than a bad one.
>
> *Feast Dates:* November 20 — St. Dacey, also known as Dacius.

Dack (nickname) See Dakota.

Dacy (variant) See Dacey.

Dad (variant) See Papa.

Daddy (variant) See Papa.

Daemon (Greek) See Damian.

Daeshawn (African-American double) See Da+Shawn.

Daevon (African-American double) See Da+Vaughn.

Daffy (nickname) See David.

Dafydd (Welsh) See David.

Dag "The Bright Day" (Old Norse).

> *Patron Saints:* There are a dozen saints named Dagain, Dagamund, Dagan, Dagobert, Dogonius, Daigh, and Daighre. Any of them can serve as patrons. St. Dagobert, 652-679, became king of ancient Austrasia (Germany) at the age of four. At age twenty-three he was driven from power by his majordomo and into a monastery. Eventually he regained his throne. He founded an abbey and many other religious institutions. However, he was murdered at the age of twenty-seven, the victim of another palace revolution.
>
> It is helpful to know that the name Delbert also means "day" or "brightness." Delbert is usually considered a form of Adelbert, and there are many Sts. Adelbert.
>
> *Feast Dates:* December 23 — St. Dagobert II; April 23 — St. Adelbert of Prague (see Adelbert).

Dagny (variant) See Dag.

Dagoberto (Spanish double) See Dag+Bert.

Daibidh (Scottish) See David.

Dain (variant) See Dana.

Daiquan (African-American double) See Da+Juan.

DaJuan (African-American double) See Da+Juan.

Dajon (African-American double) See Da+John.

Dak (nickname) See Dakota.

Dakota "Thought of as a Friend" (North American Indian).

Patron Saints: Patrons can be found once one realizes that *dakota* means "thought of as a friend." There is one great Old Testament man, St. Abraham, who is "called the friend of God" in James 2:23.

Furthermore, the Latin word for "friend" is *amicus*, and there are three Sts. Amicus and one St. Amica. One St. Amicus was a French knight, who took his faith very seriously. He followed King Charlemagne in a campaign and died in battle in 773.

Feast Dates: October 12 — St. Amicus; October 9 — St. Abraham (see Abraham).

Dal (nickname) See Dallas.

Dale "From the Valley" (Old English).

Patron Saints: There are a few ancient saints with similar names: Dallan, Dalmatius, and Dalua. A St. Dallan was born of royalty in Ireland in about 550. He was a great scholar. His greatest work was a poem in praise of St. Columban and was called the *Ambra Choluim Kille.* Dallan died at the hands of pirates, while at sea, in 598.

Feast Dates: January 29 — St. Dallan Forgaill.

Dall (nickname) See Dallas.

Dallas "The Wise One" (Scottish Gaelic).

Patron Saints: There is one with the similar name of St. Dallan. Furthermore, there are about twenty female saints named Sophia, which means "wisdom" or "the wise one." One St. Sophia was an abbess in Edessa during the time of the emperor Julian the Apostate. She and fifty of her nuns were slain by government agents.

Feast Dates: November 6 — St. Sophia; January 29 — St. Dallen Forgaill (see Dale).

Dallis (English) See Dallas.

Dalton (English double) See Dale+Town.

Damarcus (African-American double) See Da+Marcus.

Damario (African-American double) See Da+Mario.

Dame (Polish) See Damien.

Damek (Polish) See Damien.

Damek (Czech) See Adam.

Damian (variant) See Damien.

Damiano (Italian) See Damien.

Damien "The One Who Tames" (Greek).

Patron Saints: There are two dozen Sts. Damianus. Bl. Damien de Veuster, 1840-1889, is famous for serving the lepers on Molokai in Hawaii. Named Joseph de Veuster at birth in Belgium, he took the name Damien when be became a member of the Sacred Hearts of Jesus and Mary (also called the Picpus Fathers).

In 1864 he traveled to the Hawaiian Islands and while there became aware of the scourge of leprosy, which probably first appeared in Hawaii in 1823. It was popularly (and mistakenly) thought that leprosy was caused by illicit sex. In 1873, at the age of thirty-three, Damien asked permission to minister to the lepers on Molokai. He knew that to go to Molokai meant exile unto death. On Molokai he found lawlessness, immorality, brutality, and hopelessness. He also faced the smell of rotting flesh, a stench that turned his stomach. He took to smoking a pipe to help him bear it.

Slowly he attracted the lepers to church. Then he built cottages, organized farming, sports, jobs, and provided some medical relief. He died of leprosy during Holy Week, on April 15, 1889, at the age of forty-nine.

Feast Dates: April 15 — Bl. Damien de Veuster.

Damon (Russian, Ukrainian) See Damien.

Dan (nickname) See Dana, Daniel.

Dana "The One from Denmark" (Old English) or "God Is My Judge" (variant form of Daniel).

Patron Saints: Some consider Dana to be a Scandinavian name. This leads to about a half-dozen saints named Danacha, Danax, and Danda. St. Danax lived during the 100s. He served as a lector at Avlona in Albania. When his country was invaded by a foreign army, he tried to hide the sacred altar vessels. He was caught and then beheaded.

Dana can also be identified as a variant of Daniel, which means "God is my judge." There are over three dozen Sts. Daniel from which to choose.

Feast Dates: January 16 — St. Danax; October 19 — St. Antoine Daniel (see Daniel).

Dandie (nickname) See Andrew.

Dandré (African-American double) See Da+André.

Dandy (nickname) See Andrew.

Dane (nickname, Dutch) See Dana, Daniel.

Daniel "God Is My Judge" (English, German, Hebrew, French, Spanish, Swedish, Scottish).

Patron Saints: There are more than three dozen Sts. Daniel. One of them is St. Antoine Daniel, 1601-1648, of France. He studied law, joined the Jesuits, and was ordained a priest. Then he volunteered for the American missions. He was very talented at teaching the Huron Indian children their prayers and the Ten Commandments. He did it by setting the words to music. In 1647 he was in an Indian village near Hillsdale, Ontario, and had just finished Mass when the Iroquois attacked. He fearlessly faced the invaders and forbade them to enter, and they shot him in the heart. He was the first of the North American Martyrs to die. The others are Isaac Jogues, Jean de Brébeuf, Gabriel Lalemant, Charles Garnier, Noël Chabanel, René Goupil, and Jean de Lalande.

Feast Dates: October 19 — St. Antoine Daniel, S.J.

Danielek (Polish) See Daniel.

Danielle (French) See Daniel.

Danielus (Lithuanian) See Daniel.

Danill (Greek, Romanian) See Daniel.

Danilo (Serbian, Spanish) See Daniel.

Danko (Czech) See Daniel.

Dannick (Polish) See Daniel.

Dannie (nickname) See Daniel.

Danny (nickname) See Daniel.

Dante "The One Who Endures" (Italian).

Patron Saints: St. Dante was martyred in ancient Africa.

Feast Dates: February 11 — St. Dante, also known as Dantus.

Danylo (Ukrainian) See Daniel.

Daquan (African-American double) See Da+Quan.

Dar (nickname) See Darby, Darcy.

Dar (English) See Darius, Darnell, Darrell, Darren, Darwin.

Darb (nickname) See Darby.

Darbee (nickname) See Darby.

Darby "The Free Man" (Irish Gaelic) or "From the Deer Estate" (Old Norse).

Patron Saints: There are a half-dozen Sts. Darby. One is remembered to have been the son of Darerca, the sister of St. Patrick. He was ordained a priest and helped his uncle, St. Patrick.

Furthermore, the name Darby can mean "free man," which leads to an English martyr surnamed Freeman. Finally, it is also good to know that Darby can be a form of Jeremiah. This leads to six Sts. Jeremiah.

Feast Dates: January 15 — St. Darby; August 13 — Bl. William Freeman (see Freeman).

Darc (nickname) See Darcy.

D'Arcy (nickname) See Darcy.

D'arcy (nickname) See Darcy.

Darcy "From the Fortress" (Old French) or "The Dark One" (Irish Gaelic).

Patron Saints: There is one St. Darcy. He is simply remembered as an "Irish saint."

The meaning of the Old French word *darcy*, "fortress," suggests that one may ask Jesus the Rock and Fortress to serve as patron. Furthermore, knowing that the meaning of the Irish *darcy* is "dark" leads to saints named Brown, More, and Morse.

Feast Dates: February 13 — St. Darcy, also known as Darcus; September 5 — Bl. William Browne (see Browne).

Dare (English) See Darius, Darrell, Darren.

Darence (African-American double) See Darrell/Darnell/Darius+Clarence.

Darin (English) See Darren.

Dario (English, Spanish) See Darius.

Darius "The Wealthy One" (Greek).

Patron Saints: There are two Sts. Darius. One of them suffered martyrdom in ancient Bithynia.

Feast Dates: December 19 — St. Darius.

Darl (English) See Darrell.

Darn (English) See Darnell.

Darnall (English) See Darnell.

Darnell "From the Hidden Place" (Old French) or "The Little Dear [Beloved] One" (Old French).

Patron Saints: It is also helpful to know Darnell can mean "beloved," just like the name David.

Feast Dates: December 29 — St. David (see David).

Darnley (African-American double) See Darnell+Leigh.

Darrel (English) See Darrell.

Darrell "The Beloved One" (Old French).

Patron Saints: Some ancient saints with similar names may be adopted, including Sts. Darius and Daria. There are those who insist that Darrell is a form of David. This leads to two dozen Sts. David.

Feast Dates: December 19 — St. Darius (see Darius); December 29 — St. David (see David).

Darren "The Little Great One" (Irish Gaelic) or "The Gift of God" (short form of Isidore).

Patron Saints: Darren is a variant form of Isidore, meaning "gift of God." In its short form of Dore, it becomes Darren or Darrin. There are about three dozen Sts. Isidore.

Feast Dates: May 15 — St. Isidore (see Isadore).

Darrick (variant) See Derek.

Darril (English) See Darrell.

Darrin (English) See Darren, Isadore.

Darron (English) See Darren.

Darryl (English) See Darrell.

Darwin "The Beloved Friend" (Old English double).

Patron Saints: Patrons can be found once one realizes that Darwin arises from the Old English *dar*, meaning "beloved," and *win*, meaning "friend." This leads one to two Sts. Darius, a dozen Sts. Daria, and a half-dozen Sts. Wynnin, Winin, and Winnian.

Feast Dates: December 19 — St. Darius (see Darius); November 1 — St. Wynnin (see Wynn).

Daryl (English) See Darrell.

Daryle (English) See Darrell.

Daryn (African-American) See Darren.

Dashawn (African-American double) See Da+Shawn.

Davaris (African-American double) See David+Darius.

Dave (nickname) See David.

Daven (variant) See David.

Davey (variant) See David.

David "The Beloved One" (Hebrew).

Patron Saints: There are about two dozen Sts. David. In addition, King David from the Bible can also serve as a patron. The most popular is St. David, patron of Wales and of poets. He was handsome, rich, well-educated, and a priest. He studied the Bible, the religious classics, did missionary work, and built twelve monasteries and churches. Eventually he settled in Wales with a group of followers and embraced manual labor and vegetarianism. Soon he became a bishop. He ruled his diocese until he was well into his sixties. He died in 589.

Feast Dates: March 1 — St. David, also known as Dewi.

Davidde (Italian) See David.

Davide (French) See David.

Davidson (English double) See David+Son.

Davie (nickname) See David.

Davin "The Bright, Intelligent One" (Scandinavian) or "The Beloved One" (form of David).

Patron Saints: St. Davinus lived in Armenia, where he practiced a prayerful life near the Church of St. Michael. He died in 1051.

Feast Dates: June 3 — St. Davinus.

Davin (variant) See David.

Davis (English double) See David+Son.

Davon (variant) See David, Devon.

Davy (nickname) See David.

Davyd (Russian, Ukrainian) See David.

Dawan (African-American) See Davon.

Dawid (Polish, Yiddish) See David.

Dawson (Old English) See David+Son.

Dawud (Arabic) See David.

Day (Old English) See Sunny.

Dayle (English) See Dale.

Daylon (African-American) See Dillon, Dylan.

Daymian (Greek) See Damian.

Dayne (Scandinavian) See Dane.

Dayquan (African-American double) See Day+Quan.

Dayton (Old English double) See Day+Town.

Dayvon (African-American double) See Davin, Day+Vaughn.

Dax (nickname) See Dakota.

De "From" (French prefix) or "The Holy One" (Welsh).

Patron Saints: The French prefix *de* or *d'*, indicating origin, has been much used as a prefix by modern African-Americans, usually when naming males. For example: DeShaun, DeWayne, and Devonne.

But "De" can also be form of *dee*, meaning "holy one," which is the same as the Latin word *sanctus*. A St. Sanctus was a deacon who was martyred in Lyons in 177. He was put in a red-hot iron chair and then his throat was cut.

Feast Dates: June 2 — St. De, also known as Dee.

Deacon "The One Who Serves" (Greek).

Patron Saints: There are many saints who served as deacons. In fact, two of them have been named patrons of deacons. They are Sts. Philip and Stephen and were among the first deacons ordained by the Apostles. St. Philip the Deacon was a Greek who lived in Caesarea. The Book of Acts tells how he converted the Ethiopian eunuch and baptized him. Twenty-four years later, St. Paul stayed with Philip and his family as he traveled through Caesarea. Later in life, Philip became the bishop of Tralles.

A married man, Philip was the father of four daughters. It seems they were with the Apostles and Mary in the upper room on the day of Pentecost. All functioned as prophetesses in the early Church.

Feast Dates: June 6 — St. Philip, Deacon; December 26 — St. Stephen (see Stephen).

Dean "The One from the Valley" (Old English) or "The Leader of Ten" (Greek).

Patron Saints: There is one English martyr, Bl. William Dean, who was an English secular priest-martyr. He was born in Yorkshire in the 1500s and was raised Protestant. As an adult, he converted to Catholicism and then traveled to France, where he studied and was eventually ordained a priest. He immediately returned to England, was caught, and banished on pain of death. But he came back again and was sentenced to death. At his execution in 1588, when he tried to speak, he was choked into silence.

Feast Dates: August 28 — Bl. William Dean.

DeAndré (African-American double) See De+André.

Deane (English) See Dean.

DeAngelo (African-American double) See De+Angel.

Deante (African-American double) See De+Dante.

Dec (nickname) See Dexter.

Deca (English) See Dexter.

DeCarlos (Hispanic-American double) See De+Carlos.

Deck (nickname) See Dexter.

Dederick (German) See Derek, Theodoric.

Dedric (variant) See Derek.

Dedrick (German) See Derek, Theodoric.

Dee (variant) See De.

Dehart (African-American double) See De+Hart.

Deinaba (African-American double) See De+Inabel.

DeJuan (African-American double) See De+Juan.

Deke (nickname) See Deacon.

Dekovas (African-American double) See De+Clovis.

Del (nickname) See Abdul, Adelbert, Delbert, Dell, Odell.

Delano "From the Place of the Nut Trees" (Old French).

Patron Saints: The French spelling is *de-la-noye*. In Latin, *noye* ("nut") would be *nux*. This leads to the Latin idiomatic expression *Unus pibi restat nodus, sed Herculaneus*, meaning "You have only one nut to crack, but it's a tough one."

Thus *noye* leads to *nux*, which leads to *nodus*. It all leads to St. Noda, who was martyred in ancient Egypt.

Feast Dates: April 22 — St. Noda.

Delbert "The Daylight" (Old English) or "The Brilliant One" (variant of Adelbert, Albert).

Patron Saints: There are many saints who have Bert as part of their names. Furthermore, Delbert is an alternate form of Adelbert, and there are over a dozen Sts. Adelbert.

Feast Dates: April 23 — St. Adelbert, also known as Adelbert of Prague.

Delisle (variant) See Lyle.

Dell "From the Valley" (Flemish).

Patron Saints: As a name in its own right, Dell means the same thing as Dean or Glen. It can also function as a nickname for names with Del in them, such as Adelbert and Delbert.

Feast Dates: August 28 — Bl. William Dean (see Dean); February 5 — Bl. Oldeger (see Odell).

Delmar "From the Sea" (Old English).

Patron Saints: St. Maris, whose name in Latin means "sea," will make a fine patron.

Feast Dates: July 19 — St. Maris (see Marley).

Delmer (English) See Delmar.

Delmont (African-American double) See Dell/Delmar+Monty.

Delmore (English) See Delmar.

Delroy (French) See Leroy.

Delshawn (African-American double) See Del+Shawn.

Delwyn "The Proud+Friend" (Old English double).

Patron Saints: Two saints are readily available for patrons.

Feast Dates: April 23 — St. Adelbert (see Adelbert); May 28 — St. Winin (see Win).

DeMarcus (African-American double) See De+Mark.

DeMario (African-American double) See De+Mario.

Demarre (African-American) See Delmar.

DeMarus (African-American double) See De+Maris/Maurice.

Demas (variant) See Dismas.

Demetre (French) See Demetrius.

Demetri (variant) See Demetrius.

Demetrio (Italian, Spanish) See Demetrius.

Demetris (variant) See Demetrius.

Demetrius "One Who Belongs to the Fertility Goddess" (Greek).

Patron Saints: There are about fifty Sts. Demetrius. One was a deacon during the 300s in Sirmium (modern Yugoslavia). He was arrested for preaching the Gospel, shut up in a room at the public baths, and killed with a spear.

Demetrius is remembered and honored by the Church as one of the three great warrior-saints. The other two are Sts. George (with dragon) and Theodore of Tiro, also known as Theodore the Recruit.

Feast Dates: October 8 — St. Demetrius.

Demitri (variant) See Demetrius.

Demitry (variant) See Demetrius.

Demond (African-American double) See De+Mondo.

Demorris (African-American double) See De+Morris.

Dempsey "The Proud One" (Irish Gaelic).

Patron Saints: In Gaelic, Dempsey is spelled Diomasach, and there are a half-dozen ancient saints with the name of Dioma. One was a holy monk at the Iona monastery in Scotland.

Feast Dates: June 19 — St. Dioma.

Demyan (Russian, Ukrainian) See Damien.

Den (English) See Denis, Denton, Denver.

Dene (English) See Dean.

Denes (Hungarian) See Denis.

Denis "The God of Wine" (French, Irish).

Patron Saints: There are more than four dozen saints named Dionysius (or Denis). One was born and raised in Italy and became a bishop. Then in 240, he and six other bishops were sent to Gaul (France) to restore Christian worship. They settled on an island in the Seine River, now the site of Notre Dame Cathedral, where they quickly made converts. However, they also made enemies of some prominent pagans. Denis and his friends were arrested and imprisoned for a long time. Eventually Denis was beheaded in the year 250. He is patron of those who have headaches and those who are possessed.

Feast Dates: October 9 — St. Denis of Paris.

Dennet (variant) See Denis.

Denney (variant) See Denis.

Dennie (nickname) See Denis.

Dennis (variant) See Denis.

Dennison (English double) See Denis+ Son.

Denny (nickname) See Denis.

Dent (Old English double) See Dean+ Town.

Denten (Old English double) See Dean+ Town.

Denton (Old English double) See Dean+ Town.

Denver "From the Green+Valley" (Old English double).

Patron Saints: Patrons can be found once one knows that Denver is made from two words: *den*, meaning "valley," and *ver* or *verdi*, meaning "green." This leads to Bl. Dean and St. Verda. St. Verda was martyred in Persia during the persecution under King Shapur II in 344.

Feast Dates: February 21 — St. Verda; August 28 — Bl. William Dean (see Dean).

Denys (nickname) See Denis+Son.

Denzel (English) See Denis.

Denzell (English) See Denis.

Denzyle (American) See Denis.

Deodoro (Portuguese) See Theodore.

Deondray (African-American double) See De+André.

Deondre (African-American double) See De+André.

Deone (variant) See Denis, Dionysius.

Deontahe (Hispanic-American) See Denis, Dionysius.

Depak (African-American double) See De+Paco.

Der (nickname) See Dermit.

Derby (nickname) See Darby.

Derek "The Ruler of the People" (English) or "The Gift of God" (short form of Theodoric).

Patron Saints: If one accepts that Derek is a shortened form of Theodoric,

Theodoret, and Doric, then many patrons appear. They number almost one hundred fifty.

Feast Dates: July 1 — St. Theodoric, also known as Thierry (see Theodoric).

Derick (variant) See Derek.

Derile (African-American) See Darrell.

Derk (variant) See Derek.

Dermit "The Free Man" (Irish variant of Kermit).

Patron Saints: There are a few saints who have variations of the name Dermot. They are Sts. Dermit, Dermitius, Diarmaid, and Dermotia. Dermit can also be spelled as Darby or Kermit, and this leads to another half-dozen saints. A St. Dermit was a priest in Nubromy and died a martyr in medieval Ireland.

Feast Dates: March 2 — St. Dermit; January 10 — St. Kermit (see Kermit).

Dermot (variant) See Dermit, Kermit.

Derrick (German) See Derek, Theodoric.

Derrik (variant) See Derek.

Derron (English) See Darren.

Derry "The Free Man" (short form of Dermot) or "The Red-Haired One" (Irish).

Patron Saints: Sts. Dermit and Kermit will do nicely.

Feast Dates: March 2 — St. Dermit (see Dermit); January 10 — St. Kermit (see Kermit); August 13 — Bl. William Freeman (see Freeman).

Derwin (English) See Darwin.

DeShawn (African-American double) See De+Shawn.

Desmond "The Man from Munster [The South]" (Irish) or "The Gracious Protector" (English).

Patron Saints: Dacey means "one from the south" and will make a fine patron for Desmond.

Feast Dates: November 20 — St. Dacey (see Dacey).

Dev (nickname) See Devin, Devlin.
Devan (variant) See Devin.
Devaughn (African-American double) See De+Vaughn.
Devin "The Fawn" (Irish Gaelic) or "The Poet" (Irish) or "The Excellent One" (Old French).
    Patron Saints: There are plenty of patrons for Devin or Devon. Two ancient saints are Devinic and Devanick. A few English martyrs include Bls. William Way of Devan and Thomas Ford of Devon, England. To them can be added St. David, patron of poets.
    St. Devinic was a contemporary of St. Columba of Iona. He lived for a while at the monastery of Iona in Scotland. Eventually he became a missionary, but it was not an easy job. Often, his prospective converts were hostile and his life was in danger. He died in 550.
    Feast Dates: November 13 — St. Devin, also known as Devinic; May 28 — Bl. Thomas Ford of Devon (see Ford).
Devland (variant) See Devin, Devlin.
Devlen (variant) See Devin, Devlin.
Devlin "The Brave Fierce One" (Irish Gaelic).
    Patron Saints: There is a saint with a similar name. His name is St. Devinic. He is a Scotsman.
    Feast Dates: November 13 — St. Devinic (see Devin).
Devon (English) See Devin.
Devy (English) See Devin.
Dew (nickname) See David.
Dewain (variant) See Dwayne.
DeWayne (variant) See Dwayne.
Dewey (Welsh) See David.
Dewi (Welsh) See David.
Dewie (Welsh) See David.
Dewit (variant) See DeWitt.
Dewitt (variant) See DeWitt.

DeWitt "From the+White-Haired One" (Old French double).
    Patron Saints: DeWitt means "from" or "of" plus "white" (or "white-haired"), which leads to a few patrons.
    Feast Dates: December 10 — St. Eustace White (see White).
Dex (variant) See Dexter.
Dexter "The Right-Handed One" (Latin).
    Patron Saints: St. Dexter was a black African martyr from Roman times. It also helps to know that Benjamin means "son of the right hand."
    Finally, one great patron emerges from the Bible. He is Christ the King, who sits at the "right hand" of the Father. The Book of Hebrews teaches that Jesus took his seat at "the right hand" of God. Many people argue that this means that Jesus has entered his rest, having completed his sacrifice. But just the opposite is true. For Hebrews further insists that Jesus obtained a more excellent ministry and mediated a better covenant. When a king sits on his throne he begins his work, not ends it. So too, Jesus, in taking his seat at the right hand of the Father, began his ministry. The goal of his ministry is to reconcile all mankind and reunite heaven and earth. His job is to create a love affair between God and the family of God.
    Feast Dates: May 7 — St. Dexter; Thirty-fourth Sunday of the Year — Christ the High Priest.
Dez (nickname) See Desmond.
Dezmond (Irish) See Desmond.
Diarmaid (Irish) See Darby, Dermit, Kermit.
Dick (nickname) See Benedict, Richard.
Dickie (nickname) See Benedict, Richard.
Dickens (English double) See Dixon+Son.

Dickenson (English double) See Dixon+ Son.

Dickson (English double) See Dixon+ Son.

Dicky (nickname) See Benedict, Richard.

Diego "The Supplanter" (Spanish form of James).

Patron Saints: Diego is the Spanish form of James, which leads to more than eighty-five saints named James. One is Bl. Juan Diego, an Aztec Indian who lived in colonial Mexico from 1474 to 1548. In 1531 he was a childless widower and convert who took care of a sick uncle. In that same year the Blessed Virgin appeared to him on Tepeyac hill. She told him he should to tell the bishop to build a church on the spot. Juan delivered the message, but the bishop did not believe him.

December 12 found Juan on the same hill again, where once again he met the Lady. Even though it was winter, she told Juan to pick some roses growing nearby and take them to the bishop. Juan obeyed and filled his cloak with the roses. When he opened his cloak for the bishop, the roses fell out, and on the cloak was a picture of the Lady, just as Juan had described. She appeared as an Indian. The bishop had a church built on Tepeyac hill. It is a great Marian shrine. The miraculous cloak of Mary is still displayed above the main altar. It has not faded nor rotted during the more than four hundred fifty years it has been in existence.

Our Lady of Guadalupe is recognized as the "Patron of Mexico" and "Empress of the Americas."

Feast Dates: December 9 — Bl. Juan Diego.

Diermit (Irish) See Kermit.

Dieter (German) See Derek, Theodoric.

Dietrich (German) See Derek, Theodoric.

Digby "From the Town near the Dike" (Old Norse).

Patron Saints: One saint with a very similar name can be pressed into service. St. Digain was a holy priest and son of Constantine, chieftain of Cornwall in the 400s.

Feast Dates: November 21 — St. Digain.

DiJon "God Is Gracious" (French).

Patron Saints: St. William of Dijon, 962-1031, the count of Volpiano, became a Benedictine abbot.

Feast Dates: January 1 — St. William of Dijon.

Dilan (variant) See Dillon, Dylan.

Dilbert (nickname) See Adelbert, Delbert.

Dill (nickname) See Dillon, Dylan.

Dillie (nickname) See Dillon, Dylan.

Dilly (nickname) See Dillon, Dylan.

Dillon "The Faithful One" (Irish Gaelic) or "The One from the Sea" (variant of Welsh, Dylan).

Patron Saints: There is a St. Logan who ministered for a time at Dillon Castle. Additional patrons surface when one realizes that Dillon means "faithful," which in Latin is *fidelis*. This leads to many Sts. Fidelis.

Feast Dates: February 2 — St. Logan of Dillon (see Logan); October 28 — St. Fidel of Como (see Fidel).

Dimitri (Russian) See Demetrius.

Dino (nickname) See Bernard, Dean.

Dion (variant) See Denis, Dionysius.

Dione (variant) See Denis, Dionysius.

Dionigi (Italian) See Denis, Dionysius.

Dionis (Spanish) See Denis, Dionysius.

Dionisio (Spanish, Italian) See Denis, Dionysius.

Dionisiy (Russian) See Denis, Dionysius.

Dionizy (Polish) See Denis, Dionysius.

Dionys (German) See Denis, Dionysius.

Dionysios (Greek) See Denis, Dionysius.

Dionysius "The God of Wine" (Latin).

Patron Saints: There are four dozen St. Dionysius. St. Dionysius the Great, 190-264, was born of pagan parents in Alexandria, Egypt. After converting to Christianity, he became the head of the catechetical school and a short time later was elected bishop. When persecutions broke out he went into exile. He exhibited a rare combination of zeal, firmness, and charity.

Feast Dates: November 17 — St. Dionysius; October 9 — St. Denis of Paris (see Denis).

Dirk "Ruler of the People" (English short form of Derrick) or "Gift of God" (short form of Theodoric).

Patron Saints: If one accepts Dirk as a shortened form of Theodore, Theodoric, Doric, Theodoret, or Derek, then about two hundred patrons emerge. When the prefect of the Eastern Roman Empire sought to pillage the Catholic churches for their treasures, St. Theodoret, a zealous priest, did not flee. He held worship services and he also refused to turn over Church vessels and artifacts to the prefect. For this he was killed in 362.

Feast Dates: October 23 — St. Theodoret; July 1 — St. Theodoric, also known as Thierry (see Theodoric).

Dismas "The Popular One of the People" (Greek).

Patron Saints: There is at least one great saint named Dismas. The Bible reports that Jesus declared him worthy of heaven as both hung upon crosses. This was the first official canonization. And because "Jesus Christ is the same yesterday and today and for ever" (Hebrews 13:8), the Catholic Church continues canonizing saints in the name of Jesus. In Christian legend Dismas is portrayed as a Robin Hood-like char-

acter. And the Church chose March 25 for his feast day because she honors it as the actual date of the crucifixion.

Feast Dates: March 25 — St. Dismas.

Dix (nickname) See Dixon.

Dixon "The Son of+Richard [The Powerful Ruler]" (Old English double).

Patron Saints: Dixon is built out of two names, Dick and Son. This leads to two Bls. Dickenson, many Sts. Richard and Benedict, and a St. Sotonius. Bl. Francis Dickenson was a native of Yorkshire and studied for the priesthood at Rheims in France. He was ordained in 1589 and went immediately to serve in the English missions. In 1590 he was apprehended by the authorities and executed at Rochester.

Feast Dates: July 7 — Bl. Francis Dickenson; November 17 — St. Sontius (see Son).

Dixy (nickname) See Dixon.

Diz (nickname) See Dismas.

Dizzie (nickname) See Dismas.

Dizzy (nickname) See Dismas.

Doane (variant) See Dwayne.

Doby (nickname) See Robert.

Dodge "The One Who Evades" (Old English) or "The Famous Spearman" (nickname for Roger).

Patron Saints: There is one saint with a very similar name, St. Doged. He was the brother of King St. Afan Bualt. He was killed in medieval times by King Cilydd.

Furthermore, one should not forget that Dodge is also accepted as a nickname for Roger.

Feast Dates: April 22 — St. Doged; November 15 — Bl. Roger James, O.S.B. (see Roger).

Dolf (nickname) See Adolf, Rudolph.

Dolfie (nickname) See Adolf, Rudolph.

Dolph (nickname) See Adolf, Rudolph.

Dolphie (nickname) See Adolf, Rudolph.

Dom (nickname) See Dominic.

Domas (Lusatian) See Thomas.

Domenic (English) See Dominic.

Domenico (Italian, Spanish) See Dominic.

Domingo (Spanish) See Dominic.

Domingos (Portuguese) See Dominic.

Dominic "The One Belonging to God" (Latin) or "Sunday's Child" (Latin).

Patron Saints: There are about three dozen saints named Dominic. St. Dominic Savio, 1842-1857, a teenage peasant-saint, is one of the better-known ones. His parents' religious dedication made a lasting impression on him. When he was only five years old, Dominic was attending daily Mass. When he was old enough, he served Mass.

On the day of his First Communion, at the age of seven, he wrote down a rule that would govern the rest of his life: "I will go to Confession and Communion as often as my confessor allows. I will keep holy the feast days. My friends shall be Jesus and Mary. Death — not sin."

Later he went to a school operated by St. John Bosco and learned not to do great penances but rather to do good to his companions, forgive the rude, not waste food, study all his subjects, be humble, never complain about the weather, be bright and cheerful, and have love for Jesus. He died at the age of fourteen.

Feast Dates: March 9 — St. Dominic Savio.

Dominick (English) See Dominic.

Dominik (Polish, Russian) See Dominic.

Dominiks (Latvian) See Dominic.

Dominique (French) See Dominic.

Domokos (Hungarian) See Dominic.

Don (nickname) See Donahue, Donald, Donnelly, Donovan, Seldon.

Donahue "The Dark [Brown] Warrior" (Irish Gaelic).

Patron Saints: There are a few saints with Don as part of their names. They can serve as patrons. One is St. Donnan. He was a disciple of St. Columba of Iona and founded a monastery. Unfortunately, it was destroyed by pagan invaders. The end came on Holy Saturday in 618, when some raiders descended on the monastery while the abbot was celebrating the Mass. After Mass all the monks were gathered together in the refectory and it was set on fire. Those monks who tried to escape the burning building were put to death by the sword.

Feast Dates: April 17 — St. Donan; September 5 — Bl. William Browne (see Browne).

Donaido (Spanish) See Donald.

Donal (variant) See Donald.

Donalas (Lithuanian) See Donald.

Donald "The Mighty World Ruler" (Scottish Gaelic).

Patron Saints: Donald is a very popular name in Scotland. St. Donald lived at Ogilvy in Forfarshire, Scotland, in the 700s. He was married and fathered nine daughters. After his wife died, his daughters formed a kind of religious community. They lived under their father's direction.

At some point in time, Donald must have been ordained a priest because he is remembered officially as a "confessor." His daughters have been remembered, through the ages, as the "Nine Maidens."

Feast Dates: July 15 — St. Donald.

Donaldas (Lithuanian) See Donald.

Donaldo (Spanish, Italian) See Donald.

Donall (variant) See Donald.

Donalt (variant) See Donald.

Donaugh (variant) See Donald.

Donavon (variant) See Donovan.

Dondre (French double) See Dion+ André.

Donn (nickname) See Donahue, Donald, Donnelly, Donovan.

Donnell (Irish variant) See Donald, Donnelly.

Donnelly "The Brave Dark [Brown] Man" (Irish Gaelic).

Patron Saints: There is no St. Donnelly. But any saint with Don in his name can serve as a patron.

Feast Dates: April 17 — St. Donan (see Donahue); September 5 — Bl. William Browne (see Browne).

Donnie (nickname) See Donny.

Donny (nickname) See Donahue, Donald, Donnelly, Donovan, Seldon.

Donohue (variant) See Donahue.

Donovan "The Dark [Brown] Warrior" (Irish Gaelic).

Patron Saints: There is no St. Donovan. But a saint with Don in his name can be adopted as patron.

Feast Dates: April 17 — St. Donan (see Donahue); September 5 — Bl. William Browne (see Browne).

Dontae (African-American) See Dante.

Dontay (African-American) See Dante.

Donte (African-American) See Dante.

Dooley "The Dark Hero" (Irish Gaelic).

Patron Saints: Dooley is formed from two words: *dubh*, meaning "dark," and *laoch*, meaning "hero." Two saints emerge. One is St. Dubh, who is remembered as an "Irish saint." The other is St. Hero.

Feast Dates: July 18 — St. Dubh (see Doyle); September 10 — St. Hero, also known as Herosus (see Hero).

Doran "The Gift of God" (Greek) or "The Stranger" (Celtic).

Patron Saints: Doran is a short form of Isidore or Theodore. There are three dozen saints named Isidore and almost one hundred fifty named Theodore.

Feast Dates: May 15 — St. Isidore (see Isadore); November 9 — Theodore the Recruit (see Theodore).

Dore (nickname) See Doran, Dorian, Isadore.

Dorey (variant) See Dorian, Isadore.

Dorian "From the Sea" (Greek) or "Gift of God" (nickname for Isidore or Theodore).

Patron Saints: Dorian can be considered a short form of Isidore or Theodore. There are about three dozen Sts. Isidore and about one hundred fifty Sts. Theodore.

Feast Dates: May 15 — St. Isidore (see Isadore); November 9 — Theodore the Recruit (see Theodore).

Doric (variant) See Derek.

Dorie (variant) See Doran, Dorian, Isadore.

Dorin (variant) See Doran, Dorian.

Doro (variant) See Doran, Theodore.

Dorran (variant) See Doran.

Dorrell (English) See Darrell.

Dorren (variant) See Doran.

Dory (nickname) See Doran, Dorian, Isadore.

Doug (nickname) See Douglas.

Dougal (Celtic) See Doyle.

Dougald (variant) See Douglas.

Dougie (nickname) See Douglas.

Douglas "From the Dark Water" (Scottish Gaelic).

Patron Saints: There is one English martyr surnamed Douglas. Bl. George Douglas was arrested and executed for being a Catholic priest working in the English missions in 1587.

Feast Dates: May 4 — Bl. George Douglas.

Douglass (variant) See Douglas.

Dougy (nickname) See Douglas.

Dov (Hebrew) See David.

Dovydas (Lithuanian) See David.

Doy (nickname) See Doyle.

Doyle "The Dark Stranger" (Irish Gaelic).

Patron Saints: The Gaelic spelling of Doyle is Dubhghall. And there are a half-dozen saints who bear a form of this name. For example, there is St. Dubh (or Doy) McComairde who lived in medieval Ireland. He is simply remembered as an "Irish saint." And Doyle has the same meaning as Dwayne.

Feast Dates: July 18 — St. Doy, also known as Dubh McComairde.

Dragon (English) See Drake.

Drake "The Sign of the Dragon" (Middle English).

Patron Saints: It is helpful to know that Drake means "dragon." This leads to a number of patrons whose names contain the word "dragon." They are Sts. Dracona, Dracontius, Draguttin, Dragen, and Drogo. St. Dracona, a native of ancient Greece, died a martyr.

Feast Dates: November 11 — St. Dracona.

Drew (Czech, nickname) See Andrew.

Drexel "The One Who Turns a Lathe" (German).

Patron Saints: One North American saint, St. Katharine Drexel, 1858-1955, was born into a wealthy banker's family in Philadelphia, Pennsylvania. Although she never got to know her mother, who died when Katharine was only five weeks old, she and her sister lived in one of the finest homes money could buy and received the best education available. But their father and stepmother taught the sisters that riches were a gift from God and should be shared generously with the poor. When their father died in 1885, Katharine received numerous requests for financial aid. Many of the requests came from the Catholic Indian missions out West. She began funding them and she also gave financial help to local Catholic schools. But she wanted to do more.

She slowly became convinced that prejudice and unjust laws created a cycle of ignorance and powerlessness for blacks and Indians, so she made these groups her special concern. She founded the Sisters of the Blessed Sacrament for Indians and Colored People. Then she founded Xavier University in New Orleans, Louisiana, the first college on this continent for black people.

She spent her entire fortune (that is, the portion of the approximately twenty million dollars she and her sister inherited) on the mission to which she had dedicated her life. Her goal was to evangelize, educate, and help the poor raise their standard of living. She died at the age of ninety-six.

Feast Dates: March 3 — St. Katharine Drexel; June 20 — Bl. Anthony Turner (see Turner).

Dru (English) See Andrew.

Drud (variant) See Andrew.

Drugi (variant) See Andrew.

Drystan (Old English) See Tristan.

Duane (variant) See Dwayne.

Duardo (Spanish) See Edward.

Duarte (Portuguese) See Edward.

Dud (nickname) See Dudley.

Dudd (nickname) See Dudley.

Dudley "From People's+Meadow" (Old English double).

Patron Saints: Dudley comes from these words: *dud*, meaning "people," and *ley*, meaning "meadow." This leads to two saints: St. Dudo and Bl. Richard Leigh. St. Dudo was a martyr in ancient Ebstorf.

Feast Dates: February 2 — St. Dudo; August 30 — Bl. Richard Leigh (see Leigh or Lee).

Duff (nickname) See Duffy.

Duffie (nickname) See Duffy.

Duffy "The Dark-Complected One" (Irish Gaelic).

Patron Saints: There is a St. Duffy. But his name is spelled Duffus. St. Duffus was probably a black man who died for the faith in Roman Alexandria, Egypt.

Feast Dates: April 30 — St. Duffus.

Dugaid (variant) See Douglas.

Dugald (English) See Doyle.

Duke "The Royal Leader" (Old French).

Patron Saints: Many Catholic saints held the rank of "duke." There are also two English martyrs with that name, Bls. Marmaduke Bowes and Edmund Duke. Bl. Edmund Duke was executed by the English government in 1590 because he was a Catholic priest.

Feast Dates: May 4 — Bl. Edmund Duke; May 4 — Bl. Marmaduke Bowes (see Marmaduke).

Dukey (nickname) See Duke.

Dukie (nickname) See Duke.

Duky (nickname) See Duke.

Dun (nickname) See Duncan, Dunstan.

Dunc (nickname) See Duncan.

Duncan "Brown-Skinned Warrior" (Scottish Gaelic).

Patron Saints: There are a few ancient saints with very similar names. For example: Sts. Duncad, Dunchad, and Dunghadh. All can serve as patrons for Duncan. Unfortunately, very little is remembered about any of them. Most are from Scotland or Ireland. St. Duncad was an abbot at the Iona monastery in 717.

Feast Dates: May 25 — St. Duncad.

Dunkanas (Lithuanian) See Duncan.

Dunn (Old English) See Duncan.

Dunstan "The Brown Stone Fortress" (Old English).

Patron Saints: There is one St. Dunstan, 909, 988, a great figure in early English history. He was an abbot, archbishop, and statesman. He was also a fine goldsmith, a manuscript illuminator, an embroiderer, and an accomplished musician. The local king invited him to become the royal chancellor.

Soon he found he had to speak out against the illicit sexual relations that the king had embraced and immediately found himself in exile. A year later he was recalled by King Edgar. In 961, at the age of fifty-two, he became archbishop of Canterbury. He is patron of armorers, blacksmiths, goldsmiths, jewelers, and locksmiths.

Feast Dates: May 19 — St. Dunstan.

Durand (variant) See Dante.

Durante (variant) See Dante.

Durko (Czech) See George.

Durward "The Gatekeeper" (Old English).

Patron Saints: The name means "gatekeeper," and this leads directly to two saints. Jewish tradition names St. Abel the heavenly gatekeeper and Catholic tradition names St. Peter.

Feast Dates: June 29 — St. Peter, Apostle (see Peter); January 2 — St. Abel (see Abel).

Dust (nickname) See Dustin.

Dustan (variant) See Dustin.

Dustie (nickname) See Dustin.

Dustin "The Valiant Fighter" (Old German) or "Thor's Stone" (short form of Thorsteinn).

Patron Saints: There is one known St. Dustin. He served God as a bishop in Scotland in the 600s. He was also a disciple of St. Columba of Iona and he knew St. Bede. He served as abbot before becoming a hermit near Clenesk and then a monk at the Iona monastery. Eventually he founded a monastery at Deer, Aberdeenshire, Scotland.

Furthermore, it also helps to know that Dustin means "valiant fighter."

The name Louis also means "famous warrior." There are a dozen Sts. Louis.

Feast Dates: July 11 — St. Dustin, also known as Drostan; August 25 — St. Louis the King (see Louis).

Duston (variant) See Dustin.

Dusty (nickname) See Dustin.

Dutch "The German" (German).

Patron Saints: Dutch means "the German," and there is a St. Boniface, 680-754, who is patron of Germany.

St. Boniface was an Anglo-Saxon named Winfrid, born in Devon. At the age of thirty, he became a priest. Six years later he set out as a missionary to Germany but failed. Two years after that he tried again and had some success. In 723, at the age of forty-three, Boniface was consecrated bishop for all of Germany. He founded numerous abbeys, nunneries, and schools and invited nuns and priests from England to staff them. He was martyred by pagans at the age of seventy-four. He is patron of Germany and brewers.

Feast Dates: June 5 — St. Boniface, also known as Winfrid.

Dwain (variant) See Dwayne.

Dwalou (African-American double) See Dwayne+Louis.

Dwayne "The Little Dark One" (Irish Gaelic).

Patron Saints: There are a number of ancient saints, mostly from Wales, who have variants of this name. One of them is St. Dwyn, the daughter of St. Brychan. Little is known about her except that she fell passionately in love

with a man who cared deeply for her. However, they had a major disagreement and canceled their marriage plans. She settled near Llandwyn, the site of a famous Welsh shrine, and became a nun. Later she served as an abbess. She died a martyr in about 360. She is patron of true lovers and of sick animals.

Feast Dates: February 25 — St. Dwyn, also known as Dwynwen.

Dwight (variant) See Denis, DeWitt.

Dwyone (African-American) See Dwayne.

Dyl (nickname) See Dillon, Dylan.

Dylan "The One from the Sea" (Old Welsh) or "The Faithful One" (variant of Dillon).

Patron Saints: There is one saint from Wales, St. Dilwar, whose name is similar. Remembering that Dylan means "from the sea" leads directly to a half-dozen ancient Sts. Mares and Maris. *Mares* or *maris* is Latin for "from the sea." Finally, some scholars think there is a connection between Dillon and Dylan.

Feast Dates: February 2 — St. Logan of Dillon (see Logan); July 19 — St. Maris (see Marley).

Dylon (variant) See Dillon, Dylan.

Dyrol (African-American double) See Darryl, Dionysius/Tyrone+Roland.

Dysad (African-American double) See Dionysius/Dylan+Sa'id.

Dysmas (variant) See Dismas.

Dyson (English double) See Dysmas/Dennis+Son.

E

Ea (Irish) See Hugh.

Eachunn (Scottish) See Hector.

Eadmund (variant) See Edmund.

Eamon (Irish) See Edmund.

Eamund (Irish) See Edmund.

Ean (English) See Ian.

Eanraig (Scottish) See Henry.

Earl "The Noble Chief" (Old English) or "The Pledge" (variant form of Arlen).

Patron Saints: There are a few ancient saints with similar names that can serve as patrons. One is St. Erlafrid, who was the count of Calu in Swabia. With the help of his son, a bishop, he founded the monastery of Hirsau in 830. In due time, he became a Benedictine monk at this monastery.

Finally, there is an English martyr who held the title of "earl" who can also serve.

Feast Dates: November 6 — St. Erlafrid; October 19 — St. Philip Howard, Earl of Arundel and Surrey (see Howard).

Earle (variant) See Arlen, Earl.

Earlie (variant) See Arlen, Earl.

Early (variant) See Arlen, Earl.

Earvin (English) See Ervin, Irving.

Easton (English) See Estes.

Eaton "From the Riverside Estate" (Old English).

Patron Saints: St. Eata was an Anglo-Saxon and the second bishop of Hexham. He also served as abbot of Old Melrose of Lindisfarne's famous monastery. He had a great influence in medieval England.

Feast Dates: October 26 — St. Eata.

Eatun (variant) See Eaton.

Ebenezer "The Precious Healing Stone" (Hebrew).

Patron Saints: Remember, God is our "Rock and Salvation."

Feast Dates: Thirty-fourth Sunday of the Year — Jesus Christ, Our Rock and Fortress.

Eberhard (German) See Everett.

Ebert (German) See Everett.

Eberto (Italian) See Herbert.

Ecto (variant) See Hector.

Ed (nickname) See Eddy, Edgar, Edmund, Edward , Edwin.

Edd (nickname) See Ed.

Eddi (nickname) See Ed.

Eddie (nickname) See Ed.

Eddy "The Happy Protector" (Old English).

Patron Saints: St. Edi, a native of medieval Wales, is remembered not only for his prayerfulness but also for his gigantic stature. The name can also serve as a short form of Edgar, Edmund, Edward, and Edwin.

Feast Dates: November 8 — St. Edi.

Edelmar (German) See Elmer.

Edgar "The Successful Spearman" (Old English, Spanish).

Patron Saints: There is one saint named Edgar, 944-975. As king of the Anglo-Saxons, he followed the advice of St. Dunstan and was always most generous to the religious institutions in his kingdom. He was also a strong defender of law and order. He was only thirty-one years old when death claimed him.

Feast Dates July 8 — St. Edgar the Peaceful.

Edgard (French, Portuguese) See Edgar.

Edgardo (Italian, Spanish) See Edgar.

Edgars (Latvian) See Edgar.

Edik (nickname) See Edward.

Edison (Old English double) See Edward+Son.

Edlin (nickname) See Edwin.

Edmon (variant) See Edmund.

Edmond (variant) See Edmund.

Edmund "The Happy Protector" (Old English).

Patron Saints: There are many saints who have Ed as part of their names.

Feast Dates: December 1 — St. Edmund Campion, S.J. (see Carroll).

Edmundo (Spanish, Portuguese) See Edmund.

Edmunds (Latvian) See Edmund.

Edo (Czech) See Edward.

Edouard (French) See Edward.

Edson (Old English double) See Edward+Son.

Eduard (German, Estonian, Romanian, Russian, Ukrainian, Yiddish) See Edward.

Eduardo (Spanish) See Edward.

Eduardos (Greek) See Edward.

Eduino (Spanish) See Edwin.

Edvard (Danish, Norwegian, Slovenian) See Edward.

Edvardas (Lithuanian) See Edward.

Edvino (Italian, Spanish) See Edwin.

Edvins (Latvian) See Edwin.

Edvinus (variant) See Edwin.

Edward "The Rich Guardian" (Old English).

Patron Saints: There is one St. Edward, 1002-1066, son of Ethelred the Unready, who was called to be king of England in 1042 and married a beautiful, religious girl named Edith. One of his great accomplishments was the building of Westminster Abbey.

While forced to fight occasional battles, he was by nature a peace-loving person, known for his religious devotion and gentleness. Another thing that made him popular was the abolition of the army tax. He was also a great friend of the poor and strangers. His great passion was hunting and hawking, yet he never missed daily Mass.

Feast Dates: October 13 — St. Edward the Confessor.

Edwin "The Successful Friend" (Old English).

Patron Saints: St. Edwin, 585-637, was the first Catholic king of Northumbria but at the very young age of three was driven into exile by his brother-in-law, Ethelfrid. Only after Ethelfrid was killed in battle in 616 did Edwin regain his kingdom. He was thirty-one at that time.

He married, but his wife died. Then he married again, this time to a Catholic, and this led to his conversion. However, his Christian rule was short-lived. He was killed in battle in 637 fighting against King Penda of Mercia and King Cadwallon of Wales, both pagans.

Feast Dates: October 12 — St. Edwin.

Eemeli (Finnish) See Emil.

'Eesaa (Arabic) See Jesus.

Efrain (Spanish) See Ephrem.

Efrem (variant) See Ephrem.

Efren (variant) See Ephrem.

Eg (nickname) See Egan, Egbert.

Egan "The Ardent, Fiery One" (Irish Gaelic).

Patron Saints: As an adult, St. Egan became involved in a disagreement between the pope and the emperor. By agreeing with the pope, he found himself in disagreement with his abbot and he was expelled from the abbey. He then joined the abbey of St. Blaise. In 1109 he was recalled by his original abbey and made abbot. As abbot, he soon found himself in another disagreement with the local bishop, who was involved in simony. He had to flee into exile in Rome. He died in 1122.

Feast Dates: June 15 — St. Egan.

Egbert "The Bright, Shining Sword" (Old English).

Patron Saints: There are two Sts. Egbert. One of them lived from 639 to 720, becoming a monk and then a bishop. He was sent to Frisia to reform the Columbian monasteries.

Feast Dates: April 24 — St. Egbert.

Egberto (Spanish) See Egbert.

Egg (nickname) See Egbert.

Egide (variant) See Giles.

Egidio (Italian) See Giles.

Egidius (German) See Giles.

Egon (variant) See Egan.

Egor (variant) See George.

Einar "The Individual" (Scandinavian) or "The Battle Leader" (Old Norse).

Patron Saints: Einhard served as a holy abbot in France. He died in 829.

Feast Dates: July 22 — St. Einhard.

El (nickname) See any "El"name.

El "God [or Lord]" (Hebrew).

Patron Saints: St. Elli was an abbot in medieval Wales.

Feast Dates: January 23 — St. Elli.

Elbert (English) See Albert.

Elden (variant) See Eldon.

Elder (English) See Senior.

Eldin (variant) See Alden.

Eldon "From the Holy+Hill" (Old English double).

Patron Saints: Eldon can be a full Old English name or variant of Aldous, Alden, or Elton.

Feast Dates: January 10 — St. Aldus (see Aldous); January 11 — St. Elton (see Elton); May 31 — Bl. Aldo (see Alden).

Eldric (English) See Aldrich.

Eldridge (German) See Aldrich.

Eldrige (English) See Aldrich.

Eldwin (English double) See Aldwin+ Wynn.

Elfred (English) See Alfred.

Elgin "The Noble White One" (Old English).

Patron Saints: St. Elgud, a Welsh saint and the father of a saint in the 500s, will have to serve as patron here.

Feast Dates: November 1 — St. Elgud.

Eli (Italian) See Elijah.

Elia (Italian) See Elijah.

Elian (Spanish) See Elijah, Trevelyan.

Elias (Czech, English, German, Dutch, Spanish, Greek, Hungarian, Portuguese, Yiddish) See Elijah.

Eliasz (Polish) See Elijah.

Elick (African-American) See Alec.

Eligio Meaning unknown (Spanish).

Patron Saints: There are three Sts. Eligius. The one who was the bishop of Noyon and died in 659 was very popular in the Middle Ages. He was a metalworker and a great missionary.

Feast Dates: December 1 — St. Eligius.

Elihu (variant) See Elijah.

Elijah "Yahweh Is God" (Hebrew).

Patron Saints: There are three dozen Sts. Elias and Elijah. Five more Elijahs are mentioned in the Bible. The greatest is the Jewish prophet Elijah, who told King Ahab in about 876 B.C. that there was going to be a drought because Ahab and his wife, Jezebel, had led Northern Israel to worship false gods. As prophesied, the drought came, which resulted in famine. In the third year Elijah convinced King Ahab to allow a contest between him and the king's prophets to prove that God was on Elijah's side. The contest was held on Mount Carmel between himself and the four hundred fifty prophets of

Baal, and Elijah defeated them, then executed them.

This made Queen Jezebel very angry with him and he fled for his life. He hid in a cave near Mount Horeb waiting for God to make his appearance in power and majesty. However, God came to him only in silence and nothingness. It is the genius of Elijah that he found God even in this most unlikely place. Eventually the Lord commanded him to leave his place of hiding and to carry out several tasks, including naming Elisha to succeed him as prophet.

Elijah is patron against earthquakes and droughts.

Feast Dates: July 20 — St. Elijah, Jewish Prophet.

Elio (Spanish) See Elijah.

Eliot (English) See Elijah.

Eliott (variant) See Elijah.

Elisee (French) See Elisha.

Eliseo (Italian, Spanish) See Elisha.

Eliseus (variant) See Elisha.

Elisha "God Is My Salvation" (Hebrew).

Patron Saints: Christian tradition provides about a dozen Sts. Elisha, and the Bible adds one more. St. Elisha, a Jewish prophet, lived in about 850 B.C., having succeeded to the office held by St. Elijah. He was selected by God to be a prophet to Israel and inherited wonderful powers from Elijah. He, like Elijah, stopped the waters of the Jordan and raised a child back to life. He also confronted the corrupt kings and witnessed mightily for God in his day.

Feast Dates: June 14 — St. Elisha.

Elixander (Hispanic-American double) See Elio+Alexander.

Ellary (English) See Ellery.

Ellerey (English) See Ellery.

Ellery "From the Elder Tree Island" (Middle English).

Patron Saints: There is no problem finding a patron for Ellery. There are Sts. Eleri and Elerius. The latter, who became an abbot, lived in the 500s. He was the son of Dingad ab Nudd Hael, from the family of the emperor Maximus. He lived in Denbigh, Wales. He had four brothers: Lleuddad, Baglan, Tegwy, and Tyfriog. All have been officially recognized as saints.

Feast Dates: June 13 — St. Ellery, also known as Elerius.

Ellic (African-American) See Alec.

Ellick (African-American) See Alec.

Elliot (English, Hungarian) See Elijah.

Elliott (English, Hungarian) See Elijah.

Ellis (English, Hungarian) See Elijah.

Ellison (English double) See Elijah+Son.

Ellswerth (variant) See Elsworth.

Ellsworth (variant) See Elsworth.

Ellwood (variant) See Elwood.

Elly (nickname) See El.

Elmar (Hungarian) See Elmer.

Elmer "The Famous, Noble One" (Old English).

Patron Saints: There are a few Sts. Elmer. And knowing that Aymer and Aymar are variants of Elmer leads to a martyr. In 1569 Bl. Aymar Vas became a Jesuit brother in Portugal at the age of sixteen. When St. Ignacio de Azevedo appealed for volunteers for the missions in Brazil, Aymar stepped forward. In June of 1570 he sailed on the *Santiago* with Father Ignatius and thirty-eight companions. In July of the same year, the ship was captured and boarded by French Huguenot pirates. Out of hatred for the Catholic faith the pirates put all of the missionaries to death. Most were made to walk the plank. However, Aymar was first stabbed with a sword and then thrown into the sea. He was only seventeen years old when death came for him.

Feast Dates: July 15 — Bl. Aymar (or Elmer) Vas.

Elmers (Latvian) See Elmer.

Elmo "The Lovable One" (variant of Erasmus) or "The Divinely Protected One" (variant of Anselm).

Patron Saints: Elmo can be a familiar form of Anselm and Erasmus, which leads to a couple of dozen patrons. St. Elmo (also known as Erasmus) was a bishop of Formiae in Campagna, Italy, in 303. When Emperor Diocletian launched a persecution, Elmo hid in a cave in Lebanon but was soon discovered and arrested. He was beaten with clubs and whips and rolled in pitch that was then ignited and was bound into a red-hot chair. Because of the way he was tortured, he has been recognized as patron for women in labor and against cramps, stomachaches, and colic, especially in children. He is also patron of sailors and against seasickness, since medieval sailors associated the eerie blue light (St. Elmo's fire) they saw surrounding ship's masts during electrical storms with St. Elmo's being rolled in pitch and set on fire. Another saint who is referred to as St. Elmo is St. Peter González.

Feast Dates: June 2 — St. Elmo, also known as Erasmus.

Elmore (variant) See Elmo.

Elrick (variant double) See El+Richard.

Elroy (variant double) See Leroy, El+Roy.

Elsdon (English double) See Ellis+Dean.

Elstan (English double) See Elston, Ellis+Town.

Elston "From the Nobleman's+Town [Estate]" (Old English double).

Patron Saints: St. Elstan of Wilton, who served as a holy bishop in England in ancient times, will do nicely as a patron.

Feast Dates: April 6 — St. Elstan of Wilton.

Elsworth "From the Nobleman's+Estate" (Old English double).

Patron Saints: Elsworth has an almost identical meaning with Elston.

Feast Dates: April 6 — St. Elstan of Wilton (see Elston).

Elton "From the Old+Town" (Old English double).

Patron Saints: St. Elton is remembered for being a holy priest at Spancoe.

Feast Dates: January 11 — St. Elton, also known as Eltene; January 10 — St. Aldus (see Aldous).

Elvin (variant) See Alvin.

Elvio (Spanish) See Alvin.

Elvis "The All-Wise One" (Old Norse) or "The Elf Friend" (variant of Alvin).

Patron Saints: Elvis is a popular name in modern America. While the average Catholic is usually hard-pressed to find religious connections, there are a few. One is St. Elvis (also known as Elwin), who lived in the 500s. He was an Irishman who traveled to Cornwall, England, and became bishop there.

Feast Dates: August 28 — St. Elvis, also known as Elwin.

Elwin (variant) See Alvin, Elvis.

Elwood "From the Old Forest" (Old English).

Patron Saints: There is a St. Elli who was a disciple of St. Cadoc at Llancarfan. He served God as an abbot. There is also a St. Wood. Plus, there are many saints who have Wood as part of their names.

Feast Dates: January 23 — St. Elli; March 14 — St. Odo Wood (see Woody).

Em (nickname) See Emery, Emil, Emlyn, Emmett.

Emanuel (German, Spanish) See Emmanuel.

Emanuele (Italian) See Emmanuel.

Emelen (variant double) See Emery/ Emil+Lynn, Emlyn.

Emeri (French) See Emery.

Emeric (variant) See Emery.

Emerson (Old English double) See Emery+Son.

Emery "The Industrious Ruler" (English) or "The Co-Ruler" (Old German).

Patron Saints: There are a few Sts. Emeric. One St. Emeric, 1007-1031, was the only son of St. Stephen, the first Christian king of Hungary. Not long after he was born he was given into the care of St. Gerard Sagredo.

Surrounded by saints, Emeric had a fine advantage for gaining sainthood for himself. As time passed, King St. Stephen began to slowly transfer the power to rule to his son. However, this process was cut short by Emeric's untimely death in a hunting accident.

It might be interesting to note that Emery or Emeric is an alternate way to spell America.

Feast Dates: November 4 — St. Emeric.

Emil "Industrious One" (German) or "Flatterer" (Latin).

Patron Saints: There are about four dozen Sts. Emil. However, these saints often spelled their names as Aemilius, Aemilianus, Amelius, Emilianus, Emiliusa, and Emile. One of them is St. Emil, who died a martyr in 251, during the Roman persecutions.

Feast Dates: May 22 — St. Emil, also known as Aemilius.

Emile (French) See Emil.

Emilek (Czech, Polish) See Emil.

Emilio (Spanish, Italian) See Emil.

Emir "The Commander" (Arabic) or "The Prince" (Arabic).

Patron Saints: Emir has exactly the same meaning as "Harold" or "Prince."

Feast Dates: November 1 — St. Harald II (see Harold).

Emlen (variant double) See Emery/Emil+ Lynn, Emlyn.

Emlin (variant double) See Emery/Emil+ Lynn, Emlyn.

Emlyn "The Industrious [One]" (Welsh) or "The Ruler+From the Waterfall" (Welsh double).

Patron Saints: Emlyn is a combination of Emery and Lynn or Emil and Lynn.

Feast Dates: May 22 — St. Emil, also known as Aemilius; August 11 — St. Lynn (see Lynn).

Emmanuel "God Is with Us" (Hebrew).

Patron Saints: Another name for Jesus is Emmanuel. Thus Jesus is the finest patron. But there are also over a dozen saints named Emmanuel. One of the Sts. Emmanuel died a martyr's death in ancient Anatolia.

Feast Dates: March 26 — St. Emmanuel.

Emmeric (variant) See Emery.

Emmerich (German) See Emery.

Emmerie (variant) See Emery.

Emmerson (English double) See Emery+ Son.

Emmery (English) See Emery.

Emmet (English) See Emmett.

Emmett "The Industrious Strong One" (Old German) or "An Ant" (Old English) or "The Flatterer" (Latin).

Patron Saints: If Emmett is accepted as a modern variant of Emetitus, then Sts. Emetitus, Emetrius, and Emeterus emerge as patrons. St. Emetrius was an ancient Roman martyr.

Also, if Emmett is a form of Emil, then about four dozen Sts. Emil, Aemilius, and Amelius appear.

Feast Dates: January 24 — St. Emetrius; May 22 — St. Emil (see Emil).

Emmit (English) See Emmett.

Emmott (English) See Emmett.

Emmy (nickname) See Emil, Emmett.

Emory (variant) See Emery.

Engelbert "Bright as an Angel" (Old German).

Patron Saints: Any of the holy angels in heaven or a person named Angel (or variants of it, such as Angela and Angelo) can be patron.

Feast Dates: September 29 — St. Michael the Archangel (see Michael); March 26 — St. Bert (see Bert).

Englebert (variant) See Engelbert.

Ennis (nickname) See Angus, Denis, Enos.

Ennosh (variant) See Enos.

Enoch "The Consecrated One" (Hebrew) or "The Dedicated One" (Hebrew).

Patron Saints: Christian tradition provides us with three Sts. Enoch, and the Bible presents two more. The greatest is the ancient patriarch St. Enoch, who was the seventh generation of humanity upon the earth. The Bible tells us the whole lifetime of Enoch was three hundred sixty-five years and then he walked with God. This means he did not have to die.

Jewish tradition, in the Book of Enoch, tells of Enoch's trip through the heavens. It is filled with wondrous sights, multitudes of angels, and many teachings.

Feast Dates: March 1 — St. Enoch, Patriarch.

Enos "The Fallen Man" (Hebrew) or "The Unique Choice" (Scottish Gaelic variant of Angus).

Patron Saints: The Bible provides us with only one St. Enos. Christian tradition adds a St. Enostan. It is also helpful to know that the Scottish form of Enos is Angus, and there are two Sts. Angus.

The Book of Genesis teaches that Enos was the grandson of Adam and that he lived to be nine hundred five years old. It seems Adam and Eve slowly learned that Satan was an implacable enemy and that God was a reliable friend. All that was required was for each person to discipline oneself, sacrifice, repent, and pray.

Feast Dates: March 1 — St. Enos, Patriarch; March 11 — St. Angus of Keld (see Angus).

Enrico (Italian) See Henry.

Enrique (Spanish) See Henry.

Eoin (Irish) See John.

Ephraem (variant) See Ephrem.

Ephrem "The Very Faithful One" (Hebrew).

Patron Saints: There are about a dozen Sts. Ephrem. One St. Ephrem, 306-379, is remembered as "The Sun of the Syrians," "The Harp of the Holy Ghost," and as a Father and Doctor of the Church. He was a great orator and a true poet who left many writings. They include hymns and commentaries on the Bible texts.

Born at Nisibis, he converted to Christianity with the help of St. James of Nisibis and was later ordained a deacon by St. Basil. He finally ended his days in Edessa.

Feast Dates: June 9 — St. Ephrem.

Er "The One Doing, Living in, Etc." (Old English suffix).

Patron Saints: The name part connected to this English suffix will have a patron saint.

Eracio (Spanish) See Hercules.

Erasme (variant) See Erasmus.

Erasmo (variant) See Erasmus.

Erasmus "The Lovable One" (Greek) or "The Divinely Protected One" (variant of Elmo).

Patron Saints: There are a dozen Sts. Erasmus. One was martyred in ancient Pozzuoli.

Feast Dates: July 31 — St. Erasmus.

Erasmus (variant) See Elmo.

Eraste (variant) See Erastus.

Erastus "The Beloved One" (Greek).

Patron Saints: There is one St. Erastus. A disciple of St. Paul, he was treasurer of Corinth when he became a Christian. Later, he became bishop of Caesarea Philippi and died a martyr.

Feast Dates: July 26 — St. Erastus.

Erek (English) See Eric, Frederick.

Eric "The Ever-Powerful Ruler" (Old Norse) or "The Peaceful Ruler" (nickname for Frederick).

Patron Saints: There are least three saints named Eric. One St. Eric was king of Sweden for about ten years, between 1150 and 1160. He is noted for codifying all the ancient laws and spreading Catholicism. He built Old Uppsala, the first large church to be erected on Swedish land, and after fighting and winning a battle against the marauding Finns, he convinced the bishop of Uppsala to remain in Finland and convert them.

However, his zeal for the Catholic faith did not please all the nobles, so some of them entered into a conspiracy with the king of Denmark. When told at Mass that the enemy army was close, he said: "Let us finish the sacrifice, the rest of the feast I shall keep elsewhere." He finished Mass, committed his soul to God, and then went to meet his enemies. They killed him as he was leaving church.

Feast Dates: May 18 — St. Eric IX of Sweden.

Erich (German, Slovakian) See Eric, Frederick.

Erick (English) See Eric, Frederick.

Erico (Portuguese, Italian) See Eric.

Erik (Danish, Swedish) See Eric, Frederick.

Eriks (Latvian) See Eric.

Erin (American) See Aaron.

Erin "The One from Ireland" (Irish Gaelic) or "The Peaceful One" (Irish Gaelic).

Patron Saints: There is a St. Erinhard as well as Sts. Patrick, Bridgid, and Coleman, who are patrons of Ireland. Finally there are two saints named Ireland: Bls. William Ireland, S.J., and John Ireland of Kent.

Bl. William Ireland, also known as Iremonger, was a native of Lincolnshire. He became a Jesuit in 1655 and was ordained a Catholic priest. Then he went to England to work in the mission and was executed in 1679 for alleged complicity in the imaginary Popish Plot instigated by the Anglican priest Titus Oates.

Feast Dates: January 24 — Bl. William Ireland, S.J.

Erkki (Finnish) See Eric.

Erl (variant) See Arlen, Earl.

Erle (variant) See Arlen, Earl.

Erly (variant) See Arlen, Earl.

Erman (Romanian) See Herman.

Ermanno (Italian) See Herman.

Ermano (Spanish) See Herman.

Ermin (English) See Herman.

Ern (nickname) See Eric, Ervin.

Ernek (Czech) See Ernest.

Ernest "The Earnest One" (Old English).

Patron Saints: There is one Bl. Ernest, one St. Ernaeus, eight Sts. Ernan, and sixteen Sts. Ernin. Bl. Ernest died a martyr. He served for five years as Benedictine abbot, then he resigned this position in order to take part in a Crusade with Bishop Otto of Freising. However, the Crusade proved to be a disaster. He was captured by the Muslims and tortured to death at Mecca in 1148.

Feast Dates: November 7 — Bl. Ernest, O.S.B.

Ernestas (Lithuanian) See Ernest.

Ernesto (Portuguese, Italian, Spanish) See Ernest.

Ernestus (variant) See Ernest.

Ernie (variant) See Ernest.

Erno (Hungarian) See Ernest.

Ernst (German, Russian, Slovakian, Swedish, Ukrainian) See Ernest.

Erny (nickname) See Ernest.

Errick (variant) See Eric.

Errict (African-American) See Eric.

Errol (English) See Erroll.

Erroll "The Noble Chief" (German form of Earl) or "The Wandering One" (Latin).

Patron Saints: Erroll is a German form of Earl. There are a few ancient saints with names similar to Earl or Erroll. And there are many saints who held the title of "earl."

Feast Dates: November 6 — St. Erlafrid (see Earl); October 19 — St. Philip Howard, Earl of Arundel (see Howard).

Erv (nickname) See Ervin, Irving.

Ervin "The Beautiful One" (Irish Gaelic).

Patron Saints: There is one St. Ervan (also known as Eruen). Also, if one accepts the suggestion that Ervin is a form of Urban, which means "city," then three dozen more patrons are revealed. Finally, Ervin can also be a form of Irving. This leads to more patrons.

Feast Dates: November 1 — St. Eruen (see Irving); April 12 — St. Urban of Langres (see Urban).

Ervins (Latvian) See Ervin, Irving.

Erwin (English) See Ervin, Irving.

Erwinek (English) See Ervin.

Esander (Hispanic-American) See Alexander.

Esdra (variant) See Ezra.

Esdras (Spanish) See Ezra.

Esias (Danish, Swedish) See Isaiah.

Esme (variant) See Osmond.

Esperidion "The Spiritual One" (Hispanic-American) or "The Spiritual+God of Wine" (Hispanic-American double).

Patron Saints: This name may be a variant of St. Esperantius, who was a holy bishop of Lugo, Spain. It may also be a combination of Esperantius and Dionis (or Denis).

Feast Dates: May 30 — St. Esperantius; October 31 — St. Spiridon (see Spiro).

Esra (Finnish) See Ezra.

Essex "The One from the East" (Old English).

Patron Saints: There is an English martyr "from the east," which is what *essex* means. He is St. John Houghton, the Cistercian prior of the Charterhouse in Essex, England. He was also the first churchman to oppose Henry VIII's Act of Supremacy. Because of this opposition, he and four fellow monks were arrested and executed at Tyburn. He is the protomartyr of the post-Reformation English martyrs.

Feast Dates: May 4 — St. John Houghton of Essex.

Estanislao (Spanish) See Stanislaus.

Este (French, Italian) See Estes.

Estéban (Spanish) See Stephen.

Estee (variant) See Estes.

Estefon (Portuguese) See Stephen.

Estephano (Portuguese) See Stephen.

Estes (Old English double) See Essex+Town.

Estevan (Spanish) See Stephen.

Estevao (Spanish) See Stephen.

Etan (variant) See Ethan.

Ethan "The Firm, Strong One" (Hebrew).

Patron Saints: The Bible introduces four men named Ethan. One of them,

St. Ethan the Ezrahite, was thought to be most wise. Only King Solomon was wiser. In addition, Christian tradition provides a St. Ethian who was a holy bishop in medieval Ireland.

Feast Dates: November 1 — Ethan the Wiseman; May 27 — St. Ethian.

Ethe (variant) See Ethan.

Étienne (French) See Stephen.

Ett "The Little One" (French suffix).

Patron Saints: Ett is a French suffix added to boys' names, such as Gillett and Hewett. There also is a St. Etto. He was an Irishman but lived in France working as a missionary bishop. He died in 670.

Feast Dates: July 10 — St. Etto, also known as Hetto.

Etto (variant) See Hector, Ett.

Ettore (Italian) See Hector.

Eubie (nickname) See Hubert.

Euell "The One Born at Christmastime" (Old English).

Patron Saints: There is one St. Euelpistus, a native of Cappadocia who was martyred in ancient Rome.

And when one realizes that Euell is a form of Yule, Nativity, and Noël, many more patrons appear.

Feast Dates: April 14 — St. Euelpistus; October 19 — St. Noël Chabanel (see Noël).

Eugen (German, Romanian) See Eugene.

Eugene "The Well-Born One" (Greek).

Patron Saints: There are about fifty Sts. Eugene and Eugenius. The best known is St. Eugene, bishop of Carthage in the late 400s to early 500s. He was elected bishop after the Carthage see had been vacant for twenty-five years. Eugene was known for charity, learning, zeal, piety, and prudence. Even though the heretic king would not allow him to preach, he did so anyway. Opposition dogged him to the end.

Feast Dates: July 13 — St. Eugene of Carthage.

Eugenio (Portuguese, Italian, Spanish) See Eugene.

Eugenius (variant) See Eugene.

Eugeniusz (Polish) See Eugene.

Eulises (Latin) See Ulysses.

Eusebio Meaning unknown (Greek, Spanish).

Patron Saints: There are almost seventy Sts. Eusebius. One St. Eusebius was an Irish pilgrim who became a monk at the Swiss abbey of St. Gall. He was killed in 884 by a peasant with a scythe when he was admonishing a group of them about their faults.

Feast Dates: January 31 — St. Eusebius; March 15 — Ven. Eusebio Kino, S.J. (see Kino).

Eusebius (variant) See Eusebio.

Eustace "The Tranquil One" (Latin) or "The Fruitful One" (Greek).

Patron Saints: There are about a dozen Sts. Eustace. One St. Eustace, along with John and Antony, was an official in the court of Duke Olgierd, the ruler of Lithuania. Like most of their countrymen, the three had been born and raised as pagans. However, they converted to Catholicism, and this led to problems. When they refused to eat food forbidden on Church fast days, this upset the duke and he had them thrown into prison. Eustace, only a youth at the time, was tortured for eight months until he died in 1372.

Feast Dates: April 14 — St. Eustace; December 10 — St. Eustace White (see DeWitt).

Eustache (French) See Eustace.

Eustaquio (Spanish) See Eustace.

Eustasio (Spanish) See Eustace.

Eustasius (German) See Eustace.

Eustatius (Dutch) See Eustace.

Eustazio (Italian) See Eustace.

Eustis (variant) See Eustace.

Ev (nickname) See Evan, Everett.

Evan "God Is Gracious" (Welsh form of John) or "The Well-Born Young Warrior" (Welsh).

Patron Saints: Evan is a form of John and Eugene. There are more than four hundred twenty-five saints named John, whose name means "God is gracious." And there are over fifty saints named Eugene, which means "well-born one."

One saint is Philip Evans, 1645-1679, who was born in Monmouthshire, England. He traveled to France for college and he joined the Jesuits. After ordination, he went to the Welsh missions, where he was soon arrested and executed.

Feast Dates: July 22 — St. Philip Evans, S.J.

Evander (African-American double) See Evan+André.

Evarardo (Spanish, Italian) See Everett.

Evard (French) See Everett.

Evelino (Spanish) See Eve+Helen.

Even (English) See Evan, Owen.

Evengenije (Serbian) See Eugene.

Everard (English) See Avery, Everett.

Everardo (Italian) See Everett.

Evered (English) See Everett.

Everett "The One as Strong as a Boar" (Old English).

Patron Saints: There are a dozen Sts. Eberhard, three Sts. Everard, and four Sts. Evaristus. One is Bl. Everard Hanse, who was born in England and raised Protestant. He studied at the University of Cambridge. In time, he became a popular preacher and was very proud of his success.

However, in 1579 his conversion began when his brother began to make appeals to him. Then he became seriously ill, examined his conscience, converted to Catholicism, and went to France to be ordained.

He returned to England under the alias of Evans Duckett and in three months was thrown into prison. He was then hanged, drawn, and quartered.

Feast Dates: July 30 — Bl. Everard Hanse.

Everhard (German) See Everett.

Everhart (Dutch) See Everett.

Evers (Old English double) See Everett+Son.

Everson (Old English double) See Everett+Son.

Evert (Swedish) See Everett.

Evgen (Slovenian) See Eugene.

Evgeny (Russian) See Eugene.

Evin (English) See Evan.

E'Vinski (African-American double) See Evan+Vincent.

Evraud (French) See Everett.

Evyn (English) See Evan.

Ewan (variant) See Eugene, Evan, John, Owen.

Eward (nickname) See Everett.

Ewart (nickname) See Edward, Everett.

Ewell (variant) See Euell, Yule.

Ewen (English) See Eugene, Evan, John, Owen.

Eyton (African-American) See Eaton.

Ez (nickname) See Ezekiel, Ezra.

Ezechiel (English, Hebrew) See Ezekiel.

Ezekiel "The Strength of God" (Hebrew).

Patron Saints: The Bible provides one St. Ezekiel. He is the great Jewish priest-prophet who lived from 650 to 580 B.C. Ezekiel was born into the Jewish priestly family. In about 599 B.C., Jerusalem fell to the Babylonian army, and Ezekiel and his wife were among eleven thousand Jews who were deported to Babylon.

God called Ezekiel to be a prophet and to work among the exiles, combating error, defeating vices, and strengthening faith. His visions are filled with rather unusual — some might even say "grotesque" — images. In his teachings, Ezekiel taught that God could be found everywhere. Further, he insisted that everyone was responsible only for his own sins. In the end God would allow his Temple to be rebuilt.

Ezekiel's ministry lasted until about 572 when he was stoned to death by some of his own people.

Feast Dates: April 10 — St. Ezekiel, Jewish Prophet.

Ezell (African-American) See Ezekiel.

Ezequiel (Spanish, Portuguese) See Ezekiel.

Eziechiele (variant) See Ezekiel.

Ezil (African-American) See Ezekiel.

Ezra "The Helper" (Hebrew).

Patron Saints: The Bible provides two Sts. Ezras. One of them is the great Jewish scribe-priest who lived in 500-420 B.C. In 538 the Babylonian king freed the Jewish exiles. Having been raised in the royal court of the Persian king Artaxerxes I, Ezra gained an influential position. Aware of the great difficulties in Jerusalem, he secured royal permission to organize a relief caravan to Jerusalem. Arriving there, he encountered enormous problems. It seemed that the Jewish faith was dying. He solved this by having the Jewish law read to everyone and he also insisted that all Jews promise obedience to it.

He did everything with the purpose of maintaining religious purity and dedication. For this he is recognized as the "Father of Judaism."

Feast Dates: July 13 — St. Ezra, Jewish Reformer.

Ezri (variant) See Ezra.

Ezven (Czech) See Eugene.

Ezzard (African-American) See Ezra.

Ezzie (nickname) See Ezra.

F

Fabe (nickname) See Fabian.

Faber (nickname) See Fabian.

Fabian "The Bean Grower" (English).

Patron Saints There are about two dozen Sts. Fabian, Fabianus, and Fabius. When Pope Antherus died, a meeting of clergy and laity was called to elect a new pope. They prayed, and a dove flew in the window and settled upon Fabian. This united the clergy and laity, and they elected Fabian to be pope despite the fact that he was only a layman and a stranger to boot. He served for fourteen years, compiled a book of stories about the martyrs, and was martyred in the year 250.

Feast Dates: January 20 — St. Fabian.

Fabiano (Italian) See Fabian.

Fabianus (Latin) See Fabian.

Fabien (French) See Fabian.

Fabio (Italian) See Fabian.

Fabrice (African-American) See Fabian.

Fagan (Irish) See Egan.

Fagin (Irish) See Egan.

Fairleigh (English) See Farley.

Fairlie (English) See Farley.

Falconer (English) See Fowler.

Falkner (English) See Fowler.

Falkoner (English) See Fowler.

Far (nickname) See Farley.

Farlay (English) See Farley.

Farlee (English) See Farley.

Farleigh (English) See Farley.

Farley "From the Bull [or Sheep]+ Meadow" (Old English double).

Patron Saints: Farley comes from two words: *far*, meaning "bull" or "sheep," and *ley* or *leigh*, meaning "meadow." And there are two saints with these names. They are St. Faro and Bl. Richard Leigh.

St. Faro was born into a noble Burgundian family, grew up, married, and was promoted to high offices in the royal court. Then he and his wife decided to part company. She became a nun and he began a career as a Benedictine monk. Then, at the age of thirty-five, he was elected bishop of Meaux.

Feast Dates: October 28 — St. Faro; August 30 — Bl. Richard Leigh (see Leigh).

Farly (English) See Farley.

Farm (nickname) See Field.

Farmer (English) See Farm+Er.

Farris (Irish) See Peter.

Farruco (Spanish) See Francis.

Father (variant) See Papa.

Fay (nickname) See Lafayette.

Fayette (nickname) See Lafayette.

Fede (nickname) See Frederick.

Feder (Spanish) See Fred.

Federico (Spanish) See Frederick.

Federoquito (Spanish double) See Frederick+Quito.

Fedor (Russian) See Theodore.

Fee (nickname) See Felix.

Fele (nickname) See Felix.

Feles (nickname) See Felix.

Felic (variant) See Felix.

Felice (Italian) See Felix.

Felicio (variant) See Felix.

Felike (variant) See Felix.

Feliks (Polish, Russian) See Felix.

Feliksas (Lithuanian) See Felix.

Felipe "The Lover of Horses" (Spanish).

Patron Saints: There are a couple dozen Sts. Philip (or Felipe), one of them being from Mexico City. He is St. Felipe de Jesús. His parents placed him in a Franciscan seminary to study for the priesthood; but he did not want this, so he burned the seminary down. This, of course, got him expelled and he went to the Philippine Islands to make money and live high on the hog. Then a friend died and he took a serious look at life. He repented and studied for seven years in the seminary. In 1596, after completing his studies, he set sail for Mexico because he wanted to be ordained at home. However, the ship was blown off course and he ended up in Japan. With a group of friends he was crucified at Nagasaki in 1597.

Feast Dates: February 5 — St. Felipe de Jesús, O.F.M.

Felipino (Spanish) See Philip.

Felippe (Portuguese) See Philip.

Felix "The Happy Lucky One" (Latin, Spanish).

Patron Saints: Felix has been a popular name throughout Christian history. There are over one hundred seventy-five saints named Felix. One of them is the Ven. Felix DeAndreis, C.M., 1778-1820. He was born, raised, educated, and ordained in Europe and was plagued by ill health. As a priest he conducted retreats for clergy.

In 1815 he received an invitation from the bishop of New Orleans to come to America. He gathered two dozen priests and seminarians in 1816 and went to Bardstown, Kentucky. In 1817 they traveled to Kakaskia, Illinois, to serve the people there. In 1818 he became vicar general of the New Orleans diocese. Because of him, a seminary system was established in the Midwest and the Vincentian religious order was founded in the United States. He was forty-two at the time of his death.

Feast Dates: October 15 — Ven. Felix DeAndreis, C.M.

Felizio (variant) See Felix.

Felo (Spanish) See Felix.

Felt (nickname) See Felton.

Felten (English) See Felton.

Feltie (English) See Felton.

Felton "From the Town [Estate]+Near the Meadow" (Old English double).

Patron Saints: There are two English martyrs, father and son, with this name. Bl. John Felton, a layman, was living in Southwark when the Act of Uniformity of Queen Elizabeth reached London. He bravely nailed a copy of it to the door of the home of the London bishop. For this he was arrested, tried, and then executed in the churchyard of St. Paul's in 1570.

Bl. Thomas Felton, 1568-1588, was the son of John. He was only two years old when the English government murdered his father. As a teenager, he traveled to Rheims, where he became a priest and a religious, and then returned to England. He was soon arrested and then executed. He was only twenty years old.

Feast Dates: August 8 — Bl. John Felton; August 28 — Bl. Thomas Felton, O.F.M. Min.

Felty (English) See Felton.

Fen (English) See Fenton.

Fenn (English) See Fenton.

Fennie (English) See Fenton.

Fenny (English) See Fenton.

Fenton "From the Marsh+Estate Town" (Old English double).

Patron Saints: Fenton is created out of *fen*, meaning "marsh," and *ton*, meaning "town." There are two saints who have these words (or variations of them) in their names. In 1535, when Catholics in England began to be persecuted, Bl. James Fenn, a native of

Montacute, Somerset, lived the life of a married schoolmaster. However, after his wife died he went to France, where, in 1580, he was ordained a diocesan priest. Then he returned to England and ministered for four years, until he was arrested and executed by authorities for being a Catholic priest.

Feast Dates: February 12 — Bl. James Fenn; July 21 — St. Tondach (see Town).

Feodor (Slavic) See Theodore.

Ferd (nickname) See Ferdinand.

Ferdek (Polish) See Ferdinand.

Ferdie (nickname) See Ferdinand.

Ferdinand "The Adventurous Brave One" (Gothic).

Patron Saints: There are a half-dozen Sts. Ferdinand. One is St. Ferdinand III, 1200-1253. As king of Castile, he displayed great prudence and forgiveness. He also followed the advice of his wise mother and married Beatrice, a princess of Swabia. He had ten children.

His reign was mostly peaceful, and he fought only when necessary and then he refused to tax his people to pay for the military. His favorite saying was, "God will provide." He died at the age of fifty-three.

Feast Dates: May 30 — St. Ferdinand the King.

Ferdinandas (Lithuanian) See Ferdinand.

Ferdinando (Italian) See Ferdinand.

Ferdinandos (Greek) See Ferdinand.

Ferdy (nickname) See Ferdinand.

Ferdys (Czech) See Ferdinand.

Ferenc (Hungarian) See Francis.

Ferg (nickname) See Fergus.

Ferghus (variant) See Fergus.

Fergus "The Very Strong One" (Irish Gaelic).

Patron Saints: There are about a dozen Sts. Fergus and Ferghas. St. Fergus was an Irish bishop who spent all of his time preaching the Gospel in Scotland. The first thing he did upon arrival in Scotland was to found three churches, dedicating all of them to St. Patrick. He died in 725.

Feast Dates: November 27 — St. Fergus.

Ferguson (Irish double) See Fergus+Son.

Fergy (nickname) See Fergus.

Fernand (French) See Ferdinand.

Fernandino (variant) See Ferdinand.

Fernando (Spanish) See Ferdinand.

Ferni (variant) See Ferdinand.

Ferris "The Choice One" (Irish).

Patron Saints: Depending on the authority consulted, Ferris is either accepted as an Irish name in its own right, or it is an Irish variant of Fergus or Peter.

Feast Dates: November 22 — St. Fergus (see Fergus); June 29 — St. Peter, Apostle (see Peter).

Fess (nickname) See Festus.

Festus "The Steadfast One" (Latin).

Patron Saints: There are a half-dozen Sts. Festus. One of them served as a deacon in Roman times. When Festus and the lector Desiderius heard that their bishop, Januarius, had been imprisoned, they decided to visit him and comfort him. However, the minute they appeared at the jail, they were also arrested. In the end, all of them were beheaded.

Feast Dates: September 19 — St. Festus.

Feyo (Spanish) See Alfred.

Fico (nickname) See Frederick.

Fidel "The Faithful One" (Spanish).

Patron Saints: There are about a dozen saints named with variants of Fidel. One of them was a Roman army officer who converted to Christianity. He then released some Christians and retired. Because of his conversion, some members of the army tried to arrest him, but he fled. Soon caught, he was killed in 304.

Feast Dates: October 28 — St. Fidelis of Como; April 24 — St. Fidelis of Sigmaringen (see Roy).

Fidele (French) See Fidel.

Fidelio (Italian) See Fidel.

Field "From the Field [Farm]" (Old English).

Patron Saints: The Latin word for "field" or "farm" is *ager* or *agris.* There are two Sts. Agericus and one St. Ager, also known as St. Field (or Farm), who died a martyr's death for Jesus in ancient Potenza.

Feast Dates: May 13 — St. Field (or Farm), also known as Ager.

Fielding (English) See Field.

Fields (English) See Field, Garfield, Sheffield.

Filib (Scottish Gaelic) See Philip.

Filip (Scandinavian, Polish, Czech) See Philip.

Filipo (Spanish) See Philip.

Filippo (Italian) See Philip.

Filippos (Modern Greek) See Philip.

Filmer (English) See Filmore.

Filbert (English double) See Filmore+Bert.

Filberto (Spanish) See Filbert.

Filius "The Son" (Latin).

Patron Saints: The word "son" in Latin is *filius natus.* There is one St. Fillion. He died for Christ in ancient Amasea in Pontus.

Jesus, Son of God, can also be patron. Two feast days present Gospels that quote the Father calling Jesus "his Son." They are the Baptism of the Lord and the Transfiguration.

Feast Dates: August 19 — St. Fillion; First Sunday After the Epiphany — Baptism of the Lord; August 6 — Transfiguration; November 17 — St. Sontius (see Son).

Filmore "The Very Famous One" (Old English double).

Patron Saints: Filmore is built from two words, *fil* and *more* (originally spelled *fela* and *maere*). There is a St. Felan and a St. Mor. St. Felan (also known as Fillan) is a native of Ireland. He worked as a missionary there in the 700s. In time, he became an abbot of a monastery. He died in about 750.

St. Mor is a Welsh priest of the 400s who is simply remembered for his holiness.

Feast Dates: January 9 — St. Felan; November 1 — St. Mor.

Fin (nickname) See Finian, Finlay, Finn.

Findlay (variant) See Finlay.

Findley (variant) See Finlay.

Finian "The Warrior" (Irish Gaelic).

Patron Saints: There are a half-dozen Sts. Finian. One is St. Finian McCorpre, 495-572, of Ulster. He had the good fortune to study under many fine teachers. Then after making a pilgrimage to Rome, he founded his own monastery in 540. In his later years Finian served the Catholic Church as the bishop of Moville, County Down, Ireland. He died at the age of seventy-seven. He is patron of Ulster.

Feast Dates: September 10 — St. Finian McCorpre.

Finlay "The Little Fair-Haired Soldier" (Irish Gaelic).

Patron Saints: The original spelling of Finlay is Fionn-ghalc. There are a few saints whose names contain *fionn,* which is usually rendered *fin* in modern print. They include a dozen Sts. Finan, a St. Fingar, and three Sts. Finlugh. One St. Finlugh was an Irish priest in the 500s, the brother of St. Fintan McPipan.

Feast Dates: January 3 — St. Finlugh.

Finn "The Fair-Haired One" (Irish Gaelic) or "The Warrior" (short form of Finian).

Patron Saints: There are over three dozen Sts. Finne, Finnio, Finnu, Fionan, Finan, Finbar, Fingar, and Finian. Among them is St. Finne Cruimther, a medieval Irish saint who lived near Drumlease in Leitrim.

Feast Dates: February 9 — St. Finne Cruimther.

Finne (nickname) See Finian, Finlay, Finn.

Finnie (nickname) See Finian, Finlay, Finn.

Finny (nickname) See Finian, Finlay, Finn.

Fiorello (Italian) See Florian.

Fisher "The One Who Fishes" (Middle English).

Patron Saints: In 1504 St. John Fisher was appointed bishop of Rochester. When King Henry VIII wanted a divorce and made himself head of the English Church, Bishop Fisher opposed it. He was immediately imprisoned and then beheaded in 1535.

Feast Dates: June 22 — St. John Fisher.

Fito (Spanish) See Alfred.

Fitz (Old French) See Son, Mac.

Fitzgerald (Old English double) See Fitz+Gerald.

Fitzhugh (Old English double) See Fitz+Hugh.

Fitzpatrick (Old English double) See Fitz+Patrick.

Fitzroy (Old English double) See Fitz+Roy.

Flavian "The Blond [Yellow-Haired] One" (Latin).

Patron Saints: There are over two dozen saints named Flavian or Flavianus. One was a priest and sacristan at the Church of Constantinople.

In 446 he was elected to be the patriarch. Trouble dogged his every move. In 448, when he opposed the Monophysite heresy, the heretics deposed him and drove him into exile.

Feast Dates: February 18 — St. Flavian of Constantinople.

Flavio (Spanish) See Flavian.

Flavius (Latin) See Flavian.

Fleming "The One from Denmark [The Lowlands]" (Old English).

Patron Saints: In Latin, "lowlands" is *loca plana*, and there is a St. Planus. St. Canute is patron of Denmark.

Feast Dates: January 8 — St. Planus; January 19 — St. Knute, also known as Canute or Knud (see Knute).

Fletch (nickname) See Fletcher.

Fletcher "The Arrowsmith" (Middle English) or "The Arrow-Featherer" (Middle English).

Patron Saints: It helps to know that Fletcher means "arrowsmith." This leads to Edmund Arrowsmith, 1585-1628. As a boy in Lancashire, he was left shivering in his nightclothes when government agents took his parents to jail because they were Catholic. As an adult he studied in France and was ordained a priest in 1612, joining the Jesuits in 1623. He worked in the English missions from 1613 until 1628, when he was convicted of being a religious seducer. He was hanged, drawn, and quartered.

Feast Dates: August 28 — St. Edmund Arrowsmith, S.J.

Flint "The Quartz Stone" (American) or "A Stream" (Old English).

Patron Saints: Flint means "stone" or "rock," and this leads to many patrons. There is Jesus the Foundation Stone; the Apostle Peter, whom Jesus named "Rock"; three Sts. Rock (Roche); and an English martyr named St. John Stone.

Another patron is Bl. John Roche, a young Irish water-taxi operator who was arrested in 1588 for helping a Catholic priest escape prison. He was executed.

Feast Dates: August 30 — Bl. John Roche; May 12 — St. John Stone (see Stone).

Flip (Spanish) See Philip.

Floren (variant) See Florian.

Florian "The Flower" (Latin) or "The Flowering [Blooming] One" (Latin).

Patron Saints There are about a dozen Sts. Florian and Florianus. This St. Florian was a career soldier in the Roman army and eventually gained high rank. When the persecution of Emperor Diocletian broke out in 304, he hurried to Upper Austria to comfort the soldiers imprisoned for the faith. Because he refused to murder Christians, he was arrested and imprisoned. He was twice whipped and half flayed. Finally a stone was tied around his neck and he was thrown into a river. Miracles were attributed to him.

A legend about him claiming he put out a great fire with just one pitcher of water led to his becoming patron against fires. The pitcher he is shown holding in sacred art eventually made him patron of brewers. In addition, he is patron of chimney sweeps, soap makers, and against drowning and floods.

Feast Dates: May 4 — St. Florian; May 4 — Bl. Richard Flowers, also known as Lloyd (see Lloyd).

Flory (variant) See Florian.

Floyd (English) See Lloyd.

Floyde (English) See Lloyd.

Flynn "The Son of the Red-Haired Man" (Irish Gaelic).

Patron Saints: One has to turn to the Latin name Rufus, which means "red-haired," to find a patron.

Feast Dates: August 27 — St. Rufus, also known as Red (see Rufus).

Foma (Russian) See Thomas.

Foncho (nickname) See Alphonse.

Fonz (nickname) See Alphonse.

Fonzie (nickname) See Alphonse.

Fonzo (nickname) See Alphonse.

Ford "From the River Crossing" (Old English).

Patron Saints: There is one English martyr who is surnamed Ford. Bl. Thomas Ford was born and raised a Protestant in England. He then converted to Catholicism and was ordained a diocesan priest in France in 1573. Three years later he went to the English missions. He worked in Oxfordshire and Berkshire until 1582, when he was arrested and executed.

Feast Dates: May 28 — Bl. Thomas Ford.

Forest "From the Forest" (Old French).

Patron Saints: An English martyr named Bl. John Forest, born about 1500, comes to mind as a patron. After joining the Friars Minor, he was stationed at Greenwich and became the confessor of Queen Catherine of Aragon. He soon found himself in opposition to King Henry VIII because the king was seeking a divorce. Further, he refused to recognize Henry as the head of the Church. As a result, the king had a particular hatred for Father Forest. He had him burned at the stake in 1538.

Feast Dates: May 22 — Bl. John Forest, O.F.M.

Forester (English) See Forest.

Forrest (English) See Forest.

Forrester (English) See Forest.

Forster (English) See Forest.

Fort (English) See Garrison.

Fortune "One with a Destiny" (English).

Patron Saints: There are about fifty Sts. Fortunatus. One of them died a martyr in Roman Africa.

Feast Dates: February 22 — St. Fortunatus; July 15 — St. Bonaventure (see Bonaventure).

Fortuné (French) See Fortune.

Fortunio (Italian) See Fortune.

Foss (nickname) See Foster, Forest.

Fossie (nickname) See Foster, Forest.

Foster "Keeper of the Forest" (Latin) or "From the Forest" (variant of Forest).

Patron Saints: There is one St. Foster. Also, because Foster means "keeper of the woods," an English martyr surnamed Forest can be adopted as a patron. St. Foster was probably born at Périgueux in southern France. He is also known by the names of Vedast and Gaston. Upon growing up he was ordained a priest. It is said that he instructed King Clovis in the faith after the battle of Tolbiac. He also helped St. Rémi in the conversion of the Franks. In 510 Rémi consecrated Foster a bishop. He died in 540, after thirty years of service.

Feast Dates: February 6 — St. Foster; May 22 — Bl. John Forest, O.F.M.

Fowler "The Falconer" (Old English) or "The Trapper of Wild Fowl" (Old English).

Patron Saints: One religious order founder is perfect for the job. He is Bl. Alexis Falconieri.

Feast Dates: February 17 — Bl. Alexis Falconieri (see Marlon).

Fran (nickname) See Francis, Frank.

Franc (Bulgarian) See Francis, Frank.

Francesco (Italian) See Francis.

Franchot (French) See Francis.

Francis "The One from France" (English) or "The Freeman" (English).

Patron Saints There are almost fifty Sts. Francis. One of the greatest was St. Francis of Assisi, 1181-1226. After a pilgrimage to Rome, he exchanged his rich lifestyle for the life of a beggar. On one occasion he sold merchandise from his father's business to help pay for the repair of a local church. His angry father brought him to the bishop to demand the money back that Francis had donated. Francis removed his clothes and gave them back to his father, saying that even his clothes now belonged to him. The bishop then clad Francis in the rough brown tunic of a gardener. Later, Francis was ordained a deacon but never a priest.

Francis founded a religious community that embraced absolute poverty, humility, and discipline. Among his contributions to the faithful is the Christmas crèche. He died at forty-five years of age and is considered patron of animals and birds, ecologists and the ecology movement, lace makers, merchants, needleworkers, tapestry makers, and of Italy, as well as of Catholic Action and against fires and solitary death.

Feast Dates: October 4 — St. Francis of Assisi; August 13 — Bl. William Freeman (see Freeman).

Francisco (Portuguese, Spanish) See Francis.

Franciscus (Latin) See Francis.

Franciskus (Polish) See Francis.

Franciszek (variant) See Francis.

Francklin (English double) See Francis, Frank+Landon.

Francklyn (English double) See Francis, Frank+Landon.

Franco (Italian, Spanish) See Francis, Frank.

François (French) See Francis.

Franek (nickname) See Francis.

Franjo (Serbian) See Francis, Frank.

Frank "The One from France" (English nickname) or "The Freeman" (English nickname).

Patron Saints: There are about fifty Sts. Francis. Bl. Francisco Marto, 1908-1919, was the tenth of eleven children of a poor rural family in Fátima, Portugal. He led an uneventful life watching the family sheep until May 13, 1917, when the Virgin Mary appeared to him, his sister, and cousin. Then he faced hostile police and skeptical clergy. His testimony and the "Miracle of the Sun" convinced many.

The apparitions made him very pious. He did many sacrifices to save sinners. He was also fascinated by the hidden presence of Jesus in Holy Communion and would often spend hours in church. In the fall of 1918 he became ill with influenza and lingered for a half year. He received his first Holy Communion on April 3, 1919, and died the following day. He was only eleven years old.

Feast Dates: April 14 — Bl. Francisco Marto; October 4 — St. Francis of Assisi (see Francis).

Frankie (nickname) See Francis, Frank.

Franklin "From the Land+Of France" (English double) or "The Freeman+Landowner" (English double).

Patron Saints: Franklin is built out of Frank plus Land. There are about fifty Sts. Francis, a St. Lando, a St. Landry, and a North American missionary, St. Jean de Lalande.

Feast Dates: October 4 — St. Francis of Assisi (see Francis); January 16 — St. Lando (see Land).

Franklyn (English double) See Francis, Frank+Landon.

Franky (nickname) See Francis, Frank.

Frannie (nickname) See Francis.

Franny (nickname) See Francis.

Frans (Swedish) See Francis.

Frans (variant) See Francis.

Frantisek (Czech) See Francis.

Frantisekos (Greek) See Francis.

Frants (Dutch) See Francis.

Franz (German) See Francis.

Franzen (variant) See Francis.

Frasco (Spanish) See Francis.

Frascuelo (Spanish) See Francis.

Fraser (English) See Frasier.

Frasier "The Curly-Haired One" (Old English) or "The Strawberry" (Old French).

Patron Saints: Recognizing that Frasier can mean "curly-haired" leads to twelve Sts. Crispinus and Crispinianus whose names also mean "curly-haired." Note that "frizzy hair" finds its roots in Frazier.

Feast Dates: October 25 — Sts. Crispinus and Crispinianus.

Frasquito (variant) See Francis.

Fraze (English) See Frasier.

Frazer (English) See Frasier.

Frazier (English) See Frasier.

Fred (nickname) See Alfred, Frederick, Manfred, Wilfred.

Freddie (nickname) See Alfred, Frederick, Manfred, Wilfred.

Freddy (nickname) See Alfred, Frederick, Manfred, Wilfred.

Fredek (Polish) See Frederick.

Frédéric (French) See Frederick.

Frederich (variant) See Frederick.

Frederick "The Peaceful Ruler" (Old German).

Patron Saints: There are about a dozen Sts. Frederick. St. Frederick of Utrecht, a native of Frisia, was ordained a priest and given the job of instructing converts. In about 825 he was elected bishop of Utrecht. In time, he was drawn into a quarrel between the sons of the emperor and their father and stepmother. This drew the wrath of the empress. She hired assassins to kill Frederick. His time to die came on July 18, 838. Frederick had just celebrated Mass and was about to begin his thanksgiving when he was stabbed to death.

Feast Dates: July 18 — St. Frederick of Utrecht.

Frederico (Spanish, Italian, Portuguese) See Frederick.

Frederigo (Italian) See Frederick.

Frederik (Serbian) See Frederick.

Fredi (nickname) See Frederick.

Fredo (Italian, Spanish) See Alfred, Lafredo.

Fredric (English) See Frederick.

Fredrick (English) See Frederick.

Free (English) See Freeman.

Freedman (English double) See Freeman.

Freeland (English double) See Freeman+ Landon.

Freeman "The Free Man" (Old English).

Patron Saints: There is a Bl. William Freeman. He grew up Protestant in an English world hostile to Catholicism and was educated at Oxford. However, he converted to Catholicism a short time later. Then he went to Rheims College in France, where he was ordained a priest. In 1587 he returned to England. In his work in the Catholic underground he often used the alias of "William Morse." In 1595, after eight years of working among the faithful, he was arrested and convicted of being a priest. Then he was executed.

It is also helpful to know that the name Francis means "freeman," and there are fifty Sts. Francis.

Feast Dates: August 13 — Bl. William Freeman, also known as Morse.

Freemon (English) See Freeman, Fremont.

Fremont "The Free and Noble Protector" (Old German).

Patron Saints: St. Fremund was a hermit of the royal family of Mercia

who was killed by an ambitious relative in 886.

Feast Dates: May 11 — St. Fremund.

French (variant) See Francis.

Frico (nickname) See Frederick.

Friderik (variant) See Frederick.

Friedrich (German) See Frederick.

Friedrick (variant) See Frederick.

Frigyes (Hungarian) See Frederick.

Frisco (Spanish) See Francis.

Fritz "The Peaceful Ruler" (German nickname for Frederick).

Patron Saints: Fritz is a short form of Friedrich. There is one St. Fritz and a dozen Sts. Frederick. St. Fritz is remembered for being the son of King Radbod of Frisia. He became a knight, fought with Charles Martel against the Saracens, and fell in battle.

Feast Dates: January 16 — St. Fritz, also known as Frisius; July 18 — St. Frederick of Utrecht (see Frederick).

Fritzchen (nickname) See Frederick.

Frost "The Frozen One" (Middle English) or "The One Who Brags" (Welsh).

Patron Saints: The Latin word for cold is *frigidus*. This leads to St. Frigidian, who was a native of Ireland and lived in the 500s. He traveled to Italy, was consecrated a bishop, and became known for his miracles.

Furthermore, the Catholic Church has appointed two saints for cold weather. The patron of frost is St. Urban of Langres and the patron of cold is St. Valerian.

Feast Dates: November 18 — St. Frigidian; November 15 — St. Valerian (see Calder).

Fuller "The One Who Thickens Cloth" (Middle English).

Patron Saints: The name Fuller (or Tucker) means "fuller," or "thickener of cloth." Four saints have been appointed patrons of fullers. They are Homobonus,

Athanasius the Fuller, James the Younger, and Paul the Hermit. St. Paul, 229-342, a native of Egypt, became an orphan at fifteen. He inherited great wealth but feared his brother-in-law would betray him to the government for being a Christian in order to get all the money. Thus he fled to the desert. There he learned to love solitude and prayer. He also became a friend of St. Anthony. He died at the age of one hundred thirteen.

Feast Dates: January 15 — St. Paul the Hermit; May 3 — St. James the Younger (see Jimmy).

Fulop (Hungarian) See Philip.

Fulton "From the Field+Near the Town" (Old English double).

Patron Saints: Fulton is a double name that comes from "field" and "town." There is a St. Field and a St. Tondach. Bishop Fulton J. Sheen, who was a popular radio and TV evangelist and is being considered for canonization, can also be adopted as a patron.

Feast Dates: May 13 — St. Field (or Farm), also known as Ager (see Field); July 21 — St. Tondach (see Town).

Fyodor (Russian) See Theodore.

G

Gabbi (nickname) See Gabriel.

Gabbie (nickname) See Gabriel.

Gabby (nickname) See Gabriel.

Gabe (nickname) See Gabriel.

Gabi (nickname) See Gabriel.

Gabino (Spanish) See Gabriel.

Gable (Old French) See Gabriel.

Gabor (Hungarian) See Gabriel.

Gabriel "God Is My Strength" (English, French, Spanish, Hebrew) or "Hero of God" (Hebrew).

Patron Saints: There about two dozen Sts. Gabriel. The greatest is the archangel Gabriel, who is patron of childbirth, diplomats, messengers, postal workers, stamp collectors, telephone workers, television workers, and anyone involved in the communications industry.

In Luke, St. Gabriel announces the birth of Jesus. Thus Catholics feel privileged to repeat the very words that God the Father gave Gabriel to speak, when they pray the Hail Mary. And Catholic tradition adds that Gabriel announced the birth of the Baptist, explained Mary's pregnancy to Joseph, and led the singing angels who announced Christ's birth to the shepherds. He is the herald of the "end time" and is expected to mark the foreheads of the saved before the end.

Jewish tradition also identifies him as the end-time herald because in Daniel he delivers an end-time message. In addition, it calls Gabriel the "angel of judgment" because he oversaw the destruction of Sodom.

Feast Dates: September 29 — St. Gabriel the Archangel; October 19 —

St. Gabriel Lalemant (see Lamont).

Gabriele (Italian) See Gabriel.

Gabriello (Italian) See Gabriel.

Gael (English) See Gale.

Gaelan (English) See Galen.

Gage "The Pledge" (Old French).

Patron Saints: There are three Sts. Gage. However, they spelled their names Gagus. One of them died a martyr for the faith in ancient Nicomedia.

Feast Dates: April 6 — St. Gage, also known as Gagus.

Gail (English) See Gale.

Gailard (English) See Gaylord.

Gaile (English) See Gale.

Gal (nickname) See Galvin.

Gale "The Lively One" (Old English) or "The Foreigner" (Irish) or "The Intelligent One" (form of Galen).

Patron Saints: There is one St. Gale and about a dozen Sts. Gallus. St. Gale was a black layman who died a martyr for the faith in Carthage, Africa.

It should also be noted that the English name Gale means "gay, lively." In Latin the name reads as Gaius or Caius. There are a half-dozen Sts. Gajus. Also, if Gale is accepted as a short form of the Irish *galen*, meaning "intelligent," then another half-dozen Sts. Galen become available.

Feast Dates: January 24 — St. Gale, also known as Galeus.

Galen "The Little Intelligent One" (Irish Gaelic) or "The Healer" (Greek).

Patron Saints: There are a half-dozen Sts. Galen. One of them is St. Galen, a leader of a group of ten thousand martyrs who were crucified on Mount Ararat (Turkey) in ancient times.

Feast Dates: June 22 — St. Galen, also known as Galenus.

Galeno (Spanish) See Galen.

Gallard (English) See Gaylord.

Galvan (English) See Galvin.

Galven (English) See Galvin.

Galvin "The Shining White One" (Irish Gaelic) or "The Sparrow" (Irish Gaelic).

Patron Saints: The only avenues open to finding a patron are the two name meanings. These lead to Bl. James Bird and St. Alban.

Feast Dates: March 25 — Bl. James Bird (see Bird); June 20 — St. Alban (see Alban).

Gamal (variant) See Gamaliel.

Gamaliel "The Recompense of God" (Hebrew) or "The Camel" (Arabic).

Patron Saints: There is one St. Gamaliel. He was an elder of Israel, a teacher of the young St. Paul, and a member of the Jewish Sanhedrin during the time Jesus walked the earth. In the Book of Acts he advises the Sanhedrin to be careful as to how they handle the problem of the Apostles. He strongly argues that they should not be put to death for preaching Jesus. He warns the Sanhedrin that if its members are not careful, they might find themselves making war on God himself. For a few years, the Sanhedrin grudgingly followed his advice.

Christian tradition adds that Gamaliel became a convert to Christianity long before St. Paul was converted. After accepting Jesus as his Savior, Gamaliel remained a member of the Sanhedrin in order to help fellow Christians. When St. Stephen was martyred, Gamaliel buried him on his estate. Many years later Gamaliel died a martyr's death.

Feast Dates: August 3 — St. Gamaliel.

Gar (nickname) See Gardener, Garfield, Gareth, Garth, Garrett, Gary.

Garald (Russian) See Harold.

Garalde (French) See Gerald.

Garaldo (Portuguese, Italian, Spanish) See Gerald.

García "The Fox" (Spanish).

Patron Saints: St. Margarito Flores García was born in 1899 in Mexico. Upon growing up, he was ordained a priest. On November 12, 1927, the Mexican government put him to death by firing squad.

Feast Dates: November 12 — St. Margarito Flores García.

Gard (nickname) See Gardener.

Gardell (African-American) See Gardener+Tyrell.

Gardelle (African-American) See Gardener+Tyrell.

Gardener "One Who Tends a Garden" (Middle English).

Patron Saints: There is one English martyr, Bl. Jermyn Gardiner, who was executed in 1544 for refusing to take the Oath of Supremacy, which meant recognizing King Henry VIII as head of the Church.

Other patrons can be found when one realizes that the name Gardener means "one who cares for a garden." And the Catholic Church has officially appointed six saints to act as patrons of gardeners. They are Sts. Adam, Adelard, Dorothy, Fiacre, Gertrude of Nivelles, and Phocas.

Feast Dates: March 7 — Bl. Jermyn Gardiner; December 24 — Sts. Adam and Eve (see Adam).

Gardie (nickname) See Gardener.

Gardiner (English) See Gardener.

Gardner (English) See Gardener.

Gardy (nickname) See Gardener.

Garek (variant) See Gerald.

Garek (Czech, Polish) See Edgar.

Gareth (Welsh) See Garrett.

Garey (variant) See Gary.

Garfield "From the Battle+Field" (Old English double).

Patron Saints: Garfield is composed of two words: *gar*, which means "battle," and *field*, which has retained the same meaning, "field." There is a St. Garai as well as a Bl. Field.

Feast Dates: November 1 — St. Garai (see Gary); May 13 — St. Field (or Farm), also known as Ager (see Field).

Garick (Czech) See Edgar, Garrett.

Garik (Czech) See Edgar.

Garner "The Armed Defender" (Old French form of Warner).

Patron Saints: There are two Sts. Garnier. One served as provost of a Dijon monastery in the 900s.

Feast Dates: July 19 — St. Garnier.

Garnett (Old English) See Garrett.

Garold (variant) See Gerald.

Garrard (Czech) See Garrett.

Garrek (Czech) See Edgar.

Garrek (variant) See Gerald.

Garrelt (Dutch) See Gerald.

Garren (English) See Gary.

Garretson (English double) See Garrett+ Son.

Garrett "The Brave Spearman" (Irish).

Patron Saints: Garrett and Gerald mean the same thing.

Feast Dates: October 13 — St. Gerald of Aurillac.

Garrick (variant) See Gerald, Garrett.

Garrik (variant) See Edgar, Gerald.

Garrison "From the Fortified Place" (Old English).

Patron Saints: There is a St. Fort. In addition, a very powerful patron can easily be found if one remembers that Garrison means "fortified place." Just remember what Psalms 18:2 tells us: "The Lord is my rock, and my fortress, and my deliverer, . . . my stronghold." This means that God the Father is a sturdy defense against evil.

Furthermore, Jesus shares the job of being our sturdy refuge, for Isaiah 33:16 tells us that "his place of defense will be the fortresses of rocks." This passage shows that Jesus would be a strong and protective King. Acts 4:11 adds, "This is the stone which was rejected by you builders, but which has become the head of the corner." Thus Jesus as the "Cornerstone" becomes our sure guarantee of salvation. He is the "Rock of Our Salvation."

Feast Dates: Thirty-fourth Sunday of the Year — Jesus, Our Fortress; May 16 — St. Fort (see Shay).

Garrot (English) See Garrett.

Garrott (English) See Garrett.

Garry (nickname) See Gerald.

Garson (English double) See Garrison+ Son.

Garth "From the [Meadow] Enclosure" (Old Norse) or "From the Garden" (Middle English).

Patron Saints: There is only one saint with the name of Garth. He is Bl. Richard Leigh, who often traveled undercover and used the alias of "Richard Garth." There is also one saint with a similar name: St. Gartheli. Moreover, because Gareth is considered to be a variant of Gerald and Gerard, even more patrons emerge. There are about a dozen Sts. Gerald and Gerard.

Feast Dates: August 30 — Bl. Leigh, also known as Garth (see Leigh); October 16 — St. Gerard (see Gerard).

Gary "The Spear Ruler" (Old English).

Patron Saints: Gary is a short form of Garrott and an English form of Gerald or Gerard. There are a dozen Sts. Gerald and another dozen Sts. Gerard. Furthermore, there is one St. Garai. He was the holy son of Cewydd, a native of medieval Wales. He founded an abbey.

Feast Dates: November 1 — St. Garai.

Gaspar (Spanish) See Casper.

Gasparcio (Spanish) See Casper.

Gaspare (Italian) See Casper.

Gaston "The One from Gascony" (French).

Patron Saints: There is one St. Gaston. He served God as a bishop in southern France in the 500s.

Feast Dates: February 6 — St. Gaston.

Gauthier (French) See Walter.

Gautier (French) See Walter.

Gav (nickname) See Gavin.

Gavan (English) See Gavin.

Gaven (English) See Gavin, Gaylord.

Gavin "The White Hawk" (Old Welsh).

Patron Saints: There is one English patron whose name is close: Bl. John Gavan. He was born in London in the 1600s. In 1660 he traveled to the Continent and was ordained as a Jesuit. He returned to England and ministered to English Catholics until 1679. Finally he was arrested and condemned to death for alleged involvement in the bogus Oates Plot (or Popish Plot).

Feast Dates: June 20 — Bl. John Gavan, S.J.

Gavrylo (Ukrainian) See Gabriel.

Gawain (English) See Gavin, Gaylord.

Gawayne (English) See Gavin.

Gawen (English) See Gavin, Gaylord.

Gay (English) See Gaylord.

Gayelord (English) See Gaylord.

Gayle (English) See Gale, Galen.

Gayler (English) See Gaylord.

Gaylon (English) See Gale, Galen.

Gaylor (English) See Gaylord.

Gaylord "The Jailer [Gaoler]" (Old French) or "The Lively One" (Old French).

Patron Saints: The Catholic Church has officially appointed five saints as patrons of prison guards. They are Adrian, Basildes, Hippolytus, Processus, and Martinian. The last two mentioned were soldiers and the warders of Sts. Peter and Paul in the Mamertine prison. They converted and died martyrs.

Feast Dates: July 2 — Sts. Processus and Martinian.

Gearalt (variant) See Gerald.

Gearard (variant) See Gerald, Gerard.

Gellert (Hungarian) See Gerard.

Gellett (English) See Gillett.

Gellette (English) See Gillett.

Gelo (nickname) See Angel.

Gencho (Spanish) See Eugene.

Gene (nickname) See Eugene.

Geo (nickname) See George.

Geoff (nickname) See Geoffrey, Godfrey, Jeffrey.

Geoffredo (Italian) See Geoffrey, Godfrey, Jeffrey.

Geoffrey "From the Peaceful Land" (Old German) or "The Peaceful Traveler" (Old German).

Patron Saints: Godfrey, Geoffrey, and Jeffrey are all the same name.

Feast Dates: July 9 — St. Godfrey of Merville (see Merton).

Geoffroi (French) See Geoffrey, Godfrey, Jeffrey.

Geoffroy (French) See Geoffrey, Godfrey, Jeffrey.

Geoffry (French) See Geoffrey, Godfrey, Jeffrey.

Georas (Scottish) See George.

Geordie (Scottish) See George.

Georg (German, Danish, Swedish) See George.

George "The Farmer" (Old English).

Patron Saints: There are about fifty Sts. George. The most famous is St. George the Great. He was born of upper-class Christian parents in ancient

Cappadocia, became a soldier, and won promotion through bravery in battle. In time, he found himself attached to the personal staff of Emperor Diocletian. When the emperor decided to persecute Christians, George resigned his commission and bitterly complained to the emperor. Diocletian had him arrested, tortured, and executed in 303.

He was very popular among Christians in the Middle Ages, and many myths were attached to him, including the story of his killing a dragon. He is considered patron of archers, armorers, Boy Scouts, soldiers, the cavalry, equestrians, farmers, knights, saddlers, sword makers, and horses; he is also patron of England, Italy, Georgia, Germany, Lithuania, Portugal, Spain, and against fevers, the plague, leprosy, and syphilis.

Feast Dates: April 23 — St. George the Great.

Georges (French) See George.

Georghe (African-American) See George.

Georgi (English) See George.

Georgie (nickname) See George.

Georgios (Greek) See George.

Georgy (English) See George.

Geovani (Hispanic-American) See Giovanni.

Gerado (Spanish) See Gerard.

Gerald "The Spear Ruler" (Old German, English).

Patron Saints: There are about a dozen saints named Gerald. One of them is St. Gerald, the count of Aurillac and the founder of the monastery of Aurillac. As a child, he was plagued with bad health. Thus he embraced a life of prayer and spent his considerable fortune on charitable purposes. He died in 909.

Feast Dates: October 13 — St. Gerald of Aurillac.

Geralde (variant) See Gerald.

Geraldo (Spanish) See Gerald.

Geraldos (Greek) See Gerald.

Geralds (Latvian) See Gerald.

Gerard "The Spear Carrier" (Old German, English, Irish).

Patron Saints: The Church provides us with two dozen Sts. Gerard. One was a citizen of Monza in the 1200s. He is remembered for building a hospice, where he served the sick, especially lepers. He performed many miracles. He died in 1217.

Feast Dates: June 6 — St. Gerard of Tintorio.

Gerardo (Portuguese, Italian, Spanish) See Gerard.

Geraud (French) See Gerald.

Gerek (variant) See Gerald.

Geremia (Italian) See Jeremiah.

Gerhard (German, Swedish) See Gerard.

Gerhardt (variant) See Gerard.

Gerhold (Dutch, German) See Gerald.

Gerhold (variant) See Gerald.

Gerick (variant) See Gerald.

Gerik (Polish) See Gerald, Edgar.

Germain "The Warrior from Germany" (German) or "The Bud [Sprout]" (French).

Patron Saints: There is one saint who bears this name, Bl. Jermyn Gardiner. And when one realizes that Germain means "bud" or "sprout," a most important patron appears.

The Jewish prophet Isaiah was the first to speak of the Messiah as the "shoot from the stump of Jesse." The prophet's reference to the "stump" is a sobering call to responsible living. For God promised that someone from the house of David would sit on the throne only if all remained faithful to God. The Jewish kings and their nation failed to do this and the throne of David remained empty from 587 to 7 B.C. Thus the royal line was like a stump. Then with the birth of Jesus, a tender shoot budded from a seemingly dead stump. This new life came about because God always keeps his promises, even when mankind does not.

Feast Dates: March 13 — The Shoot of Jesse; March 7 — Bl. Jermyn Gardiner (see Gardener).

Germaine (variant) See Germain.

Germayne (variant) See Germain.

Gerold (German) See Gerald.

Gerome (English) See Jerome.

Geronimo (Italian) See Jerome.

Gerrard (English) See Gerard.

Gerri (nickname) See Gerald, Gerard, Jeremiah, Jerome.

Gerrie (nickname) See Gerald, Gerard, Jeremiah, Jerome.

Gerry (nickname) See Gerald, Gerard, Jeremiah, Jerome.

Gevin (African-American double) See any "G" name+Kevin.

Geyo (Latvian) See Roger.

Gherardo (Italian) See Gerard.

Giacinto (Portuguese, Spanish) See Jacinto.

Giacobbe (Italian) See Jacob.

Giacobo (Italian) See Jacob.

Giacomo (Italian) See Jacob, James.

Giacopo (Italian) See Jacob.

Gian (Italian) See John.

Giancarlo (Italian double) See Gian+ Carlo.

Gianni (Italian) See John.

Gianpaolo (Italian double) See Gian+ Paolo.

Giavani (Italian) See John.

Gib (nickname) See Gilbert.

Gibb (nickname) See Gilbert.

Gibbie (nickname) See Gilbert.

Gibby (nickname) See Gilbert.

Gibson (Old English double) See Gilbert+Son.

Gide (Provençal) See Giles.

Gideon "The Destroyer" (Hebrew).

Patron Saints: Christian tradition presents two Sts. Gideon, and the Bible presents us one more. One Christian St. Gideon is often called the "new martyr" because he had, earlier in life, apostatized. However, he repented and did his penance on Mount Athos. He was killed for his faith by Turkish Muslims in 1818.

Feast Dates: December 30 — St. Gideon.

Giermo (Italian) See William.

Gigo (German) See Roderick.

Gil (nickname) See Gilbert, Gilmore.

Gil (Portuguese, Spanish) See Giles.

Gilbert "The Trusted One" (Old English) or "The Hostage" (Old English).

Patron Saints: There are about a half-dozen Sts. Gilbert. St. Gilbert, bishop of Caithness in Scotland, was the last Scotsman canonized before the Reformation. He was a zealous pastor of souls. He died in 1245.

Feast Dates: April 1 — St. Gilbert.

Gilberto (Italian, Spanish) See Gilbert.

Gilburt (English) See Gilbert.

Gilchrist "The Servant+Of Christ" (Irish Gaelic double).

Patron Saints: Two patrons fill the bill. St. Gil (also known as Giolla) is one. The other is Jesus the Suffering Servant.

Feast Dates: March 27 — St. Gil (see Gilmore); Good Friday — Jesus the Suffering Servant (see Abdul).

Giles "The Shield Bearer" (Latin) or "The Young Downy-Bearded One" (Old French).

Patron Saints: There are about a dozen Sts. Giles. One of them was born in Greece and traveled to France as a young man. There he was ordained and spent his life in prayer. It is said that one of the French kings, while hunting deer, shot Giles by accident. Giles died of the arrow wound and the king, filled with remorse, had a great monastery built upon the site. St. Giles died in 750.

St. Giles is patron of beggars, blacksmiths, cripples, hermits, nursing mothers, and horses, as well as against lameness, leprosy, and sterility.

Feast Dates: September 1 — St. Giles.

Gilibeirt (Irish, Gaelic) See Gilbert.

Gill (Norwegian) See Giles.

Gill (nickname) See Gilbert, Gilmore.

Gilleabart (Scottish Gaelic) See Gilbert.

Gilleasbuig (Scottish Gaelic) See Archibald.

Gillecriosd (Scottish Gaelic) See Christopher.

Gilles (French) See Giles.

Gillett (Old French) See Gilbert+Ett.

Gillis (Danish) See Giles.

Gilmore "The Follower of+Mary [Bitter One]" (Irish Gaelic double).

Patron Saints: Gilmore is made up of two Gaelic words: *giolla*, meaning "follower," and *mhuire*, meaning "Mary." There is a St. Gil (also known as Giolla) and hundreds of Sts. Mary. St. Gil, 1089-1174, was elected to fill the see of Armagh left vacant by the death of St. Malachy. He had the cathedral rebuilt, which had been destroyed by fire. He also called a meeting of clergy to suppress the abuses of simony and usury. In addition he established peace between warring chiefs.

Feast Dates: March 27 — St. Gil; October 24 — St. Anthony Mary Claret (see Mary).

Gilroy (Irish double) See Gilmore+Roy.

Gino (variant) See Louis.

Giorgio (Italian) See George.

Giosia (Italian) See Josiah.

Giosue (Italian) See Joshua.

Giovanni (Italian) See John.

Giraldo (Italian) See Gerald.

Giraud (French) See Gerald.

Girolamo (Italian) See Jerome.

Giordano (Italian) See Jordan.

Giselbert (German) See Gilbert.

Gitano "The Male Wanderer" (Spanish).

Patron Saints: Gitano has the same meaning as Wendelin. This leads to a fine patron.

Feast Dates: October 21 — St. Wendelin.

Giuda (Italian) See Jude.

Giuliano (Italian) See Julian.

Giulio (Italian) See Julian, Julius.

Giuseppe (Italian) See Joseph.

Giustino (Italian) See Justin.

Giusto (Italian) See Justin.

Glen "From the Valley" (Old Welsh).

Patron Saints There is no St. Glen, but there is a St. Vale and a Bl. Dean, whose names mean "valley."

Feast Dates: August 28 — Bl. William Dean (see Dean); May 21 — St. Vales (see Valle).

Glenn (English) See Glen.

Glennie (nickname) See Glen.

Glenny (nickname) See Glen.

Glyn (Welsh) See Glen.

Glynn (Welsh) See Glen.

Godfrey "The God of Peace" (Norman French).

Patron Saints: Many scholars think that Godfrey and Geoffrey were originally two separate names. But most moderns see them as alternate forms of the same name, and both lead to the English name Jeffrey.

Feast Dates: July 9 — St. Godfrey of Merville (see Merton).

Godofredo (Portuguese, Spanish) See Geoffrey, Godfrey, Jeffrey.

Godofroy (French) See Geoffrey, Godfrey, Jeffrey.

Godwin (Old English double) See Godfrey+Wynn.

Gofredo (Italian, Spanish) See Geoffrey, Godfrey, Jeffrey.

Goldwin "The Golden+Friend" (Old English double).

Patron Saints: The Latin word for "gold" is *aurum*, which leads to about two dozen Sts. Aurelius and Aureus. St. Aureus was bishop of Mayence. In 460, when the Vandals overran what is now Germany, he and his companions were slaughtered by them. He had taken a strong stand against the Arian heretics and had become *persona non grata*. In addition, *wyn* means "friend," and there are several Sts. Winin.

Feast Dates: June 16 — St. Aureus; May 28 — St. Winin (see Kirwin).

Gomer "The Finished One" (Hebrew) or "From the Famous Battle" (English).

Patron Saints: This name leads to St. Gomez. He was a priest who served his people in Toledo, Spain, in the 800s, when it was dominated by the Muslims. They beheaded him because he insisted on being Catholic.

Feast Dates: January 13 — St. Gomez.

Gomez (Spanish) See Gomer.

Gonçalvo (Portuguese) See González.

Gonsalve (Spanish) See González.

Gontier (French) See Gunther.

Gonzaleo (Spanish) See González.

González "The Son of+The Wolf" (Spanish double) or "The Son of+Strife" (Spanish double).

Patron Saints There are three saints with variations of this name who were either natives of the Americas or missionaries to them. One is Bl. Andrew

Gonsálves. A religious brother, he was one of about forty missionaries who were murdered en route to Brazil in 1570. Their ship was boarded by French Huguenot pirates who hated the Catholic faith. All but one of this party was murdered at sea. Andrew was first wounded by the sword and then thrown into the sea and drowned.

St. Toribio Romo González was executed by firing squad on February 25, 1928, in Mexico. He was a diocesan priest.

Feast Dates: January 19 — Bl. Andrew Gonsálves; September 8 — SG Anaclete González Flores (see Anaclete); February 25 — St. Toribio Romo González.

Gonzallo (Spanish) See González.

Gonzalo (Spanish) See González.

Gonzi (nickname) See González.

Goodwin "The Good+Friend" (Old English double).

Patron Saints: In Latin the word for "good" is *bonus*, and in Old English the word for "friend" is *win*.

Feast Dates: August 1 — St. Good, also known as Bonus (see Osgood); May 28 — St. Winin (see Kirwin).

Goran (Swedish) See George.

Gordan (variant) See Gordon.

Gorden (variant) See Gordon.

Gordiano (Spanish) See Gordon.

Gordie (variant) See Gordon.

Gordon "From the Triangular Hill" (Old English) or "From the Large Fort" (Old English).

Patron Saints: There are seven Sts. Gordianus and Gordius. They all make good patrons for Gordon. St. Gordon (also known as Gordius) served in the Roman army as a centurion. Then he retired in about 303. But since he was also a Christian, he was eventually arrested and imprisoned, then put in the

Roman Circus during a festival in honor of Mars. He was beheaded in 303.

Feast Dates: January 3 — St. Gordon.

Gordy (nickname) See Gordon.

Gotfrid (Russian, Serbian) See Geoffrey, Godfrey, Jeffrey.

Gotfrids (Latvian) See Geoffrey, Godfrey, Jeffrey.

Gotfried (German) See Geoffrey, Godfrey, Jeffrey.

Gotfryd (Polish) See Geoffrey, Godfrey, Jeffrey.

Gotson (German) See Angel.

Gottfrid (Swedish) See Geoffrey, Godfrey, Jeffrey.

Gowan (Scottish) See Owen.

Gower "The Pure One" (Old Welsh).

Patron Saints: There is a St. Gower. He is remembered as the patron of Llangower, Wales.

Feast Dates: July 11 — St. Gower.

Goyo (Spanish) See Gregory.

Gozoyo (variant) See González.

Graciano "The Thankful One" (Spanish).

Patron Saints: There are three Sts. Gratianus. One was a bishop martyred by Arian heretics in 473.

Feast Dates: October 23 — St. Gratianus.

Grade (nickname) See Grady.

Gradeigh (variant) See Grady.

Gradey (variant) See Grady.

Grady "The Noble Illustrious One" (Irish Celtic).

Patron Saints: There is a medieval Welsh saint with a similar name: St. Gredfyw. He was the son of Ithel Hael of Llydaw, Wales. Later in life he migrated to Brittany.

Also, the meaning of the name, "noble" or "famous," leads to two Roman saints named Sts. Nobilis and Nobilitanus. It is also helpful to know that the name Patrick means "noble."

Feast Dates: November 11 — St. Gredfyw; April 25 and October 17 — Sts. Nobilis and Nobilitanus (see Noble).

Graehme (English) See Graham.

Graeme (English) See Graham.

Graham "From the Gray+Home" (Old English double).

Patron Saints: It is helpful to know that the name Graham comes from two words: *gra*, meaning "gray," and *ham*, which means "home." This leads to the discovery of three patrons. The first is an Irish saint, St. Ronan the Gray. He is remembered as a prayerful man from Liath-Ros, Louth, Ireland. The second is St. Hamo, a British saint. The third is Bl. Robert Grissold, an English martyr.

Feast Dates: April 30 — St. Ronan the Gray; April 30 — St. Hamo (see Hamilton).

Graig (variant) See Gregory.

Gram (nickname) See Graham.

Gran (nickname) See Granger, Grant, Grantham, Grenville.

Grande (Spanish) See Grant.

Grange (nickname) See Granger.

Granger "The Farmer" (Old English).

Patron Saints: There is one ancient saint with a similar name who can be adopted as a patron. He is St. Granus, a martyr in ancient Alexandria. He may have been a black man.

Also, realizing that Granger means "farmer" leads to more patrons. The Catholic Church has officially named four saints patrons of farmers. They are Isidore, George, Sidwell, and Walstan. Finally, it is helpful to know that the name George also means "farmer." There are many Sts. George.

Feast Dates: April 10 — St. Granus; April 23 — St. George (see George).

Grannie (nickname) See Granger, Grant, Grantham, Grenville.

Grant "The Great One" (Middle English).

Patron Saints: There is a Bl. Hugh More of Grantham. Also, because Grant means "great," another patron surfaces. He is a Spaniard, Bl. Juan Grande, whose last name also means "great." Juan Grande, 1546-1600, was employed for some time in the linen business, but he soon tired of it and looked for something better. This led him to become a hermit at Marcena. Thus he made a pun of his surname. He told everyone that he was Juan Grande Pecador, which means, "John, the great sinner." He gave much of his time to charity, especially hospital work. In time, he joined the new order founded by St. John of God. He also ministered to prisoners.

Feast Dates: June 3 — Bl. Juan Grande; April 10 — Bl. Hugh More of Grantham (see Grantham).

Grantham "From the Great+House" (Old English double).

Patron Saints: This name is based on two words: *grant*, which means "great," and *ham*, meaning "home" or "house." There is one saint who is perfect as patron of those bearing this name. Bl. Hugh was born in Grantham, raised Protestant, and educated at Oxford. Despite the anti-Catholic culture, he converted to Catholicism. Then he went to France and was ordained a priest. Returning to England, he was arrested and executed in 1588 for being a priest.

Feast Dates: April 10 — St. Hugh More of Grantham.

Granthem (English double) See Grantham, Grant+Ham.

Grantley (English double) See Grant+Leigh.

Granville (French double) See Grant+Ville.

Gray "The Gray One" (Middle English) or "The Farmer" (short form of Granger).

Patron Saints: There is one ancient saint known as St. Ronan the Gray. And there are two more saints surnamed Grisold (or variants of it), which means "gray moor." St. Grisold died a martyr in medieval Saxony. Bl. Robert Grissold was a British layman during the time when the British government considered it treason to be a Catholic. He was executed in 1604 for practicing his Catholic faith.

Feast Dates: December 30 — St. Grisold; May 4 — Bl. Robert Grissold.

Grayson "The Son+Gray One" (English double) or "The Son of+Bailiff" (Middle English double).

Patron Saints: There is one ancient saint known as St. Ronan the Gray. And there are two more saints who have Gray as part of their names. Their common name, Grisold (or Grissold), means "gray moor."

Feast Dates: April 30 — St. Ronan the Gray (see Graham); May 4 — Bl. Robert Grissold (see Gray).

Green "The Green Color" (Middle English).

Patron Saints: Two English priest-martyrs have the surname of Green. Bl. Thomas Green was a monk in the Cistercian abbey that was particularly hated by King Henry VIII. He was executed in 1537. Bl. Hugh Green came on the scene over a hundred years later and was executed in 1642.

Feast Dates: May 4 — Bl. Thomas Green, O. Cart.; August 19 — Bl. Hugh Green.

Greer (English) See Gray.

Greerson (English double) See Gray+Son.

Greg (nickname) See Gregory.

Gregg (nickname) See Gregory.

Greggory (variant) See Gregory.

Gregoire (French) See Gregory.

Gregor (Czech, German, Norwegian) See Gregory.

Gregorio (variant) See Gregory.

Gregorius (Latin) See Gregory.

Gregory "The Vigilant One" (English).

Patron Saints: There are about eighty recognized saints with the name of Gregory. St. Gregory Nazianzen was the father of three saints: Gorgonia, Gregory the Younger, and Caesarius. He was converted to Catholicism by his wife, St. Nonna, in 325. In 328 he was elected bishop of Nazianzus. For a while he fell into heresy, but his son, Gregory, eventually brought him back to the Catholic faith. He died at the age of one hundred.

Feast Dates: January 1 — St. Gregory Nazianzen the Elder.

Grenville "From the Large+Town" (Old French double).

Patron Saints: Patrons emerge when one discovers that Grenville is made from two words: *gren*, meaning "great," and *ville*, meaning "town." This leads to Bl. John Grande and St. Villicus. Villicus served as the bishop of Metz between 543 and 568. He was generally regarded as a very holy man by his people.

Feast Dates: April 17 — St. Villicus; June 3 — Bl. John Grande (see Grant).

Grey (English) See Gray.

Greyson (English double) See Gray+Son.

Griff (nickname) See Griffith, Griffin.

Griffie (nickname) See Griffith, Griffin.

Griffin "The Dedicated Protector [Savior]" (Middle English).

Patron Saints: A griffin is a mythological animal that comes from the ancient Minoans of Crete. It has the head, wings, and front legs and claws of an eagle while the rest of its body resembles that of a lion. Because of the predatory nature of the eagle and the ferociousness of the lion, the griffin in ancient times symbolized opposition to Christianity and attacks on the human soul.

However, in time, Christianity adopted and rehabilitated this creature. It began to see the griffin as a dedicated protector against evil, much like the gargoyles on church buildings. Soon Christians "baptized" the griffin to stand as a symbol of Jesus Christ, Lord and Savior. Remember, Jesus means "God saves." Also note that the name William has the same meaning as griffin, thus more patrons are available.

Feast Dates: All Sundays — Jesus, Defender and Savior; February 23 — St. William (see William).

Griffith "The One with Strong Faith" (Old Welsh) or "The Fierce Lord" (Old Welsh).

Patron Saints: There are a couple of saints whose name is Faith. One of them, St. Faith of Agen, died a martyr's death in 287. She was roasted to death because she would not deny her faith.

Feast Dates: October 6 — St. Faith of Agen.

Griffy (nickname) See Griffith, Griffin.

Grigori (Bulgarian) See Gregory.

Grisha (Russian) See Gregory.

Grove (nickname) See Grover.

Grover "From the Grove" (Old English) or "The One Who Carves" (Old English).

Patron Saints: There is one English martyr surnamed Grove. Bl. John Grove was a layman and a servant of the Jesuit priest Father William Ireland. He was executed, along with Father Ireland in 1679, after both had been convicted of being involved in the so-called Oates Plot. Also known as the Popish Plot, it was a phony conspiracy created by the Anglican priest Titus Oates and some powerful Protestants in an attempt to keep the hatred of Catholics alive.

Feast Dates: January 24 — Bl. John Grove.

Gualberto (Spanish) See Albert.

Gualterio (Spanish) See Walter.

Gualtiero (Italian) See Walter.

Guglielmo (Italian) See William.

Guido (Italian, Spanish, Portuguese) See Guy.

Guilbert (French) See Gilbert.

Guillaume (French) See William.

Guillermo (Spanish) See William.

Guillo (nickname) See William.

Guiremo (nickname) See William.

Gulielm (Romanian) See William.

Gun (nickname) See Gunther.

Gunder (Danish) See Gunther.

Gunn (nickname) See Gunther.

Gunner (Dutch, Hungarian) See Gunther.

Gunny (nickname) See Gunther.

Guntar (variant) See Gunther.

Gunter (Dutch, Hungarian) See Gunther.

Gunther "The Battle Warrior" (Old Norse, German).

Patron Saints: There is one Bl. Gunther and one Bl. Gunter. Bl. Gunther, O.S.B., lived from 955 to 1045 and was a cousin of King Stephen of Hungary. Early in life he was filled with worldly ambition, but in time, St. Godehard convinced him to become a monk. He soon became an abbot but was a failure at the job. Having learned humility, he lived the rest of his life (twenty-eight years) as a hermit devoted to prayer. He died at the age of ninety.

Feast Dates: October 9 — Bl. Gunther.

Gus (nickname) See Angus, Augustine, Fergus, Gustave.

Gussy (nickname) See Angus, Augustine, Fergus, Gustave.

Gust (nickname) See Gustave.

Gustaf (Swedish) See Gustave.

Gustave "The Staff of the Goths" (Swedish, French).

Patron Saints: There is a saint with a similar name: St. Gustan. He chose to embrace the life of a monk at the monastery of St. Gildas de Rhuys. He died in 1000.

Feast Dates: November 27 — St. Gustan.

Gustavo (Italian, Portuguese, Spanish) See Gustave.

Gustavus (Latin) See Gustave.

Gusti (nickname) See Gustave.

Gustino (Lithuanian) See Justin.

Gusts (Latvian) See Gustave.

Guthrey (variant) See Guthrie.

Guthrie "From the Windy Place" (Gaelic) or "The War Hero" (Gaelic).

Patron Saints: There is one saint with a similar name who can be adopted as a patron. He is St. Guthlac, O.S.B., 673-714. Early in life, he served as a soldier in the army of King Ethelred of Mercia, England. Soon he felt called to enter the Benedictine abbey at Repton. For the last fifteen years of his life he embraced the hermit's life in the heart of Lincolnshire. He died at the age of forty-one.

Feast Dates: April 11 — St. Guthlac, O.S.B.

Guthry (variant) See Guthrie.

Gutiérre (Spanish) See Walter.

Guy "The Warrior" (Old German) or "The Guide" (French).

Patron Saints: There are about a dozen Sts. Guido or Guy from which to choose. Guy of Anderlecht is called the "Poor Man of Anderlecht." He was born near Brussels, of poor rural parents who taught him, "For if you do what is true, your ways will prosper through your deeds. . . . Do not turn your face away from any poor man, and the face of God will not be turned away from you" (Tobit 4:6-7). Guy avoided becoming attached to things and often shared his food and money with the poor.

He soon became a sacristan and then he invested in a business and lost everything. This caused him to reexamine his life and make a pilgrimage on foot to Rome and then to Jerusalem. Seven years later, in 1012, he returned to Belgium, sick and tired, worn out by his journeys. He was admitted to the local hospital and soon died. He is patron of horses and horse-drawn cabs.

Feast Dates: September 12 — St. Guy of Anderlecht.

Gvidas (Lithuanian) See Guy.

Gvidon (Bulgarian, Croatian, Russian) See Guy.

Gwayne (Welsh) See Gavin, Wayne.

Gwilym (Welsh) See William.

Gwyn "The Fair Blond One" (Old Welsh).

Patron Saints: There is one medieval saint by the name of Gwyn. He and his five saint-brothers are known as the "Five Saints." They are all from Wales.

Feast Dates: January 7 — St. Gwyn.

Gyles (English) See Giles.

Gyorgy (Hungarian, Russian) See George.

Gyula (Hungarian) See Julius.

411

ℋ

Haabeel (Arabic) See Abel.

Haakon (Norse) See Hakon.

Haaroon (Arabic) See Aaron.

Hacine (African-American) See Hasan, Hasin.

Habib "The Beloved One" (Arabic).

Patron Saints: There are a dozen ancient saints named Habib. One St. Habib was a deacon at Thelai near Edessa when the persecution of Licinius broke out in 322. At first, he hid, but soon went to the judge to witness for the faith. He was immediately arrested and viciously whipped. Then he was condemned to be burned at the stake. Meanwhile, he constantly encouraged the others in prison to remain faithful. Because he refused to be silent about his faith, he was bound and gagged. His mother encouraged him and watched him.

Feast Dates: September 5 — St. Habib.

Had (nickname) See Hadley.

Haddad (Arabic) See Smith.

Hadlee (English double) See Hadley, Had+Leigh.

Hadleigh (English double) See Hadley, Had+Leigh.

Hadley "From Wasteland+Meadow" (Old English double).

Patron Saints: The word *had* means "wasteland" or "heath" and *ley* (or *leigh*) means "meadow." This combination leads to two patrons.

Feast Dates: May 4 — Bl. Henry Heath (see Heath); August 30 — Bl. Richard Leigh (see Leigh).

Hadrian (variant) See Adrian.

Haeley (English) See Haley.

Hailey (nickname) See Haley.

Haily (nickname) See Haley.

Hak (nickname) See Hakon.

Hakeem "The Wise One" (Arabic) or "The Ruler" (Arabic).

Patron Saints: Hakeem means "wise one." In Greek, *sophia* means "wise," and there are a few Sts. Sophia. In its second meaning, "the ruler," it matches the meanings for Kenrick and Richard.

Feast Dates: February 7 — St. Richard (see Richard).

Hakim (Arabic) See Hakeem.

Hako (Norse) See Hakon.

Hakon "From the Chosen Race" (Arabic).

Patron Saints: It is helpful to know that the Jews are called the "chosen race" and that one of their greatest leaders was the patriarch Jacob. Later, God changed his name to Israel, which means "he who wrestles with God."

Feast Dates: November 1 — St. Jacob (see Jacob).

Hal (nickname) See Haley, Hall, Halsey, Harold.

Hale (nickname) See Haley, Hall, Henry.

Haleigh (nickname) See Haley, Hall.

Haley "The Ingenious One" (Irish Gaelic) or "The Scientific One" (Irish Gaelic).

Patron Saints: There is a St. Thomas Hales and Bl. Richard Leigh. Thomas Hales was a monk of St. Martin's Priory in Dover. In 1295 the French raided Dover, and all the monks went into hiding except Thomas. He was too old and ill to flee. The raiders found him in bed and demanded he tell them where the church treasures were hidden. He refused and was murdered.

After his death, miracles occurred at his tomb. This led to his canonization.

Feast Dates: August 2 — St. Thomas Hales of Dover, O.S.B.; August 30 — Bl. Richard Leigh (see Leigh).

Hall "From the Manor" (Old English).

Patron Saints: The closest name to this is St. Hallvard. He was born near Oslo, Norway. When Hallvard was thirteen, his father began taking him on business voyages. On one occasion, a rich young man invited him to dinner, gave him gifts, and told him he was destined to do something great in his life. That rich young man was St. Botvid.

Sometime later this came true. In 1043 Hallvard tried to protect a woman who was falsely accused of theft and he was shot through the neck with an arrow. He died and his body was thrown into the sea. He is patron of the innocent and of the diocese of Oslo.

Feast Dates: May 14 — St. Hallvard.

Hallsey (variant) See Halsey.

Halsey "From Hal's Island" (Old English).

Patron Saints: Any saint with Hal in his name can serve as a patron. This leads to St. Hallvard.

Feast Dates: May 14 — St. Hallvard; August 2 — St. Thomas Hales of Dover, O.S.B. (see Haley).

Halsy (variant) See Halsey.

Ham (nickname) See Hamal, Hamid, Hamilton, Hamlet, Hamlin, Hammad, Hampton.

Hamal "The Lamb" (Arabic).

Patron Saints: The word *hamal* means "lamb"; in Latin, the word for "lamb" is *agnus*. This leads to a dozen Sts. Agnes and one St. Agnus. St. Agnus suffered martyrdom in the land of the Goths in ancient times. And then there is the best patron of all: Jesus Christ, the Lamb of God.

Feast Dates: March 26 — St. Agnus.

Hamel (nickname) See Hamilton.

Hamid "The Much Praised One" (Arabic) or "The Prophet" (short form of Muhammad).

Patron Saints: Hamid means "thank God," while "thanks" in Latin is *gratia*. This leads to six Sts. Gratianus. One of them was a Roman soldier, who with some of his soldier friends converted to the faith and were baptized in about 250. They were immediately arrested, tortured, and put to death by decapitation.

Feast Dates: June 17 — St. Gratianus.

Hamil (nickname) See Hamilton.

Hamilton "From the Home Lover's+ Estate [Town]" (Old English double).

Patron Saints: This name is derived from *ham*, which means "home," and *ton*, meaning "town" or "estate." This leads to Sts. Hamo and Tondach.

Hamo was born in Brittany, became a monk at Savigny Abbey, and ministered to lepers. After he was ordained a priest, he gave missions (retreats) in many different places. He also acted as a director of the religious brothers. A very holy man, he could read the secrets of sinners' hearts. He died in 1173.

Feast Dates: April 30 — St. Hamo; July 21 — St. Tondach (see Town).

Hamish (Scottish) See James.

Hamlet (Old French-German) See Hamilton+Ett.

Hamlin (Norman-French) See Hamlet.

Hamlin (variant) See Henry.

Hammad (nickname) See Hamid, Muhammad.

Hamp (nickname) See Hampton.

Hampton (Old English double) See Hamilton+Town.

Hanan (variant) See John.

Handy (nickname) See Hannibal.

Hanes (variant) See Hans.

Hanford (Old English double) See Hanley+Ford.

Hanibal (variant) See Hannibal.

Hank (nickname) See Henry.

Hanleigh (English) See Hanley.

Hanley "From the High+Meadow" (Old English double).

Patron Saints: Patrons can be found if one realizes that Hanley comes from two words: *han*, meaning "high," and *ley* (or *leigh*), meaning "meadow." This leads to two Sts. Han and a Bl. Leigh. One St. Han was a priest. His good friend, also named Han, was a deacon. They were martyred together in Kaskhar in ancient times.

Feast Dates: May 16 — St. Han; August 30 — Bl. Richard Lee (see Leigh).

Hannes (Afrikaans) See John.

Hannibal "The One Favored by God [Baal]" (Phoenician).

Patron Saints: The closest name to Hannibal is Hanniel, which means "favored by God (Yahweh)." The Old Testament records that God chose Hanniel to help divide the Promised Land among the twelve tribes of Israel in about 1250 B.C. (see Numbers 34:16, 23).

Feast Dates: November 1 — Holy Hanniel.

Hanoch (variant) See Enoch.

Hanraoi (Irish) See Henry.

Hans "God Is Gracious" (Dutch, Danish, German form of John).

Patron Saints: Hans is the Scandinavian form of John, and there are over four hundred Sts. John or variants of the name. Among them is Bl. Hans Wagner, O. Cart., a religious brother. He lived his life as a hermit and died in 1516.

Feast Dates: May 9 — Bl. Hans Wagner, O. Cart.

Hansel (Bavarian) See John.

Hanson (Old English double) See Anson, Hans+Son.

Harailt (Scottish) See Harold.

Harald (German, Scandinavian) See Harold.

Haraldo (Portuguese, Spanish) See Harold.

Haralds (Latvian) See Harold.

Harbert (Dutch) See Herbert.

Harcourt "From the Fortified Dwelling" (Old French-German).

Patron Saints: When one thinks of a "fortified dwelling," one thinks of a "fortress." This leads directly to Jesus, our Rock and Fortress. There is also one saint named Bl. William Harcourt. A native of Lancastershire, in 1632 he became a Jesuit and between 1645 and 1678 he ministered in London. In 1678 he was accused of being involved in the nonexistent Popish Plot (or Oates Plot) against the government. The following year Father Harcourt was executed at Tyburn with five Jesuit companions.

Feast Dates: June 30 — Bl. William Harcourt, S.J.; Thirty-fourth Sunday of the Year — Jesus, Our Fortress (see Garrison).

Harding "The Son of+The Follower of Heard [Brave One]" (Old English double).

Patron Saints: St. Stephen Harding, born at Sherborne, Dorsetshire, England, became a Benedictine monk at the monastery of Citeaux. He soon became the driving force behind reforms by insisting upon a very strict observance of poverty. In time, he was elected subprior, then prior, and finally abbot of his monastery. It was Stephen's great privilege to receive St. Bernard into the order. He died in 1134.

Feast Dates: January 26 — St. Stephen Harding, O. Cist.

Harlan "From the Army+Land" (Old English double) or "From the Hare+ Land" (Old English double).

Patron Saints: There is one St. Harlindis, which is a variant of Harlan. She was the daughter of the Austrasian count Adelard. She and her sister, St. Relindis, founded the abbey of Maaseyk in Belgium. She carried on an extensive correspondence with many saints of her time, which included Boniface and Willibrord. She died in 745.

Feast Dates: March 22 — St. Harlindis, also known as Herlindis.

Harland (English) See Harlan.

Harlee (English double) See Harley.

Harlen (English) See Harlan.

Harley "From the Hare [or Deer or Army]+Meadow" (Old English double).

Patron Saints: Harley is made up of two words: *har*, which means "hare, deer, or army," and *ley* (or *leigh*), which means "meadow." This leads to two patrons.

Feast Dates: March 22 — St. Harlindis (see Harlan); August 30 — Bl. Richard Leigh (see Leigh).

Harlin (English) See Harlan.

Harman (Danish, German, English) See Herman.

Harmon (Danish, German, English) See Herman.

Harold "The Commander" (Old Norse).

Patron Saints: There are just a handful of Sts. Harold (or variants of the name). One of them, St. Harald II, 911-986, was the king of Denmark. Nicknamed Bluetooth, he was a convert to Catholicism. His son, Sweyn,

began a war with him to return the country to paganism. Harald died of his wounds after a battle. He was seventy-five years old.

Feast Dates: November 1 — St. Harald II.

Haron (African-American) See Haroun.

Haroun (Arabic) See Aaron.

Harp (nickname) See Harper.

Harper "The Harp Player" (Old English).

Patron Saints: A *harper* is a "harpist." Four saints have been named patrons of musicians by the Catholic Church. They are Benet Biscop, Cecilia, Leo the Great, and Odo of Cluny.

Music has always been an important part of Church liturgy. It has also provided significant relief from labor. It is a way to relax and celebrate. In time, music came to be associated with heavenly bliss. This led artists to picture angels and saints playing musical instruments in heaven.

Thus it was only natural for the Bible to present images of angels singing and blowing trumpets. Furthermore, the 144,000 in the New Testament, symbolizing all the saints, are pictured being present during the playing of harps before God (see Revelation 14:1-3). The harps are symbolic of prayer.

Feast Dates: September 29 and October 2 — The Holy Seraphim (see Amber); November 1 — All the Saints of God.

Harris (English double) See Harold/ Harry+Son.

Harrison (English double) See Harold/ Harry+Son.

Harry (nickname) See Harcourt, Harold, Henry.

Hart (nickname) See Hartley.

Hartley "From the Deer+Meadow" (Old English double).

Patron Saints: Hartley is constructed out of *hart*, meaning "deer," and *ley* (or *leigh*), meaning "meadow." Bl. William Hartley of Wilne, England, was raised Protestant and was educated at St. John's College, Oxford. He became an Anglican parson. However, after a short time, he converted to Catholicism and traveled to Rheims, where he studied for the Catholic priesthood and was ordained in 1580. Eight years later he was arrested, tried, and convicted of being a Catholic priest in England. He died on the gallows.

Feast Dates: October 5 — Bl. William Hartley; March 15 — Bl. William Hart of Wells (see Hershel).

Harv (nickname) See Harvey.

Harvey "The Army Warrior" (Old German).

Patron Saints: There are three Sts. Harvey. Their names are usually given as Herveus or Hervé. St. Hervé, the son of a British troubadour, was born blind in about the year 500. His mother raised him to the age of seven years and then gave him into the care of his uncle. Soon Hervé was put in charge of his uncle's monastery and school. He had an opportunity to be ordained a priest but refused and then he founded a monastery, becoming its abbot. He is remembered for performing many miracles and was often called upon to drive out evil spirits. He is patron against blindness, demons, foxes, and wolves.

Feast Dates: June 17 — St. Harvey, also known as Hervé.

Hasan (Arabic) See Hussein, Kenneth.

Hasen (Arabic) See Isaac.

Hasin (Arabic) See Isaac.

Haskel (variant) See Haskell.

Haskell "The Understanding, Intellectual One" (Hebrew).

Patron Saints: Haskell has the same as meaning as Hugh.

Feast Dates: November 17 — St. Hugh of Lincoln (see Hugh).

Hassan (Arabic) See Kyle, Kenneth.

Hassin (Hindu) See Isaac.

Hayden "From the Hedged+Valley" (Old English double).

Patron Saints: Hayden is made up of two words: *hay*, meaning "hedged," and *den*, meaning "valley." Bl. George Haydoc was executed in England in 1584 for being a Catholic priest.

Feast Dates: May 4 — Bl. George Haydoc; August 28 — Bl. William Dean (see Dean).

Haydon (variant) See Hayden.

Haydyn (English) See Hayden.

Hayward (Old English) See Bailey.

Haywood "From the Hedged+Forest" (Old English).

Patron Saints: Two saints can serve as patrons. Bl. Nicholas Woodfen, a diocesan priest, gave his life for the faith in 1586 during the persecutions of Catholics in Great Britain.

Feast Dates: May 4 — Bl. Nicholas Woodfen; May 4 — Bl. George Haydoc (see Hayden).

Hayyim (Hebrew) See Hyman.

Heath "From Open+Wasteland" (Middle English double).

Patron Saints: Bl. Henry Heath, O.F.M., 1599-1643, a Franciscan priest, was arrested by accident. Having walked all the way to London, he had just sat down on the steps in front of his residence to rest when he was mistaken for a shoplifter. Once in custody, his Catholic religion and priesthood were discovered, and he was swiftly tried and hanged in 1643 at the age of forty-four.

Feast Dates: May 4 — Bl. Henry Heath, O.F.M.

Heathcliffe (Old English double) See Heath+Cliff.

Hebert (French) See Herbert.

Heck (nickname) See Hector.

Hector "The Steadfast One" (Greek, Spanish).

Patron Saints: There are two saints who have names that are similar. They are Bl. Hechard and St. Etto. Hechard was a priest who lived in Europe in about 1170. With two friends, Menric and Berthold, he founded Scheda Monastery near Unna. He died in about 1179.

Feast Dates: July 1 — Bl. Hechard; July 10 — St. Etto (see Ett).

Heindrik (variant) See Henry.

Heinrich (German) See Henry.

Heinrik (variant) See Henry.

Heinz (German) See Henry.

Helio (Spanish) See Apollos.

Hieronym (Slovakian) See Jerome.

Hieronymus (German, Dutch, Scandinavian) See Jerome.

Heitor (Portuguese) See Hector.

Hektor (Polish, Czech, Scandinavian) See Hector.

Hektoras (Lithuanian) See Hector.

Henderson (English double) See Henry+Son.

Hendrick (variant) See Henry.

Hendrik (Danish, Dutch) See Henry.

Henk (nickname) See Henry.

Henleigh (English) See Hanley.

Henley (English) See Hanley.

Henrey (English) See Henry.

Henri (French) See Henry.

Henrico (Swedish) See Henry.

Henrik (Swedish) See Henry.

Henry "The Ruler of the Estate" (Old German).

Patron Saints: There are over twenty Sts. Henry.

Feast Dates: May 4 — Bl. Henry Heath (see Heath); February 1 — St. Henry Morse (see Morse).

Henryk (Polish) See Henry.

Heraclido (Spanish) See Hercules.

Heraclito (Spanish) See Hercules.

Herakles (Greek) See Hercules.

Heraldo (Spanish) See Harold.

Herb (nickname) See Herbert.

Herbert "The Glorious Warrior" (Old German).

Patron Saints: There are three Sts. Herbert. One was a priest who lived on an island in the middle of Lake Derwentwater in the British Isles. He was a disciple of St. Cuthbert and once each year he would travel to Lindisfarne to receive instruction from his master. At their last meeting, Herbert was ill and both realized they would not meet again on this earth. They both wept and asked God to reassure them of life after death by granting them a vision, which was granted.

Feast Dates: March 20 — St. Herbert.

Herberto (Spanish) See Herbert.

Herbie (variant) See Herbert.

Herby (variant) See Herbert.

Herc (nickname) See Hercules.

Hercil (nickname) See Hercules, Hershel.

Herculano (Spanish) See Hercules.

Hercule (French) See Hercules.

Hercules "The Glorious Gift" (English).

Patron Saints: There are about a dozen Sts. Herculanus and Herculianus. One St. Herculanus was a Roman soldier. When it was discovered that he was a Christian, he was condemned to death. He was executed by having his neck bound to a heavy stone and was thrown into a river in about the year 100.

Feast Dates: September 26 — St. Herculanus.

Herculie (variant) See Hercules.

Heribert (German, Slovakian) See Herbert.

Heriberto (Spanish) See Herbert.

Herm (nickname) See Herman.

Herman "The Army Warrior" (Old German) or "The High-Ranked Person" (Latin).

Patron Saints: There are a half-dozen Sts. Herman. An important one is Bl. Herman the Cripple. Seriously deformed from birth, he was bedridden all his life. Yet he still made his vows as a Benedictine monk.

He had a brilliant mind and wrote books, produced a world chronicle, composed poems, authored an astronomy treatise, and made musical instruments. His greatest works are *Alma Redemptoris Mater* and the *Salve Regina.* The people of his era called him "A Wonder of the Times." He died in 1054.

Feast Dates: September 25 — Bl. Herman the Cripple, O.S.B.

Hermann (Danish, German) See Herman.

Hermie (nickname) See Herman.

Hermino (Spanish, Portuguese) See Herman.

Hermon (variant) See Herman.

Hermy (nickname) See Herman.

Hernando (Spanish) See Ferdinand.

Hero "The Very Courageous One" (Latin).

Patron Saints: The word "hero" in Latin is *heros,* and there are a few Sts. Heros and Herosus. A St. Herosus was martyred for the faith in ancient Egypt.

Feast Dates: September 10 — St. Hero, also known as Herosus.

Herold (Dutch, English) See Harold.

Herrick (variant) See Harold.

Hersch (nickname) See Hershel.

Herschel (variant) See Hershel.

Hersey (African-American) See Hershel.

Hersh (nickname) See Hershel.

Hershel "The Deer" (Hebrew).

Patron Saints: It is helpful to know that the name Hershel means "deer." The English names Hart and Hartley mean the same thing. Bl. William Hart was a native of Wells and was educated at Lincoln College in Oxford. He was ordained a priest in France in 1581 and immediately returned to England. A very short time later he was betrayed by an apostate Catholic, arrested, hanged, drawn, and quartered in 1583.

Feast Dates: March 15 — Bl. William Hart of Wells; March 15 — Bl. William Hartley (see Hartley).

Hervé (French) See Harvey.

Hervey (variant) See Harvey.

Hesus (variant) See Jesús.

Hew (nickname) See Hewett.

Hewart (variant) See Howard.

Hewe (English) See Hubert, Hugh.

Hewet (nickname) See Hewett.

Hewett "The Little Intelligent One" (Old French-German).

Patron Saints: There is one English martyr with a similar surname. Bl. John Hewitt was a native of Yorkshire who went to the Continent to study for the Catholic priesthood. He was ordained at Rheims in 1586 and immediately he returned to England to minister to his people. He functioned under the aliases of Weldon and Savell. However, he was soon arrested and executed in 1588.

Feast Dates: October 5 — Bl. John Hewitt.

Hewie (nickname) See Hewett, Hubert, Hugh.

Hewitt variant) See Hewett.

Heywood (variant) See Haywood.

Hi (nickname) See Hilary, Hill, Hillel, Hiram.

Hilaire (variant) See Hilary.

Hilario (variant) See Hilary.

Hilarion (Spanish) See Hilary.

Hilarius (Latin) See Hilary.

Hilary "The Cheerful One" (Latin).

Patron Saints: There are about forty Sts. Hilary. One, St. Hilary of Poitiers, was born into a pagan family in Gaul (France) in the early 300s. His life was a journey to discover the truth of God. His conversion came through the Bible.

Before his conversion, he had married and fathered a daughter. After embracing Christianity, he was urged by the people to serve them as bishop. He was consumed with a passion for the truth, sparing no pains and braving all dangers to discover it. Hilary was also gentle and courteous, but he found that, in defense of the Church, he often had to use the most severe language. He is a Doctor of the Church and considered patron of lawyers and slow children, of those bitten by snakes, and of the mentally ill.

Feast Dates: January 13 — St. Hilary of Poitiers.

Hilario (Spanish) See Hilary.

Hilel (Arabic) See Hillel.

Hill "From the Hill" (Old English) or "The Cheerful One" (nickname for Hilary).

Patron Saints: If Hill is accepted as a short form of Hillary, then about forty Sts. Hilary are available. But it is also good to know that at least one English saint was surnamed Hill. Father Richard Hill was arrested for being a Catholic priest. He was executed in 1590.

Feast Dates: May 4 — Bl. Richard Hill; January 13 — St. Hilary of Poitiers (see Hilary).

Hillary (English) See Hilary.

Hillel "The Greatly Praised One" (Hebrew) or "The New Moon" (Arabic form of Hilel).

Patron Saints: Two ancient saints with the similar name Hilus may serve as patrons. One of them is remembered to have died a martyr in ancient Rome.

It is also good to know that Judah means "praised one" and that Christian tradition offers three Sts. Jude.

Feast Dates: May 28 — St. Hilus; October 28 — St. Jude, Apostle (see Jude).

Hillery (English) See Hilary.

Hillie (nickname) See Hilary.

Hilly (nickname) See Hilary.

Hiram "The Most Noble One" (Hebrew).

Patron Saints: Christian tradition supplies us with only one saint whose name is only remotely similar. He is St. Hirenarchus. However, the Bible provides two Hirams, one being a Jew, the other a pagan.

The Bible, specifically 1 Kings 7:13ff, introduces Hiram, a Jewish architectural genius who lived from about 960 to 920 B.C. He was the son of a woman from the tribe of Naphtali and a pagan brassworker from Tyre. He cast the great pillars, the molten sea, the twelve oxen, and the Temple utensils.

Feast Dates: November 1 — Holy Hiram, Jewish Architect.

Hirsch (nickname) See Hershel.

Hirsh (nickname) See Hershel.

Hob (nickname) See Robert.

Hobard (variant) See Hobart, Hubert.

Hobart (Irish) See Hubert.

Hobart "The Intelligent One" (Old German) or "The Bright Mind" (Irish form of Hubert).

Patron Saints: Bert means "bright one" and can be considered a short form of Hobart. There are a few Sts.

Bert who can serve as patrons. It is also helpful to know that Hobart is a variant of Hubert.

Feast Dates: March 26 — St. Bert (see Bert); November 3 — St. Hubert (see Hubert).

Hobbie (nickname) See Robert.

Hobbs (English double) See Hob+Son.

Hobby (nickname) See Robert.

Hobert (German) See Hubert.

Hobey (nickname) See Hobart.

Hobie (nickname) See Hobart.

Hobkins (English triple) See Hob+Kin+Son.

Hobs (nickname) See Robert.

Hobson (English double) See Hob+Son.

Hodge (English) See Roger.

Hodges (English double) See Hodge+Son.

Hodson (variant) See Hudson.

Hoebart (nickname) See Hobart.

Hogan "The Youth" (Irish Gaelic).

Patron Saints: There is one saint with a similar name. St. Hoger was the archbishop of Hamburg-Bremen for six years, 909-915. He is remembered for his very strict administration and convert-making. He died in 915. The Reformation in Germany destroyed devotion to him.

Furthermore, it might be helpful to find a patron based on the meaning of the name. The name Hogan means "youth," and the Catholic Church has recognized four saints as patrons of youth. They are Aloysius Gonzaga, John Berchmans, Stanislaus Kostka, and Dominic Savio.

Feast Dates: November 1 — St. Hoger, O.S.B.; March 9 — St. Dominic Savio (see Dominic).

Hoibeard (Irish) See Hubert.

Hoireabard (Irish) See Herbert.

Holden "From the Hollow+In the Valley" (Old English double).

Patron Saints: Holden is composed of two words: *hol*, meaning "hole," and *den*, meaning "valley."

Feast Dates: August 28 — Bl. William Dean (see Dean).

Holle (nickname) See Hollis.

Hollings (variant) See Hollis.

Hollins (variant) See Hollis.

Hollis "From the Holly Tree Grove" (Old English) or "The Holy One" (Latin).

Patron Saints: Some scholars relate Holly to Christmas, and there are about a dozen Sts. Noël and Natividad. Others think Holly is s form of Holy. There are a few Sts. Sanctus.

Finally, there is one English saint surnamed Holiday. Bl. Richard Holiday was arrested for being a Catholic priest in England. He was tried, convicted, and executed in 1590.

Feast Dates: May 4 — Bl. Richard Holiday; November 1 — All Saints (see Santos).

Holly (nickname) See Hollis.

Holman "From the Island in the River" (Old German).

Patron Saints: Sts. Nwy and River fit nicely as patrons here.

Feast Dates: November 1 — St. Nwy (see Ny); May 28 — St. River, also known as Fluminus (see River).

Holmes (German double) See Holman+Son.

Homer "The Promise [Pledge]" (English).

Patron Saints: Omer can be a variant of Homer. St. Omer and his father entered religious life after Omer's mother died. He was soon elected bishop of Therouanne and dedicated himself to a life of evangelization. In his old age he became blind. He died in 667 and is patron of sore eyes.

Some other patrons are the Homerite Martyrs, who were killed about the year 500, and St. Mares of Homeron, who died in 430.

Feast Dates: September 9 — St. Omer.

Homère (French) See Homer.

Homéro (Spanish) See Homer.

Homeros (Greek) See Homer.

Homerus (Latin) See Homer.

Homo (Latin) See Mann.

Homobono (Spanish double) See Homo+ Boone.

Hondo "The Soldier" (North American Indian) or "The One Prepared for War" (South African).

Patron Saints: Hondo means the same as the name Herman.

Feast Dates: September 25 — Bl. Herman (see Herman).

Hoop (nickname) See Hooper.

Hooper (English) See Cooper.

Hopkins (English double) See Hob+Kin.

Horace "The Keeper of Time" (Latin).

Patron Saints: There is one saint who bears a variant of the name of Horace. Known as St. Racho, he served as the first French bishop of Autun. He died in 660.

Feast Dates: January 25 — St. Racho.

Horacio (Spanish) See Horace.

Horatio (Estonian, German) See Horace.

Horatius (Estonian, German) See Horace.

Horats (Dutch) See Horace.

Horse "Like a Horse" (Middle English).

Patron Saints: The Latin for "horse" is *equus*, and there is a St. Equinus. He died a martyr in ancient Antioch.

Feast Dates: May 7 — St. Equinus.

Horst "From the Thicket" (Old German).

Patron Saints: A saint with a similar name is St. Hortasius, who was a martyr in ancient Alexandria.

Feast Dates: May 8 — St. Hortasius.

Hort (nickname) See Horton.

Horten (English) See Horton.

Horton "From the Garden+Estate" (Old English double) or "From the Town+In the Ravine" (Old English double).

Patron Saints: There is an English martyr who came from the town of Horton. Bl. William Lacey of Horton was a married man from Horton in Yorkshire. He married twice. During the fourteen years of his second marriage, his home served as a refuge for Catholics. This made him and his family subject to persecution, and his wife died from these hardships.

After his wife died, William traveled to France and Italy and was ordained a priest. He then returned to England and worked as a missionary for a year. Captured by the authorities, he was tried and condemned for being a priest. In 1582 he was hanged, drawn, and quartered.

Feast Dates: August 22 — Bl. William Lacey of Horton.

Hos (English) See Horse.

Hose (variant) See Hosea.

Hosea "God Brings Salvation" (Hebrew).

Patron Saints: The Bible presents the great Jewish prophet Hosea, 760-725 B.C., born of the tribe of Issachar. He married, but his wife left him to become a prostitute. Then God called Hosea to serve as a prophet and tell the Jewish people of the Father's love for them. Hosea showed how all had been acting like prostitutes, chasing other gods or husbands. He called them back to an intimate love affair with the true God. His prophetic mission was a failure.

Feast Dates: July 4 — St. Hosea, Jewish Prophet.

Hoseia (variant) See Hosea.

Houston "From Hugh's+Town" (Scottish double) or "From the Hill+Town" (Old English double).

Patron Saints: Houston can mean "hill town" or "Hugh's town."

Feast Dates: May 4 — Bl. Richard Hill (see Hill); November 17 — St. Hugh of Lincoln (see Hugh).

Howard "The Watchman" (Old English) or "The Chief Guard" (Old English).

Patron Saints: There are two English martyrs surnamed Howard and two more with the surname of Ward. Finally, there is St. Peter of Alcántara who is recognized as patron of watchmen.

St. Philip Howard, 1557-1595, the earl of Arundel and Surrey, grew from indifference into a fervent Catholic. For his trouble, he soon found himself in the Tower of London. In 1589 he was sentenced to death. He was never executed but did remain in prison until his death.

Feast Dates: October 19 — St. Philip Howard, Earl of Arundel.

Howey (nickname) See Howard.

Howie (nickname) See Howard.

Hoyt "Of the Spirit" (Irish) or "Of the Mind" (Irish).

Patron Saints: There is one saint with a similar name, St. Aout, a hermit, who was elected bishop against his will. He is usually referred to as St. Aigulf.

Moreover, Hoyt's meaning, "of the mind," leads to a North American missionary named Magín, which has the same meaning. SG Magín Catalá, 1761-1830, was born in Spain. After being ordained he traveled to Mexico City and later to the Santa Clara mission in California. He remained there for the rest of his life, thirty-six years. He devoted himself exclusively to the spiritual care of the Indians in eleven settlements near the mission. He made constant visitations and baptized about five thousand people, mostly Indians. He did all this despite the fact that he suffered from a very painful inflammatory rheumatism. Father Catalá, who was known as "The Holy Man of Santa Clara," died at the age of sixty-nine.

Feast Dates: November 22 — SG Magín Catalá, O.F.M.; May 22 — St. Aout, also known as Aigulf.

Hoyte (variant) See Hoyt.

Hristo (Bulgarian) See Christian.

Hristofor (Macedonian) See Christopher.

Hub (nickname) See Hubert.

Hubbard (Spanish) See Hubert.

Hube (nickname) See Hubert.

Hubert "The Bright-Minded One" (Old German).

Patron Saints: There are three Sts. Hubert. One of them, St. Hubert, 656-727, of France, had little use for religion and a great interest in hunting. One Sunday while stalking a stag, it turned to face him. And Hubert saw a crucifix between its horns. He also heard a voice that said, "Unless you turn to God, you will go to hell." He fell to his knees and asked advice and was told to see the local bishop.

Hubert was only around twenty-nine years of age when his wife died in childbirth. He then studied for the priesthood and was ordained. In 705 he was made a bishop. He was credited with converting many to the faith and with having the gift of miracles. He is patron of hunters, mathematicians, machinists, and metalworkers, as well as against dog bites.

Feast Dates: November 3 — St. Hubert.

Huberto (Spanish) See Hubert.

Hubi (Spanish) See Hubert.

Hubie (nickname) See Hubert.

Hud (nickname) See Hugh, Richard.

Hudd (nickname) See Hugh, Richard.

Hudd (Danish, Dutch, German, Spanish, Swedish) See Hubert, Hugh.

Hudson (English double) See Hudd+Son.

Huet (Danish, German, Spanish, Swedish) See Hubert.

Huey (variant) See Hubert, Hugh.

Hugan (Spanish) See Hugh.

Hugbert (German) See Hubert.

Hugh "The Intelligent One" (Old English) or "The Bright-Minded One" (variant of Hugh).

Patron Saints: There are two dozen Sts. Hugh. One St. Hugh, 1140-1200, was ordained a priest at the age of nineteen and lived ten years in solitude.

At the age of forty he was asked by King Henry II to govern a newly founded Carthusian monastery in England. Later he became bishop of Lincoln. When Jew-baiting broke out, he defended the Jews. This meant that he often had to face angry, ignorant mobs.

Feast Dates: November 17 — St. Hugh of Lincoln.

Hughie (nickname) See Hubert, Hugh.

Hughy (nickname) See Hubert, Hugh.

Hugibert (German) See Hubert.

Hugo (Danish, Dutch, German, Spanish, Swedish) See Hubert, Hugh.

Hugon (Polish, Spanish) See Hubert, Hugh.

Hugonas (Lithuanian) See Hubert, Hugh.

Hugues (French) See Hubert, Hugh.

Hum (nickname) See Humphrey.

Humberto (variant) See Hubert.

Humfredo (Spanish) See Humphrey.

Humfrey (English) See Humphrey.

Humfrid (Swedish) See Humphrey.

Humfried (German, Dutch) See Humphrey.

Humfry (nickname) See Humphrey.

Hump (nickname) See Humphrey.

Humph (nickname) See Humphrey.

Humphrey "The Peaceful Hun" (Old German) or "The Supporter of Peace" (Old German).

Patron Saints: There are three English martyrs who bear the name of Humphrey. One of them, a layman named Laurence Humphrey, was hanged, drawn, and quartered in 1591 because he insisted upon practicing his Catholic faith. He was only twenty years old.

Feast Dates: July 7 — Bl. Laurence Humphrey.

Hunfredo (Spanish) See Humphrey.

Hunter "The One+Who Hunts" (Old English double).

Patron Saints: There are two English martyrs surnamed Hunt. In 1600 Father Thomas Hunt was arrested for being a diocesan Catholic priest in England. He was quickly executed.

Feast Dates: May 4 — Bl. Thomas Hunt; August 30 — Bl. Thurston Hunt (see Thurston).

Hunt (nickname) See Hunter, Huntley.

Huntley "From Hunter's+Meadow" (Old English double).

Patron Saints: Huntley is a combination of two words: *hunt*, meaning "hunter," and *ley* (or *leigh*), meaning "meadow." This leads to three English martyrs surnamed Hunt and Leigh. Furthermore, St. Hubert can also serve as a patron because he is patron of hunters.

Feast Dates: May 4 — Bl. Thomas Hunt (see Hunter); August 30 — Bl. Richard Leigh (see Leigh).

Husain (Arabic) See Hussein.

Hussein "The Little Handsome One" (Arabic).

Patron Saints: It helps to know that Hussein means "little handsome one." This leads to St. Paul, whose name means "little," and St. Kenneth, whose name means "handsome."

Feast Dates: June 29 — St. Paul, Apostle (see Paul); October 11 — St. Kenneth (see Kenneth).

Husto (Lithuanian) See Justin.

Hutch (nickname) See Hubert, Hugh.

Hutton "From the Town+On the Jutting Ledge" (Old English double).

Patron Saints: Hutton comes from *hut*, meaning "jutting ledge," and *ton*, meaning "town" or "house."

Feast Dates: July 21 — St. Tondach (see Town).

Huugo (Finnish) See Hubert, Hugh.

Hy (variant) See Hiram, Hyginus, Hyman.

Hyginus "The Healthy One" (Greek).

Patron Saints: There is at least one St. Hyginus. He was pope from 136 to 140 and fought the heresy of Gnosticism. He was also instrumental in the establishment of minor orders for the priesthood as well as the role of godparents in baptism.

Feast Dates: January 11 — St. Hyginus.

Hyman "The Living One" (Hebrew).

Patron Saints: There are about a half-dozen saints who bear variant forms of the name Hyman. They include Hymenaeus, Hymerius, and Hymeterius. St. Hymerius lived in about 400. Early in life he became a hermit, then he joined a religious order and became known for his holiness.

When a vacancy occurred in Amelia, a diocese in Umbria, Italy, the people elected him to be the next bishop. Even after becoming bishop of Amelia, he continued his monastic practices of discipline and self-denial.

Feast Dates: June 17 — St. Hymerius.

Hymie (variant) See Hyman.

Hyrum (variant) See Hiram.

J

Iacovo (Italian) See Jacob.

Iago (Spanish-Welsh) See Jacob, James.

Iain (variant) See Ian.

Iain (Scottish) See John.

Ian "God Is Gracious" (Scottish).

Patron Saints: Ian is the Scottish form of John, and there are some four hundred twenty-five Sts. John. St. Ian was consecrated a bishop and was sent by his superiors to the Slav missions. Upon his arrival, the pagans took him prisoner and tortured him for a long time. Finally, they beheaded him in 1066.

Feast Dates: November 10 — St. Ian the Scot.

Iban (Spanish) See John.

Ibraheem (Arabic) See Abraham.

Ibrahim (Arabic) See Abraham, Abram.

Idrees (Arabic) See Enoch.

Iggie (nickname) See Ignatius.

Iggy (nickname) See Ignatius.

Ignac (Czech) See Ignatius.

Ignace (French) See Ignatius.

Ignacio (Spanish) See Ignatius.

Ignacius (Latin) See Ignatius.

Ignacy (Polish) See Ignatius.

Ignat (Bulgarian) See Ignatius.

Ignatius "The Ardent, Fiery One" (Latin, Dutch).

Patron Saints: There are about a dozen-and-a-half saints named Ignatius. One of them, St. Ignatius Loyola, was born Iñigo López de Loyola in 1491. He was trained to be a soldier and saw military service. But his career was cut short when a cannonball broke his right shin and tore open his calf.

His broken leg was badly set and had to be broken again. A violent fever followed, and many thought he would die, but he did not. However, he was deformed, as the end of the bone stuck out under his knee. While confined to bed, Ignatius asked for some books on knight-errantry. None could be found, but some books on the lives of the saints were brought to him. They set him on fire for God.

After a short honeymoon with God, Ignatius entered a state of terrible depression and sadness. He was filled with fears and found no relief in prayer, fasting, self-discipline, or the sacraments. Out of this trial he wrote the *Spiritual Exercises.* After a year he regained tranquility. Sometime later he was ordained a priest. In 1534 he gathered six followers, and the group made vows of poverty and chastity and to do apostolic works. But it would be another six years before he would get papal approval to found the Order of Jesuits. He died suddenly at the age of sixty-five in 1556.

Feast Dates: July 31 — St. Ignatius Loyola.

Ignaz (German) See Ignatius.

Ignazio (Italian) See Ignatius.

Igor "The Hero" (Scandinavian, Slavic) or "The Famous One" (Old Norse).

Patron Saints: There is at least one saint with this name. St. Igor Olegowitsh was the grand duke of Russia for a mere twelve days in 1146. A rebellion placed a new grand duke in power, and Igor humbly retired to a monastery. However, some rebels still felt he was a threat and they murdered him.

Feast Dates: June 5 — St. Igor Olegowitsh.

Ike (nickname) See Isaac.

Ikey (nickname) See Isaac.

Ikie (nickname) See Isaac.

Ikoy (nickname) See Frederick.

Ilario (Italian) See Hilary.

Illis (Hungarian) See Elijah.

Imaam (Arabic) See Iman.

Iman "Leader of Prayer [or The Priest]" (Arabic) or "God with Us" (Hebrew short form of Emmanuel).

Patron Saints: Any saint who is an ordained Catholic priest can serve as patron. Probably the best choice is St. John Vianney, 1786-1859, who is patron of parish priests. The Curé of Ars spent almost his entire life serving God's people in the small town of Ars in France. He spent most of his time each day (averaging sixteen to eighteen hours) hearing confessions, and he had the ability to read souls.

Feast Dates: August 4 — St. John Vianney.

Immanuel (English) See Emmanuel.

Indiana "From the Place of the Indians" (Latin).

Patron Saints: There is one North American saint who dedicated her entire life to the service of the American Indians and blacks.

Feast Dates: March 3 — St. Katharine Drexel (see Drexel).

Indy (nickname) See Indiana.

Ingar (Scandinavian) See Igor.

Ingelbert (variant) See Engelbert.

Ingemar (Scandinavian) See Igor.

Inger (Scandinavian) See Igor.

Inglebert (variant) See Engelbert.

Inglis (English) See Ingram.

Ingmar (Scandinavian) See Igor.

Ingra (English) See Ingram.

Ingram "[Ings] The Son's+Raven" (Old Norse+English).

Patron Saints: There is one English martyr by the name of Bl. John Ingram.

He was born in Herefordshire, England. Raised a Protestant, he converted to Catholicism as an adult. He then traveled to Rheims, France, to study for the priesthood. After being ordained a diocesan priest in 1589, he went to help Catholics in Scotland. However, he was executed within five years after his ordination.

For further name explanation, see Remington.

Feast Dates: July 26 — Bl. John Ingram.

Ingrim (English) See Ingram.

Ingvar (Scandinavian) See Igor.

Iñigo (variant) See Ignatius.

Innis (Scottish-Irish) See Ny.

Ioan (Romanian) See John.

Ioannes (Greek) See John.

Iordache (Romanian) See Jordan.

Iordanos (Greek) See Jordan.

Iosef (Greek) See Joseph.

Ioseph (Gaelic) See Joseph.

Ira "The Watchful One" (Hebrew).

Patron Saints: Two ancient saints bear names similar to Ira. One is St. Irais, who died a child martyr, aged ten, in the year 310. A native of Memphis, Egypt, and a Christian, she soon found herself in prison and condemned to death.

Also knowing that the name Ira means "watchful" leads to the Latin word *vigilia*, which also means "watchful" (or "vigilant"), and St. Vigilius.

Feast Dates: September 22 — St. Irais.

Iradly (American double) See Ira+Leigh.

Irby (nickname) See Ervin, Irving.

Irv (nickname) See Ervin, Irving.

Irvin (English) See Ervin, Irving.

Irvine (English) See Ervin, Irving.

Irving "The Sea Friend" (Old English) or "The White River" (Old Welsh) or "From the City" (form of Urban).

Patron Saints: There are a few ancient saints who have names that are very similar. St. Eruen was a priest in ancient Wales. He is one of the four popular saints of Llangwm, Wales.

Moreover, some think that Irving or Irwin is a form of Urban, which leads to about three dozen saints named Urban or Urbanus.

Feast Dates: November 1 — St. Eruen; April 12 — St. Urban of Langres (see Urban).

Irwin (English) See Ervin, Irving.
Irwinn (English) See Ervin, Irving.
Irwyn (English) See Ervin, Irving.
Isa (Arabic) See Jesus.
Isaac "The One Who Laughs" (Hebrew).

Patron Saints: There are over fifty saints with the name of Isaac. In addition, the Bible presents us with the great patriarch Isaac, the son of Abraham.

Here is the story of an Isaac, who was a New World missionary. St. Isaac Jogues was born in Orléans, France, in 1607 and was ordained a Jesuit priest at the age of twenty-nine. In 1636, the year of his ordination, he traveled to the missions in New France (Canada) and was assigned to a Huron mission.

In the summer of 1642, on a one-day's journey from Three Rivers, Father Jogues and his companions became prisoners of the Iroquois. Father Jogues was subjected to mutilation, then released. After he visited Europe, he returned to the missions and was en route to the Iroquois as a peace delegate when he was captured by the Mohawks. Shortly after he was taken captive in 1646 he was killed with a tomahawk. Father Jogues was thirty-nine.

Feast Dates: October 19 — St. Isaac Jogues, S.J.

Isaak (German, Greek, Russian) See Isaac.
Isac (variant) See Isaac.
Isacco (Italian) See Isaac.
Isace (English) See Isaac.
Isador (variant) See Isadore.
Isadore "The Gift of the Goddess Isis" (Greek).

Patron Saints: There are about three dozen saints named Isidore. St. Isidore, 1090-1130, was a married day laborer. He had one son who died in childhood. Both he and his wife worked and prayed very hard. Their greatest joy was attending Mass every morning. They also shared their meager possessions with the poor. Isidore died at the age of forty. He is patron of farmers, ranchers, and laborers.

Feast Dates: May 15 — St. Isidore the Farmer.

Isaia (Italian, Romanian) See Isaiah.
Isaiah "God Is My Helper" (Hebrew) or "God Is Holy" (Hebrew).

Patron Saints: There are more than a dozen saints named Isaiah. In addition, the Bible presents us with the great Jewish prophet Isaiah. He was born into a priestly family in Jerusalem and was familiar with Temple ministry. In about 740 B.C., God called him to teach his ways to the Jewish people. Isaiah pursued this vocation for sixty years, until about 681 B.C. Then he was martyred by being sawed in half by the evil king Manasseh.

Feast Dates: July 6 — St. Isaiah, Jewish Prophet.

Isaias (variant) See Isaiah.
Isais (Spanish, Portuguese) See Isaiah.
Isavello (Spanish) See Isabel.
Ishaaq (Arabic) See Isaac.
Isiah (variant) See Isaiah.
Isidor (German) See Isadore.
Isidore (variant) See Isadore.
Isidoro (Italian) See Isadore.

Isidro (Spanish) See Isadore.

Israel "The One Who Wrestles with God" (Hebrew) or "The Prince of the Strong God" (Hebrew).

Patron Saints: Israel was the name God gave to Jacob.

Feast Dates: November 1 — St. Jacob (see Jacob).

Israele (Italian) See Israel.

Issa (Arabic, Swahili) See Jesus.

Issiah (variant) See Isaiah.

Issy (nickname) See Isadore.

István (Hungarian) See Stephen.

Ito "Little One" (Spanish, Italian).

Patron Saints: Ito is used as a diminutive suffix with many Hispanic names. St. Italus has the closest name.

Feast Dates: June 6 — St. Italus.

Itzak (Modern Hebrew) See Isaac.

Itzhak (Dutch, Polish) See Isaac.

Iuda (Bulgarian) See Jude.

Ivan "God Is Gracious" (Russian, Slavic).

Patron Saints: Ivan is the Russian form of John. There are some four hundred twenty-five Sts. John.

St. Ivan was a member of a royal Russian family. However, his uncle, Duke John, kept him in prison for thirty-two years in order to prevent him from inheriting the throne. While in prison he joined a religious order. He died in 1523.

Feast Dates: May 19 — St. Ivan of Uglitsh.

Ivano (African-American) See Ivan.

Ives (variant) See Yves.

Izaak (Dutch, Polish) See Isaac.

Izrael (Polish, Hungarian) See Israel.

Izraelis (Lithuanian) See Israel.

Izzy (nickname) See Isadore.

J

Ja "Yes" (German).

Patron Saints: Modern Hispanic-Americans seem to favor the "Ja" sound and prefix it to many names. For purposes of finding a patron saint, it can also be recognized as a short form of any name beginning with Ja.

Jaan (Estonian) See John.

Jaap (Dutch) See Jim.

Jace (nickname) See Jason.

Jacee (American) See any "J" name+any "C" name.

Jacinth (African-American) See Jacinto.

Jacinto "The Hyacinth Flower" (Spanish-Greek).

Patron Saints: Jacinto is Spanish for Hyacinth, and there are about a dozen saints by that name. The best remembered is the "Apostle of the North," St. Hyacinth, 1190-1257, a nobleman who became a religious priest and a great missionary in Cracow, Poland. He traveled extensively. To the northeast, he went to Lithuania. To the east, he went to Kiev, Russia. To the southeast, he traveled as far as the Black Sea. His southernmost point was on the Danube River in the Balkans. In the northwest, he could be found in Scandinavia. Some think he may even have gone as far as Tibet and the frontiers of China.

Feast Dates: August 17 — St. Hyacinth, O.P.

Jack (nickname) See Jacob, John.

Jackie (nickname) See Jacob, John.

Jacko (nickname) See Jacob, John.

Jackson (English double) See Jacob/Jack+Son.

Jacky (nickname) See Jacob, John.

Jacob "The Supplanter" (Hebrew) or "May God Protect Him" (Hebrew).

Patron Saints: Jacob in its English form is James, which leads to about one hundred Sts. James. The greatest St. Jacob is the Old Testament Jewish patriarch Jacob, 1900-1800 B.C., the son of Isaac. A second-born twin, he stole his brother Esau's blessing and became the father of twelve sons who fathered the twelve tribes of Israel. Jacob's whole life was a struggle. The story is told that one night Jacob wrestled with an angel of God and suffered a hip injury. After the wrestling match, the angel renamed Jacob "Israel," which means "he who wrestles with God." (See Genesis 32:24ff.) This teaches us that everyone must "struggle" with God. True faith is not a spectator sport. Each one must personally work through the struggle.

Feast Dates: November 1 — St. Jacob, Patriarch.

Jacobo (Spanish) See Jacob.

Jacobson (English double) See Jacob+Son.

Jacorey (African-American double) See Jacob+Corey.

Jacques (French) See Jacob, James.

Jae (nickname) See Jason.

Jaegar (German) See Hunter.

Jago (Cornish) See James.

Jaime (Spanish) See James.

Jaimito (Spanish double) See Jaime+Ito.

JaJuan (Hispanic-American) See Ja+Juan.

Jake (nickname) See Jacob, James.

Jakie (nickname) See Jacob, James.

Jakib (variant) See Jacob.

Jakob (German) See Jacob.

Jaleel (Arabic) See Grant.

Jalil (African-American) See Jaleel.

Jamaal (Arabic) See Jamal.

Jamaine (Arabic) See Germaine.

Jamal (Arabic) See Kenneth.

Jameel (Arabic) See Jamal.

Jamel (Arabic) See Jamal.

James "The Supplanter" (English) or "May God Protect Him" (English).

Patron Saints: There are about a hundred saints named James. The greatest is St. James the Elder, one of the Apostles. Throughout the ministry of Jesus, he, along with Peter and John, formed the inner circle of disciples. Catholic tradition tells us that he preached in India and Spain. He was also the first Apostle to suffer martyrdom. This occurred in the year 44, a scant eleven to fourteen years after the crucifixion of Jesus.

Catholic tradition goes on to say that the man who had caused James to be brought into court was so moved by his defense that he declared himself to be a Christian and was condemned to die with James. They were taken away together, and on the way he asked James to forgive him. James thought for a moment, then said, "I wish you peace," and kissed him. Both were beheaded. St. James is patron of blacksmiths, furriers, horsemen, laborers, soldiers, tanners, and veterinarians; he is also patron of Chile, Guatemala, Nicaragua, and Spain, as well as of those suffering from arthritis and rheumatism.

Feast Dates: July 25 — St. James the Elder.

Jameson (English double) See James+Son.

Jamesy (variant) See Jacob.

Jamey (nickname) See Jacob.

Jamie (nickname) See James.

Jamieson (English double) See James+ Son.

Jamir (African-American) See Jamal+ Shaakira, Jaime.

Jamison (English double) See James+Son.

Jamy (American) See Jared.

Jan (Czech, Danish, Dutch) See John.

Jandino (Spanish) See Alexander.

Jando (Spanish) See Alexander.

Janek (Czech) See John.

Janis (Latvian) See John.

Janiuszck (variant) See Jarek.

Janne (French) See John.

János (Hungarian) See John.

Januarius (Latin) See Jarek.

Januisz (variant) See Jarek.

Janus (Latin) See Jarek.

Jaquarius (African-American triple) See Jacob+Quan+Darius.

Jarad (American) See Jared.

Jared "The Descendant" (Hebrew) or "The Inheritor" (Hebrew).

Patron Saints: The Book of Genesis presents us with Jared the patriarch. He was the fifth generation from Adam and Eve and lived to the age of nine hundred sixty-two years, which many may find difficult to believe.

Some scholars insist that the ancients really did live extremely long lives. Others suggest that each patriarch's name was actually the name of a dynasty of rulers. In any case, the long life spans are the Bible's way of teaching that the first few generations of mankind walked with God. Sin did not rule their lives. The decreasing life spans further teach that sin slowly made its presence felt among our ancestors. By sinning they slowly destroyed life.

Feast Dates: March 1 — St. Jared.

Jarek "The God of Beginnings and Ends" (Slavic).

Patron Saints: Jarek is a form of Januarius or Janus. And there are two dozen Sts. Januarius. One of them, with his two friends, lived at Cordova in 305. When Emperor Diocletian began persecuting the Christians, Januarius and his companions Festus and Desiderius were quickly arrested. They were tortured on the rack to make them offer sacrifice to the pagan gods, but they steadfastly refused. Although various sources disagree as to how they died, one story points out that all three were decapitated.

Feast Dates: October 13 — St. Januarius.

Jarid (American) See Jared.

Jarmon (German) See Germain.

Jarrad (American) See Jared.

Jarrell (African-American double) See Gerald+Terrell.

Jarrett (English) See Garrett.

Jarrid (American) See Jared.

Jarrod (American) See Jared.

Jarrot (English) See Garrett.

Jarrott (English) See Garrett.

Jarvis (Old English) See Victor.

Jas (nickname) See Casper.

Jase (nickname) See Jason.

Jasen (American) See Jason.

Jasius (Lithuanian) See John.

Jason "The Healer" (Greek) or "Yahweh Saves" (German form of Joshua).

Patron Saints: There are at least three saints named Jason. The most prominent is mentioned in the Bible. It seems Sts. Paul and Silas stayed at his home in Thessalonica. However, a mob formed and accused Jason of aiding Paul and Silas. Christian tradition claims that Jason later worked with St. Paul. Still later he became a bishop and worked in Tarsus. He ended his life as a martyr.

Feast Dates: July 12 — St. Jason.

Jasper (English, Old French) See Casper.

Jasun (American) See Jason.

Javiel (Spanish) See Xavier.

Javier (Arabic, Spanish) See Xavier.

Jawaun (Hispanic-American double) See Jacob+Juan.

Jaxon (English double) See Jacob/Jack+Son.

Jay (nickname) See Jacob, James, Jason.

Jaycee (American double) See any "J" name+any "C" name.

Jaydee (American double) See any "J" name+any "D" name.

Jaye (nickname) See Jacob, James, Jason.

Jaylee (American double) See any "J" name+Leigh.

Jaylyn (American double) See any "J" name+Lynn.

Jayme (Portuguese, Spanish) See James.

Jaymie (variant) See Jacob.

Jayson (English double) See Jason+Son.

Jayvon (African-American double) See any "J" name+Vaughn.

Jazz "American-Born Music" (American).

Patron Saints: The Church-appointed patrons of musicians are Sts. Arnold, Gregory the Great, Cecilia, and Dunstan.

Feast Dates: July 8 — St. Arnold.

Jean "God Is Gracious" (French).

Patron Saints: The name Jean is a French form of John, and there are more than four hundred saints named John. One is St. Jean de Brébeuf, 1593-1649, born in Normandy, France. He entered the Jesuits, taught school for three years, was ordained a priest, and then sailed to New France (Canada). He worked among the Huron Indians for twenty-four years, converting many to Catholicism.

In 1649 he and Gabriel Lalemant were in a Huron village when it was attacked by the Iroquois. They were taken captive and subjected to one of the most inhumane tortures imaginable. The Jesuit *Relations*, a collection of annual reports spanning the years

1632 through 1672, describes it this way: "Before their death . . . these barbarians feasted on them. . . . While still full of life, pieces of their thighs, calves, and arms were removed by the butchers who roasted them on coals and ate them in their sight."

Feast Dates: October 19 — St. Jean de Brébeuf.

Jecho (variant) See Jesus.

Jed (nickname) See Jedidiah.

Jedd (nickname) See Jedidiah.

Jedediah (variant) See Jedidiah.

Jedidiah "The One Loved by God" (Hebrew).

Patron Saints: The Bible presents one Jedidiah. He is better known as King Solomon, 980-900 B.C., the second son of King David by Bathsheba. He built the first Jewish Temple and is credited with collecting and/or writing most of the books of Proverbs, Songs, Ecclesiastes, 1 and 2 Samuel, and 1 Kings.

He is also remembered as the wisest man that ever lived. However, the story told about him in the Bible is really about a most foolish king. Solomon had everything but eventually lost his special relationship with God. This led him to participate in the slow alienation of himself from his people. The tradition of the Abyssinian Orthodox Church, however, regards him as a saint. It teaches that Solomon returned to God before he died.

Feast Dates: June 17 — St. Jedidiah, also known as Solomon.

Jedy (nickname) See Jedidiah.

Jeff (nickname) See Geoffrey, Godfrey, Jeffrey.

Jefferey (English) See Geoffrey, Godfrey, Jeffrey.

Jefferson (English double) See Jeffrey+ Son.

Jeffery (nickname) See Geoffrey, Godfrey, Jeffrey.

Jeffie (nickname) See Geoffrey, Godfrey, Jeffrey.

Jeffrey "From the Peaceful Place" (English) or "The Peaceful Traveler" (English).

Patron Saints: Jeffrey is a form of Godfrey, which leads to about a dozen saints with this name.

Feast Dates: July 9 — St. Godfrey of Merville (see Merton).

Jeffry (nickname) See Geoffrey, Godfrey, Jeffrey.

Jeffy (nickname) See Geoffrey, Godfrey, Jeffrey.

Jehan (Belgian) See John.

Jem (nickname) See James.

Jemmy (nickname) See James.

Jen (Danish, Norwegian, Swedish) See John.

Jens (Danish, Norwegian, Swedish) See John.

Jerad (American) See Jared.

Jerald (variant) See Gerald.

Jeramey (variant) See Jeremiah.

Jeramie (variant) See Jeremiah.

Jere (variant) See Jeremiah, Jerome.

Jereme (variant) See Jeremiah.

Jeremey (English) See Jerome.

Jeremiah "God's Appointed One" (Hebrew) or "The One Exalted by God" (Hebrew).

Patron Saints: There are a half-dozen Sts. Jeremiah, and the Bible provides almost a dozen more. The greatest is the Jewish prophet Jeremiah, who lived from 655 to 586 B.C. He was born into a family of priests and while still in his teens was called by God to be a prophet. He was not enthusiastic about the call, but God assured him that he would stand by him (see Jeremiah 1:18-19). Then God gave Jeremiah the job of calling Israel to conversion and repentance.

Jeremiah was a man who deeply loved Jerusalem and its people, yet he had to speak of violence and punishment. Knowing that the justice and anger of God would soon overtake everyone, he refused to marry and have children. He often became frustrated and depressed and would howl at God. Then he would rededicate himself to the job God had given him.

Jewish tradition adds that after the fall of Jerusalem, the exiles took him into Egypt. There they stoned him to death.

Feast Dates: May 1 — St. Jeremiah.

Jeremias (German, Spanish) See Jeremiah.

Jeremie (French) See Jeremiah.

Jeremio (English) See Jeremiah.

Jeremy (English) See Jeremiah.

Jerid (American) See Jared.

Jermain (variant) See Germain.

Jermaine (variant) See Germain.

Jermayne (variant) See Germain.

Jerod (American) See Jared.

Jeroen (Dutch) See Jerome.

Jerome "The Sacred Holy Name" (English).

Patron Saints: There are about twenty saints with this name or variants of it. The greatest was Eusebius Hieronymus Sophronius, 342-420, of Italy. At eighteen years of age he converted to Catholicism, yet it was not until he was thirty-four that he fully chose Jesus. He did so only because he became very ill. His conversion process took more than four years living as a hermit in the desert. To overcome sinful thoughts, he disciplined himself by studying and learning Hebrew. He had already become a master of Latin, Greek, and oratory.

He felt called to become a religious monk, not a priest. However, he allowed himself to be ordained when pressed by Church authority, but he never presided at the Mass during his lifetime. When theological disputes arose, he always defended the Holy Father. In time, the pope asked him to make a Latin translation of the Bible. His translation is known as the *Vulgate*. After a stormy life, he died peacefully. He is a Doctor of the Church and patron of librarians and students.

Feast Dates: September 30 — St. Jerome.

Jeromo (Slovenian, Croatian) See Jerome.

Jeromy (variant) See Jeremiah.

Jeronim (Slovenian, Croatian) See Jerome.

Jerónimo (Spanish) See Jerome.

Jerrell (African-American double) See Gerald+Terrell.

Jerrick (African-American double) See Gerald+Richard/Derrick.

Jerrie (nickname) See Gerald, Gerard, Jeremiah, Jerome.

Jerrold (variant) See Gerald.

Jerrome (English) See Jerome.

Jerry (nickname) See Gerald, Gerard, Jeremiah, Jerome.

Jervis (nickname) See Jarvis.

Jerzy (Polish) See George.

Jeshua (Hebrew) See Joshua.

Jesito (variant) See Jesús.

Jess (nickname) See Jessie, Jester.

Jesse "The Wealthy One" (Hebrew).

Patron Saints: There seem to be only two saints with the name of Jesse. One of them was the grandson of Ruth and Boaz and the father of King David. He was a prominent married citizen and leader in Bethlehem in about 1100 B.C. A strong supporter of the Jewish faith, he entertained the prophet Samuel when he came to Bethlehem and discovered that his last son, David, would be the king of Israel and Judah.

In David's time, the term "son of Jesse" was spoken with a sneer to indicate that David came from humble (nonroyal) origins. In time, however, the title was exalted to mean "the expected Messiah."

Feast Dates: December 29 — St. Jesse, Patriarch.

Jessie (nickname) See Jesse, Jester.

Jessy (nickname) See Jessie, Jester.

Jester "The Comedian" (Middle English).

Patron Saints: A jester is a person who creates laughter, and there is a St. Genesius, known as "The Comedian." He was martyred in about 300. When Diocletian assumed the throne, he was entertained by many stage productions that included a burlesque of a Christian baptism by an actor named Genesius.

Then Genesius suddenly became very serious. He told the emperor he was a Christian. He told how he came to understand Christian teachings and converted. He made a heartrending plea for a proper understanding of Christian rites and beliefs. The emperor became enraged and ordered that Genesius be beaten and beheaded.

He is patron of actors, comedians (jesters), dancers, lawyers, printers, stenographers, and secretaries, as well as of those suffering from epilepsy and from freezing.

Feast Dates: August 25 — St. Genesius the Comedian.

Jesualdo (Spanish double) See Jesús+Aldo.

Jesus "Yahweh Saves" (Greek, Latin forms of Joshua).

Patron Saints: The name Jesus is the Greek and Latin forms of the Hebrew name Joshua. The Bible clearly declares that Jesus is the God-Man, the expected Messiah, the end-time King of Israel, the "Poor Little One" of God, and a model for all. Born of the Virgin Mary and God the Holy Spirit in Bethlehem in about 6 B.C., Jesus remained at home in Nazareth for thirty years. Then he began a ministry of preaching, healing, and founding the Catholic Church. His teachings attracted opposition, and his enemies crucified him. Then he rose from the dead and ascended to heaven as the Redeemer of all mankind.

Feast Dates: All Sundays — Jesus Christ, Son of God and Man.

Jesús (Spanish) See Jesus.

Jet (variant) See Jett.

Jeth (nickname) See Jethro.

Jethro "The Preeminent [Excellent] One" (Hebrew).

Patron Saints: The Bible has one Jethro who can be regarded as a saint. He was the priest-ruler of the Kenites who lived in about 1250 B.C. The Book of Exodus tells us that when Moses was exiled from Egypt by the pharaoh, he fled to the land of Midian, where he met Jethro. He married Jethro's daughter, Zipporah, who introduced him to the practice of circumcision. After Moses had his encounter with the "burning bush" he discussed it with Jethro. Later, during the Exodus, Jethro guided the Israelites through the desert and he advised Moses. In time, the Kenites were completely assimilated into the Jewish people.

Feast Dates: November 1 — St. Jethro.

Jett "The Glossy Black Gemstone" (English).

Patron Saints: The name Jett means "black," and thousands of Catholic saints are black. A few of have Black as part of their names. One was St. Benedict the Black, 1522-1585. He was

434

born a slave but was soon set free. All his life he was taunted because of his dark skin. One day he was being made fun of when a nobleman passed by. The nobleman was so impressed by Benedict's patience and kindness that he publicly reprimanded the persecutors. Then he invited Benedict to join him and become a Franciscan. Benedict became a cook and did everything well. In 1578 the members of this friary elected him superior even though he was neither a priest nor could he read. However, he prayed and practiced penance and observed seven Lents every year. He is patron of African-Americans.

Feast Dates: April 4 — St. Benedict the Black, O.F.M.; August 28 — St. Moses the Black (see Blackie).

Jevon (African-American double) See any "J" name+Devon.

Jibreel (Arabic) See Gabriel.

Jim (variants) See James, Jimmy.

Jimel (African-American) See Jimmy+ Darnell/Terrell.

Jimeno (Modern Hebrew) See Simon.

Jimmie (variant) See James, Jimmy.

Jimmy "The Supplanter" (Hebrew) or "May God Protect Him" (Hebrew).

Patron Saints: Jimmy is a nickname for James, and there are over a hundred Sts. James. An important one is St. James the Younger, the Apostle. He may have been a son of St. Joseph by a previous marriage and a stepbrother to Jesus. Some think he was the author of the Epistle of James. He could have been the first bishop of Jerusalem and seems to have spoken a decisive word at the Council of Jerusalem in the year 42. He probably drew up the decree that approved of "salvation by faith, but not by faith alone."

James was well known for his holiness, and because he converted so many Jews to Jesus, the Pharisees became his bitter enemies. In 62 they threw him from the heights of the Temple and then beat him to death with fuller's clubs. He was in his sixties when he died and is patron of hat makers, fullers, and of the dying.

Feast Dates: May 3 — St. James the Younger, Apostle.

Jindrich (Czech) See Henry.

Jo (nickname) See Joseph.

Joachim "The Lord Will Judge" (Hebrew).

Patron Saints: There are about a dozen saints named Joachim. The most famous one lived from 60 to 5 B.C. Catholic tradition suggests that this Joachim and his wife, Anne, were childless during the first twenty years of their marriage. Therefore, they prayed and fasted forty days. Then an angel appeared to Joachim and another to Anne and told them that God heard their prayers and they would have a child. The child would be called "blessed" by all ages.

Anne and Joachim were so happy for receiving this wonderful promise from God's messenger that they, in turn, offered to give the child as a gift to God, to do with as he saw fit. God accepted, and a little girl was born. They named her Mary, and in time she made them the grandparents of the Son of God. Joachim died after witnessing the presentation of Jesus in the Temple.

Feast Dates: July 26 — St. Joachim, Grandfather of Jesus.

Joakim (English) See Joachim.

João (Portuguese) See John.

Joaquín (Spanish) See Joachim.

Job "The Afflicted One" (Hebrew).

Patron Saints: Christian tradition provides three Sts. Job, and the Bible adds one more. St. Job the Jewish patriarch, who lived on the western border of the Holy Land, suffered through a great test from God. His story is told in the Old Testament in the Book of Job. He is patron against syphilis.

Feast Dates: May 10 — St. Job, Patriarch.

Jobo (Spanish) See Job, Joseph.

Jock (Scottish, American) See Jacob, John.

Jocko (variant) See Jacob, John.

Joda (American) See Jody.

Jodi (variant) See Jody.

Jodie (variant) See Jody.

Jody "He Shall Add" (nickname for Joseph) or "God Is Gracious" (nickname for John).

Patron Saints: St. Jodocus was the son of King Hoel III of Brittany in the mid-600s. To avoid the kingship he left Brittany and became a priest and hermit. He died in 669.

Feast Dates: December 13 — St. Jodocus, also known as Judoce or Josse.

Joe (nickname) See Joseph.

Joel "The Lord Is God" (Hebrew) or "The Lord Is Willing" (Hebrew).

Patron Saints: Christian tradition provides one St. Joel, and the Bible presents us with a dozen more. The greatest is St. Joel, the Jewish prophet who lived in about 400 to 360 B.C. He was called to preach repentance to Judah. It seems that Joel wrote while a great plague of locusts was devastating Israel. He interprets this event to be part of the judgment of God, but he also promises a new outpouring of God's "spirit" on Israel. With this statement, he brings the Jews closest to introducing the Holy Spirit as a separate Person of God. He also promised that in the end, Israel would gain salvation. St. Peter quotes Joel in the Acts of the Apostles to prove that Jesus was the fulfillment of all God's promises.

Feast Dates: July 13 — St. Joel.

Joey (nickname) See Joseph.

Joffre (French) See Geoffrey, Godfrey, Jeffrey.

Joffrey (French) See Geoffrey, Godfrey, Jeffrey.

Johan (Danish) See John.

Johann (German) See John.

Johannes (German) See John.

John "God Is Gracious" (Hebrew, English).

Patron Saints: There are some four hundred twenty-five saints named John or variants of it. One is St. John Nepomucene Neumann, C.Ss.R, 1811-1860, bishop of Philadelphia in the United States. He was born in Bohemia and at the age of twenty decided to become a priest. By 1836 he had completed his studies and traveled to America to be ordained. He was ordained a priest in June and then sent to Buffalo, New York. During his priestly years, he served in parishes from eastern Pennsylvania to western Ohio.

In 1840 he joined the Redemptorist Order and was professed two years later. At the age of forty-one he became bishop of Philadelphia and died eight years later.

Feast Dates: January 5 — St. John Nepomucene Neumann.

Johnathan (variant) See Jonathan.

Johnathon (variant) See Jonathan.

Johnnie (nickname) See John.

Johnny (nickname) See John.

Johns (English double) See John+Son.

Johnson "Son of+John [God Is Gracious]" (Old English double).

Patron Saints: There are two English martyrs with the surname of Johnson. Bl. Thomas Johnson, a Carthusian priest, was executed in 1537. King Henry VIII had him and five priest-companions chained to pillars and starved to death in Newgate Prison.

Bl. Robert Johnson was one of three priests hanged, drawn, and quartered at Tyburn on May 28, 1582, because he refused to recognize Queen Elizabeth as the head of the Church.

Feast Dates: September 20 — Bl. Thomas Johnson, O. Cart.; May 28 — Bl. Robert Johnson.

Johnston (English triple) See John+Son+Town.

Johny (nickname) See John.

Jon (nickname) See John, Jonathan.

Jona (variant) See Jonah.

Jonah "The Dove" (Hebrew).

Patron Saints: Christian tradition provides us with about two dozen Sts. Jonah. The Old Testament adds the story of Jonah, one of the prophets.

In 327 the king of Persia began a terrible persecution of Christians. Two monks, Sts. Jonas and Barachisius, hearing that several Christians were under sentence of death, went to the prison to encourage them, and they were also arrested and imprisoned. Brought before the king, they refused to deny Jesus and were condemned to death. Jonas was laid facedown on the ground with a sharp stake under his belly and he was beaten with rods. Then he was placed in an icy pond for the night. Finally, he was put in a wooden wine press and slowly crushed to death. His friend was killed by having hot pitch and sulfur poured into his mouth.

Feast Dates: March 29 — Sts. Jonas and Barachisius.

Jonas (Greek, Spanish) See Jonah.

Jonatan (Spanish, Slavic, Hungarian) See Jonathan.

Jonathan "The Gift of the Lord" (Hebrew).

Patron Saints: Christian tradition provides us with only one saint with a similar name: St. Jonatus. However, the Old Testament presents us with about twenty Jonathans. The greatest, of course, is King Saul's son and King David's best friend, who lived in about 1000 B.C.

Although he was heir to the throne of his father, Jonathan knew that David had been appointed by God to be king. Therefore, he put David ahead of his own self-interests. He died at his father's side in a final battle with the Philistines on Mount Gilboa. He was about thirty years old.

Feast Dates: November 1 — Holy Jonathan.

Jonathon (variant) See Jonathan.

Jone (variant) See John.

Jonel (African-American double) See John/Jones+Darnell/Terrell.

Jones "Son of+John [God Is Gracious]" (Old English double).

Patron Saints: There are two English martyrs with the name of Jones. Bl. Edward Jones was born in Wales and was raised a Protestant. After converting to the Catholic faith, he traveled to Rheims, France, and was ordained a priest in 1588. He returned to England and one year later he was captured and executed for being a Catholic priest.

St. John Jones was known in the English Catholic underground by the alias of Buckley. Born in Wales, he joined the Franciscans while living in Rome. He labored in the English missions for five years, between 1592 and 1597. He was martyred for his priesthood at Southwark.

Feast Dates: May 6 — Bl. Edward Jones; July 12 — St. John Jones, O.F.M.

Joop (Dutch) See Joseph.

Joquín (Spanish) See Joaquín.

Jordan "The Descending One" (Hebrew).

Patron Saints: There are about a half-dozen Sts. Jordan. A popular one is Bl. Jordan of Pisa, O.P., 1250-1311. When he was about fifty-five, he was appointed the "official teacher" of theology in Florence. He was a real genius. He knew the priest's breviary, the missal, most of the Bible with its marginal notes, the second part of the *Summa*, and other writings — by heart. He also was the best preacher of his era. In fact, he gave birth to the modern Italian language because he insisted on using the Tuscan dialect in his talks. Before Jordan's time, only bishops announced the Word of God. This was considered their office. Other clergy and religious were expected to preach only by the example of their lives. But after Jordan, priests, monks, and hermits were all expected to actually preach the Word of God.

Feast Dates: March 6 — Bl. Jordan of Pisa, O.P.

Jorden (English) See Jordan.

Jordon (English) See Jordan.

Jordy (nickname) See Jordan.

Jorgan (variant) See George.

Jorge (Portuguese, Spanish) See George.

Jory (nickname) See Jordan.

José (Spanish) See Joseph, Josiah.

Joseba (Basque) See Joseph.

Josecito (Spanish double) See José+Ito.

Josef (Czech, Dutch, German, Scandinavian) See Joseph.

Joseito (Spanish double) See José+Ito.

Joselito (Spanish double) See José+Ito.

Joseph "He Shall Add" (Hebrew).

Patron Saints: There are over sixty Sts. Joseph. The greatest is St. Joseph, the husband of the Blessed Virgin Mary and foster father of Jesus. The New Testament tells us that Joseph, who was betrothed to Mary, was about to break off their engagement when he found out she was pregnant. But an angel explained everything to Joseph, and God's plan was carried out as prophesied. Very little is known about Joseph, but there are many pious legends surrounding him.

One of the stories insists that he was married at the age of forty years and had six children before his first wife died. One year after her death, when he was ninety, a twelve-year-old named Mary was given to his care by the Temple priests. Two sons and two daughters had already married. Mary helped him raise the last two sons.

The flight to Egypt and work needed to support this family must have been hard. Tradition goes on to say that Joseph died at the age of one hundred eleven when Mary was thirty-three and Jesus was nineteen. A private revelation to Ven. Mary Agreda insists Joseph suffered illness for eight years, gradually becoming bedridden. Finally, he died in the arms of Jesus.

He is patron of families, married couples, laborers, carpenters, candy makers, engineers, pioneers, and the hesitant, as well as of a happy death, house hunting, the universal Church, and to obtain a good wife; he is also considered patron of Austria, Belgium, Canada, China, Korea, Mexico, Peru, and Vietnam, and against Communism and doubt.

Feast Dates: March 19 — St. Joseph, Foster Father of Jesus; May 1 — St. Joseph the Worker.

Josh (nickname) See Joshua, Josiah.

Joshia (variant) See Joshua.

Joshua "Yahweh Saves" (Hebrew form of Jesus).

Patron Saints: Christian tradition gives us one St. Joshua, and the Bible presents the Jewish patriarch Joshua. St. Joshua was the son of Nun, of the tribe of Ephraim, and for many years served as Moses' lieutenant during the desert wanderings. Later he succeeded Moses as the leader. He is an Old Testament foreshadowing of Jesus because he led the Jewish people into the Promised Land.

This last fact points to the best patron, Jesus. The name Jesus is the Greek form of "Joshua."

Feast Dates: September 1 — St. Joshua.

Joshuah (variant) See Joshua.

Josia (Spanish) See Josiah.

Josiah "The Lord Heals" (Hebrew).

Patron Saints: The Bible presents King Josiah, 640-609 B.C., the "third greatest king" ancient Judah ever had. He inherited the throne when he was only eight years old and was very sensitive to the need to serve God from the heart. When he became an adult he ordered the Temple rebuilt, and while this was being done, the Book of Deuteronomy was found. He had the book read to the people and rededicated himself and the people to God.

For thirteen years he worked at religious reformation. However, his reforms never really caught on with most of the masses and the nobles. This sealed Judah's fate, and King Josiah died in a battle against the Egyptian army in 609 when he was only thirty-one.

Feast Dates: June 23 — St. Josiah.

Josias (French, German, Spanish) See Josiah.

Josua (German) See Joshua.

Josue (French, Spanish) See Joshua.

Jourdain (French) See Jordan.

Jovan (Serbian) See John.

Jozef (Polish) See Joseph.

Jozsef (Hungarian) See Joseph.

Jozsias (Hungarian) See Josiah.

Juan "God Is Gracious" (Spanish).

Patron Saints: Juan is the Spanish form of John, which leads to some four hundred twenty-five Sts. John. A North American missionary, SG Father Juan de Padilla, 1492-1540, became the first martyr on future United States soil. This happened on the plains of Kansas, not quite fifty years after the discovery of America. Father Padilla had great success in converting the Quiviras Indians. Then he set out to convert the Kaws (or Kansa Indians), the enemy of the Quiviras. Some of the Quiviras did not want him to preach to their enemies, so they attacked him and his companions. Father Padilla knelt down to receive their arrows, thus giving his companions time to escape. He was forty-eight when he died.

Feast Dates: November 14 — SG Juan de Padilla; December 9 — Bl. Juan Diego (see Diego).

Juanch (Spanish) See Juan.

Juancho (Spanish) See Juan.

Juanito (Spanish double) See Juan+Ito.

Juaquín (Spanish) See Joaquín.

Jud (nickname) See Jude.

Juda (English) See Jude.

Judah (Hebrew) See Jude.

Judas (Greek) See Jude.

Judd (nickname) See Jude.

Jude "The Praised One" (English).

Patron Saints: The Bible mentions about a half-dozen men named Judah or Judas. Christian tradition presents us with three more. The most important of them is St. Jude Thaddeus, one of the Apostles. Most scholars think that he is the author of the Epistle of Jude in the New Testament. He was probably married and had children. This is deduced from the fact that ancient tradition speaks of his grandsons, Zoker and James. Tradition also insists that Jude confined his ministry to the Middle East and that he probably died with St. Simon.

He was long neglected by the faithful because his name was similar to that of the traitor Judas Iscariot. The devotion to him as patron of desperate situations and hopeless cases was begun in a Catholic parish in Chicago during the Depression in the 1930s. He is now also recognized as patron of hospitals.

Feast Dates: October 28 — St. Jude Thaddeus, Apostle.

Judge "The Law Court Presider" (Old English).

Patron Saints: There is one American saint-in-the-making who can serve as a patron. He is SG Father Thomas A. Judge, C.M., 1868-1933. He was born in Massachusetts to a family that prayed together. Thomas wanted to become a missionary to China, but tuberculosis threatened his life and he stayed in America.

He also became convinced that all Catholics should function as missionaries. He preached, gave missions, taught, and founded a lay apostolate organization with this goal in mind. He also founded both a male and a female religious congregation to help him. Often his efforts met with bigotry, opposition, and violence, such as the time he encountered the Ku Klux Klan in Alabama. But he never relaxed his efforts.

Also, it should not be forgotten that God the Father, as Judge of All, can serve as patron.

Feast Dates: November 23 — SG Thomas Augustine Judge.

Judson (English double) See Jude+Son.

Juha (Finnish) See John.

Jule (French) See Julius.

Jules (French) See Julius.

Julian "Belonging to Julius" (Latin, Spanish) or "The Downy-Bearded One" (Latin, Spanish).

Patron Saints: There are over one hundred twenty-five saints named Julian or Julianus. St. Julian the Hospitaler was born in Italy during the Middle Ages. As a young man he left home, without notice, to seek adventure. Soon he had a castle and a bride. When Julian left home his parents grieved and then set out to search for him.

One day they came upon Julian's castle. His wife learned that they were her husband's parents and treated them royally, giving them her own bed to sleep in. The next morning she went to Mass while his parents slept in her bed. Meanwhile Julian returned, saw the couple in his bed, and thought his wife had been unfaithful and he murdered the couple. Finding out he had mistakenly killed his own parents, he wept bitterly and vowed to do penance by serving others. His wife joined him in this activity. Together, they built a hospital for sick travelers and helped those who wished to cross a nearby river. He is now patron of ferry boatmen, travelers, hotelmen, innkeepers, wandering minstrels, and circus people.

Feast Dates: February 12 — St. Julian the Hospitaler.

Julianus (Finnish, German) See Julian.

Juliao (Portuguese) See Julian, Julius.

Julie (variant) See Julius.

Julien (French) See Julian.

Julio (Spanish) See Julius.

Julion (variant) See Julian.

Julius "The Youthful One [Downy-Bearded One]" (Latin) or "The Descendant of Jupiter" (Latin).

Patron Saints: Some one hundred twenty-five saints are named Julius or variants of the name. One St. Julius,

255-302, pursued a glorious career in the Roman army for twenty-six years. At one point he was sent to Dorostorum on the lower Danube River. He also became a Christian and was beheaded.

Feast Dates: May 27 — St. Julius of Dorostorum.

Juma "Born on Friday" (Swahili).

Patron Saints: There is one group of citizens from ancient Alexandria, Egypt, who were actually martyred on Good Friday in 332. This occurred when the apostate prefect ordered a great number of Catholics killed. His battalions of soldiers methodically descended upon the Catholic churches in Alexandria, where they found large groups of Catholics gathered in prayer. Without hesitation, they slaughtered everyone they could find.

Feast Dates: March 21 — Good Friday Martyrs, Alexandria.

Junior "The Younger One" (Latin).

Patron Saints: There are many saints whose names signal "youth," such as Sts. Juvenalis, Juventius, and Juvinus. In addition there is Bl. Junípero Serra, whose first name can also mean "youth" or "junior." However, the greatest saint of them all is often overlooked. He is Jesus the Teenager.

Jesus the Teenager is often overlooked by Christians but not by the Church. In fact, in Nazareth there is a Catholic church dedicated to "Christ the Teenager." Christ, as Teenager, teaches many lessons. The Bible tells us that when Jesus' parents found him in the Temple going about his Father's business, they asked him to come back home, and he was obedient. Tradition further insists that he filled his days learning the carpenter's trade and helped support his family. He also stud-

ied the Bible and learned how to pray. For a long time he was the sole support of his mother, Mary.

Feast Dates: Feast of the Holy Family — Jesus the Teenager; July 1 — Bl. Junípero Serra (see Juniper).

Juniper "The Younger One" (Latin) or "The Juniper Tree" (Latin).

Patron Saints: There are almost a dozen Sts. Juvenal and Juvenalis. However, there is one North American saint whose name, besides meaning the "juniper plant," can also mean "youth" or "younger."

Bl. Junípero Serra, 1713-1784, was born on the island of Majorca. Upon reaching his sixteenth birthday he became a Franciscan, and at the age of twenty-five he was ordained a priest. He longed to go to the New World and teach the Indians, but it was not until 1750, when he was thirty-seven that he finally got to Mexico City. Then for the next ten years he worked with the poor and Indians near Mexico City.

Only at the age of fifty-six did he get a chance to go to California. He immediately founded the Mission of San Diego, his first. For the next thirteen years Father Serra walked thousands of miles, all over California, despite an ulcerated leg. His life was one long martyrdom of labor, loneliness, and sacrifice; but he taught the Indians, provided the sacrament, and is credited with twenty-one missions (although twelve of them were built after his death). He died at the age of seventy-one.

Feast Dates: July 1 — Bl. Junípero Serra, O.F.M.

Junípero (Spanish) See Juniper.
Juozas (Lithuanian) See Joseph.
Jurard (African-American) See Gerard.
Jurgen (German) See George.

Jus (nickname) See Justin, Justus.

Just (nickname) See Justin.

Juste (French) See Justin, Justus.

Justen (French) See Justin.

Justice (English) See Justin.

Justin "The Upright One" (Old French) or "The Just One" (Latin).

Patron Saints: There are about three dozen Sts. Justin and variants of the name, including Sts. Justinianus and Justinus. Among them is St. Justin the Martyr, 105-165. He was the son of a wealthy pagan priest and received a fine education at Ephesus. At one point a wise old man suggested he study the Jewish prophets, who would lead him to Jesus. This he did and he was converted to Christianity at the age of twenty-five.

He immediately began to employ his philosophical background to help preach Jesus and he became the first Christian apologist. He logically answered the objections raised by pagans and heretics. However, his defense of the faith made him many enemies, and he died a martyr's death. He is patron of philosophers.

Feast Dates: June 1 — St. Justin the Martyr.

Justinas (Lithuanian) See Justin.

Justinian (variant) See Justin.

Justino (Spanish, Portuguese) See Justin.

Justinus (Dutch, Scandinavian) See Justin.

Justis (French) See Justin, Justus.

Justo (Spanish) See Justin, Justus.

Justus "The Just One" (Latin).

Patron Saints: There are about seventy saints named Justus. One of them was a disciple of Jesus. He is also known as Joseph Barsabas and was one of two men who were considered to take the place of Judas Iscariot after Judas killed himself. While St. Matthias was chosen instead of him, Justus remained faithful to Jesus and the Catholic Church. He eventually became bishop of Eleutheropolis and died a martyr's death.

Feast Dates: July 20 — St. Justus.

Justyn (Czech, Ukrainian) See Justin.

Jusztin (Hungarian) See Justin.

Juuso (Finnish) See Joseph.

𝒦

Kaapo (Finnish) See Gabriel.

Kacey (variant) See Casey, Casimir.

Kadeem (African-American) See Kedem.

Kahaleel (Arabic) See Kalil.

Kahlil (Arabic) See Kalil.

Kai "The Keeper of the Keys" (Welsh).

Patron Saints: St. Cai was a holy Welsh nobleman in medieval times.

Feast Dates: November 1 — St. Cai.

Kain (English) See Kane.

Kaine (English) See Kane.

Kaiser (German) See Caesar.

Kaleb (variant) See Caleb.

Kalil "The Good Friend" (Arabic).

Patron Saints: Knowing that the name Kalil means "friend" leads to patrons. In Latin the word for "friend" is *amicus*, and there are several Sts. Amicus and Amicia.

Feast Dates: October 12 — St. Amicus (see Dakota).

Kalvin (variant) See Calvin.

Kamaal "The Perfect One" (Arabic).

Patron Saints: Kamaal means "perfect one," which leads directly to St. Perfectus, a priest who served in the Church of St. Asciclus in Cordova, Spain, during the time of the Muslim occupation. He was beheaded after he spoke out against Muhammad in 850.

Feast Dates: April 18 — St. Perfectus.

Kamil "The Church Server [Acolyte]" (Latin) or "The Perfect One" (Arabic variant form of Kamaal).

Patron Saints: This leads to a dozen Sts. Camillus, one of them being St. Camillus de Lellis, 1550-1614, who grew to be more than six-and-a-half feet tall. Being very strong, he joined the Venetian army as a mercenary and fought against the Turks. Wounded in the leg, he ended up being hospitalized. The wound became infected, and he eventually received a military discharge. He returned home and became addicted to gambling, often losing heavily. By the time he was twenty-four, he had lost everything and began begging. He had hit bottom.

He vowed to change his life. Soon he began to devote himself to the sick at the hospital where he had been a patient. In time, he rose to the office of superintendent and, becoming much bothered by the laxity of the hired help, he began recruiting men who wished to serve purely out of love for their fellowmen. Following the advice of his confessor, St. Philip Neri, he started his own religious order to help the sick. He is patron of hospitals, nurses, the sick, and against gambling.

Feast Dates: July 14 — St. Camillus de Lellis.

Kane "The Tribute" (Irish Gaelic) or "The Little Warlike One" (English).

Patron Saints: Even if no saints are actually named Kane, there are others with similar-sounding names, including four Sts. Cain and one St. Keine. St. Cain Comrac served for a period of time as an abbot and as bishop of Louth. In the end, he embraced a solitary life in Ireland. He died in 898.

Feast Dates: July 23 — St. Cain Comrac.

Kaream (African-American) See Kareem.

Kareem "The Noble Exalted One" (Arabic) or "The Much Praised One" (Arabic).

Patron Saints: The meaning of the name is "the noble exalted one." This leads to the Latin word for "noble," which is *nobilis*. For "exalted" it is *laudus*. These words lead us to Sts. Nobilis, Nobilitanus, and Laudus.

St. Laudus was the son of Llewdad, an Armorican (Breton) and the dean of the College of St. Padarn in Cardigan. Then in about 529 Laudus returned to his native Brittany. There, he became the bishop of Coutances.

Feast Dates: September 22 — St. Laudus; April 25 and October 17 — Sts. Nobilis and Nobilitanus (see Noble).

Karel (variant) See Carl, Charles.

Karim (Arabic) See Kareem.

Karl (German, Russian) See Carl, Charles.

Karol (Polish) See Carl, Charles.

Karolek (Polish) See Carl, Charles.

Karolis (Lithuanian) See Carl, Charles.

Karoly (Hungarian) See Carl, Charles.

Karsten (Greek) See Christian.

Kaspar (German) See Casper.

Kato (Latin) See Cato.

Kay "The Rejoicer" (Welsh) or "The Fiery One" (Irish).

Patron Saints: The closest name that comes up is St. Cai, one of the many holy sons of Brychan in medieval Wales.

Feast Dates: November 1 — St. Cai.

Kaycee (American double) See any "K" name+any "C" name.

Kayne (English) See Kane.

Kazimir (variant) See Casimir.

Keanu "A Cool Breeze Over the Mountains" (Hawaiian).

Patron Saints: There are a few saints with similar names such as Sts. Kea and Nuad. Also, knowing that *keanu* means "cool breeze over the mountains" leads to Sts. Zephyrin and Montanus.

Zephyros is Greek for "breeze" and *montanus* is Latin for "mountain."

St. Kea was born in Wales and founded Llangynin in Carmarthen. However, he was driven away by the Welsh and he fled to Cornwall. There he founded another religious house but was soon driven away by the tyrant Tewdrig. Then he fled to Armorica (Brittany) in France. He died in 550.

St. Nuad was archbishop of Armagh, Ireland, from 812 to 816. He also served for a short time as an abbot for a local monastery. He is remembered for his prayerfulness. He died in the 800s.

Feast Dates: October 3 — St. Kea; February 19 — St. Nuad; August 26 — St. Zephyrin (see Zephyrin).

Keary (variant) See Kerry.

Kedem (Hebrew) See Essex.

Keefer (variant) See Kiefer.

Keen (variant) See Keenan.

Keenan "The Little Ancient One" (Irish Gaelic).

Patron Saints: There are about a half-dozen Sts. Keenan. However, they all spelled their names in slightly different ways: Cienan, Kienan, Keine, and Kenan.

St. Kienan, a native of Meath, Ireland, was baptized by St. Patrick. Later in life, he became the bishop of Duleek. He was the first person in Ireland to ever build a church of stone. He died in the sixth century.

Feast Dates: November 24 — St. Kienan.

Keeshon (nickname) See Kieshon.

Keifer (variant) See Kiefer.

Keishon (nickname) See Kieshon.

Keith "From the Forest Hollow" (Old Welsh) or "From the Battle [Windy] Place" (Irish Gaelic).

Patron Saints: There are very few ancient Sts. Keith and they spelled their name as Cetheus, Cethig, and Cethaid. A St. Cetheus was bishop of San Vittorino in southern Italy in about 600. It was his lot to have to face the savage cruelty of the invading Arian Lombards. Falsely accused of being a criminal, he suffered a martyr's death by being drowned in the River Aterno.

And because Keith can also mean "forest," Bl. John Forest may serve as patron.

Feast Dates: June 13 — St. Cetheus, also known as Caetheus; May 22 — Bl. John Forrest (see Forest).

Kekey (African-American) See Henry, Kiki.

Kelcey (English) See Kelsey.

Kele (variant) See Kelly.

Keleman (Hungarian) See Clement.

Kell (nickname) See Kelly.

Kelley (variant) See Kelly.

Kelly "The Warrior" (Irish Gaelic) or "From the Church" (Irish Gaelic).

Patron Saints: There are at least a half-dozen Sts. Kelly. One St. Kelly, 520-545, was the son of the king of Connaught. When he was seventeen, he succeeded to the throne, but a revolt resulted in his ouster. Then in 543, at the age of twenty-three, he became the bishop of Killala. After long service, he retired to Lough Conn. However, his royal lineage was not forgotten by his enemies, and the king of Connaught convinced a cleric at Kelly's monastery to murder him.

Feast Dates: May 1 — St. Kelly McEoghan Beul.

Kelsay (English) See Kelsey.

Kelsey "From the Ship Island" (Old Norse).

Patron Saints: There are a few ancient saints who have names that are very similar: Celsinus, Celsa, and Celsus. St. Celsinus was a priest in France in the 500s. The son of St. Balsamia, he became a disciple of St. Remi of Rheims. He died in 532.

Feast Dates: October 25 — St. Celsinus; February 3 — St. Celsa (see Kelton).

Kelsie (nickname) See Kelsey.

Kelton "From the Keel [Shipbuilding] Town" (Old English).

Patron Saints: There are a few ancient saints with similar names. One, St. Celsa, was from medieval Flanders. She was also probably the niece of St. Berlindis. She is remembered for remaining single and dedicating her life to the service of prayer and charity.

Feast Dates: February 3 — St. Celsa; July 21 — St. Tondach (see Town).

Kelvan (English) See Kelvin.

Kelvin "From the Narrow River" (Irish Gaelic double) or "The Lover of Ships" (Irish Gaelic double).

Patron Saints: Kelvin comes from two words: *kel* ("ships") and *vin* or *win* ("lover" or "friend"). Fortunately, there are several names that can be connected to Kelvin, among them Sts. Cellan, Celer, Winin, Winnian, and Wynnin.

Cellan was a holy Irish priest and Winnian was a Scottish bishop.

Feast Dates: June 17 — St. Cellan McFionnan; July 13 — St. Winnian.

Kelwin (English) See Kelvin.

Ken "The Royal Chief" (Irish Gaelic nickname) or "A Game of Chance" (short form of Keno).

Patron Saints: The word *ken* means "royalty" and is a part of many Irish names. These include Kendall, Kendrick, Kenley, Kennedy, Kenneth, Kent, and Kenton. St. Kendeus suffered martyrdom in ancient Nicomedia.

Feast Dates: January 20 — St. Kendeus.

Kenan "The Enduring One" (Irish Gaelic) or "The White-Haired One" (Irish Gaelic).

Patron Saints: There are a number of Sts. Kenan. One of them was the bishop of Connaught. Later in life, he crossed the Irish Sea and became a disciple of St. Gildas. He became a hermit. He died in Brittany.

Feast Dates: November 3 — St. Kenan Colodok.

Kendal (English) See Kendall.

Kendall "From the Bright+Valley" (Old English double) or "The Royal Chief+ Of Dale" (Old English double).

Patron Saints: Kendall is made up of two words: *ken*, meaning "chief," and *dall*, meaning "dale" or "valley," and this leads to Sts. Kenelm and Dallan. There is also a Bl. John Mason from the town of Kendal.

Feast Dates: December 10 — Bl. John Mason of Kendal (see Mason).

Kendell (English) See Kendall.

Kendrick (English double) See Ken+Rick.

Kenleigh (Irish-English double) See Ken+Leigh.

Kenley (Irish-English double) See Ken+Leigh.

Kenn (nickname) See Kendall, Kendrick, Kenley, Kennedy, Kenneth, Kent, Kenton.

Kennedy "The Helmeted Chief" (Irish Gaelic).

Patron Saints: There is only one saint with a specific connection to Kennedy. He is Bl. Bryan O'Kennedy, 941-1002, the son of the king of Munster. He was well educated and trained in combat and chivalry. At the age of thirty-six he was elected king of Munster. He died in battle in 1002 at the age of sixty-one, fighting against the Norsemen. Because he died fighting against the pagan invaders, he is considered a martyr.

Feast Dates: April 23 — Bl. Bryan Boroimha O'Kennedy.

Kennet (English) See Kenneth.

Kenneth "The Handsome One" (Irish Gaelic) or "The Royal Oath" (Irish Gaelic).

Patron Saints: Kenneth means the same thing as Adonis, "the handsome one." There is one St. Kenneth. He lived the life of a monk, later becoming an abbot and moving to different monasteries many times. After making a pilgrimage to Rome, he became a disciple of Sts. Mobhi and Finnian in Ireland. Later, in Scotland, he founded St. Andrew's and then lived at the monastery of Iona. He died in 599.

Feast Dates: October 11 — St. Kenneth.

Kennett (English) See Kenneth.

Kennet (English) See Kenneth.

Kenney (nickname) See Kendall, Kendrick, Kenley, Kennedy, Kenneth, Kent, Kenton.

Kennith (English) See Kenneth.

Kenny (nickname) See Kendall, Kendrick, Kenley, Kennedy, Kenneth, Kent, Kenton.

Keno "A Game of Chance" (French) or "The Chief" (variant Irish form of Ken).

Patron Saints: There is one American saint-in-the-making who can be pressed into service. The Ven. Eusebio Kino was born in 1645 and grew up in northern Italy and became a Jesuit. In 1681, four years after he was ordained, he sailed for Mexico. In 1683, at the age of thirty-eight, he went to southern California. A year later he went to Arizona. For the next thirty years he ministered to the Indians in the area, teaching them to farm, to care for cattle, to read and write, and to embrace the Catholic faith. And he built churches. He also made forty exploratory expeditions into the Southwest and mapped the region. He did this in order to organize successful routes of communication. He died in 1711 while celebrating Mass.

Feast Dates: March 15 — Ven. Eusebio Kino, S.J.

Kenrick (Old English double) See Ken+ Richard.

Kent "The Bright White One" (Old Welsh).

Patron Saints: The saints available include St. Kentigern Mungo, 518-603, a native of Scotland. He was ordained a priest and did missionary work and was consecrated a bishop. This led to his being driven into exile. While in exile, he founded a monastery. In the end, he was allowed to return from exile, and he made Glasgow the center of his ministries. He died at the age of eighty-five.

There is also Bl. John Ireland of Kent, who was executed by the English government in 1544 because he was a Catholic priest.

Feast Dates: January 13 — St. Kentigern Mungo; March 7 — Bl. John Ireland of Kent (see Erin).

Kenton (English double) See Kent+Town.

Kenyon (Irish Gaelic) See Kent, Kenan, Alban.

Kephas (Greek) See Peter, Rocky.

Ker (nickname) See Kermit.

Kerby (English) See Kirby.

Keresztely (Hungarian) See Christian.

Kerk (English) See Kirk.

Kermie (nickname) See Kermit.

Kermit "The Free Man" (Irish Gaelic).

Patron Saints: There are at least eight Sts. Kermit. In ancient Ireland they spelled their name Diarmaid. St. Kermit the Just served as abbot of Inis Clothrann, Longford. He is remembered for composing a metrical psalter. He died in about 530.

Feast Dates: January 10 — St. Kermit the Just.

Kermy (nickname) See Kermit.

Kerr (nickname) See Kermit.

Kerry "The Dark One" (Irish Gaelic) or "The Dark-Haired One" (Irish Gaelic).

Patron Saints: There is one St. Kerrien and a dozen Sts. Kieran. One St. Kerry, 514-549, built an abbey on the Shannon River with King Diarmaid. It served as "a retreat for the sons of noblemen."

Feast Dates: September 9 — St. Kerry, also known as Kieran.

Kerwin "The Friend+Of the Marshlands" (Old English double) or "The Little Jet-Black One" (Irish Gaelic).

Patron Saints: Two ancient saints can be adopted: Sts. Cura and Winin. St. Cura was born at Muskerry in Ireland. She founded two convents in Ireland during her lifetime. She died in 680.

Feast Dates: October 16 — St. Cura; May 28 — St. Winin (see Win).

Kerwinn (variant) See Kerwin.

Keshon (African-American double) See Kieshon.

Kester (nickname) See Christopher.

Kevan (Irish) See Kevin.

Keven (Irish) See Kevin.

Kevin "The Gentle, Lovable One" (Irish Gaelic).

Patron Saints: There is one St. Kevin, 498-618. He was born into a royal family in Leinster, Ireland, and was educated by the monks. He practiced great self-discipline and grew to love solitude. After being ordained a priest, he withdrew to a cave to live alone. Soon a small group of disciples began to gather around him. He filled his life with prayer and teaching. Near the end of his life he considered making another pilgrimage to Rome but was discouraged by a wise old friend who told him, "Birds do not hatch eggs when they are in flight." He died in 618 at the age of one hundred twenty. Although he is patron of Ireland, he is especially honored as the protector of Dublin.

Feast Dates: June 3 — St. Kevin, also known as Coemgen.

Kevon (Irish) See Kevin.

Keyshon (African-American variant) See Kieshon.

Khalil (Arabic) See Kalil.

Khan (Turkish) See Prince.

Khari (Swahili) See Royal.

Khary (African-American) See Khari.

Khephra (African-American) See Cephas, Rocky.

Khristian (Latvian) See Christian.

Khristjanis (Latvian) See Christian.

Kiefer "The Cooper [Barrelmaker]" (German).

Patron Saints: The fact that the name Kiefer means "cooper" leads directly to patrons because the Catholic Church has named three saints as patrons of coopers, or barrelmakers. They are Sts. Abdon, Nicholas of Myra, and Urban of Langres.

Feast Dates: December 6 — St. Nicholas (see Nicholas); April 12 — St. Urban of Langres (see Urban).

Kiel (variant) See Kyle.

Kienan (Irish) See Kenan.

Kieran "The Little Dark One" (Irish Gaelic).

Patron Saints: Christian tradition provides us with a dozen Sts. Kieran. St. Kieran, 446-530, was born into a noble pagan family at the southernmost point of Ireland. As a young man of thirty, he traveled to Cornwall in England and became a Catholic. Three

years later Kieran returned to Ireland and he met St. Patrick in the royal court of King Aengus, at Cashel. He was ordained a priest and eventually consecrated a bishop. He died when he was eighty-four.

Feast Dates: March 5 — St. Kieran.

Kiernan (Irish) See Kieran.

Kieshon "The Handsome One+God Is Gracious" (African-American single or double).

Patron Saints: The female form of this name, Kiesha, is often thought to be a variant of Kennera, the female form of Kenneth. Thus Kieshon could be accepted as an African-American variant of Kenneth. Furthermore, Kieshon could also be interpreted to be a compound name, Kenneth plus Shaun. Kevin may also be considered.

Feast Dates: October 11 — St. Kenneth (see Kenneth); December 27 — St. John, Apostle (see Sean).

Kijoberto "Born on Monday+The Bright One" (Hispanic-American double of West African-Spanish).

Patron Saints: Two possible patrons come to mind.

Feast Dates: July 1 — St. Lunaire (see Moon); March 26 — St. Bert (see Berto, Bert).

Kiki (Spanish) See Henry.

Kiko (nickname) See Henry.

Kilab (Arabic) See Caleb.

Kile (variant) See Kyle.

Kiley (variant) See Kyle.

Kilian (English) See Killian.

Killian "The Little Warlike One" (Irish Gaelic) or "From the Church" (Irish Gaelic).

Patron Saints: There are a half-dozen Sts. Kilian. One St. Kilian was a priest in Ireland in the late 600s. He had two very good friends: St. Coleman, a priest, and St. Totnan, a deacon. In 686 they decided to go to Franconia, where they converted the local leader, Duke Gozbert. However, the conversion cost them their lives.

It seems that Geilana, the wife of Gozbert, was angry with Kilian because he had asked the duke to part company with her, since there had been a previous marriage. So she had the missionaries killed.

Feast Dates: July 8 — St. Kilian and Companions.

Killie (nickname) See Killian.

Killion (English) See Killian.

Killy (nickname) See Killian.

Kim "The Warrior Chief" (Old English form of Kimball).

Patron Saints: There are almost fifty Welsh and English saints that have Kim in their names. There are also fifteen Korean martyrs with the surname of Kim. Twelve of them are female and three are male. One of these is St. Andrew Kim Tae-gon, the son of one of the first lay catechists and martyrs of Korea. Kim's parents sent him to Macao for studies and ordination. In 1844 the newly ordained deacon Kim sneaked into Korea for a short visit. But he had to be very careful. Leaving Korea again, he was ordained a priest in 1845 and in 1846 was arrested when he tried to reenter his own country. Three months later, after torture, he was beheaded at the age of twenty-six. He is the first native Korean Catholic priest.

Feast Dates: September 20 — St. Andrew Kim Tae-gon.

Kimball "The Warrior Chief" (Old Welsh) or "The Bold Royal One" (Old English).

Patron Saints: The original spelling of Kimball is Cyn-bel, and this leads to almost fifty ancient Welsh and En-

glish saints with similar names. One is St. Cynbryd, who was a son of St. Brychan of Wales. He was slain in battle while defending his country and the faith from the pagan Saxons.

Feast Dates: March 19 — St. Cynbryd.

Kimbell (English) See Kimball.

Kimble (English) See Kimball.

Kimmie (nickname) See Kim, Kimball.

Kimmy (nickname) See Kim, Kimball.

Kin "Little One" (Middle English suffix of endearment like Lambkin) or "A Relative" (Middle English).

Patron Saints: St. Kinath was abbot of Darrow, Kings County, Ireland, in the late 700s.

Feast Dates: August 1 — St. Kinath.

King "The Ruler" (Old English).

Patron Saints: Christian tradition provides us with many saints who ruled as kings. Some very popular ones are: St. Louis, king of France; St. Wenceslaus, king of Bohemia; St. Stephen, king of Hungary. Another way to find patrons of this name is to find saints named King, Roi, Roy, and Rey (which all mean "king"). But in any case, the greatest patron is Jesus Christ, the King of Kings.

Feast Dates: April 24 — St. Mark Rey, also known as Fidelis of Sigmaringen (see Roy); Thirty-fourth Sunday of the Year — Christ the King.

Kingsley (English double) See King+ Leigh.

Kingsly (English double) See King+ Leigh.

Kingston (English double) See King+ Town.

Kino (American) See Keno.

Kinsley (English double) See King+ Leigh.

Kiovani (Hispanic-American double) See any "K" name+Giovanni.

Kip (Scottish) See Kipp.

Kipp "From the Pointed Hill" (Scottish).
Patron Saints: A patron can be found by looking at the meaning of the name, which is "the pointed hill."
Feast Dates: May 4 — Bl. Richard Hill (see Hill).

Kippar (variant) See Kipp.

Kipper (variant) See Kipp.

Kippie (nickname) See Kipp.

Kippy (nickname) See Kipp.

Kirby "From the Church Village" (Old Norse).
Patron Saints: There is one St. Kirby. Also, since both Kirby and Kirk refer to "the Church," another saint, Bl. Richard Kirkman, can serve as a patron.
It was during a time of persecution in 1582 that St. Luke Kirby, a diocesan priest, was arrested, imprisoned, and executed. Luke converted to the Catholic faith and traveled to France to study for the priesthood. Then he went back to England and was arrested immediately. Taken to the Tower of London, he was placed in the "Scavenger's Daughter." This torture device was an iron hoop. The victim was placed inside, in a ball, and squeezed until blood came from his nose, hands, and feet. Then he was hanged.
Feast Dates: May 30 — St. Luke Kirby; May 4 — Bl. Richard Kirkman of Skipton (see Kirk).

Kiril (Bulgarian) See Cyril.

Kirill (Russian) See Cyril.

Kirk "From the Church" (Old Norse).
Patron Saints: There is a saint whose name contains the word *kirk*, and he is an English martyr. In 1582 Bl. Richard Kirkman, a diocesan priest, was arrested, imprisoned, and executed. Born in Yorkshire, he had been educated at Douai, France, and ordained in 1579. Then he went to England to serve as a tutor for the Dymoke family in Scrivelsby. He was killed because he refused to officially recognize Queen Elizabeth I as head of the Church.
Feast Dates: May 4 — Bl. Richard Kirkman of Skipton; May 30 — St. Luke Kirby (see Kirby).

Kirkwood (Old English double) See Kirk+Wood.

Kirwin (variant) See Kerwin.

Kit (nickname) See Christian, Christopher.

Klaudiusz (Polish) See Claude.

Klaus (Danish, German) See Nicholas.

Klavdii (Russian) See Claude.

Klemens (German, Latvian, Polish) See Clement.

Klemensas (Lithuanian) See Clement.

Klement (Czech, Slovakian) See Clement.

Klementos (Greek) See Clement.

Kleon (variant) See Cleon.

Kliment (Bulgarian, Russian) See Clement.

Klymentiy (Ukrainian) See Clement.

Knight "The Cavalry Rider" (Middle English).
Patron Saints: One beatified English martyr might be adopted. His surname, Knight, means the same thing as "rider." In 1596 William Knight, a layman, was arrested for making his home a shelter for priests. He was quickly tried and convicted and then executed by the English government.
Feast Dates: May 4 — Bl. William Knight.

Knoll (nickname) See Knolton.

Knolton "From the Town+On the Round Hill" (Old English double).
Patron Saints: Two saints will make fine patrons.
Feast Dates: May 4 — Bl. Richard Hill (see Hill); July 21 — St. Tondach (see Town).

Knox (Old English) See Hill.
Knut (variant) See Knute.
Knute "The Knot" (Scandinavian).

Patron Saints: St. Knute was born the son of Sweyn III, king of Denmark, and he was also a blood relative to the English monarchy. In time, he succeeded to the Danish throne. He was strongly committed to spreading the Catholic Gospel throughout Denmark. He also had to fight his share of wars.

Although he was very well liked by his people, he was murdered in church in 1086 by a group of malcontents. They were led by his brother, Olaf. Knute is patron of Denmark.

Feast Dates: January 19 — St. Knute, also known as Canute or Knud.
Kodie (American) See Cody.
Kody (American) See Cody.
Kolby (Polish) See Jacob.
Kolos (Hungarian) See Claude.
Kolya (Russian) See Nicholas.
Konrad (German) See Conrad.
Korey "From the Hollow [Valley]" (Irish-Scottish Gaelic) or "From the Heart" (English).

Patron Saints: A couple of saints fit the bill here: St. Corey and another saint from Cori. Furthermore, if one accepts that *cor* is Latin for "heart," then the Sacred Heart of Jesus may act as patron.

St. Thomas of Cori, 1655-1729, worked as a shepherd in Velletri, Italy. When he was twenty, he became an Observant Franciscan. Then he was ordained a priest and spent the next fifty-one years of his life preaching the Gospel and ministering to the inhabitants around Subiaco. He died at the age of seventy-four.

Feast Dates: January 19 — Bl. Thomas of Cori; Friday Following the Second Sunday After Pentecost — Sacred Heart.

Kori (English) See Korey.
Kornel (variant) See Cornell.
Kort (English) See Cort, Courtney.
Kory (English) See Korey.
Kosey (African) See Leo.
Kris (nickname) See Christian, Christopher.
Krisha (variant) See Krishna.
Krishah (variant) See Krishna.
Krishna "The Delightful One" (Hindu).

Patron Saints: Krishna is the name of a Hindu god. Thus it is not associated with Christianity. However, like all other names, it can be Christianized. While there is, as yet, no St. Krishna, it helps to know that the name means "delightful one." In Latin, "delightful" is *dulcedo*. And there are about a half-dozen saints with variants of this name. They are Dulcidius, Dulcissimus, Dulcissima, and Dulcitus.

St. Dulcidius was a bishop in Agen in the mid-to-late 400s. For much of his life he was a disciple of St. Phoebadius. When Phoebadius, the bishop of Agen, died, Dulcidius became bishop.

Remember, God the Father called Jesus his "delight" at the transfiguration on Mount Tabor (or, according to others, Mount Hermon).

Feast Dates: October 16 — St. Dulcidius; August 6 — The Transfiguration of Jesus (see Delight).

Kriss (nickname) See Christian, Christopher.
Kristaps (Latvian) See Christopher.
Kristian (Latvian) See Christian.
Kristof (Slovakian, Hungarian) See Christopher.
Kristofer (Swedish) See Christopher.
Kristoffer (Swedish) See Christopher.
Krizas (Lithuanian) See Christian.
Krys (nickname) See Christian, Christopher.

Krystian (Polish) See Christian.

Kurillos (Greek) See Cyril.

Kurt (nickname) See Conrad, Cort, Courtney, Curtis.

Kurtis (nickname) See Conrad, Cort, Courtney, Curtis.

Kustaa (Finnish) See Gustave.

Kwanza "The First Harvest" (African-American) or "The Firstborn" (African-American).

Patron Saints: The fact that *kwanza* means "firstborn" leads to the finest patron anyone can have. St. Paul teaches that Jesus is "the first-born of all creation" (Colossians 1:15). Being the firstborn of God the Father means the Son is God. Jesus became the firstborn of both God and mankind in order to share this privilege equally with all human beings. The chief benefit of this sharing is the resurrection of the dead. As Jesus rose, so also will all of us.

Sharing in being "firstborn sons" with Jesus, Christians receive a legal right to eternal life in heaven. Each one has the right to receive all that heaven has to give. Christians are called upon to share in being family forever (see Hebrews 12:23).

Feast Dates: All Sundays — Jesus the Firstborn of All Creation; June 9 — St. Primus (see Primo).

Kwasi "Born on Sunday" (African).

Patron Saints: Since we know of no saints named Kwasi, we must look at the meaning, which leads to one saint. St. Sunday is from Campagna, Italy. In 304 she was tortured and finally beheaded.

Feast Dates: July 6 — St. Sunday.

Kweisi "The Very Strong One" (West African).

Patron Saints: Like Kweisi, Brian also means "strong one," which points us to a patron with a similar name.

Feast Dates: April 23 — Bl. Bryan Boroimha O'Kennedy (see Kennedy).

Ky (nickname) See Kyle.

Kye (nickname) See Kyle.

Kyev (African-American) See Kevin.

Kyle "From the Strait" (Irish) or "The Handsome One" (Irish).

Patron Saints: There is one St. Kyle, a female, and it helps to know that Kyle can mean "handsome." This is the same meaning of the Irish name Kenneth. St. Kyle was also known by the name of Kennocha. She was a Scottish religious sister who belonged to a convent in Fife. She died in 1007.

Feast Dates: March 25 — St. Kyle of Fife; October 11 — St. Kenneth (see Kenneth).

Kylie (variant) See Kyle.

Kyros (Greek) See Cyrus.

Kyrylo (Ukrainian) See Cyril.

Labhrainn (Scottish) See Lawrence.

Labhras (Irish) See Lawrence.

LaBron (African-American) See Bronson.

Lad (nickname) See Ladd, Ladislaus, Latimer.

Ladarius (African-American double) See La+Darius.

Ladd "The Attendant [Youth]" (Middle English) or "The Famous Ruler" (nickname for Ladislaus).

Patron Saints: Because a lad is a "male youth," one is led to the patron of youths.

Feast Dates: June 21 — St. Aloysius Gonzaga (see Luigi); May 4 — Bl. Antony Page (see Page).

Ladde (Scottish) See Ladd.

Laddie (nickname) See Ladd, Ladislaus, Latimer.

Laderrick (African-American double) See La+Derrick.

Ladey (nickname) See Ladd, Ladislaus, Latimer.

Ladimer (variant) See Latimer.

Ladislaus "The Famous Ruler" (Slavic form of Walter).

Patron Saints: Among the half-dozen Sts. Ladislaus is a king, 1040-1095, who inherited the throne of Hungary. He accepted the kingship out of a sense of duty. Among his closest allies was Pope Gregory VII. He often found himself called upon to make war, but he also showed great charity, and he granted religious liberty to the Jews and Muslims in his kingdom. When Pope Urban need help for the First Crusade he turned to Ladislaus. The kings of France, Spain, and England elected him commander-in-chief, but his service was brief. He died suddenly while at Nitra in Bohemia at the age of fifty-five.

Feast Dates: June 27 — St. Ladislaus, also known as Laszlo.

Ladislav (Czech) See Ladislaus.

Lafayette "From the Beech Tree Grove" (French).

Patron Saints: Since Lafayette is not a saint's name, we must consider something similar, which leads us to three ancient Sts. Fay (also known as Faith). One, a teenager, was arrested and brought before a pagan judge in about 250. First, he asked her name. She signed herself with the cross and answered, "My name is Faith, and I will try to live as I have been named." He demanded she offer sacrifice to the pagan goddess Diana, which she refused to do. Then he ordered that she be tied to a red-hot bed and killed.

Feast Dates: October 6 — St. Faith of Agen; July 10 — St. Etto, also known as Hetto (see Ett).

Lafe (nickname) See Lafayette.

Lafredo (Spanish) See Alfred.

Laith (nickname) See Latham.

Lakota (variant) See Dakota.

Lal "The Beloved Boy" (Sanskrit).

Patron Saints: Lal has the same meaning as Ladd and can share its patron.

Feast Dates: June 21 — St. Aloysius Gonzaga (see Luigi).

Lalo (nickname) See Edwin.

Lamar "Famous Throughout the Land" (Old German) or "The Dweller by the Sea" (French).

Patron Saints: There is one saint with a similar name: St. Lamanus. Furthermore, the fact that Lamar means "famous" leads to a dozen Sts. Clarus, since the Latin word *clarus* means "famous." Moreover, because Lamar can also mean "by the sea," one can turn to the half-dozen Sts. Maris and Mares.

Feast Dates: May 25 — Bl. Clare Voglia (see Clare); July 19 — Bl. Maris (see Marley).

LaMarr (African-American) See Lamar.

Lambert "From the Bright Land" (Old German) or "The Fair Lamb" (English).

Patron Saints: There are about a dozen Sts. Lambert. One of them, St. Lambert, 636-708, became bishop of his hometown. However, in 675, when his friend King Childeric II was murdered, Lambert was banished to a monastery for six years. Because of political intrigue by many factions around him, he was marked for death. One day while he was praying before the altar, he was pierced by a javelin. He was seventy-two years old.

Feast Dates: September 17 — St. Lambert, O.S.B.

Lamberto (Italian) See Lambert.

Lammond (English) See Lambert.

Lamond "The Lawman [Lawyer]" (English) or "A Man of the Land" (Irish) or "The World" (French).

Patron Saints: This name leads to a North American martyr, St. Gabriel Lalemant, S.J., 1610-1649, who became a Jesuit priest and went to French Canada to minister to the Indians. In 1649, while in the village of St. Ignace with Father Jean de Brébeuf, the Iroquois attacked. Both were taken prisoner along with many Hurons.

The French missionaries were subjected to one of the most horrific tortures ever devised by man. According to the Jesuit *Relations*, a collection of annual reports, "Before their death ... these barbarians feasted on them. ... While still full of life, pieces of their thighs, calves, and arms were removed by the butchers who roasted them on coals and ate them in their sight."

Father Lalemant was only thirty-nine years old and had worked among the Hurons for only six short months.

Also, the Catholic Church has named five saints as patrons of lawyers. They are Sts. Catherine of Alexandria, Genesius, Ivo Helory of Kermartin, Raymond of Peñafort, and Thomas More.

Feast Dates: October 19 — St. Gabriel Lalemant, S.J.; June 22 — St. Thomas More (see Morley).

Lamont (Scandinavian) See Lamond.

Lance (nickname) See Lancelot.

Lancelot "The Attendant" (English) or "The Server" (Old French).

Patron Saints: Lancelot can mean "server," which leads to about a dozen Sts. Servatius and Servatus. St. Servatius, 338-384, was born into a Jewish family in Armenia. Upon growing up he converted to Catholicism and eventually became a bishop. He took an active part in repelling the Arian heresy. His stand with the truth caused him a great deal of trouble with the local rulers.

Some experts also think Lancelot is an alternate form of Ladislaus.

Feast Dates: May 13 — St. Servatius; June 27 — St. Ladislaus, also known as Laszlo (see Ladislaus).

Land "From the Land" (Old English).

Patron Saints: The name Land means just that: "land." This leads to St. Lando, an abbot and then in 731 the bishop of Rheims.

Feast Dates: January 16 — St. Lando; October 19 — St. Gabriel Lalemant, S.J. (see Lamond).

Landan (variant) See Landon.

Landbert (German) See Lambert.

Landel "The Dweller in the Valley+Land" (Old English double).

Patron Saints: There is one St. Landel and about a dozen saints with very similar names. St. Landel, 625-686, was born of a noble Frankish family and early in life fell in with robbers. However, the sudden death of one of his robber friends caused him to take another look at life, and he converted to Jesus. Then he made three pilgrimages to Rome and became a priest. Later he became a monk and a hermit.

Feast Dates: June 15 — St. Landel, also known as Landelin.

Lander (Old English double) See Land+Er.

Lando (Spanish) See Orlando.

Landon (Old English double) See Land+Town.

Landry (Old English double) See Land+Drystan.

Lane "From the Narrow Road" (Middle English).

Patron Saints: There are two saints who can qualify as patrons. One has a similar name, while the other does not. In addition, there is the finest patron of them all: Jesus Christ, the Narrow Way.

St. Frances Lanel, 1745-1798, was a member of the Ursulines in France during the French Revolution. She insisted on teaching the children their religion, which was contrary to the orders of the revolutionaries. She was guillotined.

Feast Dates: June 26 — St. Frances Lanel; September 25 — Bl. William Way of Devon (see Wayland).

Laney (nickname) See Lane.

Lang "The Long Narrow One" (Old English) or "The Tall Thin One" (Scandinavian).

Patron Saints: There is one Bl. Richard Langley. A gentleman from Yorkshire, he was hanged in 1586 in York for sheltering Catholic priests in his home.

Feast Dates: December 1 — Bl. Richard Langley.

Langdon (Old English double) See Lang+Town.

Langford (Old English double) See Lang+Ford.

Langley (Old English double) See Lang+Leigh.

Langsdon (Old English double) See Lang+Town.

Langston (Old English double) See Lang+Town.

Lanie (nickname) See Lane.

Lannie (nickname) See Landel, Landon, Lawrence, Orlando, Roland.

Lanny (nickname) See Landel, Landon, Lawrence, Orlando, Roland.

Lanz (Italian) See Lance.

LaQuarius "Born Under the Sign of Aquarius" (African-American).

Patron Saints: Aquarius is the "water carrier" and St. Matthew the Apostle is credited with giving "holy water" to the Church.

Feast Dates: September 21 — St. Matthew (see Matthew).

Larenzo (Italian, Spanish) See Lawrence.

Larkin (Scandinavian) See Lawrence.

Larnell (African-American double) See Larry+Darrell/Terrell.

Larrance (English) See Lawrence.

Larrie (nickname) See Lawrence.

Larry (nickname) See Lawrence.

Lars (Scandinavian) See Lawrence.

Lash (Romany) See Louis.

Lashon (African-American double) See La+Shawn.

Lat (nickname) See Latimer.

Latavious (African-American double) See La+Travis.

Latham "From the Barns" (Old Norse).

Patron Saints: It helps to know that the word for "barn" in Latin is *horreum*. There is one St. Horres. He and his companions met their deaths as martyrs for Jesus in ancient Rome.

In French the word for "barn" is *grange*, and a barn is cared for by a "granger" or "farmer." The Catholic Church has appointed Sts. Isidore, George Sidwell, and Walstan as patrons of farmers.

Feast Dates: March 13 — St. Horres; May 15 — St. Isidore the Farmer (see Isadore).

Lathan (African-American double) See La+Nathan.

Lathe (variant) See Latham, Lathrop.

Lathrop "From the Barn [Farmstead]" (Old English).

Patron Saints: The patrons for Lathrop are the same ones for Latham.

Feast Dates: March 13 — St. Horres; May 15 — St. Isidore the Farmer (see Isadore).

Lathrope (variant) See Lathrop.

Latimer "The Interpreter" (Middle English).

Patron Saints: There is one saint who worked as a translator-interpreter much of his life.

Feast Dates: February 9 — Bl. Marianus Scotus (see Marian).

Lattie (nickname) See Latimer.

Latty (nickname) See Latimer.

Laughton (variant) See Lawton.

Launce (variant) See Lancelot.

Launo (Finnish) See Nicholas.

Laurance (English) See Lawrence.

Laureano (Spanish) See Lawrence, Loren.

Lauren (nickname) See Lawrence, Loren.

Laurence (English) See Lawrence.

Laurencio (Spanish) See Lawrence.

Laurenço (Portuguese) See Lawrence.

Laurens (Dutch) See Lawrence.

Laurent (French) See Lawrence.

Laurentius (Latin) See Lawrence.

Laurenz (German) See Lawrence.

Lauri (Finnish) See Lawrence.

Laurie (nickname) See Lawrence.

Laurits (Danish) See Lawrence.

LaVar (African-American double) See Lamar+Vernon.

Lavern (variant) See Vernon.

Lavon (African-American double) See La+Vaughn.

Lavrentij (Russian) See Lawrence.

Law (nickname) See Lawford, Lawson, Lawton, Lawrence, Lawyer.

Lawanza (African-American double) See La+Kwanza.

Lawford (Old English double) See Law+Ford.

Lawrance (English) See Lawrence.

Lawrence "The Laurel-Crowned One" (Latin).

Patron Saints: There are about forty Sts. Lawrence. The most famous was a Spanish deacon who was martyred in Rome in 258. When Pope Sixtus and most of the Roman clergy were put to death by Emperor Valerian, Lawrence was spared for three extra days. The emperor hoped Lawrence would reveal where the Church treasure had been hidden. But when asked, Lawrence presented him with the poor of Rome, declaring, "These are the treasures of the Church."

The angry emperor ordered that Lawrence be killed by slow roasting. While roasting on the gridiron, he simply informed his torturer he "was done on this side and was ready to be turned over." Then he died. He is patron of cooks, librarians, the poor, of Ceylon, and against lumbago and fire.

Feast Dates: August 10 — St. Lawrence, Deacon.

Lawrency (variant) See Lawrence.

Lawry (nickname) See Lawrence.

Lawson (Old English double) See Lawrence+Son.

Lawton (Old English double) See Law+Town.

Lawyer "The One Trained in the Law" (Middle English).

Patron Saints: There is no St. Lawyer. However, the name Lawyer means "one trained in the law," and the Church has named five saints as patrons of lawyers. They are Catherine of Alexandria, Genesius, Ivo Helory, Raymond of Peñafort, and Thomas More.

Feast Dates: June 22 — St. Thomas More (see Chauncey, Morley); May 19 — St. Ivo Helory (see Yves).

Lay (nickname) See Latham, Lathrop.

Lazar (nickname) See Lazarus.

Lazare (French) See Lazarus.

Lazaro (Italian, Spanish) See Lazarus.

Lazarus "God Will Help" (Hebrew, English).

Patron Saints: There are over a dozen Sts. Lazarus. The most famous is Jesus' friend and the brother of Martha and Mary of Bethany. When Lazarus died, Jesus wept and then raised him from the dead. According to one story, after Jesus was executed, his enemies tried to get rid of Lazarus by putting him and his sisters in a leaky boat and set adrift at sea. However, they survived. Later, Lazarus was consecrated a bishop by all the Apostles in concelebration. He ruled as a bishop of Marseilles for thirty years. He is patron of gravediggers.

Feast Dates: July 29 — St. Lazarus of Bethany.

Lazer (nickname) See Lazarus.

Lazlo (Hungarian) See Roarke, Ladislaus.

Leander "The Lionlike One" (Greek).

Patron Saints: There are about a half-dozen Sts. Leander. One became a Benedictine monk and later an abbot. Between 579 and 582 he fell into disfavor with the king and went into exile. He returned to Spain just in time to be sent into exile again for another year. He also insisted that the Nicene Creed be recited at every Mass. One of his great victories was the conversion of the Spanish Visigoths to the Catholic Church who were brought into the Church by the sheer force of his logic. He died in 596.

Feast Dates: February 27 — St. Leander, O.S.B.

Leandre (French) See Leander.

Leandro (Italian, Spanish) See Leander.

Leao (Portuguese) See Leo.

Ledell (African-American double) See Le+Delbert/Dell.

Lee (nickname) See Leander, Leigh, Leland, Lemar, Leo, Leon, Leonard, Leroy, Leslie.

Leeland (Old English double) See Leigh+Land.

Leeroy (variant) See Leroy.

LeGrande (French) See Grant.

Leicester (English) See Lester.

Leif (Scandinavian) See David.

Leigh "From the Meadow" (Old English) or "The Poetic One" (Irish Gaelic).

Patron Saints: One English saint, Bl. Richard Leigh, 1561-1588, was born in London and traveled to Rheims and Rome to study for the Catholic priesthood. He was ordained in 1586 in Rome and was sent to the English missions.

He often used aliases such as Bart, Garth, and Earth. However, he was soon caught and banished from the country, but he immediately returned. He was arrested again and was sentenced to be hanged, drawn, and quartered at Tyburn. He was executed at the age of twenty-seven.

It should be noted that Leigh, under the short forms of Lee, Ley, and Ly, forms the second syllable of a great many English names and always means "from the meadow." Examples of such names include Ashley, Raleigh, and Wesley.

Feast Dates: August 30 — Bl. Richard Leigh.

Leland "From the Meadow+Land" (Old English double) or "From the Church Place" (Old English).

Patron Saints: Leland comes from two words: *ley* (or *leigh*), meaning "meadow," and *land*, meaning "land." One North American saint makes a fine patron. He is St. Jean de Lalande, one of a group of laymen who volunteered to serve the missionaries in Canada. They acted as carpenters, hunters, woodsmen, guides, and tradesmen. St. Jean de Lalande volunteered to take Father Jogues to the Indians, very well aware of the great danger. Sure enough, he and Father Isaac Jogues were taken captive by the Mohawks in 1646. First, the Indians killed Jogues with a tomahawk and then did the same to Lalande the following day.

Feast Dates: October 19 — St. Jean de Lalande; January 16 — St. Lando (see Land).

Lem (nickname) See Lemuel.

Lemar (variant) See Lamar.

Lemmie (nickname) See Lemuel.

Lemmy (nickname) See Lemuel.

Lemuel "The One Belonging to the Lord" (Hebrew).

Patron Saints: The Bible presents one man named Lemuel. Surprisingly, Lemuel is given as a symbolic name for King Solomon.

Feast Dates: June 17 — St. Solomon (see Jedidiah).

Len (nickname) See Lenox, Leonard.

Lenard (Hungarian) See Leonard.

Lenart (variant) See Leonard.

Lencho (Spanish) See Lorenzo, Lawrence.

Lenci (variant) See Lawrence.

Lennard (English) See Leonard.

Lennart (Scandinavian) See Leonard.

Lennie (nickname) See Lenox, Leonard.

Lennox (Scottish Gaelic) See Lenox.

Lenny (nickname) See Lenox, Leonard.

Lenox "From the Land of the Elms" (Scottish Gaelic).

Patron Saints: The fact that the first part of the name means "land" leads to many patrons.

Feast Dates: January 16 — St. Lando (see Land); June 15 — St. Landel (see Landel).

Lenz (Swiss) See Lawrence.

Leo "The Lion" (Latin) or "The Lionlike One" (short form of Leander) or "Brave As a Lion" (short form of Leonard).

Patron Saints: There are about fifty Sts. Leo. One of them, St. Leo the Great, is one of only three popes to be given the title "The Great." His reign was the second most important in antiquity. As pope, Leo faced the Pelagian, Manichaean, Monophysite, and Priscillianist heresies. He wrote a dogmatic letter teaching how Christ had two natures and he directed the proceedings of the Council of Chalcedon. Then he issued a Sacramentary to standardize Catholic worship. Hundreds of his sermons are still extant.

On the home front, he found he had to stand alone against the barbarian invasion of Attila the Hun. When Attila approached Rome with his armies, Leo met him and pleaded for the city, and the barbarian granted Pope

Leo's request. He is a Doctor of the Church.

Feast Dates: November 10 — St. Leo I, also known as Pope St. Leo the Great.

Leobardo (Spanish) See Leonard.

Leon (French, Slavic, Spanish, Irish) See Leo, Leonard.

Leon (nickname) See Napoleon.

Leonard "The One Brave As a Lion" (Old German).

Patron Saints: There are about a dozen Sts. Leonard. One was born into a rich, noble French family and raised in the court of King Clovis I. He became a monk and, in time, evangelized Gascony. He also founded the Noblac monastery and he became a hermit. He is patron of childbirth, prisoners of war, the insane, against robbery, and of horses as well as other domestic animals.

Feast Dates: November 6 — St. Leonard of Noblac.

Leonardo (Italian, Spanish, Portuguese) See Leonard.

Leonardus (Dutch) See Leonard.

Leonas (Lithuanian) See Leo.

Leone (Italian) See Leo.

Leonel (Spanish) See Leo.

Leonerd (English) See Leonard.

Leonhard (German) See Leonard.

Leonid (Russian) See Leonard.

Leonidas (Spanish) See Leonard.

Leonon (Czech, Slovakian) See Leo.

Leopold "The Patriot" (Old German).

Patron Saints: There are two Sts. Leopold. One of them, St. Leopold IV, ruled Austria in the 1100s and was very good to the Church. He died in 1136.

Feast Dates: February 15 — St. Leopold IV.

Leopoldo (Spanish) See Leopold.

Leos (Czech, Slovakian) See Leo.

LeRoi (variant) See Leroy.

Leroy "The King" (Old French).

Patron Saints: Christian tradition provides us with many saints who ruled as kings. Some very popular ones are St. Louis, king of France; St. Wenceslaus, king of Bohemia; and St. Stephen, king of Hungary.

Another way to determine a patron is to find a person named King. In French that would be Roi. In Spanish, Rey. And there is a St. Roys, who is simply remembered as an ancient "Ethiopian saint."

But, of course, the greatest patron of them all is Jesus, who is "Christ the King."

Feast Dates: July 20 — St. Roys; April 24 — St. Mark Rey, also known as Fidelis of Sigmaringen (see Roy).

Les (nickname) See Lester.

Lesley (variant) See Leslie.

Leslie "From the Gray Fortress" (Scottish Gaelic) or "The One Who Leases" (English).

Patron Saints: The meaning of Leslie, "gray fortress," leads to two patrons.

Feast Dates: May 16 — St. Fort; Thirty-fourth Sunday of the Year — Jesus, Our Fortress (see Garrison).

Lesly (variant) See Leslie.

Lester "From the Chosen Camp" (Latin).

Patron Saints: Lester is a form of Sylvester, and there are a dozen Sts. Sylvester. St. Sylvester, the pope, sent representatives to the first ecumenical council in 325. Because he reigned during the first period of peace granted the Church in three hundred years, his pontificate saw the building of many new churches and of the basilicas of St. Peter and St. John Lateran. He died in 335.

Feast Dates: December 31 — St. Sylvester I.

Levar (African-American) See LaVar.

Levi "The One Joined in Harmony" (Hebrew).

Patron Saints: There is one Catholic St. Levi and, of course, the Bible presents us with St. Levi, the great Jewish patriarch, who was the source of the Jewish priesthood. The Catholic St. Levi is remembered as a disciple of the Apostles. He preached the Gospel at Phainos in Caesarea Philippi.

Feast Dates: November 1 — St. Levi.

Levin (variant) See Levi.

Levon (variant) See Levi.

Levy (variant) See Levi.

Lew (nickname) See Louis, Llewellyn.

Lewelyn (variant) See Louis, Llewellyn.

Lewie (nickname) See Louis.

Lewis (English) See Louis, Llewellyn.

Lex "The Lawful One" (Latin, English) or "The Helper of Mankind" (nickname for Alexander).

Patron Saints: Since Lex is a nickname for Alexander, one can choose from over a hundred Sts. Alexander.

Feast Dates: August 11 — St. Alexander the Charcoal Burner (see Alexander).

Lexie (French) See Alexander.

Lexy (French) See Alexander.

Lezlie (variant) See Leslie.

Liam (Irish) See William.

Lico (Spanish) See Frederick.

Lienhard (Swiss) See Leonard.

Lionardo (variant) See Leonard.

Lile (variant) See Lyle.

Lilo (nickname) See Cyril.

Lin (variant) See Lyndon, Lynn.

Linc (nickname) See Lincoln.

Lincoln "From the Colony by the Pool" (Old English).

Patron Saints: Two saints are officially identified as coming from Lincoln, England. One was Bl. Roger Dickenson of Lincoln. He studied for the priesthood and was ordained in 1583 and then went to the English missions. He was put to death by the English government in 1591 because he was a Catholic priest.

Feast Dates: July 7 — Bl. Roger Dickenson of Lincoln; November 17 — St. Hugh of Lincoln (see Hugh).

Lind (nickname) See Lindell, Lindsey, Lynn.

Lindell "From the Linden Tree+Valley" (Old English double).

Patron Saints: A few saints with similar names can be adopted as patrons.

Feast Dates: May 3 — St. Ethelwin of Lindsey (see Lindsay); August 28 — Bl. William Dean (see Dean).

Linden (variant) See Lyndon.

Lindon (variant) See Lyndon.

Lindsay "From Linden Tree Island" (Old English) or "From Lincoln's Island" (Old English).

Patron Saints: There is one patron whose name can be connected to Lindsey. He is St. Ethelwin, bishop of Lindsey in the 700s, who was a devoted friend of St. Egbert. It also helps to know that Lindsey arises out of Lincoln, which makes two more saints available: Bl. Roger Dickenson of Lincoln and St. Hugh of Lincoln.

Feast Dates: May 3 — St. Ethelwin of Lindsey; November 17 — St. Hugh of Lincoln (see Hugh).

Lindsey (variant) See Lindsay.

Lindy (variant) See Lyndon.

Link (nickname) See Lincoln.

Linn (nickname) See Lynn.

Linus "The Flaxen-Haired One" (Greek).

Patron Saints: There are only a handful of Sts. Linus. St. Linus, the second pope, 64-76, was born in Tuscany. He is mentioned in the New Testament in 2 Timothy 4:21. It is argued whether or not he suffered martyrdom. It is well known that he preached the Gospel in Rome.

Feast Dates: September 23 — St. Linus, Pope.

Linzy (English) See Lindsay.

Lion (English) See Leo.

Lionel "The Lion Cub" (Old French) or "The Lionlike One" (variant of Leo).

Patron Saints: There are about one hundred saints named Leo, Leobard, Leonard, Leonianus, Leonidas, Leoninus, and Leonius. All can serve as patrons for Lionel.

Feast Dates: November 10 — St. Leo I (see Leo); November 6 — St. Leonard (see Leonard).

Lionell (variant) See Lionel.

Lionello (Italian) See Lionel.

Lisle (variant) See Lyle.

Lito (nickname) See Carlito.

Ljudvig (Russian, Ukrainian) See Louis.

Llewellyn "The Lionlike One" (Welsh) or "The One Like Lightning" (Welsh).

Patron Saints: There is one St. Llewellyn. And there are a few others with similar names, including Sts. Llywel and Llywen. St. Llewellyn was a medieval Welshman. He was the father of two saints, St. Gwenerth and Gwyddfarch. His brother, Mabon, has also been declared a saint. St. Mabon was a monk and founder of the monastery at Bardsey in Trallwm. Today that community is known as Welshpool.

Feast Dates: April 7 — St. Llewellyn, also known as Llywelin.

Lloyd "The Gray-Haired One" (Welsh).

Patron Saints: There are two Sts. Lloyd, and both are English martyrs. Bl. Richard Flower (alias Lloyd), a layman, was executed in 1588 for helping a Catholic priest.

St. John Lloyd, a diocesan priest, was ordained on the Continent and immediately traveled to England. Twenty years later, in 1678, he was accused of violence in the phony Oates Plot (or Popish Plot) and was tried, convicted, and executed in 1679.

Feast Dates: May 4 — Bl. Richard Flower, also known as Lloyd; July 22 — St. John Lloyd.

Llywellyn (variant) See Llewellyn.

Llywelyn (variant) See Llewellyn.

Lobo (Spanish) See Wolf.

Lodewijk (Dutch) See Louis.

Lodovico (Italian) See Louis.

Logan "From the Little Meadow" (Irish Gaelic).

Patron Saints: St. Logan was of Irish royalty, born in the late 400s to early 500s. He was born the son of Cormac, king of Leinster. After he was ordained he served for a while at Disert Illadhan in Ireland. Today this is known as Castle Dillon. In about 549 he crossed the Irish Sea to Cornwall. A little over ten years later, in about 560, he traveled to Brittany, where he probably worked as a missionary. He died at Cornwall.

Feast Dates: February 2 — St. Logan (or Illogan) of Dillon.

Lohn (variant) See Lon.

Lon "The Strong, Fierce One" (Irish Gaelic).

Patron Saints: Besides being a name in its own right, Lon can also serve as a nickname for Lawrence, Alphonse (or Alonso), and Mahlon. This leads to many patrons. In addition, there are a half-dozen Sts. Lon. One of them, St. Lon of Cillgobhra, is simply remembered as an "Irish saint."

Feast Dates: June 24 — St. Lon of Cillgobhra; July 15 — Bl. Alphonsus de Baena (see Alphonse).

Longino "The Tall One" (Spanish).

Patron Saints: There are over a dozen Sts. Longinus. The most famous is St. Longinus the Centurion, who witnessed the death of Jesus on the cross and the miracles that accompanied it. He soon after returned to his native Cappadocia and preached the Gospel. He was killed by some Jews.

Feast Dates: October 16 — St. Longinus.

Lonnard (variant) See Leonard.

Lonnie (nickname) See Alphonse/Alonso, Lawrence, Leonard, Lon, Mahlon.

Lonnt (nickname) See Alphonse.

Lonny (nickname) See Alphonse, Alonso, Lawrence, Leonard, Lon, Mahlon.

Lope (Spanish) See Wolf.

Loral (variant) See Lawrence [through Laurel].

Lorant (variant) See Lawrence.

Loren "The Laurel-Crowned One" (short form of Lawrence).

Patron Saints: Loren is a short form of Lawrence. St. Loran was a priest who ministered around County Mayo, Ireland, in the 450s. He was a disciple of the great St. Patrick.

Feast Dates: August 30 — St. Loran.

Lorencho (variant) See Lorenzo, Lawrence.

Lorenjo (variant) See Lorenzo, Lawrence.

Lorens (Scandinavian) See Lawrence.

Lorenz (German) See Lawrence.

Lorenzo (Italian, Spanish) See Lawrence.

Lorimer "The Harness Maker" (Latin).

Patron Saints: Sts. Lucy and Wolfhard have been declared patrons of saddlers by the Catholic Church. St. Wolfhard was a successful German merchant and saddler. He moved to Verona in 1098 and made it his particular mission to give all the money he had to the poor. The locals looked upon him as a living saint, and this made him very uncomfortable. So he moved away and became a hermit for a short time. Then someone suggested that he enter a nearby monastery. He did and he stayed there the rest of his life.

Feast Dates: April 30 — St. Wolfhard.

Lorin (nickname) See Loren, Lawrence.

Lorinc (Hungarian) See Lawrence.

Loring "The Son of+Famous Warrior" (Old German double).

Patron Saints: Loring and Louis mean the same thing, and there are two dozen Sts. Louis.

Feast Dates: August 25 — St. Louis IX, King (see Louis).

Lorrie (variant) See Lawrence, Lorimer, Loring.

Lorrimer (variant) See Lorimer.

Lorry (variant) See Lawrence, Lorimer, Loring.

Lotario (Spanish, Italian) See Lothair.

Lothair "From the Famous Army" (Old German).

Patron Saints: Although there seems to be no St. Lothair, there are several with similar names, including two Sts. Luthard and two Sts. Lothar. One St. Lothar was born in Lorraine and was educated at the royal court in Paris. He married, but after his wife died he chose not to marry again. Instead, he donned a penitential habit and embraced the life of a hermit, giving himself to a life of prayer. He died in 756.

Feast Dates: June 15 — St. Lothar.

Lothaire (French) See Lothair.

Lothar (German) See Lothair.

Lothario (variant) See Lothair.

Lou (nickname) See Louis.

Louie (nickname) See Louis.

Louis "The Famous Warrior" (English).

Patron Saints: There are two dozen Sts. Louis. The best known is St. Louis IX, 1214-1270, king of France. He was a deeply religious man who prayed every day and is remembered as a mild, just, and chivalrous ruler. He would not tolerate either vulgarity or profanity and was a friend of the clergy. He often invited St. Thomas Aquinas to his home. He also endowed many pious foundations and had the Sainte Chapelle built in Paris to house relics of Jesus' cross and crown of thorns. He is patron of button makers, marble workers, masons, sculptors, Third Order members of religious orders, and wig makers.

Feast Dates: August 25 — St. Louis IX, King.

Lovell (variant) See Lowell.

Lovre (Croatian) See Lawrence.

Lowe (nickname) See Barlow, Lowell.

Lowell "The Little Beloved One" (Old French) or "The Little Wolf" (Old French).

Patron Saints: A patron is available in Bl. John Lowe, who was executed in 1586 for being a diocesan Catholic priest.

Feast Dates: May 4 — Bl. John Lowe.

Lowrance (variant) See Lawrence.

Loy (variant) See Lloyd.

Loyal "The One Who Remains Faithful" (Old French).

Patron Saints: The Latin word for "loyal" is *fidelis*. This leads to a few patrons.

Feast Dates: April 24 — St. Mark Rey, also known as Fidelis of Sigmaringen (see Roy).

Loyd (variant) See Lloyd.

Loydie (variant) See Lloyd.

Luc (French) See Luke.

Luca (Italian) See Luke.

Lucais (Scottish) See Luke.

Lucas (Latin, Dutch) See Luke.

Luce (variant) See Luke.

Lucho (variant) See Louis.

Lucian (English) See Luke.

Luciano (Italian) See Luke.

Lucias (variant) See Luke.

Lucien (French) See Luke.

Lucio (Spanish) See Luke.

Lucius (Latin) See Luke.

Luck (English) See Luke.

Lucky "The Good Fortune" (Middle English) or "The Bringer of Light" (English form of Luke).

Patron Saints: Some experts suggest that Lucky comes from Lucius or Luke. This makes two dozen patrons available. Others would emphasize its meaning of "good fortune," which leads to at least fifty Sts. Fortunatus.

One St. Fortunatus was known as "The Philosopher of the Lombards" because of his great knowledge.

Feast Dates: June 18 — St. Fortunatus; October 18 — St. Luke (see Luke).

Ludis (Latvian) See Louis.

Ludlow "From the Prince's Hill" (Old English) or "The Famous Warrior" (English form of Louis).

Patron Saints: Because Ludlow can be recognized as a form of "Louis," two dozen Sts. Louis are available.

Feast Dates: August 25 — St. Louis IX (see Louis).

Ludovic (Scottish) See Louis.

Ludovicus (Latin) See Louis.

Ludvig (Scandinavian) See Louis.

Ludvik (Czech) See Louis.

Ludwig (German) See Louis.

Ludwik (Polish) See Louis.

Lugaidh (Irish) See Louis.

Luigi "The Famous Warrior" (Italian).

Patron Saints: St. Aloysius Gonzaga's real first name was Luigi. He was born to a father who wanted him to be a soldier. However, that life with its rough talk and manners was not for him. Nor were the political obligations, and he searched for a better way. When he was thirteen years old he became convinced that he should become a Jesuit. But his father disagreed.

Eventually his father gave his permission and Luigi became a novice at the age of seventeen. He filled his time with prayer, self-discipline, and study, and often became ecstatic and joy-filled. But it was not to last. When a plague struck in 1591, Luigi volunteered to help at the hospital. While tending the sick and doing the menial tasks assigned to him, he caught the plague and died.

Feast Dates: June 21 — St. Aloysius Gonzaga, S.J.

Luis (Spanish) See Louis.

Luither (variant) See Luther.

Luiz (Spanish, Portuguese) See Louis.

Lukas (German, Scandinavian, Czech) See Luke.

Luke "The Bringer of Light" (English) or "The One from Lucania" (Greek).

Patron Saints: There are two dozen saints named Luke. The most famous is the Evangelist who lived from about 10 B.C. to A.D. 74. A Greek pagan physician with an excellent education, he converted to Christianity in Antioch. The Bible tells us that he collected the testimonies of those who had known Jesus and from these accounts wrote the Gospel of Luke and the Book of Acts. Christian tradition adds that Luke never married and may have died a martyr — by crucifixion beside Andrew. He may also have painted a picture of the Blessed Mother and Jesus. He is patron of butchers, doctors, glassworkers, goldsmiths, lace makers, notaries, painters, physicians, and sculptors.

Feast Dates: October 18 — St. Luke, Evangelist.

Lute (variant) See Luther.

Lutero (Spanish) See Luther.

Luthais (Scottish Gaelic) See Louis.

Luther "From the People's Army" (Old German).

Patron Saints: Luther arises out of Lothair. Thus the patron of Lothair can also serve Luther.

Feast Dates: June 15 — St. Lothar (see Lothair).

Lutherio (variant) See Luther.

Luto (variant) See Luther.

Lutrell (African-American double) See Louis+Terrell.

Lutz (variant) See Louis.

Ly "From the Meadow" (Old English form of Leigh) or "From the Island" (nickname for Lyle).

Patron Saints: There is one St. Lyle. He worked as a shepherd at Meon near the River Meuse in France.

Feast Dates: September 14 — St. Ly; August 30 — Bl. Richard Leigh (see Leigh).

Lydell (Old English double) See Ly+Dell.

Lyel (variant) See Lyle.

Lyell (variant) See Lyle.

Lyle "From the Island" (Old French).

Patron Saints: There is one St. Lyle. He was a disciple of Sts. Dyfrig and Theilo in medieval Wales.

Feast Dates: November 1 — St. Lyle, also known as Llywel.

Lyman (Middle English double) See Ly+Mann.

Lyn (variant) See Lyndon, Lynn.

Lyndon "From Linden Tree Hill" (Old English) or "The Cheerful One" (variant of Lynn or Alan).

Patron Saints: Lyndon's patron is St. Dona of Llandona. Dona was the son of Selyf Sarffgadau, king of Powys. He became a monk at Bangor, Deiniol. Then he moved to Anglesey. For a period of time, he also worked in Brittany. Another saint with the similar name of Lynn can also be adopted.

Feast Dates: November 1 — St. Dona of Llandona; August 11 — St. Lynn (see Lynn).

Lynn "From the Pool Below the Waterfall" (Old Welsh) or "From Linden Tree Hill" (nickname for Lyndon).

Patron Saints: There is one St. Lynn, and a half-dozen more patrons appear if one realizes that Lynn can be a short form of Alan. Lynn lived in medieval Wales. He is patron of Llanllwni, Carmarthen.

Feast Dates: August 11 — St. Lynn, also known as Llwni; November 1 — St. Dona of Llandona (see Lyndon).

Lynne (variant) See Lynn.

Lyon (English) See Leo.

Lysander "The Liberator" (Greek).

Patron Saints: St. Liberator was the first bishop of Ariano, Italy, in ancient times.

Feast Dates: May 15 — St. Liberator.

Mac (Scottish) See Mack.

Macadam (Scottish Gaelic) See Mac+Adam.

MacArthur (Scottish) See Mac+Arthur.

MacAulay (Scottish Gaelic) See Macauley.

Macauley "Son of+Olaf [Ancestral Relic]" (Scottish Gaelic).

Patron Saints: There are a few saints whose names can be derived from Macauley. One of them, St. Maccallin, was an Irishman who made a pilgrimage and then entered the Benedictine abbey of Gorze before becoming a hermit. Later, he gathered followers around him and became an abbot. He died in 978.

Feast Dates: January 21 — St. Maccallin, O.S.B.

Macdonald (Scottish Gaelic) See Donald.

Mace (variant) See Mason.

Mack "Son of" (Scottish Gaelic) or "Mr. [Mister]" (English).

Patron Saints: There are about a hundred saints with names that begin with Mc, Mac, or Max. Among them is St. Mac Erc, who served as the bishop of Donoughmore, Ireland, in the 400s.

Feast Dates: July 6 — St. Mac Erc.

Mackenzie "The Son of+The Wise Leader" (Scottish Gaelic).

Patron Saints: Some patrons can be found only by adopting saints with similar names. It is helpful to know that *mac* means "son of" and *ken* means "chief." This leads the searcher to two saints with similar names: Sts. Mac Erc and Kendeus.

Feast Dates: July 6 — St. Mac Erc (see Mack); January 20 — St. Kendeus (see Ken).

Macknair (Scottish Gaelic) See Macnair.

MacLaine (Scottish Gaelic) See Mac+Lane.

MacLane (Scottish Gaelic) See Mac+Lane.

Macnair "The Son of+The Heir" (Scottish Gaelic).

Patron Saints: There is one saint with a very similar name. A St. MacNersi ruled the abbey of Clonmacnoise in Ireland as a holy abbot in the late 500s.

It is also helpful to remember that the name Jared means "inheritor," the same as Macnair.

Feast Dates: June 13 — St. MacNersi; March 1 — St. Jared (see Jared).

Maddie (nickname) See Madison.

Maddy (nickname) See Madison.

Madison "Son of+Maud [Powerful Warrior]" (Middle English double) or "Son of+Matthew [Gift of God]" (Middle English double).

Patron Saints: It is helpful to know that the name Madi means "powerful warrior" while Son means "son." Thus Sts. Maden and Sontius may be adopted. For centuries St. Maden has been remembered at the place where he lived as a hermit. It is said that healings still take place at a well on this site. It is called St. Maden's Well in Cornwall.

Feast Dates: November 1 — St. Maden of Holywood; November 17 — St. Sontius (see Son).

Madre "Mother [or Source or Origin]" (Spanish).

Patron Saints: St. Madron was a holy abbot in Cornwall. He died in 540.

Feast Dates: May 17 — St. Madron.

Mahlon "The Weak One" (Hebrew).

Patron Saints: The Book of Ruth names Mahlon as a son of Emilech and Naomi. He may have been the husband of Ruth, who left her a widow.

A saint with a similar name, St. Malard, may be pressed into service. He was a bishop of Chartres, France, in 700.

Feast Dates: January 15 — St. Malard.

Mahmud (Arabic) See Muhammad.

Mahomet (Arabic) See Muhammad.

Maison (French) See Mason.

Maje (variant) See Major.

Major "The Greater One" (Latin).

Patron Saints: There are a half-dozen saints named Major, Majorianus, and Majoricus. When the Vandal barbarians invaded Northern Africa in 484, they murdered thousands. The Vandals were Arian heretics and hated all Catholics. Thus it was that a young boy named Majoricus, his mother, his aunt, a doctor friend, a monk, a nobleman, and the bishop of Sibido died together. As death approached, Majoricus's mother urged her son to be brave and remain faithful so that, together, they might inherit eternal life.

Feast Dates: December 6 — St. Major, also known as Majoricus.

Maksymilian (Polish, Ukrainian) See Maximilian.

Mal (nickname) See Malachy, Malcolm, Malik, Mallory, Melvin.

Malachi (variant) See Malachy.

Malachy "God's Messenger [Angel]" (Hebrew).

Patron Saints: Two Sts. Malachy exist. Christian tradition provides one and the Bible provides the other. The biblical patron is Malachy, the Jewish prophet,

450-325 B.C. His Bible writing is concerned with Jewish law and proper worship in the Jewish Temple. Jewish tradition identifies him as Esdras the Priest.

Feast Dates: November 3 — St. Malachy of Armagh.

Malcolm "Follower of Columba [Dove]" (Scottish Gaelic).

Patron Saints: Two ancient, holy Scottish kings bear the name of Malcolm. They both lived in about 400.

Feast Dates: June 3 and December 3 — both Sts. Malcolm.

Malcolmb (variant) See Malcolm.

Malik "The Master" (Arabic).

Patron Saints: While the name Malik means "master," and Master was a favorite title used for Jesus in the New Testament, it is simply a term that recognizes that Jesus is "the Boss." He is the Lord and King.

The Old Testament insisted that Yahweh was the King of Israel. Thus it is not surprising to discover that the New Testament just as strongly insists that the Son of God is Master, Lord, and King. Furthermore, his kingdom is not built on politics, power, or force. Rather, the kingdom of heaven is built on vulnerability, sacrifice, charity, and service of others. Jesus' kingship is life and love. It is built on the creating of "home" and "belonging" for everyone.

To be called to reign with Christ is not a call to be a boss or to give orders. It is simply a call to share life, love, belonging, and "at-homeness" with God and with all our loved ones forever.

Feast Dates: Thirty-fourth Sunday of the Year — Christ the King.

Mallory "The Army Counselor" (Old German) or "The Armored Knight" (Old French).

Patron Saints: There are a couple of ancient saints with very similar names, such as St. Malo. A member of the famous ancient Theban Legion in the Roman army, he was martyred in 287.

Feast Dates: October 10 — St. Malo; September 22 — St. Maurice (see Maurice).

Malvin (variant) See Melvin.

Manco (Spanish-Inca) See King.

Mandel "The Almond" (German).

Patron Saints: One saint with a very similar name is St. Mandalicus, a martyr in ancient Tripoli. There is also an English martyr whose name, meaning "almond," reflects the meaning of Mandel.

St. John Almond was a native of Allerton in England. Because of the anti-Catholic sentiment prevalent at the time, he had to travel to France to study for the priesthood. He was ordained in 1598 and worked in the English missions from 1602 to 1612. Then he was caught by the English government and put to death.

Feast Dates: June 10 — St. Mandalicus; December 5 — St. John Almond.

Mando (Spanish) See Herman.

Manfred "The Man+Of Peace" (Old English double).

Patron Saints: Manfred comes from *man* (meaning "man") and *fred* (meaning "peace" or "friend"), and there is one known Bl. Manfred. He was from Milan, Italy, and after he was ordained a priest in about 1200, he gave himself to a life of prayer as a hermit. In addition, a dozen Sts. Frederick can also be adopted as patrons for Manfred.

Feast Dates: February 28 — Bl. Manfred; July 18 — St. Frederick (see Frederick).

Mango (Spanish) See Emmanuel, Manuel.

Manley (Old English double) See Mann+Leigh.

Mann "The Man" (German).

Patron Saints: St. Manius was the thirtieth bishop of Verona, Italy, in the fifth century.

Feast Dates: September 3 — St. Manius.

Mannie (nickname) See Mann, Manny.

Mannix "The Monk" (Irish).

Patron Saints and Feast Dates: There are countless monks that have been declared saints and honored on various dates of the year.

Manny (nickname) See Emmanuel, Hyman, Mandel, Manfred, Sherman, Wyman, Mann.

Mano (variant) See Emmanuel.

Manólon (Spanish) See Emmanuel.

Mansfield (Old English double) See Mann+Field.

Manue (Spanish) See Emmanuel.

Manuel (Spanish) See Emmanuel.

Mar (nickname) See Marcel, March, Marion, Mark, Marley, Marlon, Marlow, Marshall, Martin, Marvin.

Marc (French) See Mark.

Marcel (French) See Marcellus.

Marcello (Italian) See Marcellus.

Marcellus "The Little Warlike One" (Latin) or "The Little Hammer" (Latin).

Patron Saints: There are more than sixty saints named Marcellinus and Marcellus. In 304 the reigning pope was killed and for the next four years no one could decide on a new pope. Finally, Marcellus was elected. He immediately set out to reorganize and set standards for the Church. First, he divided the Roman Church into twenty-five local parishes. Then he established guidelines for readmitting fallen-away Catholics. After being pope for one year, he was sent into exile and he died a short time later.

Feast Dates: January 16 — St. Marcellus I.

Marcelo (Spanish) See Marcellus.

March "The Guardian of the Boundary" (Old English-Old French).

Patron Saints: The closest patron is St. Marchelm, although Sts. Marcellus and Marcelinus can also be pressed into service. St. Marchelm was an Anglo-Saxon who followed St. Willibrord to Holland. There he worked to evangelize the people. Sometime later he accompanied St. Boniface to Rome. He was martyred in 762.

Feast Dates: July 14 — St. Marchelm.

Marchelm (variant) See March.

Marciano (Italian) See Martin.

Marco (Italian, Spanish) See Mark.

Marcos (Spanish) See Mark.

Marcus (Czech, Polish) See Mark.

Mareece (African-American) See Maurice.

Marek (Czech, Polish) See Mark.

Maria (Latin) See Mary.

Marian (Polish) See Mark.

Mariano (Italian, Spanish) See Mark.

Marie (French) See Mary.

Marin (French) See Marino.

Marino "The Sailor" (Italian).

Patron Saints: The following qualify, since they are all patrons of sailors: Sts. Cuthbert, Brendan, Eulalia, Christopher, Peter González, Erasmus, and Nicholas.

Feast Dates: December 6 — St. Nicholas of Myra (see Nicholas).

Mario (Italian, Latin, Spanish) See Marino, Mark.

Marion "Like Mary [The Bitter One]" (French).

Patron Saints: The finest patron for anyone named Marion, Marian, or Mariano is the Blessed Virgin Mary. However, there are male saints, named after the Mother of God, who can be called upon. One is Bl. Marianus Scotus, O.S.B., 1045-1088, who in his twenties set out with some friends to make a pilgrimage to Rome. They got as far as Regensburg. There, Marianus was employed by the abbess Emma to transcribe books for her. He was a most skillful and industrious scribe and he copied all manner of texts, from the Bible to spiritual writings. Often, he would provide free texts for poor clerics and widows.

Being an author and a poet, he also composed some religious texts himself. Among them, some think, is the Epistle to the Laodiceans. This text is a skillful, pious intertwining of quotes from many of St. Paul's letters as found in the Bible. Marianus never did get to Rome. But he did become very famous for his dedication to sacred literature.

Feast Dates: February 9 — Bl. Marianus Scotus, O.S.B.

Mariono (Spanish) See Mary.

Marius (Latin) See Mark.

Mark "The Warlike One" (Latin) or "The Little Hammer" (Latin).

Patron Saints: There are some sixty-five saints named Mark or Marcus. The most famous is St. Mark the Evangelist. He converted after the resurrection of Jesus and traveled with Sts. Paul and Barnabas. Later, he became a secretary to St. Peter. The Gospel of Mark, which he wrote, is a collection of the memories of St. Peter.

Peter sent Mark to Egypt as the bishop of Alexandria. The pagans thought he was a magician and caught him while celebrating Mass in the year 68. They tied him up, dragged him through the streets, threw him into prison, and the next day tortured him to death.

He is patron of cattle breeders, notaries, and glaziers, as well as of Venice and against fly bites.

Feast Dates: April 25 — St. Mark, Evangelist.

Markese (French) See Marquis.

Markku (Finnish) See Mark.

Marko (Serb, Croatian, Ukrainian) See Mark.

Markos (Greek) See Mark.

Markus (Danish, Dutch, German, Swedish) See Mark.

Marley "From the Meadow+Near the Sea [Lake]" (Old English double).

Patron Saints: It is good to know that Marley is composed of two parts: *mar*, meaning "sea," and *ley*, meaning "meadow." This leads to many Sts. Maris, among whom one was a missionary bishop in the first century and is known as the Apostle to Assyria and Babylonia.

There is also a saint that can be pressed into service as a patron here. He is St. Theobald (also known as Thibaud), who was born in the castle of Marly, thus his name.

Feast Dates: July 19 — St. Maris; July 27 — St. Theobald of Marly (see Theobald).

Marlin (variant) See Marlon.

Marlo (variant) See Marlow.

Marlon "The Little Falcon" (Old French) or "The Hawk" (Old French).

Patron Saints: The closest we can come to Marlon are a couple of Sts. Merin. Furthermore, knowing that the name Marlon or Merlin means "falcon" leads to a few more possibilities.

Between 1225 and 1227, seven men from Florence, Italy, joined a confraternity dedicated to the Blessed Virgin. Alexis Falconieri was one of them.

Soon Mary appeared to all seven of them to ask their help. Thus they came to support a single religious goal and founded the Servite religious congregation. All became saints. St. Alexis, a brother, outlived them all. He died at the age of one hundred ten.

Feast Dates: February 17 — St. Alexis Falconieri.

Marlow "From the Hill+Near the Lake" (Old English double).

Patron Saints: There is one saint who is just perfect for the job of patron. He is St. Thomas of Hereford of Great Marlow, 1218-1282. He had the privilege to study in both Oxford and Paris. In 1261 he became chancellor of Oxford and four years later became chancellor of all England under King Henry III. But he was soon turned out of office and returned to Oxford.

In 1275, at the age of fifty-seven, he became bishop of Hereford and served for seven years. He died on a trip to Rome to appeal his excommunication by the archbishop of Canterbury. In the end, his personal holiness and pastoral zeal outweighed his short temper and he was canonized a saint.

Feast Dates: October 2 — St. Thomas of Hereford of Great Marlow.

Marlowe (variant) See Marlon.

Marly (variant) See Marley.

Marmaduke "The Stronger One" (German).

Patron Saints: Marmaduke Bowes, a layman, was arrested for helping Catholic priests. He was tried, convicted, and executed in 1585.

Feast Dates: May 4 — Bl. Marmaduke Bowes.

Marquan (African-American double) See Mark+Quan.

Marquel (African-American) See Marcellus.

Marques (Portuguese) See Mark.

Marquis "The Count of the Borderlands" (Middle Latin) or "The Warlike One" (Portuguese form of Mark).

Patron Saints: If one accepts Marquis as a form of Mark, then over sixty-five patrons become available. If one accepts it as a royal title equivalent to "Count," then another dozen patrons emerge. Finally one can search for a patron based on the name's meaning, and another patron appears.

Feast Dates: April 25 — St. Mark, Evangelist; July 14 — St. Marchelm (see March).

Marquise (African-American) See Mark, Marquis.

Marsalis (Italian) See Marcellus.

Marsh (nickname) See Marshall.

Marsh "From the Marshland" (Middle English).

Patron Saints: It is helpful to know that the Old English word for "marsh" is *fenn*, and this leads to a patron.

Feast Dates: February 12 — Bl. James Fenn (see Fenton).

Marshal (English) See Marshall.

Marshall "The Steward" (Old French) or "The Horse Keeper" (Old French).

Patron Saints: There are four Sts. Marchell and Marchelm, names that are similar to Marshall. One of them, St. Marchell, was a sister to Sts. Teyrnog, Deifer, Tudur, and Tyfrydog, and a daughter of St. Arwystli Gloff. All lived in medieval Wales.

Also, in Cologne, Germany, four saints are specially honored as stewards of the diocese. Called the Four Holy Marshals, they are Sts. Anthony Hermit, Cornelius, Quirinus of Neuss, and Hubert.

Feast Dates: September 5 — St. Marchell.

Marshawn (African-American double) See Mark+Shawn.

Mart (nickname) See Martin.

Martainn (Scottish Gaelic) See Martin.

Marten (English) See Martin.

Martez (Spanish) See Martin.

Marti (Spanish) See Martin.

Martial (French) See Mark.

Martie (nickname) See Martin.

Martijn (Dutch) See Martin.

Martin "The Warlike One" (Latin).

Patron Saints: Almost three dozen Sts. Martin can be called upon to serve as patrons. One of them was St. Martín de Porres, 1579-1639, of Lima, Peru. He became a religious and joined the Friars Preachers as a brother. He functioned as a barber, surgeon, wardrobe-keeper, and infirmarian. He also extended his care to the sick and poor in the city and worked to establish an orphanage and a foundling hospital. He took upon himself the care of the poorest and African slaves, and he practiced self-discipline and carried out sacrifices.

During his life, Martín was a good friend of St. Rose of Lima and St. John Massias. He died at the age of sixty years. He is patron of blacks, hairdressers, the poor, public health workers, people of mixed race, social justice, and of Peruvian television.

Feast Dates: November 3 — St. Martín de Porres, O.P.

Martínez (Spanish) See Martin.

Martiniano (Spanish) See Martin.

Martino (Italian) See Martin.

Marto (Spanish) See Martin.

Marty (nickname) See Martin.

Martyn (variant) See Martin.

Marv (nickname) See Marvin.

Marve (nickname) See Marvin.

Marven (variant) See Marvin.

Marvin "The Famous Friend" (Old English) or "The Sea Friend" (Old English) or "From the Ridge" (English).

Patron Saints: There is no known St. Marvin. However, Marvin comes from the following: *mar* (or *mer*), which means "sea," and *vin* (or *win*), which means "lover" or "friend." This leads directly to Sts. Maris and Winnin.

Feast Dates: July 19 — St. Maris (see Marley); May 28 — St. Winnin (see Win).

Marwin (variant) See Marvin.

Mary "The Bitter One" (Hebrew).

Patron Saints: It is the custom in many nations to give the name of Mary, Maria (María), or Marie as a second name to their sons. This is done to honor the Blessed Virgin. Thus many male saints bear the name of Mary.

Feast Dates: August 14 — St. Maximilian Mary Kolbe (see Maximilian).

Mason "The Stoneworker" (Old English).

Patron Saints: Two saints may serve as patrons for Mason. The first is St. Peter the Apostle, who is officially recognized as the patron of stoneworkers (masons). The other is a little-known saint named Bl. John Mason. He was born in Kendal, Westmorland, England, in the mid-1500s. A layman, he was arrested and condemned to death for attending Mass and helping the Catholic priests. He was executed with three diocesan priests and another layman in 1591.

Feast Dates: December 10 — Bl. John Mason of Kendal; June 29 — St. Peter, Apostle (see Peter).

Massey (nickname) See Thomas.

Massimiliano (Italian) See Maximilian.

Massimo (French) See Maximilian.

Mat (nickname) See Matthew.

Mata (Scottish) See Matthew.

Matej (Bulgarian, Slovenian) See Matthew.

Mateo (Spanish) See Matthew.

Mateusz (Polish) See Matthew.

Mathe (German) See Matthew.

Matheu (German) See Matthew.

Mathew (Hebrew) See Matthew.

Mathian (variant) See Matthew.

Mathias (German, Swedish) See Matthew.

Mathieu (French) See Matthew.

Mathis (variant) See Matthias, Matthew.

Matías (Spanish) See Matthias.

Mats (Swedish) See Matthew.

Matson (English double) See Matthew+ Son.

Matt (nickname) See Matthew.

Mattaus (German) See Matthew.

Matteo (Italian) See Matthew.

Matteus (Scandinavian) See Matthew.

Matthaeus (Danish) See Matthias, Matthew.

Matthaus (variant) See Matthias, Matthew.

Mattheus (Dutch) See Matthias, Matthew.

Matthew "The Gift of the Lord" (Hebrew, English).

Patron Saints: There about two dozen Sts. Matthew. Ancient Christian tradition tells us that St. Matthew the Apostle wrote his Gospel in Aramaic between the years 60 and 70. Matthew suggested the use of "holy water" as a holy sign. Also, Matthew preached in Judea for fifteen years and made many converts. Then he traveled to the East, to Persia. There is much confusion as to how and where he died.

He is patron of accountants, bookkeepers, bankers, customs officials, security guards, stockbrokers, and tax collectors.

Feast Dates: September 21 — St. Matthew, Evangelist.

Matthias "The Gift of the Lord" (Hebrew, Finnish).

Patron Saints: There about a dozen saints named Matthias. The most famous is the Apostle who was elected to fill the vacancy caused by Judas. Christian tradition insists that Matthias performed sacrifices and practiced self-discipline in order to control his sensual appetites. Then he traveled to Cappadocia, where he suffered martyrdom.

One ancient legend insists that Matthias was crucified soon after he was elected to fill the vacancy left by Judas. This necessitated the calling of another election. St. Paul was elected the second time. At best, this "election story" can only be classified as a legend.

St. Matthias is patron of the Holy Cross Fathers and of alcoholics and against alcoholism.

Feast Dates: May 14 — St. Matthias, Apostle.

Matthieu (variant) See Matthew.

Matthiew (variant) See Matthew.

Matti (Finnish) See Matthew.

Mattias (Swedish) See Matthias, Matthew.

Mattie (nickname) See Matthew.

Matty (nickname) See Matthew.

Matvei (Russian) See Matthew.

Matyas (Czech, Hungarian) See Matthias, Matthew.

Mauri (Finnish) See Maurice.

Maurice "The Dark-Skinned One" (Late Latin).

Patron Saints: There about twenty Sts. Maurice. The most famous was an officer who died a martyr in the Theban Legion. In about 287 the Bagaudae in Gaul revolted against Rome. Emperor Maximian marched against them with his army. One unit of it, the Theban Legion, was composed entirely of Christians. Just before joining battle, Maximian ordered all members of the army to sacrifice to the gods, praying for success. The Theban Legion refused to do this at the request of its officers.

Maximian ordered that every tenth man be killed. This was done. Then it was done a second time. Maximian threatened that they all would die unless they offered the sacrifice. The soldiers replied that they were loyal to the emperor, but they could not worship false gods, for they had taken an oath.

Maximian ordered that the legion be cut to pieces. This was done without resistance. The legionnaires, with their weapons in their hands, allowed themselves to be martyred for Christ. In all, about six thousand men died for Jesus.

St. Maurice is patron of infantrymen, sword makers, weavers, dyers, and people with cramps, as well as of Savoy and Sardinia.

Feast Dates: September 22 — St. Maurice and Companions.

Mauricio (Spanish) See Maurice.

Maurie (nickname) See Maurice.

Maurise (variant) See Maurice.

Maurits (Danish, Dutch) See Maurice.

Maurizio (Italian) See Maurice.

Maury (nickname) See Maurice.

Maurycy (Polish) See Maurice.

Maverick "One Who Strays [Not Conforms]" (English).

Patron Saints: A maverick was an animal that was owned by one person but had strayed and was then claimed by a second owner. This perfectly describes the sinner's poor condition. By straying from the path of righteousness, he distanced himself from God's protection and was claimed by the devil. Fortunately for him, God sees the rounding up of the strays as his most important job. Among those gathered by God are the souls in purgatory. We pray for them now, and they return the favor later.

Feast Dates: November 2 — The Poor Souls in Purgatory.

Mavriki (Russian) See Maurice.

Max "The Most Excellent One" (Latin) or "The Greatest One" (Latin).

Patron Saints: Although there seems to be no saint named Max, there are over a hundred Sts. Maximus. Among them is an ancient Roman martyr.

Feast Dates: January 24 — St. Maximus.

Maxi (Spanish) See Max, Maximilian.

Maxie (nickname) See Max, Maximilian, Maxwell.

Maxim (nickname) See Max, Maximilian, Maxwell.

Maximilian "The Most Excellent One" (Latin).

Patron Saints: There are almost a dozen Sts. Maximilian. Among them is St. Maximilian Kolbe, 1894-1941. In 1910, at the age of sixteen, he joined the Franciscans and began studying for the priesthood. After ordination, in 1918, he founded the Knights of the Immaculate to help young people remain chaste. In 1920 he became ill with tuberculosis and had to go into a sanatorium for two years. There he gave himself to prayer. In 1939 he was arrested by the Gestapo for the first time and then released. In 1941 he was arrested again and sent to Auschwitz. He was singled out for constant abuse because he insisted on being Catholic.

Whenever a prisoner escaped, the Nazis would arbitrarily pick ten inmates to be tortured and executed. Shortly after one of these escapes, a Polish soldier, who had a wife and family, was chosen to be killed with nine others. Father Kolbe volunteered to take the man's place. His request was granted and the priest was led off to be starved to death with nine companions. He filled the time with prayer, comforting his companions the best he could. After two weeks without food or water he was injected with carbolic acid. Father Kolbe was only forty-seven at the time of his death.

Feast Dates: August 14 — St. Maximilian Mary Kolbe.

Maximiliano (Spanish) See Max, Maximilian.

Maximilianus (Dutch) See Max, Maximilian.

Maximilien (French) See Max, Maximilian.

Maximino (Spanish) See Max, Maximilian.

Maximo (Spanish) See Max, Maximilian.

Maxwell "From Large+Spring" (Old English double) or "From the Great Man's+Well" (Old English double).

Patron Saints: Maxwell is a combination of two words, Max meaning "great," and Well meaning "a well." No patrons named Maxwell seem to exist, but there are more than one hundred twenty-five saints named Sts. Maximus, as well as St. Swithin Wells, an English martyr. St. Swithin Wells, 1536-1591, was an English gentleman who was arrested for sheltering a priest. As he was awaiting execution his executioner taunted, "See what your priests have brought you to!" He replied, "I am happy to have had so many priests under my roof." Wells was then hanged. He was fifty-five.

Feast Dates: December 10 — St. Swithin Wells; January 24 — St. Maximus (see Max).

May (variant) See Maynard.

Mayer (variant) See Major.

Mayhew (Old French) See Matthew.

Maynard "The Brave, Powerful One" (Old German).

Patron Saints: There are only two saints known to have been named Maynard. One lived in the eleventh century and was coincidentally the eleventh bishop of Urbino, Italy. In this office, he was in a position to assist Pope Nicholas II call and hold a Roman synod. Apparently, he died of old age.

Feast Dates: May 9 — St. Maynard.

Mayne (variant) See Maynard.

Mayolo (Spanish) See Major.

Mayor (variant) See Major.

Mayorico (Spanish) See Major.

Mazer (Hispanic-American) See Marcellus.

Mc (Irish Gaelic) See Mack.

McAulay (variant) See Macauley.

McCauley (variant) See Macauley.

McLean (Scottish Gaelic) See Mac+Leander.

Medardo (Spanish) See Maynard.

Medwin "The Strong Friend" (Old English).

Patron Saints: Medwin is made from two words: *med*, meaning "strong," and *win*, meaning "friend." In the Catholic Church there is a St. Meddwidd, who is remembered for being a prayerful Welsh saint, and there is a St. Winin.

Feast Dates: November 1 — St. Meddwidd; May 28 — St. Winin (see Win).

Meical (Welsh) See Michael.

Meiers (variant) See Meyers.

Meirs (variant) See Meyers.

Mel (variant) See Melbourne, Melville, Melvin.

Mel "The Chieftain" (Irish Gaelic).

Patron Saints: St. Patrick's sister, Darerca, came to Ireland to help her brother. She seems to have done this job very well, but in her own way. First, she

married Restitutus. Their children included Sts. Sechnall, Nectan, Auxilius, and Diarmaid. After Restitutus died, she married Conis. To them were born sons: Sts. Mel, Rioc, Muinis, and Moelchu (Melchu). All four sons became bishops. They also had two daughters: Sts. Eiche and Lalloc.

Melchu and Mel both helped their uncle in his missionary effort. Melchu became bishop of a church located near Kilkenney, Ireland, and Mel seems to have become bishop of Ardagh. He supported himself by farming. And what he earned, beyond the bare necessities, he shared with the poor.

A humorous story is told how once, when St. Patrick visited him, Mel prayed and then miraculously picked live fish off the ground. Patrick was impressed but then told Mel that, in the future, he should do his fishing in the sea like everybody else.

Feast Dates: February 6 — Sts. Mel and Melchu.

Melborn (English) See Melbourne.

Melbourne "From the Mill+Stream" (Old English double).

Patron Saints: There is no St. Melbourne, but it helps to know that the words *mel* and *bourne* mean "mill" and "stream" respectively. There is a St. Mel as well as a Bl. Thomas Welbourne.

Feast Dates: August 1 — Bl. Thomas Welbourne (see Bourne); February 6 — Sts. Mel and Melchu (see Mel).

Melburn (English) See Melbourne.

Melchior (Hebrew) See King.

Meldrick (African-American double) See Melvin+Dedrick.

Melville "From the Estate+Hard Worker" (Old French double).

Patron Saints: Mel can be a short form of Melville. Thus Sts. Mel and

Melchu can serve can as patrons.

Feast Dates: February 6 — Sts. Mel and Melchu (see Mel); April 17 — St. Villicus (see Grenville).

Melvin "The Sword Friend" (Old English) or "The Polished Chieftain" (Irish Gaelic).

Patron Saints: Mel can be a short form of Melvin. This leads to St. Mel. To him, any one of about sixty Sts. Vincent can be added.

Feast Dates: February 6 — St. Mel (see Mel); September 27 — St. Vincent de Paul (see Vincent).

Melvyn (English) See Melvin.

Menard (variant) See Maynard.

Mendel "The Wise and Knowledgeable One" (Semitic).

Patron Saints: There is a Bl. Mendus Valle, which is the closest name to Mendel. He gave his life for the Catholic faith in ancient Tavira.

Feast Dates: June 11 — Bl. Mendus Valle.

Mendie (nickname) See Mendel.

Mendy (nickname) See Mendel.

Menz (nickname) See Clement.

Meredith "The Guardian of the Sea" (Old Welsh).

Patron Saints: There are two Sts. Meriadec (or Meredith) who can serve as patrons. A third saint, with a very similar name, St. Meridia, may also be considered a patron.

St. Meredith (or Meriadec) was born in Wales in the early 600s. He lived much of his early priestly life as a hermit. Unfortunately, such a lifestyle was not to be his for very long, for in 666 he was elected bishop either of Vannes or of a suffragan see. This job he embraced for twenty years. He died of old age in 686. He is patron of those suffering from deafness.

Feast Dates: June 7 — St. Meredith.

Merideth (variant) See Meredith.

Merill (variant) See Merrill.

Merle "The Blackbird" (French) or "The Falcon [or Hawk or Blackbird]" (variant of Marlon, Merlin, Merrill).

Patron Saints: Merle is a short form of Merlin or Merrill. There is one male and one female St. Merle. The male St. Merle was a Roman monk at St. Andrew who is remembered for his prayers and works of charity.

Also, an additional patron can be found when one realizes that the name Merle means "blackbird," which is a raven or crow. And this leads to a Bl. Alexander Crow.

Feast Dates: January 17 — St. Merle, also known as Merulus; May 4 — Bl. Alexander Crow (see Raven).

Merlin (variant) See Marlon, Merrill.

Merrel (variant) See Merrill.

Merrell (variant) See Merrill.

Merrick "The Ruler of the Sea" (Old English).

Patron Saints: There are a dozen saints with similar names that mean "sea." They include St. Mera, who dedicated her single life to the service of God and her neighbor. A church in a diocese in France is dedicated to her.

Feast Dates: July 20 — St. Mera; July 19 — St. Maris (see Marley).

Merrill "The Falcon [or Hawk or Blackbird]" (French) or "The Famous One" (French).

Patron Saints: It is helpful to know that, depending on which scholar is consulted, Merrill means either "famous" or "falcon." This leads to a couple of patrons.

Feast Dates: February 17 — St. Alexis Falconieri (see Marlon); May 25 — Bl. Clare Voglia (see Clare).

Merry (nickname) See Meredith.

Merton "From the Estate+Near the Sea" (Old English double).

Patron Saints: It is also helpful to know that Merton comes from two words: *mer* means "by the sea" and *ton* means "from the town." This leads directly to St. Godfrey of Merville. Merville means "village by the sea." Godfrey was a painter. He joined the Franciscans as a brother and then became the *custos* of the friary in Gorkum, Holland. This means he became a kind of guardian for the religious living there.

When the Calvinist heretics gained control of Holland, they began to persecute the Catholics. In 1572 Godfrey was arrested by them because of his Catholic faith. The Calvinists hanged him at Briel.

Feast Dates: July 9 — St. Godfrey of Merville, O.F.M.; July 21 — St. Tondach (see Town).

Merv (nickname) See Merton, Mervin.

Mervin (Old English double) See Marvin, Merton+Win/Wynn.

Mervyn (Old English double) See Mervin.

Merwin (variant) See Marvin.

Merwyn (Old English double) See Mervin.

Meryl (variant) See Merle, Merrill.

Meurig (Welsh) See Maurice.

Meyers "The Farmer" (German) or "The Bringer of Light" (Hebrew) or "The Greater One" (Latin).

Patron Saints: Meyers can mean many different things depending on which root a person uses to build this name. Each of the name's meanings leads to a different patron.

Feast Dates: April 23 — St. George (see George); October 18 — St. Luke (see Luke).

Mic (variant) See Micah.

Micah "He Who Is Like God" (Hebrew, also Russian form of Michael).

Patron Saints: Christian tradition presents a half-dozen Sts. Micah. The Old Testament adds St. Micah, the Jewish prophet who lived in about 750 B.C. He was a contemporary of the prophets Hosea, Amos, and Isaiah and was called by God to denounce both the kingdoms of Judah and Israel. He warned that disaster would soon befall the people if they did not turn their lives around and honor God. However, he added, in the end, God would send a Messiah-Deliverer who would be born in Bethlehem. He was killed by his enemies who threw him off a high cliff.

Feast Dates: January 15 — St. Micah.

Michael "He Who Is Like God" (Hebrew).

Patron Saints: There are about fifty saints named Michael. However, the greatest is St. Michael the Archangel. He is named twice each in both the Old and New Testaments and is one of the three archangels whose names are mentioned in the Bible. The Book of Daniel identifies him as the guardian angel of Israel. Jewish tradition further identifies Michael as the author of Psalm 85, a prayer of protection for Israel. He is also credited with destroying the army of Sennacherib outside the gates of Jerusalem and of stopping Abraham from killing Isaac on Mount Moriah, being the fire of the burning bush, and leading the legions of angels against the powers of darkness.

Christian tradition recognizes him as a protector at the hour of death. He is patron of bankers, grocers, policemen, sailors, knights, paratroopers, radiologists, those in peril at sea, those in battle, those tempted, the sick, the dying, the Basques, Brussels, Germany,

Solomon Islands, Papua New Guinea, and cemeteries.

Feast Dates: September 29 — St. Michael the Archangel.

Michail (Russian) See Michael.

Michal (Polish) See Michael.

Michale (variant) See Michael.

Micheal (Irish, Scottish) See Michael.

Micheil (variant) See Michael.

Michel (French) See Michael.

Michele (Italian) See Michael.

Micho (Spanish) See Michael.

Mick (nickname) See Micah, Michael.

Mickael (English) See Michael.

Mickey (nickname) See Michael.

Mickie (nickname) See Michael.

Micky (nickname) See Michael.

Miguel "He Who Is Like God" (Spanish, Portuguese).

Patron Saints: Miguel is the Spanish form of Michael, and there are about fifty Sts. Michael. One is Bl. Miguel Pro, 1892-1927, who began studying to be a Jesuit priest at twenty years of age. In 1914, however, the fighting and anti-Catholicism were so great that Miguel left Mexico and went to Texas, then to California, Nicaragua, Spain, and Belgium to continue his studies. He was ordained a priest in 1925 and returned to Mexico, where all public worship had been suppressed by the Communist government.

In order to serve his people in Mexico City, he became a master of disguise. In November of 1927 he was arrested with two of his brothers and was sentenced to death. Standing before the firing squad he said, "May God forgive you all." Then he added, "Long live Christ the King." And he was shot.

Feast Dates: November 24 — Bl. Miguel Pro, S.J.

Migui (Spanish) See Michael.

Mihael (Greek) See Michael.

Mihai (Romanian) See Michael.

Mihaly (Hungarian) See Michael.

Mihhail (Estonian) See Michael.

Mikael (Swedish) See Michael.

Mike (nickname) See Micah, Michael.

Mikel (Basque) See Michael.

Mikelis (Latvian) See Michael.

Mikey (nickname) See Micah, Michael.

Mikhail (Russian) See Michael.

Miki (Spanish) See Michael.

Mikkel (Norwegian) See Michael.

Mikko (Finnish) See Michael.

Miklos (Hungarian) See Nicholas.

Mikol (variant) See Michael.

Mikolaj (Polish) See Nicholas.

Mikolas (Czech) See Nicholas.

Miksa (Hungarian) See Maximilian.

Mil (nickname) See Millard, Milton.

Milagros "A Miracle" (Spanish).

Patron Saints: The first way to find a patron with this or a similar name is to search among those saints the Church has officially described as "Wonderworkers." These include Sts. Cyril, Luke, Stephen, and Gregory.

A second way is to adopt the greatest Wonder or Miracle Worker of them all, Jesus the Christ. He is remembered for working all kinds of miracles: over nature, healing the sick, driving out devils, and raising the dead. However, he never performed miracles to entertain or for personal gain. In fact, all his miracles were performed in order to help people and to lead them to place faith in him. Then they could come to him and receive deeper healings. These consisted of the forgiveness of sin and the reception of eternal life.

Feast Dates: All Sundays — Jesus the Miracle Worker.

Milan (Czech, Hungarian) See Miles.

Milborn (English) See Melbourne.

Milburn (English) See Melbourne.

Miles "The Soldier" (English).

Patron Saints: There are about a dozen saints with this name or variants of it, including Milo, Milles, and Milius. One is Bl. Miles Gerard, 1550-1590. He was born into an anti-Catholic world at Lancashire, England. He became a schoolmaster and then traveled to Rheims in France and was ordained in 1583.

In 1589 he returned to England to serve as a missionary under the alias of William Richardson. However, his ship wrecked off the coast of Kent and he was discovered, arrested, and imprisoned. He was tried for treason and for being a Catholic priest and was hanged, drawn, and quartered in Rochester. He was forty years old when he was martyred.

Feast Dates: April 30 — Bl. Miles Gerard.

Milford (Old English double) See Miller+Ford.

Mill (nickname) See Millard, Miller.

Millard "The Flour Mill Worker" (Old English) or "The Winning Flatterer" (Old French).

Patron Saints: There is a St. Miller (or Millard), but his name is spelled Milner. Bl. Ralph Milner was an illiterate Protestant living near Winchester who supported a wife and seven children by farming. Impressed by the Catholics living around him, he converted. On the day of his First Communion he was arrested and imprisoned for many years. Eventually he was put on trial. At his trial the judge wanted to release him because of his great age and family, but Ralph refused to pray in an Anglican Church as requested. His friends, wife, and seven children begged him to relent. But he would not. He asked his children to follow his example. He was then hanged in 1591.

The Catholic Church has appointed five saints to be patrons of millers. They are Sts. Arnulph, Catherine of Alexandria, Honoratus, Meingold, and Verana.

Feast Dates: December 10 — Bl. Ralph Milner; July 18 — St. Arnulph (see Milton).

Mille (French) See Miles.

Miller "The Flour Grinder" (Old English).

Patron Saints: The Catholic Church has named several saints, including St. Arnulph, as patrons of millers.

Feast Dates: July 18 — St. Arnulph (see Milton).

Millner (English) See Millard.

Milo (Slovenian, Romanian) See Miles.

Milos (Slovenian, Romanian) See Miles.

Milt (nickname) See Milton.

Miltie (nickname) See Milton.

Milton "From the Mill+Town" (Old English double).

Patron Saints: Bl. Ralph Milner can be adopted as the patron of those named Milton, and the Catholic Church also has appointed five saints to be patrons of millers. They are Sts. Arnulph, Catherine of Alexandria, Honoratus, Meingold, and Verana.

St. Arnulph, 582-640, was of noble Frankish stock and was trained to serve in the diplomatic corps. In due time, he married and had two sons. Feeling his soul was in danger because of the political affairs that passed through his hands, he entered a monastery. His wife, Doda, entered the convent as a nun. Then at the age of thirty-one, he was elected the bishop of Metz. In later years he resigned his bishopric and spent thirteen years living in a cave as a hermit. He died at the age of fifty-eight. Besides being one of the patrons of millers, he is also patron of brewers and workers in the flour industry, as well as of music and of helping find lost articles.

Feast Dates: July 18 — St. Arnulph; December 10 — Bl. Ralph Milner (see Millard).

Milty (nickname) See Milton.

Mincho (nickname) See Benjamin.

Minel (Spanish) See Emmanuel.

Mingo (Spanish) See Dominic.

Mique (Spanish) See Michael.

Miron (variant) See Myron.

Miroslav (Russian) See Vladimir, Slava.

Mischa (Slavic) See Michael.

Misha (Slavic) See Michael.

Mishenka (variant) See Michael.

Mitch (nickname) See Michael.

Mitchel (French) See Michael.

Mitchell (Lithuanian, English) See Michael.

Modesto "The Modest One" (Spanish).

Patron Saints: There are almost two dozen Sts. Modesto. One died a martyr in ancient Nice.

Feast Dates: October 21 — St. Modesto.

Moe (nickname) See Moses.

Mohammad (Arabic) See Muhammad.

Mohammed (Arabic) See Muhammad.

Moise (variant) See Moses.

Moisei (variant) See Moses.

Moises (Spanish) See Moses.

Moishe (Hebrew) See Moses.

Moisis (Greek) See Moses.

Mojzesz (Polish) See Moses.

Mojzis (Slovakian) See Moses.

Moke (nickname) See Moses.

Monchi (Spanish) See Moses.

Moncho (Modern Hebrew) See Simon.

Mondo "From the World" (Latin, Spanish).

Patron Saints: The closest name we have as a patron is St. Mundus, who was Scottish and died in 962.

Feast Dates: April 15 — St. Mundus.

Monro (English) See Monroe.

Monroe "From the Red Swamp" (Irish Gaelic) or "From the Mouth of the Roe River" (Irish Gaelic).

Patron Saints: There are few ancient saints who have similar names. St. Mun was one of the four nephews of St. Patrick who worked with him in about 450 for the conversion of Ireland. In his younger years he served as a bishop. In his later years he lived as a hermit.

St. Roa was a companion of St. Cyrilla at Cyrene in Libya. She was martyred during the persecution of Emperor Diocletian in about 300.

Feast Dates: February 6 — St. Mun; July 4 — St. Roa.

Montague "From the Pointed Mountain" (French).

Patron Saints: Montague means "mountain" and the Latin word for "mountain" is *montanus*. This, in turn, leads to a dozen Sts. Montanus.

Feast Dates: February 24 — St. Montanus (see Montgomery).

Montana "From the Mountain" (Spanish).

Patron Saints: There are a dozen saints whose name Montanus is the Latin for "mountain."

Feast Dates: February 24 — St. Montanus.

Monte (nickname) See Lamond, Montague, Montgomery.

Montell (American) See Montreal.

Montez (Spanish) See Montana.

Montford "From the Mount+Near the River Crossing" (Old English double).

Patron Saints: Bl. Montford Scott was executed by the English in 1591 for being a Catholic priest.

Feast Dates: May 4 — Bl. Montford Scott.

Montgomery "The Rich Man's+Mountain" (Old English double).

Patron Saints: Since there is evidently no saint named Montgomery, any saint named Montanus, which means "mountain," will have to serve as patron. There are a dozen Sts. Montanus and one of them was the leader of a group of imprisoned Christians. He was a black priest who had worked with St. Cyprian. He constantly encouraged his imprisoned companions. He also repeatedly rebuked the proconsul and the jailers. After many months of suffering, he and his companions were finally beheaded for the faith in the year 259.

Feast Dates: February 24 — St. Montanus.

Monti (nickname) See Lamond, Montague, Montgomery.

Montreal (French) See Montana+Royal.

Montrell (French) See Montreal.

Monty (nickname) See Lamond, Montague, Montgomery.

Moon "The Earth's Satellite" (Middle English) or "The Separated One" (variant of Mona).

Patron Saints: If one accepts the name as meaning "single," then St. Mona will be patron. However if one insists the name refers to earth's closest neighbor, then St. Lunaire should be called upon.

St. Lunaire, 509-570, was the son of King Hoel I of Brittany and his mother was St. Pompeo. He and his brother, St. Tugdual, were educated by St. Illtyd. The brothers were then ordained priests by St. Dyfrig of Caerleon. Later, Lunaire became a bishop, went to Brittany, and founded a monastery near St. Malo. He died when he was about sixty-one.

Feast Dates: July 1 — St. Lunaire, also known as Leonore.

Moore "The Dark-Complected One" (Old French).

Patron Saints: There are several patrons with names similar to Moore, including two Sts. Mor, a St. Thomas More, and a Bl. Hugh More. There are also a dozen Sts. Maurice, whose name also means "dark-complected one."

St. Hugh More grew up as a Protestant and was educated at Cambridge. After he converted to Catholicism, he went to France and was ordained a Catholic priest. Returning to England, he was eventually arrested and executed for being a Catholic priest. He became a martyr in 1588.

Feast Dates: August 28 — Bl. Hugh More of London; June 22 — St. Thomas More (see Chauncey, Morley).

Moosaa (Arabic) See Moses.

Mooses (Estonian, Finnish) See Moses.

Mor (nickname) See Morley, Morse.

More (variant) See Moore.

Moreno "The Brown-Haired One" (Spanish) or "The Bitter One" (Irish form of Mary).

Patron Saints: There is one saint-in-the-making with this name: SG Sister Carmen Moreno, 1885-1936. In 1936 the nuns had to flee from Spain because the Red army began a severe persecution of those in religious orders. Sisters Moreno and Carbonell remained behind to help a very ill nun in the hospital. Soon after the release of the sick sister, all were arrested by army authorities. The sick nun was released, but the other two were taken to the local stadium, where they were beaten and shot in the head.

Feast Dates: September 6 — SG Carmen Moreno, F.M.A.

Morey (nickname) See Maurice, Morse, Seymour.

Morgan "The White Sea Dweller" (Scottish Gaelic) or "From the Edge of the Sea" (Scottish Gaelic).

Patron Saints: There are two Sts. Morgan and a half-dozen Sts. Pelagius. Pelagius is the Breton form of Morgan. St. Morgan was the son of Dubhtach, chief bard of King Laoghaire of Ireland. He was baptized with his father in 447. Ordained a priest, St. Morgan was named abbot in Tyr Gwyn, Wales, by St. Patrick. Morgan died in Brittany in the 400s.

Feast Dates: June 18 — St. Morgan, also known as Mawgan.

Morgen (variant) See Morgan.

Morgun (variant) See Morgan.

Moric (Hungarian) See Maurice.

Morie (variant) See Maurice, Morse, Seymour.

Moritz (German) See Maurice.

Morkus (Lithuanian) See Mark.

Morlee (variant) See Morley.

Morley "From the Meadow+Moor" (Old English double).

Patron Saints: Morley comes from two words: *mor*, meaning "moor," and *ley* (or *leigh*), meaning "meadow." This leads to three saints. The most famous is St. Thomas More, 1478-1535. He became England's leading literary light. He wrote poetry, history, devotional books, prayers, and defenses of the faith.

During the reign of King Henry VIII, he steadily rose in rank — from undersheriff in 1510 to lord chancellor in 1529, with other honors and positions in between. In time, he was faced with the problem surrounding the king's divorce and subsequent remarriage in 1533. St. Thomas resigned his post and retired to his home in Chelsea. But he was increasingly pressured to recognize the king as head of the Church. This he steadfastly refused to do. In 1534 he was arrested and imprisoned in the Tower of London. Fifteen months later he was beheaded. On the scaffold he openly declared that "he was the king's good servant, but God's first." He was fifty-seven at the time of his death.

Feast Dates: June 22 — St. Thomas More; August 30 — Bl. Richard Leigh (see Leigh).

Morly (variant) See Morley.

Morrie (variant) See Maurice, Morse, Seymour.

Morris (English) See Maurice, Morse, Seymour.

Morry (variant) See Maurice, Morse, Seymour.

Morse "The Son of+Maurice [The Dark-Skinned One]" (Old English double).

Patron Saints: There are over a dozen saints named Maurice. And there is one English saint surnamed Morse. St. Henry Morse, 1599-1649, was raised a Protestant, and as an adult he converted to Catholicism. He then traveled to the Continent and was ordained a priest. A very likable character, he worked in London for many years as a Jesuit priest. Only in 1638, at the age of thirty-nine, was he arrested. After being released, he worked in various parts of England. At the age of fifty he was arrested once again and thrown into prison before he was executed at Tyburn.

Feast Dates: February 1 — St. Henry Morse, S.J.; September 22 — St. Maurice (see Maurice).

Mort (nickname) See Mortimer, Morton.

Morten (nickname) See Morton.

Morten (Danish, Norwegian) See Martin.

Mortie (nickname) See Mortimer, Morton.

Mortimer "From the Still Water" (Old French) or "The Sea Director" (Old French).

Patron Saints: A patron can be found by recognizing that Mortimer means "from the still water." This leads to Bl. Waterson, whose name means about the same thing. Bl. Edward Waterson was born in London and converted to Catholicism. He studied at Rheims and was ordained a diocesan priest in 1592. He went to England and a year later was caught and executed.

Feast Dates: January 21 — Bl. Edward Waterson.

Morton "From the Town+Near the Moor" (Old English double).

Patron Saints: There is a saint who bears this name. Bl. Robert Morton was born at Bawtry in South Yorkshire, England. He traveled to Rheims, France, and Rome, Italy, to study for the priesthood and was ordained a diocesan priest in 1587. Immediately after ordination he sailed for England. In 1588, after only a few months of ministry, he was arrested and executed.

Feast Dates: August 27 — Bl. Robert Morton.

Morty (nickname) See Mortimer, Morton.

Mose (Spanish) See Moses.

Mosell (African-American double) See Moses+Darrell/Terrell.

Moses "The One Drawn from the Water" (Hebrew) or "A Child" (Egyptian).

Patron Saints: There are over thirty Christian saints named Moses, but the Bible presents us with the greatest St. Moses, one of the most important personalities in the Old Testament. He lived in about 1250 B.C. He had all the advantages of wealth and power and received an excellent education. But he also remained very sensitive to the plight of his people, who were in slavery. One day he killed an Egyptian for beating a Hebrew. For this he had to flee from Egypt to Midian.

God then ordered him to lead the chosen people out of Egypt to the Promised Land of Canaan. At God's command, Moses unleashed the ten plagues on the Egyptians, led the Israelites through the Red Sea and the desert, and received the law from God on Mount Sinai. He persevered in the face of great discouragement. After bringing his people to the borders of Canaan, Moses went up Mount Nebo and died.

Feast Dates: September 4 — St. Moses, Jewish Lawgiver.

Moshe (Hebrew) See Moses.

Mosie (Spanish) See Moses.

Moss (Spanish) See Moses.

Moyses (Portuguese) See Moses.

Moze (Lithuanian) See Moses.

Mozell (African-American double) See Moses+Darrell/Terrell.

Mozes (Dutch, Hungarian) See Moses.

Muhammad "The Highly Praised One" (Arabic).

Patron Saints: The name Muhammad (also spelled Mohammad, Mohammed, and Mahomet) is usually associated with Islamic Arabs. But it should be remembered that many Arabs are Christian and Catholic. Thus it can be a Christian name. It is also helpful to know that Achmed is a form of Muhammad, and there is a St. Achmed. Furthermore, Thaddeus has the same meaning as Muhammad.

St. Achmed was an architect who was of Turkish Muslim descent. He converted to the Orthodox Church because of a miracle he had seen. He was murdered by his own people in about 1682 because he had converted.

His feast is celebrated by the Orthodox Church.

Feast Dates: December 24 — St. Achmed; October 28 — St. Jude, Apostle (see Jude).

Muir "From the Moor" (Scottish Gaelic).

Patron Saints: There are a half-dozen Irish saints who have Muir as part of their names. St. Muirghen served the Church as abbot of Gleann-Uisean, Queen's County, Ireland.

Feast Dates: January 27 — St. Muirghen.

Mundek (Polish) See Edmund.

Mundo (Latin, Spanish) See Mondo, Edmund.

Munro (English) See Monroe.

Munroe (English) See Monroe.

Munrow (English) See Monroe.

Murdoch (Scottish) See Murdock.

Murdock "The Wealthy Sailor" (Scottish Gaelic).

Patron Saints: There are three saints named Murdock and they are all from Ireland. One was a disciple of St. Patrick. In time, St. Patrick appointed him to act as the bishop of Killala. He was its first bishop. Murdock concluded his life on the island of Inishmurray. He died of old age in about the year 455.

In addition, St. Brendan can be adopted as a patron because the Catholic Church officially recognizes him as patron of sailors. And, as we have seen, the name Murdock means "wealthy sailor."

Feast Dates: August 13 — St. Murdock, also known as Muredach.

Murffy (Irish Gaelic) See Murphy.

Murphy "The Sea Warrior" (Irish Gaelic).

Patron Saints: It helps to know the name's original spelling, which is Murchadh. This leads to two saints. St. Murchon is identified as a female saint who lived in ancient Sligo, Ireland. St. Murchu is remembered simply as an "Irish saint."

Feast Dates: June 12 — St. Murchon; June 8 — St. Murchu McO'Maichten.

Murray "The Sailor" (Scottish Gaelic) or "The One from the Sea" (Irish).

Patron Saints: Some think Murray is a form of Murrough. Others think it is a form of Mury, Mor, Moran, or Moroech. This leads to a half-dozen saints with similar names. St. Mury served God as an abbot of the Bangor monastery in the Middle Ages. St. Murrough served as a holy bishop in Banaghe.

Knowing that the name Murray means "sailor" leads to the Church-appointed patrons of sailors: Sts. Andrew, Barbara, Brendan, Cuthbert, Elmo, Eulalia, Francis of Paolo, Nicholas, Peter González, and Phocas.

Feast Dates: April 21 — St. Mury; November 1 — St. Murrough.

Murry (Irish Gaelic) See Murray.

Murton (nickname) See Mervin.

Murvyn (English) See Marvin.

Mustafa "The Chosen One" (Arabic).

Patron Saints: Christian is the name Christians call the "chosen one." The best patron is Jesus Christ.

Feast Dates: December 4 — St. Christianus (see Christian).

My (nickname) See Myron.

Myca (English) See Micah.

Mycah (English) See Micah.

Mychal (English) See Michael.

Myer (variant) See Meyers.

Myers (variant) See Meyers.

Mykal (American) See Michael.

Mykola (Ukrainian) See Nicholas.

Mykolas (Czech, Lithuanian) See Nicholas, Michael.

Myles (English) See Miles.

Myron "The Fragrant Ointment" (Greek).

Patron Saints: There are about a half-dozen Sts. Myron. One was born in Achaia, became a priest, and practiced his ministry in the Hellespont. He was martyred in 251 during the persecution under the Roman emperor Decius. When the imperial officers came to his church to wreck it and to arrest the Christians they found there, Myron withstood them face-to-face. He protested vigorously against the evil law of the pagan emperor aimed at the destruction of Christianity.

Feast Dates: August 17 — St. Myron.

Myrvyn (English) See Marvin.

Myrwyn (English) See Marvin.

N

Naldo (Spanish) See Reginald.

Nalin (Hispanic-American) See Reginald, Neal.

Nando (variant) See Ferdinand.

Nandor (Hungarian) See Ferdinand.

Nano (nickname) See Ferdinand.

Nap (nickname) See Napoleon.

Napoleon "The Lion of the Woodland Valley" (Greek) or "The One from Naples" (Italian).

   Patron Saints: There are two Sts. Napoleon. One was martyred in Alexandria, Egypt, during the reign of the Roman emperor Diocletian.

   Feast Dates: August 15 — St. Napoleon.

Nappie (nickname) See Napoleon.

Nappy (nickname) See Napoleon.

Narbate (West African) See Ett.

Nardo (Spanish) See Bernardo.

Nasser (Arabic) See Victor.

Nat (nickname) See Nathan, Nathaniel.

Natal (Spanish) See Noël.

Natale (Italian) See Noël.

Natalino (Spanish) See Noël.

Natan (Polish, Spanish, Italian) See Nathan.

Nataneal (Spanish) See Nathaniel.

Natanial (Spanish) See Nathaniel.

Nate (Italian, Hebrew) See Nathan, Nathaniel.

Nap (nickname) See Napoleon.

Narbeh (African-American) See Narbate.

Nate (nickname) See Nathan, Nathaniel.

Nathan "The Hopeful One" (French-Hebrew) or "The Gift of God" (short form of Nathaniel).

   Patron Saints: Christian tradition provides only two saints named Nathaniel, while the Old Testament provides us with a great prophet named Nathan who lived in about 1000 B.C., during the time of King David. Of all the men in the kingdom, Nathan was the one man who could stand up to David. When David sinned with Bathsheba, Nathan found himself in the uncomfortable position of having to reprimand the king.

   Feast Dates: November 1 — St. Nathan.

Nathanial (variant) See Nathaniel.

Nathaniel "The Gift of God" (Hebrew) or "The Lord Has Given" (Hebrew).

   Patron Saints: Christian tradition presents St. Nathaniel, an Apostle of Jesus. The Gospel of John tells us that Nathaniel was a native of Cana in Galilee and learned of Jesus through Philip.

   Christian tradition usually identifies Nathaniel as the Apostle St. Bartholomew. After all, Bartholomew was not a name but a description. It means "son of the farmer." About Nathaniel Bar Tholmai, tradition adds that he preached the Gospel throughout the Middle East and provided his converts with a copy of the Gospel of Matthew.

   He is patron of cheesemakers, tanners, and plasterers, as well as of Armenia and against nervous tics.

   Feast Dates: August 24 — St. Nathaniel.

Natty (nickname) See Nathan, Nathaniel.

Naython (American) See Nathan.

Nazario "The One from Nazareth" (Spanish).

Patron Saints: There are a dozen Sts. Nazarius. One of them died a martyr in ancient Rome.

Feast Dates: June 12 — St. Nazarius.

Neacail (Scottish Gaelic) See Nicholas.

Neal "The Champion" (Irish Gaelic) or "The Flaxen-Haired One" (variant form of Cornelius).

Patron Saints: If Neal is from Cornelius, then two patrons are available here. There are also about two dozen Sts. Cornelius. If the name arises from Nicholas, then another fifty patrons become available. There are even a few Sts. Nielchus and Nilus. A St. Nielchus was the bishop of Ardagh in medieval times.

Feast Dates: February 6 — St. Nielchus; December 6 — St. Nicholas (see Nicholas).

Neale (English) See Neal.

Neall (English) See Neal.

Nealon (variant) See Neal.

Nealson (English double) See Neal+Son.

Necho (Spanish) See Andrew, Edward.

Necolas (Italian) See Nicholas.

Ned (nickname) See Eddy, Edgar, Edmund, Edward, Edwin.

Neddie (nickname) See Eddy, Edgar, Edmund, Edward, Edwin.

Neddy (nickname) See Eddy, Edgar, Edmund, Edward, Edwin.

Needham (African-American double) See Ned+Hamilton.

Neel (English) See Neal.

Neeley (variant) See Neal.

Neely (variant) See Neal.

Nehemiah "The Compassion of the Lord" (Hebrew).

Patron Saints: Christian tradition lacks a St. Nehemiah. However, the Bible provides us with three men with that name. One of them is the great Jewish patriarch who lived in about 500 B.C. He was born in exile in Babylon.

However, sometime after the Persian king Cyrus had allowed the Jews to return to the Promised Land, it was discovered that things were not going well for them.

Nehemiah, who was a cupbearer to the king, begged for a leave of absence so that he could help his people in Jerusalem. This the king granted. Nehemiah then collected all kinds of building materials and other resources and set out for Jerusalem. There, he united the dispirited returnees and began to oversee the rebuilding of the walls around the city.

Feast Dates: July 13 — St. Nehemiah.

Neil (English) See Neal.

Neill (English) See Neal.

Neils (English double) See Neal+Son.

Nel (nickname) See Nelson, Parnell.

Nell (nickname) See Nelson, Parnell.

Nellie (nickname) See Nelson, Parnell.

Nelly (nickname) See Nelson, Parnell.

Nelo (Spanish) See Daniel.

Nels (Swedish double) See Nicholas, Neal+Son.

Nelson "The Son of+The Champion" (English double).

Patron Saints: There is an English martyr surnamed Nelson. Bl. John Nelson, S.J., 1530-1578, was the son of Sir Nelson of Yorkshire. When he was forty years old he heard about the Catholic college at Douai, France, traveled there, and was ordained a priest in 1576. He immediately returned to England and was apprehended. He was hanged, drawn, and quartered in 1578. He was forty-eight at the time of his death.

Feast Dates: February 3 — Bl. John Nelson, S.J.

Nero "The Stern One" (Spanish, Latin).

Patron Saints: There are a few Sts. Nero. One St. Nero was an ancient martyr who is still honored by the Abyssinian Church.

Feast Dates: July 11 — St. Nero.

Neron (Spanish) See Nero.

Nester "The Traveler" (Greek) or "The Wise One" (Greek).

Patron Saints: There are almost a dozen Sts. Nestor, although none seems to have the spelling "Nester." Among them is a very handsome young man who had participated in the destruction of the pagan temple of Marmion. This outraged the authorities and they arrested him and his companions. All were dragged through the streets of Gaza in Palestine, then he was left to die in the gutter. The year was 362.

Feast Dates: September 8 — St. Nestor.

Neto (Spanish) See Ernesto.

Nev (nickname) See Nevada, Neville.

Nevada "That Snowed Upon" (Spanish).

Patron Saints: The Spanish word *nevada* means "that snowed upon," and this leads to Our Lady of the Snows. Known as the Basilica of St. Mary Major (Santa Maria Maggiore or the Great St. Mary's), it was the first church in Rome, in fact, in the entire Western Church to be dedicated to the honor of our Lady.

An ancient pious legend recalls that Mary appeared to a Roman patrician named John and asked to have a church built in her honor. Then, in the middle of a hot summer, miraculous snow fell on the Esquiline Hill. John immediately funded the building project. Thus, its name, Our Lady of the Snows.

This ancient church has also been known as St. Mary at the Crib. This is because it was believed to house a relic from the manger at Bethlehem. Its most treasured possession is an icon of Our Lady, Health of the Roman People. It is popularly thought to have been painted by St. Luke.

Feast Dates: August 5 — Our Lady of the Snows.

Nevalon (African-American double) See Neville+Lon.

Nevil (English) See Neville.

Nevile (English) See Neville.

Neville "From the New+Town" (Old French double) or "The Dawn" (Old French).

Patron Saints: Two saints with similar names, Nevers and Nevolo, may be adopted as patrons. St. Nevolo was a French shoemaker who spent a rather carefree and frivolous youth. However, at the age of twenty-four he experienced a conversion and became very serious about life. He joined a Third Order and gave himself to prayer. He also became well known for his penances. He died in 1280.

Feast Dates: July 27 — St. Nevolo.

Newel (French) See Noël.

Newland (Old English double) See Newy+Land.

Newlin (Old Welsh double) See Newy+Lynn.

Newton (Old English double) See Newy+Town.

Newman (Old English double) See Newy+Manfred/Mann.

Newy "The New One" (Old English).

Patron Saints: St. New was a rich Roman layman. He responded to a call to the ministry and was ordained a priest. He spent his whole life doing works of charity. He died in 152.

Feast Dates: June 20 — St. New, also known as Novatus.

Ney (variant) See Ny.

Nial (English) See Neal.

Niall (Irish) See Neal.

Nicandro (Spanish) See Nicholas.

Nicanor (Spanish) See Nicholas.

Nicasio (Spanish) See Nicholas.

Niccolo (Italian) See Nicholas.

Nicho (Spanish) See Dennis, Nicholas.

Nichol (variant) See Nichols, Nicholas.

Nicholas "The Victorious People" (Greek, Spanish).

Patron Saints: Nicholas has been a popular name from very ancient times. There are over fifty saints known to be named Nicholas. Here is the story of a famous one.

St. Nicholas, bishop of Myra, 280-350, used the great wealth he inherited to help the poor. The story is told how he helped the three daughters of a bankrupt local citizen. They each needed a dowry for marriage and Nicholas provided it — on three separate occasions. Under the cover of darkness, he delivered bags of money to their home. From this act of charity was born the legend of Santa Claus.

He is patron of bakers, bootblacks, brewers, children, coopers (barrel-makers), dockworkers, fishermen, merchants, pawnbrokers, perfumers, prisoners, sailors, spinsters, and travelers; also of bridges, Greece, Russia, Sicily, and Switzerland.

Feast Dates: December 6 — St. Nicholas of Myra.

Nicholis (English double) See Nicholas+Son.

Nichols "The Son of+Nicholas [The Victorious People]" (Old English double).

Patron Saints: There is one martyred English saint surnamed Nichols. It was a world of anti-Catholicism in which Father Nichols was arrested, tried, and convicted of being a Catholic priest in 1589. He was then executed.

Feast Dates: May 4 — Bl. George Nichols.

Nick (nickname) See Dominic, Nicholas.

Nicki (variant) See Dominic, Nicholas.

Nickie (variant) See Dominic, Nicholas.

Nickilas (variant) See Nicholas.

Nickolaus (variant) See Nicholas.

Nicky (variant) See Dominic, Nicholas.

Nico (Greek) See Anthony, Dominic, Nicholas.

Nicol (nickname) See Nichols, Nicholas.

Nicola (Italian) See Nicholas.

Nicolaas (Dutch) See Nicholas.

Nicolai (Norwegian, Russian) See Nicholas.

Nicolao (Portuguese) See Nicholas.

Nicolas (French, Spanish) See Nicholas.

Nicolis (variant) See Nichols, Nicholas.

Nicolo (Italian) See Nicholas.

Nidzo (Serbian) See Nicholas.

Niel (variant) See Neal.

Niels (English, Danish) See Neal, Nicholas.

Nigel "The Black One" (Latin).

Patron Saints: The name Nigel means "black," and thousands of Catholic saints are black. A few of them have Black as part of their names. There is also a St. Niger, whose name also means "black." He gave his life for Christ in ancient Constantinople.

Feast Dates: May 8 — St. Niger; August 28 — St. Moses the Black (see Blackie).

Niilo (Finnish) See Nicholas.

Nik (nickname) See Dominic, Nicholas, Nikita.

Nikita "The Unconquerable One" (Russian).

Patron Saints: There are about two dozen Sts. Nikita. One is a Syrian saint known as "The Wonderworker." In ancient times Nikita was spelled Nicetas.

Feast Dates: August 4 — St. Nikita, also known as Nicetas.

Nikitas (Greek) See Nikita.

Nikki (nickname) See Dominic, Nicholas, Nikita.

Niklas (Scandinavian) See Nicholas.

Niko (Dutch, Slovenian) See Nicholas.
Nikolai (Estonian, Russian) See Nicholas.
Nikolaos (Greek) See Nicholas.
Nikolas (Greek) See Nicholas.
Nikolaus (German) See Nicholas.
Nikolos (Greek) See Nicholas.
Nikos (variant) See Nicholas.
Nil (Russian) See Neal.
Nile (variant) See Niles.
Niles "Son of+Neil [The Champion]" (Old English double).

    Patron Saints: There are about two dozen Sts. Cornelius and over fifty Sts. Nicholas from which to choose. And then there is also a St. Niles (Nilus), 910-1004. As a youth and a young adult, he was rather lukewarm, religiously speaking. It seems he was living with a young lady for a while and had a child outside of marriage. However, when he was about thirty years old, his companion and their child died. He himself almost died of sorrow and of a serious illness. These tragedies forced him to examine his life, and he entered a monastery of the Byzantine rite. His reputation for knowledge and sanctity grew. And he became an abbot.

    Feast Dates: September 26 — St. Nilus of Rossano.
Nilo (Spanish) See Niles.
Nils (English double) See Neal/Niles+Son.
Nils (Norwegian, Swedish) See Nicholas.
Nilson (English double) See Neal+Son.
Niño (Spanish) See Ladd, Page.
Nixon (Old English double) See Nicholas+Son.
Njal (Scandinavian) See Neal.
Noach (English double) See Noah.
Noah "The Rested One" (Hebrew) or "The Consoling One" (Hebrew) or "Like a Dove" (Hebrew).

    Patron Saints: Christian tradition provides a half-dozen saints named Noah. The Bible gives us the ancient prehistoric patriarch Noah, who experienced the great flood, or deluge. He was the last of the ten pre-flood patriarchs listed in the Book of Genesis. His story in the Bible teaches that God is both just and merciful. He rewards and disciplines. Furthermore, life in this world is a time of mercy given for repentance. It insists that virtue and vice can be recognized by anyone's conscience, and the self-righteous cannot save themselves. Finally, the example of one just man in a sinful world proves that one cannot blame society for one's own failures.

    Feast Dates: May 2 — St. Noah.
Noak (variant) See Noah.
Nobby (variant) See Norbert.
Nobe (nickname) See Noble.
Nobie (nickname) See Noble.
Noble "The Well-Born One" (Latin).

    Patron Saints: There are a couple of Sts. Noble. Both were martyrs in ancient times.

    Feast Dates: April 25 — St. Noble, also known as Nobilis; October 17 — St. Noble, also known as Nobilitanus.
Noby (nickname) See Noble.
Noé (Spanish) See Noah.
Noël "Born at Christmastime" (French) or "Nativity" (French).

    Patron Saints: Noël comes from *natalis*, and there are about a half-dozen ancient saints named Natalis. There is also one North American martyr-saint. He is St. Noël Chabanel, 1613-1649, a Jesuit priest who went to Canada in 1643 to convert the Indians. He spent a year studying the Huron language. Although he was very intelligent, the Huron tongue remained a mystery to him. Further, he developed a loathing for the filth found on the frontier. He became depressed and wanted to return home but thought this wrong. He persevered because he was convinced God wanted him in the New World. But God's reasons eluded him. He often worked as administrator or did domestic duties. He felt useless.

He was the "Ziggy" of American saints. Nothing ever seemed to go right for Noël. Even his death was shrouded in mystery for a long time. He was killed by his Indian guide while traveling through the frontier. Eventually this Indian confessed to the murder, committed out of hatred of the Catholic religion.

Feast Dates: October 19 — St. Noël Chabanel, S.J.

Nohely (Hispanic-American) See Noël.

Nolan "The Famous, Noble One" (Irish Gaelic).

Patron Saints: The town of Nola in Campania, southern Italy, is noted for turning out a great number of saints. All can serve as patrons for Nolan. Those mentioned here are among the better-known saints.

St. Felix of Nola served in the army for a while and then became a priest and an adviser and friend to St. Maximus, bishop of Nola. When St. Maximus died in 250, the bishopric of Nola was offered to him, but he refused. When the next bishop also died, Felix was again invited to become bishop and this time he accepted. His very long life was filled with holiness and charity. St. Felix died in 260.

Feast Dates: January 14 — St. Felix of Nola; January 15 — St. Maximus of Nola.

Noland (variant) See Nolan.

Noldy (nickname) See Arnold.

Noll (nickname) See Oliver.

Nollie (nickname) See Oliver.

Nolly (nickname) See Oliver.

Nooh (Arabic) See Noah.

Nomar (Hispanic-American) See any "N" name+Omar.

Norbert "The Brilliant Hero" (Old German) or "The Divine Brightness" (Old Norse).

Patron Saints: St. Norbert, 1080-1134, is patron of Bohemia and of those seeking peace. In his early years, he was completely consumed by worldliness. However, at the age of thirty-five he was thrown from his horse during a thunderstorm. This made him examine his life. He decided to change and immediately went to a monastery to do penance and eventually became a priest. Then he tried to bring reform to his diocese but was ridiculed. So he resigned, gave his property to the poor, and traveled barefoot to France and then to Rome.

The pope heard his confession, absolved him, and commanded him to preach the Gospel everywhere. Soon he gathered a group of disciples around him and in 1126 formed the religious Order of Premonstratensians. A short time later he was elected archbishop of Magdeburg.

Feast Dates: June 6 — St. Norbert, O. Praem.

Norberto (Spanish) See Norbert.

Norbie (variant) See Norbert.

Norby (variant) See Norbert.

Norm (nickname) See Norman.

Norman "The Northman" (Old French, Spanish).

Patron Saints: Norman means about the same thing as Norris, and there are Sts. Norrice and Nothelm. St. Nothelm was elected to be archbishop of Canterbury in 734. He served his people in this position of archbishop for six years. At one point St. Boniface turned to him for some advice; he also assisted

St. Bede in compiling his *History of the Church*. He died in 740.

Feast Dates: October 17 — St. Nothelm; November 14 — St. Norrice (see Norris).

Normand (Old French) See Norman.

Normando (Spanish) See Norman.

Normie (nickname) See Norman.

Normy (nickname) See Norman.

Norrie (nickname) See Norris.

Norris "The Northman" (Old French) or "The Northern King" (Old French).

Patron Saints: There is one ancient saint named Norrice who will make a fine patron. Another ancient saint with a similar name, Nothelm, can also be adopted. St. Norrice married and gave birth to one son at Rheims. She named him Celsinus. At about the same time, she served as a wet-nurse for a little boy named Remi. Remi was destined to become the bishop of Rheims, and Celsinus was to be his disciple. Both have been recognized officially as saints of the Catholic Church. Also recognized as saints are the birth mother and brother of Remi. She must have been a very holy woman to inspire so many to become saints. She died in about 415 and is patron of pregnant women.

Feast Dates: November 14 — St. Norrice; October 17 — St. Nothelm (see Norman).

Norry (nickname) See Norris.

Nort (nickname) See Norton.

North "From the Northern Land" (Middle English).

Patron Saints: There is no St. North, but there is one ancient saint named Norrice, whose name means "north." And there is another saint with a similar name, Nothelm. Both can be adopted as patrons of those named North.

Feast Dates: October 17 — St. Nothelm (see Norman); November 14 — St. Norrice (see Norris).

Norton "From the Northern+Town" (Old English double).

Patron Saints: There is an English saint surnamed Norton. Bl. John Norton, a layman, was arrested for giving shelter to a Catholic priest. After his arrest, he was tried, convicted, and executed in 1600.

Feast Dates: May 4 — Bl. John Norton.

Nowel (English) See Noël.

Nowell (English) See Noël.

Numps (nickname) See Humphrey.

Nunzio (Italian) See Angel.

Ny "From the Island" (Old English).

Patron Saints: The word *ny* is Old English for "island," and one saint with a similar name serves very well. St. Nwy was a priest in Wales in ancient times. He is patron of an ancient chapel in Skenfrith parish in Monmouth, Wales.

Feast Dates: November 1 — St. Nwy.

Nye (English) See Ny, Nigel.

Nyle (Irish) See Nile.

Nyles (English double) See Nile+Son.

O

Oalo (Spanish) See Paul.

Oates (English) See Otis.

Oba (Yoruba) See Roy, Regis.

Obadiah "The Servant of God" (Hebrew).

Patron Saints: Christian tradition provides almost a half-dozen Sts. Obadiah (also spelled Abdias and Abdjesus), and the Bible presents a dozen more. The greatest is the ancient Jewish prophet Obadiah, who lived in about 585 B.C. God moved him to write the shortest book in the Old Testament. It is only twenty-one verses long. It is not quoted in the New Testament. It clearly teaches that one should be careful not to become an enemy of God's chosen people.

Feast Dates: November 19 — St. Obadiah.

Obadias (Greek) See Obadiah.

Obed (nickname) See Obadiah.

Obediah (variant) See Obadiah.

Oberon (German) See Aubrey.

Obie (nickname) See Obadiah.

Oby (nickname) See Obadiah.

Octavius "The Eighth-Born Son" (Latin).

Patron Saints: There are a half-dozen Sts. Octavius. One of them was martyred in ancient Ravenna.

Feast Dates: November 11 — St. Octavius.

Ode (nickname) See Odell.

Odell "The Little Wealthy One" (Anglo-French) or "From the Forested+Hill" (Old English double) or "The Ode [Melody]" (Greek) or "The Otter" (Irish).

Patron Saints: There is one known saint with a variation of this name.

Odelger served as prior in an Augustinian monastery. Under his guidance, the religious order grew in numbers and spread from France to Spain. He died in 1037.

Feast Dates: February 5 — Bl. Odelger.

Odie (nickname) See Odell.

Odiseo (Spanish) See Ulysses.

Odey (nickname) See Odell.

Odo (Latin, Polish) See Otto.

Odoardo (Italian) See Edwin.

Odon (Portuguese) See Otto.

Odon (Hungarian) See Edmund.

Ody (nickname) See Odell.

Odysseus (Greek) See Wendelin.

Ogdan (variant) See Obadiah.

Ogden "From the Oak+Valley [or Hill]" (Old English double).

Patron Saints: Ogden is made up of two words: *og*, meaning "oak," and *den*, meaning "valley." This leads to two patrons. St. Oghan served God as a holy bishop in ancient Ireland.

Feast Dates: February 26 — St. Oghan, also known as Ogan; August 28 — Bl. William Dean (see Dean).

Ogdon (variant) See Ogden.

Ojay (American double) See any "O" name+any "J" name.

Okay "Everything Is All Right [Correct]" (American).

Patron Saints: Since there are no saints named Okay, we will have to consider another possibility. "True" in Latin is *verus*, which leads to a half-dozen Sts. Verus. One of them died a martyr in ancient Constantinople.

Feast Dates: December 30 — St. Verus.

Oke (Hawaiian) See Oscar.

Olaf "The Ancestral Relic" (Old Norse) or "From the Olive Tree" (Norwegian form of Olaf).

Patron Saints: There are at least two Sts. Olaf. One of them was the king of Norway from 995 to 1030, having ascended to the throne at the age of twenty. He conquered many neighboring lands and sent Catholic missionaries to convert the people. However, the methods he used to bring his people to Christ plus some of his policies as a ruler were unbearable for many, and a rebellion took his life. Soon miracles were reported at his grave.

Feast Dates: July 29 — St. Olaf of Norway.

Olav (Norse) See Olaf.

Ole (nickname) See Olaf.

Olen (variant) See Olaf.

Olin (variant) See Olaf.

Oliver "The Kind One" (Old Norse) or "From the Olive Tree" (Old French).

Patron Saints: Christian tradition provides us with two Sts. Oliver. One of them, St. Oliver Plunket, 1629-1681, grew up in Dublin. At the age of sixteen he went to Rome, where he studied and was ordained a priest. He taught theology and did special jobs for the pope. At forty years of age he was named archbishop of Armagh.

The Oates Plot in England made life dangerous for Catholic clergymen. (Also known as the Popish Plot, it was instigated by the Anglican priest Titus Oates.) Lord Shaftesbury vowed to convict Plunket of treason, and Plunket found himself a fugitive. In 1679 he was arrested. Two years later he was tried, but the Irish judges refused to convict him. So he was removed to London and found guilty of treason by royal decree. In 1681, at the age of fifty-two, Archbishop Oliver Plunket was hanged, drawn, and quartered. He was the last Catholic to die for the faith at the Tyburn gallows.

Feast Dates: July 11 — St. Oliver Plunket.

Olivo (variant) See Oliver.

Olley (nickname) See Oliver.

Ollie (nickname) See Oliver.

Olly (nickname) See Oliver.

Olimpo (Spanish) See Olympius.

Oliverio (Spanish) See Oliver.

Olivier (French) See Oliver.

Oliviero (Italian) See Oliver.

Olo (Spanish) See Rolando.

Olvan (variant) See Oliver.

Olympius "The Heaven of the Gods" (Greek).

Patron Saints: About a dozen male and female saints bear variations of this name. One St. Olympius died a martyr in ancient Ostia.

Feast Dates: August 24 — St. Olympius.

Omar "The Long-Lived One" (Arabic) or "The Speaker" (Hebrew) or "The Trustworthy One" (North African).

Patron Saints: The closest name to this that we can find is St. Omer, bishop of Therouanne in the 600s. He dedicated his ministry to the conversion of pagans. He is a patron against sore eyes.

Feast Dates: September 9 — St. Omer.

Omero (Italian) See Homer.

Onando (African-American) See Orlando.

Ondrej (Czech) See Andrew.

Onfré (Spanish) See Humphrey.

Onfredo (Italian) See Humphrey.

Onfroi (French) See Humphrey.

Oracio (Italian) See Horace.

Oral "From the Mouth" (Latin).

Patron Saints: Oral means "spoken from the mouth" and leads to two patrons of orators. One is St. Ambrose and the other is St. John Chrysostom, his surname being Greek for "golden-mouthed." St. John was a Doctor and Father of the Church and lived from about 349 to 407.

St. John converted to Christianity at the age of nineteen. He entered a monastery, lived as a hermit, was ordained a priest, and became a great preacher in Antioch. In the year 398 he became archbishop of Constantinople. He reformed the clergy and laity, funded hospices for the sick, sent missionaries to the Goths, and reformed the Greek liturgy. Because of his outspoken support of Christian principles, he found himself the target of those in high place. He was eventually deposed and driven into exile. He died with these words on his lips: "Glory to God for all things."

Feast Dates: September 13 — St. John Chrysostom; December 7 — St. Ambrose (see Ambrose).

Oran "The Pale One" (Irish Gaelic).

Patron Saints: There are a few ancient saints named Oran. One St. Oran was a chariot driver for St. Patrick. In time, he was ordained a priest and consecrated a bishop.

Feast Dates: September 27 — St. Oran.

Oran (variant) See Orande, Oren.

Orande "The Appointed One" (West African).

Patron Saints: There is one patron whose name is very close to Orande. She is St. Oranda, a virgin who lived in fourteenth-century Lorraine.

Feast Dates: May 3 — St. Oranda.

Orasio (Italian) See Horace.

Orazio (Italian) See Horace.

Orban (Hungarian) See Urban.

Ordando (Spanish) See Orlando.

Ordell (African-American) See Odell.

Orel (variant) See Oral.

Oren "The One from the Pines" (Hebrew).

Patron Saints: Even though no saints named Oren seem to exist, there are a couple of Sts. Orentius. One of them was the father of St. Lawrence the Deacon, who was martyred in Rome in the first century. He was married to St. Patientia.

Feast Dates: May 1 — St. Orentius.

Oreste (variant) See Orestes.

Orestes "The Mountain Man" (Greek).

Patron Saints: There are almost a dozen Sts. Orestes. One St. Orestes served as a soldier in the Roman army. When it was discovered that he was a Christian, he was put to death at Sebaste.

Feast Dates: December 13 — St. Orestes.

Ori (nickname) See Oral, Orande, Oren, Orestes, Orion, Orlando, Orman, Orson, Orville.

Orien (variant) See Orion.

Orin (variant) See Oran, Oren.

Orion "The Son of Fire [Light]" (Greek).

Patron Saints: There are a half-dozen Sts. Orion. One of them was buried alive at Heraclea when it was discovered he was a Christian.

Feast Dates: November 10 — St. Orion.

Orito (nickname) See George.

Orlan (nickname) See Orlando.

Orland (Italian) See Orlando, Roland.

Orlando "From the Pointed Land" (Old English) or "From the Famous Land" (Spanish).

Patron Saints: There are at least two saints named Orlando. A Bl. Orlando became a religious brother and did penance all of his life. He was a holy man and had great power over the devil. He died in about 1242.

Feast Dates: May 20 — Bl. Orlando; January 16 — St. Lando (see Land).

Orlee (African-American double) See any "Or" name+Leigh.

Orlo (Spanish) See Orlando.

Orman "The Rowing Sailor" (Old English) or "From Bear Mountain" (Old French) or "The Spearman" (Old English).

Patron Saints: Patrons can be found in two places. If the name is accepted as "oarman," then ten patrons of sailors can be adopted. They are Sts. Andrew, Barbara, Brendan, Cuthbert, Elmo, Eulalia, Francis of Paolo, Nicholas, Peter González, and Phocas.

If the name is accepted as a form of Orson, then a dozen Sts. Ursus become available.

Feast Dates: May 16 — St. Brendan the Voyager (see Brendan); February 1 — St. Orson, also known as Ursus (see Orson).

Ormand (English) See Orman.

Ormond (English) See Orman.

Ornell (African-American double) See any "Or" name+Darnell.

Oro (Spanish) See Aurelia.

Orran (variant) See Oran.

Orren (variant) See Oren.

Orrin (English) See Oran, Oren.

Orscinio (African-American) See Arsenio.

Orsino (Danish, French, Russian, Romanian) See Orson.

Orson "Son of+The Spearman" (Old English double) or "The Bearlike One" (Old French).

Patron Saints: There is one ancient Egyptian saint, Orsiesius, who can serve as patron. There are also a dozen Sts. Ursus who can serve as patrons for Orson. One St. Orson was a layman and an avid follower of St. Gratus, his parish priest. Following the priest's

advice in spiritual matters, he grew in holiness. He lived in the 300s.

Feast Dates: February 1 — St. Orson, also known as Ursus.

Orton (English) See Horton.

Orv (nickname) See Orville.

Orvie (nickname) See Orville.

Orville "From the Golden Estate" (Old French).

Patron Saints: It helps to know that Orville is made up of two words: *or* and *ville*, meaning "gold" and "village" or "estate." There are a few ancient saints who bear similar names, among them Sts. Ori and Villicus. Ori served as a priest in Satanuf, Egypt. He was favored with a vision of Jesus. He was arrested because he was a Christian and sent to Alexandria, where he was beheaded.

Feast Dates: August 2 — St. Ori; April 17 — St. Villicus (see Grenville).

Orzell (African-American) See Ozell.

Osborn "The Warrior of God" (Old English) or "The Divine Bear" (Old Norse).

Patron Saints: If Osborn means "divine bear," then a dozen Sts. Celestine, meaning "heavenly," and a dozen Sts. Ursus, meaning "bear," can be pressed into service. One St. Celestine died a martyr in ancient Rome.

Feast Dates: February 13 — St. Celestine, also known as Caelestinus; February 1 — St. Orson, also known as Ursus (see Orson).

Osborne (English) See Osborn.

Osbourn (English) See Osborn.

Osbourne (English) See Osborn.

Oscar "The Divine Spearman" (Old Norse).

Patron Saints: There is one medieval saint named Oscar. And there is one recent Latin American who was murdered in the service of the poor. He is SG Archbishop Oscar Romero,

1917-1980. He worked as a parish priest and then in 1970, at the age of fifty-three, he was consecrated a bishop. In 1977 he became archbishop of El Salvador. He slowly became aware of the great gulf between the rich and poor of his country and he began to make this situation known to the rich families and to the government. He used letters, newspaper articles, the pulpit, and the radio to tell of the plight of the poor.

This angered many wealthy people, and they sent the archbishop death threats and urged him to stay in his church and leave running the world to them. He was assassinated while celebrating Mass in his cathedral in 1980. He was only sixty-three. He is being considered for canonization.

Feast Dates: March 24 — SG Archbishop Oscar Romero.

Osee (Greek) See Hosea.

Osgood "The Divinely Good One" (Old Norse).

Patron Saints: The meaning of the name leads to many patrons. There are a dozen Sts. Celestine, whose name means "heavenly," and one St. Bonus, whose name means "good." St. Good was a priest who, with many friends, embraced death for the sake of Christ in Roman times.

Feast Dates: August 1 — St. Good, also known as Bonus; February 13 — St. Celestine (see Osborn).

Osip (Russian, Ukrainian) See Joseph.

Oskar (English) See Oscar.

Osmond "The Divine Protector" (Old English).

Patron Saints: The best Divine Protector is none other than Jesus the Paraclete.

Feast Dates: All Sundays — Jesus, Our Rock and Fortress (see Garrison);

Good Friday — Jesus, Our Protector (see Griffin).

Osmont (English) See Osmond.

Osmund (English) See Osmond.

Osmundo (Spanish) See Osmond.

Ossie (nickname) See Oscar, Oswald.

Ossy (nickname) See Oscar, Oswald.

Osvaldo (Spanish) See Oswald.

Oswald "The Divinely Powerful One" (Old English).

Patron Saints: There are two medieval Sts. Oswald. One was an archbishop. The other St. Oswald, 604-642, became king of Northumbria. Immediately upon gaining the throne, he imported missionaries from Scotland and Ireland and had churches built in many places. He was known for his piety. Whenever a break in his royal duties occurred, he could be counted upon to fall into prayer.

And he always cared for the poor. He and his wife had one son who, at thirty-eight years of age, was attacked by the pagan king Penda of Mercia and killed in battle.

Feast Dates: August 7 — St. Oswald.

Oswaldo (Spanish) See Oswald.

Oswell (English) See Oswald.

Otao (Portuguese) See Otto.

Otello (Italian) See Otto.

Otes (variant) See Otis.

Otey (African-American) See Otis.

Othello (Spanish) See Otto.

Otilio (Spanish) See Otto.

Otis "The Wealthy One" (Old German) or "The One with Keen Hearing" (Greek).

Patron Saints: Otis comes from Otto, and there are two medieval saints named Otto. One became a bishop and lived from 1062 to 1139. Emperor Henry IV made him chancellor of the realm. Five years later, at forty-four years of age, Otto was appointed the bishop of Bamberg. He zealously worked for peace in the face of much opposition from a fellow bishop. He also led a very prayerful and disciplined life and he baptized over twenty-two thousand people. He died at the age of seventy-eight.

Feast Dates: July 2 — St. Otto of Bamberg; February 23 — Bl. Otto of Cappenberg, O. Praem. (see Otto).

Otman (Spanish) See Otto.

Oto (Bulgarian, Croatian) See Otto.

Otón (Spanish) See Otto.

Otone (Italian) See Otto.

Otti (Estonian) See Otto.

Otto "The Rich One" (Old German).

Patron Saints: There are two medieval saints named Otto. The one who became a religious priest was a convert and died in 1172. He caused many problems by resisting the efforts of his brothers, Godfrey and Norbert, to convert him. However, he eventually converted and was filled with zeal.

Feast Dates: February 23 — Bl. Otto of Cappenberg, O. Praem.; July 2 — St. Otto of Bamberg (see Otis).

Ottone (French, Greek, Russian) See Otto.

Ovid Meaning unknown (Greek).

Patron Saints: The patron closest to this name is St. Ovidius, who was a holy bishop in Portugal in the Middle Ages.

Feast Dates: November 1 — St. Ovidius.

Ovidio (Spanish) See Ovid.

Ovie (American) See Obie, Ovid.

Owain (variant) See Owen.

Owen "The Well-Born One" (Welsh form of Eugene) or "God Is Gracious" (Welsh form of John).

Patron Saints: Owen can come from either John or Eugene. There are more than four hundred twenty-five Sts. John and some fifty Sts. Eugene. There are also a few named Owen or Evan. One St. Owen lived from 600 to 684 and was chancellor to the king. He acquired some land and had a monastery built. At the age of forty-seven he received permission from the king to be ordained a priest. Later he was elected a bishop and sent missionaries to all parts of the kingdom.

Feast Dates: August 24 — St. Owen, also known as Ouen.

Ox "The Bovid Beast of Burden" (Old English).

Patron Saints: Because St. Luke begins his Gospel with the story of the birth of Jesus in a stable, Christian art has often used the ox as a symbol for St. Luke.

Feast Dates: October 18 — St. Luke, Evangelist (see Luke).

Oxley (Old English double) See Ox+ Leigh.

Oz (nickname) See Osborn, Oscar, Osmond, Oswald.

Ozburn (English) See Osborn.

Ozell (African-American double) See Osgood/Osmond/Osborn+Denzell.

Ozzie (nickname) See Osborn, Oscar, Osmond, Oswald.

Ozzy (nickname) See Osborn, Oscar, Osmond, Oswald.

P

Paal (Estonian) See Paul.

Paavo (Finnish) See Paul.

Pablo (Spanish) See Paul.

Pace (English) See Pascal.

Packston (variant) See Paxton.

Packy (nickname) See Patrick.

Paco (Spanish, Portuguese) See Francis.

Pacomio (Spanish) See Francis.

Pacorro (Spanish) See Francis.

Paddie (nickname) See Patrick.

Paddy (nickname) See Patrick.

Padget (French) See Page.

Padgett (French) See Page.

Padraic (variant) See Patrick.

Padraig (Irish Gaelic) See Patrick.

Padrig (Welsh) See Patrick.

Page "The Young Assistant" (French).

Patron Saints: There are two English martyrs with the surname of Page. Bl. Antony Page, 1571-1598, studied at Douai, France, and was ordained a diocesan priest in 1591. He was hanged, drawn, and quartered in 1593 for being a Catholic priest. He was only twenty-seven years old.

The other martyr from England, Bl. Francis Page, met his death at Tyburn in 1602. He had converted to Catholicism and was ordained a secular priest in 1600 at Douai in France. While in prison, awaiting execution, he became a Jesuit.

Feast Dates: May 4 — Bl. Antony Page; April 20 — Bl. Francis Page, S.J.

Paige (English) See Page.

Paine (English) See Payne.

Pal (Hungarian, Scottish, Swedish) See Paul.

Paladio (Spanish) See Palladin.

Pall (variant) See Palladin, Paul.

Palladin "The One Who Fights" (North American Indian).

Patron Saints: There are no saints with the name of Palladin. However, there are more than a dozen Sts. Palladius from which to choose. One of them was the son of the count of Gevaudan. He received a fine education and was elected bishop of Saintes, France, in 570. He built many churches and often found himself at odds with the aristocracy.

Feast Dates: September 6 — St. Palladius.

Pallaten (variant) See Palladin.

Pallaton (variant) See Palladin.

Palm (nickname) See Palmer.

Palmer "The Palm-Bearing Pilgrim" (Old English).

Patron Saints: There are at least three Sts. Palmatius and Palmus. A St. Palmer died in ancient Alexandria, Egypt.

Feast Dates: May 28 — St. Palmer, also known as Palmus.

Panchito (Spanish) See Francis.

Pancho (Spanish, Portuguese) See Alphonse, Francis.

Pancholo (Spanish, Portuguese) See Francis.

Panther "The Large Carnivorous Cat" (Middle English).

Patron Saints: There is a St. Panther. He died a martyr in ancient Thessalonica.

Feast Dates: April 1 — St. Panther, also known as Pantherus.

Panzo (variant) See Francis.

Paolo (Italian) See Paul.

Papa "The Father" (Latin derivative).

Patron Saints: At least four saints were named Papa. Two saints by the name of Papa gave their lives for Jesus in ancient Persia. One of them was a deacon.

Feast Dates: September 5 — St. Papa.

Paquito (variant) See Paco, Francis.

Par (Swedish) See Peter.

Parcifal (Dutch) See Percival.

Paris "The Lover" (Greek).

Patron Saints: There is at least one saint named Paris. He was born in Athens, Greece. After he converted to the teachings of Jesus, he traveled to Italy. Eventually he became bishop of Tiano. He died in 333.

Feast Dates: August 5 — St. Paris.

Park (nickname) See Parker.

Parke (nickname) See Parker.

Parker "The Guardian of the Park" (Middle English).

Patron Saints: Among the candidates to consider for patron is St. John Gualbert, patron of park keepers; St. Peter, guardian of the gates of heaven; and St. Abel, guardian of the gateway to paradise. In addition, there is a large group of angels who guard the Garden of Eden.

Genesis teaches that after Adam and Eve had been expelled from the Garden of Eden, God placed cherubim near its entrance to keep humanity away from the tree of life (see Genesis 3:22-24). They were pictured to be like powerful winged lions whose task was to enforce God's law. The Bible also tells us that two cherubim were carved on either side of the Ark of the Covenant. Jewish tradition understands them to be the charioteers of God, the bearers of his throne.

Feast Dates: September 29 and October 2 — The Holy Cherubim; June 29 — St. Peter, Apostle (see Peter).

Parlan (Scottish) See Bartholomew.

Parlett (American double) See Parlan+ Ett.

Parnel (variant) See Parnell.

Parnell "Little Peter [Rock]" (Old French).

Patron Saints: There are more than two hundred thirty Sts. Peter from which to choose.

Feast Dates: June 29 — St. Peter, Apostle (see Peter).

Parrie (nickname) See Parrish.

Parrisch (nickname) See Parrish.

Parrish "From the Church District" (Middle English).

Patron Saints: There is Bl. Kirkman, whose name means "churchman," and a St. Ecclesius, which means "church." St. Ecclesius was the archbishop of Ravenna in the early 500s. He accompanied Pope John I to Constantinople. He also built a church that was a copy of the pagan temple of Minerva.

Feast Dates: July 27 — St. Ecclesius; May 4 — Bl. Richard Kirkman of Skipton (see Kirk).

Parry "The Dweller Near the Pear Tree" (variant of Perry) or "The Son of Harry" (variant of Harold) or "Little Peter" (variant of Peter) or "From the Church" (variant of Parish).

Patron Saints: If one accepts Harold as the root of Perry, then a couple of Sts. Harold can be adopted. On the other hand, if one thinks Parry is a variant of Peter, then some two hundred thirty patrons emerge. If the name is a form of Parrish, then two more saints qualify.

Feast Dates: June 29 — St. Peter, Apostle (see Peter); July 27 — St. Ecclesius (see Parrish).

Parsifal (Italian, Polish, Czech) See Percival.

Partricio (Spanish) See Patrick.

Parzival (German, Hungarian) See Percival.

Pascal "The One Born at Easter" (French).

Patron Saints: There are at least three Sts. Pascal. St. Pascal Baylon, 1540-1592, was born into a peasant family in an obscure corner of Spain and became a shepherd. At about the age of eighteen he joined the Franciscan Friars Minor as a brother and did the most ordinary of tasks. His care of the sick was always tender and compassionate. It seems he was infused with a deep joy.

However, he is best known for his devotion to the Eucharist. He spent long hours in prayer before the Blessed Sacrament and prayed from a homemade scrapbook of prayers saved from the rubbish heap. Pascal died at the age of fifty-two with the name of Jesus on his lips. He lived in simplicity and obscurity, and the Catholic Church has appointed him patron over Eucharistic confraternities and congresses.

Feast Dates: May 17 — St. Pascal Baylon, O.F.M.

Pascale (variant) See Pascal.
Paschal (Cornish) See Pascal.
Pascoe (Cornish) See Pascal.
Pascual (Spanish) See Pascal.
Pasquale (Italian) See Pascal.
Passi (Estonian) See Sebastian.
Pastor "One Who Shepherds" (Latin).

Patron Saints: There are about a half-dozen Sts. Pastor. One lived in the second century and was the brother of Pope Pius I. He erected the church now known in Rome as St. Prudenziana. It seems St. Pastor had the blessing of dying in peace.

Feast Dates: July 27 — St. Pastor.

Pat (nickname) See Patrick, Peyton, Patton.

Pate (nickname) See Peyton, Patton.
Paten (variant) See Peyton, Patton.
Patin (variant) See Peyton, Patton.
Paton (variant) See Peyton, Patton.
Patric (Latin) See Patrick.
Patrice (French) See Patrick.
Patricio (Spanish, Portuguese) See Patrick.
Patricius (Dutch) See Patrick.
Patrick "The Noble One" (Latin, English).

Patron Saints: There are about eighteen Sts. Patrick and Patricius. Four of them, according to one story, helped the great St. Patrick McCalpurn convert Ireland. (Since Patrick's father's name was Calpurnius, the saint can be referred to as Patrick McCalpurn to set him apart from the other four Patricks.) The four who helped him win the Irish over to Christ were Sts. Patrick Palladius, Patrick McMawon, Patrick McSannan, and Patrick McAlfryd.

Patrick was probably born in Roman Britain. However, he was captured and carried off into slavery by pagan Irish raiders. He returned to Britain when he was about twenty-two. He then traveled to Gaul, became a monk, and in 417 was ordained a priest. In 432 he was consecrated a bishop and sent to Ireland as a missionary. Earlier missions, led by two other Sts. Patrick, had failed.

During his thirty years in Ireland he made converts, raised the standards of learning, brought Ireland into a closer relationship with the rest of Europe, wrote a defense of his activities to answer detractors, and denounced raiding Welsh Catholics who were killing Irish Catholics. He died at about the age of seventy-six and is the patron of Ireland and Nigeria, as well as of those bitten by snakes.

Feast Dates: March 17 — St. Patrick, also known as Patrick McCalpurn.

Patrik (Czech, Finnish, Swedish, Hungarian) See Patrick.

Patriss (Latvian) See Patrick.

Patrizio (Italian) See Patrick.

Patrizius (variant) See Patrick.

Patryk (Polish) See Patrick.

Patsy (nickname) See Patrick.

Patten (variant) See Peyton, Patton.

Pattie (nickname) See Patrick.

Pattin (variant) See Peyton, Patton.

Patton "From the Warrior's+Town" (Irish Gaelic double).

Patron Saints: There is one English martyr, Bl. William Patenson, a convert. He was a diocesan priest who was tried, convicted, hanged, drawn, and quartered in 1592. During the hanging portion, his executioners cut him down while he was still conscious in order to make him suffer more. They were angry with him because he had convinced six of the seven men imprisoned with him to convert to Catholicism. He was in his thirties.

Feast Dates: January 22 — Bl. William Patenson of Durham; July 21 — St. Tondach (see Town).

Patty (nickname) See Patrick, Peyton, Patton.

Paul "The Small One" (Latin).

Patron Saints: There are about one hundred thirty Sts. Paul. The most famous is St. Paul the Apostle, who lived from about the years 3 to 64. He is recognized by the Catholic Church as patron of the press, authors, journalists, publishers, writers, rope makers, tentmakers, upholsterers, hospital public relations personnel, and travelers, as well as of Greece and Malta; he is also known as the Apostle to the Gentiles.

He was born a Jew and a Roman citizen. While Aramaic was his native tongue, he also spoke Greek fluently. He became a tentmaker. He was short and probably had a lisp. Some scholars think he was single; still others insist that he married but was divorced from his wife because of his conversion to Christianity. He experienced conversion probably between the years 34 and 36 when he was in his early thirties. Between 43 and 67, he made four trips, preaching throughout the Mediterranean world and converting many, during which time he suffered imprisonment, stoning, and shipwreck. It is likely that he wrote between eight to thirteen of the Epistles attributed to him in the New Testament. He made Christianity understandable to non-Jews. He died in Rome on the same day as St. Peter, having been beheaded at the age of sixty-four.

Feast Dates: June 29 — St. Paul, Apostle.

Paulie (nickname) See Paul.

Paulin (German, Polish) See Paul.

Paulino (Spanish) See Paul.

Paulo (Portuguese, Swedish, Hawaiian, Spanish) See Paul.

Paulos (Greek) See Paul.

Paulus (Latin, Dutch) See Paul.

Pauly (nickname) See Paul.

Pava (Russian) See Paul.

Paval (Russian) See Paul.

Pavao (variant) See Paul.

Pavel (Bulgarian, Slovenian, Russian) See Paul.

Pavlo (Ukrainian) See Paul.

Pawel (Polish) See Paul.

Pawley (nickname) See Paul.

Pax (Latin) See Paxton.

Paxon (English double) See Pax+Town.

Paxton "From the Peaceful+Town" (Old English double).

Patron Saints: There is no saint named Paxton. However, knowing that

Paxton is composed of two words (*pax* and *ton*, meaning "peace" and "town") leads to many patrons. Among them is St. Pacius, who died a martyr's death for the faith in ancient Spain.

Feast Dates: January 11 — St. Pacius; July 21 — St. Tondach (see Town).

Payne "The Unbaptized Pagan" (Latin) or "One from the Country" (Latin).

Patron Saints: One English martyr, St. John Payne, will make a fine patron. A native of England, he was educated for the priesthood at Douai, France, and ordained in 1576. He worked many years in the English missions at Ingatestone in Essex. He was convicted of the false charge of plotting against the queen and killed in 1600.

Feast Dates: April 20 — St. John Payne.

Payton (English) See Peyton, Patton.

Paz (Spanish) See Pax.

Peadar (Gaelic) See Peter.

Pearce (variant) See Percival, Peter.

Pearson (English double) See Peter+Son.

Peder (Danish) See Peter.

Pedrín (Spanish) See Peter.

Pedro (Spanish) See Peter.

Peeter (Estonian) See Peter.

Peirce (variant) See Percival. Peter.

Pekka (Finnish) See Peter.

Pello (Basque) See Peter.

Pen (nickname) See Penrod.

Penn (nickname) See Penrod.

Pennie (nickname) See Penrod.

Penny (nickname) See Penrod.

Penrod "The Famous Commander [General]" (Old German).

Patron Saints: The Catholic Church has named seven saints as patrons of generals. They are Sts. Adrian, Faith of Agen, Ignatius Loyola, Martin of Tours, Mercury, Sebastian, and Theodore the Recruit (Theodore of Tiro).

Feast Dates: May 31 — St. Ignatius Loyola (see Ignatius); November 9 — St. Theodore (see Theodore).

Pentti (nickname) See Benedict.

Pepe (Spanish) See Joseph.

Pepi (nickname) See Pepin.

Pepillo (Spanish) See Joseph.

Pepin "The Persevering Petitioner" (Old German, Spanish).

Patron Saints: There is one known St. Pepin. He was master of the royal palace of Austrasia in the mid-600s and became the ancestor of the Carolingian dynasty of French kings. He is remembered as serving his people as a wise and magnanimous king. Catholic teaching must have found a home in his palace because he produced two daughters who have been officially recognized as saints by the Catholic Church. They are Sts. Begga and Gertrude.

Feast Dates: February 21 — St. Pepin the Elder of Landen.

Pepito (Spanish) See Joseph.

Peppi (nickname) See Pepin.

Peppy (nickname) See Pepin.

Pequin (Spanish) See Peter.

Per (Scandinavian) See Peter.

Perce (nickname) See Percival.

Perceval (English) See Percival.

Percival "The Valley Piercer" (Old French) or "Piercer of the Veil of Religious Mystery" (Old French).

Patron Saints: There is an English martyr named Bl. Thomas Percy, 1528-1572. He was the earl of Northumberland and was condemned to death and executed at York for his part in the rising of the North against Elizabeth. Before he was executed, he spent three years in prison. During this time he was repeatedly offered his freedom on the condition that he embrace the Protestant faith. He steadfastly refused.

He was forty-four years old at the time of his death.

Feast Dates: August 26 — Bl. Thomas Percy.

Percy (French) See Percival.

Perekin (variant) See Peter.

Perequin (Spanish) See Peter.

Perico (Spanish) See Peter [through Pedro].

Perkin (English double) See Peter+Kin.

Perkins (English variant) See Perkin+Son.

Pernell (variant) See Parnell.

Pero (Spanish) See Peter [through Pedro].

Perren (variant) See Peter.

Perry (variant) See Parry, Peter.

Pershing "One Who Sells Peaches" (German) or "One Who Sorrows" (German).

Patron Saints: It is helpful to know that a "seller of peaches" is a grocer, and St. Michael is patron of grocers.

Feast Dates: September 29 — St. Michael the Archangel (see Michael).

Pervis (variant) See Purvis.

Petar (Bulgarian) See Peter.

Pete (nickname) See Peter.

Peter "The Rock" (Latin).

Patron Saints: There are more than two hundred thirty Sts. Peter. The most famous is St. Peter the Apostle, who is recognized as patron of bridge builders, clockmakers, fishermen, masons, netmakers, shipbuilders, stationers, those seeking long life, and those suffering from fevers, foot trouble, or from frenzy, as well as protection against wolves.

He was a Galilean fisherman, who married Perpetua and had one daughter, Petronilla. After the ascension of Jesus, Peter presided over the election of Matthias, received the first Jewish and Gentile converts into the Church, performed the first miracles, and guided the Council of Jerusalem to its decision. Peter was martyred in 64, just outside Rome. He was crucified upside down.

Feast Dates: June 29 — St. Peter, Apostle.

Peters (English double) See Pierson, Peter+Son.

Peterson (English double) See Pierson, Peter+Son.

Peterus (variant) See Peter.

Petey (nickname) See Peter.

Petie (nickname) See Peter.

Peto (Hungarian) See Peter.

Petr (Czech) See Peter.

Petras (Lithuanian) See Peter.

Petro (Ukrainian) See Peter.

Petronio (Spanish) See Peter.

Petros (Greek) See Peter.

Petru (Romanian) See Peter.

Petrus (Dutch, German) See Peter.

Petter (Norwegian) See Peter.

Peyo (Spanish) See Peter [through Pedro].

Peyton "From the Warrior's+Estate" (Irish Gaelic double).

Patron Saints: Peyton means the same thing as Patton or Paten, and there is a Bl. William Patenson. There is also a twentieth-century American saint-in-the-making who can be adopted as a fine patron. Father Patrick Peyton, 1909-1993, was born in Ireland and in 1928, at the age of nineteen, went to America with his brother, Tom. They lived with their sister in Scranton, Pennsylvania. A year later, both entered the seminary at Notre Dame, Indiana. He was ordained in 1941. The following year he felt called to dedicate his life to promoting the "family Rosary." In 1945 he had the opportunity to promote his idea in Hollywood. And many stars backed him with time, money, and energy. In 1947 *Father Peyton's Family Theater* made its debut on television. His teaching, "The family that prays together, stays together," became a popular saying in many households.

Feast Dates: November 1 — SG Patrick Peyton, C.S.C.; January 22 — Bl. William Patenson (see Patton).

Phil (nickname) See Filmore, Philip.

Philip "Lover of Horses" (Greek).

Patron Saints: Some fifty saints are named Philip. The greatest is St. Philip the Apostle. He was also a married man and the father of three daughters, all of whom remained single and dedicated their lives to prayer.

After the resurrection of Jesus, Philip preached in Scythia and then in Phrygia. He died the death of a martyr. He was tied to a cross and then stoned to death. He is patron of fullers.

Feast Dates: May 3 — St. Philip, Apostle.

Philipp (German) See Philip.

Philippe (French) See Philip.

Philippus (Dutch) See Philip.

Phillip (English) See Philip.

Phillips (Old English double) See Philip+Son.

Philo "The Loving, Friendly One" (Greek).

Patron Saints: There are a half-dozen Sts. Philo. One of them died a martyr in ancient Spain.

Feast Dates: January 11 — St. Philo.

Phineas "The Oracle" (Hebrew).

Patron Saints: Christian tradition provides one St. Phineas and the Old Testament provides one more. St. Phineas, who lived around the twelfth century before Christ, was the grandson of Aaron, the brother of Moses. Filled with great zeal for God, he served as a Jewish high priest. He even went to war at one point to overthrow the pagan Madianites and their worship of Baal-Phegor.

Feast Dates: August 12 — St. Phineas, Jewish High Priest.

Phoenix "The Blood-Red, Deadly One" (Greek).

Patron Saints: The phoenix was a mythical bird of great beauty that lived a life span of three hundred to five hundred years in the Arabian desert. Periodically it would burn itself on a funeral pyre and then rise from its own ashes, restored to youthfulness.

It was adopted and made a Christian symbol in the first century. At first it served as an artistic reminder of the expected resurrection of the dead. Later is was used as a symbol of the resurrected Lord.

Feast Dates: November 1 — All Saints Awaiting the Resurrection; Easter Sunday — The Resurrected Lord.

Pico (Spanish) See Peter [through Pedro].

Pierre (French) See Peter.

Pierce (English) See Percival, Peter.

Piercy (nickname) See Percival.

Piero (Italian) See Peter.

Pierre (French) See Peter.

Piers (Middle English, Dutch) See Peter.

Pierson "Son of+Peter [Rock]" (Middle English double).

Patron Saints: There is one English martyr with the surname of Pierson. In 1537 the English government began to apply pressure on the twenty-nine monks in the London Carthusian monastery. Nineteen monks, including the prior, took the Oath of Supremacy, recognizing the king as head of the Church.

However, ten others refused. This group included three priests, one seminarian, and six lay brothers. One of the religious brothers was Walter Pierson. All were imprisoned, tied to posts, and left to die of starvation. They were kept alive for a short time on account of the heroic actions of St. Thomas More's adopted daughter, Margaret Clement, who sneaked food to them. But when King Henry expressed surprise that the monks were still alive, Margaret was found out and refused admittance, and the monks slowly starved to death.

Feast Dates: May 11 — Bl. Walter Pierson, O. Cart.

Piet (Dutch) See Peter.

Pieter (Dutch) See Peter.

Pietrek (variant) See Peter.

Pietro (Italian) See Peter.

Pilib (Irish) See Philip.

Pilypas (Lithuanian) See Philip.

Pincas (variant) See Phineas.

Pinchas (variant) See Phineas.

Pincus (variant) See Phineas.

Pino (Italian) See Joseph.

Pio (Italian, Spanish) See Pius.

Piotr (Polish, Bulgarian) See Peter.

Pious (English) See Pius.

Pip (nickname) See Philip.

Pipi (Spanish) See Lucky, Happy.

Pipo (Spanish) See Lucky, Happy.

Pippin (German) See Papa.

Pippo (nickname) See Philip.

Piter (Hispanic-American) See Peter.

Piti (Spanish) See Peter, Rock.

Pitin (Spanish) See Felix.

Pito (Spanish) See Felix.

Pius "The Pious One" (Latin).

Patron Saints: There are a half-dozen saints named Pius, including St. Pius X, 1835-1914. He was named Giuseppe Sarto by very poor parents. As a boy he had no shoes, but he did get an education. After being ordained, he quickly moved up in the hierarchy of the Catholic Church. In 1903 he was elected pope. During his pontificate, the reception of First Communion was extended to children at the early age of seven. He also condemned the heresy of Modernism and saw to the codifi-cation of canon law. He died at the age of seventy-nine.

Feast Dates: August 21 — St. Pius X, Pope.

Pjotr (Slavic) See Peter.

Placi (nickname) See Placido.

Placid (English, Russian) See Placido.

Placide (French) See Placido.

Placido "The One Without Worry" (Spanish).

Patron Saints: There are about a dozen-and-half Sts. Placidus. One of them was born into the royal Rhaetian family. He founded the Dissentis monastery in Switzerland. It seems that he was quick to speak out against injustice. This ultimately attracted the attention of a man named Victor who hated Placidus so much that he had him murdered in 670.

Feast Dates: July 11 — St. Placidus.

Placidus (Latin) See Placido.

Placyd (Polish, Ukrainian) See Placido.

Plakidos (Greek) See Placido.

Plasio (nickname) See Placido.

Plato "The Broad-Shouldered One" (Greek).

Patron Saints: There are at least two Sts. Plato. One was a rich youth in Constantinople in ancient times. Because he insisted on being Catholic, he was arrested and condemned to torture and death. Red-hot iron plates were laid upon him, and his flesh was roasted and then cut off in strips. He languished in prison for eight days and then was beheaded.

Feast Dates: July 22 — St. Plato.

Platon (Spanish) See Plato.

Pol (Irish, Swedish) See Paul.

Polo (Greek) See Apollo.

Polo (Italian) See Paul.

Ponce (Spanish) See Quentin.

Ponso (nickname) See Alphonse.

Port (nickname) See Porter.

Porter "The Gatekeeper" (French).

Patron Saints: There are two saints who are universally recognized as heaven's gatekeepers.

Feast Dates: January 2 — St. Abel (see Abel); June 29 — St. Peter, Apostle (see Peter).

Portie (nickname) See Porter.

Porty (nickname) See Porter.

Poul (Danish) See Paul.

Povilas (Lithuanian) See Paul.

Powel (variant) See Powell.

Powell "Son of+Howell [Alert One]" (Old English double).

Patron Saints: There is an English martyr surnamed Powel. In 1640 a predominantly Puritan parliament began to challenge the king and again register hostility toward Catholics. And once again Catholics began to die. One of these was Bl. Philip Powel, a Benedictine priest, who had ministered to Catholics in England for twenty-four years. He was hanged at Tyburn in 1646.

Feast Dates: June 30 — Bl. Philip Powel, O.S.B.

Pranas (Lithuanian) See Francis, Frank.

Pren (nickname) See Prentice.

Prent (nickname) See Prentice.

Prentice "The Apprentice" (Middle English).

Patron Saints: Since the name Prentice means "apprentice," we can turn to St. John Bosco, 1815-1888, patron of apprentices. He entered the seminary at the age of sixteen. After ordination, he was assigned as chaplain of a girls' refuge. His time off found him entertaining and ministering to homeless boys. Then he rented some poor lodgings and asked his mother to act as his housekeeper and began to gather neglected boys to train as apprentices in various trades. Slowly,

other priests joined him, and he eventually founded the Salesian religious order to care for the children. In all, he opened almost one hundred homes for homeless children. His enemies, thinking him crazy, once sent priests to take him to an insane asylum. Being warned in time, he sent the priests off to the asylum by themselves.

Feast Dates: January 31 — St. John Bosco.

Prescott "From the Priest's+Cottage" (Old English double).

Patron Saints: Patrons can be found once one becomes aware that Prescott is made up of two words: *pres*, meaning "priest," and *cott*, meaning "cottage." One is St. Cottus, who was a citizen of ancient Besançon. He fled when the Roman persecution ordered by Emperor Aurelian arrived in town. But his flight was not successful, and he was captured and then executed near Auxerre in 274.

Feast Dates: November 1 — St. Cottus; May 30 — Bl. Thomas Cottam (see Byron).

Presley (English double) See Preston+ Lee.

Preston "From the Priest's+Estate" (Old English double).

Patron Saints: Two martyrs are from Preston, England. One of them, Bl. Richard Herst, a farmer, made his peace with Catholicism and began practicing his faith. This upset many Protestants, and they arranged to have him arrested on the false charge of murder. He was then tried on this charge. The reluctant jury was commanded by the judge to find Richard guilty. It soon became obvious that the real reason for the conviction was that he had reconciled with Catholicism. Just before his execution he was commanded to listen to an Anglican sermon. He refused, sticking his fingers in his ears. Then on the gallows he was told his life would be spared if he would recognize the king as head of the Church. He again refused and was hanged in 1628.

Feast Dates: August 29 — Bl. Richard Herst of Preston; August 24 — St. John Wall of Preston (see Walton).

Prezell (African-American double) See Prescott/Preston+Denzell.

Price "The Son of+The Ardent One" (Old Welsh double).

Patron Saints: Usually St. Brice is offered as a patron for a person named Price. It is helpful to know that the name means "ardent one." This leads one to Ignatius, whose name also means "ardent one."

Feast Dates: November 13 — St. Brice (see Brice); July 31 — St. Ignatius Loyola (see Ignatius).

Primo "The Firstborn Son" (Italian, Spanish).

Patron Saints: There are almost two dozen Sts. Primus. One was an aged citizen of Rome. Both he and his friend Felicianus refused to reject Jesus even when subjected to many torments. In the end they were both beheaded.

Feast Dates: June 9 — St. Primus.

Prince "The Chief" (Latin) or "The Leader" (Latin).

Patron Saints: The word *principis* is Latin for "prince." There are two Sts. Principinus and two Sts. Principius. One St. Principius was the bishop of LeMans and had great love for the poor and sick. He died in 501.

However, the greatest patron is Jesus the Prince of Peace. The prophet Isaiah introduced the Messiah as the Prince of Peace, the Wonderful Counselor, Mighty God, and Everlasting Father because of his perfect justice. The Gospel of Matthew insists that those who strive to live in peace will be specially blessed and be called "the sons of God."

Feast Dates: September 11 — St. Principius; Christmas Season — Jesus, Prince of Peace.

Prinz (English) See Prince.

Pritchard "The Rich, Powerful Ruler (English form of Richard).

In 1589 Bl. Humphrey Pritchard, a layman, was executed by the English government because he converted to Catholicism. He was only twenty years old.

Feast Dates: May 4 — Bl. Humphrey Pritchard.

Pryce (English) See Price.

Purcell (variant) See Percival.

Purvis "One Who Provides Food" (English-French) or "A Steward" (English-French).

Patron Saints: It is helpful to know that a steward is a domestic servant, and two saints have been appointed as patrons of domestics. One is St. Martha of Bethany and the other is St. Zita. One can also adopt St. John Rigby, who was a steward. And because a steward is a "dispenser of provisions," one is led to Bl. William Spenser.

Feast Dates: June 21 — St. John Rigby (see Steward); May 4 — Bl. William Spenser (see Spencer).

Pylyp (Ukrainian) See Philip.

Pyotr (Russian) See Peter.

Q

Qadeer (African-American) See Quaadir.

Quaadir (Arabic) See Quinlan.

Quabeel (Arabic) See Cain.

Quadarius (African-American double) See Quan+Darius.

Quade (African-American) See Quartus.

Quadeer (African-American) See Quaadir.

Quamaine (African-American double) See Quan+Jermaine.

Quan (African-American) See Quanah.

Quanah "The Fragrant One" (North American Indian).

Patron Saints: The Latin word for "fragrant" is *odoratus,* which can lead to a number of patrons, including Sts. Oderisiua and St. Odorio. There is also a St. Odoric, 1286-1331, who joined the Franciscans and traveled for three years in the Far East. He even preached the Gospel in the royal court of the Great Khan, where he was well received. He returned in 1330 with great plans for Chinese missions. However, he died before he could see the pope and inaugurate these plans.

Feast Dates: January 14 — St. Odoric.

Quandré (African-American double) See Quan+André.

Quantavious (African-American double) See Quan+Octavius.

Quartus "The Fourth-Born Son" (Latin).

Patron Saints: There are a dozen Sts. Quartus. One was a layman who died a martyr in ancient Rome.

Feast Dates: August 6 — St. Quartus.

Quashawn (African-American double) See Quan+Shawn.

Quenby (Scandinavian) See Quimby.

Quennell (African-American double) See Quan+Denzel.

Quent (variant) See Quentin.

Quenten (Latin) See Quentin.

Quentin "The Fifth-Born" (Latin) or "From the Queen's+Town" (Old English double).

Patron Saints: There are about fifty saints named Quintianus, Quintillus, Quintinus, and Quintus. St. Quentin was a Roman Christian who decided to journey to Gaul with a friend. Their purpose was to make converts for Jesus. At Amiens, France, the local prefect took exception to their activities and had Quentin thrown into prison. When Quentin would not give up his faith, the prefect had him whipped and then tortured. Quentin escaped from prison and headed directly for the marketplace to continue his preaching. He was again arrested and then beheaded.

Feast Dates: October 31 — St. Quentin, also known as Quintinus.

Quico (Spanish diminutive) See Chico.

Quill (variant) See Quillan.

Quillan "The Little Cub" (Irish Gaelic).

Patron Saints: St. Quilisinda lived as a holy Benedictine nun in Switzerland in about 650.

Feast Dates: August 22 — St. Quilisinda.

Quimby "The Dweller at the Woman's Estate" (Old Norse).

Patron Saints: The closest match that can be made is with St. Quiemad of medieval Trèves.

Feast Dates: November 6 — St. Quiemad.

Quin (variant) See Quinn.

Quina (Spanish) See Achilles.

Quinby (variant) See Quimby.

Quincy "The Dweller at the Fifth Son's Estate" (Latin).

Patron Saints: St. Quintius was born in Phrygia. A committed layman, he decided he had to tell others about Jesus. This led to his arrest and torture by the governor. Released after forty days, he continued his preaching. He was arrested and tortured again. This time, his legs were broken. Eventually he gained his freedom and worked as a physician for many years.

Feast Dates: July 2 — St. Quintius.

Quindarius (African-American double) See Quin+Darius.

Quindell (African-American double) See Quin+Dell/Denzell.

Quinlan "The Strong One" (Irish Gaelic).

Patron Saints: There are some fifty saints available for the job of patron.

Feast Dates: July 2 — St. Quintius (see Quincy).

Quinn "The Wise Counselor" (Irish Gaelic) or "The Fifth-Born Son" (short form of Quentin).

Patron Saints: Quinn can be accepted as a complete name in itself or as a short form of Quentin, Quincy, Quindell, and Quinlan.

Feast Dates: October 31 — St. Quentin, also known as Quintinus (see Quentin); July 2 — St. Quintius (see Quincy).

Quint (variant) See Quentin.

Quintavius (African-American double) See Quin+Octavius.

Quintin (variant) See Quentin.

Quinto (Spanish) See Quentin.

Quinton (variant) See Quentin.

Quiqui (Spanish) See Henry.

Quisi (African-American) See Quincy.

Quito (Spanish) See Achilles, Quentin.

$\mathcal{R}$

Raashid (Arabic) See Reynolds.
Rab (Scottish) See Rabi, Robert.
Rabbi (Arabic) See Rabi.
Rabbie (nickname) See Robert.
Rabi "Like the Breeze" (Arabic).

Patron Saints: There is an ancient saint with a similar name, St. Rabulas, who can be adopted. Also, it is helpful to know that Rabi has the same meaning as the Latin *zephyrus,* which leads to an ancient pope, St. Zephyrinus.

Rabulas converted to Christianity and was later appointed bishop of Edessa. He was also a strong force in forming the canon (Church law) for the ancient Syrian Church. He died of old age in 435.

Feast Dates: December 17 — St. Rabulas; August 26 — St. Zephyrin (see Zephyrin).
Race "The One Who Races [Goes Fast]" (English).

Patron Saints: Race means almost the same thing as the names Remus and Sherwin.

Feast Dates: September 3 — St. Remaclus (see Remus); December 1 — St. Ralph Sherwin (see Sherwin).
Racel (English) See Race.
Racho (nickname) See Horace.
Rad "The Adviser" (English) or "Happy One" (Slavic).

Patron Saints: St. Radbod served as a holy bishop in Holland. He died in 918.

Feast Dates: November 29 — St. Radbod.
Radbert (Old English double) See Rad+Bert.

Radcliff (Old English double) See Rad+Cliff.
Radford (Old English double) See Rad+Ford.
Radious "Electronic Sound Transmitter" (African-American).

Patron Saints: The Catholic Church has appointed St. Gabriel to be patron of radio workers.

Feast Dates: September 29 — St. Gabriel the Archangel.
Radislav (Slavic) See Radoslaw.
Radley (Old English double) See Rad+Leigh.
Radman (Slavic double) See Rad+Mann.
Radoslaw "The Glorious, Happy One" (Polish).

Patron Saints: St. Hilary can be pressed into service here.

Feast Dates: January 13 — St. Hilary of Poitiers.
Raemonn (variant) See Raymond.
Rafael (Spanish) See Raphael.
Rafaele (Italian) See Raphael.
Rafaello (Italian) See Raphael.
Rafail (Russian) See Raphael.
Rafal (Polish) See Raphael.
Rafe (nickname) See Rafferty, Ralph, Raphael.
Raff (nickname) See Rafferty, Ralph.
Raffaello (Italian) See Raphael.
Raffarty (variant) See Rafferty.
Rafferty "The Rich, Prosperous One" (Irish Gaelic).

Patron Saints: Rafferty means "rich," and the Latin word for "rich" is *fortunatus.* There are about sixty saints named Fortunatus, Fortunianus, and Fortunio.

Feast Dates: June 18 — St. Fortunatus (see Lucky).

Rafi (Spanish) See Raphael.

Raghnall (Irish) See Reginald, Ronald.

Ragnvald (Scandinavian) See Reginald.

Raimo (Finnish) See Raymond.

Raimondo (Italian) See Raymond.

Raimund (German) See Raymond.

Raimundo (Spanish, Portuguese) See Raymond.

Rainger (English) See Ranger.

Raleigh "From the Deer+Meadow" (Old English double).

Patron Saints: There is an English saint surnamed Hartley, whose name comes from *hart* and *ley* (or *leigh*), meaning "stag" and "meadow." This is almost identical to the meaning of Raleigh, which leads us to Bl. Richard Leigh.

Feast Dates: October 5 — Bl. William Hartley (see Hartley); August 30 — Bl. Richard Leigh (see Leigh)).

Ralf (English) See Ralph.

Ralfs (Latvian) See Ralph.

Ralph "The Wolf [Wise] Counselor" (Old English).

Patron Saints: There are a half-dozen saints named Ralph. One of them is St. Ralph of Slignac, the son of Raoul, count of Ouercy. He was given into the care of the Benedictine abbot of Slignac. In time, Ralph became a monk, then a priest, and finally an abbot. He is remembered for supporting education, founding monasteries, and promoting the welfare of the general populace. He died in 866.

Feast Dates: June 21 — St. Ralph of Slignac; December 1 — St. Ralph Sherwin (see Sherwin).

Ralphie (nickname) See Ralph.

Ralston (Old English double) See Ralph+Town.

Ram "The Ram" (Middle English) or "The Godlike One" (Hindu).

Patron Saints: Besides being a full name in its own right, Ram can also serve as a nickname for Ramadon, Ramiro, Ramón, Ramses, and Ramsey. There is a St. Ramnold, who was a holy abbot in Bavaria in the year 1000.

Feast Dates: June 17 — St. Ramnold.

Rami (Spanish) See Ramiro.

Ramírez "The Divine Judge" (Spanish).

Patron Saints: The Mexican martyr Father Peter Esqueda Ramírez was executed by firing squad on November 22, 1927. He was canonized in 2000.

Feast Dates: November 22 — St. Peter Esqueda Ramírez.

Ramiro "The Divine Judge" (Spanish).

Patron Saints: St. Ramiro was prior of a monastery in Spain when the Visigoth Arian heretic king took control of the land. The prior and his monks would not agree to the Arian heresy and were massacred by the king's men while they recited the Nicene Creed.

Feast Dates: March 11 — St. Ramiro and Companions.

Ramón (Spanish) See Raymond.

Ramos "The Branch of a Tree" (Spanish).

Patron Saints: St. Ramiro, a saint with a similar name, can be adopted here.

Feast Dates: March 11 — St. Ramiro (see Ramiro).

Ramsey (Old English double) See Ram+Dempsey.

Rance "The One Crowned with Laurel Leaves" (nickname for Lawrence) or "He Who Borrowed All" (Africa) or "Like a Dull Red [or Pale Blue or White] Marble" (Belgian).

Patron Saints: Some think Rance is a variant of Lawrence, and this leads to about forty Sts. Lawrence. Others think the name arises from a particular kind of marble. And the Catholic

Church has named two saints as patrons of marble workers: Sts. Clement and Louis.

Feast Dates: August 10 — St. Lawrence (see Lawrence); November 23 — St. Clement (see Clement).

Rancell (African) See Rance.

Ranch "From the Small Farm" (Spanish).

Patron Saints: It helps to know that the name Ranch means "farm," which leads to four saints who have been named patrons of farmers by the Catholic Church. They are Sts. Isidore, George, Sidwell, and Walstan.

Feast Dates: May 15 — St. Isidore the Farmer (see Isadore); April 23 — St. George (see George).

Rand (nickname) See Randall, Randolph.

Randal (English) See Randall, Randolph.

Randall "The Shield [Swift] Wolf" (Modern English form of Randolph).

Patron Saints: Most experts seem to think that Randall is only a modern form of Randolph.

Feast Dates: February 21 — St. Randoald (see Randolph).

Randell (Spanish) See Randall, Randolph.

Randey (Spanish) See Randall, Randolph.

Randi (nickname) See Randall, Randolph.

Randie (nickname) See Randall, Randolph.

Randle (Spanish) See Randall, Randolph.

Randolf (Spanish) See Randall, Randolph.

Randolfo (Spanish) See Randall, Randolph.

Randolph "The Shield [Swift] Wolf" (Old English) or "The Wolf [Wise] Counselor" (form of Ralph).

Patron Saints: Randolph can come from either Randolf or Ralph. The first means "swift wolf"; the other is "house wolf." Both can be translated as "wise

counselor." Furthermore, there are almost a half-dozen Sts. Ralph and a few Sts. Adolf, whose name means "hero wolf." There are also a dozen-and-a-half Sts. Lupus, which means "wolf" in Latin. Finally, there is one St. Randoald. He was martyred in ancient Grandval.

Feast Dates: February 21 — St. Randoald.

Randulfo (Spanish) See Randall, Randolph.

Randy (nickname) See Randall, Randolph.

Range (English) See Ranger, Rangle.

Ranger "The Public Lands Warden" (Old French).

Patron Saints: Knowing that a Ranger is a "guardian" or "warden of public lands" leads to two English saints surnamed Ward, which is a short form of "warden."

Father Watson was in jail because he was a Catholic priest and two of his friends came to his rescue. St. Margaret Ward furnished a rope, while her Irish servant, Bl. John Roche, provided a boat to help him escape from jail in 1588. They were both soon arrested. In prison, they were offered their freedom if they would attend a Protestant service. They refused and were hanged in 1603.

Feast Dates: August 30 — St. Margaret Ward; July 26 — Bl. William Ward, also known as Webster (see Ward).

Rangle "The Cowboy" (Spanish-American).

Patron Saints: Cowboys work with cattle, and St. Sylvester is associated with them because pious legend tells of how he raised a bull back to life.

Feast Dates: December 31 — St. Sylvester.

Ranse (nickname) See Lawrence, Ransom.

Ransell (African) See Rance.

Ransom (Old English double) See Randall+Son.

Ranolfo (Italian) See Randall, Randolph.

Raoul (French) See Ralph, Randolph, Rudolph.

Raphael "The One Healed by God" (Hebrew).

Patron Saints: The Old Testament Book of Tobit identifies him as one of the seven angels that continually worship before the throne of God. God sent him in response to the prayers of Tobit and Sarah. God always hears our prayers, no matter when or where they are said.

Jewish tradition further suggests that it is Raphael's job to bring healing to the earth. Also, Raphael was one of the three men (in reality God and two of his angels) who visited Abraham (see Genesis 18). He also healed Abraham of his circumcision and Jacob of his injured hip. He is the guardian of the West, of the evening winds, and of the tree of life in the Garden of Eden. He is one of the six angels of repentance, prayer, love, joy, and light. And he is the "angel of science and knowledge."

In Christian tradition he is the angel who stirred the waters of Bethesda. In medieval paintings he is pictured dining with the patriarchs because he is also the "sociable angel." Moreover, he is patron of apothecaries, happy meetings, druggists, health inspectors, lovers, nurses, physicians, travelers, young people leaving home, those with eye diseases (including the blind), those who raise sheep, and for a safe journey.

Feast Dates: September 29 — St. Raphael the Archangel.

Ras (nickname) See Erasmus, Erastus.

Rashad (Arabic) See Quinn.

Rashan (Arabic) See Star.

Rashawn (African-American double) See Rashad+Shawn.

Rashean (African-American double) See Rashad+Sean.

Rasheed (Arabic) See Rashad.

Rasmus (Danish) See Erasmus.

Rastus (nickname) See Erastus.

Raul (Italian, Spanish, French) See Ralph.

Rauli (Finnish) See Ralph.

Raven "Blackbird" (Old English) or "The Crow" (Old English).

Patron Saints: There is an English martyr surnamed Crow. Because a raven is really a "crow," Bl. Alexander Crow can be adopted as a patron. During the reign of Queen Elizabeth I, Father Alexander Crow was arrested for being a Catholic priest. He was executed in 1586.

Feast Dates: May 4 — Bl. Alexander Crow; May 16 — St. Brendan the Voyager (see Brendan).

Ravi "The One Like the Sun" (Hindu).

Patron Saints: This is a Hindu name, but, surprisingly, there are patrons readily available. One is St. Ravennus, who with his friend was a native of Britain in ancient times. They fled to northern France in order to live in peace as hermits and to devote their lives to prayer. However, in the end, they both suffered martyrdom. One can also adopt St. Cyrus as a patron because the name Cyrus means "sun."

Feast Dates: July 23 — St. Ravennus; January 31 — St. Cyrus (see Cyrus).

Ravid (variant) See Ravi.

Raviv (variant) See Ravi.

Rawley (variant) See Raleigh.

Rayce (English) See Race.

Ray (nickname) See Raphael, Rayburn, Raymond, Royal.

Ray "The Deer" (Old English) or "The Kingly One" (French).

Patron Saints: Ray can also be a short form of Raphael, Raymond, and RayShawn.

Feast Dates: March 15 — Bl. William Hart (see Hershel); April 24 — St. Mark Rey, also known as Fidelis of Sigmaringen (see Roy).

Rayburn (Old English double) See Ray+Bourne.

Raymond "The Mighty, Wise Protector" (Old German).

Patron Saints: There are a half-dozen Sts. Raymond. One of them, St. Raymond of Peñafort, O.P., 1175-1275, was born near Barcelona, Spain, where he completed school and subsequently taught rhetoric and logic. He is recognized as patron of canonists, lawyers, law schools, and medical records librarians.

In 1221 he joined the Order of St. Dominic. He filled his life with prayer, preaching, instructing, hearing confessions, and converting heretics, Jews, and Moors. When he was fifty-five, Pope Gregory IX called him to Rome to be his personal confessor and ordered him to collect and codify all the papal decretal letters that had been issued during the past one hundred years. This became the standard Church law until 1917. The pope tried to make him archbishop of Tarragona, Spain. But anxiety over this made Raymond ill and the pope relented. Raymond returned to Barcelona and was elected third master general of the Dominican religious order. He lived to the age of about one hundred.

Feast Dates: January 7 — St. Raymond of Peñafort, also known as Ramón.

Raymundo (Spanish) See Raymond.

Raynaldo (Spanish) See Reynolds.

Rayshawn (African-American double) See Ray+Shawn.

Raz (Hungarian) See Rufus.

Read (English) See Red.

Reade (English) See Red.

Reading (Old English double) See Red+Ingar.

Reagan (English) See Regan.

Reagen (English) See Regan.

Reamonn (Irish) See Raymond.

Rebrecht (variant) See Robert.

Red "Red [Ruddy] One" or "From the Reeds" (Old English) or "Man with Red Hair" (nickname for Rufus).

Patron Saints: There are about two dozen Sts. Red and Ruddy. However, they spelled their names Rubens, Rubentius, Rubianus, and Rufus. St. Red is known as the "Martyr of the Orient" in ancient times.

Feast Dates: January 17 — St. Red, also known as Rubentius.

Rede (English) See Red.

Redford (Old English double) See Red+Ford.

Redd (English) See Red.

Redman (Old English double) See Red+Mann.

Reece "The Ardent One" (Welsh).

Patron Saints: Reece means the same thing as Rhett, and there are two ancient saints named Rhett. One was born into a noble family at Autun and married. After the death of his wife, he was chosen to be bishop of Autun. He was a great writer and defender of the faith. Unfortunately, most of his writings have been lost. He died in 334.

Feast Dates: July 20 — St. Rhett, also known as Rheticus.

Reed (Old English) See Red.

Reese (English) See Reece.

Reeves "The Shire Officer" (Middle English) or "The Steward" (Middle English).

Patron Saints: Two saints have been appointed as patrons of domestics. One is St. Martha of Bethany; the other is St. Zita. And then there is St. John Rigby, who worked as a steward. Also, because a steward is a "dispenser of provisions," one can adopt Bl. William Spenser.

Feast Dates: June 21 — St. John Rigby (see Steward); May 4 — Bl. William Spenser (see Spencer).

Reg (nickname) See Reginald, Regis.

Regan "The Little King" (Irish Gaelic).

Patron Saints: One ancient saint who can serve as a patron is St. Regan. He was a deacon who was martyred for the faith in ancient Omer.

There are a half-dozen others named Regulus, whose name in Latin means "little" or "vassal king."

Feast Dates: May 25 — St. Regan, also known as Regenar; November 25 — St. Regulus (see Ryan).

Regen (variant) See Regan.

Reggie (nickname) See Reginald, Regis.

Reggis (English) See Reginald, Regis.

Reggy (nickname) See Reginald, Regis.

Reginald "The Mighty, Powerful One" (Old English).

Patron Saints: There are about a half-dozen saints named Reginald. One of them, Bl. Reginald of Orléans, 1183-1220, became a Church lawyer and taught canon law at the University of Paris from 1206 to 1211. At the age of twenty-nine, he was appointed dean of a collegiate chapter at Orléans. Then, just two years before his death, he met St. Dominic and became vicar of the Dominicans.

Reginald went to Bologna to found a Dominican religious house. The following year he returned to Paris to found another house. It is said that he had a vision of the Blessed Virgin, who told him that the Dominicans were to wear a white woolen scapular as a sign of their commitment. He died at the age of thirty-seven.

Feast Dates: February 12 — Bl. Reginald of Orléans, O.P.

Reginauld (French) See Reginald.

Regis "The Regal One" (Latin) or "The Kingly One" (Latin).

Patron Saints: There is a fine patron named Bl. Francis Regis Clet, 1748-1820. He was born at Grenoble and joined the Lazarist Fathers. After ordination, he was sent to China as a missionary in 1791 and worked there for the remainder of his life, nearly thirty years. He often faced great difficulties. Finally in 1820, when he was seventy-two, he was tortured and then strangled near Hankow.

One can also look to Christ the King for a patron.

Feast Dates: February 17 — Bl. Francis Regis Clet; July 20 — St. Roys (see Leroy).

Reid (English) See Red.

Reilly (variant) See Riley.

Reinald (Dutch, German) See Reginald.

Reinaldo (Spanish) See Reginald.

Reinaldos (Spanish) See Reginald.

Reinhold (Danish, Swedish) See Reginald.

Reino (Finnish) See Reginald.

Reinold (Dutch, German) See Reginald.

Reinwald (German) See Reginald.

Rem (nickname) See Remington, Remus.

Remington "From the Raven+Estate" (Old English double).

Patron Saints: There are five saints with similar names. However, it might be better to adopt two English saints to serve as patrons. Remington is composed of two words: *reming*, which means "raven," and *ton*, meaning "estate" or "town." There are at least a dozen English martyrs with "ton" in their names. Also, there is one English martyr, Bl. John Ingram, whose name means "raven."

Feast Dates: July 26 — Bl. John Ingram (see Ingram); July 21 — St. Tondach (see Town).

Remo (nickname) See Remington, Remus.

Remus "The Fast Moving One" (Latin).

Patron Saints: St. Remaclus, a saint with a similar name, was a native of Aquitaine and became an abbot of a local monastery before being named a bishop. He died in 663.

Feast Dates: September 3 — St. Remaclus; December 1 — St. Ralph Sherwin (see Sherwin).

Renado (variant) See Reynolds.

Renaldo (Spanish) See Reginald, Reynolds.

Renardo (Italian) See Reginald.

Renato (variant) See Reynolds.

Renaud (French) See Reginald, Ronald.

Renault (French) See Reginald.

René "The Reborn One" (Latin) or "The Mighty, Powerful One" (short form of Reginald).

Patron Saints: There are six ancient saints named Raynie and two ancient Sts. Renatus, also known as René. One saint is a North American martyr. St. René Goupil, 1608-1642, entered the Jesuit novitiate in Paris as soon as he could. However, he had to leave because of deafness. Then he turned to the study of medicine and in 1639 offered his services to the Jesuits to serve as a *donné* in the New World. A *donné* worked without salary, as a lay assistant. He hunted food, rowed boats, pitched tents, and fixed equipment.

The year 1640 found René Goupil assigned to a hospital in Quebec, Canada. Then Father Isaac Jogues arrived looking for an assistant. René volunteered to accompany him. On a jour-

ney from Quebec to Indian lands the men were ambushed by an Iroquois band and taken captive. They were forced to run the gauntlet and jabbed with sharp instruments and were then made slaves. During this captivity, Father Jogues received René as a religious brother. René, who had taught prayers to the Indian children, was tomahawked by a warrior when he made the Sign of the Cross over one of the children. He died in 1642 at the age of thirty-four.

Feast Dates: October 19 — St. René Goupil, S.J.

Renny (Irish) See René.

Reno "The Gambler" (American) or "The Brown-Haired One" (Spanish short form of Moreno).

Patron Saints: Two saints may serve here as patrons. One of them, St. Renus, was martyred in ancient Carthage.

Feast Dates: February 24 — St. Renus; September 6 — SG Carmen Moreno, F.M.A. (see Moreno).

Renzo (nickname) See Lorenzo, Lawrence.

Reod (English) See Red.

Reon (African-American double) See any "Re" name+Deone.

Reuben "Behold a Son" (Hebrew).

Patron Saints: Christian tradition provides us with three saints who have variants of the name Reuben. And the Bible presents us with four more men with the same name. A Christian St. Reuben was a priest and a stylite in Kartamin in Mesopotamia. A stylite was a Christian who did penance by living on top of a pillar, day and night. Such a practice was popular in ancient times.

Feast Dates: August 1 — St. Reuben.

Reuven (Hebrew) See Reuben.

Rex (Latin) See Regis.

Rexford (Old English double) See Rex+ Ford.

Rey (Spanish) See Regis.

Reyes (English) See Reece.

Reymundo (Spanish) See Raymond.

Reynaldo (Spanish) See Reynolds.

Reynold (Old English) See Reginald, Reynolds.

Reynolds "Son of+Reginald [Powerful One]" (Old English double).

Patron Saints: There are two English martyrs named Reynolds. St. Richard Reynolds of Devon, 1492-1535, became a Bridgettine monk-priest and was appointed university preacher. Then King Henry VIII insisted that all in his kingdom take the Oath of Supremacy, recognizing him as head of the Church. This was something that Father Richard Reynolds absolutely refused to do and was included in the first group of martyrs the king had executed in 1535.

Father Thomas Reynolds, 1562-1642, whose real name was Green, was born at Oxford in England. Upon growing up he traveled to Rheims in France to study for the Catholic priesthood and be ordained. Then he returned to England and ministered to his people for nearly fifty years as a diocesan priest. But, eventually, the British authorities caught him and hanged him. He was about eighty at the time of his martyrdom.

Feast Dates: May 4 — St. Richard Reynolds of Devon; January 21 — Bl. Thomas Green, also known as Reynolds.

Réz (Hungarian) See Rufus.

Rezso (Hungarian) See Rudolph.

Rhett (Welsh) See Reece.

Rhisiart (Welsh) See Richard.

Rhodes "The Dweller at the Crucifix" (Old English) or "The Place Where Roses Grow" (Greek).

Patron Saints: Although no saint seems to carry the name Rhodes, there are a dozen Sts. Rhodon. One died a martyr's death in ancient Greece.

Feast Dates: March 20 — St. Rhodon.

Rhys (variant) See Reece.

Rian (variant) See Ryan.

Riane (variant) See Ryan.

Ric (Italian, Spanish) See Richard.

Ricard (variant) See Richard.

Ricardo (Spanish) See Richard.

Riccardo (Italian) See Richard.

Ricciardo (Italian) See Richard.

Rice (variant) See Reece.

Rich (nickname) See Aldrich, Broderick, Cedric, Eric, Frederick, Richard, Roderick.

Richard "The Powerful Ruler" (Old German) or "The Very Brave One" (Old German).

Patron Saints: There are two dozen Sts. Richard from which to choose. One was an English royal prince from Wessex who never became a king. However, he did belong to a family of saints. Through marriage to his wife, Winna, Richard became the uncle of St. Boniface. Moreover, his three sons and one daughter are all recognized as saints.

In 720 Richard decided to make a pilgrimage to Rome with his entire family. He began the journey but did not finish it. He died en route to Rome and was buried in the Church of San Frediano.

It is interesting to learn that an unusual occurrence is observed each year, even to this day. For four months each year, from about October 12 to February 15, oil drips from the bones of St. Richard.

Feast Dates: February 7 — St. Richard the "King."

Richardo (variant) See Richard.

Richardson "The Son of+Richard [The Powerful Ruler]" (Old English double).

Patron Saints: There are two English martyrs with the name of Richardson. One was Bl. Laurence Richardson, who often went by the name of Johnson in the English underground of the 1500s. A native of Great Crosby, he was ordained in France in 1577 and immediately went to England. He was hanged for being a Catholic priest in 1586.

Feast Dates: May 30 — Bl. Laurence Richardson; February 17 — Bl. William Richardson (see Anderson).

Richart (Dutch) See Richard.

Richerd (English) See Richard.

Richi (Spanish) See Richard.

Richie (nickname) See Rick.

Richman (Old English double) See Richard+Mann/Manfred.

Richy (nickname) See Rick.

Rick (nickname) See Aldrich, Broderick, Cedric, Eric, Frederick, Richard, Roderick.

Rickard (variant) See Richard.

Rickert (German) See Richard.

Rickie (nickname) See Rick.

Ricky (nickname) See Rick.

Rico (Spanish) See Richard.

Rico (Italian) See Henry.

Riddick (African-American) See Riddock.

Riddock "From the Smooth Way" (Irish).

Patron Saints: One saint is available for a patron.

Feast Dates: September 25 — Bl. William Way (see Wayland).

Rider "The Horseman" (Middle English) or "The Cavalry Rider" (Old English).

Patron Saints: An English martyr surnamed Knight might be adopted as patron.

Feast Dates: May 4 — Bl. William Knight (see Knight).

Ridge "From the Area on the Ledge" (Middle English).

Patron Saints: There is a St. John Rigby. *Rigby* means "meadow" or "town" on the "ledge" or "ridge."

Feast Dates: June 21 — St. John Rigby (see Steward).

Ridgeway (Old English double) See Ridge+Way.

Ridgley (Old English double) See Ridge+Leigh.

Riel (Spanish) See Gabriel.

Riggs (nickname) See Ridge.

Ridley (Old English double) See Red+Leigh.

Rik (nickname) See Aldrich, Broderick, Cedric, Eric, Frederick, Richard, Roderick.

Rikard (Scandinavian) See Richard.

Riki (nickname) See Aldrich, Broderick, Cedric, Eric, Frederick, Richard, Roderick.

Riku (Finnish) See Richard.

Riley "The Valiant, Warlike One" (Irish Gaelic).

Patron Saints: Patrons can be found if one knows that Riley means "valiant" or "brave." In Latin the word for "brave" is *fortis*. This leads to Bl. Fortis Gabrielli, a religious priest who became a hermit and lived in the mountains near Scheggia. Sometime later, he retired to the monastery of Fontavellano. He lived there for ten years, until his death in 1040.

Feast Dates: March 13 — Bl. Fortis Gabrielli.

Rinaldo (Italian) See Reginald.

Ring "From the Circle [Ring]" (Old English) or "The Apple" (Japanese).

Patron Saints: There are a couple of Sts. Ring. However, in ancient Rome, they spelled their name as Corona. One St. Ring died for Jesus in ancient times.

She is a patron of games of chance, lotteries, and hidden treasure.

Feast Dates: May 14 — St. Ring, also known as Corona.

Ringo (English) See Ring.

Río (Spanish) See River.

Riobard (Irish) See Robert.

Riocard (variant) See Richard.

Riordan (Irish) See Teague.

Ripley "From Shouter's+Meadow" (Old English double).

Patron Saints: Ripley is really a marriage of two words: *rip* meaning "shouter" and *ley* (or *leigh*) meaning "meadow." There is no saint named Ripley, but there is a Bl. Richard Leigh.

Feast Dates: August 30 — Bl. Richard Leigh (see Leigh).

Riqui (Spanish) See Richard.

Risteard (Irish) See Richard.

Risto (Finnish) See Christopher.

Ritch (nickname) See Aldrich, Richard, Roderick.

Ritchard (English) See Richard.

Ritchie (nickname) See Aldrich, Richard, Roderick.

Ritchy (nickname) See Aldrich, Richard, Roderick.

Ritter (Old English) See Rider.

River "From the Flowing Waters" (Middle English).

Patron Saints: Flumen is Latin for "river," and there is a St. River (or Fluminus). He died a martyr's death in ancient Rome.

Feast Dates: May 28 — St. River, also known as Fluminus.

Roarke "The Famous Ruler" (Irish Gaelic).

Patron Saints: A saint with a similar name is St. Ruak, who died a martyr in ancient Egypt.

Feast Dates: October 3 — St. Ruak.

Rob (variant) See Robert.

Robart (Bulgarian) See Robert.

Robat (Welsh) See Robert.

Robb (nickname) See Robert.

Robbie (nickname) See Robert.

Robby (nickname) See Robert.

Rober (Spanish) See Robert.

Robert "The One Bright with Fame" (Old English).

Patron Saints: There are about a dozen Sts. Robert. Among the most famous ones is St. Robert Bellarmine, 1542-1621, a Doctor of the Church and patron of catechists and canonists.

He became a Jesuit and a very effective preacher. At the age of twenty-eight he was ordained a priest and given a professorship. He became the leading mind of his age. He was a friend of Galileo.

Feast Dates: September 17 — St. Robert Bellarmine.

Robertas (Lithuanian) See Robert.

Roberto (Italian, Portuguese, Spanish) See Robert.

Roberts (English double) See Robinson, Robert+Son.

Robertson (English double) See Robinson, Robert+Son.

Robin "The Little One+Bright with Fame" (Old English double).

Patron Saints: The name Robin is generally accepted as a form of Robert. And there are about a dozen Sts. Robert. There are also two Bls. Robinson. Bl. Christopher Robinson was executed by the British government in 1597 because he insisted on ministering to the Catholics in England.

Feast Dates: May 4 — Bl. Christopher Robinson.

Robinet (Old English double) See Robin+Ett.

Robinson "Son of+Robert [The One Who Shines Bright]" (Old English double).

Patron Saints: There are two English martyrs. One of them, Bl. John Robinson, was married. But after his wife died he went to France to be ordained a priest. After ordination in 1585 he went back to England, where he was arrested and executed in 1588.

Feast Dates: October 1 — Bl. John Robinson.

Robrecht (Dutch) See Robert.

Robyn (English) See Robert.

Rocco (Italian) See Rochester, Rocky, Rockwell.

Roch (French) See Rochester, Rocky, Rockwell.

Roche (Old English) See Rochester, Rock, Rocky, Rockwell.

Rochester "From the Rocky+Fortress [Camp]" (Old English double) or "The Sky Fortress" (Old English).

Patron Saints: Rochester comes from two words: *roche* and *chester*, meaning "rock" and "camp." Thus many saints can qualify as patrons for Rochester. A good candidate is Peter the Apostle, whom Jesus named "Rock." There is also Bl. John Rochester, who when faced with taking the Oath of Supremacy to King Henry VIII wrote a letter of protest. This led to his arrest, along with that of Father William Walworth. They were both swiftly tried and executed in 1537.

Feast Dates: May 11 — Bl. John Rochester, O. Cart.

Rock (Old English) See Rochester, Rocky, Rockwell.

Rockie (Old English) See Rochester, Rocky, Rockwell.

Rockwell (Old English double) See Rocky+Wells.

Rocky "The Rock" (English).

Patron Saints: There are three saints who can serve as patrons of Rock. The finest is St. Peter the Apostle, whom Jesus named "Rock." Plus, there is an English martyr, Bl. John Rochester.

There is also a St. Rock who was a native of France. In about 1348 he traveled to Italy, where a pestilence was raging, and dedicated himself to nursing the sick and dying. It is said that he cured a great many sick people simply by making the Sign of the Cross over them. Then he became ill and, not wishing to be a burden to anyone, dragged himself into the woods to die. He was discovered and helped.

He returned to France and was arrested for being a vagrant and a foreign spy. In prison for five years, he died from neglect. He is patron of cattle, dog lovers, invalids, prisoners, as well as those suffering from cholera, contagious diseases, skin diseases, and the plague.

Feast Dates: August 16 — St. Rock, also known as Roche.

Rod "The Famous One" (Old German).

Patron Saints: There is one St. Rod. He died a martyr in ancient Tomi. There are also many saints who have Rod as part of their names. They include Penrod, Roderick, Rodman, Rodney, and Rodger.

Feast Dates: January 3 — St. Rod, also known as Rodus.

Rodas (Spanish) See Rhodes.

Rodd (nickname) See Rod.

Roddie (nickname) See Rod.

Roddy (nickname) See Rod.

Roderic (English) See Roderick.

Roderich (German) See Roderick.

Roderick "The Famous Ruler" (Old German).

Patron Saints: There are a few Sts. Roderick. One of them was a convert from Islam in 857, during the time Cordova, Spain, was occupied by the Muslims. After becoming a Catholic, he was ordained a priest. But his brother denounced him to the authori-

ties and he was immediately imprisoned for being a Christian. Soon after,
he was beheaded.

Feast Dates: March 13 — St.
Roderick, also known as Rodrigo.

Roderigo (variant) See Roderick.

Roderyk (Polish, Ukrainian) See Roderick.

Rodge (nickname) See Roger.

Rodger (English) See Roger.

Rodhlann (Irish) See Roland.

Rodney "From the Famous One's Island"
(Old English).

Patron Saints: There are a couple of
Sts. Rodney once one realizes that the
original spelling of the name is
Rodanig (also known as Rodan). Furthermore, there are many ancient saints
who have Rod as part of their names.
St. Rodan is remembered as one of the
"Twelve Apostles of Ireland." He was
a follower of St. Finian of Clonard and
founded a monastery at Lorrah in
about 550. He also founded monasteries at Dare-Enech and Bonaghum and
served as abbot. He died in 584.

Feast Dates: April 15 — St. Rodney,
also known as Rodan.

Rodolfo (Spanish, Italian) See Rudolph.

Rodolph (English) See Rudolph.

Rodolphe (French) See Rudolph.

Rodrick (English) See Roderick.

Rodrigo (Italian, Spanish, Portuguese)
See Roderick.

Rodrigue (French) See Roderick.

Rodríguez (Spanish) See Roderick.

Rodzers (Latvian) See Roger.

Roeland (Dutch) See Roland.

Roelof (Dutch) See Rudolph.

Rog (nickname) See Roger.

Rogelio (Spanish) See Roger.

Roger "The Famous Spearman" (Old
English).

Patron Saints: There are about a half-
dozen saints named Roger, one of them

being Bl. Roger James. In 1539 he was
the youngest Benedictine monk at
Glastonbury Abbey. When he refused to
recognize the king as head of the Church,
he was executed with two fellow monks.
Another is Bl. Roger Filcock, a Jesuit.
He was executed in 1600 by the English
government for being a priest.

Feast Dates: November 15 — Bl.
Roger James, O.S.B.; November 15 —
Bl. Roger Filcock, S.J.

Rogerio (Spanish, Portuguese) See Roger.

Rogero (Portuguese) See Roger.

Rogers (English double) See Roger+Son.

Rohan (African-American double) See
Robert/Roland+Aaron.

Roi (French) See Roy.

Roibeard (Irish) See Robert.

Roja (Spanish) See Red.

Rojelio (German) See Roger.

Roland "From the Famous Land" (Old
German).

Patron Saints: There are about a
half-dozen saints named Roland. One
was the count of Mans under Charlemagne. He fought against the invading Muslim armies and fell in battle in
778.

Feast Dates: June 16 — St. Roland.

Rolando (Portuguese, Spanish) See
Roland.

Rolann (Irish) See Roland.

Rolant (Welsh) See Roland.

Roldan (Spanish) See Roland.

Roldao (Portuguese) See Roland.

Roley (variant) See Roland.

Rolf (Old German, English, Scandinavian) See Ralph, Rudolph.

Rolfe (variant) See Ralph, Rudolph.

Rolland (English) See Roland.

Rollie (nickname) See Rollo.

Rollin (English) See Roland.

Rollins (English) See Roland.

Rollo (nickname) See Erroll, Raleigh,
Ralph, Roland, Rolando, Rudolph.

Rollon (Spanish) See Roland.
Rolly (nickname) See Rollo.
Rolon (Spanish) See Rudolph.
Rolph (variant) See Rudolph, Ralph.
Romain (variant) See Roman.
Roman "The One from Rome" (Latin).
   Patron Saints: There are over forty saints named Romanus. A Syrian deacon named St. Roman lived during the sixth century. He is remembered as "The Melodist" and is considered the greatest Greek hymn writer of ancient times. About eighty of his hymns survive to our time. Modern critics pronounce them to be vivid and dramatic but too long and flowery.
   Another 1,250 unnamed Christians are remembered as being martyred in ancient Rome for Jesus.
   Feast Dates: October 1 — St. Roman the Melodist; November 1 — All Holy Martyrs (see Courtney).
Romano (Spanish) See Roman.
Rome (English) See Roman.
Romeo "The Pilgrim to Rome" (Italian, Spanish).
   Patron Saints: There is one St. Romeo. He lived in the fourteenth century in Italy and was known to be a holy priest.
   Feast Dates: March 4 — St. Romeo.
Romualdo (Spanish) See Romulus.
Romulus "The Citizen of Rome" (Latin).
   Patron Saints: There are about a dozen Sts. Romulus. One died a martyr in ancient Concordia.
   Feast Dates: February 17 — St. Romulus.
Ron (nickname) See Aaron, Myron, Ronald.
Ronald "The Powerful One" (Scottish form of Reginold).
   Patron Saints: There is one St. Ronald and about a half-dozen Sts. Reginald. St. Ronald, the earl of Ork-

ney, lived in the twelfth century. He was also a warrior prince because of a vow he had made in the Cathedral of St. Magnus at Kirkwall. He was murdered by rebels in 1158.
   Feast Dates: August 20 — St. Ronald, Warrior Prince.
Ronaldo (Italian, Portuguese) See Ronald.
Ronnie (nickname) See Aaron, Myron, Ronald.
Ronny (nickname) See Aaron, Myron, Ronald.
Rooney "The Red-Haired One" (Irish Gaelic).
   Patron Saints: In Latin, "red-haired" is *capillus rufus*, and there are a dozen Sts. Rufus. One can also adopt a saint with a similar-sounding name such as Rouin, Ruan, Riowen, or Ruine. St. Ruine is simply remembered as an "Irish saint."
   Feast Dates: September 25 — St. Ruine; August 27 — St. Rufus (see Rufus).
Roope (Finnish) See Robert.
Roosevelt "From the Rose Field" (Old Dutch).
   Patron Saints: Roosevelt comes from *roose* and *velt*, meaning "rose" and "field." In addition, there are a few saints with Rose as part of their names. They include St. Rosius, who was one of a group of twelve African bishops set afloat on a helmless ship during the Vandal persecutions in the 400s. He was probably black.
   Feast Dates: September 1 — St. Rosius, Bishop; May 13 — St. Field (or Farm), also known as Ager (see Field).
Roque (Spanish, Portuguese) See Rochester, Rocky, Rockwell.
Rorke (English) See Roarke.
Rory "The Red King" (Irish Gaelic) or "The Famous Ruler" (nickname for Roderick).

Patron Saints: Knowing that the name Rory means "red king" leads to a few patrons. About twenty ancient saints can be found who are named Rubianus, Rubens, Rubentius, and Rufus, whose names mean "red."

There are also many saints who reigned as kings. Some of the more popular ones are St. Louis, king of France; St. Wenceslaus, king of Bohemia; St. Stephen, king of Hungary. And, of course, the greatest patron of them all is Jesus, who is "Christ the King."

Feast Dates: January 17 — St. Red, also known as Rubentius (see Red); Thirty-fourth Sunday of the Year — Christ the King.

Rosalio (Spanish) See Rosey.

Rosario "He Who Prays the Rosary" (Spanish, Italian) or "The Garland of Flowers" (Latin).

Patron Saints: Counting one's prayers on beads is a very old practice, found in many different cultures and religions. In the Catholic Church the practice dates to the 100s with the *Jesus Prayer* prayed on each bead. In the Western Church, the use of a rosary can be traced to about 1200. At that time it became the custom to recite anywhere from fifty to one hundred fifty Our Fathers. This prayer was introduced to help the illiterate pray.

In the 1400s the Rosary devotion, preached by the Dominican Alan de la Roche, was essentially the same as that prayed today. In 1573 the pope established the feast of the Holy Rosary. It celebrated the victory of Christian forces over the Muslims at Lepanto in 1571.

Feast Dates: October 7 — Our Lady of the Holy Rosary.

Rosco (variant) See Roscoe.

Roscoe "From the Deer Forest" (Scandinavian).

Patron Saints: Knowing that Rosco means "deer forest" leads to two patrons, both English martyrs. The first is Bl. William Hart, whose surname is Old English for "deer" or "stag." The second is Bl. John Forest, whose last name means just what it says.

Feast Dates: October 5 — Bl. William Hart (see Hartley); May 22 — Bl. John Forest (see Forest).

Rosey (nickname) See Roosevelt.

Rosie (nickname) See Roosevelt.

Ross "From the Peninsula" (Scottish Gaelic) or "The Red One" (French) or "Deer Forest" (short form of Roscoe).

Patron Saints: There is one saint with a similar name. He is St. Niles of Rossano. More can by found by matching the meaning of the name. *Ross* means "red," and about twenty ancient saints can be found with names that mean "red" or "ruddy." Their names are Rubens, Rubentius, Rubianus, and Rufus.

Feast Dates: September 26 — St. Niles of Rossano (see Niles); January 17 — St. Rubentius (see Red).

Rosse (variant) See Roscoe, Ross.

Rossie (nickname) See Roscoe, Ross.

Rossy (nickname) See Roscoe, Ross.

Roth "The Red-Haired One" (Old German).

Patron Saints: There are a handful of saints who have Roth as part of their names. They include Sts. Rothald, Rothard, and Rotho. St. Rotho first served as a Benedictine abbot. Then he served as the bishop of Paderborn for sixteen years. He died in 1052.

Feast Dates: November 6 — St. Rotho of Buren.

Rourke (English) See Roarke.

Rouvin (variant) See Reuben.

Rovertos (Greek) See Robert.

Rowan (variant) See Rooney.
Rowe (nickname) See Roland.
Rowen (variant) See Rooney.
Rowland (English) See Roland.
Rowney (variant) See Rooney.
Roy "The King" (Old French).

Patron Saints: In French, "king" is *roy* (or *roi*) while in Spanish it is *rey*. This leads to St. Mark Rey, who was born at Sigmaringen, Prussia, in 1577. After he earned his doctorate, he dedicated himself to serving the poor. He became known as the "Poor Man's Lawyer." At the age of thirty-five, he became disgusted with the abuses of his profession, gave up his law practice, and gave away his wealth to the poor. Then he was ordained a Capuchin monk and took the name Fidelis.

He became a successful preacher and converted many Protestants back to Catholicism. This made him some very bitter enemies. He received hate mail and, on one occasion, a gun was fired at him but missed. Finally, in 1622, he was ambushed and murdered at the age of forty-five.

Feast Dates: April 24 — St. Mark Rey, also known as Fidelis of Sigmaringen.
Royal (Middle English) See Roy.
Royce (English) See Roy+Son.
Ruaidhri (Irish) See Roderick.
Ruark (English) See Roarke.
Rube (English) See Reuben.
Rubén (Spanish) See Reuben.
Rubin (variant) See Reuben.
Ruby (English) See Reuben.
Rudd (nickname) See Red, Rudyard.
Ruddie (nickname) See Red, Rudyard.
Ruddy (nickname) See Red, Rudyard.
Rudelle (African-American double) See Rudolph+Dell.
Rudi (Spanish) See Rudolph.
Rudie (nickname) See Rudolph, Rudyard.

Rudiger (German) See Roger.
Rudolf (German, Danish, Swedish, Dutch) See Rudolph.
Rudolfo (Spanish) See Rudolph.
Rudolph "The Famous Wolf" (Old German).

Patron Saints: There are about a half-dozen saints named Rudolph (or variations of it), including Bl. Rudolf Acquaviva, 1550-1583, who became a Jesuit at the age of eighteen. After being ordained a priest, he was sent to Goa, India, to teach philosophy. In 1580 he went to the court of the Great Mogul, Akbar, at Fatehpur Sikri, near Agra. However, three years of hard work led to no converts and he was recalled.

Upon returning to Goa, Rudolf and four other missionaries set about trying to win converts. Some of their methods, including the destruction of Hindu shrines, enraged the villagers, who attacked and killed them. He was only thirty-three at the time of his death.

Feast Dates: July 27 — Bl. Rudolf Acquaviva, S.J.
Rudy (nickname) See Rudolph, Rudyard.
Rudyard "From the Red+Enclosure" (Old English double).

Patron Saints: This English compound name leads to a couple of patrons.

Feast Dates: August 27 — St. Rufus, also known as Red.
Ruele (variant) See Rule.
Ruelle (French) See Rule.
Ruf (French, Bulgarian) See Rufus.
Rufe (Italian) See Rufus.
Ruffo (Italian) See Rufus.
Rufo (Spanish, Portuguese, Croatian) See Rufus.
Ruford (Old English double) See Rufus+Ford.
Rufus "The Man with the Red Hair" (English).

Patron Saints: There are some sixty patrons named Sts. Rufinus and Rufus. One was a high-born Roman in ancient times. He rose to the rank of general in the Roman army and was eventually named consul. Then he retired and converted to Christianity after St. Apollinaris cured his sick daughters through prayer.

This conversion led to his being exiled to Capua. But, while there, he was elected the first bishop of Capua. This did not please the government authorities either. They had Rufus beheaded.

Feast Dates: August 27 — St. Rufus, also known as Red.

Rufusz (Hungarian) See Rufus.

Ruggiero (Italian) See Roger.

Ruhan (African-American double) See Rufus+Aaron.

Rule "The One Who Rules" (English).

Patron Saints: The name Rule seems to be an English form of Regulus, which leads to one saint.

Feast Dates: November 25 — St. Regulus (see Ryan).

Rupert (German, English) See Robert.

Ruperto (Spanish, variant) See Robert.

Ruph (variant) See Ralph, Randolph.

Rupprecht (German) See Robert.

Ruprecht (variant) See Robert.

Rurik (Russian) See Roderick.

Rush "One Who Lives Among the Rushes" (Old English).

Patron Saints: One patron, whose name is the closest to Rush, can serve here. St. Russan McRodan was a disciple of St. Columba of Iona in about 563.

Feast Dates: April 29 — St. Russan McRodan.

Ruskin "The Little Red-Haired One" (French-German).

Patron Saints: The name is derived from the words *rus* (meaning "red") and *kin* (meaning "little"). This leads to

about twenty saints with names that mean "red" or "ruddy," including Rubens, Rubentius, and Rubianus. Another sixty are named Sts. Rufus and Rufinus.

Feast Dates: January 17 — St. Red, also known as Rubentius (see Red); August 27 — St. Rufus (see Rufus).

Russ (nickname) See Cyrus, Rosario, Russell.

Russel (variant) See Russell.

Russell "The Red-Haired One" (French) or "The Fox-Colored One" (French).

Patron Saints: Since the root word of this name is *rus*, which means "red" or "ruddy," we can call on about twenty patrons (among them Rubens, Rubentius, and Rubianus) whose names mean the same thing. An additional sixty Sts. Rufus and Rufinus can be added as patrons.

Feast Dates: January 17 — St. Red (see Red); August 27 — St. Rufus (see Rufus).

Rustie (nickname) See Russell.

Rustin (nickname) See Russell.

Rusty (nickname) See Russell.

Rutger (Dutch, German) See Roger.

Rutherford "From the Cattle+River Crossing" (Old English double).

Patron Saints: The name Rutherford means "cattle ford," and this leads to a patron. He is Bl. Thomas Ford.

Feast Dates: May 28 — Bl. Thomas Ford (see Ford).

Ruttger (variant) See Roger.

Ruy (Spanish) See Roderick.

Ryan "The Little King" (Irish Gaelic) or "The Vassal King" (Irish Gaelic).

Patron Saints: Patrons can be found if one remembers that Ryan means "little king." The Latin word for "little king who rules" is *regulus*. And there are a few Sts. Regulus from which to choose. One St. Regulus was the twenty-sixth archbishop of Rheims in France. He also belonged to the Benedictine religious order and founded the Orbais monastery. He died in 698.

Feast Dates: November 25 — St. Regulus.

Rydder (variant) See Rider.

Ryder (variant) See Rider.

Rye (variant) See Rider, Ryan, Rylan.

Ryeland (Old English double) See Rylan.

Ryerson (Old English double) See Rylan+Son.

Ryffe (Finnish) See Rufus.

Rylan "From the Rye+Farm [Land]" (Old English double).

Patron Saints: Two saints with similar names may help. They are Sts. Ryddoch and Lando. St. Ryddoch was a son of St. Brychan of Wales. This medieval family produced many saints. Ryddoch traveled to France and became a monk.

Feast Dates: November 1 — St. Ryddoch; January 26 — St. Lando (see Land).

Rylee (variant) See Riley.

Ryley (variant) See Riley.

Ryon (variant) See Ryan.

Ryszard (Polish) See Richard.

Ryun (variant) See Ryan.

S

Sabastian (Greek) See Sebastian.

Saber "The Sword" (French).

Patron Saints: In poetic Latin "sword" is *acinaces*, which leads to a St. Acindynus, who was martyred in ancient Thrace.

Feast Dates: August 22 — St. Acindynus.

Sachar (Russian) See Zachariah.

Sage "The Wise Man" (Middle English).

Patron Saints: The fact that Sage means "wise man" leads to three very popular ancient saints. The Gospel of Matthew tells of the Magi, the three wise men from the East who followed a star and came to offer homage to Jesus shortly after his birth. They presented him with gifts of gold, frankincense, and myrrh. The gifts reveal Jesus. Gold indicates he is a king. Frankincense points to his priesthood and divinity. Myrrh indicates that Jesus is united to humanity in its sin and suffering.

In time, Christian tradition produced the Magi's names and places of origin. Melchior came from Persia, Gaspar was from India, and Balthasar came from Arabia. After visiting Jesus, each returned to his homeland, and all became Catholic bishops and made many converts.

Feast Dates: January 6 — Three Wise Men.

Sahar (Estonian) See Zachariah.

Sa'id (Arabic) See Hilary.

Sailbheastar (Irish Gaelic) See Sylvester.

Sakarias (Finnish) See Zachariah.

Sal (variant) See Salvador.

Salamon (Spanish) See Solomon.

Saleem (variant) See Solomon.

Salem (variant) See Solomon.

Salim "The Peaceable One" (Arabic) or "The Lamb" (Arabic).

Patron Saints: There is a St. Solomon whose name means "peace" and a St. Norbert who has been officially named the patron of peace.

Feast Dates: June 17 — St. Solomon (see Jedidiah); June 25 — St. Solomon (see Solomon).

Sallie (variant) See Salvador.

Salmon "The Peaceable One" (Old French).

Patron Saints: There is an English martyr with this name. Bl. Patrick Salmon was the servant of Bl. Thomas Bosgrave. He died with his master in 1594 because they gave shelter to a Catholic priest.

Also, the fact that Salmon means "peaceful" leads to many other patrons.

Feast Dates: July 4 — Bl. Patrick Salmon; June 17 — St. Solomon (see Jedidiah).

Salomo (Dutch, German) See Solomon.

Salomone (Italian) See Solomon.

Salvador "The One Who Brings Redemption" (Spanish).

Patron Saints: There are three saints whose name is a variation of Salvador. One of them is St. Salvator of Horta, 1520-1567, who was a poor shoemaker. In his twentieth year, he became a Franciscan brother and pursued a life of prayer and strict observance of the order's rule. He advanced in spiritual gifts. Soon the blind, deaf, and lame were coming to him seeking healings. He also seemed to possess the gift of prophecy. His devotion to the Blessed

Virgin and to St. Paul was exemplary. He died at the age of forty-seven.

Of course, the greatest patron is Jesus Christ, Our Lord and Savior.

Feast Dates: March 18 — St. Salvator of Horta, O.F.M.

Salvatore (Italian) See Salvador.

Salwator (Polish) See Salvador.

Sam (nickname) See Samson, Samuel.

Samahl (Arabic) See Hilary.

Samahl (nickname) See Samson, Samuel.

Sami (Arabic) See Samuel.

Sammie (nickname) See Samson, Samuel.

Sammy (nickname) See Samson, Samuel.

Sampson (variant) See Samson.

Samson "The One Like the Sun" (Hebrew).

Patron Saints: Christian tradition provides two Sts. Samson, and the Bible adds St. Samson, the judge. St. Samson of Constantinople lived in the middle of the fifth century and was a very rich, philanthropic man. He was also a medical doctor and served all who asked for his services. Moreover, he founded a hospital in Constantinople and in time came to be known as "The Hospitable" and "The Father of the Poor."

Feast Dates: June 27 — St. Samson of Constantinople.

Samu (Hungarian) See Samuel.

Samuel "The Name of God" (Hebrew) or "The One Who Listens" (Arabic).

Patron Saints: Christian tradition provides about a half-dozen Sts. Samuel, and the Bible adds the great prophet Samuel. One St. Samuel and his brother were devout Christians. At one point, they made a pilgrimage to the tomb of the holy martyrs Abdas and companions. While praying there in 375, the brothers were attacked and killed by soldiers under orders from the Persian emperor Shapur II.

Feast Dates: May 18 — St. Samuel.

Samuele (Italian) See Samuel.

Samuelo (Russian, Greek, Bulgarian) See Samuel.

Samuil (Russian, Greek, Bulgarian) See Samuel.

San (Spanish) See Santos.

Sanborn (Old English double) See Sand+Bourne.

Sanchez (Latin) See Santos.

Sancho (Spanish) See Santos.

Sand (nickname) See Alexander.

Sand (Old English) See Sandy.

Sander (English) See Alexander, Sandy.

Sanders (English double) See Sandy/Alexander+Son.

Sanderson "The Son of+Alexander [The Helper of Humanity]" (Old English double).

Patron Saints: Bl. Thomas Holland used different names in the English Catholic underground in the 1600s, including Sanderson and Hammond. He became a Jesuit priest in 1624 and ministered to the Catholics in England until 1642. He was then executed by the government because he was a Catholic priest.

Feast Dates: December 12 — Bl. Thomas Holland of Sutton, also known as Sanderson.

Sándor (Hungarian) See Alexander, Sandy.

Sandro (Italian, Spanish) See Alexander, Sandy.

Sandy "The Helper of Humanity" (short form of Alexander) or "The Loose Beach Soil" (Middle English).

Patron Saints: There are over one hundred twenty saints named Alexander from which to choose. There is also one English martyr, Bl. John Sandys. He was executed for his Catholic priesthood and faith in 1586.

Feast Dates: May 4 — Bl. John Sandys; August 11 — St. Alexander the Charcoal Burner (see Alexander).

Sanford (Old English double) See Sand+Ford.

Sanjay (African-American double) See any "San" name+Jay.

Sansón (Spanish) See Samson, Sunny.

Santana (Spanish) See Santos.

Santiago (Spanish) See James, Santos.

Santino (Spanish double) See San+Antonio.

Santos "The Saintly Holy One" (Spanish).

Patron Saints: The Spanish word *santo* means "saint" or "holy," and *sanctus* is the Latin equivalent. There are a dozen Sts. Sanctianus, Sanctinus, and Sanctus. In the ancient Roman Church the feast of All Saints was celebrated on May 13. Then in 741 Pope Gregory III dedicated a chapel in the Vatican basilica to honor "All the Saints." He also moved the date of the celebration to November 1.

Slowly, most of the other branches (rites) of the Catholic Church adopted the date of November 1 to honor all the saints in heaven, especially those known to God alone. It now allows us to recognize and honor our holy ancestors, relatives, and friends who live with God. It also gives a well-founded hope to all of us on earth that we will soon join our loved ones in an eternal celebration of family.

Ven. Pierre Toussaint, who was born in Haiti but moved to New York, can be added to those mentioned above.

Feast Dates: November 1 — All Saints; June 30 — Ven. Pierre Toussaint (see Toussaint).

Santtwan (Hispanic-American double) See Santos+Antonio/Juan.

Santtwon (Hispanic-American double) See Santos+Antonio/Juan.

Santuan (Hispanic-American double) See Santos+Juan.

Sarge (nickname) See Sargent.

Sargent "The Military Attendant" (Middle English) or "The Army Officer" (Middle English).

Patron Saints: There is an English martyr, Bl. Richard Sargeant, who was imprisoned, tried, convicted, and executed in 1586 because he was a diocesan Catholic priest.

Feast Dates: May 4 — Bl. Richard Sargeant.

Sarito (Spanish) See Caesar.

Saul "The One Asked For" (Hebrew).

Patron Saints: There is one St. Saul. He died a martyr in ancient Africa.

Feast Dates: February 16 — St. Saul.

Saunder (Old English double) See Sandy/Alexander+Son.

Saunderson (Old English double) See Sandy/Alexander+Son.

Saverio (Italian) See Xavier.

Savon (Spanish) See Savannah.

Saw (nickname) See Sawyer.

Sawel (Welsh) See Samuel.

Sawyer "The Sawer of Wood" (Middle English) or "The Carpenter" (Middle English).

Patron Saints: Since a "sawer of wood" is a "carpenter," this leads to four saints who have been named patrons of carpenters. They are Sts. Eulogius of Cordova, Thomas, Wolfgang, and Joseph.

There are also two saints whose name, Sawyl, is similar to Sawyer. One of them, St. Sawyl Benuchel, was the son of St. Pabo, a Welsh king. He married Gwenasedd and became the father of St. Asaph. He was defeated by the pagan Picts, escaped to Wales, and became a religious monk.

Feast Dates: November 1 — St. Sawyl Benuchel; May 1 — St. Joseph the Worker (see Joseph).

Sawyere (English) See Sawyer.

Say (nickname) See Sayer.

Sayer "The Sawer of Wood" (Welsh-Cornish) or "The Carpenter" (Welsh-Cornish).

Patron Saints: Although there seem to be no saints named Sawyer, we can call on other saints with similar names. This includes St. Sawyl Feljin, who was the grandson of King Meurig. History also records that he was one of the four kings who bore the magic sword Excalibur before King Arthur of the Round Table.

Feast Dates: January 15 — St. Sawyl Feljin the Tawny; July 3 — St. Thomas, Apostle (see Thomas).

Sayre (Welsh) See Sayer.

Sayyid (Arabic) See Malik.

Schad (Punjabi) See Happy, Hilary.

Schuyler (Dutch) See Skylar.

Scot (English) See Scott.

Scott "The One from Scotland" (Old English).

Patron Saints: There are two English martyrs with the name of Scott. One is Bl. William Scott, O.S.B., a Benedictine priest who was executed in 1612 because he had converted to Catholicism and became a monk in 1604. The other is Bl. Montford Scott.

Feast Dates: May 30 — Bl. William Scott, O.S.B.; May 4 — Bl. Montford Scott (see Clifford).

Scotti (nickname) See Prescott, Scott.

Scottie (nickname) See Prescott, Scott.

Scotty (nickname) See Prescott, Scott.

Scully "The Town Crier [Herald]" (Irish Gaelic).

Patron Saints: St. Bernardine of Siena is patron of the communications industry and St. Gabriel is patron of radio and television workers. These occupations would include newscasters, the modern equivalent of the medieval herald.

Feast Dates: September 29 — St. Gabriel the Archangel (see Gabriel).

Seafus (African-American variant double) See Cephas/Seton+Rufus.

Seainin (Irish) See John.

Seamas (Irish) See James.

Seamus (Irish) See James.

Sean "God Is Gracious" (Irish form of John).

Patron Saints: Sean is an Irish form of John, and there are more than four hundred saints named John. The greatest is St. John the Apostle. 1 B.C.-A.D. 100, who has been named patron of art dealers, booksellers, compositors, engravers, lithographers, papermakers, printers, publishers, writers, as well as of Turkey and against poisoning.

With Peter and his brother, James, he witnessed the transfiguration of Jesus and the raising of the daughter of the Jewish official Jarius. He was the only Apostle who did not abandon Jesus on the cross and he was the first to believe, on Easter morning, that Jesus had risen as promised.

Christian tradition teaches that John took care of the Blessed Virgin and never married. He founded many churches in Asia Minor and was exiled to the island of Patmos. After he returned to Ephesus, he wrote his Gospel. Tradition states that he died at the age of one hundred one.

Feast Dates: December 27 — St. John, Apostle.

Seaton (Old English double) See Seton.

Seb (Italian) See Sebastian.

Sebastian "The Venerable Revered One" (Latin).

Patron Saints: There are about a dozen Sts. Sebastian. Bl. Sebastian Aparicio, O.F.M., 1502-1600, can be numbered among them. Born to peasants in Spain, the handsome young man was pursued by the ladies. However, at the age of thirty-one, he set sail for the recently discovered New World to make his fortune. First, he worked as a field laborer, then made plows and wagons and transported grain. Finally, he was hired by the government to build the road between Zacatecas and Mexico City. He became very rich and used his money to help the poor. He himself lived very simply.

He married twice and, after the death of his second wife, he gave all his possessions to the poor and to a convent of Poor Clare nuns. Then, at the age of seventy-three, he became a Franciscan brother and performed the most menial of tasks. To this, he added prayer and sacrifices and worked miracles.

Feast Dates: February 25 — Bl. Sebastian Aparicio, O.F.M.

Sebastiano (Italian) See Sebastian.

Sebastien (French) See Sebastian.

Sedale (African-American double) See any "Se" name+Dale.

Segismundo (Spanish) See Sigmund.

Segundo "The Second Son" (Spanish) or "The Second-Hand One" (Spanish).

Patron Saints: There are over three dozen saints named Secundus or variants of the name. One is Father Segundo Montes, a Jesuit priest who was murdered in El Salvador in 1989 and is being considered for canonization.

It was in the early morning hours of November 16, 1989, that government troops forced their way into the Jesuit house of the Central American University in San Salvador. They killed six priests and two housekeepers. One of them was Father Segundo Montes. The others were Fathers Ignacio Martín-Baro, Amando López, Ignacio Ellacuría, Juan Ramón Moreno, and Joaquín López y López; in addition, Elba Ramos and Celina Ramos were killed. All were shot in the head with M-16 rifles at close range.

Feast Dates: November 16 — SG Segundo Montes, S.J.

Selden (variant) See Seldon.

Seldon "From the Willow Tree+Valley" (Old English double).

Patron Saints: There is no saint named Seldon. However, the name arises from two words: *salax*, which means "willow," and *den*, meaning "valley." There is a St. Salès and a Bl. Dean.

St. James Salès, S.J., 1556-1593, was sent with Brother William Saultemouche to preach at Aubenas in the Cévennes. In his sermons he attacked Protestant beliefs and inspired many to embrace Catholicism. This did not make him friends among the Huguenot heretics. One day in February of 1593, James and William were dragged before an improvised court of Calvinist ministers. A heated theological debate followed. It ended with Father Salès being shot to death and Brother Saultemouche being fatally stabbed.

Feast Dates: February 7 — Bl. James Salès, S.J.; August 28 — Bl. William Deane (see Dean).

Semaj (African-American) See James (here spelled backward).

Senior "The Old One" (Old French).

Patron Saints: When St. James, the son of Zebedee, is called "the Greater" in the Bible, it means "the Elder," to distinguish him from the other Apostle by the same name, who was his junior. Furthermore, in Latin, "the Elder" is rendered *senior*. This leads to another patron.

St. Senior McMaeldalus ruled in Armaugh as primate of Ireland from 598 to 609.

Feast Dates: April 11 — St. Senior McMaeldalus; July 25 — St. James the Elder (see James).

Señor "Sir [Mister]" (Spanish) See Senior, Elder.

Seosamh (Irish) See Joseph.

Sepp (German) See Joseph.

Serenc (Hungarian) See Francis.

Serge (French, Finnish) See Sergius.

Sergeant (variant) See Sargent.

Sergei (Russian) See Sergius.

Sergent (variant) See Sargent.

Sergio (variant) See Sergius.

Sergius "The Attendant" (Latin).

Patron Saints: There are about three dozen Sts. Sergius. One of them was a Roman army officer in the household of Emperor Maximian. In 290 he converted to Christianity. This brought him into conflict with Maximian. When ordered to offer sacrifice to the pagan gods, he refused.

He was immediately dressed in women's clothing and paraded through the streets of Arabis in Cappadocia. After being scourged, Sergius, still in feminine apparel, was then marched to Resapha in Syria. There he was shod in sandals that had nails that entered the bottom of his feet and was made to run the distance between the cities. Having arrived in Resapha, he was tortured until he died.

Feast Dates: October 7 — St. Sergius.

Servando (Spanish) See Steward.

Sessylt (Welsh) See Cecil.

Seth "The Substitute" (Hebrew) or "The Appointed One" (Hebrew).

Patron Saints: Christian tradition fails to provide us with a St. Seth. However, the Bible makes up for this and presents St. Seth, the third son of Adam and Eve. Chapters 4 and 5 of Genesis teach that Seth was given to Adam and Eve by God to replace Abel, who had been killed by Cain. Seth died at the age of nine hundred twelve years.

Jewish tradition adds that Seth learned how to defeat the devil by being obedient to his parents' pious teachings. Adam and Eve had taught him that prayer and sacrifice were his most powerful weapons against evil. When tempted by Satan, he would automatically turn to God in prayer. When gravely tempted, he would flee to an altar he had built for the Lord. There he would beg God's aid.

Feast Dates: March 1 — St. Seth, Patriarch.

Sethard (African-American) See Seth.

Seton "From the Town+By the Sea" (Old English double).

Patron Saints: One North American qualifies, and it is St. Elizabeth Bayley Seton. She died in 1821.

Feast Dates: January 4 — St. Elizabeth Bayley Seton (see Bailey).

Seumas (Irish) See James.

Sevastian (Romanian, Russian) See Sebastian.

Sevastianos (Greek) See Sebastian.

Seymore (English) See Seymour.

Seymour "From the Town of St. Maur [The Dark-Skinned One]" (Old French).

Patron Saints: Seymour is a form of Maurice, and there are about a dozen-and-a-half saints named Maurice.

Feast Dates: September 22 — St. Maurice (see Maurice).

Shadoe (variant) See Shadow.

Shadow "The Dark Image" (Middle English).

Patron Saints: Since *umbria* is the Latin word for "shadow," one can say that there is a St. Shadow, a male known as St. Umbrius. The name Umbria is also a province in Italy from which a great number of saints have come. St. Shadow is remembered for giving his life for the faith in ancient Constantinople.

Feast Dates: December 30 — St. Shadow, also known as Umbrius.

Shae (Irish) See Shay.

Shaine (English) See John, Sean.

Shakeel (Arabic) See Kenneth.

Shakeith (African-American double) See Shaun+Keith.

Shakir "The Content One" (Arabic) or "The Thankful One" (North African form of Shakir).

Patron Saints: The Latin word *gratia* or *gratiae* means "thanks," and there are a dozen Sts. Gratus and Gratianus. One St. Gratianus worked as a simple shepherd in France when he was martyred in 303.

Feast Dates: October 23 — St. Gratianus.

Shalom (variant) See Solomon.

Shamus (Irish) See James.

Shanan (English) See Shannon.

Shandue (African-American) See Shannon.

Shane (Irish) See John, Sean, Shannon.

Shannan (English) See Shannon.

Shannon "The Small Old Wise One" (Irish Gaelic).

Patron Saints: There is one Irishman with a similar name who can serve as patron. St. Patrick McSannon was the nephew of the great St. Patrick. He was ordained a priest and later was consecrated a bishop. He helped his uncle convert Ireland to the Catholic faith. He is one of five Sts. Patrick who converted Ireland. He died in about 450.

Feast Dates: March 17 — St. Patrick McSannon (see Patrick).

Shaquille (African-American) See Shakeel.

Shaughn (African-American double) See Shaun+Vaughn.

Shaun (American-Irish) See John, Sean.

Shavon (African-American double) See Shaun+Vaughn.

Shaw "From the Grove of Trees" (Old English).

Patron Saints: The name Shaw means "grove," and this leads to Bl. John Grove, an English martyr.

Feast Dates: January 24 — Bl. John Grove (see Grover).

Shawn (American-Irish) See John, Sean.

Shay "From the Fairy Fort" (Irish Gaelic) or "The Courteous One" (variant form of Shea).

Patron Saints: A patron can easily be found if one remembers that Shay means "fairy fort." There is one St. Fort. He was a bishop who gave his life for Jesus in Roman times.

Also, one can ask the question "Who is our mighty fortress and refuge?" This leads to Jesus.

Feast Dates: May 16 — St. Fort; Thirty-fourth Sunday of the Year — Jesus, Our Fortress (see Garrison).

Shayn (English) See John, Sean.

Shayne (English) See John, Sean.

Shea "The Majestic, Scientific, Ingenious One" (Irish Gaelic) or "The Courteous One" (Irish).

Patron Saints: The Latin word for "ingenious" can be gleaned from *ingenuim*, and there is a St. Ingenuinus.

Feast Dates: February 5 — St. Ingenuinus (see Cassidy).

Sheahan (Irish) See Sheehan.

Shean (Irish) See Sheehan.

Sheehan "The Peaceful One" (Irish Gaelic).

Patron Saints: Sheehan means "peaceful," which leads to St. Norbert, who has been officially appointed the patron of peace. It also leads to a half-dozen Sts. Solomon because Solomon also means "peace."

Feast Dates: June 6 — St. Norbert (see Norbert); June 25 — St. Solomon (see Solomon).

Sheff (nickname) See Sheffield.

Sheffie (nickname) See Sheffield.

Sheffield "From the Crooked Field" (Old English double).

Patron Saints: Two words make up this name: *shef,* meaning "crooked," and *field,* meaning "field" or "farm."

Feast Dates: May 13 — St. Field (or Farm), also known as Ager (see Field).

Sheffy (nickname) See Sheffield.

Shehan (Irish) See Sheehan.

Shelby "From the Ledge+Estate" (Old English double).

Patron Saints: There is one English martyr with the similar name of Shelley.

Feast Dates: August 30 — Bl. Edward Shelley (see Sheldon).

Sheldon "From the Ledge Hill+Farm [Town]" (Old English double) or "From the Spring in the Valley" (variant of Seldon).

Patron Saints: Although there is no saint named Sheldon, there is an English martyr whose surname is Shelley, which can be accepted as a short form of Sheldon.

Bl. Edward Shelley was a lay gentlemen from Warminghurst in Sussex. He was hanged at Tyburn after it was discovered that he had been allowing Catholic priests to stay in his house.

Feast Dates: August 30 — Bl. Edward Shelley.

Shell (nickname) See Shelby, Sheldon.

Shelley (nickname) See Shelby, Sheldon.

Shelly (nickname) See Shelby, Sheldon.

Shelton (Old English) See Sheldon.

Shem (variant) See Samson, Samuel.

Shep (nickname) See Shepherd.

Shepard (English) See Shepherd.

Shepherd "Protector [Leader]+Of Sheep" (Old English double).

Patron Saints: There are almost a dozen Sts. Shepherd. However, they are usually listed under the name of Pastor, which is the Latin form of "shepherd." Furthermore, there are a number of saints who have been named patrons of shepherds. They include Sts. Bernadette, Dominic of Silos, Drogo, Mamas, Pascal Baylon, Simeon Stylites, Solangia, and Wolfgang. The best patron, of course, is the Good Shepherd.

In the Book of Ezekiel, God the Father compares his relationship to Israel as that of a shepherd to his sheep. Psalm 23 rejoices because the Lord is our Shepherd. Jesus specifically identified himself as the "good shepherd" (John 10:11) and said he would lay down his life for his sheep.

The image of the Good Shepherd teaches us that God the Son is deeply in love with us and identifies with us. He is filled with compassion and always searches for the lost. The Book of Revelation reminds us that Jesus is not only a shepherd but also a sheep. Thus he identifies completely with us.

Feast Dates: Fourth Sunday of Easter — Jesus the Good Shepherd; July 27 — St. Pastor (see Pastor).

Sheppard (variant) See Shepherd.

Sherlock "The Fair+Haired One" (Old English double).

Patron Saints: The original spelling is Scir-locc. This leads to Sts. Scire and Lochen. St. Scire was a holy Irish virgin from the sixth century. St. Lochen was a holy abbot in Kildare who died in 694.

Feast Dates: March 24 — St. Scire; June 12 — St. Lochen.

Sherlocke (variant) See Sherlock.

Sherm (nickname) See Sherman.

Sherman "Shearer" (Old English) or "Wool Cutter" (Old English).

Patron Saints: A saint with the very similar name of Sherwin can be adopted as a patron. Also, because Manny is an acceptable nickname for Sherman, St. Manfred might also qualify.

Feast Dates: December 1 — St. Ralph Sherwin (see Sherwin); February 28 — St. Manfred (see Manfred).

Shermie (nickname) See Sherman.

Shermy (nickname) See Sherman.

Sherwin "The Swift Runner" (Middle English).

Patron Saints: There is one patron who has this surname: St. Ralph Sherwin. He lived during the time of the persecution of Catholics in England. He grew up in England and attended Oxford and in 1575, a year after receiving his master's degree, he reconciled to the Catholic Church. He then traveled to Douai in France and was ordained a priest in 1577. In 1580 he returned to England disguised in secular clothes. Unfortunately, he was soon arrested and imprisoned in the Tower of London. He was tortured on the rack many times and made to lie in the snow for long periods. He was also offered a bishopric if he would apostatize. When he refused to give up the faith, he was hanged at the age of thirty-one.

Feast Dates: December 1 — St. Ralph Sherwin.

Sherwood "From the Sunny Clearing+In the Forest" (Old English double).

Patron Saints: There is one English martyr surnamed Sherwood. Bl. Thomas Sherwood, 1551-1578, a Catholic layman, was preparing to travel to France in 1577 to study for the Catholic priesthood when he was arrested for attending a Catholic Mass. He was tortured for six months, but he would not disclose where the Mass took place. He was hanged in 1578 at the age of twenty-seven.

Feast Dates: February 7 — Bl. Thomas Sherwood.

Sherwynd (variant) See Sherwin.

Shevin (Hispanic-American double) See any "Sh" name+Kevin.

Shimon (Modern Hebrew) See Simon.

Shlomo (Hebrew) See Solomon.

Shmuel (Modern Hebrew) See Samuel.

Sholom (variant) See Solomon.

Shurlock (variant) See Sherlock.

Shurlocke (variant) See Sherlock.

Shurwood (variant) See Sherwood.

Si (nickname) See Silas, Simon.

Sid (nickname) See Sidney.

Sidnee (variant) See Sidney.

Sidney "From St. Denis [The Holy God]" (Old French).

Patron Saints: Four dozen Sts. Dionysius (or Denis) are available to be patrons. Furthermore, there is an English martyr named Sidney. Bl. Sidney Hodgson, a layman and a convert, was arrested for giving shelter to a Catholic priest. He was imprisoned, tried, and convicted, then executed at Tyburn in 1591.

Feast Dates: December 10 — Bl. Sidney Hodgson; October 9 — St. Denis of Paris (see Denis).

Sidonio (Spanish) See Sidney.

Siemen (Dutch) See Simon.

Sierra "Black One" (Irish) or "The Sawtoothed One" (Spanish).

Patron Saints: One North American saint qualifies, Bl. Junípero Serra.

Feast Dates: July 1 — Bl. Junípero Serra (see Juniper).

Sig (nickname) See Sigmund.
Sigfredo (Spanish) See Sigfried.
Sigfrido (Spanish) See Sigfried.
Sigfried "The Victorious, Peaceful One" (Old German).

Patron Saints: There are two Sts. Sigfried. One was a missionary from England to Scandinavia in 1000.

Feast Dates: February 15 — St. Sigfried.
Sigismond (French) See Sigmund.
Sigismondo (Italian) See Sigmund.
Sigmund "The Victorious Protector" (Old German).

Patron Saints: There is at least one patron whose name is similar: St. Sigismund. He is recognized as a patron against fever and hernia.

He was the king of Burgundy from 516 to 523, having converted to Catholicism from Arianism before he became king. He is remembered for having a great monastery built. He is also remembered for having his son strangled, but he repented of this and did penance. Later an enemy king captured him and his whole family and had them thrown into a well, where they all drowned together.

Feast Dates: May 1 — St. Sigismund.
Silas "The Forest God" (Latin).

Patron Saints: Christian tradition presents us with four Sts. Silas and almost fifty Sts. Silvanus. One St. Silas was a Greek Jew and one of the seventy-two original disciples of Jesus. He served as an elder of the Jerusalem Church. The Council of Jerusalem sent Silas along with Paul and Barnabas to announce its decision on circumcision. St. Paul consecrated Silas as the first bishop of Corinth. Furthermore, Silas may be the Silvanus who acted as a secretary for St. Peter and wrote the First Epistle of Peter. Apparently, Silas died a natural death.

Feast Dates: July 13 — St. Silas, also known as Silvanus.
Silvain (French) See Silvanus.
Silvan (variant) See Silvanus.
Silvano (Spanish, Italian) See Silvanus.
Silvanus "The One from the Forest" (Latin).

Patron Saints: There are a dozen Sts. Silvanus. One died a martyr in ancient Ancyra.

Feast Dates: November 4 — St. Silvanus.
Silvester (variant) See Sylvester.
Silvestre (French, Spanish) See Sylvester.
Silvestro (Italian) See Sylvester.
Silvestru (Romanian) See Sylvester.
Silvio (Italian) See Silvanus.
Silvo (Finnish) See Sylvester.
Sim (Scottish Gaelic) See Simon.
Simao (Portuguese) See Simon.
Simba (South African) See Leo.
Simeon (Italian, English) See Simon.
Simmonds (variant) See Simon.
Simon "The One Who Hears" (Hebrew).

Patron Saints: There are at least thirty saints bearing the name of Simon. The greatest is St. Simon the Apostle, the patron of woodcutters. He is called "the Canaanite" and "the Zealot" because he belonged to that Jewish faction of troublemakers who were spoiling for a war with Rome. Christian tradition suggests that it was his wedding that Jesus attended at Cana and that he was the third bishop of Jerusalem (from 60 to 83).

The Greek Catholic Church insists that Simon preached in Egypt, near the Black Sea in Asia, in Britain, and among the Armenians in Persia. Some think he died in peace in Edessa. Others insist he was martyred in Armenia with St. Jude or he died by crucifixion after preaching the Gospel in Samaria.

Feast Dates: October 28 — St. Simon the Apostle.

Simone (Italian) See Simon.

Simonson (Old English double) See Simon+Son.

Simpson "The Son of+Simon [He Who Hears]" (Old English double).

Patron Saints: There is one English martyr with this name. Bl. Richard Simpson was executed by English authorities in 1588 because he chose to function as a diocesan Catholic priest in Great Britain.

Feast Dates: May 4 — Bl. Richard Simpson.

Sims (Scottish) See Simon.

Simson (Old English double) See Simon+Son.

Sinclair "From St. Claire [The Brilliant One]" (Old French).

Patron Saints: Sinclair means "St. Clare," which leads to about a half-dozen female saints named Clair or Clare. There are also about the same number of male Sts. Clarus.

Feast Dates: May 25 — Bl. Clare Voglia, also known as Claritus (see Clare).

Sinclare (variant) See Sinclair.

Siomon (Irish Gaelic) See Simon.

Siomonn (Irish Gaelic) See Simon.

Sir "A Man of Rank" (Middle English).

Patron Saints: Sir is a polite title used in addressing males. There are many saints that have Sir as part of their name. One of them is St. Sirus, who died a martyr in ancient Egypt. Another is St. Sirinus, son of King Abgar of Edessa, who allegedly wrote a letter to Jesus.

Also, any saint who can serve as a patron who has Sir as his official title. Such a one is Sir Thomas More.

Feast Dates: November 1 — St. Sirinus; September 11 — St. Sirus.

Sirmarkus (African-American double) See Sir+Marcus/Mark.

Skeet (nickname) See Skeeter.

Skeeter "The Swift One" (Middle English) or "The One Who Is Like a Mosquito" (Modern English).

Patron Saints: The name Skeeter means "swift," which leads to an English martyr whose name indicates fast movement. There are also a half-dozen saints who spent their lives in the Skete Desert in Egypt. St. Poemon is one of these hermits. He became the abbot of a group of hermits who lived nearby. He died in about 450.

Feast Dates: August 27 — St. Poemon of Skete; February 4 — St. John Speed, also known as Spence (see Speed).

Skete (nickname) See Skeeter.

Skip "The Shipmaster" (Scandinavian).

Patron Saints: There appears to be no St. Skip, but there are a number of patrons whose names can be derived from Skip. First, there is an English martyr, Bl. Richard Kirkman of Skipton. Then, there are the Church-appointed patrons of seafarers (which would include skippers). Among them are Sts. Andrew, Barbara, Brendan, Christopher, Cuthbert, Elmo, Erasmus, Eulalia, Francis of Paolo, Michael, Nicholas, Peter González, and Phocas. To them can be added the Blessed Virgin Mary, Star of the Sea, patron of navigators and yachtsmen. Then there is St. Peter the Apostle, patron of fishermen and shipbuilders and "the captain of the Bark of Peter."

Finally, *The Recognitions of Clement,* written in about 360, pictures the Church like a great ship, traveling to heavenly Jerusalem. God is the Shipmaster (Skipper). Christ is the Pilot. The bishop is the mate. The presbyters and deacons are sailors. The catechists are midshipmen. The laity are the passengers. The sea is the world. The foul winds are temptations and persecutions. The waves are afflictions. The squalls are false teachings. The hidden rocks are anti-Christian state officials. The pirates are the hypocrites. The whirlpool is sin. Seasickness is "sin-sickness." The crossing is very uncomfortable, but it is better than being left behind. All should obey the words of the Pilot (Jesus) for a peaceful voyage.

Feast Dates: Trinity Sunday — God the Shipmaster; May 4 — Bl. Rich Kirkman of Skipton (see Kirk).

Skipp (variant) See Skip.

Skipper (variant) See Skip.

Skippie (variant) See Skip.

Skippy (variant) See Skip.

Skipton (variant) See Skip.

Skully (Irish) See Scully.

Sky (variant) See Skylar.

Skylar "The Teacher" (Dutch) or "The Sheltering One" (Dutch).

Patron Saints: There is no saint with this name. However, the name Skylar means "teacher," and the Catholic Church has appointed five patrons of teachers. They are Sts. Cassian of Imola, Catherine of Alexandria, Gregory the Great, John Baptist de la Salle, and Ursula.

Feast Dates: November 25 — St. Catherine of Alexandria (see Wheeler).

Skyler (variant) See Skylar.

Slade "The Child from the Valley" (Old English).

Patron Saints: There is one English martyr with the name of Bl. John Slade. He studied at New College, Oxford, and became a schoolmaster. He was executed by the British government in 1583 because he refused to take the

oath acknowledging the queen as head of the Church.

Feast Dates: October 30 — Bl. John Slade.

Slav (variant) See Slava.

Slava "Famous or Glorious One" (Russian nickname).

Patron Saints: Slava is a pet name often added to Russian and Slavic names. See Vadislav, Vladislav, and Vladimir.

Feast Dates: July 15 — St. Vladimir the Great.

Slava (Russian) See Stanislaus, Vladislav.

Sly (nickname) See Sylvester.

Smedley "From the Flat+Meadow" (Old English double).

Patron Saints: Since *ley* (or *leigh*) means "meadow," there is one patron available for the second half of this double name.

Feast Dates: August 30 — Bl. Richard Leigh.

Smith "The Blacksmith" (Old English).

Patron Saints: Bl. Richard Newport often used the alias Smith when ministering in the English Catholic underground in the 1600s. Ordained in Rome in 1597, he was executed in England in 1612.

Feast Dates: May 30 — Bl. Richard Newport, also known as Smith.

Smitty (nickname) See Smith.

Smokey "The Mist Rising from the Fire" (Middle English).

Patron Saints: There is no St. Smokey, not even an ancient saint with a name similar to Smokey. However, that does not mean patrons are lacking, for Isaiah 6:4 states, "And the foundations of the threshold shook at the voice of him who called and the house was filled with smoke." The Book of Revelation pictures Jesus offering the prayers of the saints, like smoke rising from burning incense. Thus the best patron is Jesus Christ, the Eternal High Priest. Also, the smoke and prayers point to all the saints of God as patrons.

Feast Dates: November 1 — All Saints (see Santos); Thirty-fourth Sunday of the Year — Jesus the High Priest (see Dexter).

Smythe (English) See Smith.

Sol (nickname) See Saul, Solano, Solomon.

Solamh (Gaelic) See Solomon.

Solano "From the Sunny Place" (Spanish).

Patron Saints: There are two modern American saints who bear this name. One of them is Ven. Solanus Casey, a North American. The other is St. Francis Solano, 1549-1610, a South American who began his life in Spain and entered the Order of Friars Minor. He came to America in 1589 and worked in Argentina, Paraguay, and Peru, always working to convert the Indians. In time, he baptized some nine thousand converts.

Always bubbling over with energy, he cheered the sick with song and his beloved violin. After twenty years of labor in South America, he died in peace at the age of sixty-one.

Feast Dates: July 14 — St. Francis Solano, O.F.M. Min.; January 6 — Ven. Solanus Casey (see Barney).

Solanus (Latin) See Solano.

Sollie (nickname) See Saul, Solano, Solomon.

Solly (nickname) See Saul, Solano, Solomon.

Solomon "Peaceful One" (French, English, Polish, Spanish).

Patron Saints: The Bible provides King Solomon, the son of King David, and Christian tradition provides a half-dozen Sts. Solomon. One of them was king of Armorica (Brittany) at the turn

of the fifth century. He was married to St. Gwen and was the father of St. Cybi. He was killed by some rebellious subjects.

Feast Dates: June 25 — St. Solomon; June 17 — St. Jedidiah, also known as Solomon (see Jedidiah).

Somers "From the Place of the Summer Settlers" (Old English).

Patron Saints: There is an English martyr with the surname of Somers. He was born in Westmoreland, England, and worked as a schoolmaster. Later he went to Douai, France, and was ordained a Catholic priest. He returned to England and ministered to his people under the alias of Thomas Wilson, working in the London mission until he was arrested by government authorities. He was hanged in 1610 at Tyburn for being a Catholic.

Feast Dates: December 10 — Bl. Thomas Somers, also known as Wilson.

Somerset (variant) See Somers.

Sommer (variant) See Somers.

Son "The Male Offspring" (Old English) or "Mountain" (Vietnamese) or "The Star" (North American Indian).

Patron Saints: There are a few ancient saints who have very similar names. One of them is St. Sontius. He died a martyr in ancient times in southern Italy. However, the best "son" patron is Jesus the Son of God. His sonship can be celebrated on the feast of the Baptism of the Lord or on the feast of the Transfiguration.

Feast Dates: November 17 — St. Sontius; August 6 — Transfiguration; First Sunday After Epiphany — Baptism of the Lord.

Sonnie (nickname) See all English male names that end in "son."

Sonny (nickname) See Sonnie.

Spalding "From the Split+Meadow" (Old English double).

Patron Saints: Spalding springs from *speld* ("split" or "divided") and *ing* ("meadow" or "field"). The closest match is St. Inghen, who is remembered for being a holy "Irish virgin."

Feast Dates: April 16 — St. Inghen.

Sparke (English) See Sparky.

Sparkie (English) See Sparky.

Sparks (Old English double) See Sparky+Son.

Sparky "The Happy One" (Middle English) or "The One Who Sparkles" (Middle English).

Patron Saints: Knowing that Sparky means "happy" helps lead to a patron. One is reminded of the forty Sts. Hilary and the half-dozen Sts. Alan. Both names mean "cheerful."

Feast Dates: November 1 — St. Alan (see Alan); January 13 — St. Hilary of Poitiers (see Hilary).

Spas (Russian, Belgian, Ukrainian) See Salvador.

Speed "The Successful One" (Middle English) or "The One Who Moves Fast" (Modern English).

Patron Saints: There are two English martyrs whose names indicate swift movement. One of them is Bl. John Speed, a layman from Durham, England. He was executed in 1594 because he befriended some Catholic priests. The other is St. Ralph Sherwin, whose surname means "swift runner."

Feast Dates: February 4 — Bl. John Speed, also known as Spence; December 1 — St. Ralph Sherwin (see Sherwin).

Speedy (English) See Speed.

Spejus (Lithuanian) See Salvador.

Spence (nickname) See Spencer.

Spencer "The Dispenser of Provisions" (Old English).

Patron Saints: There are three martyred English saints who can be patrons. One is Bl. John Speed, who used the alias of Spence. And then there is St. John Rigby, who actually worked as a steward. Finally, there is Bl. William Spenser, who was arrested because he was ministering as a Catholic priest in England. He was quickly executed in 1589.

Feast Dates: May 4 — Bl. William Spenser; February 4 — Bl. John Speed, also known as Spence (see Speed).

Spense (nickname) See Spencer.

Spenser (nickname) See Spencer.

Spergon "The Seed of Life" (Latin, Greek, African-American).

Patron Saints: This seems to be a truly unique modern African-American invention. It finds no root in English, Arabic, or African names. Probably the only people who may know its meaning are the parents who created it.

Lacking this insight, many suggestions come to mind. For example, it could be a combination of "sperm" plus "gonad," and this leads to the meaning cited above. However, it could also be created out of mispronunciations of "Spear Gun," "Spur Gear," "Splurge On" or "Sturgeon," "Spur On," and the like.

In any case, two patron saints stand at the ready. The first is St. Sperus, a holy bishop of Metz who died in 538. To him add St. Goneri, who was a holy priest in Wales in the 500s and is a patron of sailors.

Feast Dates: November 22 — St. Sperus; July 19 — St. Goneri.

Spider "The One Who Weaves a Web" (Latin-Greek).

Patron Saints: "Spider" in Latin is *aranea*, and there is a St. Arandus. He died a martyr in ancient France.

Feast Dates: October 21 — St. Arandus.

Spike "The Large Pointed Nail" (Middle English) or "Like an Ear of Grain" (English).

Patron Saints: Spike has been used as a nickname for boys for many years, but there are no saints with this name. Thus we must turn to the meaning of the name, "large nail." This leads directly to St. Cloud, a medieval saint who is patron of nail makers. He was the grandson of Clovis, the first Catholic king of the Franks. One day, an evil uncle killed his two brothers. Cloud escaped and hid. To fill his time, he gave himself to prayer, and this led to sanctity. He became a disciple of St. Severinus, a recluse who lived not far from Paris. St. Cloud went about instructing those willing to listen to the teachings of the Church. He died at the age of thirty-six in 560.

Feast Dates: September 7 — St. Cloud.

Spiro "The Breath [Spirit]" (Greek) or "The Round Basket" (Greek).

Patron Saints: Although there seem to be no saints named Spiro, there are three with a similar name: Spiridon. One of them was a holy monk in a twelfth-century Kiev monastery.

Feast Dates: October 31 — St. Spiridon; January 2 — St. Abel (see Abel).

Spud "The Small Dagger" (Middle English) or "The One Who Digs with a Spade" (Middle English).

Patron Saints: Spud has been used for years as a nickname for male children. One must turn to the meaning of the name to find a patron. The fact that *spud* means "dagger" leads to St. Maurice, patron of knife sharpeners. Because it can also mean "spade," the

name leads to St. Isidore the Farmer.

Feast Dates: September 22 — St. Maurice (see Maurice); May 15 — St. Isidore (see Isadore).

Spyros (Greek) See Spiro.

Squire "The Knight's Attendant" (Middle English) or "The Country Gentleman" (Middle English) or "The Local VIP" (Middle English).

Patron Saints: Since there are no saints named Squire, the word "attendant" must be used to find a patron. This leads to a modern sergeant, who can be defined as a military attendant. Certainly, as a noncommissioned officer he commands troops at the service of the military officers.

Feast Dates: May 4 — Bl. Richard Sargeant (see Sargent); October 7 — St. Sergius (see Sergius).

Srul (Yiddish) See Israel.

Stacey (nickname) See Eustace, Stacy.

Stacie (nickname) See Eustace, Stacy.

Stacy "The Stable, Prosperous One" (Latin) or "The Tranquil One" (nickname for Eustace).

Patron Saints: There are a couple of martyrs by the name of St. Statianus, whose name comes from *status*, meaning "stable" or "fixed." One of them died for the faith in ancient Sebaste.

Stacy can also be accepted as a nickname for Eustace, and there are a few Sts. Eustace.

Feast Dates: July 24 — St. Statianus; April 14 — St. Eustace (see Eustace).

Staffard (variant) See Stafford.

Stafford "From the River Crossing+ Landing Place" (Old English double).

Patron Saints: There is a patron for Stafford. When St. Philip Howard, the earl of Arundel and Surrey, died in prison for the faith, he left behind a wife and family. They were devout Catholics, and the faith survived to produce another saint in a later generation. He is William Howard, 1616-1680, the grandson of Philip, Viscount Stafford. He was falsely accused of being involved in the nonexistent Popish Plot, which was the brainchild of Titus Oates, an Anglican priest. After two years' imprisonment, he was beheaded in 1680 at the age of sixty-four. He was one of the last martyrs to die for the Catholic faith in England.

Feast Dates: December 29 — Bl. William Howard, Viscount Stafford.

Staford (variant) See Stafford.

Stan "From the Rocky Place" (Old English) or "From the Camp of Glory" (English nickname for Slavic Stanislaus).

Patron Saints: There is one English martyr named Stone. There are also four saints who can serve as patrons of Rocky. And there are at least three saints named Stanislaus.

Feast Dates: May 12 — St. John Stone (see Stone); August 16 — St. Rock (see Rocky); November 13 — St. Stanislaus Kostka (see Stanislaus).

Standford (Old English double) See Stafford, Stan+Ford.

Standish (Old English double) See Stan+Park.

Stanfield (Old English double) See Stan+Field.

Stanford (Old English double) See Stafford, Stan+Ford.

Stanislas (variant) See Stanislaus.

Stanislaus "From the Camp of Glory" (Slavic).

Patron Saints: There are at least three saints named Stanislaus. The most famous St. Stanislaus, 1550-1568, was the second son of a Polish senator. His older brother often treated his sensitivity and religious devotion with con-

temptuous amusement. But no matter, Stanislaus always remained faithful.

When he was seventeen, he applied for entrance in the Jesuit Society and was admitted. This did not make his father happy, and he threatened the Jesuits with persecution. But neither Stanislaus nor the Jesuits relented. Stanislaus intensified his efforts at prayer, and his devotion to the Eucharist grew and grew. But he also found the heat of Rome too much, which adversely affected his health. He died at the age of eighteen.

Feast Dates: November 13 — St. Stanislaus Kostka, S.J.

Stanislav (Slavic) See Stanislaus.

Stanislaw (Polish) See Stanislaus.

Stanley (English form of Stanislaus) See Stanislaus.

Stanley (Old English double) See Stan+Leigh.

Stanton (Old English double) See Stan+Town.

Stanwood (Old English double) See Stan+Wood.

Star "The Heavenly Guiding Light" (Middle English).

Patron Saints: The two most powerful patrons with Star as a descriptive part of their names are the Blessed Virgin, Star of the Sea, and Jesus Christ, Morning Star. The Book of Numbers uses the image of a star to foretell the coming of the Messiah. In the New Testament, Jesus himself declares that he is "the root and the offspring of David, the bright morning star" (Revelation 22:16). Connecting Jesus with the "bright morning star" identifies him as the Victor of life over death, of God over Satan. We must keep our eyes on the Morning Star.

Feast Dates: Fifth and Eighteenth Sundays of the Year — Jesus the Morning Star.

Starbuck "The Challenger of Fate" (English).

Patron Saints: One of the most powerful of all patrons can be adopted here.

Feast Dates: Fifth and Eighteenth Sundays of the Year — Jesus the Morning Star (see Star).

Starr (variant) See Star.

Steaphan (Scottish Gaelic) See Stephen.

Steef (Dutch) See Stephen.

Stefan (Scandinavian, German, Polish) See Stephen.

Stefano (Italian) See Stephen.

Stefanos (Greek) See Stephen.

Steffan (Welsh) See Stephen.

Stein (German) See Stone.

Stepan (Russian) See Stephen.

Stephan (French) See Stephen.

Stephen "The Crowned One" (Greek).

Patron Saints: There are some eighty saints named Stephen or variations of it. The greatest of them is St. Stephen, the Church's first deacon and martyr. He was stoned to death probably between the years 30 and 33 by Jewish leaders because they simply could not withstand his wisdom and logic. The Church recognizes him as patron of bricklayers, builders, casketmakers, and stoneworkers, as well as of Austria and horses.

Feast Dates: December 26 — St. Stephen the Deacon.

Sterling "The Valuable One" (Middle English) or "From the Yellow House" (Middle English).

Patron Saints: One English martyr can be adopted as patron. His name is Bl. William Walworth, whose surname means "great worth," which is very similar to the meaning of the name Sterling.

In 1837, when a monk who had taken the Oath of Supremacy was placed in charge of a London monastery by the king, Bls. John Rochester and William Walworth protested in a letter. This led to their arrest and execution.

Feast Dates: May 11 — Bl. William Walworth, O. Cart.

Steve (nickname) See Stephen.

Steven (English) See Stephen.

Stevie (nickname) See Stephen.

Stew (nickname) See Steward.

Steward "The Steward" (Old English) or "The Caretaker" (Old English).

Patron Saints: It is helpful to know that the name Steward means "steward" or "domestic servant." Two saints have been appointed as patrons of domestics: Martha of Bethany and Zita. There is also St. John Rigby, who was a steward. And because a steward is a "dispenser of provisions," one is also led to Bl. William Spenser.

John Rigby, 1570-1600, was a domestic in the home of Sir Edmund Huddleston. Being a Catholic employed in a Protestant home, John often attended Protestant services with his employer's family. However, he soon came to understand that this was wrong, went to confession, and stopped attending Protestant services. He was arrested. He said he could not attend a church that was headed by the queen. He was tried and convicted of treason, then executed shortly thereafter.

Feast Dates: June 21 — St. John Rigby; May 4 — Bl. William Spenser (see Spencer).

Stewart (English) See Steward.

Stiofan (Irish) See Stephen.

Stirling (variant) See Sterling.

Stoffel (nickname) See Christopher.

Stone "A Hard Mineral" (Middle English).

Patron Saints: There is an English martyr named Stone. He is St. John

Stone, a doctor of theology and an Augustinian friar at Canterbury. He was arrested in 1538 because he refused to recognize Henry VIII as the head of the English Church. The lone dissenter of his friary, he was thrown into prison. Eventually he was hanged, drawn, and quartered.

Feast Dates: May 12 — St. John Stone.

Storm "From the Tempest" (Old English).

Patron Saints: Two saints have been named patrons of storms. One is St. Barbara, who lived in the fourth century. She was a beautiful woman and a convert to Catholicism. Marriage proposals piled up, and her pagan father pressed her to choose, but she did not wish to marry. Heated words followed. He accused her of the "crime" of being a Christian before a judge, and the judge ordered her to be beaten and tortured and then killed. At this point her father secured her release, took her up a high mountain, and killed her himself. He, in turn, was killed by lightning.

She was a very popular saint in medieval times and is considered patron of architects, builders, brass workers, miners, stoneworkers, ammunition workers, artillerymen, gunners, prisoners, the impenitent, fortifications, and warehouses. She is also patron for protection from lightning, thunder, storms, fire, accidents, and sudden death.

Feast Dates: December 4 — St. Barbara.

Strange "The Unknown Foreign One" (Latin) or "The Unusual Miraculous One" (Latin).

Patron Saints: If one means "foreigner, stranger, or traveler," then St. Christopher, patron of travelers, qualifies as patron saint. But if one means the "odd or unusual one," then this

leads to "Wonderworker." Some saints are officially described as wonderworkers. They include Sts. Cyril, Luke, Stephen, and Gregory. And then there is Jesus the Healer and Miracle Worker (see Milagros).

Feast Dates: All Sundays — Jesus the Miracle Worker; July 25 — St. Christopher the Giant.

Strom "From the Stream" (German) or "From the Bed" (Greek).

Patron Saints: There are no patrons named Strom, but there are a couple of Sts. River, whose surname is a synonym for "stream."

Feast Dates: May 28 — St. River (see River); August 1 — Bl. Thomas Welbourne (see Bourne).

Strong "The Powerful One" (Old English).

Patron Saints: Brian also means "strong one," which leads to at least one patron with a variant of that name.

Feast Dates: April 23 — Bl. Bryan Boroimha O'Kennedy (see Kennedy).

Stu (nickname) See Steward.

Stuart (English) See Steward.

Studs "The One with Nail-Headed Ornaments" (Old English).

Patron Saints: St. Studius, the closest name to Studs, was martyred in ancient Constantinople.

Feast Dates: December 30 — St. Studius.

Sulaimaan (Arabic) See Solomon.

Sulayman (Arabic) See Solomon.

Sullivan "The Black-Eyed One" (Irish Gaelic).

Patron Saints: Only one saint with a vaguely similar name is available. He is St. Sulien. He was born in Brittany and went to Wales to preach the Gospel in medieval times.

Feast Dates: November 1 — St. Sulien.

Sully (Irish) See Sullivan.

Sumner "One Who Summons to Court" (Middle English).

Patron Saints: It is helpful to know that it is the job of the bailiff to summon one to court. And there is a saint who bears a name that means "bailiff": St. Balay. Furthermore it might be helpful to note that St. Ivo Helory is officially appointed patron of all law court workers.

Feast Dates: July 12 — St. Balay (see Bailey); May 13 — St. Ivo Helory (see Yves).

Sumnor (variant) See Sumner.

Sutherlan (variant) See Sutherland.

Sutherland "From the Southern+Land" (Scandinavian double).

Patron Saints: Bl. William Southerne was executed in 1618 for being a practicing Catholic.

Feast Dates: May 4 — Bl. William Southerne.

Sutton "From the Southern+Town" (Old English double).

Patron Saints: There are two English martyrs who can serve as patrons. One is Bl. Thomas Holland of Sutton (also known as Sanderson). The other is Bl. Robert Sutton, who was arrested for being reconciled to the Catholic Church. Born at Kegwell in Leicestershire, he had been raised Protestant and worked as a schoolmaster in London. When he refused to acknowledge Queen Elizabeth as head of the Church, it was enough to convict him. He was hanged in 1588.

Feast Dates: October 5 — Bl. Robert Sutton; December 12 — Bl. Thomas Holland of Sutton (see Sanderson).

Sven "The Youth" (Scandinavian).

Patron Saints: There is no known saint named Sven. But the fact that the name means "youth" leads to St. Aloysius Gonzaga, officially appointed patron of youth by the Catholic Church.

Feast Dates: June 21 — St. Aloysius Gonzaga (see Luigi); Feast of the Holy Family — Jesus the Teenager (see Junior).

Svend (variant) See Sven.

Sweeney "The Little Hero" (Irish Gaelic) or "God Is Gracious" (Irish Gaelic form of John).

Patron Saints: There are a half-dozen Sts. Sweeney. One is St. Sweeney McCrunmall, a holy archbishop of Armagh who died in 730. However, if one accepts the suggestion that Sweeney is a Gaelic form of Sean (or John), then there are more than four hundred twenty-five Sts. John to claim as patrons.

Feast Dates: June 21 — St. Sweeney McCrunmall.

Swen (variant) See Sven.

Sweyne (variant) See Sweeney.

Sy (nickname) See Sylvester, Simon.

Syd (nickname) See Sidney.

Sydny (variant) See Sidney.

Sylas (variant) See Silas, Silvanus.

Sylvan (variant) See Silvanus.

Sylvanus (Latin) See Silvanus.

Sylvester "From the Woods" (Latin).

Patron Saints: There are about a dozen Sts. Sylvester. One of them ruled the Church as pope from 314 to 335. The only information available revolves around a few legends.

Feast Dates: December 31 — St. Sylvester.

Sylvio (Italian) See Silas, Silvanus.

Sylwester (Polish) See Sylvester.

Syman (variant) See Simon.

Symon (variant) See Simon.

Szalvator (Hungarian) See Salvador.

Szczepan (Polish) See Stephen.

Szymon (Polish) See Simon.

T

T Seventh-to-the-last letter of the alphabet (English).

Taariq (Arabic) See Star.

Taaveti (Finnish) See David.

Tab (nickname) See Tabburt.

Tabb (nickname) See Tabburt.

Tabburt "Brilliant Among the People" (Old German) or "The Drummer" (Middle English).

Patron Saints: Since Tabburt evidently is not a patron's name, St. Bert will have to be pressed into service here.

Feast Dates: March 26 — St. Bert (see Bert).

Tabby (nickname) See Gustave.

Taber (nickname) See Tabburt.

Tabo (Spanish) See Gustave.

Tabor (nickname) See Tabburt.

Tad (nickname) See Thaddeus.

Tadarius (African-American double) See any "Ta" name+Darius.

Tadd (nickname) See Thaddeus.

Taddeo (Italian) See Thaddeus.

Tadeo (Spanish) See Thaddeus.

Tadeo (variant) See Thaddeus.

Tadeusz (Polish) See Thaddeus.

Tadhg (Irish) See Thaddeus.

Tadj (nickname) See Taj.

Tadzio (Polish, Spanish) See Thaddeus.

Tag (nickname) See Taggart.

Taggart "The Son of the Prelate" (Irish Gaelic).

Patron Saints: There is no St. Taggart, but there is a saint who is a "son of a prelate." St. Landry (also known as Landericus) was the oldest son of Sts. Madelgarus and Waldetrudis. After his mother died, his father served as the abbot of Soignies in Belgium. Thus St. Landry became the "son of a prelate." Landry served as bishop of Meaux, but after his father died he became the abbot of Soignies. He also regularly helped the poor and sick. He died in the 650s.

Feast Dates: April 17 — St. Landry.

Tailer (English) See Taylor.

Tailor (English) See Taylor.

Tait (English) See Tate.

Taite (English) See Tate.

Taj "The Exalted One" (Urdu).

Patron Saints: St. Tadjat Guthuni was a Persian satrap who fell in battle in 450 while defending Armenia and Christianity.

Feast Dates: August 31 — St. Tadjat Guthuni.

Takis (Greek) See Peter.

Takota (North American Indian) See Dakota.

Talbert (English double) See Tally+Bert.

Talbot "The Bloodhound" (Old English) or "The Pillager" (Old French) or "The Bootmaker" (French).

Patron Saints: There are two Bls. Talbot. One is Bl. John Talbot, an English martyr. The other is Bl. Matt Talbot, 1856-1925, the patron of alcoholics.

At the age of twelve, Matt got his first job bottling wine, and he also began to come home drunk. His alcoholism found him, at age twenty-eight, begging in the streets. One day he collapsed outside a church. He had finally hit bottom and decided to take "the pledge" (that is, to quit drinking).

He recovered with God's help, went to confession often, attended Mass regularly, and made evening visits to the Blessed Sacrament. He received Communion daily, and read the religious classics and the Bible. He gave up tobacco and added acts of self-denial to gain mastery over his body.

Then he turned his attention to helping others. His extra money went to help neighbors in distress. During his last two years, his health failed and Matt found himself the object of charity. In 1925 he died of heart failure while on his way to attend Mass. He was sixty-nine years old.

Feast Dates: June 7 — Bl. Matt Talbot.

Tallie (nickname) See Talbot.

Tally (nickname) See Talbot.

Tam (Scottish) See Thomas.

Tamar "The Palm Tree" (Hebrew).

Patron Saints: St. Tammarus was an African bishop who fled to Campania, Italy, in about 430, when the barbarian Vandals began persecuting Christians in Africa.

Feast Dates: October 15 — St. Tammarus.

Tamas (Lithuanian) See Thomas.

Tammie (nickname) See Thomas.

Tammy (nickname) See Thomas.

Tan (nickname) See Tanner.

Tandy (nickname) See Andrew.

Tanix (Spanish) See Stanislaus.

Tann (nickname) See Tanner.

Tanner "The Leather Worker" (Old English).

Patron Saints: There is no saint named Tanner. However, a tanner is a "leather worker," and five saints have been named by the Church as patrons of leather workers. They are Sts. Bartholomew, Clement, Crispinianus, Crispinus, and Simon Stock.

Feast Dates: October 25 — Sts. Crispinus and Crispinianus (see Frasier).

Tanney (nickname) See Tanner.

Tannie (nickname) See Tanner.

Tanny (nickname) See Tanner.

Tano (Spanish) See Stanislaus.

Taran "From the Rocky Pinnacle" (Irish Gaelic) or "Heaven" (Sanskrit).

Patron Saints: The name Taran means "rocky pinnacle." The finest candidate for patron is St. Peter the Apostle, whom Jesus named "Rock." There are also a few Sts. Rocky (Roche).

Feast Dates: August 16 — St. Rock (see Rocky); June 29 — St. Peter, Apostle (see Peter).

Tariq (African-American) See Taariq.

Tarleton (English double) See Thor+ Town.

Tarrance (variant) See Terence.

Taro (Japanese) See Primo.

Tate "The Cheerful One" (Middle English).

Patron Saints: There is one St. Tate, O.S.B. She was the daughter of King St. Ethelbert of Kent and married King St. Edwin of Northumbria. After his death she founded a nunnery and became its abbess. She died in 647.

It also helps to know that Tate means "cheerful." Other names that mean "cheerful" are Alan and Hilary. There are forty Sts. Hilary and a half-dozen Sts. Alan.

Feast Dates: April 5 — St. Tate, O.S.B.; January 13 — St. Hilary of Poitiers (see Hilary).

Tatum (English) See Tate.

Tav (nickname) See Thomas.

Tavian (nickname) See Octavius.

Tavis (Scottish) See Thomas.

Tavish (Scottish) See Thomas.

Tavito (nickname) See Gustave.

Tavo (nickname) See Gustave.

Tayler (English) See Taylor.

Taylor "The Tailor" (Middle English).

Patron Saints: Knowing that Taylor means "tailor" leads to five saints who have been named patrons of tailors. They are Sts. Boniface of Crediton, Homobonus, Martin of Tours, Quentin, and Ursula.

There are also two martyrs named Taylor. Bl. Hugh Taylor was arrested in England for being a Catholic priest. He was tried and convicted, then hanged, drawn, and quartered in 1585.

Bl. Francis Taylor came from a family of wealthy Irish merchants. At one point the mayor's office of Dublin became vacant. No Catholic came forward for the job because the new mayor would have to take the Oath of Allegiance, acknowledging the English king as head of the Church. Bl. Francis Taylor eventually was elected. The Protestant faction immediately had him arrested and condemned to life in prison. This was all done without any charges filed or trial held. He died in prison in 1621.

Feast Dates: May 4 — Bl. Hugh Taylor; January 30 — Bl. Francis Taylor.

Te (nickname) See Clement.

Teague "The Poet" (Irish Gaelic).

Patron Saints: There is one St. Teague, an "Irish saint."

Feast Dates: September 15 — St. Teague, also known as Tadhg.

Teb (Spanish) See Stephen.

Tecumseh "The One Who Springs" (North American Indian) or "The Shooting Star [Meteor]" (North American Indian).

Patron Saints: One saint has a similar name. St. Tecusa suffered martyrdom in ancient Galatia.

Feast Dates: May 18 — St. Tecusa; Fifth and Eighteenth Sundays of the Year — Jesus the Morning Star (see Star).

Ted (nickname) See Eddy, Edgar, Edmund, Edward, Edwin, Theobald, Theodore, Theodoric.

Tedd (nickname) See Ted.

Teddie (nickname) See Ted.

Teddy (nickname) See Ted.

Tegan (Irish) See Teague.

Tejas (Spanish) See Tex.

Tel (English) See Terence.

Temp (nickname) See Templeton.

Temple (nickname) See Templeton.

Templeton "From the Town+With the Temple" (Old English double).

Patron Saints: There is a saint who came from Eccleston, which means the same as Templeton. Because of certain laws, a farmer by the name of John Finch was executed in 1584. He was killed because he reconciled with the Catholic Church and let priests sleep in his home.

Feast Dates: April 20 — Bl. John Finch of Eccleston.

Tennessee "The Mighty Warrior" (North American Indian).

Patron Saints: One saint with a similar name, St. Tenestina, was cured of an illness by St. Rigomar. Then she built an oratory.

Feast Dates: August 24 — St. Tenestina.

Tennyson (English double) See Denis+Son.

Tente (nickname) See Clement.

Teodomiro (Spanish) See Theodore.

Teodor (Polish, Serbian) See Theodore.

Teodorick (variant) See Theodoric.

Teodorico (variant) See Theodoric.

Teodoro (Italian, Spanish) See Theodore.

Teodosio (Spanish) See Theodosius.

Teofilo (Spanish) See Theophilus.

Terace (African-American) See Terrance.

Terance (Latin) See Terence.

Terence "The Smooth-Polished One" (Latin) or "Like Thor" (Irish Gaelic).

Patron Saints: There are over a dozen Sts. Terentianus and Terentius, which are the equivalent of the name Terence. One of the Sts. Terence, who lived in the first century, was the commander of the imperial bodyguard and witnessed the sentencing to death of Sts. John and Paul. Eventually he converted to Christianity and had to face martyrdom himself. It is said that his son died with him.

Feast Dates: June 26 — St. Terence, also known as Terentianus; December 23 — St. Thorlák Thórhallsson (see Thor).

Terencio (Spanish) See Terence.

Terentui (Romanian) See Terence.

Terenzio (Italian) See Terence.

Teresk (Estonian) See Terence.

Tero (Finnish) See Terence.

Terrance (English) See Terence.

Terrel (African-American double.) See Terrell, Terry/Terence+Darryl.

Terrell "The Beloved One+Who Is Like Thor [With Thunder]" (German double).

Patron Saints: Terrill seems to be a mix of Terry or Terence plus Darryl. Thus the dozen Sts. Terence can be adopted as patrons. St. Thorlák Thórhallsson and the ancient martyrs of Tyre may also be called upon to act as patrons.

Feast Dates: June 26 — St. Terence (see Terence); February 20 — Saints of Tyre (see Tyrus).

Terrence (English) See Terrance.

Terri (nickname) See Terrance.

Terrie (nickname) See Terrance.

Terrill (African-American double) See Terrell, Terry/Terence+Darryl.

Terris (African-American double) See Terrill/Terence+Son.

Terron (African-American) See Tyrone.

Terry (nickname) See Terence.

Terryal (African-American) See Terry.

Teuvo (Finnish) See Theodore.

Tevin (African-American double) See any "Te" name+Kevin.

Tevis (Scottish) See Thomas.

Tex "The Allies" (Spanish).

Patron Saints: There is no St. Tex, but there is a North American saint-in-the-making who is recognized officially as the "Apostle of Texas." He is Ven. Antonio Margil, O.F.M., 1657-1726. Born in Spain, he became a Franciscan priest and volunteered to become a missionary in Mexico.

He was twenty-six when he traveled to the New World, arriving at Veracruz, Mexico, in 1683. During the next forty-three years his work took him as far south as Panama and as far north as present-day Louisiana and Texas. He also founded the College of Our Lady of Guadalupe at Zacatecas, Mexico, in 1708. In Texas he founded the Missions of Dolores and San Miguel.

In 1719 he went to the Mission of San Antonio (later known as the Alamo). Recalled to Mexico in 1726, he died in Mexico City at the age of sixty-nine.

Feast Dates: August 6 — Ven. Antonio Margil, O.F.M.

Texas (English) See Tex.

Thad (nickname) See Thaddeus.

Thaddaus (German) See Thaddeus.

Thaddeus "The Praiser" (Latin) or "The One Given by God" (Greek).

Patron Saints: There are about a half-dozen saints named Thaddeus. The Thaddeus presented here is not the Apostle but rather a disciple of Christ. Christian tradition tells us that Thaddeus was one of the seventy-two disciples of Jesus.

After the death of Jesus, Thaddeus traveled to Edessa in Mesopotamia and converted King Abgar and his nation to Jesus. The Syrian Church insists that he brought with him a "miraculous picture of Christ." It also presents us with a mystery that will have to await eternity to be solved. According to one story, there are two very ancient letters that were exchanged between Jesus and Abgar, popularly called *The Letters of Abgar and Jesus.* They give evidence that King Abgar, while still a pagan, had heard about Jesus. He wrote Jesus a letter asking him to come to his kingdom in Edessa. Jesus wrote back that he could not come because he needed to preach to Israel first. But after his death and resurrection, the story continues, Jesus promised to send a disciple (Thaddeus) to Edessa. Thaddeus died or was martyred in about the year 47.

Feast Dates: October 28 or August 21 — St. Thaddeus.

Thaine (English) See Thane.

Thane "The Warrior's Attendant" (Old English).

Patron Saints: St. Thane died a martyr in ancient Egypt.

Feast Dates: November 17 — St. Thane, also known as Thanus.

Thaniel (Hebrew) See Nathaniel.

Thayne (English) See Thane.

Thebault (variant) See Theobald.

Thedrick (variant) See Theodoric.

Theo (nickname) See Theobald, Theodore, Theodoric, Theotis.

Theobald "The People's Prince" (Old German).

Patron Saints: There are a dozen Sts. Theobald, including St. Theobald of Marly, 1200-1247, who was educated in the royal court school and embraced the career of a knight. However, he soon converted to Catholicism, renounced all worldly prospects, and took the vows of a Cistercian monk in 1220.

He became a great example by practicing simplicity, humility, charity, and poverty. He was forty-seven years old at the time of his death.

Feast Dates: July 27 — St. Theobald of Marly.

Theodor (German, Swedish) See Theodore.

Theodore "The Gift of God" (Greek).

Patron Saints: There are some one hundred twenty-five saints named Theodore. The most famous is St. Theodore of Tiro (also known as Theodore the Recruit), who joined the Roman army and got the name Tiro because it means "recruit."

In 306, after becoming Catholic, he refused to sacrifice to the idols. His superiors asked him why he did not make these offerings, then they dismissed him. Upon being released he set fire to a pagan temple and was promptly arrested again. This time he was beaten with whips, thrown into prison, and condemned to be burned alive in a fiery furnace. He is usually remembered by Christians as one of the three great warrior-saints, the other two being St. George and St. Demetrius.

Feast Dates: November 9 — St. Theodore of Tiro.

Theodoric "Ruler of a Powerful People" (Old German).

Patron Saints: There is one St. Theodoric and more than one hundred fifty Sts. Theodore from which to choose. One St. Theodoric had a rather evil father who made Theodoric's life a kind of hell. Theodoric married because his family forced him. However, after the wedding, he and his wife agreed to part company, and he became a priest. Soon he founded a religious community. He was a persuasive preacher and he became known for the many conversions he inspired. Among the repentant was his own father. Theodoric died in 533.

Feast Dates: July 1 — St. Theodoric, also known as Thierry.

Theodorus (Dutch) See Theodore.

Theodosius "From the Knolls [Little Round Hills]" (Greek).

Patron Saints: There are two dozen Sts. Theodosius. One died a martyr in ancient Anatolia.

Feast Dates: March 26 — St. Theodosius.

Theophilus "The Lover+Of God" (Greek double).

Patron Saints: There are more than two dozen Sts. Theophilus. One was bishop of Caesarea. He wanted to keep the Easter celebration on Passover, whether of not it occurred on Sunday. He died in 195.

Feast Dates: March 5 — St. Theophilus.

Theotis "The One Like God" (Greek).

Patron Saints: There is one St. Theotus and a half-dozen Sts. Theotimus. St. Theotus is remembered for dying a martyr's death in ancient Persia in the 200s.

Feast Dates: September 19 — St. Theotus.

Theotus (variant) See Theotis.

Thibaud (variant) See Theobald.

Thibaut (variant) See Theobald.

Thom (nickname) See Thomas.

Thoma (German) See Thomas.

Thomas "The Twin" (Greek).

Patron Saints: Although there are some eighty Sts. Thomas, the best known is St. Thomas the Apostle. He is considered patron of architects, builders, construction workers, carpenters, geometricians (or geometers), masons, and surveyors, as well as of Pakistan and the East Indies and against blindness and doubt. He is also called the Apostle of India.

The most famous Bible story about him is found in John 20:24-29. The risen Jesus appears to the Apostles, but Thomas is absent. When he returns, he is told of Jesus' resurrection, but he does not believe. Jesus appears to Thomas later and challenges him to put his finger and hand into his hand and side and become a believer. Thus, because Thomas doubted, we received certain proof that Jesus had risen from the dead as he promised.

Christian tradition testifies that Thomas later preached in Parthia and then carried the Gospel to India. He was speared to death in the year 53 at Mylapore, near Madras in India. He would have been about sixty-five years of age.

When Portuguese explorers reached India in the 1500s, they discovered Christians there who traced their faith back to Thomas. Today they make up the Malabar rite in the Catholic Church.

Feast Dates: July 3 — St. Thomas, Apostle.

Thompkins (English variant double) See Tomkin+Son.

Thompson (English double) See Thom+Son.

Thor "The Thunderer" (Old Norse).

Patron Saints: Although there seems to be no saint who goes by the name of Thor, there is one with a similar name. St. Thorlák Thórhallsson, 1133-1193, was born in Iceland and was ordained a priest at the age of eighteen. Then he was sent to study in Paris, France, and Lincoln, England. In 1177, at the age of forty-four, he became bishop of Skálholt in Iceland. He worked hard to stamp out simony.

It should also be noted that an English form of Thor is Tyrus, which is another way of spelling Tyre.

Feast Dates: December 23 — St. Thorlák Thórhallsson, O.S.A.; February 20 — Saints of Tyre (see Tyrus).

Thorbert (English double) See Thor+Bert.

Thorin (Scandinavian) See Thor.

Thorley (English double) See Thor+Leigh.

Thorn (nickname) See Thorndike, Thornton.

Thorndike "From Thorny+Embankment" (Old English double).

Patron Saints: There is a Bl. John Thorne. He was a Benedictine monk at Glastonbury abbey at the time of its dissolution by King Henry VIII. He was also its treasurer and would not allow the sacred vessels and various other treasures to be confiscated. Rather, he hid everything and refused to reveal the location. He was charged with sacrilege by government authorities and was convicted and executed in 1539.

Feast Dates: November 15 — Bl. John Thorne, O.S.B.

Thorne (nickname) See Thorndike, Thornton.

Thornie (nickname) See Thorndike, Thornton.

Thornton "From Thorny+Farm [Town]" (Old English double).

Patron Saints: There is an English saint, Bl. Richard Rolle of Thornton, 1300-1349, who embraced the life of a hermit and became known as a mystic. He wrote many spiritual books, and some are still in print. The most popular is *The Fire of Love.* He died at the age of forty-nine.

Feast Dates: September 29 — Bl. Richard Rolle of Thornton.

Thorny (nickname) See Thorndike, Thornton.

Thorpe "The Dweller in the Village" (Old English).

Patron Saints: Bl. Robert Thorpe was arrested for being a Catholic priest. He was tried, convicted, and executed in 1591.

Feast Dates: May 4 — Bl. Robert Thorpe.

Thorstein (variant) See Thurston.

Thorsten (variant) See Thurston.

Thorvald (Scandinavian) See Thor.

Thurgood (English double) See Thor+Osgood.

Thurlow (English double) See Thor+Lowe.

Thurstan (variant) See Thurston.

Thurston "Thor's+Jewel [Stone]" (Old English double).

Patron Saints: There is one English martyr, Bl. Thurston Hunt, who was arrested in 1601 and quickly convicted and executed by the English government.

Feast Dates: August 30 — Bl. Thurston Hunt.

Tiago (Spanish) See Jacob.

Tiberius "From the Tiber River" (Latin).

Patron Saints: There are about a half-dozen Sts. Tiberius. One of them gave his life for belief in Jesus and his Church in ancient Pinerolo.

Feast Dates: April 24 — St. Tiberius.

Tibold (variant) See Theobald.

Ticho (Spanish) See Patrick.

Tiebold (variant) See Theobald.

Tiebout (variant) See Theobald.

Tiger "The Strong Hunting Cat" (Middle English).

Patron Saints: The Latin word for the name Tiger is *tigris,* and two Sts. Tiger can be found. One was a priest in 406 who was a strong supporter of St. John Chrysostom. After St. John was sent into exile, St. Tiger was falsely accused of starting a fire in the cathedral. He was tortured and then sent into exile.

Feast Dates: January 12 — St. Tiger.

Til (nickname) See Tilden.

Tilden "From the Fertile Valley" (Old English).

Patron Saints: Tilden comes from two words: *til* and *den*, meaning "fertile" and "valley." There seem to be no patrons named Tilden, but there is a St. Tilman. He was born in Saxony but had the misfortune to be sold as a slave. However, it was his good luck to be bought by St. Eligius of Noyon, who gave him a fine education. As an adult, he first worked as a goldsmith, but later he was ordained a priest. In time, he became an abbot. As old age approached, he retired to become a hermit and give his life to prayer. He died in 700. He is patron against children's fevers and illnesses.

Feast Dates: January 7 — St. Tilman; August 28 — Bl. William Dean (see Dean).

Tiler (nickname) See Tyler.

Tilo (Spanish) See Stanislaus.

Tim (nickname) See Timothy.

Timmie (nickname) See Timothy.

Timmy (nickname) See Timothy.

Timofei (Russian) See Timothy.

Timot (Hungarian) See Timothy.

Timotej (Czech) See Timothy.

Timoteo (Italian, Portuguese, Spanish) See Timothy.

Timothee (French) See Timothy.

Timotheos (Greek) See Timothy.

Timotheus (German) See Timothy.

Timothy "The One Who Honors God" (Greek).

Patron Saints: More than fifty Sts. Timothy are known. The best known

lived probably between the years 15 and 97 and is now patron of those suffering from stomach diseases. He was a convert of St. Paul and eventually became the first bishop of Ephesus. In about the year 65 Paul wrote the First Letter to Timothy. The Second Letter to Timothy was written approximately two years later. These New Testament letters show how Church authority passed to the next generation in a three-ranked priesthood: bishop, priest, and deacon.

A group of pagans attacked Timothy during a festival in honor of the goddess Diana and stoned him to death. He was more than eighty years of age when he was martyred.

Feast Dates: January 26 — St. Timothy.

Tino (nickname) See Christopher.

Tioboid (Irish) See Tobias.

Tiomoid (Irish) See Timothy.

Tirel (variant) See Tyrell.

Tirrell (variant) See Terrill.

Tito (nickname) See Albert, Andrew, Titus.

Titos (nickname) See Titus.

Titus "One of the Giants" (Greek).

Patron Saints: There are a half-dozen Sts. Titus. Among them is a Carmelite priest named Titus Brandsma. Born Anno Sjoerd in 1881 in Holland, he earned a doctorate at the age of twenty-eight, four years after he was ordained. Three of his four sisters became nuns and his brother became a Franciscan priest.

He taught philosophy at the Catholic University of Nijmegen in the Netherlands, and when the Nazis came to power in 1935 he, as a journalist, spoke out against the Nazi anti-Semitic laws. This made him an enemy of the state, but he refused to go into hiding. Soon he was arrested and sent to Dachau. For five weeks he was beaten every day, given extra work, and harassed by the guards. He became so weak that he was sent to the infirmary, where inhumane experiments were performed upon him. Then on July 26, 1942, he gave his rosary to the nurse, a lapsed Catholic, who injected him with the poison that killed him. Titus was sixty-one years old.

Feast Dates: July 26 — Bl. Titus Brandsma.

Tivadar (Hungarian) See Theodore.

Tobal (Spanish) See Christopher.

Tobalito (Spanish) See Christopher.

Tobe (nickname) See Tobias.

Tobia (Italian) See Tobias.

Tobiah (Hebrew) See Tobias.

Tobias "The Lord Is Good" (Spanish) or "The Twin" (Welsh form of Thomas).

Patron Saints: Christian tradition provides us with three Sts. Tobias, and the Old Testament presents one more. It is also helpful to note that Toby is accepted as a Welsh form of Thomas.

The Old Testament Book of Tobit introduces us to Tobias, a Jewish exile who was deported to Nineveh during the reign of King Salmanasar (Shalmaneser) V, 727-722 B.C. At that time Jews were often murdered if they practiced their faith, but this did not stop Tobias. He said his daily prayers, observed religious feasts, helped the poor, buried the dead, and taught his son the correct beliefs and practices. When he became blind, he cried out to God. The Lord heard his prayer and sent the archangel Raphael to cure Tobias of his blindness.

Feast Dates: September 13 — St. Tobias, Patriarch.

Tobie (French) See Tobias.

Tobin (nickname) See Tobias.

Tobit (nickname) See Tobias.

Toby (English) See Todd.

Todd "The Fox" (Scottish) or "The Wiley One" (English).

Patron Saints: Todd can mean "fox," and "fox" in Latin is *vulpes*. This leads to two patrons. One is named St. Vulpian. The other, St. Blaise (of throat-blessing fame), is patron of wild animals.

St. Todd was a Christian youth who lived at Tyre in Phoenicia during the time of the Roman Empire. When Emperor Maximian began persecuting Christians in about 300, Vulpian was arrested, tried, and convicted. He was executed by being placed in a sack with a dog and a snake and thrown into the sea.

Feast Dates: April 3 — St. Todd, also known as Vulpian.

Todde (English) See Todd.

Toddie (nickname) See Todd.

Toddy (nickname) See Todd.

Todor (Bulgarian) See Theodore.

Toibout (variant) See Theobald.

Tola (nickname) See Bartholomew.

Toli (nickname) See Bartholomew.

Tom (nickname) See Thomas.

Toma (Romanian) See Thomas.

Tomas (Irish Gaelic, Lithuanian, Spanish) See Thomas.

Tomaso (variant) See Thomas.

Tomasz (Polish) See Thomas.

Tomaz (Slovenian) See Thomas.

Tome (variant) See Thomas.

Tomkin "Little Thomas" (Old English double).

Patron Saints: More than eighty Sts. Thomas can be patron.

Feast Dates: July 3 — St. Thomas, Apostle (see Thomas).

Tomkins (English variant) See Tomkin+Son.

Tomlin (English) See Thomas.

Tommaso (Italian) See Thomas.

Tommie (nickname) See Thomas.

Tommy (nickname) See Thomas.

Tomo (variant) See Thomas.

Tomos (Welsh) See Thomas.

Tompkins (English variant double) See Tomkin+Son.

Toms (Latvian, German) See Thomas.

Toncho (nickname) See Anthony.

Tonek (nickname) See Anthony.

Toni (nickname) See Anthony.

Tonico (nickname) See Anthony.

Tonio (nickname) See Anthony.

Tony (nickname) See Anthony, Hamilton, and other names ending in "ton."

Tore (variant) See Thor, Torrance.

Torey (variant) See Thor, Torrance.

Torin (variant) See Thor, Torrance.

Torquil (Danish) See Thor.

Torr (nickname) See Thor, Torrance.

Torrance "From the Knolls [Little Round Hills]" (Anglo-Irish).

Patron Saints: There is no known saint named Torrance. However, the fact that *torrance* means "knolls" or "round hills" leads to a patron.

Feast Dates: May 4 — Bl. Richard Hill (see Hill).

Torre (English) See Thor, Torrance.

Torrence (English) See Thor, Torrance.

Torrey (English) See Thor, Torrance.

Torrin (English) See Thor, Torrance.

Torry (English) See Thor, Torrance.

Toussaint "The Holy One" (French).

Patron Saints: Ven. Pierre Toussaint was a black slave on a plantation in Haiti. Conflicting records show that he could have been born anytime between 1766 and 1778, although his death certainly did occur in 1853. He was introduced to voodoo, but his Catholic relatives and friends led him to the Church. Because of unrest in Haiti, Pierre's master, Jean Berard, moved his family and two of his house slaves to New York City. The two were Pierre and his sister Rosalie. Their master returned to Haiti to see if he could recover his estate and ended up dying on the Caribbean island. His widow, who had encouraged Pierre to take up hairdressing, fell into a deep depression.

In time, Pierre was able to purchase his sister's freedom. And although Pierre could have become a free person himself, he chose to remain a slave so that he could dedicate his life to the support of his former master's ill wife. He worked long hours at his trade of doing women's hair and doing charitable works. When Marie Berard was dying, she thanked Pierre for his loyalty to her over the years and granted him his freedom. Only after his mistress died, when Pierre was probably in his forties, did he feel free to marry. Then he doubled his efforts to serve the poor, orphaned, sick, and refugees in New York City. One orphan, his niece, he raised. He died two years after his wife passed away.

Feast Dates: June 30 — Ven. Pierre Toussaint.

Town "From the Town [or Village or Estate]" (Old English).

Patron Saints: There appear to be no saints named Town, so we must consider the next best alternative, which is *ton* (meaning "town" or "estate"). Attached to many English male names and surnames, it can be applied here to at least one saint: St. Tondach. He is remembered for being a holy bishop in medieval Ireland.

Feast Dates: July 21 — St. Tondach.

Townly (English double) See Town+Leigh.

Trace (English) See Tracey.

Tracey "The Battler" (Irish Gaelic) or "From the Pathway" (Old English).

Patron Saints: There is one St. Tracey. He served the ancient Church as bishop of Eumenia in Phrygia. He was much praised by his contemporaries for defending the true faith against the Montanist heretics. He died a martyr's death in about 171 near Smyrna.

It is also helpful to know that one of the meanings of *tracey* is "a pathway." And there is an English martyr whose name means the same thing.

Feast Dates: October 5 — St. Tracey, also known as Thraseas; September 25 — Bl. William Way (see Wayland).

Tracie (English) See Tracey.

Tracy (English) See Tracey.

Tragan (American) See Trajan.

Trajan "The Beginning and End" (variant of the Latin name Janus).

Patron Saints: There are two Sts. Trajan. One died a martyr in ancient Rome.

Feast Dates: December 23 — St. Trajan.

Traveler "One Who Makes Trips" (English).

Patron Saints: The Catholic Church has appointed Sts. Anthony of Padua, Nicholas, Christopher, and Gabriel as patrons of travelers.

Feast Dates: December 6 — St. Nicholas of Myra.

Traver (English) See Travis.

Travers (Old French) See Travis.

Travis "From the Crossroads" (English) or "The Crossing Guard" (Old English).

Patron Saints: Travis is really a combination of two words: *trans*, meaning "to cross," and *via*, meaning "way." There are a few saints who use these words as part of their names, among them Tranus and Visa.

St. Tranus lived the life of a hermit in Sardinia in ancient times, while St. Visa is remembered as being a bishop and abbot in ancient Egypt.

Feast Dates: June 21 — St. Tranus; July 30 — St. Visa.

Travus (English) See Travis.

Treach (English) See Treat.

Treacher (English) See Treat.

Treat "The Treacherous, Unreliable One" (Old English).

Patron Saints: The name Treat arises from *treacher*, and there is one ancient saint who bears a variant spelling of this name. St. Treche served God and the Catholic Church as an abbot in medieval France.

Feast Dates: October 17 — St. Treche.

Treatch (English) See Treat.

Treet (English) See Treat.

Trefor (Welsh) See Trevor.

Tremain "From the House at the Rock" (Old Cornish).

Patron Saints: There are two saints whose names, when put together, equal Tremain. They are Tremeur and Mayne. St. Tremeur was the infant son of St. Trifina. He was murdered at Carhaix by his stepfather, Count Conmore. The other patron, St. Cuthbert Mayne, joined the Church after meeting St. Edmund Campion.

Feast Dates: November 7 — St. Tremeur; November 29 — St. Cuthbert Mayne (see Cuthbert).

Tremaine (English) See Tremain.

Tremayne (English) See Tremain.

Trent "From the Flooding Torrent" (Welsh) or "From the Rapids" (Old English).

Patron Saints: There are a few Sts. Trent. One has a story that is most unusual and challenges everyone to be fair-minded and to work against racism and for the brotherhood of mankind. The year was 1475 and the crime committed was that of child abduction and murder.

It seems that a Jewish physician enticed and then kidnapped a little Christian boy who was about two-and-a-half years old. He bound, gagged, crucified, and later threw the body of this child into the canal. What made the crime even worse was that it was done on Holy Thursday and out of hatred for the faith. Simon of Trent was considered for canonization only after miracles began to occur for those who visited his grave.

Feast Dates: March 24 — St. Simon of Trent.

Trenton (English double) See Trent+ Town.

Trev (nickname) See Trevelyan, Trevor.

Trevar (English) See Trevor.

Trevelyan "House of Elian [Lord God]" (Old Cornish).

Patron Saints: Trevelyan comes from *trev* ("house") and *Elian* ("the Lord is God"). Eleyan is an English form of Elijah, which leads to the numerous Catholic martyrs of Trèves. They were murdered by Rictiovarus in 287.

Feast Dates: October 6 — The Martyrs of Trèves; July 20 — St. Elijah (see Elijah).

Trever (English) See Trevor.

Trevor "The Prudent, Discreet One" (Irish Gaelic).

Patron Saints: There is one St. Trevor. He was born into a noble Roman family in northern France. He became a monk, but he soon left the monastery and embraced the life of a hermit. He died in 550.

Feast Dates: January 16 — St. Trevor, also known as Treverius.

Trey "The Third-Born" (Middle English).

Patron Saints: There seems to be only a female St. Trey, a convert of St. Patrick who dedicated her single life to prayer and solitude in the 450s.

There are also a few ancient saints with similar names. They include Sts.

Trian and Trinio. However, the finest patron is the Triune God himself.

Feast Dates: August 3 — St. Trey, also known as Trea.

Trian (English) See Trey.

Trini (Spanish) See Trinidad.

Trinidad "The Threefold One" (Spanish).

Patron Saints: The first patron of Trinidad is the Triune God. In addition, there are a few saints named after the Trinity. They include Sts. Trea, Trian, and Trinio.

The fact of the Trinity is presented in the Gospels. Matthew commands that baptisms be done in the "name of the Father and of the Son and of the Holy Spirit" (Matthew 28:19). Matthew, Mark, and Luke also make it clear that the Father and Son are God, and John reveals the divinity of the Spirit. Eventually the Catholic Church coined the word "Trinity" to speak of this Bible truth. Of all doctrines, that of the Trinity is most important for Christian belief. For without the Trinity there would be no Jesus Christ, nor could anyone explain the existence of love and the need for relationships or charity.

Feast Dates: The Sunday After Pentecost — The Blessed Trinity.

Trinio (variant) See Trey, Trinidad.

Trip (English) See Tripper.

Tripp (English) See Tripper.

Tripper "The Traveler" (Old English) or "The Dancer [Wall Climber]" (English).

Patron Saints: It helps to know that Tripper can mean either "traveler" or "dancer." The Catholic Church has named eight saints as patrons of travelers. They are Christopher, Eulalia, Gertrude of Nivelles, Joseph, Julian the Hospitaler, The Magi, Nicholas, and Raphael. Furthermore, St. Julian the

Hospitaler is also patron of wandering minstrels and entertainers (dancers). To these there must be added St. Vitus as patron of dancers.

Feast Dates: February 12 — St. Julian the Hospitaler (see Julian); June 15 — St. Vitus (see Vito).

Tris (nickname) See Tristan, Tristram.

Tristam (English) See Tristan.

Tristan "The Noisy One" (Celtic).

Patron Saints: Tristan comes from the Celtic word *drystan*. The saint with the most similar name is Drostan (or Dustin). He was a disciple of St. Columba of Iona. For a time, he ruled as abbot of the Dal-Congaile monastery. He then became a hermit. Later, he became a member of the famous Iona monastery. Finally, he again became an abbot, this time at Deer, Aberdeenshire, Scotland. He lived in the 500s.

Feast Dates: July 11 — St. Drostan.

Tristin (English) See Tristan, Tristram.

Tristram "The Sorrowful One" (Latin) or "The Melancholy One" (Latin).

Patron Saints: There is no St. Trista. But the name means "sorrowful" or "melancholy," which leads to two patrons. One is Jesus the Man of Sorrows. The other is the Blessed Virgin.

Feast Dates: Good Friday — Jesus the Man of Sorrows.

Troy "The Place of Curly-Haired People" (Old French) or "The Foot Soldier" (Irish Gaelic).

Patron Saints: The fact that Troy can mean "foot soldier" leads to a dozen saints. Remember that *miles* in Latin also means "soldier." This leads to a few patrons with the same name or variants of it, including Miles, Milo, Milles, and Milius.

Feast Dates: April 30 — Bl. Miles Gerard (see Miles).

True (nickname) See Truman.

Truemain (English) See Truman.

Trueman (English) See Truman.

Truemann (English) See Truman.

Truman "The Faithful [Honest] Man" (Old English).

Patron Saints: Truman permits us to appreciate the "true man." The Bible tells us that before creation, before anything material existed, there was with God, his Son. This Word of God served as God the Father's agent and workman in the creation of the world. At the time of the annunciation, this Divine Word united himself with a true human body, a true human soul, and a true human will. The Word was made flesh, the Light shone in the darkness, and Jesus came to be.

The Son embraced all human characteristics, except sin, so that he could become a channel of life or light for us. God assumed a human nature to make intimacy with him possible, without blinding us with his splendor. The true God descended and became a true man so that we might be embraced by divinity. Jesus is our Light, or Torch, to set the world on fire so that we can rise to share divine life and light.

Feast Dates: March 25 — The Word Incarnate, Feast of the Annunciation.

Tuck (nickname) See Tucker.

Tucker "The Fuller" (Middle English) or "The Thickener of Cloth" (Middle English).

Patron Saints: Tucker means "fuller," and this leads to four patrons officially appointed by the Church. They are Sts. Homobonus, Athanasius the Fuller, James the Younger, and Paul the Hermit.

Feast Dates: January 15 — St. Paul the Hermit (see Fuller); May 3 — St. James the Younger (see Jimmy).

Tuckie (nickname) See Tucker.

Tucky (nickname) See Tucker.

Tudor (Old Welsh) See Theodore.

Tug "The One Who Pulls" (Scandinavian).

Patron Saints: The most similar name belongs to St. Tugal, who was from a royal Brittany family. He founded a monastery and died in 559.

Feast Dates: December 1 — St. Tugal.

Tuki (nickname) See Tucker.

Tulio "A Friend to All" (Spanish) or "The Lively One" (Italian).

Patron Saints: Since there seems to be no patron with exactly this name, we must call upon Tullius to serve as patron. St. Tullius was a black man who died a martyr in ancient Africa.

Feast Dates: February 10 — St. Tullius.

Tully "The One Devoted to God's Will" (Irish Gaelic) or "The Quiet, Peaceful One" (Irish Gaelic).

Patron Saints: There was a St. Tully who was a martyr in ancient Africa.

Feast Dates: February 19 — St. Tully, also known as Tullius.

Tuomo (Finnish) See Thomas.

Tupac (African-American double) See Tulio+Paco.

Turi (nickname) See Arthur.

Turner "The One Who Turns a Lathe" (Middle English).

Patron Saints: There is one English martyr whose surname is Turner. Bl. Anthony Turner was the son of a Protestant clergyman. He converted to Catholicism, studied in Rome, and at the age of twenty-four became a Jesuit. After his ordination he was sent to the English missions, where he was arrested for conspiring to murder the king. His trial was a travesty of justice. On the scaffold he was offered a pardon if he would admit to the con-

spiracy. He refused and was hanged in 1679. His body was butchered and sent to his family.

St. Katharine Drexel can also be adopted because Drexel means the "one who turns a lathe."

Feast Dates: June 20 — Bl. Anthony Turner, S.J.; March 3 — St. Katharine Drexel (see Drexel).

Tuto (nickname) See Arthur.

Tutu (Spanish) See Justin.

Ty (nickname) See Tiberius, Tiger, Tye, Tyler, Tynan, Tyrell, Tyrone, Tyrus, Tyson.

Tybalt (variant) See Theobald.

Tye "From the Enclosure" (Old English) or "The Bound One" (Middle English).

Patron Saints: For the most part, Tye serves as a nickname for many names beginning with "Ty" or "Ti." They include Tiberius, Tyler, Tynan, Tyrell, Tyrone, Tyrus, and Tyson. These lead to a number of patrons.

Feast Dates: June 5 — St. Tyneio (see Tynan); February 20 — The Saints of Tyre (see Tyrus).

Tyger (American) See Tiger.

Tylan (African-American double) See Ty+Land.

Tyler "The Tile Maker" (Middle English) or "The Roofer" (Middle English).

Patron Saints: Tyler means "tile maker or layer." A tile maker is a person who works in stone and/or ceramics. There are four saints named patrons of masons: Sts. Louis of France, Reinhold, Stephen, and Thomas. The patron of stoneworkers is St. Peter the Apostle, and Bl. John Mason can be added to them all.

Also, the two Bl. Taylors may be pressed into service. If, in the past, the Catholic Church allowed St. Brice to serve as a patron for a person named

Bruce, then surely the two Bl. Taylors may be called upon to act as patrons of a person named Tyler.

Feast Dates: December 10 — Bl. John Mason (see Mason); December 26 — St. Stephen, Deacon (see Stephen).

Tymon (variant) See Timothy.

Tymoteusz (Polish) See Timothy.

Tymothy (English) See Timothy.

Tynan "The Dark One" (Irish Gaelic) or "The Gray One" (Irish Gaelic).

Patron Saints: There is one ancient Welsh saint with a similar name who can be adopted as a patron. St. Tyneio was one of the sons of Seithenin Frenin in Wales in the 500s. When his inheritance was destroyed by a flood, he became a monk at Bangor. Three of his brothers joined him in his religious commitment.

Also, knowing that Tynan means "dark" leads to a half-dozen Sts. Dwayne.

Feast Dates: June 5 — St. Tyneio; February 25 — St. Dwyn (see Dwayne).

Tyne (nickname) See Tynan.

Tyoka (African-American double) See Ty+Okay.

Tyreese (African-American) See Terence.

Tyrel (African-American double) See Tyrell, Terrill, Terry/Terence+Darryl.

Tyrell "The Stubborn Person" (Old French) or "Sovereign One+Beloved by Thor" (African-American).

Patron Saints: Some think Tyrell is an African-American mix of Tyrone and Terrell, which leads to a few Sts. Terrence. Others accept it as an Old French name meaning "the stubborn one." This leads to St. Barbara, the patron of the impenitent. Surely the impenitent are among the most stubborn of people.

Feast Dates: June 26 — St. Terence.

Tyrick (African-American double) See Tyrell, Terrill, Terry/Terence+Richard.

Tyrone "From the Land of Owen [Warrior]" (Irish) or "The Sovereign One" (Greek).

Patron Saints: One ancient saint, Tyrannio, can be pressed into service as patron. He was bishop of Tyrus in about 304. During a local persecution, he was arrested along with three companions. All were whipped and then thrown to the wild beasts. Apparently he survived because this incident was followed by many years spent in prison. Finally, he was taken under guard to Antioch. He was sentenced to death and was drowned in a river in 310.

Furthermore, when one realizes that Tyrone is a form of Owen, about a half-dozen saints named Owen appear.

Feast Dates: February 20 — St. Tyrannio; August 24 — St. Owen (see Owen).

Tyrrel (variant) See Tyrell.

Tyrus "One Like Thor" (Latin form of Thor) or "The Thunderer" (Latin form of Thor).

Patron Saints: There are many saints from ancient Tyre (Tyrus). During the reign of Emperor Diocletian in about 300, a great many Christians were martyred in Tyre. Usually they were thrown to the beasts in the arena. Those people whom the beasts did not kill were beheaded and their corpses were thrown into the sea.

Feast Dates: February 20 — The Saints of Tyre (or Tyrus); December 23 — St. Thorlák Thórhallsson (see Thor).

Tyson "The Firebrand [Torch]" (Old French) or "The Son of+Thor [or The German]" (Old French).

Patron Saints: Tyson can mean "son of Thor," and this leads to Sts. Thorlák Thórhallsson and Sontius. Furthermore, it also means "firebrand, torch, or light." Did not Jesus the Light of the World once tell how he came to light a fire on the earth? And he called Sts. James and John "Boanerges," meaning "The Sons of Thunder." He recognized them to be "firebrands," useful for spreading the fire, the Light of Christ.

Feast Dates: November 17 — St. Sontius (see Son); December 23 — St. Thorlák Thórhallsson (see Thor); December 27 — St. John, Apostle (see Sean); July 25 — St. James, Apostle (see James).

Trystan (English) See Tristan.

𝒰

Ualan (Scottish Gaelic) See Valentine.

Ualtar (Irish) See Walter.

Uberto (Italian) See Hubert.

Ugo (Italian) See Hubert, Hugh.

Ugon (Greek) See Hugh.

Uilleam (Scottish) See William.

Uilliam (Irish) See William.

Uinseann (Irish Gaelic) See Vincent.

Ulises (Spanish) See Ulysses.

Ulisse (Italian) See Ulysses.

Ulysses "The One Who Is Full of Anger" (Latin).

Patron Saints: Two ancient saints have names that, when put together, approximate Ulysses. They are Sts. Ulo and Ysice. St. Ulo is remembered as a "Welsh saint." St. Ysice was a bishop of Vienna, who died in 490.

Feast Dates: November 1 — St. Ulo; March 16 — St. Ysice.

Upton "From the Upper+Town [Estate]" (Old English).

Patron Saints: Knowing that Upton means "from the upper town or estate" leads directly to a very fine patron. All one needs to know is that *uppsala* in Swedish means "from the upper estate." St. Henry of Uppsala worked with King St. Eric to make Catholic converts of the Swedes. Later, after King Eric marched against the Finns and conquered them, he asked St. Henry to bring about their conversion. Then King Eric went back to Sweden and built a church at Nousis. Henry was killed in 1150 by an angry excommunicated soldier. After his death, miracles began to be reported at St. Henry's tomb.

Feast Dates: January 19 — St. Henry of Uppsala.

Urbain (French) See Urban.

Urbaine (French) See Urban.

Urban "From the Town [City]" (English) or "The Courteous One" (English).

Patron Saints: There are about three dozen Sts. Urban. One is patron of coopers (barrelmakers) and vintners (winemakers), as well as against blight and frost. He was the sixth bishop of Langres, located in Burgundy, the winemaking area of France. He ruled between 430 and 450. His stewardship witnessed the restoration of many ancient church buildings and a reform of clerical discipline and liturgy. He also performed many miracles.

Feast Dates: April 12 — St. Urban of Langres.

Urbano (Italian, Spanish) See Urban.

Urbanus (German, Dutch) See Urban.

Uri (nickname) See Uriah, Uriel.

Uriah "Yahweh Is My Light" (Hebrew).

Patron Saints: Christian tradition lacks a St. Uriah. However, the Old Testament presents a half-dozen patrons. The Second Book of Samuel tells of the most saintly one, who lived in about 980 B.C. He is the Hittite soldier and husband of Bathsheba. King David had him killed because he wanted Uriah's wife for himself. The Bible contrasts the sinfulness of King David, a Jew, with the sinlessness and dedication of Uriah, a lowly pagan. It seems virtue can be found anywhere, even outside God's chosen people.

Feast Dates: November 1 — Holy Uriah; January 22 or July 15 — St. Uriel (see Uriel).

Uriel "Yahweh Is My Light" (Hebrew) or "The Justice of God" (Hebrew).

Patron Saints: The Old Testament provides us with three men named Uriel. Jewish tradition presents Uriel, thought to be a seraph, a cherub, an angel of the presence, or an archangel. Qumran texts identify him as the "Prince of Lights." His name identifies him as the "Fire of God" or "God's Justice."

The *First Book of Enoch* (also known as the *Ethiopic Book of Enoch*), which is not included in any canon of Scripture, presents Uriel as the angel who watches over thunder and the planets. In other writings he is identified as the angel who presides over the lower regions. He announced to Noah the coming of the flood and helped bury Adam and Abel in Paradise. Other writings identify Uriel as the dark angel who wrestled with Jacob and as the angel who destroyed the pagan army of Sennacherib outside Jerusalem and presides over repentance. Catholic tradition reveres Uriel as the angel who stands guard at the Garden of Eden.

Feast Dates: January 22 or July 15 — St. Uriel.

Urpo (Finnish) See Urban.

Urshel (Latin) See Orson.

Ursin (Danish, French, Russian, Romanian) See Orson.

Ursino (Italian, Spanish) See Orson.

Urson (Ukrainian) See Orson.

Ursyn (Ukrainian) See Orson.

Urvan (Russian) See Urban.

$\mathcal{V}$

Vaclav (Bohemian) See Wenceslaus.

Vadim "Famous Ruler" (Russian).

Patron Saints: Vadim is probably a short form of Vladimir.

Feast Dates: July 15 — St. Vladimir the Great.

Vadislav (Russian double) See Vadislava.

Vadislava "Glorious Ruler" (Russian double).

Patron Saints: Vadislava might be a combination of *volat*, meaning "rule," and *slava*, meaning "famous or glorious." And although no saint seems to go by this name, there is one with a similar name.

Feast Dates: July 15 — St. Vladimir the Great.

Vail (variant) See Valle.

Val (nickname) See Valentine, Valle.

Vale (English) See Valle.

Valente (Italian) See Valentine.

Valentijn (Dutch) See Valentine.

Valentin (French, German, Spanish) See Valentine.

Valentine "The Strong, Healthy One" (Latin, English).

Patron Saints: There are some forty saints named Valentine, Valentinianus, Valentinus, and Valentus. Some believe that the most famous St. Valentine was only a priest-physician in ancient Rome, while others insist that he eventually became a bishop. All agree that he helped many Christians and their families who were being persecuted. Thus the authorities had him arrested and beheaded in 269.

During the Middle Ages, St. Valentine became very popular with the faithful. Medieval people believed that birds began to pair every year on February 14. Since Valentine's feast was celebrated on this day, a connection was made in their minds. Thus they began to call the greetings of love that they sent on this day "Valentines." He is now patron of lovers, greetings, and the greeting-card industry, as well as against blindness and epilepsy.

Feast Dates: February 14 — St. Valentine.

Valentino (Italian) See Valentine.

Valerian (Latin) See Valentine.

Valery (English) See Valentine.

Valle "From the Valley" (Old English).

Patron Saints: There is at least one patron with a variant of this name: St. Vales. He served God as a priest in fourth-century France.

Feast Dates: May 21 — St. Vales.

Van (nickname) See Evan.

Van "The Son of" (Dutch) or "Of Noble Descent" (Dutch).

Patron Saints: Any saint with "Van" in his name can serve as a patron. Among them are Sts. Vanna, Vanne, Vandalet, Vando, and Vandrille. St. Vando served as the thirteenth abbot of Saint-Vandrille, near Vaudebec in Normandy, France. He died in 756.

Also remember that Jesus Christ is the Son of God, which makes him the perfect patron.

Feast Dates: April 17 — St. Vando.

Vanarva (Russian) See Barnabas.

Vance "The Thresher" (Middle English) or "From the Marshes" (Old English).

Patron Saints: The name Vance arises from *fenn*, and there is a Bl. James Fenn. In addition, Vance can also mean "one who threshes." Threshing is part of the activity of the harvest. The Catholic Church has appointed six saints as patrons of the harvest (threshing). They are Sts. Ansovinus, Anthony of Padua, Barnabas, Josse (also known as Jodocus or Judoce), Martin, and Médard.

Feast Dates: February 12 — Bl. James Fenn (see Fenton); March 13 — St. Ansovinus (see Anson).

Vann (variant) See Van.

Vanni (Italian) See John.

Vanny (nickname) See Van.

Vanya (Russian) See John.

Varn (nickname) See Varney.

Varne (nickname) See Varney.

Varney "The Dweller by the Alder Grove" (Old French).

Patron Saints: There are about a half-dozen ancient saints with similar names. These include Varus, Varinus, and Verenus. St. Varinus served as an abbot and eventually was named bishop of Sion.

Feast Dates: January 6 — St. Varinus.

Varrek "From the Harbor Settlement" (Old English).

Patron Saints: A patron with a similar name is St. Variacus, who died a martyr in ancient northern Africa.

Feast Dates: November 15 — St. Variacus.

Varrick (English) See Varrek.

Vartolomej (Bulgarian) See Bartholomew.

Vartolomeu (Romanian) See Bartholomew.

Vas (nickname) See Basil, Vasilis, Vassily.

Vasileior (variant) See Basil, Vasilis.

Vasilek (variant) See Vassily.

Vasili (Greek) See Vasilis, Vassily.

Vasilios (Greek) See Basil, Vasilis.

Vasilis "The Knightly, Magnificent One" (Greek form of Basil).

Patron Saints: There is one saint with a very similar name, and there is an English martyr whose name reflects the meaning of this name.

Feast Dates: May 4 — Bl. William Knight (see Rider); April 16 — St. Vasius (see Vassily).

Vasos (variant) See Basil, Vasilis.

Vassily "The Unwavering Protector" (Slavic, German, Russian form of Vasilis).

Patron Saints: There is one saint with a very similar name who can be adopted as patron. St. Vasius, a layman, lived in Saintonge, France. When it came time for him to die, he directed that all he had should be given to the poor. But his relatives disagreed and took his possessions away from him. He appealed to the local Visigoth ruler, Alaric. For his trouble, Alaric had him killed in 490.

Feast Dates: April 16 — St. Vasius.

Vasska (Russian) See Basil.

Vasya (variant) See Vassily.

Vaughan (Welsh) See Vaughn.

Vaughn "The Small One" (Welsh).

Patron Saints: There is a saint whose name, though spelled differently, is pronounced the same as "Vaughn." He is St. Vaun and he served as bishop of Verdun between 500 and 525. He was so highly thought of that sometime later a Benedictine monastery was dedicated in his honor.

It should also be noted that Vaughn means "small," which leads to St. Paul, whose name also means "small."

Feast Dates: November 9 — St. Vaun; June 29 — St. Paul, Apostle (see Paul).

Vazul (Hungarian) See Basil.
Velten (German-Swiss) See Valentine.
Venable "The Revered [Venerable] One" (Latin).
  Patron Saints: The patron who serves nicely here is St. Bede the Venerable, as will St. Sebastian, whose name means "venerable."
  Feast Dates: May 25 — St. Bede the Venerable.
Venceslao (Spanish) See Wenceslaus.
Venediktos (Greek) See Benedict.
Veniamin (Russian) See Benjamin.
Venya (Russian) See Benjamin.
Venyamin (Russian) See Benjamin.
Verdell "The Flourishing Green+Valley" (French double).
  Patron Saints: One saint, Adjutor of Vernon, makes a fine patron, since Vernon means "springlike."
  Feast Dates: February 20 — St. Adjutor of Vernon (see Vernon).
Verge (nickname) See Virgil.
Vergil (variant) See Virgil.
Vern (variant) See Vernon.
Vernal (variant) See Vernon.
Vernaldo (Spanish) See Bernard.
Vernardino (Spanish) See Bernard.
Vernardinos (Greek) See Bernard.
Vernay (Old French) See Varney.
Verne (variant) See Vernon.
Vernell (African-American) See Verdell, Verney.
Verney (Old French) See Varney, Vernon.
Vernie (nickname) See Vernon.
Vernon "The Springlike One" (Latin) or "From the Alder Trees" (Old French).
  Patron Saints: There is one St. Vernon. St. Adjutor was the lord of Vernon and served as a knight fighting against the Saracens in the Middle East. After seventeen years of service, he was captured by the enemy and imprisoned. Upon regaining his freedom he became a monk. In time, he retired to his estate, where he lived a life devoted to prayer. He died in 1131 and is patron against danger of drowning.
  And because Vernon means "springlike" or "youthful," this leads to the greatest patron of all, Jesus.
  Feast Dates: February 20 — St. Adjutor of Vernon; All Sundays — Jesus the Teenager (see Junior).
Vic (nickname) See Victor, Vito.
Vicellous (African-American double) See Vincent+Marcellus.
Vicente (Spanish) See Vincent.
Vicho (Spanish variant) See Victor.
Vick (nickname) See Victor.
Vicko (Croatian) See Vincent.
Vico (nickname) See Victor.
Victo (Spanish) See Victor.
Victor "The Conqueror" (Latin).
  Patron Saints: There are more than one hundred thirty saints named Victor. One of them was a black man who ruled as pope from 189 to 199. Pope St. Victor I dealt with some very serious problems, including a heresy called Adoptionism. This error taught that Jesus only became God at his baptism.
  St. Victor also ordered all churches to adopt the celebration of Easter on the same Sunday. On another front, Victor had to deal with the trouble caused by a man named Montanus, who had declared himself a prophet and taught that the Church had no power to forgive the sins of idolatry, murder, and adultery.
  Some think Victor died a martyr, while others think he died in his bed in 199.
  Feast Dates: June 28 — St. Victor.
Victoriano (Spanish) See Victor.
Victorio (Spanish) See Victor.
Vihelm (Scandinavian) See William.

Vihtori (Finnish) See Victor.
Vikent (Ukrainian) See Vincent.
Vikentij (Russian, Bulgarian) See Vincent.
Viktor (German, Scandinavian, Czech, Russian) See Victor.
Viktoras (Lithuanian) See Victor.
Vila (variant) See William.
Vilem (Czech) See William.
Vili (variant) See William.
Vilmos (Hungarian) See William.
Vilppu (Finnish) See William.
Vin (nickname) See Calvin, Vinton.
Vincas (Lithuanian) See Vincent.
Vince (nickname) See Vincent.
Vincenc (Czech) See Vincent.
Vincent "The Conquering One" (English, Latin).

Patron Saints: There are approximately sixty Sts. Vincent. One of them, St. Vincent de Paul, 1580-1660, was born in France of very poor parents. He struggled for an education and was ordained a priest at the age of twenty. In 1605 he was captured by some Corsairs and sold into slavery. He converted his third master to Catholicism and then fled with him to Avignon, France.

In 1609 he was put in charge of the Queen's Royal Charities in Paris. Between 1612 and 1617 he became a pastor and a tutor. In 1617 he was appointed pastor of a very poor parish and immediately organized relief from the rich. In 1619 he took charge of all the "royal charitable affairs." He seemed to have a talent for organizing and getting the rich to help the poor.

Then he gathered some priests to help him form the Vincentians (or Lazarists), formally known as the Congregation of the Mission. With the collaboration of St. Louise de Marillac he also founded the Sisters of Charity. St.

Vincent's various works included giving aid to the blind, the insane, sick children, and pregnant girls. Vincent was a frail man, but he had a sunny, smiling disposition and great faith. He is patron of charitable societies, hospital workers, lepers, and prisoners, as well as of Madagascar and of those seeking spiritual help.

Feast Dates: September 27 — St. Vincent de Paul.

Vincente (Italian, Portuguese) See Vincent.
Vincentius (Dutch) See Vincent.
Vincentui (Romanian) See Vincent.
Vincenzo (Italian) See Vincent.
Vinn (nickname) See Calvin, Melvin, Vincent, Vinton.
Vinnie (nickname) See Calvin, Melvin, Vincent, Vinton.
Vinny (nickname) See Calvin, Melvin, Vincent, Vinton.
Vinson (Old English double) See Vincent+Son.
Vinton "From the Vineyard+Town [Estate]" (Old English double).

Patron Saints: It helps to know that Vinton comes from two words: *vin* means "vineyard" and *ton* means "estate" or "town." The patron whose name comes closest to Vinton is St. Vintillas, a hermit noted for his prayerfulness. He lived in Spain in the late 800s and died at Pugino in the diocese of Orense. Also, the Blessed Virgin is honored since 1484 in Dettelbach, Germany, as Our Lady of the Vineyard.

Feast Dates: December 23 — St. Vintillas; September 15 — Our Lady of the Vineyard.

Vinzenz (German) See Vincent.
Virge (nickname) See Virgil.
Virgie (nickname) See Virgil.

Virgil "Staff Bearer" (Latin) or "The Virgin" (Latin).

Patron Saints: There are at least two ancient saints named Virgil or Virgilius. One St. Virgil, 700-789, was born in Ireland and became the abbot of Aghadoe in Kerry. He eventually became the bishop of Salzburg and worked hard to convert the people of Carinthia. Once he had an argument with St. Boniface over the correct form for baptism. He also got into trouble with Pope Zachary because Virgil believed in an underground world with a sun and moon of its own and that elves and gnomes lived in the hearts of mountains. He died at the age of eighty-nine.

Feast Dates: November 27 — St. Virgil, also known as Virgilius.

Virgilio (Italian, Spanish) See Virgil.

Vite (nickname) See Vito.

Vito "The Living One" (Latin).

Patron Saints: There are about a dozen saints named Vitus, on which the name Vito is based. The most popular is a teenage saint who died a martyr in about 300. St. Vitus converted to Christianity at the age of twelve without his parents' knowledge. However, this did not remain a secret for long, and he quickly became a great inspiration for conversions. He was soon noticed by the local Roman governor, who had Vitus arrested. However, all the governor's promises and threats failed to bring the boy back to paganism. Then Vitus escaped and was recaptured.

Because he would not worship the pagan gods, he was accused of sorcery and was condemned to death. He was racked until his limbs were dislocated, succumbing to his wounds at the age of thirteen or fourteen.

The medieval faithful had a great regard for him, and he was made the patron of many things, which included actors, comedians, dancers, and Sicily, as well as against epilepsy, oversleeping, nervous disorders, muscular motor disease, rheumatic chorea (St. Vitus's dance), snakebites, storms, and wild animals.

Feast Dates: June 15 — St. Vitus.

Vitorio (Portuguese) See Victor.

Vittore (Italian) See Victor.

Vittorio (Italian) See Victor.

Vitus (Latin) See Vito.

Vlade (nickname) See Vladimir.

Vladamir (variant) See Vladimir, Vadislava.

Vladimir "The Powerful+Prince" (Russian double) or "Famous+Ruler" (Russian double).

Patron Saints: Vladimir might be a combination of *volat*, meaning "rule," and *meri*, meaning "famous." There are about a half-dozen Sts. Vladimir, one of them being the first ruler of Russia to become Christian. In the beginning he was a very zealous pagan, but upon converting he became an even more ardent Catholic. To show his disdain for paganism, he had the image of Perun, the Slav god of thunder, scourged through the streets and then thrown into the river. He also imported Christian priests from Constantinople and urged his subjects to become Christian.

He even married a saint, St. Ann, sister of the Christian emperor of the Greeks, and he had a couple of great churches built. He also founded the first school in Russia. Despite his faith and good works, he suffered much from his twelve pagan sons and died while making a journey to Novgorod in 1014.

Remember, the most "powerful prince" remains, for all times, Jesus Christ.

Feast Dates: July 15 — St. Vladimir the Great; All Sundays — Jesus Christ, Prince of Peace (see Prince).

Vladimiro (Spanish) See Vladimir, Vadim, Vladislav.

Vladislav (Slavic) See Vadislava/Vadim+ Slava.

Von (variant) See Vaughn.

Vondie (African-American) See Vaughn.

W

Wade "The One Who Goes Ahead" (Old English) or "From the River Crossing" (Old English).

Patron Saints: The fact that Wade can mean "a river crossing" or "ford" leads to one English martyr.

Feast Dates: May 28 — Bl. Thomas Ford (see Ford).

Wadell "From the River Crossing+In the Valley" (Old English double).

Patron Saints: Wadell comes from *wade*, meaning "river crossing" or "ford," and *dell*, meaning "valley." This leads to Bl. Thomas Ford and St. Vales.

Feast Dates: May 28 — Bl. Thomas Ford (see Ford); May 21 — St. Vales (see Valle).

Wadsworth (English double) See Wade+Worth.

Wagner (German) See Wainwright, Wayne.

Wahad (African-American) See Waheed.

Waheed (Arabic) See Unique.

Wain (variant) See Wainwright.

Wainwright "The Wagonmaker" (Old English).

Patron Saints: The patron we can press into service here is Bl. Peter Wright, a martyr of England. Peter Wright was born of Catholic parents in the early 1600s. As a young man he became a Protestant, and as an adult he reconciled with the Catholic Church. He then went to France, became a Jesuit, and was ordained. Then he was sent to minister to the English soldiers in Flanders. He made a very good impression on the colonel, Sir Henry Gage, and the colonel made him his constant companion, both in the Netherlands and in England.

After Sir Henry died, Father Wright lived at the home of the marquis of Winchester. There he was arrested by priest-catchers in 1650. He was condemned to death and hanged in 1651. His body was butchered after he had died. Father Wright's composure on the scaffold led to the conversion of many of those watching the proceedings.

Feast Dates: May 19 — Bl. Peter Wright, S.J.

Wait (Middle English) See Walter, Ward.

Wake "The Alert, Watchful Man" (Old English) or "The Wet One" (Old English).

Patron Saints: If Wake means "watchful," three Sts. Ward and Warin become available. If Wake means "wet," then one St. Maden appears. The word *maden* is Latin for "wet," and St. Maden is a medieval Breton saint who performed miracles and lived near a holy well.

Feast Dates: November 1 — St. Maden; August 30 — St. Margaret Ward (see Ranger).

Wakefield (Old English double) See Wake+Field.

Wakeley (Old English double) See Wake+Leigh.

Wakeman (Old English double) See Wake+Mann.

Walcott "From the Wall-Enclosed Cottage" (Old English).

Patron Saints: Two saints are available: St. John Wall of Preston and St. Cottus.

Feast Dates: August 22 — St. John Wall of Preston (see Walton); November 1 — St. Cottus (see Prescott).

Wald (nickname) See Oswald, Walden, Waldo.

Waldemar (German) See Waldo, Walter.

Walden "From the Woods+In the Valley" (Old English double).

Patron Saints: There is one saint available, Bl. Thomas Netter of Walden, 1375-1430. He joined the Carmelites, was ordained a priest, and became a prominent member of the council of Constance and an active opponent of the heresy of Lollardism. King Henry V chose him for his confessor and died in Thomas's arms. Thomas himself died at Rouen at the age of fifty-five.

Feast Dates: November 2 — Bl. Thomas Netter of Walden.

Waldo "The Ruler" (Old German) or "The Divinely Powerful One" (short form of Oswald).

Patron Saints: There are three possible patrons. One is named Walde and two are named Oswald. St. Walde was the second bishop of Evreux, France. He is remembered for his holiness and his zeal in defeating paganism. He died in 491.

Feast Dates: January 31 — St. Walde, also known as Gaudus; August 7 — St. Oswald (see Oswald).

Waldon (Old English double) See Wald+Dean.

Walford (Old English double) See Wallace+Ford.

Walgierz (Polish) See Walter.

Wali (nickname) See Oswald, Walden, Waldo, Walker, Wallace, Walter, Walton.

Walker "The Fuller [or The Thickener of Cloth]" (Old English).

Patron Saints: Because the name Walker means "fuller," or "thickener of cloth," four patrons emerge: Sts. James the Younger, Homobonus, Athanasius the Fuller, and Paul the Hermit.

Feast Dates: May 3 — St. James the Younger (see Jimmy); January 15 — St. Paul the Hermit (see Fuller).

Wallace "The One from Wales" (Old English).

Patron Saints: There is no St. Wallace. However, since the name Wallace means "Welshman," the officially appointed patron of Wales, St. David, can serve as patron.

Feast Dates: — St. David (see David).

Wallache (variant) See Wallace.

Wallas (variant) See Wallace.

Wallie (nickname) See Oswald, Walden, Waldo, Walker, Wallace, Walter, Walton.

Wallis (variant) See Wallace.

Wally (nickname) See Oswald, Walden, Waldo, Walker, Wallace, Walter, Walton.

Walsh (variant) See Wallace.

Walt (nickname) See Walter, Walton.

Walter "The Powerful Warrior" (Old German) or "The Army Commander" (Old German).

Patron Saints: There are about a half-dozen saints named Walter. One of them is St. Walter of Brabant, who died in 1222. Early in life he became a knight and for years was a familiar figure at the tournaments.

Then one day he found his way to a Cistercian abbey. There he deepened his faith in Jesus and gave himself to the service of the abbey. He was appointed guestmaster, and his cheerful, good example attracted many to the monastic life. He died at Villers.

Feast Dates: January 22 — St. Walter.

Walther (German) See Walter.

Walton "The Town+Near the Ruined Wall" (Old English double) or "From the Wooden+Town" (Old English double).

Patron Saints: Knowing that Walton means "walled town" leads to St. John Wall, an English martyr. St. John was born in 1620 near Preston in England and studied for the priesthood in France and Rome. He was ordained in 1645 and a few years later, in 1651, joined the Friars Minor at Douai, taking the name Joachim of St. Anne. Some six years later he began working in the Worcestershire mission, which lasted for the next twenty-two years. He was arrested in 1678 for being a priest and was executed in 1679.

Feast Dates: August 22 — St. John Wall of Preston, O.F.M.; July 21 — St. Tondach (see Town).

Walworth (Old English double) See Wallace+Worth.

Walwyn (Old English double) See Wallace+Wynn.

Ward "The Watchman [Guardian]" (Old English) or "The Chief Guardian" (short form of Howard).

Patron Saints: There are two English saints surnamed Ward. Both were martyred during the Protestant Reformation in England. Bl. William Ward (also known as Webster) was executed for being a Catholic priest in 1641. Ordained in 1608, he had spent thirty-three years in the English missions, twenty of them in prison.

Feast Dates: July 26 — Bl. William Ward, also known as Webster; August 30 — St. Margaret Ward (see Ranger).

Warde (English) See Ward.

Wardell (Old English double) See Ward+Hill.

Warden (English) See Ward.

Ware (English) See Warren.

Warefield (Old English double) See Warren+Field.

Wareford (Old English double) See Warren+Ford.

Waring (English) See Warren.

Warner "The Armed Defender" (Old German).

Patron Saints: Warner is a form of Werner, and there are two Sts. Werner. One of them was born in Germany in 1273 and orphaned a short time later. Being poor and an orphan, he was forced to seek employment. This led him to take a job as a house servant in the home of a Jew in Oberwesel.

As a teenager, he received the sacrament of Holy Communion on April 19, 1287. Soon after, he was murdered, and his body was thrown into the river. It is thought that he was killed because of hatred for the Eucharist.

Feast Dates: April 18 — St. Werner.

Warren "The Park Guardian" (Old German) or "The Watchman" (Old German).

Patron Saints: There are three ancient saints who bear variations of the name Warren. One of them is St. Warin. He was the son of Count Egbert. His mother, Ida of Hovestadt, and his brother, Ludolf, duke of Saxony, have both been officially recognized as saints by the Catholic Church. Warin was elected abbot of Corvey Monastery in Westphalia in 826 and died that same year.

Feast Dates: September 26 — St. Warin.

Warrick (English) See Varrick.

Warton (Old English double) See Warren+Town.

Wash (nickname) See Washington.

Washington "The Town+Of the Astute One" (Old English double) or "From the Town+On the River" (Old English double).

Patron Saints: Despite the fact that there are no saints with the name of Washington, there is one who can serve as patron.

On December 8, 1854, Pope Pius IX infallibly declared the doctrine of the Immaculate Conception, which states that the Blessed Virgin Mary was conceived without sin, unlike the rest of us who come into this world with the stain of original sin on our souls.

This is based upon the tradition of the Church and Scripture. St. Luke relates that the message of Gabriel to Mary was that she was "full of grace." To be "full of grace" means "never to be touched by sin." It was the constant tradition of the Church that Mary was ever-virgin and, in the Bible, "virgin" is symbolic of commitment. To be "ever-virgin" is to "always say yes" and "never sin." Finally, the Immaculate Conception provides an answer to the problem of abortion.

What God did for Mary, at the first moment of her conception, he does for all of us at baptism. He defeats sin and fills us with his presence. Only a person can be saved from sin. Thus preservation from sin, from conception, is another way of saying that persons really begin to exist at conception.

Feast Dates: December 8 — The Immaculate Conception of the Blessed Virgin Mary.

Wasili (Russian) See Basil.

Wat (nickname) See Walter.

Waterio (Spanish) See Walter.

Watkin (English) See Walter.

Watkins (English double) See Watkin+Son.

Watkinson "Son of+Walter [Powerful Warrior]" (Old English double).

Patron Saints: Because Watkins is an alternate form of Walter, any of the half-dozen Sts. Walter can also serve as patrons. To these can be added two English martyrs named Watkinson.

Bl. Thomas Watkinson, a layman, was executed in 1591 because he insisted on practicing his Catholic faith.

Bl. Robert Watkinson, 1579-1602, a native of Yorkshire, went to France to study. He was ordained a Catholic priest, returned to England, was captured and executed, all in 1602. He was only twenty-three at the time of his martyrdom.

Feast Dates: May 4 — Bl. Thomas Watkinson; April 20 — Bl. Robert Watkinson.

Watson (Old English double) See Wat+Son.

Wawrzyniec (Polish) See Lawrence.

Way (nickname) See Wayland.

Wayland "From the Land+Near the Road" (Old English double).

Patron Saints: Wayland is made up of two words: *way* ("path" or "road") and *land*, meaning "land." A couple of patrons should fit the bill here nicely.

One of them is Bl. William Way, 1561-1588. He attended college in Rheims, France, where he was ordained in 1586. He sailed for England immediately after becoming a priest. However, his ministry was destined to be short-lived. Six months after his arrival, he was in jail in London. From about the middle of 1587 to the latter part of 1588 he languished in prison. Finally, he was convicted of being a Catholic priest and was hanged, drawn, and quartered. He was only twenty-seven years old.

Feast Dates: September 25 — Bl. William Way of Devon; January 16 — St. Lando (see Landon).

Waylan (English) See Wayland.

Waylen (English) See Wayland.

Waylin (English) See Wayland.

Waylon (English) See Wayland.

Wayne "The Dark One" (short form of Dwayne) or "The Wagoner" (short form of Wainwright).

Patron Saints: About a half-dozen saints can qualify as patrons for Wayne. Not much is known about any of them. Among them is St. Dwynan, who was an envoy of Pope St. Eleutherus. He died in about 360.

Feast Dates: April 8 — St. Dwynan.

Webb (nickname) See Webster.

Weber (nickname) See Webster.

Webster "The Weaver" (Old English).

Patron Saints: There are two English martyrs named Webster. Furthermore, six more saints have been named patrons of weavers. They are Sts. Anthony Claret, Barnabas, Benno, Onuphrius, Maurice, and Paul the Hermit.

The first English Catholic martyrs began climbing English scaffolds in 1535. Among them was Father Augustine Webster, prior of the monastery of Axholme. He had traveled to London to meet with other priors of his order to consider how to respond to the increasing government pressure. While the meeting was in progress, government agents appeared and demanded that the Oath of Supremacy be taken by all. The London prior and his guest priors refused. All were arrested. They were publicly hanged while wearing their habits in order to humiliate them before the people.

Feast Dates: May 4 — Bl. August. Webster, M.O. Cart.; July 26 — Bl. William Ward, also known as Webster (see Ward).

Welbourne (English double) See Wells+Bourne.

Welby (English double) See Wells+By.

Welch (variant) See Wallace.

Weldon (English double) See Wells+Don.

Welford (English double) See Wells+Ford.

Wellington (English double) See Wells+Town.

Wells "From the Spring [Well]" (Old English).

Patron Saints: There is one English martyr with the surname of Wells. There are also a few English martyrs who were natives of Wells, England.

Feast Dates: December 10 — St. Swithin Wells (see Maxwell).

Welsh (variant) See Wallace.

Wenceslaus "The Garland of Glory" (Old Slavic).

Patron Saints: There is one great St. Wenceslaus, 907-935. He was raised by his grandmother, St. Ludmilla, who was very holy and pious. After his father died in 922, Ludmilla was murdered, and the pagans drove out all the Catholic missionaries. Murders of prominent people and neglect of Catholic churches followed.

Upon growing up, Wenceslaus in 928 took over the reigns of government. He made peace, recalled priests, and raised the moral, religious, and cultural standards of his people. Still, some of the Bohemian nobles did not agree with him. His brother killed him at the door of his church. His dying words were, "Brother, I forgive you." Wenceslaus was only twenty-eight years old at the time of his murder.

Feast Dates: September 28 — St. Wenceslaus.

Wendall (English) See Wendel.

Wendel "The Dweller at the Boundary" (Old English) or "The Wanderer" (Old German).

Patron Saints: There is a St. Wendelin, 554-607, even if no saints are named Wendel. He was born in Ireland, the son of a Scottish king. Wendelin was not as interested in fighting as in reading, and his father sent him away because of this. Thus Wendelin found himself a wanderer or pilgrim. Eventually he arrived in Bliess and was employed as a shepherd.

His holiness was noticed by some monks, and in the 590s they elected him to be their superior. He served as abbot for this order until his death.

Only after his death was any notice taken of him. This occurred because of the miracles that began to happen for those who visited his burial place. He is now patron of peasants, shepherds, and swineherds, and against sickness in cattle.

Feast Dates: October 21 — St. Wendelin.

Wendelin (English) See Wendel.

Wendell (English) See Wendel.

Wentworth (English double) See White+Worth.

Werner (variant) See Warner.

Wernher (variant) See Warner.

Wes (nickname) See Wesley.

Wesley (Old English double) See West+Leigh.

West "The One from the West" (Old English).

Patron Saints: The word *wessex* is Old English for "west," and this leads to St. Swithun of Wessex. Upon reaching adulthood, he was ordained a priest. He became chaplain to Egber, king of the West Saxons, and tutor to the young prince. Later he became bishop of Wessex. Many miracles connected to him occurred after his death, not the least of which was the gift of much needed rain. This led to the popular saying "If it rains on St. Swithun's day, it will rain forty days more." Swithun died in 862.

Feast Dates: June 2 — St. Swithun of Wessex.

Westbrook (Old English double) See West+Brook/Brooke.

Westby (English double) See West+By.

Westleigh (English double) See West+Leigh.

Westley (English double) See West+Leigh.

Weston (English double) See West+Town.

Wetherby "From the Sheep+Farm" (Old English double).

Patron Saints: Two patrons serve adequately.

Feast Dates: March 26 — St. Agnus (see Hamal); August 13 — St. Ager (see Field).

Wetherly (English double) See Wetherby+Leigh.

Weylin (English) See Wayland.

Wheeler "The Wheelmaker" (Old English).

Patron Saints: St. Catherine of Alexandria is patron of wheelmakers. A Roman martyr in 310, she was very popular in the Middle Ages. She is also patron of jurors, lawyers, librarians, millers, nurses, philosophers, preachers, rope makers, schoolgirls, secretaries, stenographers, single women, students, and teachers, as well as of universities and for healing ailments of the tongue.

She was a black woman of great courage from Alexandria, Egypt. A convert, she denounced the emperor to his face because of his persecution of Christians, and her testimony converted fifty pagan philosophers. Then the emperor discovered that Catherine was the reason why his wife and two hundred of his personal guard had converted to Christianity. This made him very angry, and he had her tied to a wheel full of spikes. But when the wheel broke, he ordered her to be beheaded.

Feast Dates: November 25 — St. Catherine of Alexandria.

Whilloughby (variant) See Willoughby.

Whit (English) See DeWitt, Whitney, Whittaker.

Whitaker (English) See DeWitt, Whittaker.

Whitby (English double) See White+By.

Whitcomb "From the White+Valley" (English double).

Patron Saints: St. Wita will have to serve as patron here. She was a matron of Whitechurch in Dorsetshire. There is also at least one St. Vales. He served God as a priest in France in the 300s.

Feast Dates: November 1 — St. Wita; May 21 — St. Vales.

White "The White-Haired [Blond] One" (Old English).

Patron Saints: There are a few patrons, the chief of whom is the English martyr Father Eustace White. While working in the English missions in 1591, St. Eustace was arrested, convicted, and executed for being a Catholic priest. Father White had been born in Lincolnshire. Upon reaching adulthood, he converted to the Catholic Church. Then he traveled to France, where he studied for the priesthood because such study was outlawed in England. He was ordained in 1588 and returned to England, where he worked among the faithful for a few years until he was arrested and put to death.

Feast Dates: December 10 — St. Eustace White.

Whitey (Old English) See White.

Whitford (English double) See White+Ford.

Whitman (Old English) See White.

Whitney (Old English double) See White+Ny.

Whittaker "From the White+Field" (Old English double) or "From the North Part of the Graveyard+Allotted for Criminals and the Poor" (Old English double) or "From the Northeast Part+Of the Middle Ground" (Old English double).

Patron Saints: There is an English martyr, Bl. Thomas Whittaker, who was executed by the British government in 1646 because he insisted on functioning as a Catholic priest.

Feast Dates: May 4 — Bl. Thomas Whittaker.

Wiatt (English) See Wyatt.

Wickliffe (English double) See White+Cliff.

Wiktor (Polish) See Victor.

Wil (nickname) See Wilbert, Wilfred, Willard, William, Willoughby, Wilson, Wilton.

Wilbert (German) See Gilbert.

Wilbur (German) See Gilbert.

Wilburt (German) See Gilbert.

Wilek (variant) See William.

Wiley "From the Tricky Stream" (Old English) or "The Sly One" (Old English) or "From the Water Meadow" (Old English).

Patron Saints: Wiley can be an English form of William, which leads to some seventy Sts. William. However, St. Wye and Bl. Leigh will also make fine patrons.

St. Wye (also known as Wyden or Guido) worked as a day laborer and also served as a sacristan for his parish church. After trying to build a business and failing, he set out on a pilgrimage to Rome. Then, accompanied by a deacon friend, he went to Jerusalem. He returned home very sick and tired. He died a short time later.

Feast Dates: September 12 — St. Wye; August 30 — Bl. Richard Leigh (see Leigh).

Wilford (English double) See Will+Ford.

Wilfred "The Resolute Peacemaker" (Old German).

Patron Saints: There are at least two saints named Wilfred. One St. Wilfrid, 634-709, was raised in the court of King Oswy of Canterbury. Queen Eanfleda took special care of his education and sent him to a monastery. He was ordained at the age of twenty-nine and a year later was elected archbishop of York. He spent much of his daily energy introducing the Roman rule to the Celtic Church and he introduced the rule of St. Benedict to local monasteries.

On another front, he worked for the conversion of pagans. On one occasion, he had to flee England in order to escape being murdered by his enemies. He died in England at the age of seventy-five.

Feast Dates: October 12 — St. Wilfrid.

Wilfredo (Spanish) See Wilfred.

Wilfrid (variant) See Wilfred.

Wilhelm (German) See William.

Wilkes (Old English double) See Wilkie+Son.

Wilkie (English) See William.

Will (nickname) See Wilbert, Wilfred, Willard, William, Willoughby, Wilson, Wilton.

Willard "The Resolute, Brave One" (Old English).

Patron Saints: There are two saints with names very similar to Willard. St. Willehad, 745-789, was probably educated at York and was ordained a priest. In 765 he set out to preach Catholicism in Frisia. He had some success. He also suffered from some opposition and had to flee.

Then in 780 Charlemagne asked him to preach and organize a church in Lower Weser. Upon arriving, he faced a Saxon revolt and had to flee to Frisia. From there he went to Rome and was consecrated a bishop. He occupied himself with finishing the building of his cathedral in Bremen.

Feast Dates: November 8 — St. Willehad.

Willem (Dutch) See William.

Willet (variant) See William.

Willets (variant double) See Will+Son.

Willey (nickname) See Willy.

Willi (nickname) See Willy.

William "The Resolute Defender" (Old German).

Patron Saints: There are about seventy saints named William. One of the Sts. William was a baker in Perth, Scotland. Early in life he took in a foundling and raised him. Later, while making a pilgrimage to Rome in the 1100s, his servant murdered him. Miracles at his tomb prompted his canonization.

Feast Dates: February 23 — St. William of Scotland.

Williamson (Old English double) See William+Son.

Willie (nickname) See Willy.

Willis (Old English double) See William+Son.

Willoughby "From the Willow Farm" (Old English double).

Patron Saints: Although his name is not Willoughby, there is at least one saint available for the job of patron: St. Wyllow. He lived the life of a hermit at Llanteglos-by-Fowey in ancient Wales.

Feast Dates: November 1 — St. Wyllow.

Willy (nickname) See Wilbert, Wiley, Wilfred, Willard, William, Willoughby, Wilson, Wilton.

Wilmar (variant) See William.

Wilmer (German) See William.

Wilmot (Old German) See William.

Wilson "The Son of+Williard or William [The Resolute One]" (Old English double).

Patron Saints: There is one English martyr surnamed Wilson. And because Wilson means "son of William (or Will)," any of more than eighty saints can also serve as patrons.

Feast Dates: December 10 — Bl. Thomas Wilson (see Somers); February 23 — St. William of Scotland (see William).

Wilt (nickname) See Wilton.

Wilton "From the Town+Near the Spring" (Old English double).

Patron Saints: Two English saints bear the name of Wilton. St. Edith of Wilton, 961-984, was the daughter of King Edgar of England. Her mother was Wulfreda. While Edith was still a child, her mother became a religious sister, taking Edith to Wilton Abbey with her. In time, Edith also became a nun. She refused the throne, which was offered to her after her brother's death. Instead, she had a church built there in honor of Sts. Peter and Paul. She died at Wilton at the young age of twenty-two.

Feast Dates: September 16 — St. Edith of Wilton; April 6 — St. Elstan of Wilton (see Elston).

Wim (Dutch) See William.

Win "The Friendly One" (Old English).

Patron Saints: Evidently no saint with the name Win exists. But there is one that can be pressed into service as

a patron: St. Winin. He is remembered as being a holy priest who served in Cantire, Scotland.

Win can also serve as a short form of Godwin, Goldwin, Kerwin, Winchester, Winfield, Winfred, Winslow, Winston, Winthrop, Winton, and Wynn.

Feast Dates: May 28 — St. Winin.

Wincenty (Polish) See Vincent.

Winchell "From the Wine Shop" (Old English).

Patron Saints: Saints whose names are similar to Winchell include Winin and Chellinus. St. Chellinus was a holy priest in medieval Meaux.

Feast Dates: December 7 — St. Chellinus; May 28 — St. Winin (see Win).

Winchester (English double) See Win+Chester.

Winfield (English double) See Win+Field.

Winfred "The Peaceful+Friend" (Old English double).

Patron Saints: Winfred springs from *win* ("friend") and *fred*, meaning "peaceful."

Feast Dates: May 28 — St. Winin (see Win); June 5 — St. Boniface, also known as Winfred (see Boniface).

Wing "The One Who Flies" (Middle English).

Patron Saints: The Latin word for "winged" or "flying" is based on *volucer*. This leads to St. Volutianus. He died a martyr in ancient Alexandria.

Feast Dates: March 21 — St. Volutianus.

Winifield (Old English double) See Win+Field.

Winn (nickname) See Win.

Winnie (nickname) See Win.

Winny (nickname) See Win.

Winslow (Old English double) See Win+Lowe.

Winston "From the Friendly [Wine]+ Town" (Old English double).

Patron Saints: Two patrons will do nicely here: Sts. Wistan and Tondach. Wistan was the king of Mercia (Britain) in the mid-ninth century. He was murdered by his godfather, Berferth, in 850.

Feast Dates: June 1 — St. Wistan; July 21 — St. Tondach (see Town).

Winthrop "From the Wine+Village" (Old English double).

Patron Saints: There are a couple of medieval saints whose names contain references to wine. One even worked in the wine region of France. St. Winebald worked as a shepherd in the Champagne area of France in the 600s. He is remembered for his prayerfulness.

Feast Dates: April 1 — St. Winebald.

Winton (Old English double) See Win+ Town.

Wit (English) See DeWitt.

Witby (English double) See White+By.

Witcomb (English) See Whitcomb.

Witey (English) See White.

Witney (Old English double) See White+ Ny.

Witold (Polish) See Vito.

Witti (English) See DeWitt.

Wittie (English) See DeWitt.

Witty (English) See DeWitt.

Wity (English) See DeWitt.

Wladimir (variant) See Vladimir.

Wolf "The Doglike Animal" (Old German).

Patron Saints: There is a St. Wolf and almost two dozen Sts. Lupus (which is Latin for "wolf"). St. Wolf was born in Lombardy. After a pilgrimage to the tomb of St. Martin, he became a monk and preached the Gospel in the Ardennes. Then he led a hermit's life. Also, for a short time, he tried to live atop a pillar like the Ori-

ental saints of old. However, his bishop commanded him to stop and he did. He died in 594.

Feast Dates: October 21 — St. Wolf.

Wolfgang "The Advancing Wolf" (Old German).

Patron Saints: There is a St. Wolfgang. There are also a dozen-and-half Sts. Lupus and at least one St. Wolf.

St. Wolfgang, 924-994, was born in Swabia. When his friend Henry became bishop of Trèves, he followed him there and taught in the cathedral school. Upon the death of Henry, he became a Benedictine monk. In 970, at the age of fifty-six, Wolfgang was elected prior. The following year he went to Hungary and a year later was elected bishop of Ratisbon. He supported the reform of monasteries and raising the standard of education.

Feast Dates: October 31 — St. Wolfgang.

Wolfie (nickname) See Wolf, Wolfgang.

Wolfy (nickname) See Wolf, Wolfgang.

Wood (nickname) See Elwood, Haywood, Woodrow, Woody.

Woodie (nickname) See Elwood, Haywood, Woodrow, Woody.

Woodman (Old English double) See Wood+Mann.

Woodrow "From the Passage+In the Woods" (Old English double).

Patron Saints: There is one St. Wood and almost a half-dozen saints who have Wood as part of their names.

Feast Dates: May 14 — St. Odo Wood (see Woody); September 23 — Bl. William Way of Devon (see Wayland).

Woodruff "Keeper+Of the Woods" (Old English double).

Woodward (Old English double) See Wood+Ward.

Patron Saints: There is one St. Wood

and almost half a dozen saints with Wood as part of their names.

Feast Dates: May 14 — St. Odo Wood (see Woody).

Woody "From the Forest Place" (Old English).

Patron Saints: There is at least one St. Wood. Odo Wood was prior of Christ Church in Canterbury and then abbot of Battle Abbey in Sussex, England. He died in 1200.

Feast Dates: May 14 — St. Odo Wood.

Wooley "From the Uncultivated Lands" (Old English).

Patron Saints: There is one saint whose name is the closest to Wooley: St. Woolo, which is the corrupted form of Gwynllyw. He is better known as St. Gundleus (the Latin form of Gwynllyw). He was a chieftain of Wales in the sixth century. His wife was St. Gladys (also known as Gwladys), who was the daughter of St. Brychan. He was also the father of Sts. Cadoc, Cammarch, Cynfyw, Glywys, Cernyw, Gwyddlew, Cyflewyr, Cannen, Maches, and Hywge. His early years were filled with reckless living. In time his wife convinced him to embrace the Christian faith. His final years were spent in repentance and prayer.

Feast Dates: March 29 — St. Woolo, also known as Gundleus.

Woolley (English) See Wooley.

Worden (English) See Ward.

Wordsworth (English double) See Ward+Worth.

Wornie (English) See Worth, Worton, Worrell.

Worrell "From the True Man's Manor" (Old English).

Patron Saints: One saint can be

pressed into service here as patron. He is St. Woronus, a holy hermit who lived in medieval Cornwall, England.

Feast Dates: April 7 — St. Woronus, also known as Guran.

Worth "From the Farmstead [Town]" (Old English).

Patron Saints: It helps to know that the name Worth means "farm." In Latin the word for "land" (or, loosely, "farm") is *ager*. This leads to St. Agericus. St. Agericus was born of poor parents, but he had King Thierry of Austrasia (Germany) for his godfather. As an adult he was ordained and then became bishop of Verdun. He was very holy and had great influence over the kings of Thierry. He died in 588.

Feast Dates: December 1 — St. Agericus.

Worthington (Old English double) See Worth+Town.

Worthy (nickname) See Worth.

Worton (English double) See Worth+Town.

Wright (variant) See Wainwright.

Wyatt "The Little Warrior" (Old French).

Patron Saints: There is no St. Wyatt. However, two saints have very similar names, Sts. Wiho and Wye. Because Wyatt means "little warrior," this fact leads to forty Sts. Marcellus, since the name Marcellus is the name of a famous Roman warrior.

Feast Dates: January 16 — St. Marcellus (see Marcellus); September 12 — St. Wye (see Wiley).

Wycliff (Old English double) See White+Cliff/Clyde.

Wye (nickname) See Wiley, Wyatt, Wyman.

Wyl (English) See William.

Wylie (Old English) See Wiley, William.

Wyman "The Warrior" (Old English).

Patron Saints: Two saints can be adopted as patrons, Sts. Wye and Mannius.

Feast Dates: September 12 — St. Wye (see Wiley); September 3 — St. Mannius (see Lyman).

Wyn (nickname) See Godwin, Godwin, Kerwin, Win, Winchester, Winfield, Winfred, Winthrop, Winston, Winton, Wynn.

Wynn "The Fair White One" (Welsh).

Patron Saints: There are about a half-dozen ancient saints with very similar names who can serve as patrons. One is St. Wynnin, a Scotsman and patron of Kilwinning Abbey in Ayrshire, Scotland.

Feast Dates: November 1 — St. Wynnin.

Wynston (Old English double) See Winston, Win+Town.

Wythe "The Dweller by the Willow Tree" (Old English).

Patron Saints: St. Wyllow, whose name means "willow," can serve as patron.

Feast Dates: November 1 — St. Wyllow (see Willoughby); September 3 — St. Mannius (see Lyman).

Wynton (Old English double) See Winton, Win+Town.

X

X Third-to-the-last letter of the alphabet (English).

Patron Saints: Hispanic-Americans and others sometimes use "X" as a suffix to names, which will usually lead to a patron saint.

Xabiel (Czech, German, Swedish, Hungarian) See Xavier.

Xabier (Czech, German, Swedish, Hungarian, Spanish) See Xavier.

Xaver (Czech, German, Swedish, Hungarian) See Xavier.

Xavier "The New House Owner" (Spanish Basque) or "The Bright One" (Arabic).

Patron Saints: There are about a half-dozen Sts. Xavier. The greatest is St. Francis Xavier, S.J., 1506-1552. He was born near Pamplona, Spain, at the castle of Xavier, and was sent to Paris for his education. There he met St. Ignatius Loyola and joined him in founding the Society of Jesus. He was ordained a priest in 1537 with St. Ignatius and five others. After four years of service in Italy, St. Ignatius sent him to India.

He preached the Gospel, converted and baptized thousands for God in Goa, Ceylon, and the Spice Islands. Eventually he journeyed to China, then Japan, and back to Goa. He again set sail for China in 1552, but he became ill and died just off the Chinese mainland. He was only forty-six years of age. He is patron of foreign missions, Australia, Asia, China, Goa, India, Japan, Outer Mongolia, and some Italian cities, as well as of tourism.

Feast Dates: December 3 — St. Francis Xavier, S.J.

Xeno (variant) See Xenos.

Xenos "The Stranger [Foreigner]" (Greek).

Patron Saints: Although there seem to be no Sts. Xenos, there are about four dozen Sts. Zeno. One of them died a martyr in ancient Rome.

Feast Dates: February 14 — St. Zeno.

Xever (Spanish) See Xavier.

Ximénes (Spanish) See Simon.

Ximénez (Spanish) See Simon.

Ximon (Spanish) See Simon.

Xylon (Greek) See Silvanus.

𝒴

Yahya (Arabic) See John.

Yahyaa (Arabic) See John.

Yakov (Russian) See Jacob.

Yanaton (variant) See Jonathan.

Yance (variant) See Yancy.

Yancey (English) See Yancy.

Yancy "The Englishman" (North American Indian).

Patron Saints: There is no St. Yancy, nor are there any saints with similar names. However, the fact that Yancy means "Englishman" does lead us to a patron. He is St. George, the patron of England.

Feast Dates: April 23 — St. George the Great (see George).

Yank (nickname) See Yancy.

Yankee (American) See Yancy.

Yaphet "The Comedian" (Hebrew).

Patron Saints: One saint is called "The Comedian."

Feast Dates: August 25 — St. Genesius (see Jester).

Ya'qoob (Arabic) See Jacob.

Yarden (Hebrew) See Jordan.

Yaron "The One Who Sings" (Hebrew) or "The One Who Cries Out" (Hebrew).

Patron Saints: The Church has appointed two patrons of singers. They are Sts. Cecilia and Gregory. St. Gregory I, 540-604, was chosen to be pope in 590. What he accomplished during the next fifteen years has marked him as one of the most influential personages of ancient Church history. Thus he is called "The Great."

Feast Dates: September 3 — St. Gregory the Great.

Yasiel "One Created by God" (Hispanic-American double).

Patron Saints: Yasiel is created from Y plus Asiel. This leads to St. Asiel. Jewish tradition has spoken of him for thousands of years. He is believed to be one of four angels who delivered seventy books of wisdom to mankind. He also helps catch thieves on earth.

Feast Dates: September 29 — The Holy Archangels.

Yasir "The Rich One" (Arabic).

Patron Saints: The Latin word for "rich" is *dives*, which leads to a St. Divus. He was a priest who died for the faith in Roman Caesarea in Cappadocia.

Feast Dates: July 11 — St. Divus.

Yeardley "From Enclosed+Meadow" (Old English double).

Patron Saints: Since the words *yeard* and *ley* (or *leigh*) mean "enclosed" and "meadow," Bl. Leigh can represent the second half of the name and serve as patron.

Feast Dates: August 30 — Bl. Richard Leigh (see Leigh).

Yehochanan (Modern Hebrew) See John.

Yehoshua (Modern Hebrew) See Joshua.

Yehudi "Praise the Lord" (Modern Hebrew form of Judah).

Patron Saints: This name means the same as "hosanna," and there is one St. Hosanna.

Feast Dates: June 18 — St. Hosanna.

Yehudit (Hebrew) See Yehudi.

Yevgeni (Russian) See Eugene.

Yirmeya (Modern Hebrew) See Jeremiah.

Yishai (Modern Hebrew) See Jesse.

Yitzchak (Modern Hebrew) See Isaac.

Yitzhak (Modern Hebrew) See Isaac.

Yocenio (Hispanic-American) See Yosenio.

Yochanan (Yiddish) See John.

Yoosuf (Arabic) See Joseph.

York "From the Boar Estate" (Old English) or "From the Yew Tree Estate" (Celtic).

Patron Saints: There is a St. William, archbishop of York, who died in 1154. Also, the meaning of York, "from the yew tree estate," matches the meaning of Yves.

Feast Dates: June 8 — St. William of York; May 19 — St. Ivo Hélory (see Yves).

Yorke (English) See York.

Yorker (English) See York.

Yosef (Hebrew) See Joseph.

Yosenio "The Flower" (Arabic-Panamanian).

Patron Saints: This name became popular among Hispanic-Americans and was used for both boys and girls in the 1980s. Many patrons can be found, even if none of them has the exact name of Yosenio. Among the patrons are Bl. Richard Flowers and at least a dozen Sts. Arsenio.

St. Arsenio the Great was a Roman deacon whom Emperor Theodosius ordered to Constantinople in 383 to tutor his children. Ten years later he abandoned this thankless task and became a hermit in the Egyptian desert of Skete. He died in 449.

Feast Dates: July 19 — St. Arsenio the Great; May 4 — Bl. Richard Flowers (see Lotus).

Yossi (Palestinian) See Joseph.

Yosu (Modern Hebrew) See Jesus.

Yoyi (nickname) See George.

Yoyo (nickname) See George.

Yrjo (Finnish) See George.

Ysaac (variant) See Isaac.

Ysac (variant) See Isaac.

Ytzchak (Modern Hebrew) See Isaac.

Ytzhak (variant) See Isaac.

Yul (variant) See Euell, Julius, Yule.

Yule "The One Born at Christmastime" (Old English).

Patron Saints: Yule seems to be a variant of Euell, and it means the same as "Noël" and "Natalis." There are about a half-dozen ancient Sts. Natalis and two Sts. Noël.

Feast Dates: April 14 — St. Euelpistus (see Euell); October 19 — St. Noël Chabanel (see Noël).

Yuma "The Son of the Chief" (North American Indian).

Patron Saints: Although no saints go by the name of Yuma, there is an ancient martyr called Yona who was beheaded in Egypt. Also, since Harrison (from "Harold" plus "Son") means "son of the commander," we can press St. Harald, whose name is a variant of Harold, into service as another patron.

Feast Dates: November 1 — St. Harald II.

Yuri (Russian, Ukrainian) See George, Uriah, Uriel.

Yuria (variant) See Uriah.

Yurik (variant) See George.

Yusef (Arabic) See Joseph.

Yusuf (Arabic) See Joseph.

Yvaine (variant) See Evan.

Yves "From the Yew Trees" (French-German) or "The Knight of the Lion" (French).

Patron Saints: Yves is a form of Ives, which leads to about a half-dozen saints with these names or variants of them. St. Ivo Hélory, 1253-1303, was born in Brittany and received an excellent education. Then he embarked on the practice of law. In time, he became a judge on the diocesan court. In this capacity he protected orphans, defended the poor, and administered justice with great kindness. It was well known that he could not be bribed. He could often be found struggling to reconcile people and trying to settle their problems out of court.

In 1284, at the age of thirty-one, he was ordained a priest. Three years later he resigned his legal practice and devoted himself entirely to his parishioners. He built a hospital and tended the poor and the sick, especially beggars. Often he would give them the clothes off his own back. He also fasted on bread and water during Lent and only slept on a straw mat with a stone for a pillow. The Church has named him patron of judges, lawyers, and notaries.

Feast Dates: May 19 — St. Ivo Hélory.

Yvon (Old French) See Yves.

Z

Z "The End of All" (Hispanic-American).

Patron Saints: Hispanic-Americans seem to favor the letter "Z" as the beginning letter for many of their names. "Zee" is the final letter in the Roman alphabet, while Omega in the Greek alphabet is the last letter. Thus it can be used to identify the Divine Creator who is "The End of All That Is."

Feast Dates: Trinity Sunday — God the Father, The A Through Z (Alpha Through Omega).

Zac (nickname) See Zachariah.

Zacarias (Spanish) See Zachariah.

Zacario (Spanish variant) See Zachariah.

Zaccaria (Italian) See Zachariah.

Zach (nickname) See Isaac, Zachariah.

Zachar (Bulgarian, Czech, Russian, Ukrainian) See Zachariah.

Zacharia (variant) See Zachariah.

Zachariah "God Remembers" (Hebrew).

Patron Saints: About three dozen Catholic saints bear the name of Zachariah, and the Bible provides another three dozen men. One of the latter was the great Jewish prophet who lived in about 520 B.C. St. Zachariah was born into a priestly family in Babylon during the exile. He finally went to Jerusalem when he was an old man. He urged the inhabitants to prepare for the coming of the Messiah.

Feast Dates: September 6 — St. Zachariah.

Zacharias (German) See Zachariah.

Zachariasz (Polish) See Zachariah.

Zacharie (French) See Zachariah.

Zachary (English) See Zachariah.

Zacherie (variant) See Zachariah.

Zachery (variant) See Zachariah.

Zack (nickname) See Zachariah.

Zackariah (variant) See Zachariah.

Zaharius (Greek) See Zachariah.

Zain (English) See John.

Zak (nickname) See Isaac, Zachariah.

Zakarias (Swedish, Hungarian) See Zachariah.

Zakarij (Slavic) See Zacharia.

Zalman (Yiddish) See Solomon.

Zander (Greek) See Alexander.

Zane (English) See John.

Zarko (Serbo-Croatian) See Zachariah.

Zarrett (African-American double) See Z+Garrett.

Zavier (variant) See Xavier.

Zayn (English) See John.

Zayne (English) See John.

Zeb (nickname) See Zebadiah, Zebulon.

Zebadiah "The Gift of the Lord" (Hebrew).

Patron Saints: There are three saints with this name. Two are Apostles of Jesus: Sts. James and John Zebedee. The third is their father. He was a fisherman and was married to a woman named Salome.

Feast Dates: March 15 — St. Zebedee; December 27 — St. John Zebedee (see Sean).

Zebedee (variant) See Zebadiah.

Zebron (African-American) See Zebulon.

Zebulen (variant) See Zebadiah.

Zebulon "From the Dwelling Place" (Hebrew) or "The Honored One" (Hebrew).

Patron Saints: Christian tradition provides no saints named Zebulon or variants of the name. However, the Bible names one man, the Jewish patriarch Zebulun, who lived in about 1800 B.C. He was the youngest of six sons born to Jacob (Israel) and Leah. (Jacob also fathered six other sons through Rachel, Bilhah, and Zilpah.)

From Zebulun came the tribe that occupied territory in south Galilee. In addition, his family produced Elon, one of the twelve judges of Israel.

Feast Dates: November 1 — Holy Zebulun.

Zebulun (Hebrew) See Zebulon.

Zechariah (Hebrew) See Zachariah.

Zed "The Lord Is Righteous" (Hebrew).

Patron Saints: Zed is a short form of Zedekiah. Only one saint can be found with a similar name. Bl. Zdislava belonged to a noble Bohemian family, got married, and had four children. However, her acts of charity caused difficulties between her and her husband. She died in 1252.

Feast Dates: January 1 — St. Zdislava.

Zeke (nickname) See Ezekiel, Zachariah.

Zenas "The Living One" (Greek).

Patron Saints: There are two Sts. Zenas and more than fifty Sts. Zeno. One St. Zenas is a lawyer, mentioned by St. Paul in his Letter to Titus. He later became a bishop in Palestine.

Feast Dates: September 27 — St. Zenas.

Zenon (Greek) See Xenos.

Zeph (nickname) See Zephaniah, Zephyrin.

Zephan (nickname) See Zephaniah.

Zephaniah "The One Treasured by the Lord" (Hebrew).

Patron Saints: Christian tradition provides one St. Zephon, and the Bible gives us the great Jewish prophet Zephaniah, who lived in about 630 B.C. and is one of the twelve minor proph-

ets of the Jewish Old Testament. He was a descendant of King Hezekiah and warned repeatedly that the "Day of the Lord" was very near. He called the people to repentance, but they did not listen. Zephaniah knew that the time of reckoning was inevitable. The people of his day would have to give an account to God for their sinful deeds. It is not known how he died.

Feast Dates: December 3 — St. Zephaniah, Jewish Prophet.

Zephyr (nickname) See Zephyrin.

Zephyrin "The Father of the Gods" (Greek) or "The Living One" (Greek).

Patron Saints: St. Zephyrinus served the Catholic Church as pope from 199 to 217. He had his hands full responding to many heresies about Christ.

Feast Dates: August 26 — St. Zephyrinus, Pope.

Zero "The Empty One" (Arabic).

Patron Saints: There are almost a half-dozen ancient saints who bear names that are very similar to Zero. One of them, St. Zeoras, was a priest who served in ancient Amida. He sought to gain holiness by living on top of a pillar. This was a popular pious practice in some Middle Eastern countries in ancient times. The practitioners were called stylites.

Feast Dates: March 16 — St. Zeoras.

Zeus "The Father of the Gods" (Greek) or "The Living One" (Greek).

Patron Saints: Sts. Vitus and Zenas both have names that mean the "living one." Moreover, the best possible patron for someone named Zeus would be God the Father.

Feast Dates: Feast of the Holy Trinity — God the Father; September 27 — St. Zenas (see Zenas).

Zig (nickname) See Sigmund.

Ziggie (nickname) See Sigmund.
Ziggy (nickname) See Sigmund.
Zigmund (variant) See Sigmund.
Zindel (Yiddish) See Alexander.
Ziv (Old Slavic) See Vito.
Zollie (nickname) See Saul, Solomon.
Zolly (nickname) See Saul, Solomon.
Zolton (Hungarian) See Vito.
Zorba "Live Each Day" (Greek).

Patron Saints: Since Sts. Vitus and Zenas both have names that mean the "living one," they can be called patrons of anyone name Zorba.

Feast Dates: June 15 — St. Vitus (see Vito); September 27 — St. Zenas (see Zenas).

Zubin (Israeli) See Zebulon.
Zuriel "God Is My Foundation [Rock]" (Hebrew).

Patron Saints: Jewish tradition introduces St. Zuriel, the chief angel of the order of principalities.

Feast Dates: September 29 — The Holy Archangels; October 2 — The Holy Guardian Angels.

Zygmunt (Polish) See Sigmund.

Bibliography

Often in this book, under the heading of "Patron Saints," statements are made to the effect that "there is only one known saint with this name" or "there are only about a half-dozen saints named such-and-such" or "two dozen saints exist with this name" or similarly worded descriptions. The actual number of saints available for any given name is usually far greater. However, the compiler has limited his estimates to those saints that can be found in hagiographies (books on lives of the saints) that are generally available to the American public. He has also utilized a number of sources specializing in the etymology of names. They are listed below.

Books on Saints

Ball, Ann. *Faces of Holiness*. Huntington, Ind.: Our Sunday Visitor Publishing, 1998.

————. *Modern Saints: Their Lives and Faces*. Rockford, Ill.: TAN Books, 1980.

————. *Modern Saints: Their Lives and Faces, Book Two*. Rockford, Ill.: TAN Books, 1990.

Barker, William P. *Everyone in the Bible*. Ada, Mich.: Fleming H. Revell Co., 1966.

Benedictine Monks of Ramsgate. *Book of Saints*. Harrisburg, Pa.: Morehouse Publishing, 1989.

Chang-seok, Rev. Kim Thaddeus. *Lives of 103 Martyr Saints of Korea*. Seoul, Korea: Catholic Publishing, 1984.

Cruz, Joan Carroll. *Secular Saints*. Rockford, Ill.: TAN Books, 1989.

Daughters of St. Paul. *Patron Saints*. Boston: Pauline Books, 1981.

Delaney, John J. *Dictionary of Saints*. Garden City, N.Y.: Doubleday and Co., 1980.

Dunne, Rev. William P. *Is It a Saint's Name?* Chicago: Integrity Supply, 1950.

Habig, Marion, O.F.M. *Franciscan Book of Saints*. Chicago: Franciscan Herald Press, 1959.

Hanley, Boniface, O.F.M. *Ten Christians*. Notre Dame, Ind.: Ave Maria Press, 1979.

Harney, Martin P. *Magnificent Witnesses*. Boston: Pauline Books, 1970.

Heerey, Sister Frances, S.C.H. *Biographies: God at Their Sides*. Melville, N.Y.: Regina Press, 1984.

Hoagland, Victor, C.P. *The Book of Saints*. Melville, N.Y.: Regina Press, 1986.

Hoever, Hugo, S.O. Cist. *Lives of the Saints*. Totowa, N.J.: Catholic Book Publishing, 1993.

_____. *Lives of the Saints II*. Totowa, N.J.: Catholic Book Publishing, 1992.

Holtzclaw, Robert F. *Black Citizens of Heaven*. Shaker Heights, Ohio: Keeble Press, 1988.

_____, *Saints Go Marching In*. Shaker Heights, Ohio: Keeble Press, 1980.

Holweck, Rt. Rev. F. G. *A Biographical Dictionary of Saints*. St. Louis, Mo.: B. Herder Book Co., 1924 (republished by Omnigraphics, Detroit, Mich., 1990).

Kelly, Sean and Rogers, Rosemary. *Saints Preserve Us!* New York: Random House, 1993.

Liturgy Documents, Series 6. *Norms Governing Liturgical Calendars*. Washington, D.C.: U.S. Catholic Conference, 1984.

Lodi, Enzo. *Saints of the Roman Calendar*. Staten Island, N.Y.: Alba House, 1992.

Lord, Bob and Penny. *Saints and Other Powerful Men in the Church*. Fair Oaks, Calif.: Journeys of Faith, 1990.

Maynard, Theodore. *Great Catholics in American History*. New York: All Saints Press, 1957.

McKenzie, John, S.J., ed. *Dictionary of the Bible*. New York: Macmillan Publishing Co., 1965.

O'Malley, Vincent, C.M. *Ordinary Suffering of Extraordinary Saints*. Huntington, Ind.: Our Sunday Visitor, 2000.

Ryan, George E., ed. *Figures in Our Catholic History*. Boston: Pauline Books, 1979.

Sellner, Edward C. *Wisdom of the Celtic Saints*. Notre Dame, Ind.: Ave Maria Press, 1993.

Thurston, Herbert, S.J., and Attwater, Donald, eds. *Butler's Lives of the Saints, Revised and Supplemented*, four volumes. Westminster, Md.: Christian Classics, 1981.

Tylenda, Joseph N. *Jesuit Saints & Martyrs*. Chicago: Loyola University Press, 1984.

_____. *Portraits in American Sanctity*. Chicago: Franciscan Herald Press, 1982.

Weidnehan, Joseph L., S.T.L. *Baptismal Names*. Baltimore, Md.: Kenmore Productions, 1931.

Books on Names

Abadie, M.J. *Multicultural Baby Names*. Stamford, Conn.: Longmeadow Press, 1993.

Arthur, William, M.A. *Etymological Dictionary of Family and Christian Names*. New York: N.p., 1857.

Boyd, Elza D. *Proud Heritage*. New York: Avon Books, 1994.

Consumer Guide magazine editors, *Ultimate Baby Name Book*. Lincolnwood, Ill.: Publications International, 1994.

Lansky, Bruce. *Best Baby Name Book*. New York: Simon and Schuster, 1979.

Nevins, Albert J., with Ann Ball. *A Saint for Your Name, Revised and Updated: Saints for Boys*. Huntington, Ind.: Our Sunday Visitor Publishing, 2000.

_____. *A Saint for Your Name, Revised and Updated: Saints for Girls*. Huntington, Ind.: Our Sunday Visitor Publishing, 2000.

Rule, Lareina. *Name Your Baby*. New York: Bantam Books, 1986.

About the Author

Thomas W. Sheehan is a priest of the diocese of Cleveland, having been ordained in 1970.

Father Sheehan has served as an associate pastor and pastor during his priestly ministry. He has also taught in elementary and high schools as well as at the college level; however, his main thrust has been in adult education.

Although this is his first published work, he has several audio- and videotapes to his credit.

Notes

Notes

Notes

Notes

Notes

Notes

Notes

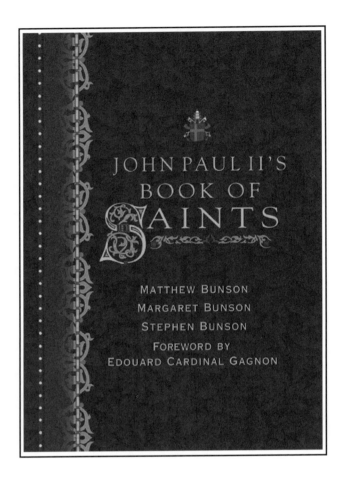

To date, the most complete list of the faithful
who have been declared saints for the entire Church.
0-87973-934-7 (934), hardcover, 368 pp.

To order from Our Sunday Visitor:
Toll free: 1-800-348-2440
E-mail: osvbooks@osv.com
Website: www.osv.com

Prices and availability of books subject to change without notice.

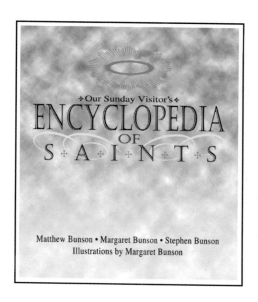

Some ten thousand saints and beati are included
in this reference, which is also available on CD-ROM.
0-87973-588-0 (588), hardcover, 798 pp.
0-87973-291-1 (291), CD-ROM

To order from Our Sunday Visitor:
Toll free: 1-800-348-2440
E-mail: osvbooks@osv.com
Website: www.osv.com

Prices and availability of books subject to change without notice.

Nearly three hundred biographies of contemporary
holy men and women are found in these two volumes.
0-87973-950-9 (950), paper, 272 pp. (first volume)
0-87973-409-4 (409), paper, 448 pp. (second volume)

To order from Our Sunday Visitor:
Toll free: 1-800-348-2440
E-mail: osvbooks@osv.com
Website: www.osv.com

Prices and availability of books subject to change without notice.

Our Sunday Visitor. . .

Your Source for Discovering
the Riches of the Catholic Faith

Our Sunday Visitor has an extensive line of materials for young children, teens, and adults. Our books, Bibles, booklets, CD-ROMs, audios, and videos are available in bookstores worldwide.

To receive a FREE full-line catalog or for more information, call **Our Sunday Visitor** at 1-800-348-2440. Or write, **Our Sunday Visitor** / 200 Noll Plaza / Huntington, IN 46750.

- -

Please send me: ___A catalog

Please send me materials on:

___Apologetics and catechetics   ___Reference works

___Prayer books   ___Heritage and the saints

___The family   ___The parish

Name_____

Address_____Apt._____

City_____State_____Zip_____

Telephone (   ) _____

A19BBABP

- -

Please send a friend: ___A catalog

Please send a friend materials on:

___Apologetics and catechetics   ___Reference works

___Prayer books   ___Heritage and the saints

___The family   ___The parish

Name_____

Address_____Apt._____

City_____State_____Zip_____

Telephone (   ) _____

A19BBABP

- -

Our Sunday Visitor
200 Noll Plaza
Huntington, IN 46750
Toll free: 1-800-348-2440
E-mail: osvbooks@osv.com
Website: www.osv.com